GLOBAL EPIDEMIOLOGY OF CANCER

Randall E. Harris, MD, PhD

Professor, Colleges of Medicine and Public Health
Director, Center of Molecular Epidemiology and Environmental Health
Division of Epidemiology and Department of Emergency Medicine
The Ohio State University Medical Center
Columbus, Ohio

JONES & BARTLETT
LEARNING

World Headquarters
Jones & Bartlett Learning
5 Wall Street
Burlington, MA 01803
978-443-5000
info@jblearning.com
www.jblearning.com

Jones & Bartlett Learning books and products are available through most bookstores and online booksellers. To contact Jones & Bartlett Learning directly, call 800-832-0034, fax 978-443-8000, or visit our website, www.jblearning.com.

Substantial discounts on bulk quantities of Jones & Bartlett Learning publications are available to corporations, professional associations, and other qualified organizations. For details and specific discount information, contact the special sales department at Jones & Bartlett Learning via the above contact information or send an email to specialsales@jblearning.com.

Production Credits

VP, Executive Publisher: David D. Cella
Publisher: Michael Brown
Associate Editor: Lindsey Mawhiney
Production Manager: Carolyn Rogers Pershouse
Senior Marketing Manager: Sophie Fleck Teague
Manufacturing and Inventory Control Supervisor: Amy Bacus

Composition: Cenveo Publisher Services
Cover Design: Michael O'Donnell
Rights and Media Research Coordinator: Mary Flatley
Cover Image: © www.royaltystockphoto.com/Shutterstock
Printing and Binding: Edwards Brothers Malloy
Cover Printing: Edwards Brothers Malloy

Library of Congress Cataloging-in-Publication Data
Harris, Randall E., author.
  Global epidemiology of cancer / Randall E. Harris.
    p. ; cm.
  Includes bibliographical references and index.
  ISBN 978-1-284-03445-5 (pbk.)
  I. Title.
  [DNLM: 1. Global Health—statistics & numerical data. 2. Neoplasms—epidemiology. 3. Epidemiologic Methods. 4. Neoplasms—etiology. QZ 220.1]
  RA645.C3
  614.5'999—dc23
                          2014047062

6048

Printed in the United States of America
19 18 17 16 15   10 9 8 7 6 5 4 3 2 1

Contents

Chapter 25   Epidemiology of Classic Sarcoma and Kaposi Sarcoma   319

Chapter 26   Epidemiology of Lymphoma: Non-Hodgkin's Lymphoma, Hodgkin's Lymphoma, and Multiple Myeloma   343

Chapter 27   Epidemiology of Leukemia   371

Chapter 28   Epidemiology of Brain Tumors: Glioma, Meningioma, Acoustic Neuroma, and Pituitary Tumors   393

Preface

Global Epidemiology of Cancer is written for all students and teachers of the health sciences, particularly those in epidemiology, public health, and medicine. Its main purpose is to present current and comprehensive information on the epidemiology, etiology, pathogenesis, risk factors, and preventive factors of common malignant neoplasms. In writing the book, I have made liberal use of the Internet and drawn upon worldwide information to address the global landscape of cancer.

The initial chapters of the book review molecular concepts of carcinogenesis and the global burden of cancer. Chapter 1 gives the reader a basic understanding of the molecular mechanisms critical to malignant transformation. Chapter 2 discusses the worldwide pandemics of tobacco abuse, alcohol abuse, obesity, and certain infections that have increased the incidence and mortality of many forms of cancer and pose unprecedented threats to the health of the human population. Standard epidemiologic methods and measures are also briefly addressed. Subsequent chapters of the book are arranged by human anatomy and physiology and discuss the diagnostic criteria, incidence, mortality, etiology, molecular pathogenesis, risk factors, preventive factors, therapies, and controversial issues for individual types of cancer.

Specific chapters address malignancies of the respiratory system (cancers of the lung, larynx, lip, oral cavity, and pharynx), the digestive system (cancers of the esophagus, stomach, colon, rectum, anus, pancreas, and liver), the female reproductive system (cancers of the breast, ovary, endometrium, cervix, vagina, and vulva), the male reproductive system (cancers of the prostate, testis, and penis), the urinary tract (cancers of the bladder, ureter, and kidney), the endocrine system (cancers of the thyroid and adrenal glands), the skin (melanoma and nonmelanoma skin cancers), connective tissues (sarcomas of soft tissue and bone), the immune system (lymphomas and leukemias), and the central nervous system (brain tumors).

Each chapter that is devoted to a specific type of cancer follows a similar format with subsections describing basic anatomy; diagnostic criteria; historical perspectives; the global burden of incidence and mortality; population differences and time trends in incidence, prevalence, and mortality; mechanisms of pathogenesis; risk factors; preventive factors; and opportunities for cancer prevention and control. Key epidemiologic studies and findings are presented in chronological order, with supporting evidence and references selected to guide readers to further study. It is assumed that readers are building on a fundamental knowledge base of human biology and have a strong sense of curiosity about medical science and cancer research. The text blends the traditional elements of cancer epidemiology with human anatomy, physiology, and molecular biology.

It is my hope that the text will provide a forum for examining current hypotheses regarding cancer epidemiology. Special sections of each chapter focus on controversial topics in cancer epidemiology with detailed information about the "pros" and "cons" of the controversy. This format facilitates active student discussion of molecular mechanisms of carcinogenesis and the relevant epidemiologic issues pertaining to the prevention and control of cancer.

I am deeply indebted to mentors, colleagues, and particularly students who have contributed to my education, research, and teaching over the past 4 decades. In essence, the book is an amalgamation of a longstanding continuum of exchange of information and ideas with many colleagues in the fields of medicine, public health, epidemiology, biostatistics, genetics, pathology, and molecular biology. The book also reflects the outstanding expertise of the editorial and production staff of Jones & Bartlett Learning; any errors or omissions in content or opinions on controversial issues are my responsibility. Finally, I am most grateful to my family for their support and understanding during the writing of this book.

Randall E. Harris

1

Pathogenesis of Cancer

With Zachary M. Harris

BIOLOGICAL BASIS OF CANCER

Cancer is the uncontrolled growth and spread of abnormal cells in the body. Cancers (malignant neoplasms) can arise from virtually any tissue and are usually named by the anatomic site of origin. Examples include breast cancer, prostate cancer, colon cancer, and lung cancer, the four cancers responsible for the majority of cancer deaths in many developed nations such as the United States. Cancer cells have the ability to divide continuously, invade other tissues, and spread (metastasize) to other organs through the blood and lymph. These primary features (uncontrolled cell division, invasion of contiguous tissue, and metastasis) distinguish cancerous growths from noncancerous (benign) cellular growths, the latter being self-limiting with no ability to invade tissue or metastasize.

Cancer is further defined according to the cell of origin based on microscopic examination by pathologists. Adenocarcinomas arise from the cuboidal epithelial cells that line the ducts of glandular tissue (e.g., adenocarcinomas of the breast, prostate, colon, or lung). Squamous cell carcinomas arise from the flat pavement cells that cover the skin and line portals of entry or exit in the human body (e.g., squamous cell carcinomas of the oral cavity, upper airways, esophagus, uterine cervix, urinary tract, or anus). Sarcomas arise from connective tissue (fibrosarcoma) or bone (osteosarcoma). Malignant gliomas arise from glial cells that provide vital support to neurons in the central nervous system. Adenocarcinomas, squamous cell carcinomas, sarcomas, and gliomas are solid tumors, as opposed to cancerous growths of immune cells that arise in the bone marrow (leukemias) or the lymph nodes (lymphomas) and circulate in the blood or the lymphatic system.

EVOLUTION OF CANCER

Solid cancerous growths (tumors) develop most often from cells of the epithelial lining of organs of the body (e.g., lungs, colon, breast, prostate), and less often from dividing cells of muscle, bone, and the central nervous system. The evolution of solid tumors is thought to be a long-term process spanning many years and often decades.

The hematopoietic (blood) cancers (leukemias, lymphomas) arise from lymphocytes, granulocytes, or other dividing cells of the bone marrow and the lymphatic system. Leukemias and lymphomas develop much more rapidly than solid tumors, perhaps over the span of a few months or even weeks.

CELL DIVISION (MITOSIS) AND CANCER

Approximately 90% of all cancers are solid tumors that originate in the epithelial lining of various organs of the gastrointestinal tract (oral cavity, esophagus, stomach, liver, pancreas, colon, rectum), the genitourinary tract (kidney, urinary bladder, uterine cervix, vagina), and the reproductive tract (breast, ovary, prostate). Solid tumors called *basal cell carcinomas* can also arise from the stratified (layered) epithelial covering of the skin. Collectively, all epithelial-derived tumors are called *carcinomas*.

In sharp contrast to epithelial-derived carcinomas, only about 8% of malignant neoplasms arise from cells of the immune system (lymphomas and leukemias), less than 2% arise from connective tissues (sarcomas of muscle, bone, and fat), and less than 1% develop in the central nervous system (gliomas and meningiomas). This distinct histologic pattern of cancer appears to be driven to a large extent by the relatively high cell division rates of epithelial and hematopoietic cell populations compared to connective tissue and the central nervous system. Periods of increased cell division during the life span also increase the likelihood of cancer development; for example, sarcomas of connective tissues arise in conjunction with bursts of cell division in fat and muscle cell populations and the elongation of bones during the early developmental years. Clearly, cancer is more likely to develop in those cell populations with higher rates of cell division. "In general, the greater the replicative activity, the greater the cancer risk" (Robbins & Cotran, 1979).

CANCER AND THE CELL CYCLE

Cancer can be succinctly defined as "deranged cell division." In cancer research, it is thus important to understand fundamental characteristics of the cell division cycle. In humans, normal cell division is an extraordinarily complex process whereby a progenitor (mother) cell forms two replicate daughter cells. In this remarkable miracle of nature, amino acids are efficiently transformed into millions of proteins and enzymes necessary for DNA replication, chromosomal formation, and reproduction of all of the working parts of the newly created cells.

Normal Cell Division and Cell Cycle

The human cell cycle consists of a preparatory phase of nutrient and energy buildup (G1 phase), DNA synthesis and replication of double-stranded DNA (S phase), condensation of DNA into 46 chromosomes and preparation for mitosis (G2 phase), and segregation of chromosomes to create two genetically equivalent daughter cells (mitosis or M phase) (**Figure 1.1**). Cytokinesis takes place after the segregation of chromosomes and is the final event in the cell division cycle. During cytokinesis, the cytoplasm and cytoplasmic organelles (e.g., mitochondria, Golgi apparatus, endoplasmic reticulum, ribosomes, lysosomes) are equally distributed to create two daughter cells with chromosomes, cytoplasm, organelles, nuclear and plasma membranes, and microtubular cytoskeletons that are virtual mirror images.

Progression through the cell cycle is tightly regulated by a family of genes called *cyclins* and the proteins they encode. Cyclins are activated by the docking of hormones, growth factors, and other extracellular *signaling molecules* to cell-surface receptors that trigger events inside the cell, a process known as *signal transduction*. Extracellular signaling molecules that modulate cell division include hormones of the endocrine system (e.g., estrogen, progesterone, testosterone, and thyroxine), paracrine factors that act locally (e.g., growth factors, cytokines, and prostaglandins),

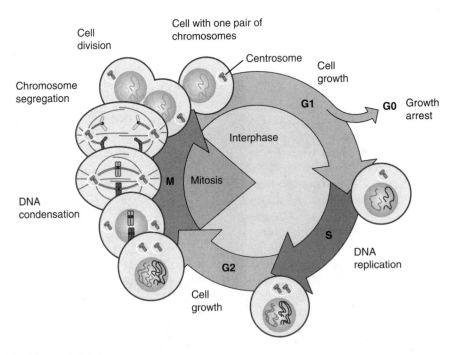

Figure 1.1 Model of Human Cell Cycle.

and autocrine factors released by the cells themselves (e.g., certain interleukins) (Hancock, 2010).

The cyclin proteins bind to cyclin-dependent kinases (CDKs), which modulate the passage of the cell through the sequential phases of the cell division cycle. The cyclins and CDKs function by phosphorylation of signaling proteins that regulate transcription and translation of genes essential for cell division. Furthermore, inhibitors of CDK encoded by specific genes (e.g., p53, RB, p27, APC, CHEK1, CHEK2) function as *gatekeepers* of error-free DNA synthesis by facilitating repair of any DNA coding errors that occurred during the S phase of the cell division cycle (Deninger, 1999).

One very important gatekeeper gene, p53, encodes a protein that checks for errors or damage in newly replicated DNA near the end of the S phase of the cell division cycle. As shown in the schematic of **Figure 1.2**, the p53 protein prompts the enzymatic repair of DNA damage before the cell progresses through the final steps of cell division. If excess DNA damage is detected, the cell undergoes apoptosis (programmed cell death), thereby preventing the proliferation of abnormal cells. In the absence of normal p53 function, cells with DNA damage (or mutations that predispose to cancer development) may continue to grow and divide (Figure 1.2). Because of its important role in eliminating mutant cells and conserving genomic stability, the p53 gene has been deemed the "guardian of the human genome" (Efeyan & Serrano, 2007).

G0 (Functional) Phase of the Cell Cycle

The G0 phase of the cell cycle is the nonreplicating "functional" period of the cell. During G0, newly formed cells undergo differentiation and carry out their designated functions; for example, epithelial cells produce and secrete proteins and glycoproteins, inflammatory cells produce and secrete prostaglandins and cytokines, immune cells produce and secrete antibodies, muscle cells exert contractile energy, skeletal cells provide structural support, fat cells store energy, endocrine cells secrete hormones, endothelial cells maintain blood pressure and water balance, neurons conduct impulses, and so on. The human body consists of trillions of cells that respond synchronously to changes in environmental conditions in order to maintain internal equilibrium (homeostasis) of life-sustaining functions.

LIFE SPANS OF HUMAN CELLS

The life spans and G0 phases of different types of cells are highly variable. In recent studies, isotopic (C^{14}) carbon dating has been used to accurately estimate the life spans of different cell types. These investigations confirm the wide range of normal cell life spans; for example, intestinal epithelial cells live only a few days, skin epithelial cells live a few weeks, lymphocytes live for months, macrophages live for years, muscle and fat cells live for decades, and nerve cells (neurons) live for the entire life span of the human

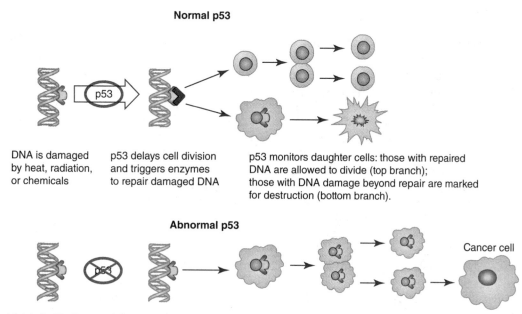

Figure 1.2 Mechanism of Action of p53 in Cell Division.

host (Spalding, Bhardwaj, Buchholz, Druid, & Frisén, 2005).

TURNOVER OF HUMAN CELLS

Populations of cells with relatively short life spans continuously undergo rapid self-renewal and have considerable regenerative capacity. The turnover rate of a given cell population depends on the delicate balance between the rate of programmed cell death (apoptosis) and the rate of cell replacement by cell division (mitosis) of progenitor cells (stem cells). Factors that upset this balance may lead to malignant transformation (Pellettieri & Alvarado, 2007).

Most epithelial cell populations continuously self-renew during adult life and have relatively short turnover times. Under normal physiologic conditions, intestinal epithelium turns over (is replaced) within about 5 days, skin epithelium within about 1 month, and lung epithelium within about 6 months. In general, cell populations that have fast and furious rates of cell turnover are more prone to cancer development than those that turn over more slowly (Blanpain, Horsley, & Fuchs, 2007).

Cells of the immune system are continuously formed from progenitor cells (stem cells) in the bone marrow by a process called *hematopoiesis*. However, mature immune cells ordinarily do not divide unless stimulated by inflammation or infection, and have relatively long life spans (months or years). It is during periods of accelerated cell division that cells of the immune system are most likely to undergo malignant transformation.

Throughout the early years of life, and especially during puberty, the cell populations of bone, muscle, and fat show high mitotic rates in conjunction with rapid growth and development, after which cell populations stabilize and cell division subsides. Indeed, cells of mature connective tissues divide infrequently and tend to have long life spans. Fat cells (adipocytes) and muscle cells divide only occasionally to replace about 5% of their respective cell populations every year. Bone undergoes continuous remodeling throughout life whereby old bone is resorbed by cells called osteoclasts and new bone is formed by osteoblasts; however, this process replaces less than 10% of skeletal cells annually. Some cells do not undergo mitotic division and therefore rarely form malignant neoplasms (e.g., neurons of the central nervous system and cells of cardiac and skeletal muscle) (Spalding et al., 2005).

EVOLUTION OF CANCER IN THE HUMAN HOST

In epithelial cell populations, normal cell division is restricted to stem cells that are in contact with the basement membrane. Mitosis of an epithelial stem cell produces one new stem cell, which remains in contact with the basement membrane and therefore retains replicative potential, and one new daughter cell that loses contact with the basement membrane and matures and differentiates into a functional cell. As newly formed daughter cells migrate to higher layers of stratified epithelium, they eventually undergo programmed cell death, which is called *apoptosis*, and are sloughed off at the surface (Marshman, Booth, & Potten, 2002).

The normal pattern of epithelial cell replacement is distinctly different from carcinomas, where the cancer cells divide indefinitely and fail to undergo apoptosis. The evolution of a solid cancerous tumor proceeds through a continuum of steps, wherein cells undergo visible morphological changes of the nucleus and cytoplasm (Holowaty, Miller, Rohan, & To, 1999; Kumar, Abbas, & Aster, 2014). The following paragraphs provide a brief description of the cell types that appear during the evolution of cancer. The progression of normal epithelial cells to invasive cancer is depicted for the epithelium of the uterine cervix in **Figure 1.3**.

Dysplasia (Premalignant Lesions)

Dysplasia is a distinct benign growth that arises from the epithelial cells lining various organs. In dysplasia, the cell nucleus becomes prominent, the cytoplasm appears swollen and vacuolated, and the cells exhibit increased rates of cell division and disordered maturation.

Dysplasia invariably precedes the development of cancer, and dysplastic lesions that serve as precursors of cancer can be detected at a number of anatomic sites. Examples of premalignant lesions include actinic keratosis of the skin, leukoplakia of the oral cavity, Barrett's esophagus, fibrocystic disease with atypia of the breast, adenomatous polyps of the colon, dysplasia of the prostate, and intraepithelial neoplasia of the uterine cervix. Fortunately, all such dysplastic lesions do not have the ability to invade or metastasize and they are curable by surgical excision or other methods of ablation. Clearly, the early detection and treatment of such lesions is an important component of effective cancer control.

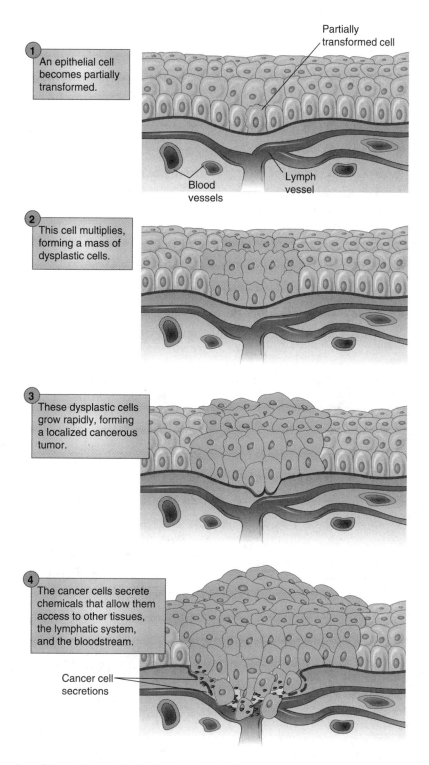

1 An epithelial cell becomes partially transformed.

Partially transformed cell

Blood vessels

Lymph vessel

2 This cell multiplies, forming a mass of dysplastic cells.

3 These dysplastic cells grow rapidly, forming a localized cancerous tumor.

4 The cancer cells secrete chemicals that allow them access to other tissues, the lymphatic system, and the bloodstream.

Cancer cell secretions

Figure 1.3 Progression of Normal Cervical Epithelium to Invasive Cancer.

Carcinoma in Situ

When solid cancerous tumors arise, they are at first confined to their original location and have not broken through the basement membranes into surrounding tissues. A confined neoplasm of the epithelial cell layer is thus called *carcinoma in situ (CIS)*. Such in situ lesions represent a defined step in cancer evolution. They exhibit all of the features of malignancy except invasiveness and metastasis; namely, the cells of in situ neoplasms manifest unchecked mitosis and proliferation, maturation failure and resistance to death, and disordered organization of the cell population. And yet, the in situ neoplasm is theoretically curable by excision because it has not spread beyond its original location and is contained by the basement membrane.

Invasive Cancer

In contrast to in situ neoplasms, invasive cancers have broken through the basement membrane to spread beyond their original location into contiguous tissues. This is a critical step in the evolution of cancer because surgical excision may no longer be effective as a form of cancer therapy. The breach of the basement membranes by cancer cells requires acquisition of certain new functions (e.g., the secretion of proteolytic enzymes that degrade basement membranes).

Metastatic Cancer

Metastatic disease represents the final step in the evolution of cancer. Cancer cells first invade contiguous tissues, and then spread through lymphatic channels and blood vessels to other anatomic sites. Cancer causes death by metastasizing (spreading) to vital organs such as the liver, brain, and spine. It is within these vital organs that the cancer cells overwhelm the normal cellular constituency, resulting in the collapse of their life-sustaining functions. Early detection prior to the development of invasive cancer and metastasis is therefore vitally important to the successful treatment and survival of cancer patients. The entire process of cancer development often goes unheeded and undetected by the human immune system over a period of many years; hence the term *silent killer* has been aptly applied to describe cancer in its various forms.

THEORIES OF CARCINOGENESIS

Cancerous growths result from a complex process known collectively as *carcinogenesis*. Although numerous theories of carcinogenesis have been proposed, considerable controversy exists as to which one is correct. Nevertheless, there is reasonable consensus that carcinogenesis is definable as a disease of the genes or a "DNA disease." Although genetic changes are ultimately responsible for the uncontrolled cell division and aberrant growth dynamics that characterize all forms of cancer, this does not infer that cancer-predisposing genetic alterations are heritable. In fact, about 95% of malignant neoplasms arise due to nonheritable genetic alterations acquired during the life span rather than inherited cancer-predisposing genes. Two main theories of carcinogenesis are discussed in this text: the *somatic mutation theory* and the *epigenetic theory*.

Somatic Mutation Theory of Cancer

Because a variety of genetic (DNA) mutations have been identified through molecular studies of cancerous tissues (Fearon & Vogelstein, 1990), the process of carcinogenesis is considered by many to result from the accumulation of two or more somatic mutations that impact upon control of the cell cycle or other features of neoplastic development (Knudson, 2001). This idea was first proposed in 1953 by Carl Nordling in Sweden, who stated that "the cancerous cell contains not one but a number of mutated genes. The occurrence of such accumulations of mutations may be expected to increase according to a certain exponent of age as well as according to the increase of cell proliferation" (Nordling, 1953).

In 1971, Alfred Knudson published a study of 48 cases of retinoblastoma, a devastating tumor of the retina that occurs primarily in children under 5 years of age. Based on the time sequence of tumors in these cases, Knudson hypothesized that retinoblastoma arises from two sequential mutational events. In the heritable form, a mutated gene is inherited from one parent and the second occurs in somatic cells of the retina. In the nonheritable form, both mutations occur in somatic cells of the retina (Knudson, 1971). The mutated retinoblastoma gene, Rb1, was later discovered by a team of investigators in Boston (Dryja, Friend, & Weinberg, 1986). The Rb1 gene was the first tumor suppressor gene ever discovered, and Knudson's two-hit mutation theory of retinoblastoma has been generalized as the *somatic mutation theory of cancer*.

Somatic mutations are base pair changes in DNA that occur during the human life span in cells of the body, in contrast to mutations that are "inherited" from parents through the germline. The somatic mutation theory of cancer is based on the premise that cancer arises from a single somatic cell and that tumor progression and development involve the accumulation of multiple DNA mutations that occur as the abnormal cells continue to replicate over time. It is postulated (but not proven) that with each successive mutation, the evolving clone of cancer cells acquires new properties that favorably impact tumor growth, invasion of contiguous tissues, and eventually metastasis to other anatomic sites.

Although the somatic mutation theory of cancer is the dominant paradigm of carcinogenesis, the emerging molecular evidence is not entirely consistent with this model. For example, many cancers arise without evidence of accumulating somatic mutations, and studies of precancerous and cancerous tissues often fail to disclose either chromosomal aberrations or mutated tumor suppressor genes and oncogenes (Soto & Sonnenschein, 2004). Furthermore, mutational events that are identified in cancerous tissues may have occurred late in tumor development as the result of cancer development, rather than being the cause (Lijinsy, 1989; Loeb, Loeb, & Anderson, 2003; Prehn, 1994).

Epigenetic Theory of Cancer

The existing scientific evidence is inconsistent with the hypothesis that cancer always arises from a single "mutated" cell and progresses due to accumulation of subsequent mutations that confer a survival advantage to cancer cells. An alternative hypothesis, the *epigenetic theory of cancer*, proposes that cancer develops due to activation or deactivation of certain genes that have a major impact on mechanisms of cell survival and cell division, *but in the absence of mutations that alter the DNA sequence* (Momparler, 2003; Verma, Maruvada, & Srivastara, 2004). Any process that modifies the expression of genes that control major mechanisms of cancer development (e.g., mitosis, apoptosis, angiogenesis, mutagenesis, immunosuppression, and metastasis) could obviously fuel the process of cancer development.

In the epigenetic theory there is no change in the underlying base pair sequence of the DNA; rather, nongenetic factors of the cellular microenvironment cause genes to be expressed differently. Epigenetic programming involves chemical reactions such as the addition or removal of methyl groups (CH_3) or acetyl groups (NH_2) to/from DNA or histones that alter the conformation of the DNA and determine whether genes are expressed or suppressed.

The best known example of programmed epigenetic changes in human biology is the process of cellular differentiation that occurs during embryogenesis. During embryogenesis, a single fertilized egg with a fixed genotype undergoes continuous mitosis and cell differentiation, leading to cell lineages consisting of billions of cells with extraordinarily diverse phenotypes (e.g., neurons, blood vessels, muscles, bones, epithelium). Cell differentiation produces such phenotypic diversity through programmed activation and inactivation of different sets of genes. Thus, differentiated cells in multicellular organisms express only the genes that are necessary for their own phenotypic activity. Furthermore, once a cell lineage becomes fully differentiated and mature, its inherent epigenetic pattern of genetic expression is usually preserved over multiple generations of cell division throughout the human life span. Nevertheless, certain molecular factors are capable of disrupting the normal epigenetic phenotype of a cell population, giving rise to mechanisms that initiate and promote the development of malignant tumors. Molecular mechanisms responsible for the genesis of specific forms of cancer are addressed in the next section.

MOLECULAR MECHANISMS OF CARCINOGENESIS

Several molecular mechanisms, acting either alone or in combination, are likely responsible for the initiation and promotion of carcinogenesis in a given individual. These mechanisms can be broadly categorized into six distinct groups: *mutagenesis, mitogenesis, angiogenesis, metastasis, inhibition of apoptosis*, and *immunosuppression* with reduced antineoplastic activity of T and B lymphocytes. A brief overview of each of these mechanisms is given in the following sections. More thorough reviews can be found in the literature (Howe, Subbaramaiah, Brown, & Dannenberg, 2001; Shiff & Rigas, 1999).

Mutagenesis
Germline and Somatic Mutations

Gene mutations can be either inherited from a parent or acquired during a person's lifetime. Mutations that are passed from parent to offspring are called hereditary mutations or *germline mutations* (because they are present in the egg and sperm cells, which are also called germ cells).

Somatic mutations occur in the DNA of individual cells at some time during the life span. Somatic mutations can be caused by environmental factors such as ionizing radiation from the sun or free radical compounds formed by physiologic processes such as lipid peroxidation, or they can result from spontaneous errors that occur during DNA replication in the cell cycle. Acquired mutations in somatic cells (cells

Somatic Mutation
Occurs in nongermline cells
Nonheritable
Mutation present in tumor only

Germline Mutation
Occurs in egg or sperm
Heritable
Mutation present in all cells of offspring

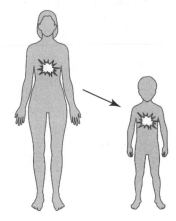

Nonheritable mutation

Heritable mutation

Figure 1.4 Somatic and Germline Mutations.

other than germ cells) cannot be passed on to the next generation (**Figure 1.4**).

Mutations that occur only in an egg or a sperm cell, or those that occur just after fertilization, are called *de novo mutations*. A genetic disorder in which an affected individual has a mutation in every cell but has no family history of the disorder may be attributable to a de novo mutation.

Mutations and Cancer

Accumulated mutagenic damage to DNA is believed to contribute substantially to the etiology of cancer; and it is indeed true that hundreds of genetic alterations have been identified that appear to influence carcinogenesis. Nevertheless, the form and timing of genetic alterations that spur the initiation, growth, and development of neoplastic cell populations remain elusive (Ames, Durston, Yamasaki, & Lee, 1973; Armitage & Doll, 1956; Cairns, 1975; Knudson, 1971; Loeb et al., 2003).

Subtypes of Genetic Alterations

Genetic alterations that have been found to influence carcinogenesis are divisible into distinct subtypes. They include (1) subtle base pair changes that alter gene function, (2) cytogenetically observable alterations in chromosome number (gain or loss of chromosomes) that produce genetic instability, (3) chromosomal translocations that create fusion genes that enhance neoplastic transformation, and (4) gene amplification whereby multiple copies of

cancer-promoting genes are overexpressed. It is notable that genetic alterations are a common feature of most forms of cancer but not of normal cell populations (Lengauer, Kinzler, & Vogelstein, 1998).

Causes of Mutagenesis

Mutations may be caused by exposure to both intrinsic and extrinsic factors. Several natural intrinsic physiologic processes generate reactive oxygen species that have mutagenic potential. Chief among them are aerobic respiration (oxidative phosphorylation), anaerobic respiration (glycolysis), lipid peroxidation, and chronic inflammation.

Intrinsic Mutagens. *Aerobic respiration (oxidative phosphorylation)* converts glucose to the high-energy compound adenosine triphosphate (ATP) in the mitochondria of the cytoplasm. The process of oxidative phosphorylation, which involves the flow of high-energy electrons through the electron transport chain, continuously generates DNA-damaging reactive oxygen species such as hydrogen peroxide, superoxide, and hydroxyl radicals. Because mitochondria contain haploid DNA unprotected by histones, mitochondrial DNA is highly vulnerable to oxidative damage mediated by persistent exposure to these compounds (Griffiths, Doudican, Shadel, & Doetsch, 2009).

The *Warburg Effect*, discovered by Otto Warburg and colleagues in 1924, describes the switch from oxidation phosphorylation to anaerobic respiration (glycolysis and lactate fermentation) for energy production in a wide spectrum of cancer cells (Warburg, 1956; Warburg, Posener, & Negelein, 1924). Warburg observed that cancer cells exhibit a high rate of glycolysis even in the presence of oxygen (*aerobic glycolysis*), a process that supplies energy for rapid cancer cell proliferation (Lunt & Vander Heiden, 2011). Although rapid cell proliferation per se may enhance mutagenesis of nuclear DNA, recent studies suggest that the diminution of reactive oxygen species with transition from oxidative phosphorylation to aerobic glycolysis may actually protect the mitochondrial DNA from damage (Ericson et al., 2012).

It is well known that the oxidative biodegradation of lipids (*lipid peroxidation*) in the human system generates reactive electrophilic compounds that have mutagenic potential. For example, malondialdehyde is a naturally occurring product of lipid peroxidation that is both mutagenic and carcinogenic (Marnett, 1999). Lipid peroxidation of polyunsaturated fatty acids is a self-propagating chain reaction that generates a variety of reactive oxygen species that are capable of interacting with DNA to cause mutations (Burcham, 1998).

Chronic inflammation stimulates the release of reactive oxygen species and reactive nitrogen species, which can interact with DNA to cause mutations. Furthermore, spontaneous breakdown of prostaglandins of the prostaglandin cascade produce the mutagenic agent malondialdehyde, which reacts with DNA under physiological conditions to form DNA adducts. Prolonged chemical exposures, persistent foreign bodies, chronic infection, and obesity are all causes of chronic inflammation (Ferguson, 2010).

The normal process of cell division has an intrinsic form of mutagenesis (Burnett, 1974). With every cell division there is incomplete duplication of the chromosomal tips (called telomeres). Successive cell divisions in a cell lineage therefore result in shortening of DNA until a point is reached where the daughter cells are no longer capable of dividing (called the *Hayflick limit*). This intrinsic mutational event is the basis for the *telomere theory of aging*—namely, as an ever-increasing percentage of cells reach their Hayflick limit and are unable to replicate, the defense, maintenance, and repair mechanisms of the body become increasingly impaired (Hayflick, 1985; 2007).

Extrinsic Mutagens Exogenous mutagenic factors include ionizing radiation, infectious agents, and certain chemicals found in some foods, beverages, drugs, and complex mixtures such as tobacco smoke and polluted air. Ionizing radiation carries enough kinetic energy to cause breaks and other damage in double-stranded DNA. Sources of ionizing radiation include cosmic rays from the sun, radon decay products from rock, medical x-rays, fallout from nuclear weapons, and discharges of radioactive waste from nuclear reactors. Light from the sun that reaches the earth is primarily nonionizing because ionizing rays are largely filtered out by ozone and other gases in the atmosphere. However, nonionizing ultraviolet rays may also induce DNA mutations by photochemical reactions (Doll, 1995; Gilbert, 2009).

Various infectious agents have strong mutagenic potential, particularly viruses that use the host DNA for replication (e.g., human immunodeficiency virus [HIV], human papillomaviruses [HPVs], hepatitis viruses, Kaposi's sarcoma virus, and Epstein–Barr virus). Such viruses have the ability to incorporate their genomes into human DNA, thereby causing structural changes and modification of gene expression. For example, integrated viral genes may encode proteins that bind to and inactivate the host tumor suppressor gene products that normally provide checks and balances on the cell cycle and thereby regular cell growth (zur Hausen, 1991). Furthermore, some viruses such as simian virus 40 (SV40) contain *oncogenes* that induce cancerous changes in the host cell (Bocchetta, Miele, Pass, & Carbone, 2003).

Tobacco smoke is a complex mixture of more than 5,000 gases and compounds, many of which are carcinogenic and/or mutagenic. Tobacco smoke contains three major classes of mutagenic substances: polycyclic aromatic hydrocarbons, nitrosamines, and heterocyclic amines. The metabolism of tobacco carcinogens is complex and involves activation versus detoxification by liver enzymes. The carcinogens of tobacco smoke, their uptake and metabolism, and the mechanisms by which they cause DNA mutations and DNA damage have been thoroughly discussed elsewhere (Hecht, 1999).

Food and beverages may also contain mutagenic agents. Notably, thermic reactions during cooking of meat can form mutagenic compounds such as heterocyclic amines and polycyclic aromatic hydrocarbons. Metabolic activation of such compounds by liver enzymes may increase their mutagenic potency. Grains and other foods may be contaminated with molds, fungal organisms, or bacteria that produce toxic substances with mutagenic properties; for example, ingestion of grain contaminated by the mold *Aspergillus flavus* results in exposure to the mycotoxin aflatoxin B1, which is highly mutagenic to hepatocytes. Food preservatives such as sodium nitrite may be metabolized in the stomach to form nitrosamines with mutagenic and carcinogenic properties. Ethanol present in alcoholic beverages has been classified as a human carcinogen by the International Agency for Research on Cancer (IARC). Dioxins with carcinogenic properties have been identified in foods and beverages. Heavy salt intake may damage the gastric epithelium and promote mutagenesis and carcinogenesis. Finally, excessive consumption of omega-6 polyunsaturated fatty acids may promote mutagenesis and carcinogenesis by enhancing chronic activation of the inflammatory cascade and the formation of reactive oxygen species (Sugimura, 2000).

Mitogenesis

Mitogens are factors that stimulate cell division (mitosis). There are a multitude of such factors that are both intrinsic and extrinsic to the human system. Intrinsic mitogens include hormones of the endocrine system and growth factors and cytokines that exert primarily paracrine effects. Whereas *endocrine* factors (hormones) travel through the blood to exert their effects, *paracrine* factors are secreted into the microenvironment in close proximity to the cell producing them to elicit local cellular responses. A special form of cell signaling involves *autocrine* factors that bind to receptors on the secreting cell to elicit cell division or changes (**Figure 1.5**). Hormones can be either steroids or polypeptides, whereas virtually all growth factors and cytokines are polypeptides.

Endocrine Factors

The human endocrine system is highly complex and consists of multiple secreting and responding organs and tissues (e.g., the central nervous system, the hypothalamic-pituitary axis, the thyroid and parathyroid glands, the thymus, the adrenal glands, the lungs, the gastrointestinal tract, the liver, the pancreas, the kidneys, the bone marrow, gonadal organs of the reproductive tract, and the immune system). A few examples of important endocrine factors with mitogenic activity are presented here.

Steroidal hormones (estrogen, progesterone, testosterone, glucocorticoids, vitamin D_3, and retinoids) are all small lipophilic molecules that easily penetrate both the cellular and nuclear membranes to enter the nucleus, where they bind to their respective receptors that are ligand-dependent transcription factors. These ligand–receptor complexes bind to specific DNA response elements in the promoter regions of genes to regulate gene expression and cell division in target cell populations.

Polypeptide hormones secreted by specific endocrine organs travel through the blood bound to carrier proteins and elicit their responses in distant cell populations. Pituitary hormones with mitogenic impact on their target tissues include growth hormone (GH), thyroid-stimulating hormone (TSH), follicular-stimulating hormone (FSH), luteinizing hormone (LH), and adrenocorticotropic hormone (ACTH). Hormones are released from the pituitary under the influence of releasing hormones secreted by the hypothalamus.

Insulin is a polypeptide hormone secreted by the beta cells in the pancreas that regulates carbohydrate and fat metabolism and induces glucose uptake for energy in muscle cells and storage in fat cells. Insulin also can stimulate the proliferation of fat and smooth muscle cells. Compounds with close homology to insulin, *insulin-like growth factors (IGFs)*, are synthesized and secreted by the liver under the influence

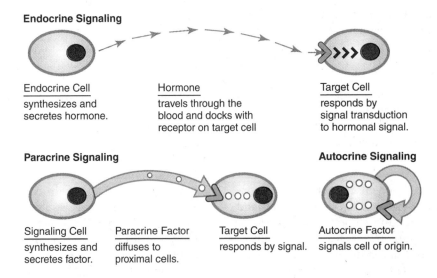

Figure 1.5 Types of Intercellular Signaling.

of pituitary GH. The IGF compounds make up the *IGF axis*, which promotes cell proliferation and the inhibition of cell death (apoptosis) in a variety of tissues (Le Roith, 1997).

Glucagon is a polypeptide hormone secreted by the alpha cells in the pancreas that induces the breakdown of glycogen and release of glucose into the bloodstream by the liver. The effects of glucagon and insulin therefore counterbalance one another in maintaining normal levels of blood glucose. Glucagon and *glucagon-like factors (GLFs)* have been found to stimulate the proliferation of intestinal epithelium (Keiffer & Habener, 1999).

Calcitonin and parathyroid hormone are polypeptide hormones synthesized by the thyroid and parathyroid glands, respectively. These hormones coordinate bone remodeling and maintain calcium homeostasis. Calcitonin stimulates bone formation by osteoblasts whereas parathyroid hormone induces bone resorption by osteoclasts (Carter & Schipani, 2006).

Erythropoietin is a hormone that is essential for red blood cell (erythrocyte) production. This glycoprotein is secreted by the kidneys and induces the differentiation and growth of erythrocytes from progenitor cells in the bone marrow.

Paracrine Factors

A number of paracrine factors called *growth factors* can also stimulate cell division in certain tissues, particularly sites of wound healing and inflammation. Examples include epidermal growth factor (EGF), fibroblast growth factor (FGF), transforming growth factors (TGFα and TGFβ), and platelet-derived growth factor (PDGF); there are many others. Each of these mitogens elicits cellular responses through interaction with specific receptor molecules on cell membranes. For example, PDGF induces proliferation of fibroblasts, smooth muscle cells, and monoctyes; EGF is mitogenic for fibroblasts and many types of epithelial cells; FGF induces growth and development of blood vessels; and TGFα has mitogenic effects similar to EGF, whereas TGFβ has growth inhibitory effects in many cell populations.

Cytokines are proteins secreted by immune cells that help orchestrate both the induction and effector phases of all immune and inflammatory responses, including cell proliferation, intercellular communication, and cell death. The term *cytokine* is often used specifically to refer to a wide variety of locally acting immunomodulating agents (e.g., interleukins, interferons, tumor necrosis factor) that facilitate the immune response. Nevertheless, certain cytokines effectively spur the proliferation of other cells. For example, specific interleukins secreted by activated T lymphocytes (IL-2 and IL-4) stimulate the clonal expansion of other immune cells in response to viral infection (Dinarello, 2007).

Prostaglandins and *leukotrienes* are short-lived compounds derived from fatty acids that modulate important physiological functions. Prostaglandins, particularly PGE1 and PGE2, are the principal mediators of the inflammatory response, whereas leukotrienes are involved in allergic and asthmatic reactions. Some prostaglandins have potent mitogenic activity in epithelial cell populations; for example, PGE2, the chief prostaglandin of the inflammatory response, stimulates proliferation of the mammary epithelium (Harris, 2007).

Mitogen-Activated Protein Kinase (MAPK) Cascade

Mitogenic hormones and growth factors stimulate cell division by a process known as *signal transduction* in which the mitogen activates specific receptors on the cell membranes of target cells that, in turn, initiate tightly regulated cascades of intracellular signaling by mitogen-activated protein kinases (MAPKs) (**Figure 1.6**). Human cells contain multiple MAPK pathways, each consisting of specific cytoplasmic protein kinases that are sequentially phosphorylated. Certain of these protein kinases are translocated into the nucleus, where they induce the expression of genes necessary for cell division. Each MAPK pathway consists of a specific profile of protein kinases that ultimately control cell differentiation, cell proliferation, and cell death in a specific tissue. In humans, more than 500 different protein kinase genes and approximately 50 distinct MAPK cascades have now been identified (Manning, Whyte, Martinez, Hunter, & Sudarsanam, 2002; Pearson et al., 2001).

Extrinsic Factors

In general, any form of cellular injury can result in a mitogenic response by the afflicted tissue. Causative

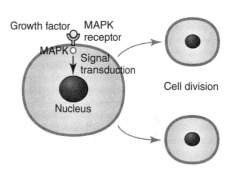

Figure 1.6 Mitogen-Activated Protein Kinase (MAPK) Cascade.

factors of cell injury include microbial infection, physical agents (burns, radiation, trauma), chemical exposures (toxins, caustic substances), ischemia, necrosis, and all types of immunological reactions. All such exposures elicit an immediate inflammatory response of the innate immune system. Although acute inflammation is self-limited and of short duration, chronic inflammation is associated histologically with the persisting presence of immune cells and is nearly always accompanied by the proliferation of blood vessels and involved tissues.

Chronic inflammation is maintained by constitutive overexpression of cyclooxygenase-2 (COX-2), which is the rate-limiting enzyme of the prostaglandin cascade. The COX-2 enzyme efficiently catalyzes the conversion of essential dietary fats (principally arachidonic acid and unconjugated linoleic acid) into prostaglandins. Chronic inflammation and continuous overexpression of COX-2 markedly amplify the biosynthesis of PGE-2, which is the chief prostaglandin of the inflammatory cascade. This short-lived intercellular hormone is capable of inducing the transcription of specific genes in the nucleus of nearby cells. In particular, PGE-2 has been found to stimulate the transcription of genes that have powerful mitogenic effects (Harris, 2007).

Contact inhibition is a special form of growth control by which cells ordinarily do not divide when in close contact with one another. This phenomenon is regulated by the density of the cell population, the access of cells to nutrients, and protein complexes of beta-catenin and cadherins that control cell-to-cell adhesion. In general, an intact *E-cadherin-catenin complex* maintains normal intercellular adhesion and limits cell division, whereas loss of function of this complex permits or enhances cell proliferation and leads to invasion and metastasis by malignant cells (Wijnhoven, Dinjens, & Pignatelli, 2000).

Angiogenesis

Angiogenesis is a normal and vital physiological process by which new blood vessels develop from pre-existing vessels. *Vascular endothelial growth factor (VEGF)* is a potent stimulant of de novo blood vessel formation (angiogenesis) in a variety of tissues. Once believed to be present only in the endothelial lining of blood vessels, VEGF has now been discovered in virtually all types of cancers. Indeed, the process of angiogenesis is fundamental to the growth, development, and metastatic spread of cancerous tumors (Folkman, 2006; Folkman & Klagsbrun, 1987).

When a tumor outgrows its blood supply, cancer cells secrete VEGF to signal nearby blood vessels, which respond by sprouting new vessels that grow into the tumor (**Figure 1.7**). This sprouting process involves the secretion of proteolytic enzymes by the

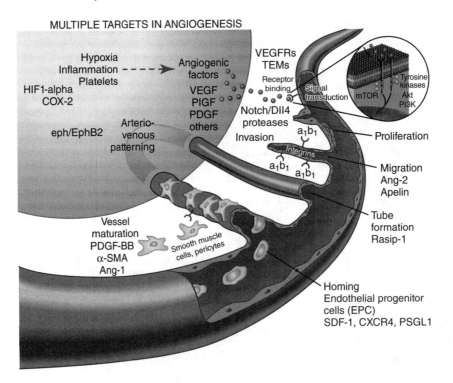

Figure 1.7 Angiogenesis Cascade in Tumor Growth and Development.

parent vessel to enable the formation of new capillaries. As a consequence, the new blood vessels are immature and "leaky," thereby providing a doorway for cancerous cells to enter the bloodstream and spread to other organs (Folkman, 2006).

Suppression of Apoptosis

Apoptosis, or controlled cell death, is an important regulatory mechanism for the maintenance of homeostasis in cell populations. Dysfunctional apoptosis results in immortalization of cells, a key feature of cancer cells. Apoptosis is regulated by an intrinsic pathway that originates inside the cell and an extrinsic pathway that originates outside the cell.

The intrinsic pathway involves mitochondrial release of cytochrome c and activation of caspase 9 and other enzymes that destroy the cell. Intrinsic apoptosis is triggered when the expression of two nuclear genes, Bcl-2 and BAX, favors BAX. The extrinsic pathway involves activation of death receptors on the cell membrane by tumor necrosis factors alpha and beta, and other epigenetic factors. This results in activation of caspase 8 and other enzymes that destroy the cell (Lowe & Lin, 2000).

Telomeres are sequences of DNA that cap the ends of eukaryotic chromosomes. In normal cell populations, as mentioned earlier, telomeres are lost from the chromosomal tips with each successive cell division, and eventually cell division ceases and apoptosis occurs. However, in abnormally proliferating cells, a special reverse transcriptase enzyme called *telomerase* replicates the terminal DNA sequence of chromosomes and restores telomeres to the chromosomal tips (**Figure 1.8**). Telomerase

activity is amplified in cancer cells that proliferate indefinitely, but is virtually undetectable in normal somatic cells that undergo programmed apoptosis. Maintenance of telomere integrity by telomerase therefore protects cancer cells from apoptosis, and reciprocally, inhibition of telomerase and loss of telomeres elicits an apoptotic response. For this reason, apoptotic factors that selectively target cancer cells may be of value in cancer therapy (Mondello & Scovassi, 2004).

Metastasis

Metastatic spread of cancer occurs by direct invasion of proximal tissues, lymphatic invasion, and hematogenous dissemination. Epithelial carcinomas develop from cells that are anchored by the basement membrane, a thin collagenous membrane that serves as a mechanical barrier to invasion of underlying tissues by malignant cells. Obviously, a key initial step in the metastatic spread of epithelial tumors is penetration of the basement membrane by cancer cells. Proteolytic enzymes called *matrix metalloproteinases (MMPs)* secreted by cancer cells facilitate penetration of the basement membrane. These zinc-dependent enzymes are important for normal tissue remodeling and repair and are capable of degrading collagen, proteins, and other components of the basement membrane. By secreting MMPs, cancer cells can break through the basement membrane as well as other cell membranes and gain access to underlying tissues, lymphatics, and blood vessels, thereby facilitating cancer metastasis (Deryugina & Quigley, 2006; Itoh & Nagase, 2002) (**Figure 1.9**).

The HER-2/neu oncogene is a member of the epidermal growth factor receptor (EGFR) family. It is an important mediator of cancer cell growth and metastasis. When the HER-2/neu receptor protein is

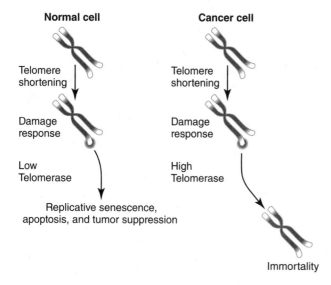

Figure 1.8 Telomeres and Apoptosis.

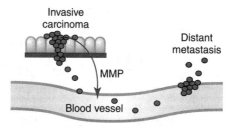

Cancer cells breach the basement membrane, enter the bloodstream, and invade distant tissues by secreting *matrix metalloproteinases* (MMPs) that biodegrade cell membranes.

Figure 1.9 Matrix Metalloproteinase (MMP) Activity in Metastatic Cancer.

activated, multiple other factors are activated that promote tumor development and metastatic spread of cancer cells. For example, VEGF is secreted to promote the sprouting of new blood vessels (angiogenesis) and MMPs are produced that degrade cell membranes and basement membranes and are thus associated with tumor invasiveness, metastasis, and poor survival. Overexpression of HER-2/neu is now widely used by clinicians as a biomarker of poor prognosis and metastasis for patients with invasive breast cancer, and the HER-2/new receptor is a molecular target for breast cancer therapy (Coussens et al., 1985; Olayioye, 2001).

Immunosuppression

Immunosuppression is a characteristic feature of cancer patients that correlates with disease promotion and progression. Prostaglandins, particularly PGE-2, are important modulators of immunosuppression. Pockaj et al. (2004) found that increased levels of PGE-2 suppress the immunocompetence of helper T-cells and dendritic cells in newly diagnosed breast cancer patients. Specifically, elevated levels of PGE-2 were associated with reduced secretion of anti-tumor factors by T-cells (interferon gamma, tumor necrosis factor alpha, and interleukins IL-2 and IL-12) and loss of immunocompetence in dendritic cells (reduced secretion of stimulatory molecules, loss of antigen-sensitizing function, reduced phagocytic activity, and lack of maturation potential). Defective T-cell and dendritic cell function due to COX-2–driven PGE-2 biosynthesis is therefore an important mechanism by which tumors evade immunosurveillance.

Inflammogenesis of Cancer

One microenvironmental process capable of inducing untoward epigenetic changes in gene expression leading to cancer development is *chronic inflammation*. More than 150 years ago the famous German pathologist, Rudolph Virchow, suggested that chronic inflammation leads to cancer development by increasing uncontrolled cellular proliferation (Balkwill & Mantovani, 2001; Virchow, 1863). In 1992, molecular biologists discovered that the process of inflammation is primarily under the control of an inducible gene called cyclooxygenase-2 (COX-2) (Herschman, 2002). The COX-2 gene is normally silent in noninflamed tissue but is readily "turned on" by a variety of inflammatory environmental stimuli known to cause cancer including tobacco smoke, reactive oxygen species (ROS), polyunsaturated fatty acids, radiation, certain infectious bacteria and viruses, hypoxia, endotoxins, and many

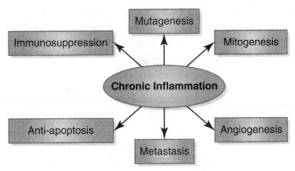

Figure 1.10 Chronic Inflammation and Carcinogenesis.

other agents (Harris, 2007; Harris, Beebe-Donk, & Alshafie, 2007). Overwhelming molecular evidence has linked induction of the COX-2 gene and overexpression of certain molecules of inflammation (called prostaglandins) to all of the essential features of carcinogenesis (mutagenesis, mitogenesis, angiogenesis, reduced apoptosis, metastasis, and immunosuppression). Indeed, carcinogenesis often evolves as a progressive series of highly specific cellular and molecular changes in response to induction of constitutive overexpression of COX-2 and the prostaglandin cascade in the *inflammogenesis of cancer* (**Figure 1.10**).

• • • REFERENCES

Ames, B. N., Durston, W. E., Yamasaki, E., & Lee, F. D. (1973). Carcinogens are mutagens: A simple test system combining liver homogenates for activation and bacteria for detection. *Proceedings of the National Academy of Sciences*, 70(8), 2281–2285.

Armitage, P., & Doll, R. (1956). The age distribution of cancer and a multi-stage theory of carcinogenesis. *British Journal of Cancer*, 8, 1–12.

Balkwill, F., & Mantovani, A. (2001). Inflammation and cancer: Back to Virchow? *Lancet*, 357, 539–545.

Blanpain, C., Horsley, V., & Fuchs, E. (2007). Epithelial stem cells: Turning over new leaves. *Cell*, 128, 445–458.

Bocchetta, M., Miele, L., Pass, H. I., & Carbone, M. (2003). Notch-1 induction, a novel activity of SV40 required for growth of SV40-transformed human mesothelial cells. *Oncogene*, 22(1), 81–89.

Burcham, P. C. (1998). Genotoxic lipid peroxidation products: Their DNA damaging properties and role in formation of endogenous DNA adducts. *Mutagenesis, 13*(3), 287–305.

Burnett, M (1974). *Intrinsic mutagenesis.* Lancaster, England: Medical and Technical Publishing Company.

Cairns, J. (1975). Mutation selection and the natural history of cancer. *Nature, 255,* 197–200.

Carter, P. H., & Schipani, E. (2006). The roles of parathyroid hormone and calcitonin in bone remodeling: Prospects for novel therapeutics. *Endocrine, Metabolic and Immune Disorders—Drug Targets, 6*(1), 59–76.

Coussens, L., Yang-Feng, T. L., Liao, Y. C., Chen, E., Gray, A., McGrath, J., … Francke, U. (1985). Tyrosine kinase receptor with extensive homology to EGF receptor shares chromosomal location with neu oncogene. *Science, 230*(4730), 1132–1139.

Deninger, P. (1999). Genetic instability in cancer: Caretaker and gatekeeper genes. *Ochsner Journal, 1*(4), 206–209.

Deryugina, E. I., & Quigley, J. P. (2006). Matrix metalloproteinases and tumor metastasis. *Cancer Metastasis Review, 25*(1), 9–34.

Dinarello, C. A. (2007). Historical review of cytokines. *European Journal of Immunology, 37*(Suppl 1), S34–S45.

Doll, R. (1995). Hazards of ionizing radiation: 100 years of observations on man. *British Journal of Cancer, 72*(6), 1339–1349.

Dryja, T. P., Friend, S, & Weinberg, R. A. (1986). Genetic sequences that predispose to retinoblastoma and osteosarcoma. *Symposium on Fundamental Cancer Research, 39,* 115–119.

Efeyan, A., & Serrano, M. (2007). p53: Guardian of the genome and policeman of the oncogenes. *Cell Cycle, 6*(9), 1006–1010.

Ericson, N. G., Kulawiec, M., Vermulst, M., Sheahan, K., O'Sullivan, J., Salk, J. J., & Bielas, J. H. (2012). Decreased mitochondrial DNA mutagenesis in human colorectal cancer. *PLoS Genetics, 8*(6), e1002689.

Fearon, E. R., & Vogelstein, B. A. (1990). A genetic model for colorectal tumorigenesis. *Cell, 61*(5), 759–767.

Ferguson, L. R. (2010). Chronic inflammation and mutagenesis. *Mutation Research, 690*(1–2), 3–11.

Folkman, J. (2006). Angiogenesis. *Annual Review of Medicine, 57,* 1–18.

Folkman, J., & Klagsbrun, M. (1987). Angiogenic factors. *Science, 235*(4787), 442–447.

Gilbert, E. S. (2009). Ionising radiation and cancer risks: What have we learned from epidemiology? *International Journal of Radiation Biology, 85*(6), 467–482.

Griffiths, L. M., Doudican, N. A., Shadel, G. S., & Doetsch, P. W. (2009). Mitochondrial DNA oxidative damage and mutagenesis in Saccharomyces cerevisiae. *Methods in Molecular Biology, 554,* 267–286.

Hancock, J. T. (2010). *Cell signaling* (3rd ed.). New York: Oxford University Press.

Harris, R. E. (2007). Cyclooxygenase-2 (COX-2) and the inflammogenesis of cancer. *Subcellular Biochemistry, 42,* 63–126.

Harris, R. E., Beebe-Donk J., & Alshafie, G. A. (2007). Cancer chemoprevention by cyclooxygenase 2 (COX-2) blockade: Results of case control studies. *Subcellular Biochemistry, 42,* 193–212.

Hayflick, L. (1985). The cell biology of aging. *Clinics in Geriatric Medicine, 1*(1), 15–27.

Hayflick, L. (2007). Entropy explains aging, genetic determinism explains longevity, and undefined terminology explains misunderstanding both. *PLoS Genetics, 3*(12), e220.

Hecht, S. S. (1999). Tobacco smoke carcinogens and lung cancer. *Journal of the National Cancer Institute, 91*(14), 1194–1210.

Herschman, H. R. (2002). Historical aspects of COX-2. Cloning and characterization of the cDNA, protein and gene. In R. E. Harris (Ed.), *COX-2 blockade in cancer prevention and therapy* (pp. 13–32). Totowa, NJ: Humana Press.

Holowaty, P., Miller, A. B., Rohan, T., & To, T. (1999). Natural history of dysplasia of the uterine cervix. *Journal of the National Cancer Institute*, 91(3), 252–258.

Howe, L. R., Subbaramaiah, K., Brown, A. M. C., & Dannenberg, A. J. (2001). Cyclooxygenase-2: A target for the prevention and treatment of breast cancer. *Endocrine-Related Cancer, 8*, 97–114.

Itoh, Y., & Nagase, H. (2002). Matrix metalloproteinases in cancer. *Essays in Biochemistry, 38*, 21–36.

Kieffer, T. J., & Habener, J. F. (1999). The glucagon-like peptides. *Endocrine Reviews, 20*, 876–913.

Knudson, A. G. (1971). Mutation and cancer: Statistical study of retinoblastoma. *Proceedings of the National Academy of Sciences, 68*, 820–823.

Knudson, A. G. (2001). Two genetic hits (more or less) to cancer. *Nature Review Cancer, 1*(2), 157–162.

Kumar, V., Abbas, A. K., & Aster, J. C. (2014). *Robbins & Cotran pathologic basis of disease* (9th ed.) Philadelphia, PA: Mosby & Saunders.

Lengauer, C., Kinzler, K. W., & Vogelstein, B. (1998). Genetic instabilities in human cancers. *Nature, 396*, 643–649.

Le Roith, D. (1997). Insulin-like growth factors. *New England Journal of Medicine, 336*, 633–640.

Lijinsy, W. (1989). A view of the relation between carcinogenesis and mutagenesis. *Environmental and Molecular Mutagenesis, 14*(Suppl 16), 78–84.

Loeb, L. A., Loeb, K. R., & Anderson, J. P. (2003). Multiple mutations and cancer. *Proceedings of the National Academy of Sciences, 100*, 776–781.

Lowe, S. W., & Lin, A. W. (2000). Apoptosis in cancer. *Carcinogenesis, 21*(3), 485–495.

Lunt, S. Y., & Vander Heiden, M. G. (2011). Aerobic glycolysis: Meeting the metabolic requirements of cell proliferation. *Annual Review of Cell and Developmental Biology, 27*, 441–464.

Manning, G., Whyte, D. B., Martinez, R., Hunter, T., & Sudarsanam, S. (2002). The protein kinase complement of the human genome. *Science, 298*(5600), 1912–1934.

Marnett, L. J. (1999). Lipid peroxidation-DNA damage by malondialdehyde. *Mutation Research, 424*(102), 83–95.

Marshman, E., Booth, C., & Potten, C. S. (2002). The intestinal epithelial stem cell. *Bioessays, 24*, 91–98.

Momparler, R. L. (2003). Cancer epigenetics. *Oncogene, 22*(42), 6479–6483.

Mondello, C., & Scovassi, A. I. (2004). Telomeres, telomerase, and apoptosis. *Biochemistry and Cell Biology, 82*(4), 498–507.

Nordling, C. O. (1953). A new theory on the cancer-inducing mechanism. *British Journal of Cancer, 7*, 68–72.

Olayioye, M. A. (2001). Update on HER-2 as a target for cancer therapy: Intracellular signaling pathways of ErbB2/HER-2 and family members. *Breast Cancer Research, 3*(6), 385–389.

Pearson, G., Robinson, F., Beers Gibson, T., Xu, B. E., Karandikar, M., Berman, K., & Cobb, M. H. (2001). Mitogen-activated protein (MAP) kinase pathways: Regulation and physiological functions. *Endocrine Review, 22*(2), 153–183.

Pellettieri, J., & Alvarado, A. S. (2007). Cell turnover and adult tissue homeostasis: From humans to planarians. *Annual Review of Genetics, 41*, 83–105.

Pockaj, B. A., Basu, G. D., Pathangey, L. B., Gray, R. J., Hernandez, J. L., Gendler, S. J., & Mukherjee, P. (2004). Reduced T-cell and dendritic cell function is related to cyclooxygenase-2 overexpression and prostaglandin E2 secretion in patients with breast cancer. *Annals of Surgical Oncology, 11*, 328–339.

Prehn, R. T. (1994). Cancers beget mutations versus mutations beget cancers. *Cancer Research*, *54*(5), 296–300.

Robbins, S. L, & Cotran, R. S. (1979). Neoplasia. In Robbins S. L., & Cotran R. S., *Pathologic basis of disease* (pp. 141–187). Philadephia, PA: W. B. Saunders Company.

Shiff, S. J., & Rigas, B. (1999). The role of cyclooxygenase inhibition in the antineoplastic effects of nonsteroidal anti-inflammatory drugs (NSAIDs). *Journal of Experimental Medicine*, *190*, 445–450.

Soto, A. M., & Sonnenschein, C. (2004). The somatic mutation theory of cancer: Growing problems with the paradigm? *Biosessays*, *26*(10), 1097–1107.

Spalding, K. L., Bhardwaj, R. D., Buchholz, B. A., Druid, H., & Frisén, J. (2005). Retrospective birth dating of cells in humans. *Cell*, *122*(1), 133–143.

Sugimura, T. (2000). Nutrition and dietary carcinogens. *Carcinogenesis*, *21*(3), 387–395.

Verma, M., Maruvada, P., & Srivastara, S. (2004). Epigenetics and cancer. *Critical Reviews in Clinical Laboratory Sciences*, *41*, 5–6.

Virchow, R. (1863). Aetiologie der neoplastischen Geschwulst/Pathogenie der neoplastischen Geschwulste. In: *Die Krankhaften Geschwulste* (pp. 57–101). Berlin, Germany: Verlag von August Hirschwald.

Warburg, O. (1956). On the origin of cancer cells. *Science*, *123*(3191), 309–314.

Warburg, O., Posener, K., & Negelein, E. (1924). Über den Stoffwechsel der Carcinomzelle. *Biochemische Zeitschrift*, *152*, 309–344.

Wijnhoven, B. P. L., Dinjens, W. N. M., & Pignatelli, M. (2000). E-cadherin-catenin cell-cell adhesion complex and human cancer. *British Journal of Surgery*, *87*, 992–1005.

zur Hausen, H. (1991). Viruses in human cancers. *Science*, *254*(5035), 1167–1173.

2

Global Epidemiology of Cancer

GLOBAL BURDEN OF CANCER

"There is no term in the entire lexicon of medicine that strikes more terror than the word 'cancer,' and with considerable justification" (Robbins & Cotran, 1979). That quote from the classic text *Pathologic Basis of Disease* written in 1974 by Stanley L. Robbins and Ramzi S. Cotran still rings true with the writing of this book 40 years later. Despite unprecedented medical and public health efforts, many forms of cancer still remain incurable and prematurely strike down millions of people each year. The metastatic spread of cancer to vital organs of the body usually results in massive tissue destruction, loss of life-sustaining functions, and ultimately, the untimely death of the human host.

Based on data recently published by the International Agency for Research on Cancer (IARC) and the World Health Organization (WHO), 14.1 million new cases of cancer and 8.2 million cancer deaths occurred in the world population during 2012. These estimates reflect increases of 11.9% in new cases of cancer and 7.9% in cancer deaths since 2008 (Boyle & Levin, 2008; Ferlay et al., 2010, 2013).

Among the 14.1 million new cases of cancer diagnosed in 2012, 1.82 million (12.9%) were cancers of the lung. Cancers of the breast (1.68 million), colon and rectum (1.36 million), prostate (1.11 million), stomach (0.95 million), liver (0.78 million), and cervix (0.54 million) accounted for an additional 45.5% of all new cases.

Lung cancer was by far the deadliest malignancy, causing 1.59 million deaths (19.4% of the total cancer deaths), more than double the number of deaths from any other malignancy. Cancers of the liver (0.75 million), stomach (0.72 million), colon and rectum (0.69 million), breast (0.52 million), pancreas (0.33 million), prostate (0.31 million), cervix (0.27 million), leukemias (0.27 million), and lymphomas (0.23 million) caused an additional 50% of the total cancer deaths. The ratio of mortality to incidence (a crude measure of case fatality) was highest for pancreatic cancer (98%), liver cancer (94%), lung cancer (85%), and esophageal cancer (83%) (Ferlay et al., 2013).

Cancer deaths now constitute approximately 13.5% of the 60 million annual deaths in the world population. Among people of all ages, cancer is the third leading cause of death (behind heart disease and infectious conditions); in people living in economically developed countries such as the United States and Great Britain, cancer has now surpassed heart disease as the leading cause of death in people under the age of 85 years (Ferlay et al., 2010, 2013; Jemal et al., 2011; Thun, DeLancey, Center, Jemal, & Ward, 2010). According to a recent estimate by investigators at the IARC, "nearly 170 million years of healthy life were lost due to cancer worldwide in 2008" (Soerjomataram et al., 2012).

GLOBAL BURDEN OF CANCER IN MEN AND WOMEN

The global burden of cancer is markedly higher in men than in women. In 2012, the number of cancer deaths among men (4.65 million) was 31% higher than among women (3.55 million). In the same year, the age-standardized cancer incidence in men was 24% higher than in women (205.4 per 100,000 versus 165.3 per 100,000), and the age-standardized cancer mortality in men was 52% higher than in women (126.3 per 100,000 versus 82.9 per 100,000) (Ferlay et al., 2013).

The deadliest cancers differ in men and women. Of the 4.65 million deaths from cancer in men during 2012, approximately 25% (1.17 million) were caused by lung cancer and other malignancies of the respiratory

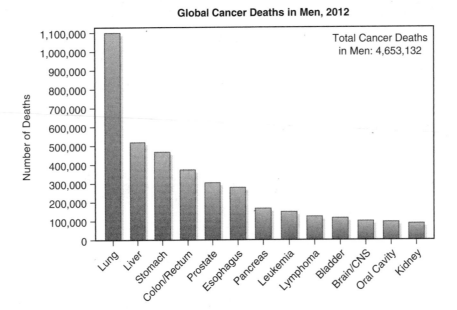

Global Cancer Deaths in Men, 2012

Total Cancer Deaths
in Men: 4,653,132

Figure 2.1 Deaths from Cancer in Men Worldwide, 2012.

Source: Data from Ferlay, J., Shin, H. R., Bray, F., Forman, D., Mathers, C., & Parkin, D. M. (2010). Estimates of worldwide burden of cancer in 2008: GLOBOCAN 2008. *International Journal of Cancer, 127,* 2893–2917; Ferlay, J., Soerjomataram, I., Ervik, M., Dikshit, R., Eser, S., Mathers, C., . . . Bray, F. (2013). *GLOBOCAN 2012 v1.0. Cancer incidence and mortality worldwide: IARC CancerBase No. 11* [Internet]. Lyon, France: International Agency for Research on Cancer.

tract (larynx, trachea) and 40% (1.88 million) were caused by malignancies of the gastrointestinal tract (stomach, liver, esophagus, colon/rectum, gallbladder, pancreas, and oral cavity). An additional 11% of male cancer deaths (0.53 million) were caused by malignancies of the genitourinary tract (prostate, testes, kidneys, bladder), and 7% (0.33 million) were due to lymphomas and leukemias (Ferlay et al., 2013) (**Figure 2.1**).

In 2012, nearly 3.55 million women died from cancer in the world population. Breast cancer caused the most deaths (0.52 million), followed closely by lung cancer (0.49 million). Gastrointestinal cancers (stomach, liver, esophagus, colon/rectum, gallbladder, pancreas, and oral cavity) together accounted for 1.20 million deaths, and malignancies of the genitourinary tract (uterus, cervix, and ovaries) caused 0.49 million deaths. Lymphomas and leukemias caused an additional 0.21 million deaths among women worldwide (Ferlay et al., 2013) (**Figure 2.2**).

HISTOLOGICAL PROFILE OF GLOBAL CANCER

Carcinomas arising from epithelial cells lining various anatomic organs make up the vast majority of malignant neoplasms. The site-specific global cancer data for 2012 suggest that more than 90% of new cases were carcinomas; other forms of cancer (leukemias, lymphomas, myelomas, sarcomas, germ cell

tumors, and brain tumors) accounted for the remainder (Ferlay et al., 2013). This 9 to 1 prominence of carcinomas relative to other forms of cancer reflects the markedly higher rates of cell division in epithelial cell populations compared to other cell populations (e.g., muscle, fat, bone, brain, nervous system, and immune system).

GLOBAL TRENDS IN CANCER

Estimated numbers of new cancer cases and deaths from cancer have increased steadily in the 21st century (Boyle & Levin, 2008; Ferlay et al., 2010, 2013; Parkin, Bray, Ferlay, & Pisani, 2001; World Health Organization [WHO], 2004) (**Figure 2.3**). During the period 2000–2012, the annual number of new cases increased by nearly 40% (from 10.1 million to 14.1 million), and the annual number of cancer deaths increased by 32% (from 6.2 million to 8.2 million). However, it is important to realize that these startling increases in new cancer cases and deaths from cancer have been driven largely by the growth and aging of the world population. During the time period 2000–2012, the world population increased from 6 to 7 billion (~17%) and life expectancy increased from 68 to 71 years (~4%) (World Bank, 2014). Because the majority of malignancies are diagnosed late in life (e.g., 55–60% of new cases are diagnosed after age 65 years), elderly populations

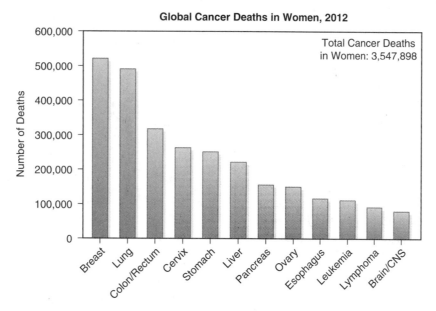

Figure 2.2 Deaths from Cancer in Women Worldwide, 2012.

Source: Data from Ferlay, J., Shin, H. R., Bray, F., Forman, D., Mathers, C., & Parkin, D. M. (2010). Estimates of worldwide burden of cancer in 2008: GLOBOCAN 2008. *International Journal of Cancer, 127,* 2893–2917; Ferlay, J., Soerjomataram, I., Ervik, M., Dikshit, R., Eser, S., Mathers, C., . . . Bray, F. (2013). *GLOBOCAN 2012 v1.0. Cancer incidence and mortality worldwide: IARC CancerBase No. 11* [Internet]. Lyon, France: International Agency for Research on Cancer.

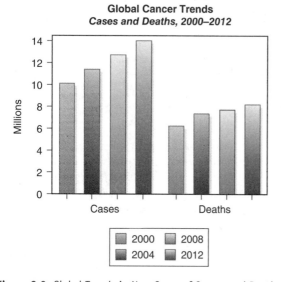

Figure 2.3 Global Trends in New Cases of Cancer and Deaths from Cancer During the 21st Century.

Source: Data from Boyle, P., & Levin, B. (Eds.). (2008). *IARC world cancer report.* Lyon, France: International Agency for Research on Cancer (IARC) Publications; Ferlay, J., Shin, H. R., Bray, F., Forman, D., Mathers, C., & Parkin, D. M. (2010). Estimates of worldwide burden of cancer in 2008: GLOBOCAN 2008. *International Journal of Cancer, 127,* 2893–2917; Ferlay, J., Soerjomataram, I., Ervik, M., Dikshit, R., Eser, S., Mathers, C., . . . Bray, F. (2013). *GLOBOCAN 2012 v1.0. Cancer incidence and mortality worldwide: IARC CancerBase No. 11* [Internet]. Lyon, France: International Agency for Research on Cancer; Parkin, D. M., Bray, F., Ferlay, J., & Pisani, P. (2001). Estimating the world cancer burden: GLOBOCAN 2000. *International Journal of Cancer, 94,* 153–156; World Health Organization. (2004). *Global burden of disease 2004 update.* Geneva, Switzerland: Author.

are expected to have higher crude (unadjusted) rates of cancer than younger populations.

METHODOLOGY

Incidence and Mortality

Incidence is the number of new cases arising during a specific period of time in a defined population. *Mortality* is the number of deaths occurring during a defined period of time in a specified population. Incidence and mortality are often expressed as rates per 100,000 persons per year. Incidence and mortality rates can be estimated for specific age groups or exposure groups within populations.

Age-Standardized Cancer Rates

Age-standardization is a technique that adjusts cancer rates for differences in the age distributions of populations being compared. This technique is very useful in examining trends in rates of cancer over time or comparing rates in different populations. This is because the incidence and mortality rates for most cancers increase rapidly with age, so that populations containing a high proportion of old people will tend to have a higher overall (crude) rate than one with mainly young people. Age standardization adjusts the age-specific rates of populations being compared to the age structure of a

(continues)

Age-Standardized Cancer Rates (continued)

reference population. In the direct method of age standardization, age-specific rates for successive 5-year age intervals (e.g., 0–4, 5–9, 10–14, 15–19, 20–24) are weighted by the age distribution of a standard (reference) population (e.g., the standard world population). The formula for calculating an age-standardized rate from a set of age-specific rates estimated for a population using the age distribution of the world population is

$$ASR(W) = \Sigma \, r f$$

where r is the age-specific rate and f is the frequency of the world population in the corresponding 5-year age interval (Ahmad et al., 2001; Stewart & Kleihues, 2003).

Global Trends in Cancer Incidence and Mortality

The age-standardized rates of annual cancer incidence and mortality estimated for the world population during 2000–2012 reflect distinctly different patterns and much smaller changes than the dramatically increased numbers of new cancer cases and cancer deaths (40% and 32%, respectively) observed during the same time period. In men, annual cancer incidence rates increased by 1.7% during 2000–2012 (from 201.9 to 205.4 cases per 100,000), whereas in women, rates increased by 4.8% (from 157.8 cases to 165.3 cases per 100,000). In contrast, annual cancer mortality rates peaked for both men and women in 2002 and have since declined (from 137.7 to 126.3 deaths per 100,000 in men and from 92.1 to 82.9 deaths per 100,000 in women, *decreases* of 8% and 10%, respectively) (**Figure 2.4**). The age-standardized rates thus reflect decreasing cancer mortality in the face of slight increases in cancer incidence and marked increases in the numbers of new cases of cancer and cancer deaths in the world population since the turn of the century (Boyle & Levin, 2008; Ferlay et al., 2010, 2013; Parkin, Bray, Ferlay, & Pisani, 2005; Parkin et al., 2001).

Although the examination of combined data from national registries and surveillance systems is critical in establishing global trends and patterns of cancer, such ecological studies must be supplemented by intensive epidemiologic and molecular investigations of individual forms of malignancy in order to elucidate causation. Indeed, there is considerable variation in the incidence and mortality of different cancers by geographic area of the world, which is a consequence not only of growth and aging of the inherent populations, but also of many other factors such as exposure to causative agents (e.g., tobacco

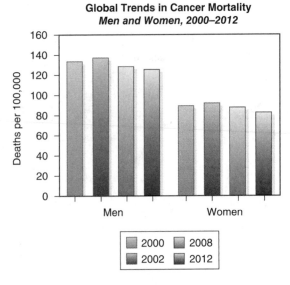

Global Trends in Cancer Mortality
Men and Women, 2000–2012

Figure 2.4 Global Trends in Age-Standardized Mortality Rates of Cancer for Men and Women During the 21st Century.

Rates are standardized to the world standard population.

Source: Data from Boyle, P., & Levin, B. (Eds.). (2008). *IARC world cancer report.* Lyon, France: International Agency for Research on Cancer (IARC) Publications; Ferlay, J., Shin, H. R., Bray, F., Forman, D., Mathers, C., & Parkin, D. M. (2010). Estimates of worldwide burden of cancer in 2008: GLOBOCAN 2008. *International Journal of Cancer, 127,* 2893–2917; Ferlay, J., Soerjomataram, I., Ervik, M., Dikshit, R., Eser, S., Mathers, C.,... Bray, F. (2013). *GLOBOCAN 2012 v1.0. Cancer incidence and mortality worldwide: IARC CancerBase No. 11* [Internet]. Lyon, France: International Agency for Research on Cancer; Parkin, D. M., Bray, F., Ferlay, J., & Pisani, P. (2005). Global cancer statistics, 2002. *CA: A Cancer Journal for Clinicians, 55,* 74–108; Parkin, D. M., Bray, F., Ferlay, J., & Pisani, P. (2001). Estimating the world cancer burden: GLOBOCAN 2000. *International Journal of Cancer, 94,* 153–156.

and alcohol), development of predisposing conditions (e.g., obesity, inflammation, infection, and other chronic conditions), and access to screening and health care. For example, overall cancer incidence rates estimated from 45 cancer registries were found to vary by sixfold in men (82 per 100,000 in Algerians to 453 per 100,000 in African Americans) and fourfold in women (80 per 100,000 in Algerians to 302 per 100,000 in Caucasian Americans) (Jemal, Center, DeSantis, & Ward, 2010). Furthermore, incidence and mortality rates of many forms of cancer are decreasing in populations of developed countries such as the United States but are surging in populations of less-developed countries with their adoption of unhealthy lifestyles that increase cancer risk (e.g., addiction to tobacco and alcohol, lack of exercise, chronic exposure to infectious agents, and consumption of diets high in fat and calories) (Jemal et al., 2010; Stewart & Wild, 2014). Factors that increase or decrease cancer risk are discussed in the following sections of this chapter.

CANCER IN DEVELOPING VERSUS DEVELOPED NATIONS

Profiles of cancer differ dramatically in developing versus developed nations (Garcia et al., 2007; Jemal et al., 2010, 2011). Among men living in developing nations, the total number of deaths due to either liver cancer or stomach cancer is more than four times higher than in developed nations, reflecting high rates of infection by liver viruses (hepatitis B virus [HBV] and hepatitis C virus [HCV]) and stomach bacteria (e.g., *Helicobacter pylori*), plus contamination of food supplies by molds that produce highly carcinogenic aflatoxins. Reciprocally, deaths from colorectal cancer or prostate cancer occur more frequently in men living in developed nations, partly due to diets high in fat and calories and low in fiber, fruits, and vegetables. Lung cancer, caused predominantly by chronic tobacco smoking, is the leading cause of cancer death in men of developing and developed nations (**Figure 2.5**).

Breast cancer is the leading cause of death from cancer among women in both developing and developed nations. Among women living in developing nations, cancer of the uterine cervix is the second leading cause of death from cancer, principally due to lack of screening for premalignant dysplastic lesions of the cervical mucosa. Lung cancer causes nearly as many deaths as breast cancer in developed nations, and rising rates of smoking among women worldwide have resulted in increasing numbers of female lung cancer deaths in all populations. Death from stomach cancer or liver cancer occurs more frequently in developing nations, whereas cancers of the colon and rectum, pancreas, and ovaries cause relatively more deaths in developed nations (**Figure 2.6**).

The contrasting patterns of cancer in the populations of developing and developed nations reflect the impact of major differences in lifestyles, environmental exposures, and access to health care. Developing nations are characterized by poverty and as a consequence, large segments of their populations suffer from inadequate nutrition, poor sanitation and hygiene, polluted environments, and lack of access to preventive, diagnostic, and therapeutic health care resources. Environmental conditions in impoverished populations favor transmission of infectious diseases that predispose to cancers of the stomach, liver, uterine cervix, and other exposed tissues. Without resources for prevention, screening, and early detection, case fatality rates are high and survival short for all forms of cancer in such populations.

In developed nations, advanced public health systems have been designed and implemented to ensure food and water safety, improve sanitation and personal hygiene, reduce pollution, and provide timely access to health care. Notably, such measures have resulted in higher standards of living and increased life spans in these populations. Nevertheless, the obesity pandemic arising from dietary excesses and sedentary lifestyles has contributed to high rates of cancers of the colon, rectum, pancreas, breast, and prostate in developed nations.

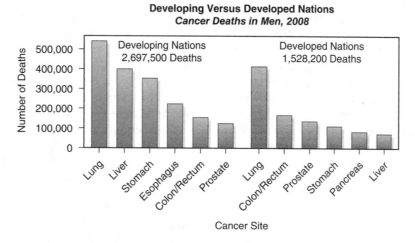

Figure 2.5 Deaths from Cancer Among Men in Developing Versus Developed Nations, 2008.

Developing nations include populations of Africa, the Caribbean, Central America, South America, Asia (less Japan), and Oceania (Melanesia, Micronesia, and Polynesia). Developed nations include populations of North America, Europe, the Russian Federation, Japan, and Australia/ New Zealand.

Source: Data from Jemal, A., Center, M. M., DeSantis, C., & Ward, E. M. (2010). Global patterns of cancer incidence and mortality rates and trends. *Cancer Epidemiology, Biomarkers and Prevention, 19*, 1893–1907; Jemal, A., Bray, F., Center M. M., Ferlay, J., Ward E., & Forman, D. (2011). Global cancer statistics. *CA: A Cancer Journal for Clinicians, 61*(2), 69–90.

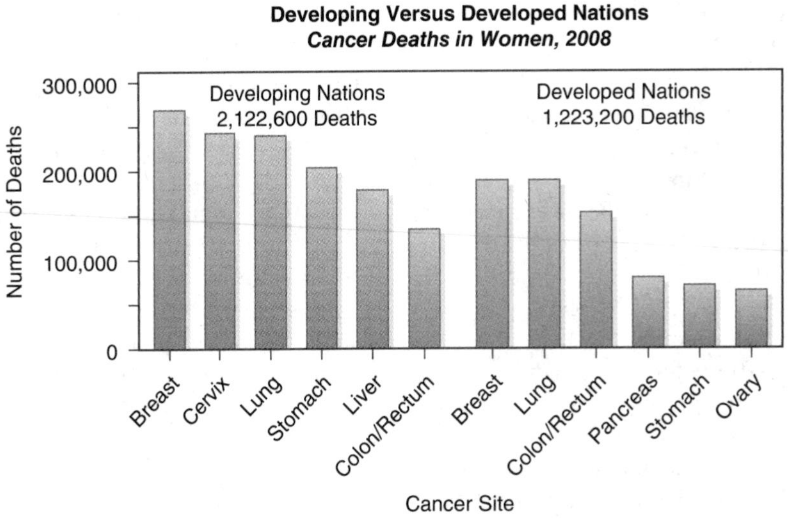

Figure 2.6 Deaths from Cancer Among Women in Developing Versus Developed Nations, 2008.

Developing nations include populations of Africa, the Caribbean, Central America, South America, Asia (less Japan), and Oceania (Melanesia, Micronesia, and Polynesia). Developed nations include populations of North America, Europe, the Russian Federation, Japan, and Australia/ New Zealand.

Source: Data from Jemal, A., Center, M. M., DeSantis, C., & Ward, E. M. (2010). Global patterns of cancer incidence and mortality rates and trends. *Cancer Epidemiology, Biomarkers and Prevention, 19*, 1893–1907; Jemal, A., Bray, F., Center M. M., Ferlay, J., Ward E., & Forman, D. (2011). Global cancer statistics. *CA: A Cancer Journal for Clinicians, 61*(2), 69–90.

One common theme in both developing and developed nations is the continuing addiction of many people to tobacco smoking. Most disturbingly, the total number of smokers is rising globally, and it is indeed startling that worldwide, more than 1 billion men and women smoke cigarettes. While smoking rates have declined in some developed countries such as the United States and Australia that have instituted antismoking campaigns, smoking bans in public places, and higher cigarette taxes, smoking rates are rising sharply in many populations, especially in low- and middle-income nations where there is virtually no education about the specific health risks of tobacco use. It is estimated that 80% of current smokers live in the developing world, a fact that heralds an impending global epidemic of lung cancer and other tobacco-related diseases (WHO, 2008, 2013). More details on tobacco and cancer appear in a later section of this chapter.

CANCER MORTALITY IN THE UNITED STATES

Despite the declaration of war on cancer by President Richard Nixon in 1971, new cases of cancer and deaths from cancer continue to increase in the United States. Shortly after this presidential declaration, the U.S. National Cancer Institute (NCI) established the Surveillance, Epidemiology, and End Results (SEER) program in order to monitor the impact of cancer in the United States. Data collection by member tumor registries of SEER began January 1, 1973. The SEER program currently collects and publishes cancer incidence and survival data from 18 population-based cancer registries covering approximately 26% of the U.S. population including all ethnic groups. The SEER registries routinely collect data on patient demographics, primary tumor site, tumor morphology and stage at diagnosis, first course of treatment, and follow-up for vital status. The SEER program is the only comprehensive source of population-based information in the United States that includes stage of cancer at the time of diagnosis and patient survival data (Horner et al., 2009; SEER, 2014).

Based on recent estimates, approximately 1.66 million new cases of invasive cancer are being diagnosed annually in the United States (excluding carcinomas in situ, and basal and squamous cell carcinomas of the skin), and more than 580,000 Americans die from cancer annually (about 1,600 people each day). Lung cancer is the leading cause of cancer deaths in both men and women (American Cancer Society, 2013).

Figures 2.7 and **2.8** show chronological trends in cancer mortality for U.S. men and women for the period 1930–2010 (American Cancer Society, 2013). Among men, more than half of cancer deaths are

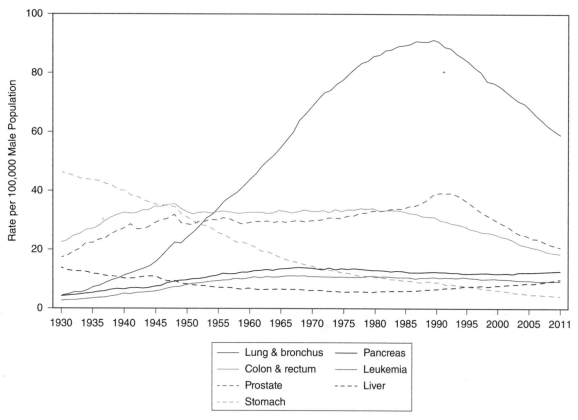

Note: Per 100,000, age adjusted to the 2000 U.S. standard population. Due to changes in ICD coding, numerator information has changed over time. Rates for cancer of the liver, lung and bronchus, and colon and rectum are affected by these coding changes.

Figure 2.7 Trends in Cancer Mortality Among U.S. Men, 1930–2011.

Reprinted from American Cancer Society. Cancer Facts and Figures 2015. Atlanta: American Cancer Society, Inc.

due to cancers of the lung and bronchus, prostate, colon, and rectum. Although lung cancer mortality has declined slightly since about 1990, the male death rates from this malignancy are still more than double that of any other anatomic site. In 1987, prostate cancer surpassed colorectal cancer as the second leading cause of cancer deaths in men. During the past two decades, the mortality rates for both prostate and colorectal cancer show evidence of a gradual decline. Mortality rates for other malignancies have remained fairly constant, with the exception of the rates for stomach cancer, which have declined dramatically beginning in about 1930, similar to the pattern for women (American Cancer Society, 2015).

Among women, cancers of the lung and bronchus, breast, and colon and rectum account for more than half of all cancer deaths. In 1987, lung cancer surpassed breast cancer as the leading cause of cancer death in women. Since 1950, lung cancer mortality among U.S. women has increased by more than 600%; it now accounts for about 25%

of all female cancer deaths. Breast cancer mortality remained remarkably constant throughout the 20th century but appears to be declining slightly in recent years. Mortality rates for cervical cancer and stomach cancer steadily declined from high to low levels during the same time period. Colorectal cancer mortality has also gradually declined since the 1950s from rates above 30 per 100,000 to rates now lower than 20 deaths per 100,000 (American Cancer Society, 2015).

The declines in mortality for some forms of cancer in the U.S. population reflect reductions in smoking and other risk factors plus earlier detection and better therapies; however, not all demographic groups have benefitted equally. Indeed, cancer mortality and incidence rates vary considerably by race and by gender. In particular, men have about 30% higher cancer death rates than women, and African American men have the highest death rates from cancers of the lung and bronchus, prostate, and colon and rectum compared to any of the other racial or ethnic groups in the United States.

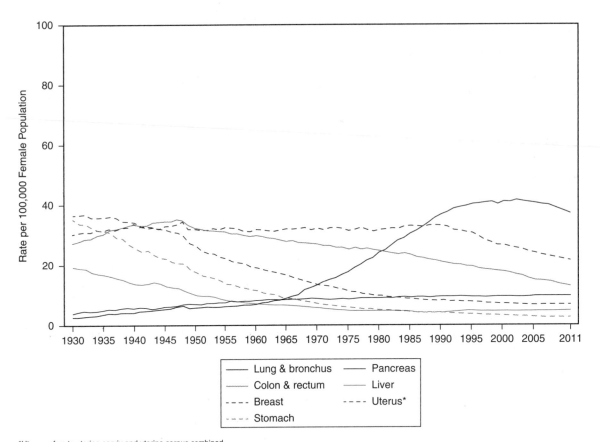

*Uterus refers to uterine cervix and uterine corpus combined.
Note: Due to changes in ICD coding, numerator information has changed over time. Rates for cancer of the lung and bronchus, colon and rectum, and ovary are affected by these coding changes.

Figure 2.8 Trends in Cancer Mortality Among U.S. Women, 1930–2011.

Reprinted from American Cancer Society. Cancer Facts and Figures 2015. Atlanta: American Cancer Society, Inc.

EPIDEMIOLOGIC TRANSITION OF CANCER

The 2014 World Cancer Report released by the World Health Organization warns of an impending "tidal wave" of cancer in many populations of the world (Stewart & Wild, 2014). The rising global burden of cancer is a prominent feature of the *epidemiologic transition* whereby chronic diseases are gradually replacing acute diseases in the world population. This phenomenon is undoubtedly a consequence of the improving economic standards of many nations, which has translated into better health and greater longevity for their native populations. But although good health coupled with increasing longevity is generally viewed as beneficial, it is also clear that the epidemiologic transition has produced a concomitant risk of chronic pathogenic processes that are typically manifested later in life. Such is the case for most adult forms of cancer, which are usually diagnosed after years and often decades of growth and development during which there are no detectable clinical symptoms.

Figure 2.9 shows the increasing proportion of incident cancers in older versus younger adults since 1980 and the corresponding data for developing versus developed regions of the world. During the period 1980–2010, the proportion of incident cancers diagnosed among people living in economically developing regions increased from 50% to 65%, and the proportion of new cases diagnosed in people over 65 years of age increased from 35% to 55% (Bray & Moller, 2006; Thun et al., 2010). Clearly, the greatest increases in cancer rates have occurred in the elderly populations of low and middle income nations (e.g., the developing regions). Based on the latest available global cancer statistics, approximately 60% of new cancer cases and 70% of all cancer deaths now occur in Africa, Asia, Central America, and South America (Stewart & Wild, 2014). Such populations have a virtual "perfect storm" of increasing longevity coupled with predisposing behavioral factors and conditions that increase cancer risk (e.g., addiction to tobacco and alcohol, unhealthy nutrition, obesity, physical

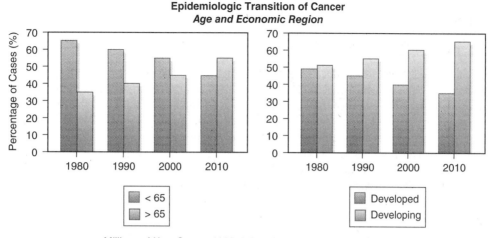

Epidemiologic Transition of Cancer
Age and Economic Region

Millions of New Cases: 1980: 6.6, 1990: 8.1, 2000: 10.1, 2010: 13.3

Figure 2.9 Relative Frequency of New Cases of Cancer by Age and Economic Region, 1980–2010.

Source: Data from Bray, F., & Moller, B. (2006). Predicting the future burden of cancer. *Nature Reviews Cancer, 6,* 63–74.

inactivity, and widespread exposure to certain sexually transmitted infectious agents that predispose to malignant transformation).

WEB OF CAUSATION OF CANCER

Most (if not all) cancers are caused by the cumulative effects of multiple causal factors that interact in a *web of causation*. As a consequence, establishing definitive proof of causality and quantifying the contribution of an individual risk factor to causation are challenging. In 1964, in the U.S. Surgeon General's Report to the Nation on Smoking and Lung Cancer, an international panel of imminent scientists formulated the "criteria of judgment" for establishing causality of a disease (U.S. Surgeon General, 1964). In a subsequent paper, British epidemiologist Bradford Hill (1965) expounded on these criteria and developed a general framework for establishing causal inference from associations observed in epidemiologic investigations. The criteria of judgment include (1) consistency of the association across independent studies, (2) strength of the association and dose response of increasing risk with increasing exposure, (3) a temporal relationship between exposure and pathogenesis, (4) biological plausibility of the association, and (5) coherence of the association when the totality of evidence is considered. Fulfillment of these criteria is essential in establishing the causal significance of a risk factor.

Evidence for or against causality of disease by a putative disease-modifying factor may come from different types of epidemiologic investigations. In prospective cohort studies, enrolled individuals are examined and queried at baseline to gather information about exposures and conditions that may influence their cancer risk; these individuals are then followed over time to determine who develops disease and who remains healthy. Such studies provide direct estimates of *relative risk (RR)* for specific factors and conditions. In retrospective case control studies, cases with a specific form of cancer are compared to matched controls without cancer to assess differences in exposure variables. In these studies, risk is quantified by estimating the *odds ratio (OR)* for specific factors and conditions.

Consistency, strength of association, and dose response can be examined simultaneously by a *meta-analysis* of independent epidemiologic studies. Homogeneity of relative risk estimates and heightened disease risk with increasing exposure (dose response) favor causality. Proof of biological plausibility and establishing the temporal sequence of exposure and pathogenesis rely on laboratory and molecular studies. It is important that such studies reveal a biologically plausible molecular mechanism of pathogenesis associated with exposure to the risk factor. Coherence infers that all evidence "sticks together" and that the proposed causal relationship is supported by the totality of evidence.

In summary, causal inference requires fulfillment of all of the criteria of judgment: observational studies of individuals and populations showing that exposure significantly elevates disease risk, laboratory and molecular studies of exposed human tissues and specimens that reveal a biologically plausible molecular mechanism of pathogenesis, and if available, randomized clinical trials and field trials of prevention and therapy targeting the causal risk factor that effectively reduce disease risk.

Methodology

Incidence and Relative Risk

The standard measure of effect in a *prospective* epidemiologic study is the relative risk (RR), which quantifies the increase or decrease in the incidence of disease with exposure to a putative disease-modifying factor. Prospective cohort studies are designed to track health outcomes in defined samples of individuals (cohorts) who are disease-free at baseline. Individuals in the cohort are initially classified according to factors that may influence disease risk and are then followed over time to detect new cases of the disease under study. The *RR* is calculated from a prospective cohort study as the ratio of disease incidence among those exposed to a factor to the disease incidence among those not exposed to the factor: $RR = i_e / i_o$, where i_e = the incidence rate with exposure and i_o = the incidence rate without exposure. Estimates of RR are interpreted as follows:

- RR = 1.0 suggests that the factor has no effect.
- RR > 1.0 suggests that the factor increases the risk.
- RR < 1.0 suggests that the factor decreases the risk.

Hazard Ratio

A related measure of risk is the *hazard ratio (HR)*, a parameter that is estimated by regression analysis of prospective data in which the *time to event* from baseline is recorded. Like the RR, HR = 1.0 suggests no effect, HR > 1.0 suggests increased risk, and HR < 1.0 suggests decreased risk. The difference between RR and HR is that the RR is a cumulative measure of risk at a single point in time (usually at the end of the follow-up period) whereas the HR measures the ratio of disease risk among subjects with exposure to a factor compared to subjects without exposure *at any point in time during the entire follow-up period*. Hence, HR = 1.50 indicates that those with exposure are at 50% greater risk than those without exposure *at any point in time during follow-up*, whereas RR = 1.50 indicates that those with exposure are at 50% greater risk than those without exposure *at the end of the follow-up period*.

Odds and Odds Ratio

The standard measure of effect in a retrospective epidemiologic study is the *odds ratio (OR)*. The OR is estimated from retrospective case control studies wherein cases with a disease are compared to controls without the disease. In case control studies, it is very important to assemble a sample of controls that are matched to the cases by age, gender, location, and other factors to assure that they have the same opportunity for exposure to putative disease-modifying factors as the cases. The OR is calculated as the ratio of the odds of exposure to a putative disease-modifying factor among cases to the odds of exposure among controls: OR = Exposure odds among cases / Exposure odds among controls. For diseases with low incidence rates, the odds ratio approximates the relative risk (OR ≈ RR). The OR and the RR are interpreted in similar fashion:

- OR = 1.0 suggests that the factor has no effect.
- OR > 1.0 suggests that the factor increases the risk.
- OR < 1.0 suggests that the factor decreases the risk.

Meta-Analysis of Risk Estimates

Meta-analysis is a procedure designed to formally evaluate the consistency of RR estimates from k independent studies and give an unbiased estimate of RR across all studies. Each estimate of RR with its 95% confidence interval (CI) is first converted to ln(RR) with a corresponding variance estimate (v). A combined estimate is then obtained in logarithmic form by weighting individual estimates by $w = 1 / v$. The formula for the combined estimate is ln(RR*) = Σw ln(RR) / Σw. This is simply the weighted average of the k logarithmic RR estimates where the weights (w) are the inverse of the corresponding error variances ($w = 1 / v$). The combined estimate is given by taking the antilog of ln(RR*), RR* = $e^{\ln RR^*}$. A chi square test of heterogeneity called *Cochran's Q test* can be utilized to test for differences among studies. The test statistic for this procedure is

$$Q = \Sigma w (\ln RR - \ln RR^*)^2$$

which is compared to a critical chi square value with $k - 1$ degrees of freedom (Borenstein, Hedges, Higgins, & Rothstein, 2009).

LIFESTYLE AND ENVIRONMENT IN CANCER DEVELOPMENT

British epidemiologists Richard Doll and Richard Peto first quantified the relative contribution of lifestyle and environmental factors to overall cancer mortality (Colditz, Selelrs, & Trapido, 2006; Doll & Peto, 1981). It is notable that only 5–10% of cancers can be attributed to germline (heritable) genetic defects, whereas the remaining 90–95% are attributable to environment and lifestyle. **Figure 2.10** shows the relative importance of broad classes of environmental and lifestyle factors as percentages of global cancer mortality. Of all cancer-related deaths, approximately 30% are due to chronic tobacco smoking, 30–35% are due to dietary factors (in particular, the excess consumption of calories resulting in obesity), 15–20% are due to cancer-causing infectious agents, and 3–4% are due to alcohol abuse (American Association for Cancer Research [AACR], 2012).

Various approaches have been used to quantify the impact of lifestyle and environmental factors on the risk of developing various forms of cancer. These include literature reviews, estimates of risk from prospective and retrospective studies, analysis of pooled data, and meta-analysis of published data (Colditz et al., 2006).

One widely used measure of the overall impact of an individual risk factor on a specific disease is the *population attributable risk* (also called the *population attributable fraction*). The population attributable risk quantifies the fraction of disease that is due to the presence of a particular risk factor in the population under investigation (e.g., the fraction of lung cancer due to cigarette smoking is about 85%). This parameter can also be thought of as the proportion of cancer cases that could be avoided if exposure to the risk factor was completely eliminated. It is important to remember that such estimates do not account for synergism between multiple factors in disease causation.

A recent investigation examined estimates of the population attributable cancer risk for selected lifestyle and environmental factors in the United Kingdom. Study results suggested that 43% of all incident cancers diagnosed in the U.K. population during 2010 were attributable to 14 major lifestyle and environmental factors. Smoking alone accounted for about 20% of all incident cases, and dietary factors (lack of fruits and vegetables, deficient fiber intake, excess consumption of red and processed meat, and high salt intake) and lack of exercise accounted for an additional 16% of cases (Parkin, Boyd, & Walker, 2011).

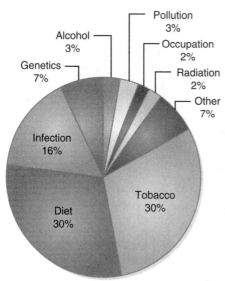

Risk Factors and Cancer

Figure 2.10 Lifestyle and Environmental Factors in Cancer Risk.

Source: Data from American Association for Cancer Research. (2012). AACR cancer progress report 2012. *Clinical Cancer Research, 18*, S1–S100.

METHODOLOGY

Population Attributable Risk

The standard formula for estimating the population attributable risk is PAR $= f_e(I_e - I_o) / I$, where f_e = frequency of exposure, I_e = incidence with exposure, I_o = incidence without exposure, and I = overall incidence. Note that because the relative risk (RR) $= I_e / I_o$ and overall incidence $= f_e I_e + (1 - f_e) I_o$, an alternative formula is PAR $= f_e(RR - 1) / (f_e[RR - 1] + 1)$.

TOBACCO AND CANCER

Tobacco smoking is the most important cancer risk factor. The World Health Organization reports that during the 20th century approximately 50 million people died from tobacco-associated cancers (WHO, 2006, 2008). It is estimated that approximately 50% of regular chronic smokers eventually succumb to tobacco-related cancer, and most die prematurely (International Agency for Cancer Research [IARC], 1986, 2004; Parkin et al., 2005; Peto, Lopez, Boreham, & Thun, 2006; Peto, Lopez, Boreham, Thun, & Heath, 1992; WHO, 2008). Multiple forms of cancer have been linked to chronic exposure of various organs to tobacco smoke, predominantly from smoking cigarettes but also from smoking tobacco in pipes, cigars, and bidis (thin cigarettes consisting of a small amount of tobacco wrapped in the leaf of the *tendu* tree, commonly used in India and South Asia). Tobacco smoking causes about 30% of all cancer deaths, making tobacco smoke the single most lethal source of carcinogens.

1964 U.S. Surgeon General's Report on Smoking and Health

The 1964 Surgeon General's Report on Smoking and Health was a landmark study that unequivocally linked tobacco to lung cancer, laryngeal cancer, and a number of other severe adverse health outcomes (Terry, 1964). This report was developed by a special committee of experts convened by U.S. Surgeon General Luther Terry to examine the existing evidence on smoking and disease. The report highlighted a number of deleterious health consequences of chronic cigarette smoking. Specifically, the report found that chronic smoking was etiologically linked to lung cancer, laryngeal cancer, chronic bronchitis, emphysema, and coronary heart disease. The 1964 Surgeon General's report and many subsequent reports have had a major impact on public attitudes and policy about smoking in the United States and most other developed nations. In the United States, the percentage of adults who smoke cigarettes has declined from 42% in 1964 to 18% in 2012, a trend that has occurred in the face of continuing concerted efforts by the tobacco industry to promote cigarette smoking and the use of other tobacco products. As a consequence of the declining prevalence of smoking, it is estimated that 8 million premature smoking-related deaths have been prevented in the U.S. population during the past half-century (Holford et al., 2014).

Despite the success of tobacco control in reducing premature deaths in the United States and some developed countries, tobacco use has continued to rise globally resulting in a "tobacco pandemic" that has become one of the greatest public health challenges of all time. Recent survey data compiled from the 193 member nations of the World Health Organization revealed the startling statistic that 1 in 3 adults in the world population smoke (**Figure 2.11**). An even more disturbing fact is that at least 5.4 million of the 1.1 billion adults who are chronically addicted to the smoking habit die annually from lung cancer and other smoking-related diseases such as heart disease, chronic obstructive pulmonary disease (COPD), stroke, and several other cancers (**Figure 2.12**) (WHO, 2006, 2008, 2013).

Compared to individuals who avoid the smoking habit, chronic smokers have a 15- to 30-fold increased risk of dying from lung cancer (Peto et al., 1992). Worldwide, approximately 85–90% of lung cancers in both men and women are attributable to cigarette smoking. Chronic tobacco use also markedly increases the risk of cancer development at many other anatomic sites, including the oral cavity, larynx, pharynx, nasal cavity, esophagus, stomach,

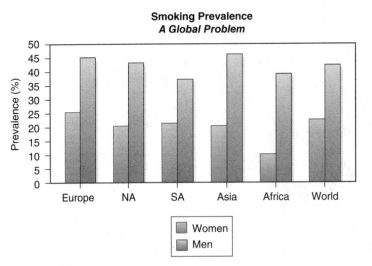

WHO: One-third of adults in the world population smoke.

Figure 2.11 Global Tobacco Addiction.

NA: North America; SA: South America.

Source: Data from World Health Organization. (2008). *WHO report on the global tobacco epidemic, 2008: The MPOWER package.* Geneva, Switzerland: Author.

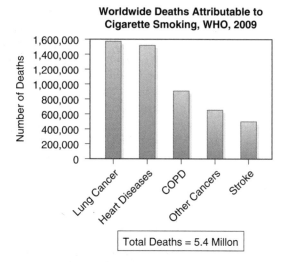

Worldwide Deaths Attributable to Cigarette Smoking, WHO, 2009

Total Deaths = 5.4 Million

Figure 2.12 Global Deaths and Tobacco Addiction.

Source: Data from World Health Organization. (2012). *WHO global report: Mortality attributable to tobacco.* Geneva, Switzerland: Author.

kidney, urinary bladder, pancreas, liver, and uterine cervix (**Figure 2.13**). Smoking has also been implicated in the development of certain types of leukemia, such as acute myelocytic leukemia (Gandini et al., 2008; IARC, 1986; Peto et al., 1992, 2006; Terry, 1964; Vineis et al., 2004; WHO, 2008).

The rise in female smoking prevalence is a critical public health concern. In the United States, more women now die from smoking-induced lung cancer than from breast cancer, and in some Nordic countries such as Iceland and Denmark, more women than men die from lung cancer. In several European countries, up to 50% of young women are regular smokers, and such high rates will inevitably produce an incredible burden of lung cancer and other smoking-related diseases in women for decades to come (Satcher, 2001).

Cigarette smoke contains three major classes of human carcinogens—polycyclic aromatic hydrocarbons, nitrosamines, and heterocyclic amines—all of which initiate tumors by causing DNA mutations; it also contains a variety of compounds that promote tumor growth and development. The interested reader is referred to a thorough review of tobacco carcinogenesis that discusses the carcinogens of tobacco smoke, carcinogen uptake and metabolism, and mechanisms by which tobacco carcinogens cause DNA mutations and DNA damage due to the formation of free radicals and reactive oxygen species (Hecht, 1999). Furthermore, cigarette smoke contains powerful stimulants of inflammation and sustained overexpression of inflammatory prostaglandins that upregulate most (if not all) of the molecular mechanisms involved in the genesis and metastasis of malignant neoplasms (Harris, 2007).

Other types of tobacco exposure also have been linked to the development of malignant neoplasms. Pipe and cigar smoking, chewing tobacco, and snuff dipping are all causes of oral cavity cancer, and chronic involuntary (passive) inhalation of tobacco smoke is a risk factor for lung cancer, particularly in women. In counseling individuals about the risk

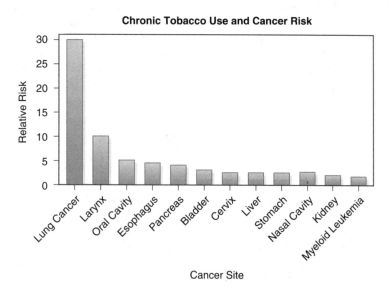

Chronic Tobacco Use and Cancer Risk

Figure 2.13 Relative Risk of Cancer and Chronic Tobacco Smoking.

Source: Data from Peto, R., Lopez, A. D., Boreham, J., Thun, M., & Heath, C. (1992). Mortality from smoking in developed countries: Indirect estimates from national vital statistics. *Lancet, 229,* 1268–1278; Peto, R., Lopez, A. D., Boreham, J., & Thun, M. (2006). *Mortality from smoking in developed countries 1950–2000* (2nd ed.). Geneva, Switzerland: Union for International Cancer Control (UICC).

of tobacco use, it is important to keep in mind that tobacco is a major risk factor not only for cancer, but also for a variety of other chronic life-threatening diseases, including cardiovascular disease, myocardial infarction, stroke, chronic bronchitis, emphysema, and asthma.

DIET AND CANCER

Only diet rivals tobacco smoke as a cause of cancer, accounting for a comparable number of deaths throughout the world each year. In developed nations, animal (saturated) fat and certain polyunsaturated fatty acids (PUFAs) are associated with cancers of the breast, prostate, and lower gastrointestinal tract (colon and rectum). In developed nations, high-fat diets are linked to the pathogenesis of colorectal cancer, prostate cancer, breast cancer, endometrial cancer, and several other malignancies. In developing nations, diets contaminated by inflammatory and carcinogenic substances often lead to the development of stomach cancer, esophageal cancer, or liver cancer.

The westernized diet of many affluent nations is characterized by the intake of excessive calories from fat, refined carbohydrates, sugar, and animal protein. The westernized diet combined with a sedentary lifestyle can quickly lead to energy imbalance associated with a multitude of chronic diseases such as obesity, type 2 diabetes, cardiovascular disease, arterial hypertension, and cancer. Obesity due to metabolic overload and lack of exercise has been linked to a number of malignancies in the United States and other developed nations. These include colorectal cancer, postmenopausal breast cancer, prostate cancer, endometrial cancer, ovarian cancer, kidney cancer, biliary cancer, and certain forms of esophageal cancer (Calle, Rodriguez, Walker-Thurmond, & Thun, 2003).

Certain types of polyunsaturated fats show differential effects on cancer development. For example, the inflammatory omega-6 polyunsaturated fatty acid (linoleic acid), which is abundant in the American westernized diet, has been linked to tumor initiation, promotion, and metastasis of colon cancer, breast cancer, endometrial cancer, ovarian cancer, and prostate cancer, whereas the anti-inflammatory omega-3 polyunsaturated fatty acid (linolenic acid), which is prominent in marine diets, shows antitumor effects.

Gastric esophageal reflux disease (GERD) is a distressing condition of the esophagus that is associated with obesity in the populations of developed nations. In GERD, reflux of stomach acid into the lower esophagus produces morphological changes and dysplasia of the squamous cell lining, a condition known as *Barrett's esophagus*. If left untreated, Barrett's esophagus can progress to invasive esophageal cancer, a highly lethal form of malignancy.

Among non-nutrient food additives, salt is a causal risk factor for stomach cancer, and the decline in stomach cancer mortality throughout the world is largely due to the replacement of salt as a food preservative by refrigeration and other techniques. Nevertheless, many developing nations continue to consume diets high in sodium, thereby resulting in high incidence and mortality rates of stomach cancer.

Aflatoxins are naturally occurring mycotoxins produced by many species of the fungus *Aspergillus*, most notably *Aspergillus flavus* and *Aspergillus parasiticus*. Molds that produce aflatoxins grow on whole grains such as corn, rice, and wheat, as well as on peanuts, almonds, walnuts, sunflower seeds, and spices such as black pepper and coriander. Aflatoxins can contaminate food and food products during processing, storage, or transport when conditions are favorable for mold growth.

Aflatoxin exposure occurs by the ingestion of contaminated foods. On entering the body, aflatoxins are metabolized by the liver into highly carcinogenic epoxides. Chronic exposure to aflatoxins produces liver cancer, a leading cause of death in populations of Southern China, Southeast Asia, and the eastern coastal regions of Africa. Furthermore, aflatoxins and hepatitis viruses (HBV and HCV) interact synergistically in the pathogenesis of liver cancer.

Regular exposure to burning hot beverages, alcohol, and other irritating substances may cause chronic inflammation and the development of dysplastic lesions of the squamous cell lining of the esophagus, a condition known as esophagitis. With continued exposure, such dysplastic changes often progress to esophageal cancer, which is frequently fatal. The practice of ingesting burning hot beverages is commonplace in many cultures of the Far East and the Middle East, where esophageal cancer is a leading cause of cancer death.

Links between diet and cancer may have as much to do with what is *not* in the diet as with what is. For example, low fiber coupled with high fat predisposes to colorectal cancer and perhaps other forms of cancer as well. Many fruits and vegetables contain antioxidants that neutralize free radicals and lessen carcinogenesis, so a lack of fruits and vegetables may contribute to many different types of cancer.

ALCOHOL AND CANCER

Consumption of alcoholic beverages is a major risk factor for malignancies of certain anatomic sites including the oral cavity, the larynx, the esophagus, the liver, and the pancreas. Alcohol abuse in conjunction with chronic cigarette smoking synergistically increases the risk of developing cancer at these anatomic sites. Many epidemiologic studies have also found that regular alcohol consumption independently increases the risk of colon cancer and breast cancer. In 1988, acetaldehyde, the main metabolite of ethanol, was classified as a potent human carcinogen by the International Agency for Research on Cancer and the World Health Organization (IARC & WHO, 1988). More recently, a team of international investigators examined associations between alcohol consumption and cancer risk on a global scale and estimated that 3.6% of all cancers and 3.5% of all cancer deaths are attributable to regular intake of alcoholic beverages (Boffetta, Mashibe, La Vecchia, Zatonski, & Rehm, 2006).

INFECTION AND CANCER

Chronic infections by specific viruses, bacteria, or parasites are responsible for a significant fraction of human cancer (Parkin, 2006). In a recent review and synthesis of global cancer data from 2008, it was estimated that 16.1% of the 12.7 million incident cancers were caused by infectious agents (de Martel et al., 2012).

In developing countries, more than 20% of malignancies and related deaths are caused by infectious agents that cause cervical cancer, liver cancer, stomach cancer, and certain other malignancies. Three pathogens account for a large proportion of the cancer burden in the populations of China, Asia, and Africa: hepatitis viruses (HBV and HCV), which cause liver cancer; sexually transmitted human papillomavirus (HPV) strains 16 and 18, which cause cervical cancer and certain other malignancies; and the food contaminant *Helicobacter pylori*, which causes stomach cancer.

In many regions of Central America, Southeast Africa, and India, where HPV infection rates are high and cervical screening programs are nonexistent, cervical cancer ranks first as a cause of cancer death. These populations also have high rates of human immunodeficiency virus (HIV), which predisposes to chronic HPV infection and the development of invasive cervical cancer. Today, more than 80% of all cervical cancer deaths occur in developing countries.

In populations of Eastern and Middle Africa where sexually transmitted diseases (STDs) are rampant, Kaposi's sarcoma due to co-infection by HIV and human herpes virus 8 (HHV-8, also known as Kaposi's sarcoma-associated herpesvirus or KSHV) has become the leading cause of cancer death. In the wetlands of China, India, and the Middle East, parasitic infections by schistosome worms are responsible for high rates of bladder cancer.

In sharp contrast to developing countries, chronic infections account for less than 10% of all malignancies in more developed nations. Stomach cancer has declined in many nations due to replacement of irritating preservatives by refrigeration and ready access to fresh fruits and vegetables and other food products that are free of contamination by *Helicobacter pylori*. Early cytological detection of cervical cancer by the Pap test has led to impressive reductions in cervical cancer mortality. Liver cancer rates have also declined in many nations, including China and Thailand, due to effective immunization programs to prevent viral hepatitis and improved storage conditions of staple foods to reduce aflatoxin exposure. Well-designed vaccination programs may prove effective in preventing other cancers arising from known infectious agents; for example, it is likely that vaccination against HBV and high-risk HPV strains may help prevent the development of liver cancer and cervical cancer, respectively.

GLOBAL CANCER PREVENTION AND CONTROL

Prevention of disease, including cancer, is often categorized into primary prevention, secondary prevention, and tertiary prevention. Primary prevention refers to avoidance of exposure to disease-causing risk factors. Secondary prevention refers to screening for the detection of antecedent conditions that predispose to disease and are curable by effective treatment or detection of disease at an early stage when effective treatment is likely to restore health. Tertiary prevention involves behavioral changes that limit the progression of disease and improve the quality of life after diagnosis.

A statement from the World Cancer Report, 2008, published by the International Association of Cancer Research (IARC), succinctly captures the essential objectives of effective cancer control:

The aim of cancer control is a reduction in both the incidence of the disease and the associated morbidity and mortality, as well as improved life for cancer patients and their families.

In addition to substantial opportunities for primary prevention, the World Cancer Report also emphasizes the potential of early detection, treatment, and palliative care. It urges all countries to establish comprehensive national cancer control programs, aimed at reducing the incidence of the disease and improving the quality of life for cancer patients and their families. In developing countries in particular, where a large proportion of cancers are detected late in the course of the disease, efforts to achieve earlier diagnosis and delivery of adequate palliative care and pain relief deserve urgent attention. (Boyle & Levin, 2008)

Despite intensive medical and public health efforts, cancer has now surpassed cardiovascular disease as the leading cause of death in people under age 85 years in highly developed nations such as the United States (Parkin et al., 2005). Although some progress has been made in cancer therapy, particularly in the treatment of leukemia in children, conventional methods of surgery, chemotherapy, and radiotherapy have not impacted greatly on the general morbidity and mortality due to many forms of cancer in adults. It is also important to realize that as developing countries succeed in achieving lifestyles similar to Europe, North America, Australia, New Zealand, and Japan, their populations will encounter much higher cancer rates, particularly cancers of the lung, breast, colon, prostate, and other malignancies that tend to appear later in life.

As pointed out by Dr. Moon Chen, Jr., in his review of cancer prevention and control for Asian and Pacific Islander Americans: "In order to achieve the full benefit of cancer prevention, attention must be directed to the unique cultural, linguistic, and behavioral attributes of Asian and Pacific Islander Americans." It is essential that this concept be extended to all target populations. In the words of Dr. Chen: "Effective cancer prevention and control initiatives must incorporate scientific validity, linguistic appropriateness, and cultural competence" (Chen, 1998).

Primary Cancer Prevention

At the core of all cancer prevention and control strategies are the following key elements of primary prevention (see also **Table 2.1**):

- Abstinence from tobacco and smoking cessation
- Limiting alcohol intake
- Regular exercise
- Maintaining optimum weight
- Eating a healthy diet with daily fruits and vegetables
- Limiting salt intake
- Practicing safe sex to avoid sexually transmitted diseases such as HPV strains 16 and 18 and HIV
- Avoiding exposure to hepatitis viruses such as HBV and HCV
- Vaccination against HPV and HBV
- Avoidance or early treatment of parasitic infections such as schistosomiasis
- Avoiding excessive exposure to sunlight and other sources of radiation such as radon

Table 2.1	Cancer Risk Factors and Preventive Strategies	
Risk Factor	**Cancer Sites**	**Prevention**
Tobacco use	Lung, pharynx, larynx, uterine cervix, bladder	Abstinence, cessation
Obesity, high fat and high calorie diet, sedentary lifestyle	Breast, prostate, colon, kidney, ovary, lower esophagus	Exercise, weight control, healthy diet with daily fruits and vegetables
Alcohol abuse	Oral cavity, esophagus, pancreas, liver	Limit alcohol intake to one drink or less daily
HPV STD	Uterine cervix, oral cavity, vulva, penis	Avoid exposure, vaccination
Hepatitis virus	Liver and biliary tract	Avoid exposure, vaccination
Helicobacter pylori and high salt intake	Stomach	Antibiotics, limit salt intake
Radiation	Skin (melanoma)	Limit sun exposure
Infectious disease	Lymphoma, leukemia	Good personal hygiene, safe sex practices, antibiotics and antivirals

- Infection control by good personal hygiene and judicious use of antibiotics and antiviral drugs
- Avoiding known chemical carcinogens such as asbestos (occupational hazard), arsenic (water contaminant), aflatoxins (food contaminant), and dioxin (environmental contaminant).

Keep in mind that this list of preventive strategies is far from inclusive and will require continual updating to keep pace with the identification of other carcinogenic factors present in the environment.

Secondary Cancer Prevention

Premalignant lesions and conditions that herald the development of cancer can usually be treated with a much higher likelihood of success than cancer itself. Effective cancer control therefore includes comprehensive cancer screening for the timely diagnosis and effective treatment of cellular lesions that could progress to invasive cancer. Proven screening methodologies with good sensitivity and specificity include mammograms for carcinoma in situ (CIS) of the breast, Papanicolaou (Pap) tests for cervical dysplasia, endoscopies for Barrett's esophagus and stomach ulcers, dental examination for oral leukoplakia, colonoscopy for colorectal adenomas and prostate-specific antigen (PSA), and ultrasound for noninvasive adenocarcinoma of the prostate gland. All of these lesions, if detected early, can be cured by limited surgical resection. Refinements in tissue imaging such as magnetic resonance (MR) and computed tomography (CT) have also led to improvements in the early detection of tumors.

Well-designed population screening programs coupled with skilled surgical excision or ablation of premalignant lesions have already been tremendously successful in reducing the mortality rates of certain cancers in developed nations. Currently, only about half of cancer patients in these populations eventually die from their disease. This differs markedly from developing nations wherein 80% of cancer victims already have late-stage (incurable) tumors when they are diagnosed.

These findings point out the need for development of much better early detection programs in many nations. Such screening modalities must be accurate, safe, inexpensive, and acceptable to the general public. Secondary prevention also mandates regular (annual) physical examinations for identification and treatment of chronic symptomatic medical conditions in individuals with inherent cancer risk factors such as chronic smoking and nicotine addiction, alcohol abuse, COPD, obesity, GERD, and chronic infections such as hepatitis and HIV.

Tertiary Cancer Prevention

Tertiary prevention emphasizes beneficial behavioral changes that limit disease progression and subsequent disability for patients after they have been diagnosed with cancer. Fundamental tertiary preventive practices include smoking cessation, limiting alcohol intake, regular exercise, improved diet, maintenance of optimum weight, and compliance with prescribed treatment regimens. Pain control and palliative care should be implemented when necessary. The ultimate goal of tertiary prevention is to improve the quality of life among cancer survivors and their families.

CANCER EDUCATION

Global cancer control polices have been adopted by the WHO, the IARC, the American Cancer Society (ACS), the NCI, and many other national and international health organizations. Nevertheless, there is an urgent need for all countries to establish comprehensive national cancer control programs with the objective of reducing cancer incidence and mortality through prevention.

Educational programs should be designed and implemented where they are needed in order to create a high degree of disease awareness regarding the risk factors and early symptoms of cancer and to disseminate accurate information on the cost, safety, and accuracy of cancer screening tests and the availability and effectiveness of cancer treatment modalities. In developing countries in particular, where a large proportion of cancers are detected late in the course of the disease, efforts to achieve earlier diagnosis and delivery of adequate treatment, palliative care, and pain relief deserve immediate attention.

Comprehensive programs of cancer prevention and control must also incorporate effective and carefully evaluated school education programs for early health promotion and disease prevention. Finally, it is imperative that such programs provide continued support of cancer research with particular focus on the molecular biology and molecular genetics of cancer in order to identify etiologic mechanisms of carcinogenesis that translate to effective interventions for the eradication of the disease.

• • • **REFERENCES**

Ahmad, O., Boschi-Pinto, C., Lopez, A. D., Murray, C. J. L., Lozano, R., & Inoue, M. (2001). *Age standardization of rates: A new WHO standard*. Geneva, Switzerland: World Health Organization.

American Association for Cancer Research. (2012). AACR cancer progress report 2012. *Clinical Cancer Research*, *18*, S1–S100.

American Cancer Society. (2007). *Global cancer facts and figures, 2007*. Atlanta, GA: Author. Retrieved from www.cancer.org/acs/groups /content/@nho/documents/document /globalfactsandfigures2007rev2p.pdf

American Cancer Society. (2015). *Cancer facts and figures, 2015*. Atlanta, GA: Author. Retrieved from http://www.cancer.org/research /cancerfactsstatistics/cancerfactsfigures2015 /index

Boffetta, P., Mashibe, M., La Vecchia, C., Zatonski, W., & Rehm, J. (2006). The burden of cancer attributable to alcohol drinking. *International Journal of Cancer*, *119*(4), 884–887.

Borenstein, M., Hedges, L. V., Higgins, J. P. T., & Rothstein, H. R. (2009). *Introduction to meta-analysis*. Hoboken, NJ: John Wiley & Sons.

Boyle, P., & Levin, B. (Eds.). (2008). *IARC world cancer report*. Lyon, France: International Agency for Research on Cancer (IARC) Publications.

Bray, F., & Moller, B. (2006). Predicting the future burden of cancer. *Nature Reviews Cancer*, *6*, 63–74.

Calle, E. E., Rodriguez, C., Walker-Thurmond, K., & Thun, M. J. (2003). Overweight, obesity, and mortality from cancer in a prospectively studied cohort of U.S. adults. *New England Journal of Medicine*, *348*, 1625–1638.

Chen, M. (1998). Cancer prevention and control among Asian and Pacific Islander Americans. *Cancer*, *83*(S8), 1856–1864.

Colditz, G. A., Selelrs, T. A., & Trapido, E. (2006). Epidemiology—identifying the causes and preventability of cancer? *Nature Reviews Cancer*, *6*, 75–83.

de Martel, C., Ferlay, J., Franceschi, S., Vignat, J., Bray, F., Forman, D., & Plummer, M. (2012). Global burden of cancers attributable to infections in 2008: A review and synthetic analysis. *Lancet Oncology*, *13*(6), 607–615.

Doll, R., & Peto, R. (1981). The causes of cancer: Quantitative estimates of avoidable risks of cancer in the United States today. *Journal of the National Cancer Institute*, *66*(6), 1191–1308.

Ferlay, J., Shin, H. R., Bray, F., Forman, D., Mathers, C., & Parkin, D. M. (2010). Estimates of worldwide burden of cancer in 2008: GLOBOCAN 2008. *International Journal of Cancer*, *127*, 2893–2917.

Ferlay, J., Soerjomataram, I., Ervik, M., Dikshit, R., Eser, S., Mathers, C., . . . Bray, F. (2013). *GLOBOCAN 2012 v1.0. Cancer incidence and mortality worldwide: IARC CancerBase No. 11* [Internet]. Lyon, France: International Agency for Research on Cancer.

Gandini, S., Botteri, E., Iodice, S., Boniol, M., Lowenfels, A. B., Maisonneuve, P., & Boyle, P. (2008). Tobacco smoking and cancer: A meta-analysis. *International Journal of Cancer*, *122*(1), 155–164.

Garcia, M., Jemal, A., Ward, E. M., Center, M. M., Hao, Y., Siegel, R. L., & Thun, M. J. (2007). *Global cancer facts and figures 2007*. Atlanta, GA: American Cancer Society.

Harris, R. E. (2007). Cyclooxygenase 2 (COX-2) and the inflammogenesis of cancer. *Subcellular Biochemistry*, *42*, 93–126.

Hecht, S. S. (1999). Tobacco smoke carcinogens and lung cancer. *Journal of the National Cancer Institute*, *91*(14), 1194–1210.

Hill, A. B. (1965). The environment and disease: Association or causation? *Proceedings of the Royal Society of Medicine*, *58*, 295–300.

Holford, T. R., Meza, R., Warner, K. E., Meernik, C., Jeon, J., Moolgavkar, S. H., & Levy, D. T.

(2014). Tobacco control and the reduction in smoking-related premature deaths in the United States, 1964-2012. *Journal of the American Medical Association, 311*(2), 164–171.

Horner, M. J., Ries, L. A. G., Krapcho, M., Neyman, N., Aminou, R., Howlader, N., . . . Edwards, B. K. (Eds.). (2009). *SEER Cancer Statistics Review, 1975–2006.* Bethesda, MD: National Cancer Institute.

International Agency for Research on Cancer. (1986). Tobacco smoking. *IARC Monographs on the Evaluation of Carcinogenic Risks to Humans. Vol. 38.* Lyon, France: Author.

International Agency for Research on Cancer. (2004). Tobacco smoke and involuntary smoking. *IARC Monographs on the Evaluation of Carcinogenic Risks to Humans. Vol. 83.* Lyon, France: Author.

International Agency for Research on Cancer and World Health Organization. (1988). *Alcohol drinking. Vol. 44.* Lyon, France: Author.

Jemal, A., Bray, F., Center M. M., Ferlay, J., Ward E., & Forman, D. (2011). Global cancer statistics. *CA: A Cancer Journal for Clinicians, 61*(2), 69–90.

Jemal, A., Center, M. M., DeSantis, C., & Ward, E. M. (2010). Global patterns of cancer incidence and mortality rates and trends. *Cancer Epidemiology, Biomarkers and Prevention, 19,* 1893–1907.

Parkin, D. M. (2006). The global health burden of infection-associated cancers in the year 2002. *International Journal of Cancer, 118*(12), 3030–3044.

Parkin, D. M., Boyd, L., & Walker, L. C. (2011). The fraction of cancer attributable to lifestyle and environmental factors in the UK in 2010. Summary and conclusions. *British Journal of Cancer, 105*(S2), S77–S81.

Parkin, D. M., Bray, F., Ferlay, J., & Pisani, P. (2001). Estimating the world cancer burden: GLOBOCAN 2000. *International Journal of Cancer, 94,* 153–156.

Parkin, D. M., Bray, F., Ferlay, J., & Pisani, P. (2005). Global cancer statistics, 2002. *CA: A Cancer Journal for Clinicians, 55,* 74–108.

Peto, R., Lopez, A. D., Boreham, J., & Thun, M. (2006). *Mortality from smoking in developed countries 1950–2000* (2nd ed.). Geneva, Switzerland: International Union Against Cancer (UICC).

Peto, R., Lopez, A. D., Boreham, J., Thun, M., & Heath, C. (1992). Mortality from smoking in developed countries: Indirect estimates from national vital statistics. *Lancet, 229,* 1268–1278.

Robbins, S. L., & Cotran, R. S. (1979). *Pathologic basis of disease* (2nd ed.). Philadelphia, PA: W. B. Saunders.

Satcher, D. (2001). *Women and smoking: A report of the surgeon general.* Atlanta, GA: Office on Smoking and Health, Centers for Disease Control and Prevention.

Soerjomataram, I., Lortet-Tieulent, J., Parkin, D. M., Ferlay, J., Mathers, C., Forman, D., & Bray, F. (2012). Global burden of cancer in 2008: A systematic analysis of disability-adjusted life-years in 12 world regions. *Lancet, 380*(9856), 1840–1850.

Stewart, B. W., & Kleihues, P. (Eds.). (2003). *IARC World Cancer Report 2003.* Lyon, France: International Agency for Research on Cancer (IARC) Publications.

Stewart, B. W., & Wild, C. P. (Eds.). (2014). *IARC World Cancer Report 2014.* Lyon, France: International Agency for Research on Cancer (IARC) Publications.

Surveillance, Epidemiology, and End Results Program. (2014). Bethesda, MD: National Cancer Institute. Retrieved from http://seer.cancer.gov.

Terry, L. (1964). *Smoking and health: Report of the advisory committee to the surgeon general of the Public Health Service.* Washington, DC: U.S. Department of Health, Education and Welfare.

Thun, M. J., DeLancey, J. O., Center, M. M., Jemal, A., & Ward, E. M. (2010). The global burden of cancer: Priorities for prevention. *Carcinogenesis,* *31*(1), 100–110.

U.S. Surgeon General. (1964). *Smoking and health.* Washington, DC: U.S. Department of Health, Education, and Welfare.

Vineis, P., Alavanja, M., Buffler, P., Fontham, E., Franceschi, S., Gao, Y. T., . . . Doll, R. (2004). Tobacco and cancer: Recent epidemiological evidence. *Journal of the National Cancer Institute, 96*(2), 99–106.

World Bank. (2014). *World bank open data.* Washington, DC: World Bank Group. Retrieved from http://data.worldbank.org/data-catalog /world-development-indicators

World Health Organization. (2004). *Global burden of disease 2004 update.* Geneva, Switzerland: Author.

World Health Organization. (2006). *Cancer.* Geneva, Switzerland: Author.

World Health Organization. (2008). *WHO report on the global tobacco epidemic, 2008: The MPOWER package.* Geneva, Switzerland: Author.

World Health Organization. (2012). *WHO global report: Mortality attributable to tobacco.* Geneva, Switzerland: Author.

Epidemiology of Lung Cancer

ANATOMY AND FUNCTION OF THE LUNGS

The human lungs are paired organs that perform the cardinal function of exchanging carbon dioxide in the blood for oxygen in inspired air. The left lung is divided into two lobes and the right lung into three lobes. Together, they contain approximately 1,500 miles of airways and 300–500 million alveoli where the carbon dioxide and oxygen exchange occurs. The total surface area of adult human lungs is approximately 70 square meters (roughly the same area as one side of a tennis court). If all of the capillary vessels that envelop the alveoli were unwound and laid end to end, they would extend for more than 600 miles.

Inspired air is conducted into the lungs through the trachea, the bronchi, and the bronchioles (**Figure 3.1**). This *conducting zone* is not involved in gas exchange and is reinforced with cartilage to maintain patency for the inhalation and exhalation of air. Its function is to warm the inspired air to 98.6°F (37°C) and humidify the air. Small projections known as *cilia* effectively cleanse inspired air by wave-like motions that propel foreign material back into the larger bronchi and trachea, where the cough reflex completes the expulsion. Furthermore, mucus-secreting cells and immune cells line the airways and help protect the lungs by trapping viruses, bacteria, pollen, dust, and other foreign material.

Exchange of gases occurs in the *respiratory zone*, which consists of respiratory bronchioles, the alveolar ducts, and the alveoli (Figure 3.1). The alveolar epithelium is a continuous layer of cells consisting of two principal cell types: type I pneumocytes that cover 95% of the alveolar surface and granular type II pneumocytes that secrete pulmonary surfactant (the major lubricant in the lungs) and that are involved in

repairing damage to the alveoli. Type I pneumocytes interface with the endothelial cells lining the pulmonary capillaries to facilitate the diffusion of carbon dioxide and oxygen across the alveolar–capillary membrane.

Total lung capacity ranges between 4 and 6 liters and is contingent upon age, height, weight, and gender. On average, females have 20–25% less capacity than males. The typical adult resting respiratory rate is 10–20 breaths per minute, and with each breath about 500 milliliters of air is exchanged (the tidal volume). Nevertheless, the lungs have a tremendous reserve volume, and the amount of air that can be exchanged by *forced* inspiration and expiration is about 4 liters (the vital capacity). The average human breathes approximately 11,000 liters of air containing 2.31 liters of oxygen per day (Kumar, Abbas, & Aster, 2014; Weinberger, 2004).

GLOBAL LUNG CANCER MORTALITY

Lung cancer, the deadliest of all malignancies, caused 1.59 million deaths in 2012 (1.24 million in men and 491,000 in women), more than double that of any other form of cancer. In the same year, over 1.82 million new cases of lung cancer were diagnosed (1.24 million in men and 583,000 in women), an overall increase of 13.2% since 2008. Nearly 90% of lung cancer patients die from the disease, most within only a few months of diagnosis. Even in developed countries, 25–30% of all cancer deaths are due to lung cancer. More people die from lung cancer than breast cancer, prostate cancer, and colon cancer combined (Boyle & Levin, 2008; Ferlay et al., 2010, 2013).

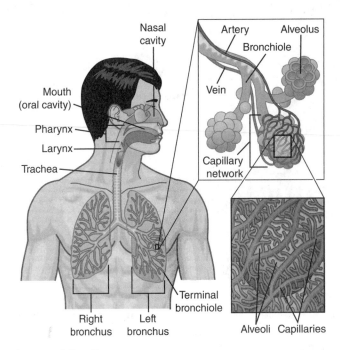

Figure 3.1 Diagram of Human Lungs and Alveoli.

The death toll from lung cancer in the 20th century exceeded 25 million, and already in the 21st century, 18 million more people have died from lung cancer. Based on the current trajectory of smoking patterns around the globe, it is estimated that 250 million people will die from lung cancer and other smoking-related cancers in the 21st century (Proctor, 2001).

Tobacco smoking is the dominant etiologic factor of lung cancer and is responsible for approximately 87% of cases. The highest rates of lung cancer therefore occur in nations with the highest prevalence rates of chronic smoking such as North America, Europe, and China (**Figure 3.2**) (International Agency for Research on Cancer [IARC], 2002). However, in evaluating the global lung cancer incidence and mortality maps in Figure 3.2, it must be kept in mind that lung cancer develops over a long period of time, perhaps decades from initiation until diagnosis. The world lung cancer mortality rates of today are therefore the consequence of many years of past smoking exposure. Indeed, young people throughout the world are taking up the smoking habit with alarming alacrity (greater than 50% in populous countries such as China, India, and Russia), and unless reversed, this unfortunate trend will have devastating health consequences in generations to come. A particularly disturbing global trend is the rising prevalence of chronic smoking among women, which

has produced sharp increases in lung cancer incidence and mortality rates among women. For example, the prevalence of smoking among adult women in the United States increased from about 6% in 1924 to 30% by 1980, which caused a 600% increase in lung cancer mortality among U.S. women during the last half of the 20th century (Satcher, 2001). The following statement from officials of the American Cancer Society succinctly describes the global marketing expansion of tobacco throughout the world by the tobacco industry: "Globally, the data are very clear in indicating that the tobacco epidemic has now expanded to and become more focused in the world's low- and middle-income countries, due largely to the expansion of the multinational tobacco industry's marketing efforts in Eastern Europe, Asia, Africa, and Latin America" (Glynn et al., 2010, p. 51).

Notably, the world's most populous country, China, is also the largest producer of tobacco and has the greatest number of smokers. The Chinese tobacco industry produces 42% of the world's cigarettes, and in China's population of 1.35 billion, there are 350 million people who smoke, which accounts for one-third of all smokers on the planet. Approximately 60% of Chinese men smoke and 4% of Chinese women. Recent estimates suggest that 1.3 million of the 5.4 million people in the world who die annually of smoking-related diseases are Chinese (Li, 2012).

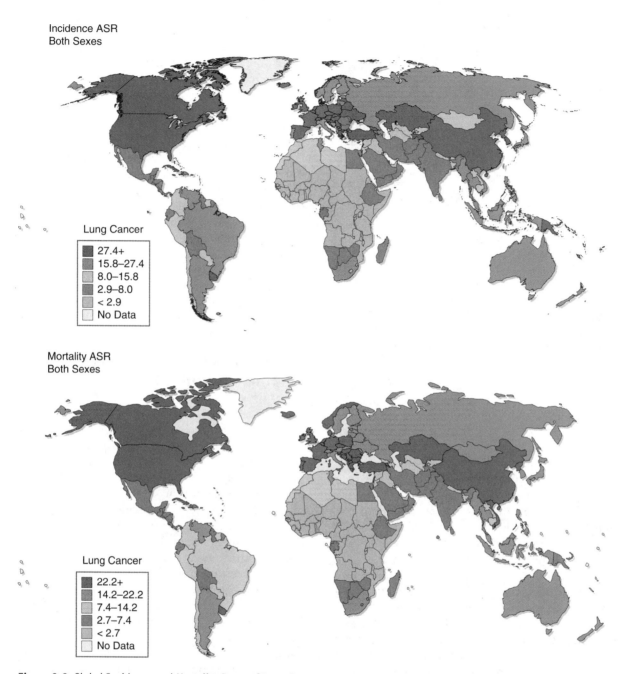

Figure 3.2 Global Incidence and Mortality Rates of Lung Cancer, 2012.

ASR: Rates per 100,000 are age-standardized to the world population, 2000–2025.

Source: Reproduced from Ferlay, J., Soerjomataram, I., Ervik, M., Dikshit, R., Eser, S., Mathers, C., . . . Bray, F. (2013). *GLOBOCAN 2012 v1.0. Cancer incidence and mortality worldwide: IARC CancerBase No. 11* [Internet]. Lyon, France: International Agency for Research on Cancer. Retrieved from http://globocan.iarc.fr

CIGARETTE SMOKING AND LUNG CANCER

The dominant risk factor for lung cancer is cigarette smoking. Early epidemiologic studies by Ernst Wynder and Evarts Graham in the United States and Richard Doll and Bradford Hill in Great Britain clearly demonstrated the etiologic link between cigarette smoking and cancer of the lung (Doll & Hill, 1950; Wynder & Graham, 1950). As shown by the data published by Wynder and Graham in 1950, lung cancer risk steadily rises with increasing smoking intensity; for example, compared to people who have never smoked, the odds of developing lung cancer is 30-fold higher in women and 50-fold higher

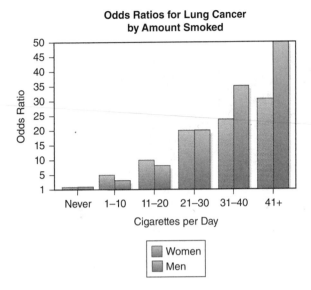

Figure 3.3 Lung Cancer Risk and Chronic Cigarette Smoking.

Source: Data from Wynder, E. L., & Graham, E. A. (1950). Tobacco smoking as a possible etiologic factor in bronchiogenic carcinoma. *Journal of the American Medical Association, 143,* 329–336.

in men who smoke at least two packs of cigarettes per day (**Figure 3.3**).

Since the pioneering studies of Wynder and Graham in the United States and Doll and Hill in Great Britain, hundreds of subsequent investigations have confirmed the causal role of tobacco smoking in the genesis of lung cancer. A landmark study was the 1964 Surgeon General's Report on Smoking and Health, which provided unequivocal evidence that chronic cigarette smoking causes lung cancer. In a pooled analysis of seven prospective studies cited in the report, lung cancer mortality among chronic smokers was 11-fold higher than for nonsmokers, and the mortality ratio increased progressively with the amount of smoking. For example, lung cancer mortality among those who smoked two or more packs per day was more than 20-fold higher than for nonsmokers. Similar results were noted for nine case control studies cited in the report (Terry, 1964).

In a recent voluminous investigation of the epidemiologic evidence on smoking and lung cancer, 16,616 estimates of risk ascertained from 287 studies conducted between 1950 and 2000 were examined by meta-analysis. The overall risk of developing any histologic type of lung cancer was markedly elevated in current smokers compared to nonsmokers (relative risk [RR] = 8.4), and the risk for squamous cell carcinoma (RR = 16.9) was higher than for adenocarcinoma (RR = 4.2). The data showed increasing risk with various measures of exposure including

increasing amount smoked, duration of smoking, tar level, and earlier age of starting to smoke, and decreasing risk with duration of smoking cessation. Risk increases were noted for ever smoking, current smoking, and ex-smoking; for smoking pipes and cigars; and for all types of cigarettes studied. Significant risk increases were evident for men and women, in younger and older subjects, in all continents studied, and in prospective and retrospective studies. The causal association was clearly evident for each of the major histological types of lung cancer studied, being stronger for squamous and small cell carcinoma, intermediate for large cell carcinoma, and weakest for adenocarcinoma (Lee, Forey, & Coombs, 2012). Similar results of meta-analyses have been reported by several other investigators, underscoring the dominant causal role of exposure to tobacco smoke in the development of cancer of the human lung (Gandini et al., 2008; Khuder, 2001; Vineis et al., 2004).

CIGARETTE SMOKING AND LUNG CANCER MORTALITY IN THE UNITED STATES

The cause and effect pattern of smoking and lung cancer is clearly visible on examination of ecologic time trend data in the United States (**Figure 3.4**). In the early years of the 20th century, lung cancer occurred infrequently and was considered a reportable disease in most medical research journals (Wynder & Stellman, 1977). As shown in the figure, the rates began to increase after the advent of cigarette smoking in the 1930s, and thereafter lung cancer incidence and mortality have continually climbed, reaching epidemic proportions during mid-century and overwhelming other forms of cancer as the leading cause of cancer death. Note the close parallelism of lung cancer mortality and cigarette use in the United States that has persisted since 1930. The time interval between the exposure curve and the mortality curve reflects an approximate average development time of 20 years or more for lung carcinogenesis. In recent years, annual incidence rates of lung cancer in the U.S. population have declined slightly (2.6% in men and 1.1% in women during 2005–2009). This encouraging trend reflects some success in the prevention and control of tobacco use (Henley et al., 2014). Nevertheless, during 2012, more than 160,000 people died from lung cancer (88,000 men and 73,000 women) in the U.S. population, which exceeded the total number of deaths from the next four most deadly cancers. (Colorectal cancer, breast cancer, pancreatic cancer, and prostate cancer caused a total of 157,000 deaths.)

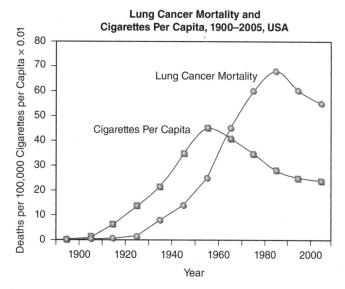

Figure 3.4 Lung Cancer Mortality and Cigarettes Per Capita, United States.

Source: Data from American Cancer Society. (2014). *Cancer facts and figures 2014.* Atlanta, GA: Author. Retrieved from http://www.cancer.org/research/cancerfactsstatistics/cancerfactsfigures2014/index (annual mortality rates are the averages for men and women); American Lung Association. (2011). *Trends in tobacco use.* Chicago, IL: Author. Retrieved from http://www.lung.org/finding-cures/our-research/trend-reports/Tobacco-Trend-Report.pdf (annual cigarettes per capita × 0.01)

SMOKING AND HISTOLOGIC CHANGES IN LUNG TISSUES

An important confirmatory study of the role of cigarette smoking in the development of lung cancer was published in 1961 by Oscar Auerbach and colleagues. The investigation presented the results of microscopic examination of lung specimens taken at autopsy from 402 men, 63 who died from lung cancer and 339 who died from causes other than lung cancer at the Veterans Administration Hospital in East Orange, New Jersey. For each autopsy case, data on smoking history were ascertained from the family and the frequencies of histological changes observed in smokers and nonsmokers were compared. The *Auerbach protocol* involved histological examination of specimens taken from 208 anatomic sites of each tracheobronchial tree. Results were based on the microscopic examination of 20,665 randomized and coded slides, which clearly showed that the frequency and severity of cellular alterations in the lungs were directly related to the intensity and duration of cigarette smoking by the patient. Lung tissues from smoking cases had significantly higher frequencies of carcinoma in situ, squamous metaplasia, hyperplasia, and loss of cilia than lung tissues from nonsmoking patients. Furthermore, the frequency of lesions increased with the level of smoking. For example, among 65 men who never smoked regularly, 16.8% of 3,324 specimens showed at least one histological change in the epithelium, whereas one or more

epithelial changes were found in 98.0% of the 13,689 specimens from 274 men who regularly smoked cigarettes and died of causes other than lung cancer and in 99.8% of the 2,784 specimens from 63 men who died of lung cancer. Most notably, the frequency of carcinoma in situ was 0% in nonsmokers, 20% in those who smoked less than one pack of cigarettes per day, 48% in those who smoked 1–2 packs per day, 75% in those who smoked more than 2 packs of cigarettes per day, and 83% in those who died from lung cancer. Based on these results, the investigators concluded the following: "In our opinion the histologic evidence from this study greatly strengthens the already overwhelming body of epidemiologic evidence that cigarette smoking is a major factor in the causation of bronchogenic carcinoma" (Auerbach, Stout, Hammond, & Garfinkel, 1961, p. 267).

TRANSITION OF LUNG CANCER CELL TYPES

Major changes have occurred in the profile of histologic cell types of lung cancer being diagnosed during the past several decades. Specifically, rates of adenocarcinoma of the lung have increased dramatically with corresponding decreases in squamous cell and small (oat) cell carcinoma (**Figure 3.5**).

Concurrent with the changing histologic profile of lung cancer, the composition of U.S. cigarettes has also changed dramatically in recent decades. Filtered

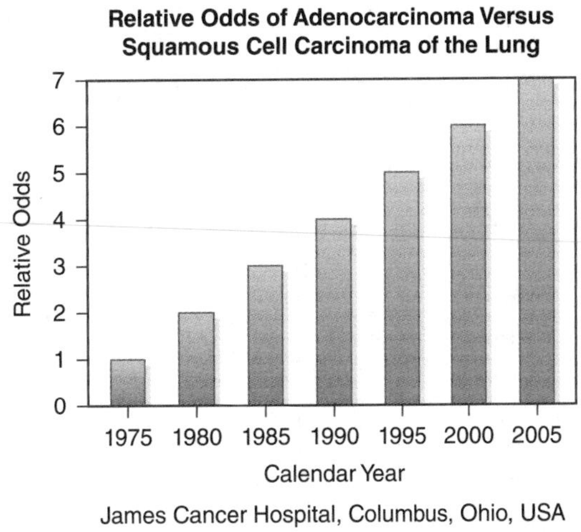

Relative Odds of Adenocarcinoma Versus Squamous Cell Carcinoma of the Lung

James Cancer Hospital, Columbus, Ohio, USA

Figure 3.5 Changing Histological Profile of Lung Cancer.

brands now dominate the market and currently comprise over 85% of all cigarettes manufactured in the United States. This trend is reflected by decreases in the average tar and nicotine yields per cigarette. Among smokers in the United States, about 96% of women and 92% of men smoke filter cigarettes. Despite this transition to "low yield" cigarettes, smokers tend to inhale deeper and compensate by smoking more cigarettes, which may account for the drastic increase in lung adenocarcinoma among cigarette smokers in recent years (Augustine, Harris, & Wynder, 1989). As pointed out by Wynder and Muscat (1995):

> *Smokers of low-yield (filtered) cigarettes compensate for the low delivery of nicotine by inhaling the smoke more deeply and by smoking more intensely; such smokers may be taking up to 5 puffs/min with puff volumes up to 55 ml. Under these conditions, the peripheral lung is exposed to increased amounts of smoke carcinogens that are suspected to lead to lung adenocarcinoma. (p. 143)*

There is also evidence from epidemiologic studies that women have a greater predisposition to smoking-induced lung carcinogenesis than men (Harris, Zang, Anderson, & Wynder, 1993; Risch et al., 1993; Zang & Wynder, 1992). The results of these studies indicate that the risk of lung cancer, particularly adenocarcinoma, is approximately two-fold higher in women who smoke than in men of the same age who smoke the same amount. Although it has been suggested that the greater susceptibility of women may relate to estrogens or estrogen receptors in the lung epithelium, the biological basis of the observed differential gender predisposition to tobacco carcinogenesis remains to be clarified.

CIGARETTE SMOKING AND LUNG CANCER HISTOLOGY

A team of international investigators recently explored associations of smoking with the major histologic cell types of lung cancer using one of the largest epidemiologic datasets on lung cancer ever assembled. The dataset included 13,169 lung cancer cases and 16,010 controls ascertained from the SYNERGY database of eight European case control studies in 11 European countries and one case control study in Canada during 1985–2005. Controls were frequency-matched to the cases by age, gender, and location. Lung cancer risks were quantified by estimating odds ratios for squamous cell carcinoma, small cell carcinoma, and adenocarcinoma of the lung. Although all histologic types of lung cancer were strongly associated with smoking, the risk estimates were markedly higher for squamous cell and small cell carcinomas compared to adenocarcinomas. As shown in **Figure 3.6**, among men and women who smoked 30 or more cigarettes daily, the odds of developing either squamous cell carcinoma or small cell carcinoma were four to five times higher than the odds of developing adenocarcinoma. There were also differences in the histologic profile of lung cancer in men and women and among smokers versus

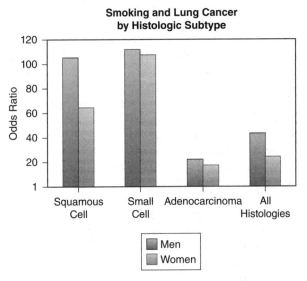

Figure 3.6 Odds Ratios for Chronic Smoking by Histologic Subtype of Lung Cancer.

Average level of current smoking: 30 or more cigarettes per day.

Source: Data from Pesch, B., Kendzia, B., Gustavsson, P., Jöckel, K. H, Johnen, G., Pohlabeln, H.,... Brüning, T. (2012). Cigarette smoking and lung cancer—relative risk estimates for the major histological types from a pooled analysis of case–control studies. *International Journal of Cancer, 131*(5), 1210–1219.

nonsmokers. Among men, the majority of tumors (53%) were squamous cell carcinomas, 20% were small cell carcinomas, and 27% were adenocarcinomas. Among women, the majority of tumors (50%) were adenocarcinomas, 28% were squamous cell carcinomas, and 22% were small cell carcinomas. Notably, among 889 cases who reported no smoking history, pulmonary adenocarcinoma was the leading subtype (58% and 70% in men and women, respectively). The authors suggest their findings of steeper dose-response gradients in the risk of squamous cell carcinoma and small cell carcinoma compared to adenocarcinoma with increasing exposure to tobacco smoke "may reflect different response pathways of the lung depending on the exposure to pulmonary carcinogens and the extent of tissue damage" (Pesch et al., 2012). Nevertheless, the two- to fourfold higher relative frequencies of nonsmokers among cases of pulmonary adenocarcinoma likely contributed to odds ratios of smaller magnitude than for other subtypes.

TOBACCO CARCINOGENESIS

Tobacco smoke is a complex mixture of more than 5,000 gases and compounds, many of which are carcinogenic (Rodgman & Perfetti, 2009). While nicotine is the addictive component of tobacco smoke, multiple carcinogens are also present with the potential to induce cancer-causing mutations in critical genes. Three major classes of carcinogens are present in tobacco smoke: polycyclic aromatic hydrocarbons, nitrosamines, and heterocyclic amines (National Toxicology Program, 2005). The metabolism of carcinogens is complex, involving activation versus detoxification by liver enzymes. The carcinogens of tobacco smoke, their uptake and metabolism, and mechanisms by which they cause DNA mutations and DNA damage have been thoroughly reviewed elsewhere (Hecht, 1999).

In addition to the carcinogens of tobacco smoke, multiple other chemical compounds are present that are highly inflammatory to lung tissue. One of the most damaging and inflammatory of the substances in tobacco smoke is the tobacco residue called *tar*. Tar is the common name given to the particulate matter of tobacco smoke, minus the nicotine and water content. Essentially, tar is a complex mixture of thousands of compounds resulting from the combustion of tobacco and tobacco resins. It is estimated that the lungs of a chronic smoker of 20 or more cigarettes per day for 40 years are exposed to 8–10 kilograms of tar (Harris et al., 1993). Tar is

by nature a sticky substance that is difficult, if not impossible, for the lungs to clear. Adherence to the cilia slows their wave-like motions and eventually stifles their ability to cleanse the airways. With the accumulation of tar in the smoker's lungs, chronic inflammation is inevitable, which in turn stimulates the critical mechanisms of cancer development: mutagenesis, mitogenesis, angiogenesis, inhibition of apoptosis, immunosuppression, and eventually metastasis (Harris, 2007).

CHRONIC OBSTRUCTIVE PULMONARY DISEASE (COPD) AND LUNG CANCER

Chronic obstructive pulmonary disease (COPD) is recognized as a chronic obstructive inflammatory condition of the lungs. Multiple studies have established a strong link between COPD and cancer of the lung (Raviv, Hawkins, DeCamp, & Kalhan, 2011). The dominant risk factor for both lung cancer and COPD is chronic tobacco smoking. Furthermore, the impaired lung function of COPD patients may also increase their lung cancer risk.

Swedish investigators studied the association of COPD and lung cancer in a large cohort of individuals (*n* = 176,997) for whom spirometry measurements were available at baseline. The stage of COPD was determined using spirometric measures of lung function. During 1971–2001, 834 incident cases of lung cancer were detected in the cohort through linkage with the Swedish National Cancer Registry. As shown in **Figure 3.7**, the relative risk of lung cancer

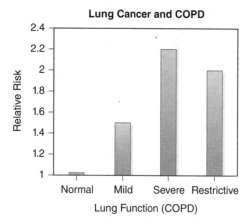

Figure 3.7 Chronic Obstructive Pulmonary Disease (COPD) and Lung Cancer.

Source: Data from Purdue, M. P., Gold, L., Järvholm, B., Alavanja, M. C. R., Ward, M. H., & Vermeulen, R. (2007). Impaired lung function and lung cancer incidence in a cohort of Swedish construction workers. *Thorax, 62,* 51–56.

is significantly increased in patients with COPD, and more severe disease accentuates the risk (Purdue et al., 2007).

COPD independently causes nearly 3 million deaths annually in the world population. Overall, COPD ranks fifth in cause-specific mortality and is projected to climb even higher in the coming years. The vast majority of deaths from COPD (nearly 90%) occur in developing countries. In developed countries, COPD currently ranks third in mortality, behind only cardiovascular disease and cancer (WHO, 2008a, 2008b, 2009).

COPD actually refers to the presence of either of two conditions, emphysema or chronic bronchitis, which may exist simultaneously or separately in a given individual. The diagnosis of COPD is initially suggested by chronic repeated episodes of dyspnea (shortness of breath), wheezing, and coughing with or without mucous production.

In emphysema uncompromised by chronic bronchitis, the patient is typically barrel-chested and dyspneic with obviously prolonged expiration due to air trapping in the lungs. Significant weight loss is a common presenting symptom. Such patients remain well oxygenated and are thus referred to as "pink puffers." Pathologically, the lungs are characterized by permanent enlargement of the air spaces distal to the terminal bronchioles accompanied by significant destruction of the alveolar walls (Weinberger, 2004).

Chronic bronchitis is clinically defined as persistent cough with sputum production for at least 3 months in at least 2 consecutive years. This condition in its pure form involves chronic bacterial or viral infection and inflammation of the lungs. Patients characteristically are obese and may be cyanotic and hypercapnic due to lack of oxygen and excess carbon dioxide in the blood, respectively. Due to the bluish tinge of skin and lips from cyanosis and fluid retention from congestive right heart failure (cor pulmonale), such patients are referred to as "blue bloaters."

The diagnosis of COPD is confirmed using spirometry, a test that measures the ratio of the forced expiratory volume of air in 1 second by the patient (FEV1) to the forced vital capacity of the lungs (FVC). Ratios less than 0.70 are diagnostic of COPD. Radiographic images of the lungs may aid in the diagnosis, and biopsy specimens are sometimes ascertained to microscopically assess the degree of alveolar destruction in emphysema.

It is important to realize that emphysema and chronic bronchitis are often superimposed in the same patient. Indeed, the coexistence of both conditions in the same individual is the rule rather than the exception. However, chronic bronchitis is diagnosed according to clinical parameters (productive cough for 3 months in 2 consecutive years). Consequently, chronic bronchitis is easier to diagnose, giving rise to higher prevalence rates. Nevertheless, pathologic studies of biopsy specimens from COPD patients with late stage disease invariably reflect the presence of components of both emphysema and chronic bronchitis (Weinberger, 2004).

The majority of COPD cases are caused by chronic exposure to the thousands of noxious chemicals in tobacco smoke and the deposition of tobacco residue (tar) in the lungs (Marsh, Aldington, Shirtcliffe, Weatherall, & Beasley, 2006). Chronic pulmonary inflammation ensues with the influx of inflammatory cells leading to the pathologic changes characteristic of both emphysema and chronic bronchitis. Sustained recursive injury to the pulmonary epithelium coupled with impaired mucociliary clearance of tobacco carcinogens and inflammatory agents may serve to accelerate malignant transformation.

LUNG CANCER RISK FACTORS OTHER THAN TOBACCO

Factors that are synergistic with cigarette smoking in heightening the risk of lung cancer include exposure to asbestos fibers, inhalation of decay products of radon gas, and certain chemical exposures related to specific occupations (e.g., arsenic, cadmium, lead, dioxins). Other factors such as genetic predisposition and diet may also modify the risk of lung cancer. In particular, exposures that lead to chronic inflammation in lung tissues have been found to increase the risk.

Radon Gas and Lung Cancer

Radon is a colorless and odorless gas generated by the breakdown of radioactive radium, the decay product of uranium that is found in rocks and soil of the Earth's crust. Radiation decay products can reach the lungs by inhalation, where they are capable of ionizing DNA to produce mutations that could lead to carcinogenesis and the development of lung cancer. In an early ecological study of lung cancer in Maine, estimates of radon levels in domestic water supplies were found to be significantly correlated with county rates of lung cancer across the state (Hess, Weiffenbach, & Norton, 1983). In several studies of uranium miners, exposure to radon particles appeared to increase the risk of lung cancer (Hornung & Meinhardt, 1987; Samet & Hornung, 1990).

Evidence supporting an etiologic link between radon and lung cancer was strengthened by results of the Iowa Radon Study, which evaluated residential exposures among women and found a significant dose response in lung cancer risk with cumulative radon exposures exceeding 4 picocuries per liter (Field et al., 2000). In 1994, the U.S. Environmental Protection Agency (EPA) issued a warning that radon *could be* the second most frequent cause of lung cancer after cigarette smoking, responsible for up to 21,000 lung cancer deaths per year in the United States (Lubin et al., 1994). Nevertheless, the EPA estimates are based on linear extrapolation of high radon exposure in miners to much lower levels of exposure. Currently, the totality of scientific evidence suggests that radon exposure poses an independent risk, albeit small compared to that of tobacco. Furthermore, although not proven, chronic exposure to both tobacco smoke and radon could synergistically elevate the risk of lung cancer. Radon levels vary greatly by locality and the composition of the underlying soil and rocks. This makes the accurate evaluation of individuals' radon exposure extremely difficult; studies sufficiently powered to detect effects of low levels of exposure and interactions are lacking.

Asbestos and Lung Cancer

Asbestos causes mesothelioma, a malignancy of the pleura surrounding the lung, as well as other forms of lung cancer. The etiologic link between lung cancer and asbestos exposure is well established through the studies of Selikoff and colleagues (Selikoff, Hammond, & Churg, 1968). Inhaled asbestos fibers migrate to the periphery of the lung where they become entrapped and cause recursive inflammatory insult and carcinogenesis. Asbestos exposure has been found to significantly increase the risk of cancer of the lung and pleura (mesothelioma) in both men and women (Berry, Newhouse, & Turok, 1972). Furthermore, some investigators have observed a synergistic multiplicative effect between tobacco smoking and asbestos exposure in the development of lung cancer (**Figure 3.8**). In a longitudinal study of smoking and asbestos exposure in a cohort of male asbestos insulation workers in the United States and Canada, smoking alone increased the death rate from lung cancer by 10-fold and asbestos alone increased the rate by 5-fold, whereas the combination of asbestos exposure and smoking increased the rate by more than 50-fold compared to subjects with neither exposure (Hammond, Selikoff, & Seidman, 1979). However, there is considerable controversy as to whether the impact of both factors fits an additive model or a multiplicative

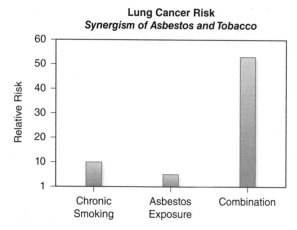

Figure 3.8 Asbestos Exposure, Smoking, and the Risk of Lung Cancer.

Source: Data from Hammond, E. C., Selikoff, I. J., & Seidman, H. (1979). Asbestos exposure, cigarette smoking and death rates. *Annals of the New York Academy of Sciences, 330*(1), 473–490.

model (Liddell, 2001). In a meta-analysis of 18 epidemiologic studies that reported relative risk estimates for smoking alone, asbestos alone, and exposure to both factors, the overall estimates of lung cancer risk were RR = 5.5 for smoking, RR = 3.1 for asbestos exposure, and RR = 13.7 for combined exposure, which approximates a simple multiplicative model of synergism slightly better than an additive model (Wraith & Mengersen, 2007).

In developed countries such as Great Britain and the United States, where asbestos has traditionally been widely used in construction and building, asbestos exposure is estimated to account for 2–3% of lung cancer deaths. A number of global committees have reviewed the cancer-causing potential of common occupational substances such as asbestos. For example, the International Agency for Research on Cancer (IARC) and the International Union Against Cancer (IUCC) have identified many workplace materials, including asbestos, that are possible lung carcinogens (McCulloch & Tweedale, 2008).

Wood Smoke and Lung Cancer

Wood smoke contains a mixture of harmful chemical substances in the form of gases and particulate matter such as carbon monoxide, ozone, nitrous oxides, sulfur dioxide, volatile organic compounds, dioxin, potential carcinogens, and inhalable particles. Certain of these compounds, such as benzo[a]pyrene and other polycyclic aromatic hydrocarbons are not only irritating and toxic, but also potent carcinogens. It has been estimated that residential wood combustion may account for up to 75% of the exposure to particle-associated organics and account for a significant fraction (up to 20%) of the cancer risk in the upper respiratory tract of nonsmokers (Lewtas, Lewis, Zweidinger, Stevens, & Cupitt, 1992).

Exposure to wood smoke may increase the risk of lung cancer via a mechanism similar to that of tobacco. Delgado and colleagues (2005) studied blood samples from patients with and without lung cancer and found that wood smoke exposure in nonsmokers significantly increased the expression of genes that control cell division such as p53, similar to the effects of tobacco exposure. Based on results, they suggested that wood smoke exposure is a possible risk factor for the development of lung cancer in nonsmokers.

Air Pollution and Lung Cancer

The role of air pollution in the genesis of lung cancer was examined in a prospective cohort study of more than 1 million American men and women conducted by investigators at the American Cancer Society. Air pollution was measured as the concentration of particulate matter in ambient air. Study results showed that each 1% increase in the concentration of particles in the air produced a 14% increase in the risk of developing a lung cancer (Krewski et al., 2005; Pope et al., 2002). Lung cancer risk was highest for inhalation of ultrafine particles (less than 2.5 micrometers in diameter) that penetrate further into the lungs (Valavanidis, Fiotakis, & Vlachogianni, 2008).

Dioxins and Lung Cancer

Dioxins and structurally related dioxin-like compounds are environmentally and biologically persistent and induce a spectrum of disease processes. Dioxins are produced by industrial processes, including incineration, chlorine bleaching of paper and pulp, and the manufacture of some pesticides, herbicides, and fungicides. Dioxin is readily absorbed by sediments and soils and persists for decades. Common sources of dioxin included backyard burning of trash, wood stoves, wood-fired commercial boilers, municipal waste incinerators, and pulp and paper mill discharges. Humans are exposed through diet and close proximity to contaminated environments.

In a follow-up study of the population of Seveso, Italy, which was exposed to dioxin after an industrial accident that occurred in 1976, lung cancer mortality among men in high-exposure zones was significantly increased (RR = 1.3, 95% confidence interval [CI] = 1.0–1.7) (Bertazzi et al., 2001). Dioxins are metabolized by liver enzymes CYP-1A1 and CYP-1B1 into compounds with carcinogenic potential in lung cells and other tissues (MacPherson, Lo, Ahmed, Pansoy, & Matthews, 2009). Results support continued evaluation of dioxin as a lung carcinogen and underscore the need to also study interactions with tobacco and other risk factors.

Arsenic and Lung Cancer

Arsenic occurs naturally in soil and bedrock and is also used in pressure-treated wood and as an ingredient in pesticides. Long-term exposure to low levels of arsenic in drinking water has been linked to human health risks associated with cancer at multiple sites including the lung, bladder, and skin. DiPaolo and Casto (1979) first demonstrated the malignant transformation of mammalian cells by inorganic arsenic; subsequently, many other studies have confirmed that arsenic exposure is both mutagenic and carcinogenic in humans (Barrett, Lamb, Wang, & Lee, 1989; Roy & Saha, 2002).

In a 50-year study of a population exposed to arsenic-contaminated drinking water in Chile, Marshall and colleagues (2007) found that toxic arsenic exposure greatly increased lung cancer risk when exposure occurred in utero or early in life. The investigators stated that "the impact of arsenic in drinking water on this large population is without precedent for environmental causes of human cancer, and it points to the public health priority of ensuring that arsenic concentrations in drinking water are controlled worldwide" (p. 927).

Environmental Tobacco Smoke (ETS) and Lung Cancer

Over the last several years, much research has focused on the dangers of exposure to environmental tobacco smoke (ETS) or secondhand smoke. Such exposure is also known as passive smoking or involuntary smoking due to breathing in the tobacco smoke from nearby smokers.

Secondhand tobacco smoke arises from the dilution of sidestream smoke from smoldering cigarettes and from the residues of mainstream smoke exhaled by active smokers. More than 4,000 chemicals have been identified in ETS and many of them are carcinogenic, including arsenic, benzene, beryllium, cadmium, nickel, chromium, ethylene oxide, polonium, and dioxin (National Toxicology Program, 2005). Furthermore, the ETS inhaled by nonsmokers has higher levels of nitrosamines and smaller particle sizes, leading to easier deposition within the bronchial tree. Specifically, smaller ETS particles are more likely to reach and be held in the lungs, where they dissolve more readily than larger particles. Therefore, the pattern of deposition of smoke particles in the respiratory tract differs between active and passive smokers.

It is estimated that approximately one-third of lung cancer in nonsmokers results from passive exposure to secondhand cigarette smoke (U.S. Environmental Protection Agency [EPA], 1992; IARC, 2004). Furthermore, ETS has been found to increase the risk of developing heart disease and myocardial infarction in adults and is also linked to various conditions in children, including sudden infant death syndrome, ear infections, and asthmatic attacks. Clearly, there is no safe level of exposure to ETS (U.S. Department of Health and Human Services [DHHS], 2006).

Within the United States, many state and local governments have passed laws prohibiting smoking in public facilities such as schools, hospitals, airports, and bus terminals. Increasingly, state and local governments are also requiring private workplaces, including restaurants and bars, to be smoke free. At the national level, several laws restricting smoking have also been passed; for example, federal U.S. law bans smoking on domestic airline flights, most international flights, and interstate buses and trains, and in federal buildings and facilities. Internationally, several nations, including France, Ireland, New Zealand, Norway, and Uruguay, have also implemented laws requiring workplaces, bars, and restaurants to be smoke free (DHHS, 2000, 2006).

Diet and Lung Cancer

For many years, an unresolved puzzle that has faced epidemiologists is the discrepant lung cancer rates in Japan versus the United States. Despite the fact that the prevalence of chronic cigarette smoking among Japanese men is approximately twice that of U.S. men, their lung cancer rates are substantially lower. For example, an early international case control study of smoking and lung cancer in Japan and the United States found that the relative risk of lung cancer development among chronic smokers is 10-fold higher in U.S. men compared to Japanese men (Wynder, Taioli, & Fujita, 1992). This phenomenon is known as the *Japanese smoking paradox*.

Although considerable research has addressed potential causes of the Japanese smoking paradox, a completely satisfactory explanation has not been forthcoming. Wynder and colleagues suggested that several factors may be involved: Japanese smokers are exposed to lower concentrations of carcinogens in their cigarettes (tobacco blends used in formulating cigarettes differ in the United States and Japan, and most Japanese cigarettes are made with charcoal filters that more effectively filter out nitrates and nitrosamines); Japanese men begin smoking at a later age than U.S. men (2–3 years on average); Japanese men consume less alcohol than U.S. men; and perhaps most importantly, the Japanese consume markedly less fat in their diet compared to Americans. Each of these factors could contribute to enhanced protection against carcinogenesis by tobacco smoke among Japanese compared to U.S. smokers (Stellman et al., 2001; Takahashi et al., 2008; Wynder et al., 1992).

Another important dietary difference between Japan and the United States is in fish consumption. Japan has one of the highest annual levels of fish consumption in the world (70 kg per capita), which is more than fourfold higher than the U.S. level (16 kg per capita) (EPA, 2002; Josupeit, 1996). To examine the role of diet in lung cancer development, Takezaki and colleagues conducted a case control study within Japan and found that consumption of cooked or raw fish reduced the risk of lung cancer in both men and women by about 50%. Eating fresh fish provides an excellent source of complex polyunsaturated fatty acids that are known to have potent anti-inflammatory effects, so it is possible that regular fish consumption by Japanese smokers inhibits or delays lung carcinogenesis by tobacco smoke (Takezaki et al., 2001).

Viruses and Lung Cancer

It is well known that chronic lung infections due to certain viruses cause lung cancer in animals; for example, the Jaagsiekte Sheep Retrovirus (JSRV) causes pulmonary adenocarcinoma in sheep (Leroux et al., 2007). However, the role of viral infections in human lung cancer development has not been definitively proven. Certain viruses have been implicated in lung carcinogenesis by virtue of their presence in lung cancer specimens (e.g., human papillomavirus strains, John Cunningham [JC] virus, simian virus 40 [SV40], BK virus, and cytomegalovirus have been found in cancerous lung tissues) (Cheng et al., 2001; Giuliani et al., 2007). However, it is highly likely that an acute viral infection present at the time of lung cancer diagnosis is an effect of the lowered susceptibility of such patients rather than the cause of a protracted course of carcinogenesis over many years.

Genetics and Lung Cancer

Sir Ronald Aylmer Fisher, the renowned "father of statistics," invented many of the maximum likelihood statistical methods that are still being used in hypothesis testing and the analysis of data. He also founded the field of quantitative genetics, developed methods for genetic linkage analysis, and proposed the concept of additive genetic variance for genes with small effects. Despite his genius for statistics and genetics, Fisher strongly opposed the conclusions of Ernst Wynder, Richard Doll, and Bradford Hill in the early 1950s that smoking caused lung cancer. Fisher compared the correlations in their papers to the "import of apples and the rise of divorce" in order to show that "correlation does not prove causation." In his view, the cause of lung cancer was largely attributable to genetic factors. However, his analysis of the causal association between lung cancer and smoking was flawed by an unwillingness to examine the entire body of available evidence that clearly demonstrated the etiologic link between cigarette smoking and cancer of the lung (Cornfield et al., 1959). It has also been pointed out that Dr. Fisher was employed as a consultant by the tobacco firms and that he himself was a smoker, thereby raising the specter of bias and casting huge doubt on the value of his arguments against the early epidemiologic findings (Stolley, 1991).

In recent years, linkage studies of multigenerational familial aggregations of lung cancer and genome-wide association studies (GWAS) have identified a number of genetic polymorphisms and mutant forms of genes that regulate key mechanisms of lung carcinogenesis. Most of these candidate genes modify effects of exposure to tobacco smoke, thereby increasing the susceptibility or resistance to tobacco carcinogenesis. Effects have been observed for genes that regulate the cell cycle and cell division (K-ras, p53, p16), genes that control DNA repair enzymes (BER, NER), genes that control the inflammatory cascade and cellular response to the plethora of highly inflammatory elements in tobacco smoke (COX-2), and genes that modulate phase I and phase II liver enzymes (CYP-1A1, CYP-1B1) resulting in heightened activation or dysfunctional metabolism of carcinogenic compounds in tobacco smoke, including polycyclic aromatic hydrocarbons (PAHs), nitrosamines, and aromatic amines (Aviel-Ronen, Blackhall, Shepherd, & Tsao, 2006; Schwartz, Prysak, Bock, & Cote, 2007). Tobacco smoke may also stimulate epigenetic events that induce or suppress gene expression without changing the DNA base pair sequence, such as DNA methylation, histone deacetylation, and phosphorylation, and these changes in gene expression may in turn influence susceptibility to lung carcinogenesis.

Cyclooxygenase-2 (COX-2), Inflammation, and Lung Cancer

More than a century ago, the German pathologist Rudolf Virchow (Virchow, 1863) suggested that chronic inflammation leads to cancer development by increasing cellular proliferation. In 1989, an inducible enzyme called cyclooxygenase-2 (COX-2) that initiates the inflammatory cascade was discovered in the laboratories of Dr. Phil Needleman at Monsanto Corporation in St. Louis, Missouri (Fu, Masferrer, Seibert, Raz, & Needleman, 1990; Masferrer, Zweifel, Seibert, & Needleman, 1990; Raz, Wyche, & Needleman, 1989). In 1991, the human version of the COX-2 gene was cloned in the laboratories of Dr. Harvey Herschman at UCLA (Fletcher, Kujubu, Perrin, & Herschman, 1992). Several investigators working in different laboratories were instrumental in the discovery and ultimate cloning of COX-2 (Herschman, 2002).

The COX-2 gene is normally silent in noninflamed tissues, but when stimulated by inflammatory factors (such as those found in tobacco smoke), COX-2 transcription is triggered, leading to the enzymatic conversion of arachidonic acid into molecules called prostaglandins that are highly inflammatory. Discovery of the inducible COX-2 gene that initiates the inflammatory cascade rekindled interest in the causal link between inflammation and cancer.

Since discovery of the inducible COX-2 gene, a huge volume of cohesive scientific evidence from molecular, animal, and human investigations supports the hypothesis that continuous aberrant induction of COX-2 and up-regulation of the prostaglandin cascade by chronic exposure to a wide variety of inflammatory agents promotes the development of cancer, including cancer of the lung. Indeed, there is evidence that chronic exposure to many highly inflammatory constituents of cigarette smoke plays a significant role in lung carcinogenesis, and reciprocally, that blockade of the process has strong potential for cancer prevention and therapy (Harris, 2002, 2007; Harris, Beebe-Donk, & Alshafie, 2007).

LUNG CANCER DIAGNOSIS, TREATMENT, AND SURVIVAL

Despite intensive medical efforts involving surgical resection, chemotherapy, and radiation therapy, the survival of patients with pathologically confirmed lung cancer has remained dismally low for decades (**Figure 3.9**). The primary reason for the failure of treatment protocols to improve survival is the lack of early detection of lung tumors. Standard chest x-rays and most other imaging techniques have shown little value in detecting lung tumors prior to their invasion of the blood, lymphatics, contiguous tissue, and more distant anatomic sites.

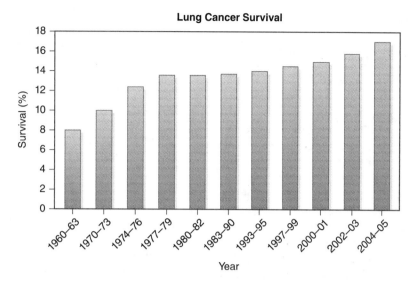

Figure 3.9 Trend in 5-Year Lung Cancer Survival, 1960–2000, United States.

Source: Data from National Cancer Institute. (2014). Cancer statistics. Lung and bronchus. Surveillance, Epidemiology, and End Results program. Retrieved from http://seer.cancer.gov/faststats

One relatively new imaging technique, low-dose helical computerized tomography (CT), was recently evaluated in a large multicenter screening program involving 31,567 asymptomatic men and women 40 years of age or older, all of whom were at risk for lung cancer because of a history of cigarette smoking or other environmental exposures. Results demonstrated identification of 412 (85%) of 484 lung cancer cases with small clinical stage I lesions having a projected 10-year survival rate of 85% (Henschke et al., 2006). However, other centers were not able to replicate this result (Bach et al., 2007), and a subsequent meta-analysis of data from 15 studies did not establish that low-dose CT reduced mortality from lung cancer (Yau, Lock, & Rodrigues, 2007).

To resolve the issue, the U.S. National Cancer Institute launched a large randomized National Lung Screening Trial (NLST) comparing the effects of low-dose helical CT and chest x-ray for the early detection and treatment of lung cancer. A total of 53,454 persons ages 55 to 74 years who were at high risk for lung cancer due to current heavy smoking were enrolled in the trial during 2002–2004. Of these, 26,722 subjects were randomized to the arm receiving screening by low-dose helical CT and 26,732 were randomized to the arm receiving screening by chest x-ray. During the follow-up period (2002–2009), 1,060 lung cancers were detected in the low-dose CT group (645 cases per 100,000 person years) versus 941 lung cancers in the x-ray group (572 cases per 100,000), and there was a 20% reduction in mortality in subjects screened by helical low-dose CT compared to chest

x-ray. A major issue with both forms of screening was the high false positive rate (96.4% in the low-dose CT group and 94.5% in the x-ray group). The NLST investigators concluded that low-dose helical CT was effective in reducing lung cancer mortality among heavy smokers, but cautioned against its routine use until additional studies rigorously examine methods to reduce the high false positive rate and cost versus benefit of such screening (National Lung Screening Trial Research Team, 2011).

PRIMARY PREVENTION OF LUNG CANCER

The primary prevention of lung cancer depends to a large extent on the prevention of cigarette smoking among adolescents and young adults. The National Cancer Institute (NCI), the National Heart, Lung and Blood Institute (NHLBI), and many other public health agencies have developed presentations and other resources designed to disseminate accurate information to elementary-age schoolchildren on the dangers of implementing the smoking habit. Such programs appear to have had some beneficial impact in reducing prevalence rates of smoking in adolescents from 30–40% to 20–25% in the United States over the past 20 years. Paradoxically, the tobacco industry has also sponsored tobacco prevention programs for kids. Nevertheless, most efforts by the tobacco industry are intended to diminish media interventions for tobacco control and oppose national, state, and county tobacco control ballot initiatives and referenda (National Cancer Institute, 2008).

In June 2009, the U.S. Senate approved bill H.R. 1256/S. 982, known as the Family Smoking Prevention and Tobacco Control Act. The new law grants the U.S. Food and Drug Administration (FDA) the authority to regulate tobacco products by eliminating tobacco marketing for kids, requiring health warnings and a complete listing of contents on the packaging of cigarettes and other tobacco products, and requiring changes in tobacco products, such as removal or reduction of harmful ingredients. Despite these public health efforts, a huge segment of the world population continues to smoke, as evidenced by recent data from the World Health Organization suggesting that 1 in 3 adults continues to smoke (WHO, 2008b). As a consequence of this addictive habit, 5.4 million people are dying annually from tobacco-related diseases such as lung cancer, heart disease, stroke, COPD, and other forms of cancer (see Figures 3.3 and 3.4 earlier in the chapter).

NONSTEROIDAL ANTI-INFLAMMATORY DRUGS (NSAIDS) AND LUNG CANCER

In 1988, Richard Peto and colleagues reported the results of a randomized prospective study of daily aspirin use among 5,139 British physicians. The study was designed to determine if 500 mg aspirin daily would reduce the incidence of and mortality from stroke, myocardial infarction, or other vascular conditions. In the study, 3,429 of the enrolled subjects were randomly assigned to receive aspirin and 1,710 were randomly assigned to avoid taking any aspirin or aspirin products. After 6 years of follow-up, the results provided little evidence of protective benefit of aspirin against vascular diseases; however, the observed death rate from lung cancer was 7.4 per 10,000 person-years in the group treated with aspirin and 11.6 per 10,000 person-years in the control group (relative mortality = 0.64) (Peto et al., 1988). Many subsequent investigations have also observed significant protective effects of aspirin and other nonsteroidal anti-inflammatory drugs (NSAIDs) against the development of lung cancer. For example, in a case control study of lung cancer and NSAIDs, Harris and colleagues observed a risk reduction of 60% (OR = 0.40) with use of selective COX-2 inhibitors, and comparable risk reductions with regular use of ibuprofen (odds ratio [OR] = 0.40) or aspirin (OR = 0.53). Notably, the comparison group in the study consisted of controls that smoked but did not have lung cancer (Harris et al.,

2007). In a meta-analysis of 18 studies of lung cancer and NSAIDs, the combined relative risk estimate for regular NSAID use was RR = 0.72 with no evidence of heterogeneity among studies (Harris, 2009).

SMOKING CESSATION AND LUNG CANCER

The 1990 Report of the U.S. Surgeon General is devoted to the health benefits of smoking cessation. Smoking cessation has major and immediate health benefits for men and women of all ages. Though there is typically a small weight gain with smoking cessation with some adverse psychological impact, the health benefits of smoking cessation far exceed any risks.

On average, former smokers live longer than continuing smokers, and the benefits of quitting extend to those who quit at older ages. For example, persons who quit smoking before age 50 have one-half the risk of dying in the next 15 years compared to continuing smokers. Furthermore, women who stop smoking before or early during pregnancy reduce their risk of having a low-birth-weight baby.

Smoking cessation reduces the risk of heart attack and stroke by 50% within the first year after quitting and also rapidly improves pulmonary function in patients with established COPD by reducing respiratory symptoms such as cough, sputum production, and wheezing, and enhancing immune defense mechanisms against respiratory infections such as bronchitis and pneumonia.

Sustained smoking cessation produces a gradual decrease in the risk of developing lung cancer as well as other tobacco-related cancers (Higgins & Wynder, 1988). Paradoxically, there is a slight increase in the risk of lung cancer diagnosis within the first few years after quitting smoking, which is apparently related to the modified growth characteristics of existing lung tumors that enhance their detection (**Figure 3.10**).

ELECTRONIC CIGARETTES (E-CIGARETTES)

The electronic cigarette (e-cigarette) is a battery-powered device designed to simulate cigarette smoking. The device heats a liquid solution containing nicotine and flavoring and the vapor is inhaled into the lungs to deliver nicotine to the blood. These delivery systems have gained popularity as substitutes for cigarettes and possible aids for smoking cessation. Nevertheless, a recent study suggests that e-cigarette use (known as *vaping*) causes an immediate increase in airway resistance (Vardavas et al., 2011). It is well known that pyrolysis of nicotine produces

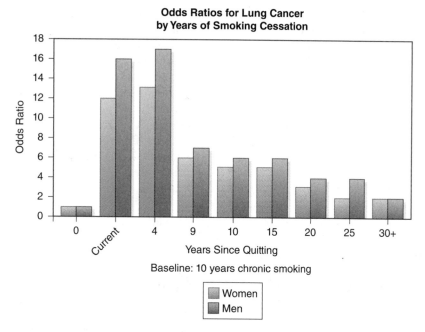

Figure 3.10 Smoking Cessation and Lung Cancer Risk.

Source: Data from Higgins, I. T., & Wynder, E. L. (1988). Reduction in risk of lung cancer among ex-smokers with particular reference to histologic type. *Cancer, 62,* 2397–2401.

formaldehyde, acetaldehyde, and a variety of other heterocyclic amines and polycyclic aromatic hydrocarbons with carcinogenic potential. Furthermore, endogenous metabolism of nicotine by liver enzymes produces carcinogenic nitrosamines (Hecht, 1999; Hecht, Adams, & Hoffmann, 1983). Nicotine itself is a powerful vasoconstrictor with mood-altering effects, and the absorption, distribution, metabolism, and excretion of nicotine and related compounds is complex and highly variable from individual to individual (Hukkanen, Jacob, & Benowitz, 2005). Given these concerns, it is important that e-cigarettes be regulated and their health effects carefully monitored because there is currently very little scientific evidence on their efficacy for smoking cessation and they are likely to have adverse long-term health effects (Etter, Bullen, Flouris, Laugesen, & Eissenberg, 2011).

● ● ● **REFERENCES**

American Cancer Society. (2014). *Cancer facts and figures 2014.* Atlanta, GA: Author. Retrieved from http://www.cancer.org/research/cancerfactsstatistics/cancerfactsfigures2014/index

American Lung Association. (2011). *Trends in tobacco use.* Chicago, IL: Author. Retrieved from http://www.lung.org/finding-cures/our-research/trend-reports/Tobacco-Trend-Report.pdf

Auerbach, O., Stout, A. P., Hammond, E. C., & Garfinkel, L. (1961). Changes in bronchial epithelium in relation to cigarette smoking and in relation to lung cancer. *New England Journal of Medicine, 265,* 253–267.

Augustine, A., Harris, R. E., & Wynder, E. L. (1989). Compensation as a risk factor for lung cancer in smokers who switch from nonfilter to filter cigarettes. *American Journal of Public Health, 79*(2), 188–191.

Aviel-Ronen, S., Blackhall, F. H., Shepherd, F. A., & Tsao, M. S. (2006). K-ras mutations in non-small-cell lung carcinoma: A review. *Clinical Lung Cancer, 8*(1), 30–38.

Bach, P. B., Jett, J. R., Pastorino, U., Tockman, M. S., Swensen, S. J., & Begg, C. B. (2007). Computed tomography screening and lung cancer outcomes. *Journal of the American Medical Association, 297,* 953–961.

Barrett, J. C., Lamb, P. W., Wang, T. C., & Lee, T. C. (1989). Mechanisms of arsenic-induced cell transformation. *Biological Trace Element Research, 21,* 421–429.

Berry, G., Newhouse, M. L., & Turok, M. (1972). Combined effect of asbestos and smoking on mortality from lung cancer and mesothelioma in factory workers. *Lancet, 2*, 476–479.

Bertazzi, P. A., Consonni, D., Bachetti, S., Rubagotti, M., Baccarelli, A., Zocchetti, C., & Pesatori, A. C. (2001). Health effects of dioxin exposure: A 20-year mortality study. *American Journal of Epidemiology, 153*(11), 1031–1044.

Boyle, P., & Levin, B. (Eds.). (2008). *IARC world cancer report.* Lyon, France: International Agency for Research on Cancer (IARC) Publications.

Cheng, Y. W., Chiou, H. L., Sheu, G. T. Hsieh, L. L., Chen, J. T., Chen, C. Y.,... Lee, H. (2001). The association of human papillomavirus 16/18 infection with lung cancer among nonsmoking Taiwanese women. *Cancer Research, 61*(7), 2799–2803.

Cornfield, J., Haenszel, W., Hammond, E. C., Lilienfeld, A. M., Shimkin, M. B., & Wynder, E. L. (1959). Smoking and lung cancer: Recent evidence and a discussion of some questions. *Journal of the National Cancer Institute, 22*, 173–203.

Delgado, J., Martinez, L. M., Sanchez, T. T., Ramirez, A., Iturria, C., & Gonzalez-Avila, G. (2005). Lung cancer pathogenesis associated with wood smoke exposure. *Chest, 128*, 124–131.

DiPaolo, J. A., & Casto, B. C. (1979). Quantitative studies of in vitro morphological transformation of Syrian hamster cells by inorganic metal salts. *Cancer Research, 39*(3), 1008–1013.

Doll, R., & Hill, A. B. (1950). Smoking and carcinoma of the lung. Preliminary report. *British Medical Journal, 2*, 739–748.

Etter, J.-F., Bullen, C., Flouris, A. D., Laugesen, M., & Eissenberg, T. (2011). Electronic nicotine delivery systems: A research agenda. *Tobacco Control, 20*, 243–248.

Ferlay, J., Shin, H.-R., Bray, F., Forman, D., Mathers, C., & Parkin, D. M. (2010). Estimates of worldwide burden of cancer in 2008: GLOBOCAN 2008. *International Journal of Cancer, 127*(12), 2893–2917.

Ferlay, J., Soerjomataram, I., Ervik, M., Dikshit, R., Eser, S., Mathers, C.,... Bray, F. (2013). *GLOBOCAN 2012 v1.0. Cancer incidence and mortality worldwide: IARC CancerBase No. 11.* Lyon, France: International Agency for Research on Cancer. Retrieved from http://globocan.iarc.fr

Field, R. W., Steck, D. J., Smith, B. J., Brus, C. P., Fisher, E. L., Neuberger, J. S.,... Lynch, C. F. (2000). Residential radon gas and lung cancer: The Iowa Radon Lung Cancer Study. *American Journal of Epidemiology, 151*, 1091–1152.

Fletcher, B. S., Kujubu, D. A., Perrin, D. M., & Herschman, H. R. (1992). Structure of the mitogen-inducible TIS10 gene and demonstration that the TIS10-encoded protein is a functional prostaglandin G/H synthase. *Journal of Biological Chemistry, 267*, 4338–4344.

Fu, J., Masferrer, J. L., Seibert, K., Raz, A., & Needleman, P. (1990). The induction and suppression of prostaglandin H2 synthase (cyclooxygenase) in human monocytes. *Journal of Biological Chemistry, 265*, 16737–16740.

Gandini, S., Botteri, E., Iodice, S., Boniol, M., Lowenfels, A. B., Maisonneuve, P., & Boyle, P. (2008). Tobacco smoking and cancer: A meta-analysis. *International Journal of Cancer, 122*(1), 155–164.

Giuliani, L., Jaxmar, T., Casadio, C., Gariglio, M., Manna, A., D'Antonio, D.,... Ciotti, M. (2007). Detection of oncogenic viruses (SV40, BKV, JCV, HCMV, HPV) and p53 codon 72 polymorphism in lung carcinoma. *Lung Cancer, 57*(3), 273–281.

Glynn, T., Seffrin, J. R., Brawley, O. W., Grey, N., & Ross, H. (2010). The globalization of tobacco use: 21 challenges for the 21st century. *CA: A Cancer Journal for Clinicians, 60*, 50–61.

Hammond, E. C., Selikoff, I. J., & Seidman, H. (1979). Asbestos exposure, cigarette smoking and death rates. *Annals of the New York Academy of Sciences, 330*(1), 473–490.

Harris, R. E. (2002). COX-2 blockade in cancer prevention and therapy: Widening the scope of impact. In: R. E. Harris (Ed.), *COX-2 blockade in cancer prevention and therapy* (pp. 341–365). Totowa, NJ: Humana Press.

Harris, R. E. (2007). COX-2 and the inflammogenesis of cancer. *Subcellular Biochemistry*, 42, 193–212.

Harris, R. E. (2009). Cyclooxygenase-2 (COX-2) blockade in the chemoprevention of cancers of the colon, breast, prostate, and lung. *Inflammopharmacology*, 17, 1–13.

Harris, R. E., Beebe-Donk, J., & Alshafie, G. A. (2007). Reduced risk of human lung cancer by selective cyclooxygenase-2 (COX-2) blockade: Results of a case control study. *International Journal of Biological Sciences*, 3(5), 328–334.

Harris, R. E., Zang, E. A., Anderson, J. I., & Wynder, E. L. (1993). Race and sex differences in lung cancer risk associated with cigarette smoking. *International Journal of Epidemiology*, 22(4), 592–599.

Hecht, S. S. (1999). Tobacco smoke carcinogens and lung cancer. *Journal of the National Cancer Institute*, 91(14), 1194–1210.

Hecht, S. S., Adams, J. D., & Hoffmann, D. (1983). Tobacco-specific nitrosamines in tobacco and tobacco smoke. *IARC Scientific Publications*, 45, 93–101.

Henley, S. J., Richards, R. B., Underwood, J. M., Eheman C., R., Plescia, M., McAfee, & T. A. (2014). Lung cancer incidence trends among men and women—United States, 2005–2009. *Mortality and Morbidity Weekly Report*, 63(01), 1–5.

Henschke, C. I., Yankelevitz, D. F., Libby, D. M., Pasmantier, M. W., Smith, J. P., Meittinen, O. S., & the International Early Lung Cancer Action Program Investigators. (2006). Survival of patients with stage I lung cancer. *New England Journal of Medicine*, 355(17), 1763–1771.

Herschman, H. R. (2002). Historical aspects of COX-2. In R. E. Harris (Ed.), *COX-2 blockade in cancer prevention and therapy* (pp. 13–32). Totowa, NJ: Humana Press.

Hess, C. T., Weiffenbach, C. V., & Norton, S. A. (1983). Environmental radon and cancer correlations in Maine. *Health Physics*, 45(2), 339–348.

Higgins, I. T., & Wynder, E. L. (1988). Reduction in risk of lung cancer among ex-smokers with particular reference to histologic type. *Cancer*, 62, 2397–2401.

Hornung, R. W., & Meinhardt, T. J. (1987). Quantitative risk assessment of lung cancer in U.S. uranium miners. *Health Physics*, 52(4), 417–430.

Hukkanen, J, Jacob III, P., & Benowitz, N. L. (2005). Metabolism and disposition kinetics of nicotine. *Pharmacological Reviews*, 57(1), 79–115.

International Agency for Research on Cancer. (2004). *Tobacco smoke and involuntary smoking*. IARC Monographs on the Evaluation of Carcinogenic Risks to Humans, *Vol. 83*. Lyon, France: Author.

Josupeit, H. (1996). Global overview on fish consumption. Marketing of aquaculture products. *Zaragoza, CIHEAM, Options Méditerranéennes*, No. 17, pp. 9–23. Retrieved from http://om.ciheam.org/om/pdf/c17/96605669.pdf

Khuder, S. A. (2001). Effect of cigarette smoking on major histological types of lung cancer: A meta-analysis. *Lung Cancer*, 31(2–3), 139–148.

Krewski, D., Burnett, R., Jerrett, M., Pope, C. A., Rainham, D., Calle, E.,… Thun, M. (2005). Mortality and long-term exposure to ambient air pollution: Ongoing analyses based on the American Cancer Society cohort. *Journal of Toxicology and Environmental Health*, 68(13–14), 1093–1099.

Kumar, V., Abbas, A. K., & Aster, J. C. (2014). *Robbins and Cotran pathologic basis of disease* (9th ed.). Philadelphia, PA: Mosby & Saunders.

Lee, P. N., Forey, B. A., & Coombs, K. J. (2012). Systematic review with meta-analysis of the epidemiologic evidence in the 1900s relating smoking to lung cancer. *BMC Cancer*, 12, 385.

Leroux, C., Girard, N., Cottin, V., Greenland, T., Mornex, J. F., & Archer, F. (2007). Jaagsietkte sheep retrovirus (JSRV): From virus to lung cancer in sheep. *Veterinary Research*, 38(2), 211–228.

Lewtas, J., Lewis, C., Zweidinger, R., Stevens, R., & Cupitt, L. (1992). Sources of genotoxicity and cancer risk in ambient air. Review. *Pharmacogenetics, 2*(6), 288–296.

Li, C. (2012). The political mapping of China's tobacco industry and anti-smoking campaign. In: *John L. Thornton China Center Monograph Series* (No. 5). Washington, DC: Brookings Institution.

Liddell, F. D. K. (2001). The interaction of asbestos and smoking in lung cancer. *Annals of Occupational Hygiene, 45*(5), 341–356.

Lubin, J. H., Boice, J. D., Edling, C., Hornung, R. W., Howe, G., & Kunz, E. (1994). *Radon and lung cancer risk: A joint analysis of 11 underground miner studies.* NIH publication no. 94–3644. Rockville, MD: National Institutes of Health.

MacPherson, L., Lo, R., Ahmed, S., Pansoy, A., & Matthews, J. (2009). Activation function 2 mediates dioxin-induced recruitment of estrogen receptor alpha to CYP1A1 and CYP1B1. *Biochemical and Biophysical Research Communications, 385*(2), 263–268.

Marsh, S., Aldington, S., Shirtcliffe, P., Weatherall, M., & Beasley, R. (2006). Smoking and COPD: What really are the risks? *European Respiratory Journal, 28,* 883–884.

Marshall, G., Ferreccio, C., Yua, Y., Bates, M. N., Steinmaus, C., Selvin, S., … Smith, A. H. (2007). Fifty-year study of lung and bladder cancer mortality in Chile related to arsenic in drinking water. *Journal of the National Cancer Institute, 99*(12), 920–928.

Masferrer, J. L., Zweifel, B. S., Seibert, K., & Needleman, P. (1990). Selective regulation of cellular cyclooxygenase by dexamethasone and endotoxin in mice. *Journal of Clinical Investigation, 86,* 1375–1379.

McCulloch, J., & Tweedale, G. (2008). The challenge of mesothelioma and Irving J. Selikoff. In McCulloch, J., & Tweedale, G. (Eds.), *Defending the indefensible: The global asbestos industry and its fight for survival* (pp. 84–118). Oxford, UK: Oxford University Press.

National Cancer Institute. (2008). *Tobacco monograph 19: The role of the media in promoting and reducing tobacco use.*

Washington, DC: U.S. Department of Health and Human Services, National Institutes of Health.

National Cancer Institute. (2014). Cancer statistics. Lung and bronchus. Surveillance, Epidemiology, and End Results program. Retrieved from: http://seer.cancer.gov/faststats

National Lung Screening Trial Research Team. (2011). Reduced lung-cancer mortality with low-dose computed tomographic screening. *New England Journal of Medicine, 365,* 395–409.

National Toxicology Program. (2005). *Report on carcinogens* (11th ed.). Research Triangle Park, NC: Author.

Pesch, B., Kendzia, B., Gustavsson, P., Jöckel, K. H, Johnen, G., Pohlabeln, H., … Brüning, T. (2012). Cigarette smoking and lung cancer—relative risk estimates for the major histological types from a pooled analysis of case–control studies. *International Journal of Cancer, 131*(5), 1210–1219.

Peto, R., Gray, R., Collins, R., Wheatley, K., Hennekens, C., Jamrozik, K., … Norton, S. (1988). Randomised trial of prophylactic daily aspirin in British male doctors. *British Medical Journal (Clinical Research Edition), 296*(6618), 313–316.

Pope, C. A. III, Burnett, R. T., Thun, M. J., Calle, E. E., Krewski, D., Ito, K., & Thurston, G. D. (2002). Lung cancer, cardiopulmonary mortality, and long-term exposure to fine particulate air pollution. *Journal of the American Medical Association, 287*(9), 1132–1141.

Proctor, R. N. (2001). Tobacco and the global lung cancer epidemic. *Nature Reviews Cancer, 1,* 82–86.

Purdue, M. P., Gold, L., Järvholm, B., Alavanja, M. C. R., Ward, M. H., & Vermeulen, R. (2007). Impaired lung function and lung cancer incidence in a cohort of Swedish construction workers. *Thorax, 62,* 51–56.

Raviv, S., Hawkins, K. A., DeCamp, M. M., & Kalhan, R. (2011). Lung cancer in chronic obstructive pulmonary disease. *American Journal of Respiratory and Critical Care Medicine, 183*(9), 1138–1146.

Raz, A., Wyche, A., & Needleman, P. (1989). Temporal and pharmacologic division of fibroblast cylcooxygenase expression into transcriptional and translational phases. *Proceedings of the National Academy of Sciences, 86*, 1657–1661.

Risch, H. A., Howe, G. A., Jain, M., Burch, J. D., Holowaty, E. J., & Miller, A. B. (1993). Are female smokers at higher risk than male smokers? A case-control analysis by histologic type. *American Journal of Epidemiology, 138*(5), 281–293.

Rodgman, A., & Perfetti, T. A. (2009). *The chemical components of tobacco and tobacco smoke.* London, England: CRC Press.

Roy, P., & Saha, A. (2002). Metabolism and toxicity of arsenic: A human carcinogen. *Current Science, 82*(1), 38–45.

Samet, J. M., & Hornung, R. W. (1990). Review of radon and lung cancer risk. *Risk Analysis, 10*(1), 65–75.

Satcher, D. (2001). *Women and smoking: A report of the surgeon general.* Atlanta, GA: Centers for Disease Control and Prevention.

Schwartz, A. G., Prysak, G. M., Bock, C. H., & Cote, M. L. (2007). The molecular epidemiology of lung cancer. *Carcinogenesis, 28*(3), 507–518.

Selikoff, I. J., Hammond, E. C., & Churg, J. (1968). Asbestos exposure, smoking and neoplasia. *Journal of the American Medical Association, 204*, 104–110.

Stellman, S. D., Takezaki, T., Wang, L., Chen, Y., Citron, M. L., Djordjevic, M. V.,... Aoki, K. (2001). Smoking and lung cancer risk in American and Japanese men: An international case-control study. *Cancer Epidemiology, Biomarkers and Prevention, 10*, 1193–1199.

Stolley, P. D. (1991). When genius errs: R. A. Fisher and the lung cancer controversy. *American Journal of Epidemiology, 133*(5), 416–425.

Takahashi, I., Matsuzaka, M., Umeda, T., Yamai, K., Nishimura, M., Danjo, K.,... Nakaji, S. (2008). Differences in the influence of tobacco smoking on lung cancer between Japan and the USA: Possible explanations for the "smoking paradox" in Japan. *Public Health, 122*(9), 891–896.

Takezaki, T., Hirose, K., Inoue, M., Hamajima, N., Yatabe, Y., Mitsudomi, T.,... Tajima, K. (2001). Dietary factors and lung cancer risk in Japanese: With special reference to fish consumption and adenocarcinomas. *British Journal of Cancer, 84*(9), 1199–1206.

Terry, L. (1964). *Smoking and health: Report of the Advisory Committee to the Surgeon General of the Public Health Service.* Washington, DC: U.S. Department of Health, Education and Welfare.

U.S. Department of Health and Human Services. (2000). *Healthy people 2010: Understanding and improving health* (2nd ed.). Washington, DC: U.S. Government Printing Office.

U.S. Department of Health and Human Services. (2006). *The health consequences of involuntary exposure to tobacco smoke: A report of the surgeon general.* Rockville, MD: Author.

U.S. Environmental Protection Agency. (1992). *Respiratory health effects of passive smoking (also known as exposure to secondhand smoke or environmental tobacco smoke—ETS).* Washington, DC: Author.

U.S. Environmental Protection Agency. (2002). *Estimated per capita fish consumption in the United States.* Washington, DC: Author.

Valavanidis, A., Fiotakis, K., & Vlachogianni, T. (2008). Airborne particulate matter and human health: Toxicological assessment and importance of size and composition of particles for oxidative damage and carcinogenic mechanisms. *Journal of Environmental Science and Health Part C, Environmental Carcinogenesis and Ecotoxicology Reviews, 26*(4), 339–362.

Vardavas, C. I., Anagnostopoulos, N., Kougias, M., Evangelopoulou, V., Connolly, G. N., & Behrakis, P. K. (2011). Short-term pulmonary effects of using an electronic cigarette: Impact on respiratory flow resistance, impedance, and exhaled nitric oxide. *Chest, 141*(6), 1400–1406.

Vineis, P., Alavanja, M., Buffler, P., Fontham, E., Franceschi, S., Gao, Y. T.,... Doll, R. (2004).

Tobacco and cancer: Recent epidemiological evidence. *Journal of the National Cancer Institute, 96*(2), 99–106.

Virchow, R. (1863). Aetiologie der neoplastischen Geschwulst/Pathogenie der neoplastischen Geschwulste. In: *Die Krankhaften Geschwulste* (pp. 57–101). Berlin: Verlag von August Hirschwald.

Weinberger, S. E. (2004). *Principles of pulmonary medicine* (4th ed.). Philadelphia: W. B. Saunders.

World Health Organization. (2008a). *The global burden of disease: Update 2004*. Geneva, Switzerland: Author.

World Health Organization. (2008b). *WHO report on the global tobacco epidemic, 2008: The MPOWER package*. Geneva, Switzerland: Author.

World Health Organization. (2009). *WHO report on the global tobacco epidemic, 2009*. Geneva, Switzerland: Author.

Wraith, D. Y., & Mengersen, K. (2008). A Bayesian approach to assess interaction between known risk factors: The risk of lung cancer from exposure to asbestos and smoking. *Statistical Methods in Medical Research, 17*, 171.

Wynder, E. L., & Graham, E. A. (1950). Tobacco smoking as a possible etiologic factor in bronchiogenic carcinoma. *Journal of the American Medical Association, 143*, 329–336.

Wynder, E. L., & Muscat, J. E. (1995). The changing epidemiology of smoking and lung cancer histology. *Environmental Health Perspectives, 103*(Suppl 8), 143–148.

Wynder E. L., & Stellman S. D. (1977). The comparative epidemiology of tobacco-related cancers. *Cancer Research, 37*, 4608–4622.

Wynder, E. L., Taioli, E., & Fujita, Y. (1992). Ecologic study of lung cancer risk factors in the U.S. and Japan, with special reference to smoking and diet. *Japanese Journal of Cancer Research, 83*, 418–423.

Yau, G., Lock, M., & Rodrigues, G. (2007). Systematic review of baseline low-dose CT lung cancer screening. *Lung Cancer, 58*(2), 161–170.

Zang, E. A., & Wynder, E. L. (1992). Cumulative tar exposure. A new index for estimating lung cancer risk among cigarette smokers. *Cancer, 70*(1), 69–76.

4

Epidemiology of Laryngeal Cancer

ANATOMY OF THE LARYNX

The larynx has three anatomic divisions: the supraglottis, glottis, and subglottis. The supraglottis consists of the epiglottis, the false vocal cords, the ventricles, and the aryepiglottic folds. The glottis includes the true vocal cords and the anterior commissure. The subglottis is located below the vocal cords and extends approximately 5 millimeters into the trachea (Fried & Ferlito, 2009). Some epidemiologic studies of laryngeal cancer have subdivided laryngeal tumors into those arising in the supraglottis and those arising in the glottis (**Figure 4.1**).

HISTOLOGY

Virtually all malignancies of the vocal cords are squamous cell carcinomas. Of these, 75% arise from the true vocal cords (glottis), and the remainder arise from other laryngeal sites.

GLOBAL EPIDEMIOLOGY

Cancer of the larynx occurs over *seven times* more often in men than in women. Globally in 2012, laryngeal cancer was diagnosed in 138,102 men compared to 18,775 women and caused 73,126 deaths in men compared to 10,115 deaths in women. Among men, cancer of the larynx comprised approximately 1.9% of all cancers and was responsible for 1.6% of all cancer deaths, whereas among women this malignancy accounted for only 0.3% of all cancers and cancer deaths (Ferlay et al., 2013).

The incidence and mortality rates of laryngeal cancer are highest in populations with the highest rates of chronic tobacco smoking and alcohol abuse. In particular, male populations characterized by heavy smoking and drinking (Cuba, Poland, Hungary, Romania, Turkey, Turkmenistan, Kazakhstan, Croatia, Russian Federation, Spain, Italy, Portugal, Brazil) have incidence rates that are 4 to 7 times higher than the average global rate of 1.9 per 100,000 (**Figure 4.2**).

LARYNGEAL CANCER IN THE UNITED STATES

The annual incidence of laryngeal cancer has declined by about 40% in the United States since 1990. This trend has occurred concurrent with sharp declines in the prevalence of cigarette smoking in U.S. men and women. During 1980–2011, the prevalence of smokers decreased by 40% in men (from 35% to 21%) and by 43% in women (from 30% to 17%). Although the relative declines are similar by gender, the data continue to reflect a four- to fivefold excess of incident cases in men compared to women (**Figure 4.3**).

AGE AT DIAGNOSIS OF LARYNGEAL CANCER

Most cases (~97%) of laryngeal cancer are diagnosed after the age of 45 years. The peak years of onset are between 55 and 75 years of age, during which time about 58% of cases are diagnosed (**Figure 4.4**).

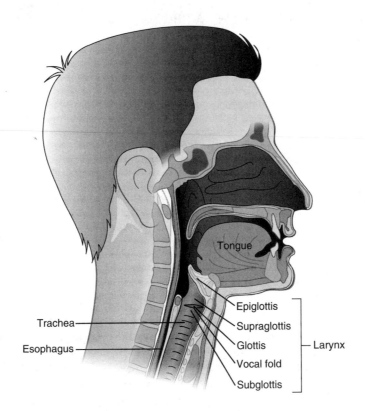

Figure 4.1 Anatomy of the Larynx.

Nevertheless, certain subtypes of laryngeal cancer are being diagnosed at earlier ages; for example, those related to human papillomavirus (HPV) infection manifest on average about 4 years earlier than those associated with tobacco and alcohol (Gillison et al., 2000).

RISK FACTORS FOR LARYNGEAL CANCER

Tobacco and Laryngeal Cancer

Chronic cigarette smoking markedly increases the risk of developing laryngeal cancer, particularly in combination with chronic alcohol consumption. The risk increases with increasing duration and intensity of exposure to each factor. Cigarette smoking is the dominant independent risk factor.

In 1956, Wynder and colleagues conducted a case control study of 209 cases of laryngeal cancer and matched controls ascertained primarily from Memorial Sloan Kettering Hospital in New York. They noted that nearly all cases (99.5%) reported a history of chronic tobacco smoking, and many reported excessive regular consumption of alcoholic beverages. Derived odds ratios (ORs) from their study show a dose response in risk with increasing intensity of chronic cigarette smoking (OR = 2.7 for

about one pack per day and OR = 5.2 for at least two packs per day) (Wynder, Bross, & Day, 1956).

In 1964, the U.S. Surgeon General Report on Smoking and Health presented data comparing the death rates from cancer and other causes from seven large prospective cohort studies of men in the United States, Great Britain, and Canada. This landmark report provided overwhelming evidence that smoking increases mortality from lung cancer, laryngeal cancer, oral cavity cancer, esophageal cancer, stomach cancer, bladder cancer, chronic bronchitis, emphysema, and heart disease. The estimated mortality from laryngeal cancer among chronic smokers was 5.4 times the expected rate, suggesting a cause and effect relationship (Terry, 1964).

In 1970, Auerbach and colleagues reported the results of microscopic examination of formalin-fixed laryngeal tissues from 942 men who were autopsied at the Veterans Administration Hospital in East Orange, New Jersey. These men died of causes unrelated to laryngeal cancer. Data on smoking habits of the decedents were collected from spouses or next of kin. Cellular atypia was observed in 99% of laryngeal specimens from smokers compared to 25% of specimens from nonsmokers, and carcinoma in situ was present in 16% of specimens from smokers but was

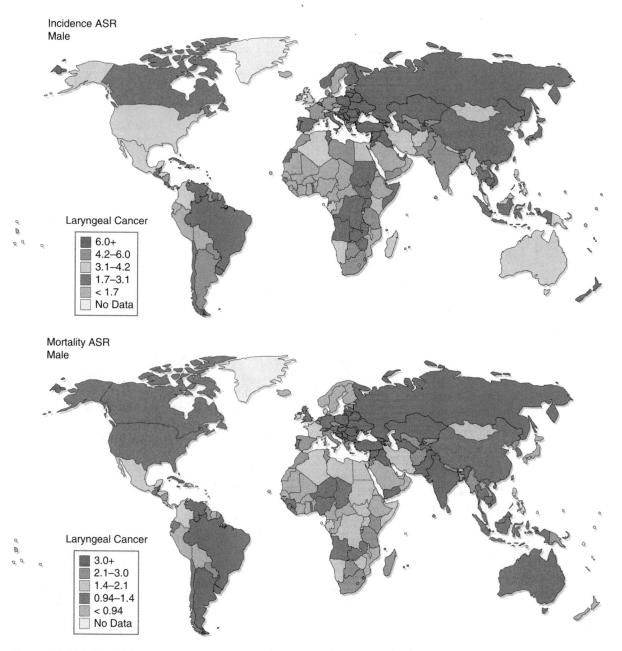

Figure 4.2 Global Incidence and Mortality Rates of Laryngeal Cancer in Men, 2012.

ASR: Rates per 100,000 are age-standardized to the world population, 2000–2025.

Source: Reproduced from Ferlay, J., Soerjomataram, I., Ervik, M., Dikshit, R., Eser, S., Mathers, C., . . . Bray, F. (2013). *GLOBOCAN 2012 v1.0. Cancer incidence and mortality worldwide: IARC CancerBase No. 11* [Internet]. Lyon, France: International Agency for Research on Cancer. Retrieved from http://globocan.iarc.fr

not observed among specimens from nonsmokers. The most significant histological change associated with smoking was "the occurrence of cells with atypical nuclei which are infrequent in nonsmokers, always found in cigarette smokers and increase in numbers with amount of cigarette smoking" (Auerbach, Hammond, & Garfinkel, 1970). These histological findings provided strong pathological evidence that exposure to tobacco smoke is in the causal pathway of the development of laryngeal cancer.

In 1976, Wynder and colleagues conducted a second hospital-based case control study of laryngeal cancer designed to examine the effects of smoking filter or nonfilter cigarettes and alcohol consumption.

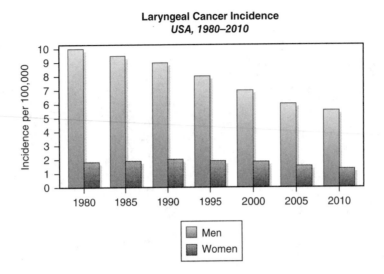

Figure 4.3 Incidence of Laryngeal Cancer in Men and Women, United States, 1980–2010.

Annual incidence rates per 100,000 are adjusted to the 2000 U.S. population.

Source: Data from National Cancer Institute. (2011). *Surveillance Epidemiology, and End Results*. SEER Stat Fact Sheets.

The study compared the smoking and drinking habits of 258 men and 56 women with laryngeal cancer to 516 men and 168 women with other conditions group-matched to the cases by gender, age, and year of interview. Results demonstrated a dramatic dose response of risk with increasing smoking of either filter or nonfilter cigarettes. Among men, chronic smoking at least two packs per day of filter cigarettes for 10 years or more produced a 30-fold risk increase, and smoking two packs per day of nonfilter cigarettes increased the risk nearly 80-fold compared to never smokers (**Figure 4.5**). The investigation also showed that heavy alcohol consumption (seven or more drinks daily) increased the risk by about three-fold and that the cancer risk in former smokers began to decline after about 6 years of smoking cessation. This investigation also found risk increases among pipe and cigar smokers and greater than additive effects for the combined use of tobacco and alcohol (Wynder, Covey, Mabuchi, & Mushinski, 1976).

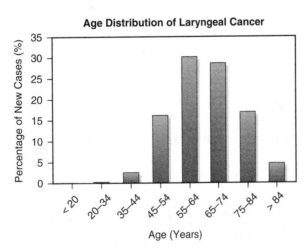

Figure 4.4 New Cases of Laryngeal Cancer by Age, United States: 2006–2010.

Source: Data from National Cancer Institute. (2011). *Surveillance Epidemiology, and End Results*. SEER Stat Fact Sheets.

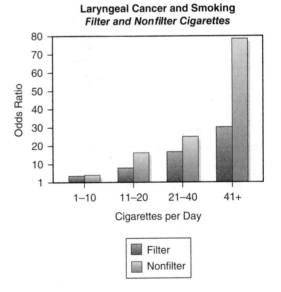

Figure 4.5 Cigarette Smoking and Laryngeal Cancer Risk.

Source: Data from Wynder, E. L., Covey, L. S., Mabuchi, K. M., & Mushinski, M. (1976). Environmental factors in cancer of the larynx, a second look. *Cancer, 38,* 1591–1601.

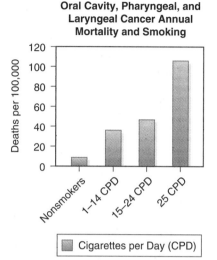

Figure 4.6 Annual Mortality from Cancers of the Oral Cavity, Pharynx, and Larynx in Men by Amount Smoked.

Source: Data from Doll, R., Peto, R., Boreham, J., & Sutherland, I. (2004). Mortality in relation to smoking: 50 years' observation on male British doctors. *British Medical Journal, 328*(7455), 1519.

Several subsequent studies have confirmed the causal role of tobacco smoking in the development of laryngeal cancer. In an important prospective cohort study, 34,439 male British physicians were followed for 50 years (1951–2001) to determine cause-specific mortality rates for cigarette smokers versus nonsmokers. The results revealed a striking dose response in combined mortality from cancers of the mouth, pharynx, and larynx with increasing smoking intensity (**Figure 4.6**). Compared to individuals who avoided the smoking habit, heavy smokers were found to have an approximately 11-fold increased risk of dying from a malignancy of the upper aerodigestive tract (Doll, Peto, Boreham, & Sutherland, 2004).

In 1986, a working group of the International Agency for Research on Cancer (IARC) found a 10-fold increase in the average risk of developing laryngeal cancer among tobacco smokers versus nonsmokers. This study examined data from 30 studies (25 case control and 5 cohort studies) and found risk increases for tobacco smoking in various forms, including cigarettes, pipes, cigars, and bidis (tobacco wrapped in the leaf of the tendu tree) (IARC, 1986).

Several investigators have conducted meta-analyses of published data on cigarette smoking and laryngeal cancer. The combined data reflect a strong overall effect of tobacco smoking and a significant dose response in the risk with increased amount of smoking (Ansary-Moghaddam, Huxley, Lam, & Woodward, 2009; Gandini et al., 2008; Peto et al.,

1992, 1994, 2006; Vineis et al., 2004; Zeka, Gore, & Kriebel, 2003).

In a meta-analysis of 10 studies that used current smoking as the measure of exposure, current smokers were seven times more likely to develop laryngeal cancer than never smokers (Gandini et al., 2008). In a meta-analysis of 15 studies that reported risk estimates for either fatal or nonfatal laryngeal cancer, the combined estimated risk among chronic smokers was increased by ninefold compared to nonsmokers (Ansary-Moghaddam et al., 2009).

Alcohol and Laryngeal Cancer

Alcohol consumption is also an independent risk factor for laryngeal cancer, but it has a weaker impact than smoking. A meta-analysis of 20 studies of alcohol and laryngeal cancer revealed an approximate fourfold increase in risk among heavy drinkers (100 grams of ethanol per day) compared to nondrinkers, as well as a significant dose response of risk with increasing levels of consumption (**Figure 4.7**) (Corrao, Bagnardi, Zambon, & La Vecchia, 2004).

Tobacco and Alcohol: Laryngeal Cancer

Wynder and colleagues first examined the synergism of tobacco and alcohol in the genesis of laryngeal cancer. Their case control study found independent increases in risk for heavy smoking (OR = 7.0) and chronic alcohol abuse (OR = 3.3), as well as a risk increase among individuals with both risk factors consistent with a multiplicative model (OR = 22.1) (Wynder et al., 1976).

As shown in Figure 4.2, incidence rates of laryngeal cancer in certain populations of Central and

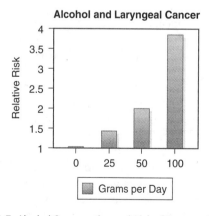

Figure 4.7 Alcohol Consumption and Risk of Laryngeal Cancer.

Source: Data from Corrao, G., Bagnardi, V., Zambon, A., & La Vecchia, C. (2004). A meta-analysis of alcohol consumption and the risk of 15 diseases. *Preventive Medicine, 38*(5), 613–619.

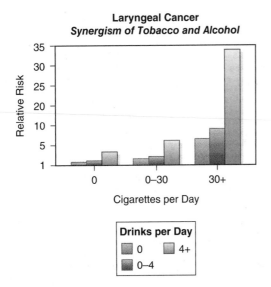

Figure 4.8 Risk of Laryngeal Cancer: Synergism of Tobacco and Alcohol.

Source: Data from Zeka, A., Gore, R., & Kriebel, D. (2003). Effects of alcohol and tobacco on aerodigestive cancer risk: A meta-regression analysis. *Cancer Causes and Control, 14*, 897–906.

Eastern Europe are among the highest in the world. Because these populations have high rates of cigarette smoking and consumption of alcoholic beverages, an international team of investigators conducted a large multicenter case control study, the Central and Eastern Europe Study, to explore the independent effects and interactions of tobacco and alcohol in the development of laryngeal cancer. During 2000–2002, 384 incident cases and 918 controls frequency-matched by age, gender, and location of residence were ascertained from medical centers in Bucharest (Romania), Budapest (Hungary), Lodz (Poland), Moscow (Russia), and Banksa Bystrika (Slovakia). Dose responses in laryngeal cancer risk by various measures, including cigarette smoking and alcohol consumption, were estimated. Compared to nonsmokers, 20 pack years of cigarette smoking increased laryngeal cancer risk by threefold, and 40 pack years of smoking increased the risk by nearly eightfold. Alcohol consumption in the absence of smoking also increased the risk compared to non-drinkers: The relative risk (RR) was 1.56 for those consuming 20–29 grams of alcohol daily and 1.85 for those consuming 40 or more grams of alcohol daily. Interactions of cigarette smoking and alcohol consumption were examined that revealed the presence of multiplicative rather than additive effects; for example, individuals who had smoked or consumed alcoholic beverages for 40 or more years were 14 times more likely to develop laryngeal cancer than those with neither exposure. The investigators estimated that 87% of cases of laryngeal cancer were attributable to tobacco smoking, with a substantial fraction (39%) attributable to the combination of smoking and drinking (Hashibe et al., 2007).

Meta-analysis has also been used to characterize the independent and interactive effects of tobacco and alcohol in the development of laryngeal cancer. In a meta-analysis of 14 studies published between 1966 and 2001 that reported risk estimates for both factors alone and in combination, the effects of smoking and drinking were found to be multiplicative on the relative risk scale. As shown in **Figure 4.8**, the estimated risk increases for heavy smoking alone (RR = 7.7) and heavy drinking alone (RR = 4.5) when multiplied together yield a close approximation to the 35-fold risk increase for high exposure to both cigarette smoking and alcohol consumption (Zeka et al., 2003).

Human Papillomavirus and Laryngeal Cancer

Recent studies suggest that chronic infection of laryngeal tissues by certain strains of human papillomavirus (HPV) increases the risk of neoplastic development. Infection by low-risk HPV strains such as HPV-6 and HPV-11 are predominantly found in benign (noncancerous) papillomas whereas high-risk strains such as HPV-16 and HPV-18 are characteristic of squamous cell carcinomas.

The link between HPV and the development of squamous cell neoplasms of the larynx and other tissues of the upper aerodigestive tract came from the clinical observation that children of mothers who manifested genital condylomata acuminata (genital warts) occasionally developed juvenile laryngeal papillomas (Quick, Faras, & Krzyzek, 1978). Subsequently, laryngeal papillomas were found to contain HPV-6 and/or HPV-11, the same HPV strains that cause genital condylomata acuminata (Franceschi, Munoz, Bosch, Snijders, & Walboomers, 1996; Gissmann et al., 1983).

Using DNA hybridization techniques, investigators at the Long Island Jewish Medical Center in New York detected HPV-16 DNA in six patients with verrucous carcinoma of the larynx. This form of laryngeal cancer is a variant of squamous cell carcinoma with a papillary wart-like appearance (Abramson, Brandsma, Steinberg, & Winkler, 1985; Brandsma, Steinberg, Abramson, & Winkler, 1986).

The early investigations of HPV in papillomas and verrucous carcinomas of the larynx prompted many subsequent molecular studies of cancer development related to HPV infection in tissues of the larynx as well as other anatomic sites of the upper aerodigestive tract (Maden et al., 1992; Schwartz et al., 1998). Gillison and colleagues tested for HPV in fresh frozen tumor specimens from 253 patients with newly diagnosed or recurrent squamous cell carcinomas of the head and neck using reverse transcriptase polymerase chain reaction (RT PCR) assays. Smoking and drinking histories were also recorded for each case. The RT PCR assays detected HPV in 62 (25%) of the 253 cases and HPV-16 was present in 56 (90%) of the positive cases. Among the 86 cases with laryngeal cancer, 16 (19%) of the cases were positive for HPV. Notably, cases with HPV-positive tumors were *less likely* to be heavy smokers or heavy drinkers than cases with HPV-negative tumors (Gillison et al., 2000).

A team of Scandinavian investigators conducted a nested case control study of head and neck cancer using serum samples from a cohort of 900,000 individuals living in Norway, Finland, and Sweden. Serum samples were tested for selected strains of HPV among 292 cases with squamous cell carcinoma of the head and neck and 1,568 controls matched on age, gender, and time of serum collection. Blood samples were collected, on average, 9.4 years prior to cancer diagnosis. Antibodies against HPV strains were detected by enzyme-linked immunosorbent assay (ELISA). Odds ratios were adjusted for serum cotinine levels (a metabolite of nicotine and a biochemical marker of exposure to tobacco smoke). Within the study, 76 patients with laryngeal cancer were compared to 411 matched controls. The overall results revealed that HPV-16 seropositive individuals were 2.2 times more likely to develop squamous cell carcinoma of the head and neck than seronegative individuals, and stratification by anatomic site revealed that HPV-16 infection significantly increased the risk of laryngeal cancer (OR = 2.4). Analysis of 160 tumor specimens using RT PCR revealed that 50% of the oropharyngeal tumors contained HPV-16. These data suggest that HPV-16 infection detectable several years prior to diagnosis heightens the risk of developing squamous cell carcinoma of the larynx and other anatomic sites of the upper aerodigestive tract, including the tongue (OR = 2.7), the oral cavity (OR = 3.6), the oropharynx (OR = 14.4), and the paranasal sinuses (OR = 3.4) (Mork et al., 2001).

Hobbs and colleagues conducted a meta-analysis of case control studies of HPV-16 infection and cancers of the head and neck with stratification by anatomic site within the upper aerodigestive tract. Twenty studies that identified site-specific head and neck cancer were identified, eight of which reported data on HPV-16 and cancer of the larynx. Significant associations were found between HPV-16 and squamous cell carcinoma at several anatomic sites, but the risk increases were greater for the tonsils (OR = 15.1) and the oropharynx (OR = 4.3) than for the oral cavity (OR = 2.0) and the larynx (OR = 2.0). Results of the investigation suggested that the methodology for detection of HPV infection, ELISA versus RT PCR analysis, was a source of heterogeneity among studies (Hobbs et al., 2006).

A team of investigators in Beijing, China, used meta-analysis to examine the role of HPV infection in the development of squamous cell carcinoma of the larynx. Among 55 eligible studies, the overall HPV prevalence in laryngeal cancer tissues was 28.0% and, most notably, 26.6% were infected with HPV-16, HPV-18, or other high-risk strains. Data from 12 case control studies were utilized to estimate summary odds ratios for HPV-16 (OR = 6.1) and HPV-18 (OR = 4.2). The investigators concluded that HPV infection, especially HPV-16 infection, significantly increases the risk of developing laryngeal cancer (Li et al., 2013).

The evidence clearly suggests there is a subset of laryngeal cancers that develop due to infection by HPV-16 and possibly other oncogenic strains of HPV. Cases with HPV-16–positive squamous cell carcinomas of the larynx or other tissues of the upper aerodigestive tract are characterized by high promiscuity consistent with heightened sexual transmission of the virus. Such cases tend to be diagnosed at younger ages than those with tumors arising from exposure to tobacco and alcohol.

Other Risk Factors for Laryngeal Cancer

Several other risk factors have been linked to the development of laryngeal cancer. Laryngeal tumors occasionally arise after incidental radiation exposure either by x-rays taken of the throat early in life or radiotherapy for malignancies of the head and neck (Glanz, 1976; Miyahara, Sato, & Yoshino, 1998). In a follow-up study of 109 patients whose first primary laryngeal cancer was treated by irradiation, eight patients developed a second primary laryngeal cancer in the previously irradiated area after 7–15 years (Martin, Glanz, & Kleinsasser, 1979).

Familial aggregations of laryngeal cancer have been observed, suggesting that some individuals may be genetically susceptible. In a study conducted at the Pomeranian Medical University in Poland, 44 (5.8%) of 753 index cases (probands) with laryngeal cancer reported at least one first-degree relative with laryngeal cancer. Pooled analysis of data from 15 case control studies involving 2,464 probands with laryngeal cancer showed a doubling of the risk in individuals with a family history in one or more first-degree relatives (Negri et al., 2008).

Various medical conditions have been found to increase the risk of laryngeal cancer. These include gastroesophageal reflux disease (GERD), immunosuppression either due to HIV disease or organ transplant, and a previous primary malignancy of the head or neck (Qadeer, Colabianchi, & Vaezi, 2005). Certain environmental exposures may also increase the risk, including chronic exposure to coal dust, wood dust, and asbestos (Muscat & Wynder, 1992). There is also some evidence that certain dietary factors may play a role in the development of laryngeal cancer. Specifically, modest risk increases have been observed among individuals with high intakes of processed meats (De Stefani et al., 1987, 2012; Levi, Pasche, Lucchini, Besetti, & La Vecchia, 2004).

PRIMARY PREVENTION OF LARYNGEAL CANCER

It is estimated that over 90% of laryngeal cancers are preventable by avoidance of tobacco and alcohol. Because tobacco and alcohol independently and synergistically increase the risk, it is obviously important to avoid exposure to both risk factors. Recent epidemiologic evidence suggests that certain strains of HPV are involved in the genesis of a subset of laryngeal carcinomas as well as several other malignancies (e.g., oropharyngeal, genital, and anal cancers). Avoidance of exposure through safe sexual practices and/or vaccination against oncogenic HPV strains is therefore critical for the primary prevention of all HPV-related malignancies, including laryngeal cancer (D'Souza & Dempsey, 2011).

• • • REFERENCES

Abramson, A. L., Brandsma, J., Steinberg, B., & Winkler, B. (1985). Verrucous carcinoma of the larynx: Possible human papillomavirus etiology. *Archives of Otolaryngology, 111,* 709–715.

Ansary-Moghaddam, A., Huxley, R. R., Lam, T. H., & Woodward, M. (2009). Risk of upper aerodigestive tract cancer associated with smoking with and without concurrent alcohol consumption. *Mount Sinai Journal of Medicine, 76,* 392–403.

Auerbach, O., Hammond, E. C., & Garfinkel, L. (1970). Histologic changes in the larynx in relation to smoking habits. *Cancer, 25*(1), 92–104.

Brandsma, J. L., Steinberg, B. M., Abramson, A. L., & Winkler, B. (1986). Presence of human papillomavirus type 16 related sequences in verrucous carcinoma of the larynx. *Cancer Research, 46,* 2185–2188.

Corrao, G., Bagnardi, V., Zambon, A., & La Vecchia, C. (2004). A meta-analysis of alcohol consumption and the risk of 15 diseases. *Preventive Medicine, 38*(5), 613–619.

De Stefani, D., Boffetta, P., Ronco, A. L., Deneo-Pellegrini, H., Correa, P., Acosta, G.,... Silva, C. (2012). Processed meat consumption and risk of cancer: A multisite case-control study in Uruguay. *British Journal of Cancer, 107,* 1584–1588.

De Stefani, E., Correa, P., Oreggia, F., Leiva, J., Rivero, S., Fernandez, G.,... Fontham, E. (1987). Risk factors for laryngeal cancer. *Cancer, 60,* 3087–3091.

Doll, R., Peto, R., Boreham, J., & Sutherland, I. (2004). Mortality in relation to smoking: 50 years' observation on male British doctors. *British Medical Journal, 328*(7455), 1519.

D'Souza, G., & Dempsey, A. (2011). The role of HPV in head and neck cancer and review of the HPV vaccine. *Preventive Medicine, 52*(1), S5–S11.

Ferlay, J., Soerjomataram, I., Ervik, M., Dikshit, R., Eser, S., Mathers, C.,... Bray, F. (2013). *GLOBOCAN 2012 v1.0, cancer incidence and mortality worldwide: IARC CancerBase No. 11 [Internet].* Lyon, France: International Agency for Research on Cancer. Retrieved from http://globocan.iarc.fr

Franceschi, S., Munoz, N., Bosch, X. F., Snijders, P. J. F., & Walboomers, J. M. M. (1996). Human papillomavirus and cancer of the upper aerodigestive tract: A review of epidemiological and experimental evidence. *Cancer Epidemiology Biomarkers and Prevention, 5,* 567–575.

Fried, M. P., & Ferlito, A. (2009). *The larynx* (3rd ed.). San Diego, CA: Plural.

Gandini, S., Botteri, E., Iodice, S., Boniol, M., Lowenfels, A. B., Maisonneuve, P., & Boyle, P. (2008). Tobacco smoking and cancer: A meta-analysis. *International Journal of Cancer, 122*(1), 155–164.

Gillison, M. L., Koch, W. M., Capone, R. B., Spafford, M., Westra, W. H., Li, W.,...

Sidransky, D. (2000). Evidence for a causal association between human papillomavirus and a subset of head and neck cancers. *Journal of the National Cancer Institute, 92,* 709–720.

Gissmann, L., Wolnik, L., Ikenberg, H., Koldovsky, U., Schnurch, H. G., & Zur Hausen, H. (1983). Human papillomavirus types 6 and 11 DNA sequences in genital and laryngeal papillomas and in some cervical cancer. *Proceedings of the National Academy of Sciences, 80,* 560–563.

Glanz, H. (1976). Late recurrence or radiation induced cancer of the larynx. *Clinical Otolaryngology and Allied Sciences, 1*(2), 123–129.

Hashibe, M., Boffetta, P., Zaridze, D., Shangina, O., Szeszenia-Dabrowska, N., Mates, D.,… Brennan, P. (2007). Contribution of tobacco and alcohol to the high rates of squamous cell carcinoma of the supraglottis and glottis in Central Europe. *American Journal of Epidemiology, 165*(7), 814–820.

Hobbs, C. G. L., Sterne, J. A. C., Bailey, M., Heyderman, R. S., Birchall, M. A., & Thomas, S. J. (2006). Human papillomavirus and head and neck cancer: A systematic review and meta-analysis. *Clinical Otolaryngology, 31*(4), 259–266.

International Agency for Research on Cancer. (1986). Tobacco smoking. *IARC Monograph Evaluating Carcinogenic Risk of Chemicals to Humans, 38,* 1–421.

Levi, F., Pasche, C., Lucchini, F., Besetti, C., & La Vecchia, C. (2004). Processed meat and the risk of selected digestive tract and laryngeal neoplasms in Switzerland. *Annals of Oncology, 15*(2), 346–349.

Li, X., Gao, L., Li, H., Gao, J., Yang, Y., Zhou, F.,… Jin, Q. (2013). Human papillomavirus infection and laryngeal cancer risk: A systematic review and meta-analysis. *Journal of Infectious Diseases, 207*(3), 479–488.

Maden, C., Beckmann, A. M., Thomas, D. B., McKnight, B., Sherman, K. J., Ashley, R. L.,… Daling, J. R. (1992). Human papillomaviruses, herpes simplex viruses, and the risk of oral cancer in men. *American Journal of Epidemiology, 135*(10), 1093–1102.

Martin, G., Glanz, H., & Kleinsasser, O. (1979). Ionising rays and laryngeal carcinomas. *Laryngologie, Rhinologie, Otologie, 58*(3), 187–195.

Miyahara, H., Sato, T., & Yoshino, K. (1998). Radiation-induced cancers of the head and neck region. *Acta Otolaryngolica, 533*(Suppl), 60–64.

Mork, J., Lie, A. K., Glattre, E., Hallmans, G., Jellum, E., Koskela, P.,… Dillner, J. (2001). Human papillomavirus infection as a risk factor for squamous-cell carcinoma of the head and neck. *New England Journal of Medicine, 344*(15), 1125–1131.

Muscat, J. E., & Wynder, E. L. (1992). Tobacco, alcohol, asbestos, and occupational risk factors for laryngeal cancer. *Cancer, 69*(9), 2244–2251.

Negri, E., Boffetta, P., Berthiller, J., Curado, M. P., Dal Maso, L., Daudt, A. W.,… Hashibe, M. (2009). Family history of cancer: Pooled analysis in the International Head and Neck Cancer Epidemiology consortium. *International Journal of Cancer, 124*(2), 394–401.

Peto, R., Lopez, A. D., Boreham, J., & Thun, M. J. (2006). *Mortality from smoking in developed countries 1950–2000* (2nd ed.). Geneva, Switzerland: International Union Against Cancer (UICC).

Peto, R., Lopez, A. D., Boreham, J., Thun, M., & Heath Jr., C. (1992). Mortality from tobacco in developed countries: Indirect estimation from national vital statistics. *Lancet, 339,* 1268–1278.

Peto, R., Lopez, A. D., Boreham, J., Thun, M., & Heath Jr., C. (1994). *Mortality from smoking in developed countries 1950–2000.* Oxford, UK: Oxford University Press.

Qadeer, M. A., Colabianchi, N., & Vaezi, M. F. (2005). Is GERD a risk factor for laryngeal cancer? *Laryngoscope, 115*(3), 486–491.

Quick, C. A., Faras, A., & Krzyzek, R. (1978). The etiology of laryngeal papillomatosis. *Laryngoscope, 88,* 1789–1795.

Schwartz, S. M., Daling, J. R., Doody, D. R., Wipf, G. C., Carter, J. J., Madeleine, M. M.,... Galloway, D. A. (1998). Oral cancer risk in relation to sexual history and evidence of human papillomavirus infection. *Journal of the National Cancer Institute, 90,* 1626–1636.

Terry, L. (1964). *Smoking and health: Report of the Advisory Committee to the Surgeon General of the Public Health Service.* Washington, DC: U.S. Department of Health, Education, and Welfare.

Vineis, P., Alavanja, M., Buffler, P., Fontham, E., Franceschi, S., Gao, Y. T.,... Doll, R. (2004). Tobacco and cancer: Recent epidemiological evidence. *Journal of the National Cancer Institute, 96*(2), 99–106.

Wynder, E. L., Bross, I. J., & Day, E. (1956). A study of environmental factors in cancer of the larynx. *Cancer, 9,* 86–110.

Wynder, E. L., Covey, L. S., Mabuchi, K. M., & Mushinski, M. (1976). Environmental factors in cancer of the larynx, a second look. *Cancer, 38,* 1591–1601.

Zeka, A., Gore, R., & Kriebel, D. (2003). Effects of alcohol and tobacco on aerodigestive cancer risk: A meta-regression analysis. *Cancer Causes and Control, 14,* 897–906.

5

Epidemiology of Cancers of the Lip, Oral Cavity, and Pharynx

ANATOMY OF THE ORAL CAVITY

The oral cavity (or mouth) is the initial portion of the alimentary canal. The digestive process begins when food enters the oral cavity and is mechanically masticated by chewing, moistened by saliva, and undergoes reactions with salivary enzymes to initiate chemical digestion. Anatomic structures of the oral cavity include the lips, teeth, hard and soft palate, upper and lower gingiva (or gums), tongue, uvula, tonsils, and pharynx. The pharynx is a channel situated behind the oral cavity and beneath the nasal cavity that extends to the level of the larynx. The oropharynx is continuous with the back of the oral cavity, extending from the soft palate to the epiglottis. A closely related structure is the nasopharynx, a channel that connects the nasal cavity and paranasal sinuses to the upper portion of the oropharynx. The laryngopharynx is the portion of the pharynx between the oropharynx and the larynx (**Figure 5.1**). The oral cavity and pharynx are lined by stratified squamous epithelium.

Global Epidemiology of Oral Cavity and Lip Cancer

Malignancies of the oral cavity and lip caused 145,328 deaths in 2012 (97,919 in men and 47,409 in women). In the same year, 300,373 new cases of oral cavity and lip cancer were diagnosed (198,975 in men and 101,398 in women), an overall increase of 14.1% since 2008. Cancers of the oral cavity and lip constitute approximately 2.1% of all malignant neoplasms and account for about 1.8% of cancer deaths in the human population (Boyle & Levin, 2008; Ferlay et al., 2010, 2013).

Globally, more than 60% of oral cavity malignancies occur in the populations of developing nations and nearly two-thirds of cases occur in men; however, the incidence and male-to-female ratio vary considerably according to the risk factors in specific populations. In most populations, there is a predominance of male cases due primarily to the higher prevalence of chronic tobacco and alcohol exposure among men; nevertheless, the changing patterns of exposure to certain risk factors, particularly sexually transmitted infection of the oral cavity by human papillomaviruses (HPVs), have markedly reduced the rate differences in men and women in certain populations (American Cancer Society, 2007).

Global patterns of incidence and mortality rates of oral cavity and lip cancer in 2012 are shown in **Figure 5.2**. High incidence rates were observed in developing nations such as India, Pakistan, Southeast Asia, and Melanesia (the southern coastal islands of Southeast Asia). The region with the highest incidence in the world is Melanesia (31.5 per 100,000 in men and 20.2 per 100,000 in women). In these populations, it is customary for both men and women to chew a mixture of tobacco, areca nut, and betel leaf called "betel quid," which has potent carcinogenic properties (Parkin, Bray, Ferlay, & Pisani, 2005). Also, in certain rural populations of Southern India, *reverse smoking* of tobacco rolled into cigars (called chutta) is particularly popular among women and can lead to the development of cancer of the hard palate (Gupta, Mehta, & Pindborg, 1984). (Reverse smoking refers to holding the lighted end of the cigar inside the mouth.) As a consequence of such practices, the mortality rates of oral cavity cancer are high in both men and women of developing nations; the male-to-female mortality ratio is approximately 1.6:1 (American Cancer Society, 2007).

The 2012 incidence rates of oral cavity and lip cancer were also high in several developed nations,

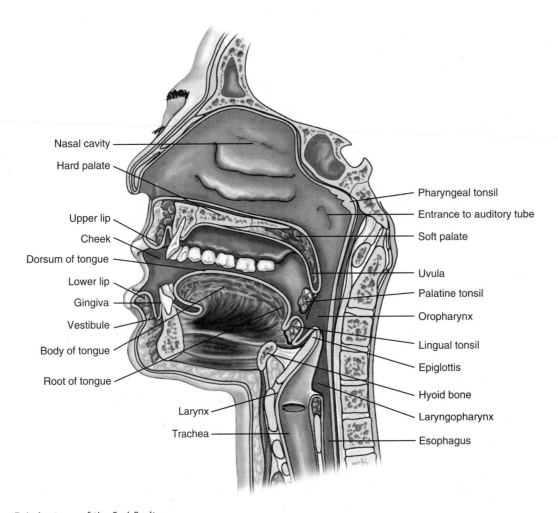

Figure 5.1 Anatomy of the Oral Cavity.

including the United States, Canada, Great Britain, Brazil, Spain, France, Germany, Austria, Norway, Denmark, and the Russian Federation. Rates were particularly high in men of Central and Eastern Europe (9.1 per 100,000), presumably due to high rates of chronic smoking and alcohol abuse. The high incidence rate in Australia and New Zealand (8.3 per 100,000) is partially due to lip cancer caused by solar irradiation.

Males in developed nations have inordinately higher mortality rates than females. In 2012, the mortality rate in men (2.3 per 100,000) was about four times the rate in women (0.6 per 100,000). This gender difference likely reflects the higher prevalence of specific risk factors among men, most often the chronic exposure of the oral mucosa to both tobacco and alcohol (American Cancer Society, 2007).

Premalignant Lesions of the Oral Cavity

Cancer of the oral cavity may begin as a dysplastic lesion such as leukoplakia (a white patch) or erythroplakia (a red patch) or any other sore that fails to

heal and persists in the mouth for a matter of weeks. Leukoplakia and erythroplakia are caused by chronic exposure to tobacco, alcohol, certain HPV strains (e.g., HPV-16), *Candida albicans* (particularly in immunosuppressed individuals with human immunodeficiency virus [HIV]), or any combination of these exposures, all of which are risk factors for the development of oral cavity cancer. These lesions usually precede the diagnosis of invasive cancer by 5–10 years. Progression of precancerous lesions to invasive oral cavity cancer can thus be interrupted by their early detection and complete surgical excision. Regular dental care and careful visual inspection of the oral cavity for such lesions is obviously paramount for cancer prevention.

Histology of Oral Cavity Cancer

The vast majority (~90%) of malignancies arising in the oral cavity are squamous cell carcinomas. An additional 5% are adenocarcinomas arising from the salivary glands within the mouth (Shklar, 1979). In a large series

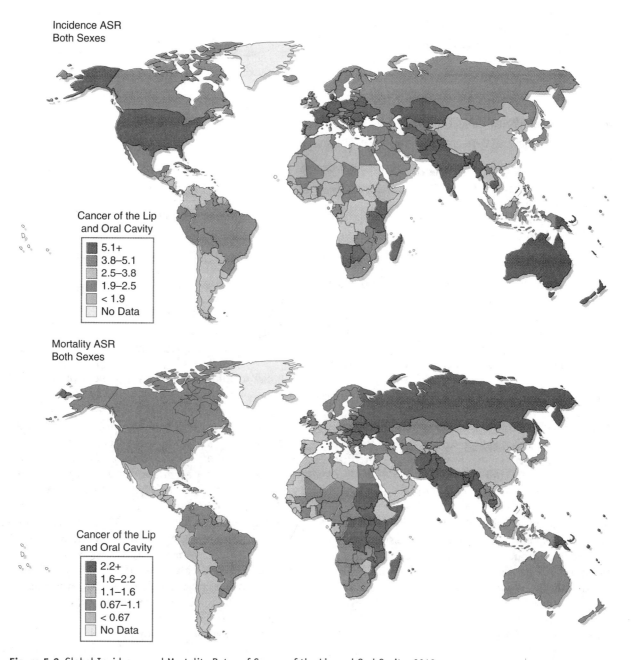

Figure 5.2 Global Incidence and Mortality Rates of Cancer of the Lip and Oral Cavity, 2012.

ASR: Rates per 100,000 are age-standardized to the world population, 2000–2025.

Source: Reproduced from Ferlay, J., Soerjomataram, I., Ervik, M., Dikshit, R., Eser, S., Mathers, C., . . . Bray, F. (2013). *GLOBOCAN 2012 v1.0. Cancer incidence and mortality worldwide: IARC CancerBase No. 11* [Internet]. Lyon, France: International Agency for Research on Cancer. Retrieved from http://globocan.iarc.fr

of 14,253 cases of oral cavity cancer, 38% developed in the lower lip, 22% in the tongue, 17% in the floor of the mouth, and the remaining 23% at other locations within the oral cavity (Krolls & Hoffman, 1976).

ORAL CAVITY CANCER RISK FACTORS

Oral cavity neoplasms are typically diagnosed between the ages of 40 and 70 years and predominate in men. (The male-to-female ratio is 2:1.) In general, the risk factors for oral cavity cancer include conditions that chronically irritate and inflame the gums, tongue, oral mucosa, and lips. The major risk factors are chronic alcohol consumption, chronic cigarette smoking, and chronic infection of the oral cavity by oncogenic strains of HPV. Other risk factors include chronic marijuana smoking, chronic use of smokeless tobacco (snuff and chewing tobacco), poor dental hygiene, and antecedent nutritional deficiencies in iron, vitamin B, and vitamin C (La Vecchia, Tavani, Franceschi, Levi, & Negri, 1997). Immunosuppression due to HIV infection has also been found to increase the risk (Beachler & D'Souza, 2013).

The pathogenesis of oral cavity cancer has recently been linked to infection by certain strains of sexually transmitted HPV. In particular, strains of HPV known to cause cervical cancer (e.g., HPV-16) also profoundly increase the risk of malignant transformation when they infect the oral cavity. As discussed later in this chapter, oropharyngeal cancers that are HPV-positive have a distinctly different risk profile than those that are HPV-negative (Gillison et al., 2008).

Though grouped with other malignancies of the oral cavity, lip cancers comprise another distinct subset of malignancies with their own profile of risk factors. Fair-skinned individuals who are chronically exposed to solar ultraviolet radiation are at increased risk of developing lip cancer (Johnson, Jayasekara, & Amarasinghe, 2011; National Cancer Institute, 2014).

Synergism of Alcohol and Tobacco in Oral Cavity Cancer

The two well-established major risk factors predisposing to oral cavity cancer are alcohol and tobacco. Many independent studies have shown elevated risk in heavy drinkers and heavy smokers (or users of smokeless tobacco) and strongly indicate a synergistic effect between these two risk factors in promoting squamous cell carcinoma of the oral cavity. As an example, an epidemiologic investigation by Blot and colleagues (1988) determined that chronic smoking and drinking had independent odds ratios of 5.8 and 7.4, respectively, whereas the odds ratio for the combination of chronic smoking and drinking increased the odds ratio more than 35-fold, reflecting a multiplicative synergistic effect (Blot et al., 1988) (**Figure 5.3**). Epidemiologic studies in developed countries also suggest that long-term use of alcohol-containing mouthwash is a risk factor. Constant exposure to these alcohol-containing rinses, even in the absence of smoking and drinking, is associated with a significant increase in the risk of developing oral cancer (Kabat & Wynder, 1989).

Although it is well known that tobacco smoke and tobacco juice contain powerful carcinogens and inflammatory substances that are linked to carcinogenesis, the mechanism by which alcohol promotes oral cavity cancer remains elusive. Animal studies do not clearly indicate that pure alcohol acts as a direct carcinogen; rather, the studies seem to indicate that alcohol may promote the transport of other carcinogens through

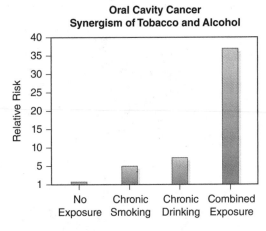

Figure 5.3 Combined Exposure to Tobacco and Alcohol Synergistically Increase the Risk of Oral Cavity Cancer.

Source: Data from Blot, W. J., McLaughlin, J. K., Winn, D. M., Austin, D. F., Greenberg, R. S., Preston-Martin, S.,... Fraumeni, J. F. (1988). Smoking and drinking in relation to oral and pharyngeal cancer. *Cancer Research, 48*, 3282–3287; Kabat, G. C., & Wynder, E. L. (1989). Type of alcoholic beverage and oral cancer. *International Journal of Cancer, 43*, 190–194.

the cell membrane either as a solvent or by acting on the cell membrane directly (Seitz & Stickel, 2007).

Though alcohol per se is not carcinogenic, *acetaldehyde*, the major product of alcohol metabolism, is classified as a human carcinogen. In the liver, the enzyme *alcohol dehydrogenase* oxidizes ethanol (alcohol) to form acetaldehyde, which is then oxidized by *acetaldehyde dehydrogenase* to produce *acetic acid* for excretion. Notably, microflora of the saliva can also produce acetaldehyde from ethanol and furthermore, many alcoholic beverages contain acetaldehyde (Homann, Jousimies-Somer, Jokelainen, Heine, & Salaspuro, 1997). Thus, sustained acetaldehyde exposure is likely to play a mechanistic role in the malignant transformation of the oral mucosa (Salaspuro, 2009).

Other possible mechanisms include the induction of microsomal enzymes in the liver that promote the formation of polycyclic aromatic hydrocarbons and/or benzopyrene, interference with DNA repair mechanisms, and epigenetic effects on DNA methylation resulting in epigenetic deregulation of tumor suppressor genes (Poschl & Seitz, 2004). Furthermore, alcohol may be a vehicle for the induction of contaminating carcinogens into the oral cavity (i.e., various alcoholic beverages may contain nitrosocompounds, phenols, or a variety of polycyclic aromatic hydrocarbons). Chronic alcohol consumption may also promote nutritional deficiency simply by substituting empty calories and reducing the dietary consumption of important micronutrients and minerals such as vitamins A and B, and iron. Heavy alcohol consumption coupled with poor nutrition may therefore result in immunosuppression, which may also increase the predisposition to oral cavity cancer (Testino & Borro, 2009).

HPV and Oral Cavity Cancer

It has been shown that chronic infection with high-risk strains of HPV (e.g., HPV-16) is an independent risk factor for the development of oral cavity cancer (D'Souza et al., 2007; Gillison et al., 2000, 2008; La Vecchia et al., 1997).

Maden and colleagues conducted an early case control study to investigate the potential role of HPV infection in the development of squamous cell carcinoma of the oral cavity. They compared HPV seropositivity and other risk factors, principally tobacco and alcohol use, in 131 male cases of oral cancer to 136 controls that were frequency-matched to the cases by age and location of residence. Seropositivity for HPV was based on reverse transcription polymerase chain reaction (RT PCR) assays of tumor specimens in the cases and oral mucosal specimens in the controls. Odds ratios (ORs) were estimated with adjustment for age, cigarette smoking, and alcohol consumption. Results revealed increases in the risk associated with seropositivity for HPV-6 (OR = 2.9) and HPV-16 (OR = 6.2) (Maden et al., 1992).

Schwartz and colleagues used similar methodology to investigate the potential role of HPV infection in the development of malignancies of the oral cavity. They conducted a case control study of 284 patients with squamous cell carcinomas of the head and neck and 477 control subjects from the general population similar in age and gender to the cases. Serum samples were tested for the presence of HPV-16 antibodies and tumor specimens from the cases, and samples of the oral mucosa from the control subjects were tested for HPV DNA. Data were also collected on the patients' history of cigarette smoking and alcohol consumption. Among 248 tumor specimens, 64 (26%) were positive for HPV and 43 (67%) of the 64 HPV-positive strains were positive for a high-risk HPV strain. Overall, 16.5% of cases (41 of 248) were positive for HPV-16, a strain that is oncogenic in other tissues such as the uterine cervix. Positivity for HPV-16 increased the risk of developing squamous cell carcinoma of the oral cavity nearly sevenfold (OR = 6.8). This association was not confounded by age, gender, cigarette smoking, or alcohol consumption. The investigators concluded that HPV-16 may contribute to the development of some oral squamous cell carcinomas, possibly in combination with cigarette smoking (Schwartz et al., 1998).

Gillison and colleagues tested for HPV in fresh frozen tumor specimens from 253 patients with newly diagnosed or recurrent squamous cell carcinomas using polymerase chain reaction–based assays (PCR-based assays). Smoking and drinking histories were also recorded for each case. The PCR assays detected HPV in 62 (25%) of the 253 cases, and HPV-16 was present in 56 (90%) of the positive cases. Notably, cases with HPV-positive tumors were *less likely* to be heavy smokers or heavy drinkers than cases with HPV-negative tumors (Gillison et al., 2000).

Mork and colleagues conducted a nested case control study of head and neck cancer using serum samples from a cohort of 900,000 individuals living in Norway, Finland, and Sweden. Serum samples were tested for selected strains of HPV among 292 cases with squamous cell carcinoma of the head and neck and 1,568 controls matched on age, gender, and time of serum collection. Blood samples were collected, on average, 9.4 years prior to cancer diagnosis. Odds ratios were adjusted for serum cotinine levels (a metabolite of nicotine and biochemical marker of exposure to tobacco smoke). Results revealed that HPV-16–seropositive individuals were 2.2 times more likely to develop squamous cell carcinoma of the head and neck than seronegative individuals. Analysis of 160 tumor specimens using RT PCR revealed that 50% of the oropharyngeal tumors contained HPV-16. Anatomic stratification of the data revealed that HPV-16 increased the risk of cancer development at multiple sites, including the oral cavity (OR = 3.6), the tongue (OR = 2.8), the oropharynx (OR = 14.2), the paranasal sinuses (OR = 3.4), and the larynx (OR = 2.2). These data suggest that HPV-16 infection detectable several years prior to diagnosis significantly heightens the risk of developing squamous cell carcinoma at multiple anatomic sites of the upper aerodigestive tract (Mork et al., 2001).

In a hospital-based case control study conducted in Baltimore, Gillison and colleagues studied 100 cases with squamous cell carcinoma of the head and neck and 200 control patients without cancer matched to the cases by age, gender, and location. The investigators examined mucosal specimens for serum antibodies to the L1 capsid protein of HPV-16 and its oncogenic proteins (E6 and E7). They also collected data on sexual practices, tobacco smoking, alcohol consumption, and other potential risk factors. Results showed that oral infection by HPV-16 increased the risk more than 14-fold, and seropositivity for the HPV-16 L1 capsid protein increased the risk more than 32-fold compared to seronegative individuals. Strikingly, seropositivity for E6 and/or E7 increased the risk nearly 60-fold. Analysis by PCR detected HPV-16 DNA in 72% of tumor specimens and HPV-16 E6 and/or E7 proteins in 64% of specimens. Sexual activity conducive to HPV exposure also increased the risk (e.g., more than 25 lifetime vaginal-sex partners or more than 5 oral-sex partners more than tripled the risk). Heavy tobacco and alcohol use also increased the risk of oropharyngeal cancer *but primarily among cases without exposure to HPV-16* (D'Souza et al., 2007).

These findings clearly show that the demographic profile of HPV-16–infected patients who develop oral cavity cancer differs markedly from that of patients whose cancer developed from chronic exposure to tobacco and alcohol. In the latter group, the disease is typically diagnosed after age 60, the ratio of African Americans to Caucasians is 2:1, and the ratio of men to women is nearly 3:1. In HPV-16–related disease, chronic exposure to tobacco and alcohol may be absent, the age at diagnosis is much earlier (age 20–50 years), the male-to-female ratio is close to 1:1, and tumors are most likely to develop on the tonsils and base of the tongue (Gillison et al., 2008). Most notably, HPV-16 and HPV-18 are the same viruses responsible for the vast majority of cervical cancers, and HPV is the most common sexually transmitted infection in the United States and elsewhere. Furthermore, infection by high-risk HPV strains is preventable by vaccination (Kenter et al., 2009).

Malignant Transformation by HPV

Oncogenic strains of HPV appear to cause malignant transformation of the oral mucosa in much the same way as in the cervix. The viral DNA integrates into human DNA in the nuclei of healthy cells and uses the cellular machinery to produce two harmful proteins, E6 and E7. These bind to, and shut down, two important tumor-suppressor proteins, p53 and pRb. Active pRb prevents excessive cell growth; without it, cells proliferate unchecked. Active p53 arrests the cell-division cycle when DNA is damaged, and then either activates DNA repair or initiates cell death. Without p53, a cell replicates wildly even if it has DNA damage (Gillison et al., 2008).

Synergism of HPV and Marijuana in Oral Cavity Cancer

Gillison and colleagues conducted a case control investigation to explore potential differences in the risk factors for HPV-16–positive and HPV-16–negative oral cavity malignancies (Gillison et al., 2008). Their study compared 240 cases with squamous cell carcinomas of the head and neck with 322 matched controls without cancer ascertained at the Johns Hopkins Hospital in Baltimore during 2000

through 2006. Among tumor specimens taken from the 240 cases, 92 (38%) were found to be positive for HPV-16 utilizing *in situ hybridization* methodology. Results revealed marked differences in the risk factors for HPV-16–positive versus HPV-16–negative cases. Sexual behavior (number of oral sex partners) was strongly associated with HPV-16–positive cases, whereas tobacco use, alcohol use, and poor oral hygiene were associated with HPV-16–negative cases. Surprisingly, use of tobacco and/or alcohol had no effect on the risk of developing HPV-16–negative cancer. An interesting finding was the association of marijuana smoking with cancer risk. The association of marijuana smoking was more pronounced among HPV-16–positive cases than HPV-negative cases, suggesting the possibility of synergism between cannabis and viral exposure (**Figure 5.4**).

HIV and Oral Cavity Cancer

The North American AIDS Cohort Collaboration on Research and Design (NA-ACCORD) was created as a part of the International Epidemiologic Databases to Evaluate AIDS (IeDEA) initiative. Investigators with NA-ACCORD are currently monitoring health outcomes among more than 90,000 patients, the majority of whom are HIV-positive, from more than 50 sites throughout the United States and Canada. Recently, investigators with NA-ACCORD examined incidence rates of oral cavity and pharyngeal cancer among 51,151 HIV-positive people in 14 cohorts across North America during the time period 2006–2010. Age-adjusted rates among HIV-positive individuals were compared with rates for the Surveillance, Epidemiology, and End Results (SEER) population during the same time period. Results revealed that the annual incidence rate of oral cavity and pharyngeal cancer in HIV-positive individuals was nearly double the rate in the general population (30.1 per 100,000 versus 15.9 per 100,000). The investigators also noted an approximate twofold increase in the incidence of these malignancies among older HIV-positive individuals with a low CD4 count (below 350 helper T lymphocytes per microliter of blood). Notably, all incident cases observed in the HIV-positive cohort were chronic cigarette smokers. These findings suggest that immunosuppression due to HIV infection may increase susceptibility to carcinogenesis in tissues of the oral cavity and pharynx, particularly among smokers (Beachler & D'Souza, 2013).

Lip Cancer and Solar Radiation

Lip cancers account for 30–40% of all malignancies of the oral cavity. These tumors are predominately squamous cell carcinomas that arise in the lower lip

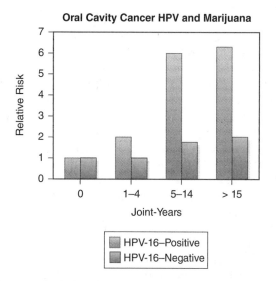

Figure 5.4 Relative Risk (RR) of Oral Cavity Cancer with Increasing Joint-Years of Marijuana Smoking in HPV-16–Positive and HPV-16–Negative Squamous Cell Carcinoma of the Head and Neck.

Source: Data from Gillison, M. L., D'Souza, G., Wester, W., Sugar, E., Ziao, W., Begum, S., & Vascidi, R. (2008). Distinct risk factor profiles for human papillomavirus type 16–positive and human papillomavirus type 16–negative head and neck cancers. *Journal of the National Cancer Institute, 100*(6), 407–420.

following chronic and excessive exposure to solar ultraviolet radiation. Incidence rates of lip cancer and other forms of skin cancer are highest in Caucasian populations residing in regions with high levels of solar radiation (Johnson et al., 2011).

Ozone (O_3) is an unstable oxygen molecule that effectively filters ultraviolet radiation in the stratosphere (the atmosphere 10–50 kilometers above the Earth). In recent decades, significant thinning of the ozone layer has been noted, particularly over the Earth's polar regions. Ozone depletion is caused by increased levels of chlorofluorocarbons, bromofluorocarbons, and other manmade chemicals that dissociate into reactive molecules at the Earth's surface. These molecules are transported into the stratosphere where they destroy ozone by catalytic reactions (Jones, 1987). The largest "ozone hole" ever recorded was imaged by the U.S. National Aeronautics and Space Administration (NASA) over Antarctica in 2006 (Carlowicz & Lindsey, 2009). Notably, Caucasian populations of Australia and New Zealand that live in closest proximity to the Antarctic ozone hole have the highest rates of lip cancer and skin cancer in the world (Anderson, Wilmouth, Smith, & Sayres, 2012; Moore, Johnson, Pierce, & Wilson, 1999; Moore, Allister, Roder, Pierce, & Wilson, 2001; Narayanan, Saladi, & Fox, 2010; Staples et al., 2006). Epidemiologic data on lip cancer collected by the South Australian Central Cancer Registry during 1977–1996

revealed age-standardized annual incidence rates of 15 per 100,000 in men and 4 per 100,000 in women, whereas the rates observed for the same time period in the U.S. population of Connecticut were less than 1 per 100,000 for both men and women (Moore et al., 2001; Morse, Pendrys, Neely, & Psoter, 1999).

Global recognition of ozone destruction by chlorofluorocarbons and bromofluorocarbons led to the Montreal Protocol of 1989, which banned the production of ozone-depleting chemicals. Predictive models of ozone depletion by manmade substances suggest that ozone depletion and heightened solar radiation will continue to increase over many decades (Carlowicz, 2009).

Cancer of the lip most often develops in the epithelium of the vermillion, a transition zone between the inner labial mucosa and the outer skin of the lower lip (Molnar, Ronay, & Tapolcsanyi, 1974). The lower lip is 5–10 times more likely to be affected owing to its greater exposure to sunlight. In a recent 25-year retrospective study of 2,152 patients from Western Australia with lip cancer, 81% occurred on the lower lip and over 75% developed in men (Abreu, Kruger, & Tennant, 2009). The risk of lip cancer is inversely related to the level of skin pigmentation (i.e., fair-skinned people have the highest risk and dark-skinned individuals the lowest). Chronic abuse of tobacco (particularly pipe and cigar smoking), chronic alcohol abuse, and certain viral infections (e.g., HPV-16) have also been found to increase the risk (Maruccia et al., 2012; Moore et al., 1999; Perea-Milla et al., 2003).

Recent studies indicate that lip cancer occurs at markedly increased rates after organ transplantation and exposure to immunosuppressive drugs. In a population-based nationwide cohort of 8,162 kidney transplant recipients, squamous cell lip cancer was diagnosed in 203 patients during periods of receiving immunosuppressive drugs at rates 41 times higher than expected in men and 72 times higher than expected in women (van Leeuwen et al., 2009).

Lip cancer and other forms of skin cancer can be prevented by using sunscreen, avoiding sunburn, limiting other sources of radiation (e.g., tanning salons), and wearing protective clothing, sunglasses, and hats. Most lip cancers are squamous cell carcinomas that have potential for metastatic spread. Nevertheless, because of their highly visible location, the majority of lip cancers are detected and excised at an early stage and mortality rates are quite low (Stebbins & Hanke, 2014).

Other Risk Factors for Oral Cavity Cancer

Plummer–Vinson syndrome (iron deficiency anemia, dysphagia, and atrophy of the oral cavity mucosa) is associated with predisposition to oral cavity cancer. Other conditions that may be associated with oral cavity neoplasms include sprue (malabsorption of wheat germ) and scurvy (deficiency in vitamin C).

Rare malignant neoplasms of the oral cavity include cancers of the salivary glands, including the parotid glands and submandibular glands. These are typically glandular carcinomas with mixed histologic features. A salivary gland carcinoma mixed with marked lymphocytic invasion is called a Warthin's tumor. The risk of salivary gland cancer is increased by ionizing radiation (e.g., in atomic bomb survivors and after radiotherapy) (Boukheris, Curtis, Land, & Dores, 2009), but other risk factors have not been identified.

Malignant melanomas may also present initially in the oral cavity. Risk factors for oral cavity malignant melanomas include certain genetic syndromes, such as Peutz-Jeuger syndrome and Addison's disease, both of which lead to melanotic pigmentation of the oral cavity mucosa (Boardman et al., 1998).

CANCER OF THE OROPHARYNX AND LARYNGOPHARYNX

During 2012, 142,387 new cases were diagnosed and 96,060 individuals died from cancer of the oropharynx or laryngopharynx in the world population. Approximately 81% of the new cases and deaths occurred in men (115,131 new cases and 77,585 deaths). Cancers of the oropharynx and laryngopharynx constitute approximately 1.0% of all malignant neoplasms and account for about 1.2% of cancer deaths in the human population (Ferlay et al., 2010, 2013).

Pathologic and epidemiologic features of malignancies of the oropharynx and laryngopharynx are similar to oral cavity cancer. Tumors arising in these tissues are predominantly squamous cell carcinomas. The global distributions of incidence and mortality rates are similar to the patterns for oral cavity cancer in Figure 5.2.

Neoplasms of the oropharynx and laryngopharynx are typically diagnosed in the elderly and occur more often in men than women. The major risk factors are tobacco smoking, alcohol consumption, and infection by oncogenic strains of HPV (e.g., HPV-16 and HPV-18). Minor risk factors include marijuana smoking; nutritional deficits of iron, vitamin B, and vitamin C; and chronic use of smokeless tobacco (La Vecchia et al., 1997). Immunosuppression due to HIV infection also increases carcinogenesis in tissues of the oral cavity and pharynx (Beachler & D'Souza, 2013).

CANCER OF THE NASOPHARYNX

During 2012, 86,691 new cases were diagnosed and 50,828 individuals died from cancer of the nasopharynx in the world population. Approximately 70% of the new cases and deaths occurred in men (60,896 new cases and 35,753 deaths). Cancer of the nasopharynx constitutes approximately 1.2% of all malignant neoplasms and accounts for about 0.6% of cancer deaths in the human population (Ferlay et al., 2010, 2013).

Figure 5.5 shows the global patterns of incidence and mortality rates of nasopharyngeal cancer in 2012. Nasopharyngeal carcinoma is rare in most regions of the world, and the low-risk populations in these regions had annual incidence rates less than 1 per 100,000. In contrast, markedly higher rates are evident for the populations of China, the nations of Southeast Asia, and the islands of Oceania. The highest incidence and mortality rates reported in 2012 were in men of Malaysia (10.6 and 3.9 per 100,000) and Indonesia (8.3 and 5.0 per 100,000) (Ferlay et al., 2013).

Certain populations within nations have very high rates of nasopharyngeal carcinoma. High-risk populations include the Cantonese of Southern China, Hong Kong, and Taiwan; the Inuits (Eskimos) in Greenland and Alaska; the Vietnamese in North Vietnam; and the Arabians of North Africa. Within these populations, several major risk factors for nasopharyngeal carcinoma have been identified.

Histology of Nasopharyngeal Cancer

Malignancies of the nasopharynx are predominantly squamous cell carcinomas that arise from the squamous epithelial lining of the organ. Nasopharyngeal carcinoma has been classified into three distinct histologic types: keratinizing squamous cell carcinoma (Type I) and nonkeratinizing squamous cell carcinoma (Types II and III). Nonkeratinizing malignancies are further classified as either differentiated (Type II) or undifferentiated (Type III). The nonkeratinized Type II and Type III malignancies constitute nearly all of the nasopharyngeal carcinomas in high-risk populations, whereas the keratinized Type I malignancies predominate in low-risk populations. The age-specific incidence of Type I malignancies of the nasopharynx increases exponentially with age beginning at about 50 years of age, whereas the age-specific incidence of Type II and Type III malignancies peaks at about age 50 years and then declines.

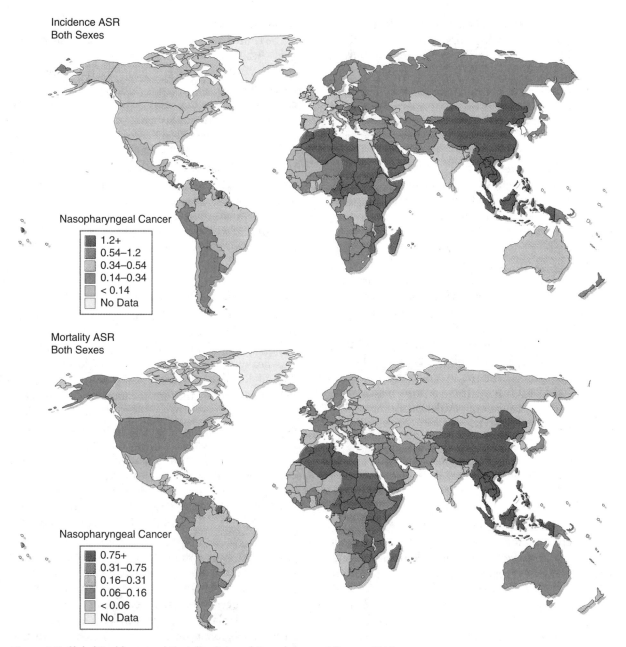

Figure 5.5 Global Incidence and Mortality Rates of Nasopharyngeal Cancer, 2012.

ASR: Rates per 100,000 are age-standardized to the world population, 2000–2025.

Source: Ferlay, J., Soerjomataram, I., Ervik, M., Dikshit, R., Eser, S., Mathers, C., . . . Bray, F. (2013). *GLOBOCAN 2012 v1.0. Cancer incidence and mortality worldwide: IARC CancerBase No. 11* [Internet]. Lyon, France: International Agency for Research on Cancer. Retrieved from http://globocan.iarc.fr

Risk Factors for Nasopharyngeal Carcinoma

Nasopharyngeal carcinoma is influenced by a web of causation that includes certain dietary factors, tobacco smoking, alcohol intake, and viral infection. The risk factors are discussed in the following sections.

Dietary Factors and Nasopharyngeal Carcinoma

In 1971, John Ho, a radiation oncologist in Hong Kong, postulated that intake of Cantonese-style salted fish may contribute to the development of nasopharyngeal carcinoma (Ho, 1971). His hypothesis was subsequently confirmed by the results of several case control studies. For example, an international team of investigators examined the effects of salted foods and other dietary factors in a study of 282 cases of nasopharyngeal carcinoma ascertained from medical centers in Malaysia and an equal number of age- and gender-matched disease-free controls from the general population. Compared to nonconsumers, individuals consuming salted fish at least weekly increased their risk of developing laryngeal carcinoma by more than fourfold (OR = 4.4). Risk increases also were also noted for heavy consumption of other salted foods (leafy vegetables, roots, and eggs) as well as alcoholic beverages. Conversely, individuals who regularly consumed fresh fruits and vegetables lowered their risk (Armstrong et al., 1998). The carcinogenic potential of salt-preserved fish is supported by experiments in laboratory rats, which develop malignant nasal and nasopharyngeal tumors after salted fish consumption (Zheng, Luo, Christensson, & Drettner, 1994).

Jeannel and colleagues examined the effects of diet in a study of 80 cases of nasopharyngeal carcinoma ascertained from the Institute Salah Azaiz in Tunisia and 160 disease-free controls matched on age, gender, and place of residence. Compared to nonconsumers, those who regularly consumed pickled vegetables, quaddid (dried mutton in oil), harissa (a very spicy condiment), salted anchovies, or pickled olives were found to be at increased risk (Jeannel et al., 1990).

Tobacco Smoking and Nasopharyngeal Carcinoma

Several epidemiologic studies have noted that chronic tobacco smoking elevates the risk of developing nasopharyngeal carcinoma. In Taiwan, exposure to tobacco and alcohol were studied in 375 cases with histologically confirmed nasopharyngeal carcinoma and 327 healthy community controls matched to the cases on gender, age, and residence. Compared to nonsmokers, those who smoked 25 or more years had a modest increase in risk (OR = 1.7). Consumption of alcoholic beverages had no influence on the risk in this sample of cases and controls from a high-risk population (Cheng et al., 1999). These results are characteristic of a number of case control studies conducted in high-risk populations: a modest risk increase in chronic smokers but no effect associated with ingestion of alcohol at any level (Yu & Yuan, 2002).

Alcohol Consumption and Nasopharyngeal Carcinoma

Although studies of alcohol and nasopharyngeal carcinoma have been uniformly null in high-risk populations, investigations conducted in low-risk populations do find effects of alcohol. Investigators in the United States studied 231 cases of nasopharyngeal carcinoma ascertained from population registries in Washington, Detroit, Connecticut, Iowa, and Utah and 246 disease-free controls matched to the cases on age, gender, and residence. Compared to nonsmokers, individuals who smoked more than 60 pack-years had a sixfold increase in risk (OR = 6.5). Compared to nondrinkers, individuals who reported the heaviest alcohol consumption (21 or more drinks per week) had a threefold increase in risk (OR = 2.9). The magnitude of risk estimates increased for persons 50 years of age or older, suggesting that a large fraction of elderly cases of nasopharyngeal carcinoma arise due to chronic smoking and alcohol intake (Vaughan et al., 1996).

Formaldehyde and Nasopharyngeal Carcinoma

In 1986, a team of U.S. investigators reported the results of a historical cohort study of mortality among 27,561 workers employed in 10 facilities where there was heavy occupational exposure to formaldehyde. Although overall cancer mortality was not influenced by formaldehyde exposure, the mortality due to nasopharyngeal cancer was significantly increased (Blair et al., 1986). In a subsequent analysis of this same cohort, formaldehyde exposure increased the standardized mortality ratio (SMR) for nasopharyngeal cancer by more than twofold (SMR = 2.1) (Hauptmann, Lubin, Stewart, Hayes, & Blair, 2004). In 2006, the International Agency for Research on Cancer (IARC) classified formaldehyde as carcinogenic to humans (IARC, 2006). Nevertheless, a recent meta-analysis revealed significant heterogeneity among published estimates of risk due to inclusion of a single plant in Connecticut with an unexplained cluster of nasopharyngeal cancers, thereby diminishing support for a causal relationship between formaldehyde exposure and nasopharyngeal cancer (Blanchard, Mundt, Mundt, & Montgomery, 2010).

Other occupational exposures have also been examined, including exposure to wood dust, wood solvents, cotton dust, combustion products, agrichemicals, and pesticides. Of these, exposure to wood dust shows the greatest consistency as a risk factor among studies (Chang & Adami, 2006; Vaughan & Davis, 1991).

Epstein–Barr Virus (EBV) and Nasopharyngeal Carcinoma

Epstein–Barr virus (EBV) is a herpes virus containing doubled-stranded DNA that infects 90–95% of the world population. In Hong Kong, EBV infects 80%

of children by the age of 5 years, 90% by the age of 8 years, and almost 100% by the age of 10 years without causing symptoms. In London, EBV infection usually occurs during the teenage years and can cause infectious mononucleosis (Kangro et al., 1994). Transmission occurs through contact with contaminated saliva. The virus initially infects the epithelium of the nasal cavity, the nasopharynx, and the oropharynx, after which it spreads into B lymphocytes. In infected individuals, EBV persists throughout life as a latent virus in resting memory B lymphocytes. In this state, EBV is dormant and replicates together with the chromosomal DNA of host cells. Latency results in limited expression of EBV genes and concealment from host immunity. Reactivation of EBV is triggered when memory B cells differentiate into plasma cells in response to specific antigenic stimuli (e.g., infection by other microbes). Reactivation leads to replication of viral DNA, assembly and budding of virions from infected cells, and dissemination to other tissues (Draborg, Duus, & Houen, 2013).

Involvement of EBV in the genesis of nasopharyngeal carcinoma was suspected as early as 1966 when cases were found to express antibodies against EBV. Later studies revealed that patients with nasopharyngeal cancer had elevated IgG and IgA antibody titers specific for the viral capsid, viral nuclear antigens, and viral DNA. Viral DNA, RNA, and gene products have also been detected in the tumor cells of most patients. Notably, the titers of IgA antibodies precede the development of nasopharyngeal carcinoma by several years and correlate with tumor burden, remission, and recurrence. The totality of evidence clearly indicates a causal role of EBV infection in the development of nasopharyngeal carcinoma. However, EBV infection alone is not a sufficient cause of nasopharyngeal carcinoma because virtually all adults worldwide are infected, yet only a small fraction develop the malignancy. Therefore, it is apparent that environmental and/or genetic cofactors also contribute to carcinogenesis (Chang & Adami, 2006; Yu & Yuan, 2002).

Immunosuppression and Inflammation in Nasopharyngeal Carcinoma

Immunosuppressive and inflammatory conditions have been found to increase the risk of developing nasopharyngeal carcinoma. In a follow-up study of a large cohort of patients with HIV/AIDS in the United States, the incidence of nasopharyngeal carcinoma was elevated more than twofold compared to the general population (Shebl, Bhatia, & Engels, 2009).

Using data from a registry of national health insurance claims, investigators in Taiwan examined incidence rates of cancer in patients with inflammatory myopathies. A startling finding was a 66-fold increase in the incidence of nasopharyngeal carcinoma among 1,059 patients with dermatomyositis compared to the general Taiwanese population (Huang et al., 2009). Dermatomyositis is a rare, systemic autoimmune disease characterized by a distinct skin rash, and inflammation and weakness of skeletal muscles. Some cases of this condition have been linked to reactivation of latent EBV and other viral or bacterial infections (Callen & Wortmann, 2006).

Genetic Predisposition to Nasopharyngeal Carcinoma

Familial clustering of nasopharyngeal carcinoma has been demonstrated in a number of studies. Compared to individuals without a family history of nasopharyngeal carcinoma, subjects with an affected first-degree relative (parent, sibling, or child) have a 4- to 10-fold elevation in risk. Notably, certain alleles of the human leukocyte antigen (HLA) locus have been identified that appear to modify genetic susceptibility (Burt et al., 1996). In a meta-analysis of studies in Southern Chinese populations, HLA-A2, -B14, and -B46 were found to be associated with increases in risk, whereas HLA-A11, -B13, and -B22 were associated with decreases in risk (Goldsmith, West, & Morton, 2002).

Molecular studies of nasopharyngeal tumors have revealed a variety of genomic abnormalities, including loss of heterozygosity, chromosomal gains and losses, and epigenetic modification of tumor suppressor genes and oncogenes. Nevertheless, additional studies will be needed in order to elucidate specific genetic factors that are related to carcinogenesis of the nasopharynx.

Carcinogenesis in the Nasopharynx

Nearly all humans are infected with latent EBV, so carcinogenesis may involve an immunocompromised human host who is predisposed to the reactivation of latent EBV and dissemination of the virus to produce an active EBV infection of the nasopharyngeal epithelium. Active infection of the nasopharynx in combination with exposure to tobacco carcinogens, nitrosamines from salted fish, or other irritating/inflammatory agents may induce DNA damage, episomal changes, and viral integration into the chromosomes of epithelial cells. The expression of specific viral genes might also disable tumor suppressor genes or amplify tumor oncogenes that spur mechanisms of carcinogenesis such as increased cell replication, dysregulation of apoptosis, angiogenesis, and metastasis (Raab-Traub, 2002).

Prevention of Nasopharyngeal Carcinoma

Specific strategies for the primary prevention of nasopharyngeal carcinoma are speculative. However, avoiding regular intake of salt-preserved fish or other foods, tobacco, and regular intake of any substance that causes irritation/inflammation in the upper alimentary canal; limiting alcohol consumption; and increasing regular intake of fresh fruit and vegetables may lower the risk.

● ● ● REFERENCES

Abreu, L., Kruger, E., & Tennant, M. (2009). Lip cancer in Western Australia, 1982–2006: A 25-year retrospective epidemiological study. *Australian Dental Journal, 54,* 130–135.

American Cancer Society. (2007). *Global cancer facts and figures, 2007.* Atlanta, GA: Author.

Anderson, J. G., Wilmouth, D. M., Smith, J. B., & Sayres, D. S. (2012). UV dosage levels in summer: Increased risk of ozone loss from convectively injected water vapor. *Science, 337*(6096), 835–839.

Armstrong, R. W., Imrey, P. B., Lye, M. S., Armstrong, M. J., Yu, M. C., & Sani, S. (1998). Nasopharyngeal carcinoma in Malaysian Chinese; salted fish and other dietary exposures. *International Journal of Cancer, 77,* 228–235.

Blanchard, A. M., Mundt, K. A., Mundt, D. J., & Montgomery, R. R. (2010). Epidemiological studies of formaldehyde exposure and risk of leukemia and nasopharyngeal cancer: A meta-analysis. *Critical Reviews in Toxicology, 40*(2), 85–100.

Beachler, D. C., & D'Souza, G. (2013). Oral HPV infection and head and neck cancers in HIV-infected individuals. *Current Opinion in Oncology, 25*(5), 503–510.

Blair, A., Stewart, P., O'Berg, M., Gaffey, W., Walrath, J., Ward, J., . . . Cubit, D. (1986). Mortality among industrial workers exposed to formaldehyde. *Journal of the National Cancer Institute, 76*(6), 1071–1084.

Blot, W. J., McLaughlin, J. K., Winn, D. M., Austin, D. F., Greenberg, R. S., Preston-Martin, S., . . . Fraumeni, J. F. (1988). Smoking and drinking in relation to oral and pharyngeal cancer. *Cancer Research, 48,* 3282–3287.

Boardman, L. A., Thibodeau, S. N., Schaid, D. J., Lindor, N. M., McDonnell, S. K., Bugart, L. J., . . . Hartmann, L. C. (1998). Increased risk for cancer in patients with the Peutz-Jeghers syndrome. *Annals of Internal Medicine, 128*(11), 896–899.

Boukheris, H., Curtis, R. E., Land, C. E., & Dores, G. M. (2009). Incidence of carcinoma of the major salivary glands according to the WHO classification, 1992 to 2006: A population-based study in the United States. *Cancer Epidemiology, Biomarkers and Prevention, 18,* 2899–2906.

Boyle, P., & Levin, B. (Eds.). (2008). *IARC world cancer report.* Lyon, France: International Agency for Research on Cancer (IARC) Publications.

Burt, R. D., Vaughan, T. L., McKnight, B., Davis, S., Beckmann, A. M., Smith, A. G., . . . Berwick, M. (1996). Associations between human leukocyte antigen type and nasopharyngeal carcinoma in Caucasians in the United States. *Cancer Epidemiology, Biomarkers and Prevention, 5,* 879–887.

Callen, J. P, Wortmann, R. L. (2006). Dermatomyositis. *Clinics in Dermatology, 24*(5), 363–373.

Carlowicz, M. (2009). Climate change and atmospheric circulation will make for uneven ozone recovery. Retrieved from http://www.nasa.gov/topics/earth/features/ozone_recovery.html

Carlowicz, M., & Lindsey, R. (2009). *Earth observatory: The world we avoided by protecting the ozone layer.* Greenbelt, MD: Earth Observatory, Goddard Space Flight Center, NASA.

Chang, E. T., & Adami, H.-O. (2006). The enigmatic epidemiology of nasopharyngeal carcinoma. *Cancer Epidemiology, Biomarkers and Prevention, 15,* 1765–1777.

Cheng, Y. J., Hildesheim, A., Hsu, M. M., Chen, I. H., Brinton, L. A., Levine, P. H., . . . Yang, C. S. (1999). Cigarette smoking, alcohol consumption and risk of nasopharyngeal carcinoma in Taiwan. *Cancer Causes & Control, 10*(3), 201–207.

Draborg, A. H., Duus, K., & Houen, G. (2013). Epstein-Barr virus in systemic autoimmune diseases. *Clinical and Developmental Immunology, 2013.* Retrieved from http://www .hindawi.com/journals/jir/2013/535738

D'Souza, G., Kreimer, A. R., Viscidi, R., Pawlita, M., Fakhry, C., Koch, W. M., . . . Gillison, M. L. (2007). Case-control study of human papillomavirus and oropharyngeal cancer. *New England Journal of Medicine, 356*(19), 1944–1956.

Ferlay, J., Shin, H.-R., Bray, F., Forman, D., Mathers, C., & Parkin, D. M. (2010). Estimates of worldwide burden of cancer in 2008: GLOBOCAN 2008. *International Journal of Cancer, 127*(12), 2893–2917.

Ferlay, J., Soerjomataram, I., Ervik, M., Dikshit, R., Eser, S., Mathers, C., . . . Bray, F. (2013). GLOBOCAN 2012 v1.0, cancer incidence and mortality worldwide: IARC CancerBase No. 11. Lyon, France: International Agency for Research on Cancer. Retrieved from http://globocan.iarc.fr

Gillison, M. L., D'Souza, G., Wester, W., Sugar, E., Ziao, W., Begum, S., & Vascidi, R. (2008). Distinct risk factor profiles for human papillomavirus type 16–positive and human papillomavirus type 16–negative head and neck cancers. *Journal of the National Cancer Institute, 100*(6), 407–420.

Gillison, M. L., Koch, W. M., Capone, R. B., Spafford, M., Westra, W. H., Wu, L., . . . Sidransky, D. (2000). Evidence for a causal association between human papillomavirus and a subset of head and neck cancers. *Journal of the National Cancer Institute, 92,* 709–720.

Goldsmith, D. B., West, T. M., & Morton, R. (2002). HLA associations with nasopharyngeal carcinoma in Southern Chinese: A meta-analysis. *Clinical Otolaryngology, 27,* 61–67.

Gupta, P. C., Mehta, F. S., & Pindborg, J. J. (1984). Mortality among reverse chutta smokers in south India. *British Medical Journal (Clinical Research Edition), 289*(6449), 865–866.

Hauptmann, M., Lubin, J. H., Stewart, P. A., Hayes, R. B., & Blair, A. (2004). Mortality from solid cancers among workers in formaldehyde industries. *American Journal of Epidemiology, 59*(12), 1117–1130.

Ho, J. H. C. (1971). Genetic and environmental factors in nasopharyngeal carcinoma. In W. Nakahara, K. Nishioka, T. Hirayama, & Y. Ito (Eds.). *Recent advances in human tumor virology and immunology* (pp. 275–295). Tokyo, Japan: University of Tokyo Press.

Homann, N., Jousimies-Somer, H., Jokelainen, K., Heine, R., & Salaspuro, M. (1997). High acetaldehyde levels in saliva after ethanol consumption: Methodological aspects and pathogenetic implications. *Carcinogenesis, 18*(9), 1739–1743.

Huang, Y. L., Chen, Y. J., Lin, M. W., Wu, C. Y., Liu, P. C., Chen, T. J., . . . Liu, H. N. (2009). Malignancies associated with dermatomyositis and polymyositis in Taiwan: A nationwide population-based study. *British Journal of Dermatology, 161*(4), 854–860.

International Agency for Research on Cancer (IARC). (2006). Formaldehyde, 2-butoxyethanol and 1-tert-butoxypropan-2-ol. *IARC Monographs on the Evaluation of Carcinogenic Risks, 88,* 39–325.

Jeannel, D., Hubert, A., De Vathaire, F., Ellouz, R., Camoun, M., Ben Salem, M., . . . De-Thi, G. (1990). Diet, living conditions and nasopharyngeal carcinoma in Tunisia—a case control study. *International Journal of Cancer, 46,* 421–425.

Johnson, N. W., Jayasekara, P., & Amarasinghe, A. A. H. K. (2011). Squamous cell carcinoma and precursor lesions of the oral cavity: Epidemiology and aetiology. *Periodontology 2000, 57,* 19–37.

Jones, R. R. (1987). Ozone depletion and cancer risk. *Lancet, 330*(8556), 443–446.

Kabat, G. C., & Wynder, E. L. (1989). Type of alcoholic beverage and oral cancer. *International Journal of Cancer, 43,* 190–194.

Kangro, H. O., Osman, H. K., Lau, Y. L., Heath, R. B., Yeung, C. Y., & Ng, M. H. (1994). Seroprevalence of antibodies to human herpes viruses in England and Hong Kong. *Journal of Medical Virology, 43*, 91–96.

Kenter, G. G., Welters, M. J., Valentijn, A. R., Lowik, M. J. G., Berends-van der Meer, D. M. A., Vloon, A. P. G., . . . Melief, C. J. M. (2009). Vaccination against HPV-16 oncoproteins for vulvar intraepithelial neoplasia. *New England Journal of Medicine, 361*, 1838–1847.

Krolls, S. O., & Hoffman, S. (1976). Squamous cell carcinoma of the oral soft tissues: A statistical analysis of 14,253 cases by age, sex and race of patients. *Journal of the American Dental Association, 92*, 571–574.

La Vecchia, C., Tavani, A., Franceschi, S., Levi, F., & Negri, M. (1997). Epidemiology and prevention of oral cancer. *Oral Oncology, 33*(5), 302–312.

Maden, C., Beckmann, A. M., Thomas, D. B., McKnight, B., Sherman, K. J., Ashley, R. L., . . . Daling, J. R. (1992). Human papillomaviruses, herpes simplex viruses, and the risk of oral cancer in men. *American Journal of Epidemiology, 135*(10), 1093–1102.

Maruccia, M., Onesti, M. G., Parisi, E., Cigna, A., Toccola, A., & Scuder, N. (2012). Lip cancer: A 10-year retrospective epidemiological study. *Anticancer Research, 32*(4), 1543–1546.

Molnar, L., Ronay, P., & Tapolcsanyi, L. (1974). Carcinoma of the lip. Analysis of the material of 25 years. *Oncology, 29*, 101–121.

Moore, S., Johnson, N., Pierce, A., & Wilson, D. (1999). The epidemiology of lip cancer: A review of global incidence and aetiology. *Oral Disease, 5*(3), 185–195.

Moore, S. R., Allister, J., Roder, D., Pierce, A. M., & Wilson, D. F. (2001). Lip cancer in South Australia, 1977–1996. *Pathology, 33*(2), 167–171.

Mork, J., Lie, A. K., Glattre, E., Clark, S., Hallmans, G., Jellum, E., . . . Dillner, J. (2001). Human papillomavirus infection as a risk factor for squamous-cell carcinoma of the head and neck. *New England Journal of Medicine, 344*, 1125–1131.

Morse, D. E., Pendrys, D. G., Neely, A. L., & Psoter, W. J. (1999). Trends in the incidence of lip, oral, and pharyngeal cancer: Connecticut, 1935–1994. *Oral Oncology, 35*(1), 1–8.

Narayanan, D. L., Saladi, R. N., & Fox, J. L. (2010). Ultraviolet radiation and skin cancer. *International Journal of Dermatology, 49*(9), 978–986.

National Cancer Institute. (2014). Oral cancer. National Institutes of Health. Retrieved from http://www.cancer.gov/cancertopics/types/oral

Parkin, M. D., Bray, F., Ferlay, J., & Pisani, P. (2005). Global cancer statistics, 2002. *CA: A Cancer Journal for Clinicians, 55*, 74–108.

Perea-Milla López, E., Miñarro-Del Moral, R. M., Martínez-García, C., Zanetti, R., Rosso, S., Serrano, S., . . . Redondo, M. (2003). Lifestyles, environmental and phenotypic factors associated with lip cancer: A case–control study in southern Spain. *British Journal of Cancer, 88*, 1702–1707.

Poschl, G., & Seitz, H. K. (2004). Alcohol and cancer. *Alcohol, 39*, 155–165.

Raab-Traub, N. (2002). Epstein-Barr virus in the pathogenesis of NPC. *Seminars in Cancer Biology, 2*(6), 431–441.

Salaspuro, M. (2009). Acetaldehyde as a common denominator and cumulative carcinogen in digestive tract cancers. *Scandinavian Journal of Gastroenterology, 44*(8), 912–925.

Schwartz S. M., Daling J. R., Doody D. R., Wipf G. C., Carter J. J., Madeleine M. M., . . . Galloway D. A. (1998). Oral cancer risk in relation to sexual history and evidence of human papillomavirus infection. *Journal of the National Cancer Institute, 90*, 1626–1636.

Seitz, H. K., & Stickel, F. (2007). Molecular mechanisms of alcohol-mediated carcinogenesis. *Nature Reviews Cancer, 7*, 599–612.

Shebl, F. M., Bhatia, K., & Engels, E. A. (2009). Salivary gland and nasopharyngeal cancers in individuals with acquired immunodeficiency syndrome in United States. *International Journal of Cancer, 126*(10), 2503–2508.

Shklar, G. (1979). The oral cavity, jaws, and salivary glands. In Robbins S. L., Cotran R. S., *Pathologic basis of disease* (pp. 886–917), Philadelphia, PA: W. B. Saunders.

Staples, M. P., Elwood, M., Burton, R. C., Williams, J. L., Marks, R., & Giles, G. G. (2006). Non-melanoma skin cancer in Australia: The 2002 national survey and trends since 1985. *Medical Journal of Australia, 184*(1), 6–10.

Stebbins, W., & Hanke, C. W. (2014). *Lip cancer: Not uncommon, often overlooked.* New York, NY: Skin Cancer Foundation.

Testino, G., & Borro, P. (2009). Carcinogenesis and alcohol. *Mediterranean Journal of Nutrition and Metabolism, 2,* 89–91.

van Leeuwen, M. T., Grulich, A. E., McDonald, S. P., McCredie, M. R., Amin J, Stewart, J. H., . . . Vajdic, C. M. (2009). Immunosuppression and other risk factors for lip cancer after kidney transplantation. *Cancer Epidemiology Biomarkers & Prevention, 18*(2), 561–569.

Vaughan, T. L., & Davis, S. (1991). Wood dust exposure and squamous cell cancer of the upper respiratory tract. *American Journal of Epidemiology, 133*(5), 560–564.

Vaughan, T. L., Shapiro, J. A., Burt, R. D., Sanson, G. M., Berwick, M., Lynch, C. F., & Lyon, J. L. (1996). Nasopharyngeal cancer in a low-risk population: Defining risk factor by histological type. *Cancer Epidemiology, Biomarkers and Prevention, 5,* 587–593.

Yu, M. C., & Yuan, J. M. (2002). Epidemiology of nasopharyngeal carcinoma. *Seminars in Cancer Biology, 12*(6), 421–429.

Zheng, X., Luo, Y., Christensson, B., & Drettner, B. (1994). Induction of nasal and nasopharyngeal tumours in Sprague-Dawley rats fed with Chinese salted fish. *Acta Otolaryngolica, 114,* 98–104.

6

Epidemiology of Esophageal Cancer

ANATOMY AND FUNCTION OF THE ESOPHAGUS

The esophagus is a muscular tube that transports saliva, food, and liquids from the mouth to the stomach. In the human adult, the esophagus is about 20 centimeters (8 inches) long. The organ is lined by stratified squamous epithelium. The upper esophageal sphincter, which is located just below the pharynx, allows passage of food and liquids during swallowing. The lower esophageal sphincter, located at the junction of the lower esophagus with the stomach, regulates the passage of food and liquids into the stomach. Just before entering the stomach, the esophagus passes through the diaphragm (see **Figure 6.1**) (Kumar, Abbas, & Aster, 2014).

GLOBAL EPIDEMIOLOGY OF ESOPHAGEAL CANCER

During 2012, 455,784 new cases of esophageal cancer were diagnosed in the world population, and 400,156 people died from this malignancy (281,212 men and 118,944 women). Approximately 5% of all cancer deaths are due to esophageal cancer, making it the sixth leading cause of death from cancer (Ferlay et al., 2010, 2013).

About 80% of all new cases reported in 2012 occurred in less-developed regions of the world. In the populations of these regions, esophageal cancer accounted for 7.4% of all cancer deaths in men (225,118 deaths) and 4.6% in women (103,703 deaths) (Ferlay et al., 2013).

Once diagnosed, invasive cancer of the esophagus does not respond well to treatment and has very poor survival (only 16% of cases in the United States and 10% of cases in Europe survive at least 5 years). As a consequence, esophageal cancer has a very high ratio of mortality to incidence (~0.88) (American Cancer Society, 2007; Ferlay et al., 2010, 2013; Parkin, Bray, Ferlay, & Pisani, 2005).

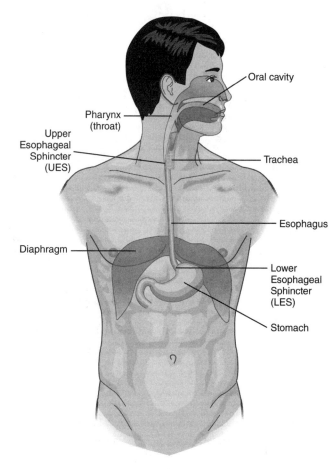

Figure 6.1 Anatomy of the Human Esophagus.

Esophageal cancer displays some of the most striking international epidemiologic characteristics of all diseases. In the United States, the incidence rates per 100,000 are 4.1 for Caucasian men and 1.2 for Caucasian women. The corresponding rates for African American men and women are threefold higher, 15.6 and 3.6, respectively.

In sharp contrast, the incidence is considerably higher in certain areas of the world. For example, in northern Iran the incidence rates are 115 for males and 131 for females, a female preponderance. Iranian women are affected almost 100 times more often than U.S. women (Day, 1975). As depicted in **Figure 6.2**, the "esophageal cancer belt" extends

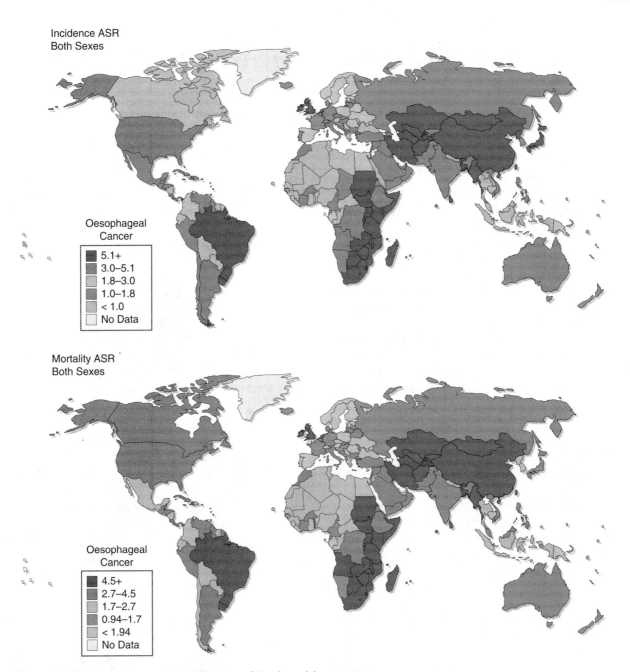

Figure 6.2 Global Incidence and Mortality Rates of Esophageal Cancer, 2012.

ASR: Incidence rates per 100,000 are age standardized to the world population, 2000–2025.

Source: Reproduced from Ferlay, J., Soerjomataram, I., Ervik, M., Dikshit, R., Eser, S., Mathers, C., ... Bray, F. (2013). *GLOBOCAN 2012 v1.0. Cancer incidence and mortality worldwide: IARC CancerBase No. 11* [Internet]. Lyon, France: International Agency for Research on Cancer. Retrieved from http://globocan.iarc.fr

from northeastern China to the Middle East; in certain populations of this region (e.g., northern Iran and certain provinces in eastern China) the cumulative lifetime risk of esophageal cancer is nearly 25%.

PATHOGENESIS OF ESOPHAGEAL CANCER

Esophageal cancer is usually diagnosed during the sixth or seventh decade of life. Male cases far outnumber female cases in most regions; for example, the male-to-female ratio is 7:1 in Eastern Europe. Historically, the majority of esophageal tumors have been squamous cell carcinomas arising from the squamous cell epithelium in the middle or upper third of the esophagus. However, in recent decades, there has been a marked increase in the incidence of adenocarcinomas of the lower esophagus near the gastroesophageal junction, particularly among men of the United States, the United Kingdom, and other developed nations (Eslick, 2009). Indeed, adenocarcinomas of the lower esophagus are now diagnosed more often than squamous cell carcinomas in the United States, the United Kingdom, and Western European nations (Umar & Fleischer, 2008).

Adenocarcinomas of the lower esophagus arise by a sequence of metaplastic and dysplastic changes in the esophageal epithelium known as Barrett's esophagus (Barrett, 1957). Such changes are due to chronic gastroesophageal reflux of acidic stomach fluid into the normally basic environment of the lower esophagus (**Figure 6.3**). Barrett's esophagus is a premalignant lesion that must be aggressively treated to halt its progression to invasive esophageal cancer, a condition that is life threatening. Effective screening strategies have been proposed for high-risk populations using endoscopy with mucosal iodine staining and biopsy to identify severe dysplastic lesions and carcinomas in situ that are curable by radical mucosectomy (Dong, Tank, Li, & Wang, 2002).

RISK FACTORS FOR ESOPHAGEAL CANCER

The risk factors for esophageal cancer differ according to histologic subtype (squamous cell carcinoma versus adenocarcinoma) and anatomic location in the esophagus (**Table 6.1**). Among the environmental risk factors for both histologic types, chronic alcoholism and cigarette smoking contribute most heavily to the development of esophageal cancer. This malignancy is 25 times more common among heavy drinkers than among controls. Habitual smokers of cigarettes also have a six- to sevenfold increased frequency of esophageal cancer after adjustment for alcohol consumption (Wynder & Mabuchi, 1973).

RISK FACTORS FOR SQUAMOUS CELL CARCINOMAS OF THE ESOPHAGUS

In the esophageal cancer belt of the Middle East and China, most of the cases are squamous cell carcinomas that are related to tobacco and alcohol addiction. However, recent epidemiologic studies have identified additional major risk factors that independently and synergistically elevate the risk. In northern Iran and other populations in the Middle East and India, the cultural practice of consuming steaming hot black

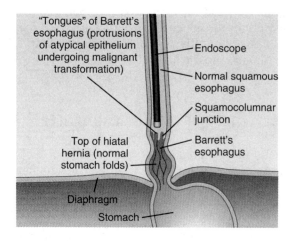

Figure 6.3 Barrett's Esophagus.

Table 6.1	Esophageal Cancer Epidemiology	
Characteristic	**Squamous Cell Carcinoma**	**Adenocarcinoma**
Age (years)	60–70	50–60
Anatomic site	Middle and upper	Lower
Risk factors	Alcohol and tobacco	Alcohol and tobacco
	Betel quid	GE reflux (GERD)
	Mycotic contamination	Obesity
	Nutritional deficits	Hiatal hernia
	Hot beverages	Asthma

GE: gastroesophageal junction; GERD: gastroesophageal reflux disease.

tea at temperatures exceeding 70°C (158°F) beginning early in life coupled with nutritional deficiencies in essential vitamins (beta carotene, folate, vitamin C, and vitamin E) are associated with the extraordinarily high rates observed (Islami et al., 2009).

Epidemiologic investigations conducted in the high-risk populations of northern China have also identified multiple factors other than tobacco and alcohol that synergistically enhance the development of squamous cell carcinoma of the esophagus (Yang, 1980). The web of causative factors includes mycotic (fungal) contamination of food and water, fungal conversion of secondary amines and nitrites to potent carcinogens (nitrosamines), fungal toxins (aflatoxins), and nutritional deficiencies in certain vitamins and minerals (selenium, molybdenum) (Chu & Li, 1994).

In Africa, the observed high rates of squamous cell esophageal cancer, particularly in men, are attributed to a web of causative risk factors involving chronic smoking and alcohol consumption, diets poor in fresh fruits and vegetables, and consumption of foods contaminated with *Fusarium verticilloides* (Day, 1975; Dlamini & Bhoola, 2005). During the 20th century there was a gradual transition of the staple diet of South Africa from sorghum to maize (corn), which was associated with the rising rates of this malignancy. Fusarium fungi grow readily on maize, producing fumonisins that reduce nitrates to nitrites and produce nitrosamines that may induce and promote esophageal carcinogenesis (Hendricks & Parker, 2008).

RISK FACTORS FOR BARRETT'S ESOPHAGUS AND ESOPHAGEAL ADENOCARCINOMA

As noted previously, Barrett's esophagus is a premalignant lesion that develops proximal to the gastroesophageal junction, primarily due to reflux of acidic stomach fluid into the lower esophagus. If left untreated, Barrett's esophagus can progress through a sequence of cellular metaplastic and dysplastic changes leading to the development of invasive adenocarcinoma of the esophagus. Patients with Barrett's esophagus have a 30- to 125-fold increased risk of developing invasive adenocarcinoma of the esophagus compared to the general population (Umar & Fleischer, 2008; Yousef et al., 2008). Barrett's esophagus develops in approximately 10% of individuals with longstanding gastroesophageal reflux disease (GERD). Major risk factors for GERD include obesity, hiatal hernia, pregnancy, smoking, alcohol abuse, and asthma (Wong & Fitzgerald, 2005).

The bacterium *Helicobacter pylorus* is a common contaminant of the stomach that can cause stomach ulcers and gastric adenocarcinoma. Gastric infection by *H. pylori* can be treated with antibiotics plus proton pump–inhibiting drugs to counteract excessive secretion of stomach acid. Paradoxically, people who have had such treatment to rid the stomach of *H. pylori* are more prone to develop adenocarcinoma of the esophagus. The biological explanation is that certain strains of *H. pylori* reduce stomach acid, which makes the stomach fluids less harmful to the esophagus (in people with reflux). Thus, *H. pylorus* infection, although causing precancerous and cancerous lesions in the stomach, may actually protect against the development of Barrett's esophagus and esophageal cancer (Blaser & Atherton, 2004; Delaney & McColl, 2005).

GENETIC RISK FACTORS FOR ESOPHAGEAL CANCER

Genetic polymorphisms of certain tumor suppressor genes that modulate cell division may also contribute to the genesis of esophageal cancer. Bani-Hani and colleagues (2000) found genetic polymorphisms in cyclin D1 and p53 that increased the risk by sixfold and threefold, respectively, and Reid and colleagues (2001) observed a 16-fold increase in the risk of esophageal cancer with loss of heterozygosity in p53.

Genetic syndromes involving malformations in esophageal structure also increase the risk of developing cancer of the esophagus. Achalasia due to dysfunction of the gastrointestinal sphincter interrupts the passage of food from the esophagus into the stomach and elevates the risk of esophageal cancer by 15-fold. Plummer–Vinson syndrome consists of iron deficiency anemia coupled with muscle atrophy, dysphagia, and the formation of esophageal rings or webs in the upper esophagus. This syndrome is associated with the development of squamous cell carcinomas proximal to the upper esophageal webs (Wynder, Hultberg, Jacobsson, & Bross, 1957).

PREVENTION OF ESOPHAGEAL CANCER

The primary prevention of esophageal cancer obviously involves avoiding exposure of the esophagus to alcohol, tobacco, boiling hot beverages, and other caustic substances. In developing nations, intake of moldy grains and other foods or beverages fermented from moldy grain should be avoided. International efforts are now being directed to the obesity

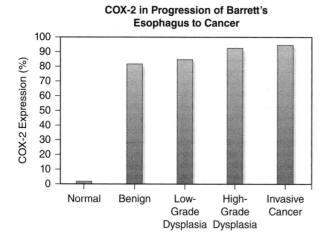

Figure 6.4 COX-2 in Progression of Barrett's Esophagus to Cancer.

Source: Data from Harris, R. E. (2007). COX-2 and the inflammogenesis of cancer. *Subcellular Biochemistry, 42,* 193–212.

pandemic in order to reduce the burden of obesity-related diseases.

Multiple epidemiologic studies have examined the potential role of aspirin and other nonsteroidal anti-inflammatory drugs (NSAIDs) in the prevention of esophageal cancer. In a recent meta-analysis of these studies, Corley and colleagues (2003) determined that regular use of NSAIDs was associated with a 40% reduction in the risk of esophageal cancer. The NSAIDs are known to reduce inflammation by inhibiting the cyclooxygenase enzymes, COX-1 and COX-2, that are responsible for the synthesis of prostaglandins of the inflammatory cascade. It is therefore notable that the inducible inflammatory gene cyclooxygenase-2 (COX-2), which is silent in normal esophageal mucosa, becomes markedly overexpressed throughout the progression of Barrett's esophagus to esophageal cancer (Harris, 2007) (**Figure 6.4**).

In high-risk populations, endoscopic screening for Barrett's esophagus or other dysplastic changes in the esophageal mucosa coupled with ablative treatment have proven effective in preventing the development of esophageal cancer (Dong et al., 2002; Spechler, 2001). Treatments found effective include administration of proton pump inhibitors (Yeh, Gerson, & Triadafilopoulos, 2003) and ablation by radiofrequency energy (Shaheen et al., 2009). Patients with Barrett's esophagus or other premalignant lesions should thus seek immediate treatment to prevent progression to esophageal cancer.

● ● ● REFERENCES

American Cancer Society. (2007). *Global cancer facts and figures, 2007.* Atlanta, GA: Author.

Bani-Hani, K., Martin, I. G., Hardie, L. J., Mapstone, N., Briggs, J. A., Forman, D., & Wild, C. P. (2000). Prospective study of cyclin D1 overexpression in Barrett's esophagus: Association with increased risk of adenocarcinoma. *Journal of the National Cancer Institute, 92,* 1316–1321.

Barrett, N. (1957). The lower esophagus lined by columnar epithelium. *Surgery, 41*(6), 881–894.

Blaser, M. J., & Atherton, J. C. (2004). *Helicobacter pylori* persistence: Biology and disease. *Journal of Clinical Investigation, 113,* 321–333.

Chu, F. S., & Li, G. Y. (1994). Simultaneous occurrence of fumonisin B1 and other mycotoxins in moldy corn collected from the People's Republic of China in regions with high incidences of esophageal cancer. *Applied and Environmental Microbiology, 60*(3), 847–852.

Corley, D. A., Kerlikowske, K., Verma, R., & Buffler, P. (2003). Protective association of aspirin/NSAIDs and esophageal cancer: A systematic review and meta-analysis. *Gastroenterology, 124,* 47–56.

Day, N. E. (1975). Some aspects of the epidemiology of esophageal cancer. *Cancer Research, 35,* 3304–3307.

Delaney, B., & McColl, K. (2005). Review article: *Helicobacter pylori* and gastro-oesophageal reflux disease. *Alimentary Pharmacology and Therapeutics, 22*(Suppl 1), 32–40.

Dlamini, Z., & Bhoola, K. (2005). Esophageal cancer in African blacks of Kwazulu Natal, South Africa: An epidemiological brief. *Ethnicity and Disease, 15*(4), 786–789.

Dong, Z., Tank, P., Li, L., & Wang, G. (2002). The strategy for esophageal cancer control in high-risk areas of China. *Japanese Journal of Clinical Oncology, 32,* 10–12.

Eslick, G. D. (2009). Epidemiology of esophageal cancer. *Gastroenterology Clinics, 38*(1), 17–25.

Ferlay, J., Shin, H.-R., Bray, F., Forman, D., Mathers, C., & Parkin, D. M. (2010). Estimates of worldwide burden of cancer in 2008: GLOBOCAN 2008. *International Journal of Cancer, 127*(12), 2893–2917.

Ferlay, J., Soerjomataram, I., Ervik, M., Dikshit, R., Eser, S., Mathers, C., . . . Bray, F. (2013). *GLOBOCAN 2012 v1.0, cancer incidence and mortality worldwide: IARC CancerBase No. 11* [Internet]. Lyon, France: International Agency for Research on Cancer. Retrieved from http://globocan.iarc.fr

Harris, R. E. (2007). COX-2 and the inflammogenesis of cancer. *Subcellular Biochemistry, 42*, 193–212.

Hendricks, D., & Parker, M. I. (2008). Oesophageal cancer in Africa. *International Union of Biochemistry and Molecular Biology Life, 53*(4–5), 263–268.

Islami, F., Pourshams, A., Nasrollahzadeh, D., Kamangar, F., Fahimi, S., Shakeri, R., . . . Boffetta, P. (2009). Tea drinking habits and oesophageal cancer in a high risk area in northern Iran: Population based case-control study. *British Medical Journal, 338*, b929.

Kumar, V., Abbas, A. K., & Aster J. C. (2014). *Robbins and Cotran pathologic basis of disease* (9th ed.). Philadelphia, PA: Mosby & Saunders.

Parkin, M. D., Bray, F., Ferlay, J., & Pisani, P. (2005). Global cancer statistics, 2002. *CA: A Cancer Journal for Clinicians, 55*, 74–108.

Reid, B. J., Prevo, L. J., Galipeau, P. C., Sanchez, C. A., Longton, G., Levine, D. S., & Rabinovitch, P. S. (2001). Predictors of progression in Barrett's esophagus II: Baseline 17p (p53) loss of heterozygosity identifies a patient subset at increased risk for neoplastic progression. *American Journal of Gastroenterology, 96*, 2839–2848.

Shaheen, N. J., Sharma, P., Overholt, B., Wolfsen, H. C., Sampliner, R. E., Wang, K. K., . . . Lightdale, C. J. (2009). Radiofrequency ablation in Barrett's esophagus with dysplasia. *New England Journal of Medicine, 360*, 2277–2288.

Spechler, S. J. (2001). Screening and surveillance for complications related to gastroesophageal reflux disease. *American Journal of Medicine, 111*(Suppl 8A), 130–136.

Umar, S. B., & Fleischer, D. E. (2008). Esophageal cancer: Epidemiology, pathogenesis and prevention. *Nature Reviews Clinical Practice Gastroenterology and Hepatology, 5*, 517–526.

Wong, A., & Fitzgerald, R. C. (2005). Epidemiologic risk factors for Barrett's esophagus and associated adenocarcinoma. *Clinical Gastroenterology and Hepatology, 3*(1), 1–10.

Wynder, E. L., Hultberg, S., Jacobsson, F., & Bross, I. J. (1957). Environmental factors in cancer of the upper alimentary tract. A Swedish study with special reference to Plummer-Vinson (Paterson-Kelly) syndrome. *Cancer, 10*, 470–482.

Wynder, E. L., & Mabuchi, K. (1973). Etiological and environmental factors in esophageal cancer. *Journal of the American Medical Association, 226*, 1546–1548.

Yang, C. S. (1980). Research on esophageal cancer in China: A review. *Cancer Research, 40*, 2633–2644.

Yeh, R. W., Gerson, L. B., & Triadafilopoulos, G. (2003). Efficacy of esomeprazole in controlling reflux symptoms, intraesophageal, and intragastric pH in patients with Barrett's esophagus. *Diseases of the Esophagus, 16*(3), 193–198.

Yousef, F., Cardwell, C., Cantwell, M. M., Galway, K., Johnston, B. T., & Murray, L. (2008). The incidence of esophageal cancer and high-grade dysplasia in Barrett's esophagus: A systematic review and meta-analysis. *American Journal of Epidemiology, 168*(3), 237–249.

Epidemiology of Stomach Cancer

ANATOMY AND FUNCTION OF THE STOMACH

The stomach is a hollow muscular organ juxtaposed between the esophagus and the duodenum with a resting volume ranging from 45 to 75 milliliters in the human adult. The stomach is lined by specialized epithelium that secretes proteases (enzymes that digest protein) and hydrochloric acid. The acidic nature of the stomach inhibits bacterial growth and facilitates the correct acid environment for activation of the enzymes secreted by the gastric epithelium. The stomach lining is folded into rugae to allow expansion and contraction. On expansion, the stomach easily holds 1 liter of food. The outer stomach wall consists of three layers of striated smooth muscle innervated by branches of the vagus nerve. Bolus (masticated food) entering the stomach at the gastro-esophageal sphincter is churned by muscular contractions of the stomach wall (called peristalsis). Chyme (partially digested food) passes from the stomach through the pyloric sphincter into the duodenum of the small intestine where the extraction of nutrients begins (see **Figure 7.1**) (Kumar, Abbas, & Aster, 2014).

GLOBAL EPIDEMIOLOGY OF STOMACH CANCER

Stomach cancer is the fifth most commonly diagnosed malignancy worldwide and the third leading cause of

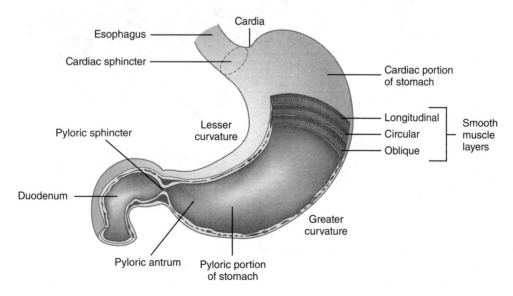

Figure 7.1 Anatomy of the Stomach.

cancer death, ranking behind only lung cancer and liver cancer. During 2012, 951,594 new cases were diagnosed (631,293 men and 320,301 women) and 723,027 persons died from stomach cancer (468,931 men and 254,096 women). About 70% of the cases and deaths occurred in developing countries. The incidence and mortality rates are highest in China and Mongolia, Eastern Asia, the Andean regions of South America, Eastern Europe, and Mali and Zaire in Africa (**Figure 7.2**) (Ferlay et al., 2010, 2013).

Mortality rates of stomach cancer are declining worldwide, and in many nations the declines have been dramatic (Ferlay et al.,2010, 2013). In the United States, death rates from stomach cancer have declined by nearly 90% in men and women since 1930 (**Figure 7.3**).

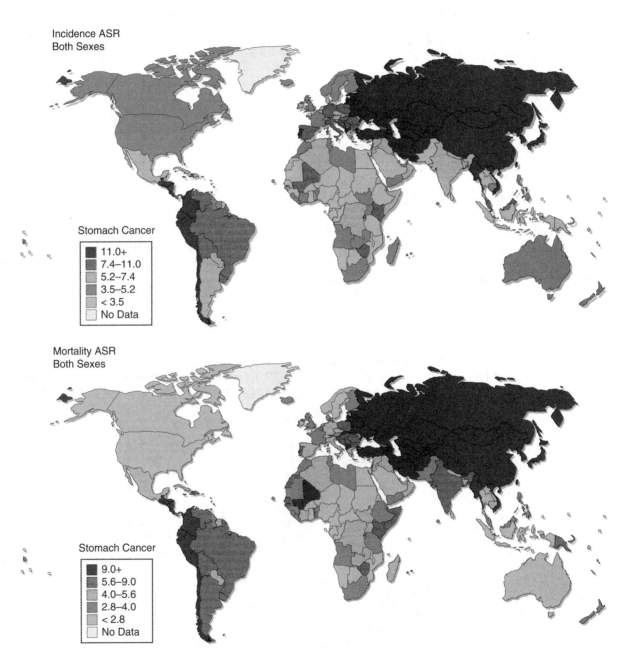

Incidence ASR
Both Sexes

Stomach Cancer

■	11.0+
■	7.4–11.0
■	5.2–7.4
■	3.5–5.2
■	< 3.5
□	No Data

Mortality ASR
Both Sexes

Stomach Cancer

■	9.0+
■	5.6–9.0
■	4.0–5.6
■	2.8–4.0
■	< 2.8
□	No Data

Figure 7.2 Global Incidence and Mortality Rates of Stomach Cancer, 2012.

ASR: Rates per 100,000 are age-standardized to the world population, 2000–2025.

Source: Reproduced from Ferlay, J., Soerjomataram, I., Ervik, M., Dikshit, R., Eser, S., Mathers, C.,... Bray, F. (2013). *GLOBOCAN 2012 v1.0. Cancer incidence and mortality worldwide: IARC CancerBase No. 11* [Internet]. Lyon, France: International Agency for Research on Cancer. Retrieved from http://globocan.iarc.fr

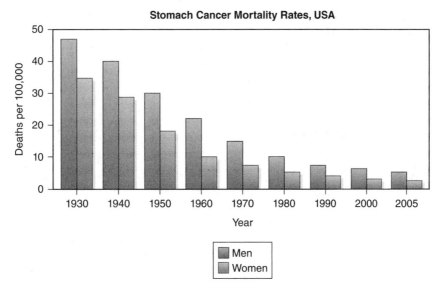

Figure 7.3 Stomach Cancer Mortality Rates in the United States, 1930–2005.

Mortality rates are age-adjusted to the U.S. population of 2000.

Source: Data from American Cancer Society. (2009). *Cancer statistics*. Atlanta, GA: Author.

A similar pattern has emerged in Japan, the nation with the highest stomach cancer mortality in the world in 1950 (nearly 100 deaths per 100,000 in men) (**Figure 7.4**). Since then, mortality rates from stomach cancer have declined by nearly 70% in Japanese men and 90% in Japanese women (Inoue & Tsugane, 2005; Tajima, Kuroishi, & Oshima, 2004). In Switzerland and neighboring European countries, stomach cancer mortality has fallen by 60% within one generation (Crew & Neuget, 2006).

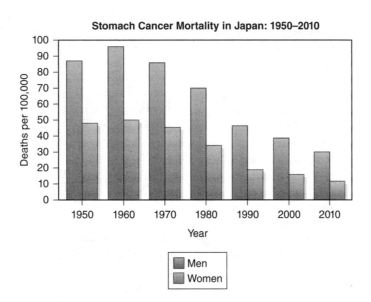

Figure 7.4 Stomach Cancer Mortality Rates in Japan, 1950–2010.

Mortality rates are age-adjusted to the Japanese population of 1985.

Source: Data from Inoue, M., & Tsugane, S. (2005). Epidemiology of gastric cancer in Japan. *Postgraduate Medical Journal, 81,* 419–424.

STOMACH CANCER PREVENTION: EPIDEMIOLOGY OF AN UNPLANNED TRIUMPH

Howson, Hiyama, and Wynder (1986) described the decline in stomach cancer incidence and mortality among developed countries within the past 50 years as the "epidemiology of an unplanned triumph." The major reason for the decline in stomach cancer in developed countries is the rapid and widespread escalation of refrigeration since 1900. Expansion of industrial refrigeration has meant fresher produce for the consumer and, in turn, has resulted in higher per capita intake of vitamins A, C, and E, which protect against gastric carcinogenesis. Furthermore, the increase in refrigeration has reduced the need for salting and pickling, two traditional means of food preservation associated with increased gastric cancer risk.

Considerable experimental evidence suggests that high salt concentration enhances gastric carcinogenesis. High salt consumption damages the stomach mucosa and can induce severe gastritis, heightening the predisposition to nitrosamines and other carcinogens. Chronic atrophic gastritis and its associated lesion, intestinal metaplasia, are the precursor conditions most closely linked to increased gastric cancer risk (Joosens et al., 1996).

Due to the widespread use of refrigeration, fish and meat can be readily preserved without salting. Reductions in the incidence and mortality rates are therefore particularly impressive in Nordic countries in which fish consumption is traditionally high (e.g., Iceland). In populations that still prefer salty food (e.g., Portugal and Brazil [salted cod, bacalao], Japan and Korea [salted pickles and salad]), stomach cancer rates remain high but have also declined significantly in recent years (Howson et al., 1986).

Another important reason for the reduction in stomach cancer mortality is that improved food sanitation through better techniques of processing, handling, and refrigeration has reduced exposure to the infectious microbe *Helicobacter pylorus*, particularly among children. This bacterium is known to cause chronic stomach inflammation, and bacterial infiltrates of the organism are commonly found associated with gastric adenocarcinoma and its precursor lesions. Studies combining methods of epidemiology and microbiology clearly suggest that *Helicobacter pylorus* should be considered as a major causal factor of gastric carcinoma (Kelley & Duggan, 2003).

An additional factor contributing to the declining rates of stomach cancer is the availability in many countries of fresh fruits and vegetables throughout the year. Technological advances in production, storage, packaging, and transportation over the past several decades have facilitated the global transport of fresh produce to consumers in a timely manner at affordable prices (Huang & Huang, 2004). There is considerable evidence suggesting that diets high in fruits and vegetables and low in salt, nitrites, and starch reduce the risk of developing stomach cancer (Bertuccio et al., 2013; Campbell, Sloan, & Kreiger, 2008).

Certain nitroso-compounds are carcinogenic in animal models and can induce glandular stomach adenocarcinomas resembling human gastric cancer. Conceivably, nitrosamides can be formed in the human stomach through an interaction between nitrite and suitable substrates. From 1925 to 1981, the content of nitrates and nitrites in cured meats in the United States decreased by 75% while gastric cancer mortality rates declined by two-thirds (Howson et al., 1986).

Cigarette smoking and other forms of tobacco addiction are also significant risk factors for the development of stomach cancer. A recent comprehensive review and meta-analysis of the available data found a twofold increase in the risk of stomach cancer among male chronic smokers (Ladeiras-Lopes et al., 2008). There is also consistent evidence that tobacco addiction in combination with chronic alcohol consumption synergistically heightens the risk by fivefold (Sjödahl et al., 2007).

Ecological studies have shown an inverse association between gastric cancer risk and socioeconomic status. These observations led to the hypothesis that high carbohydrate intake at an early age predisposes to increased gastric cancer risk. However, intracountry and time-trend comparisons have shown little association between carbohydrate intake and gastric cancer risk (Larsson, Bergkvist, & Wolk, 2006). Some studies suggest that the dietary glycemic load, a measure of the impact of total carbohydrate intake on blood sugar, is linked to the risk of stomach cancer (Augustin, Gallus, Negri, & La Vecchia, 2004); however, other studies do not support the view that a high-starch diet and related measures such as the glycemic index or glycemic load enhance predisposition to gastric carcinoma (Lazarevic, Nagomi, & Jermic, 2009).

HELICOBACTER PYLORUS AND STOMACH CANCER

In 1984, two Australian scientists, Drs. Barry J. Marshall and J. Robin Warren, made the remarkable discovery that a bacterium naturally inhabits the strong acid environment in the stomachs of patients with gastritis and stomach ulcers (Marshall & Warren,

1984). The bacterium was named *Helicobacter pylorus* due to its spiraled flagella that make it highly motile and able to avoid the severe acidity of the stomach fluids. In recognition of this remarkable discovery, Marshall and Warren were awarded the 2005 Nobel Prize for Medicine and Physiology.

Subsequent investigations have found that *H. pylorus* contaminates the stomachs of approximately 50% of humans (Pounder & Ng, 1995). The bacterium appears to be readily transmitted by oral–oral and oral–fecal routes, and infection is associated with conditions of poor sanitation (Brown, 2000).

Persistent colonization of the stomach by *H. pylori* results in chronic gastritis, an inflammatory condition of the stomach lining. The severity of the inflammation underlies the genesis of *H. pylori*–related diseases, including peptic ulcer, duodenal ulcer, and stomach cancer (Shiotani & Graham,

2002). Specifically, certain strains of *H. pylorus* that are seropositive for the CagA antigen are highly inflammatory and carcinogenic and are often present in specimens of gastric ulcers and gastric carcinomas (National Institutes of Health, 1994). Molecular epidemiologic studies have determined that severe chronic atrophic gastritis due to infection by CagA-positive strains of *H. pylorus* increases the risk of gastric cancer by more than 10-fold (Palli et al., 2007). Perhaps the most compelling evidence supporting *H. pylorus* as the major etiologic factor in the genesis of gastric cancer comes from a prospective study of 1,526 Japanese participants in which gastric cancers developed in 2.9% of infected individuals and in none of the noninfected individuals (Uemura et al., 2001). A model of gastric carcinogenesis involving the progression of inflammatory *H. pylorus* infection to gastric ulceration and cancer is shown in **Figure 7.5**.

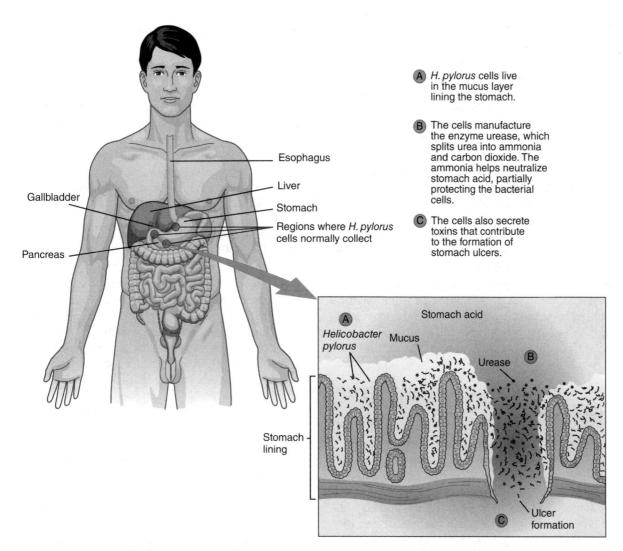

Figure 7.5 Model of *Helicobacter Pylorus* Infection in Gastric Carcinogenesis.

It is also important to realize that chronic *H. pylorus* infection interacts synergistically with other factors in the progression of carcinogenesis in the gastric mucosa. Such interactions are particularly evident in certain regions of China and Mongolia where consumption of salted and smoked foods is commonplace and conditions are ideal for the transmission of *H. pylorus* infections (e.g., crowded living conditions, family size, sharing a bedroom, low socioeconomic status, low educational level, poor sanitation, and infrequent hand washing) (Yang, 2006). High rates of smoking and alcohol consumption further exacerbate the risk. This web of causative factors is responsible for the high rates of stomach cancer in China and the staggering fact that more than 50% of stomach cancer deaths worldwide occur in this region.

Interactions involving multiple strains of *H. pylorus* and other infectious and parasitic agents have also been explored. For example, certain regions of Africa with high rates of stomach cancer (e.g., Mali and Zaire) are also prone to multiple gastrointestinal infections and mosquito-borne malarial infections that could further compromise host immunity, thereby promoting more severe *H. pylorus* infections (Blaser, 1993; Blaser & Atherton, 2004).

Gastric carcinogenesis is thus a multifactorial, multistep process, in which chronic inflammation due to *H. pylorus* infection is most often the major determinant. Indeed, any factor or condition that causes chronic tissue damage and a persisting cycle of inflammation, necrosis, and regeneration carries an increased cancer risk. Examples of the "inflammogenesis of cancer" are present throughout the gastrointestinal tract—e.g., consumption of very hot beverages and squamous cell carcinoma of the esophagus, gastroesophageal reflux of stomach acid and adenocarcinoma of the esophagus, chronic gastritis induced by *H. pylorus* infection and stomach cancer, Crohn's disease and cancer of the small intestine, and ulcerative colitis and colon cancer (Harris, 2007).

HISTOLOGIC AND ANATOMIC SUBTYPES OF STOMACH CANCER

More than 90% of gastric cancers are adenocarcinomas, which are divisible pathologically and anatomically into two subtypes: (1) poorly differentiated or *diffuse* adenocarcinomas arising near the cardia (just distal to the gastroesophageal junction) and (2) well-differentiated or *intestinal* adenocarcinomas that arise elsewhere in the corpus of the stomach (noncardia adenocarcinomas) (Crew & Neuget, 2006).

Well-differentiated (intestinal) noncardia adenocarcinomas of the stomach are thought to develop primarily as a consequence of environmental factors such as chronic *H. pylorus* infection, particularly due to CagA-positive strains, resulting in chronic severe atrophic gastritis that progresses to invasive cancer. Synergism of *H. pylorus* with other environmental factors including high-salt diets, nutritional deficits, and chronic tobacco and alcohol exposure can exacerbate the risk. The noncardia intestinal subtype of gastric cancer predominates in high-risk regions of the world, and its rates have declined dramatically in many developed nations, primarily due to refrigeration replacing salt preservation of fish and meat, better access to fresh fruits and vegetables, improved sanitation, reductions in tobacco and alcohol addiction, and effective antibiotic therapy for *H. pylorus* infections.

In contrast to the decline in noncardia intestinal gastric cancer, the rates of diffuse gastric adenocarcinomas arising near the cardia are increasing in many developed nations, particularly among Caucasian males. The increasing incidence of the diffuse type of adenocarcinomas arising near the cardia of the stomach is related to obesity and other conditions that predispose to gastroesophageal reflux disease (GERD) and Barrett's esophagus (Crew & Neuget, 2006). It has been hypothesized that ablation of colonization of the stomach by *H. pylorus* has accentuated the development of these conditions in some developed populations (Blaser & Atherton, 2006).

GENETIC PREDISPOSITION TO STOMACH CANCER

Evidence for a genetic predisposition to gastric cancer comes from both epidemiologic studies and reports of multigenerational pedigrees with excess cases of gastric cancer among relatives. Systematic case-control and cohort analyses of gastric cancer patients have shown that the risk of gastric cancer in first-degree relatives of index cases (probands) is increased two- to threefold.

Mutations, polymorphisms, and epigenetic changes in the expression of certain genes have been implicated in gastric carcinogenesis, particularly for the diffuse type of adenocarcinoma that arises in the cardia near the gastroesophageal junction. Familial clusters of hereditary diffuse gastric carcinoma have been discovered. Such families manifest key germline mutations in the CDH1 gene that encodes E-cadherin, an important calcium-dependent cell adhesion molecule (Lynch, Grady, Suriano, & Huntsman, 2005).

Excess cases of gastric cancer have also been observed in families with the adenomatous polyposis coli (APC) gene, which predisposes to familial adenomatous polyposis (FAP), and in families with hereditary nonpolyposis colorectal cancer (also called the Lynch syndrome), which is due to mutated mismatch DNA repair genes (Lynch et al., 2005). Other genetic and familial factors are also known to influence gastric cancer risk. Blood group A has been reported to be more prevalent among gastric cancer cases than among controls and appears to be associated with the development of the diffuse type of disease. Patients with pernicious anemia are also at increased risk for the development of gastric cancer. Pernicious anemia is due to the lack of intrinsic factor and failure to absorb vitamin B_{12} (Bevan & Houlston, 1999).

PREVENTION OF STOMACH CANCER

Present knowledge suggests that gastric carcinoma is caused by interactions among carcinogens and inflammatory factors derived from chronic *H. pylorus* infection, nitrate/nitrite-rich diets, and gastric mucosa irritation and damage by salt or other factors such as tobacco and alcohol. Salt restriction (less than 6 grams per day), avoidance of processed meats, abstinence from tobacco, and limitation of alcohol intake are all important for prevention and control.

Notably, infection by the bacterium *Helicobacter pylorus* causes chronic stomach inflammation that can initiate and promote cancerous lesions. Elimination of the bacterium through antibiotic therapy is therefore paramount for the prevention and control of gastric cancer. For example, a recent intervention study in high-risk rural populations in the province of Nariño in the Andes Mountains of Colombia demonstrated that administration of antibiotics for *H. pylorus* produced regression of precancerous gastric lesions (Correa et al., 2000). In the same study, supplemental administration of vitamin C or beta carotene also showed benefit, suggesting that both disease initiation and progression may be counteracted by sufficient year-round ingestion of fresh fruits and vegetables.

• • • REFERENCES

American Cancer Society. (2009). *Cancer statistics*. Atlanta, GA: Author.

Augustin, L. S. A., Gallus, S., Negri, E., & La Vecchia, C. (2004). Glycemic index, glycemic load and risk of gastric cancer. *Annals of Oncology, 15*(4), 581–584.

Bertuccio, P., Rosato, V., Andreano, A., Ferraroni, M., Decarli, A., V. Edefonti, V., & La Vecchia, C. (2013). Dietary patterns and gastric cancer risk: A systematic review and meta-analysis. *Annals of Oncology, 24*, 1450–1458.

Bevan, S., & Houlston, R. S. (1999). Genetic predisposition to gastric cancer. *Quarterly Journal of Medicine, 92*, 5–10.

Blaser, M. J. (1993). Malaria and the natural history of *Helicobacter pylori* infection [letter]. *Lancet, 342*, 551.

Blaser, M. J., & Atherton, J. C. (2004). *Helicobacter pylori* persistence: Biology and disease. *Journal of Clinical Investigation, 113*, 321–333.

Brown, L. M. (2000). *Helicobacter pylori*: Epidemiology and routes of transmission. *Epidemiology Review, 22*(2), 283–297.

Campbell, P., Sloan, M., Kreiger, N. (2008). Dietary patterns and risk of incident gastric adenocarcinoma. *American Journal of Epidemiology, 167*, 295–304.

Correa, P., Fontham, E. T. H., Bravo, J. C., Bravo, L. E., Ruiz, B., Zarama, G., . . . Mera, R. (2000). Chemoprevention of gastric dysplasia: Randomized trial of antioxidant supplements and anti-*Helicobacter pylori* therapy. *Journal of the National Cancer Institute, 92*(23), 1881–1888.

Crew, K. D., & Neuget, A. I. (2006). Epidemiology of gastric cancer. *World Journal of Gastroenterology, 12*(3), 354–362.

Ferlay, J., Shin, H.-R., Bray, F., Forman, D., Mathers, C., & Parkin, D. M. (2010). Estimates of worldwide burden of cancer in 2008: GLOBOCAN 2008. *International Journal of Cancer, 127*(12), 2893–2917.

Ferlay, J., Soerjomataram, I., Ervik, M., Dikshit, R., Eser, S., Mathers, C., . . . Bray, F. (2013). *GLOBOCAN 2012 v1.0. Cancer incidence and mortality worldwide: IARC CancerBase No. 11* [Internet]. Lyon, France: International Agency for Research on Cancer. Retrieved from http://globocan.iarc.fr

Harris, R. E. (2007). Cyclooxygenase 2 (COX-2) and the inflammogenesis of cancer. *Subcellular Biochemistry, 42*, 93–126.

Howson, C. P., Hiyama, T., & Wynder, E. L. (1986). The decline in gastric cancer: Epidemiology of an unplanned triumph. *Epidemiology Reviews, 8*, 1–27.

Huang, S., & Huang, K. (2007). Increased U.S. imports of fresh fruits and vegetables. *A Report from the Economic Research Service, FTS-328-01*. Washington, DC: United States Department of Agriculture. Retrieved from http://www.ers.usda.gov/media/187841/fts32801_1_.pdf

Inoue, M., & Tsugane, S. (2005). Epidemiology of gastric cancer in Japan. *Postgraduate Medical Journal, 81*, 419–424.

Joosens, J. V., Hill, M. J., Elliott, P., Stamler, R., Stamler, J., Lesaffre, E., . . . Kesteloot, H. (1996). Dietary salt, nitrate and stomach cancer mortality in 24 countries. *International Journal of Epidemiology, 25*(3), 494–504.

Kelley, J. R., & Duggan, J. M. (2003). Gastric cancer epidemiology and risk factors. *Journal of Clinical Epidemiology, 56*, 1–9.

Kumar, V., Abbas, A. K., & Aster, J. C. (2014). *Robbins and Cotran pathologic basis of disease* (9th ed.). Philadelphia, PA: Mosby & Saunders.

Ladeiras-Lopes, R., Pereira, A. K., Nogueira, A., Pinheiro-Torres, T., Pinto, I., Santos-Pereira, R., & Lunet, N. (2008). Smoking and gastric cancer: Systematic review and meta-analysis of cohort studies. *Cancer Causes and Control, 7*, 689–701.

Larrson, S. C., Bergkvist, L., & Wolk, A. (2006). Glycemic load, glycemic index and carbohydrate intake in relation to risk of stomach cancer: A prospective study. *International Journal of Cancer, 188*(12), 3167–3169.

Lazarevic, K., Nagomi, A., & Jermic, M. (2009). Carbohydrate intake, glycemic index, glycemic load and risk of gastric cancer. *Central European Journal of Public Health, 17*(2), 75–78.

Lynch, H. T., Grady, W., Suriano, G., & Huntsman, D. (2005). Gastric cancer: New genetic developments. *Journal of Surgical Oncology, 90*(3), 114–133.

Marshall, B. J., & Warren, J. R. (1984). Unidentified curved bacilli in the stomach of patients with gastritis and peptic ulceration. *Lancet, 1*(8390), 1311–1315.

National Institutes of Health. (1994). NIH consensus statement: *Helicobacter pylori* in peptic ulcer disease. NIH Consensus Development Panel on *Helicobacter pylori* in Peptic Ulcer Disease. *Journal of the American Medical Association, 272*(1):65–69.

Palli, D., Masala, G., Del Giudice, G., Plebani, M., Basso, D., Berti, D., . . . Gonzalez, C. A. \ (2007). CagA+ *Helicobacter pylori* infection and gastric cancer risk in the EPIC-EURGAST study. *International Journal of Cancer, 120*(4), 859–867.

Pounder, R. E., & Ng, D. (1995). The prevalence of *Helicobacter pylori* infection in different countries. *Alimentary Pharmacology and Therapeutics, 9*(Suppl 2), 33–39.

Shiotani, A., & Graham, D. Y. (2002). Pathogenesis and therapy of gastric and duodenal ulcer disease. *Medical Clinics of North America, 86*(6), 1447–1466.

Sjödahl, K., Lu, Y., Nilsen, T. I., Ye, W., Hveem, K., Vatten, L., & Lagergren, J. (2007). Smoking and alcohol drinking in relation to risk of gastric cancer: A population-based, prospective cohort study. *International Journal of Cancer, 120*(1), 128–132.

Tajima, K., Kuroishi, T., & Oshima, A. (Eds.). (2004). *Monograph on cancer research, No. 51. Cancer mortality and morbidity statistics. Japan and the world*. Tokyo, Japan: Japanese Cancer Association/Karger.

Uemura, N., Okamoto, S., Yamamoto, S., Matsumura, N., Yamaguchi, S., Yamakido, M., . . . Schlemper, R. J. (2001). *Helicobacter pylori* infection and the development of gastric cancer. *New England Journal of Medicine, 345*, 784–789.

Yang, L. (2006). Incidence and mortality of gastric cancer in China. *World Journal of Gastroenterology, 12*(1), 17–20.

8

Epidemiology of Colorectal Cancer

GLOBAL EPIDEMIOLOGY OF COLORECTAL CANCER

During 2012, colorectal (large bowel) cancer was diagnosed in 1.36 million individuals and caused 693,881 deaths in the world population. In that year, 746,298 new cases were detected in men and 614,304 new cases in women, and colorectal cancer caused 8% of all cancer deaths in men (373,631 deaths) and 9% in women (320,250 deaths). Colorectal cancer is more common in developed countries (736,867 new cases and 333,113 deaths in 2012) compared to developing countries (347,395 new cases and 198,242 deaths). In developed countries, colorectal cancer mortality (11.6 per 100,000) ranks third behind only lung cancer and breast cancer, whereas in developing nations, it ranks sixth (6.6 per 100,000) (Ferlay et al., 2013).

The male-to-female ratio of colorectal cancer deaths for developed nations (1.06) is slightly lower than for developing nations (1.22). Survival rates over 5 years after diagnosis show wide international variability ranging from 30% in India to 65% in the United States (Ferlay et al., 2010, 2013; Parkin, Bray, Ferlay, & Pisani, 2005).

Figure 8.1 depicts the extreme international variability in colorectal cancer incidence and mortality rates. Colorectal cancer is the second most frequently diagnosed malignancy in affluent societies but remains relatively uncommon in many developing countries. Regions with high incidence and mortality rates include North America; Northern and Western Europe, including Greenland; Northern Asia (Russia); Australia and New Zealand; and the southernmost nations of South America and Africa. Low rates are observed in the nations of Central Africa, Central America, and Southern Asia. Nevertheless, colorectal cancer incidence rates are increasing in economically transitioning countries (Garcia et al., 2007; Center & Jemal, 2009; Ferlay et al., 2010, 2013).

PATHOGENESIS OF COLORECTAL CANCER

As with most other solid cancerous tumors, colorectal cancer evolves over a period of years and even decades. Approximately 65–70% of large bowel cancers develop in the descending sigmoid colon and rectum and the remainder develop in the transverse and ascending portions of the colon (Figure 8.2). More than 95% of colorectal cancers are adenocarcinomas, and many of them secrete mucin. Carcinomas of the sigmoid colon and rectum often grow in an annular fashion producing a so-called "napkinring" constriction and obstruction of the bowel. Carcinomas of the ascending colon tend to extend along the bowel wall and are much less likely to cause obstruction. Colorectal cancer often develops as a sequential series of steps beginning with focal dysplasia and hyperplasia of the epithelial lining and progressing to the formation of adenomatous and villous polyps, carcinoma in situ, and ultimately invasive cancer (Kumar, Abbas, Fausto, & Astor, 2009). It is notable that colon carcinogenesis invariably progresses in the presence of inflammation (Harris, 2007).

RISK FACTORS FOR COLORECTAL CANCER

Comprehensive scientific evidence suggests that colorectal cancer is largely influenced by a number of

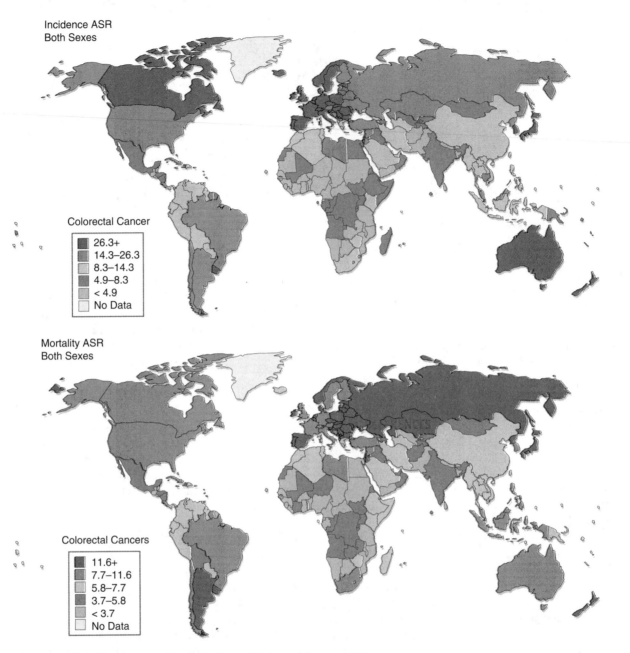

Figure 8.1 Global Incidence and Mortality Rates of Colorectal Cancer, 2012.

ASR: Rates per 100,000 are age-standardized to the world population, 2000–2025.

Source: Reproduced from Ferlay, J., Soerjomataram, I., Ervik, M., Dikshit, R., Eser, S., Mathers, C.,... Bray, F. (2013). *GLOBOCAN 2012 v1.0. Cancer incidence and mortality worldwide: IARC CancerBase No. 11* [Internet]. Lyon, France: International Agency for Research on Cancer. Retrieved from http://globocan.iarc.fr

lifestyle factors. The risk of colorectal cancer development is increased by diets high in fat and low in fiber, sedentary lifestyle, obesity, alcohol and tobacco addiction, and deficiencies in vitamin D, calcium, and possibly selenium. Genetic syndromes involving mutant mismatch repair genes and tumor suppressor genes account for only a small percentage of cases.

The following sections discuss each of these risk factors individually.

Dietary Fat and Colorectal Cancer

The wide geographic variation in the rates of colorectal cancer is most likely a consequence of differences in diet. Ernst Wynder and colleagues initially

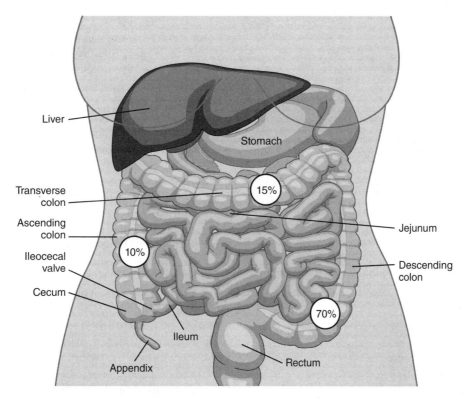

Figure 8.2 Anatomic Distribution of Colorectal Cancer.

postulated that colon cancer development is linked to high intake of dietary fat that upsets the balance of gut flora (Wynder et al., 1969). This hypothesis was based on the historic low rates of colorectal cancer in Japan compared to high rates in the United States corresponding to their low- and high-fat diets, respectively. Many subsequent epidemiologic investigations have consistently found that the risk of colorectal cancer increases with high intake of saturated fat and animal fat and reciprocally, that the risk is reduced with increased intake of fish and fish oil (Boyle & Langman, 2000; Lipkin, Reddy, Newmark, & Lamprecht, 1999). For example, Willett and colleagues found that U.S. women who ate beef, pork, or lamb daily had a 2.5-fold higher risk compared to women reporting little consumption (Willett, Stampfer, Colditz, Rosner, & Speizer, 1999). In an investigation conducted in 24 European nations, increasing the intake of omega-3 fatty acids from fish and fish oil conferred significant protection against colon cancer development, even in populations consuming diets high in total fats (Caygill & Hill, 1995). Animal studies are in general agreement with the epidemiologic evidence in finding that a high amount of omega-6 fatty acids from beef, corn oil, or lard in the diet enhances chemically induced tumor development

in laboratory animals, and reciprocally that increasing the intake of omega-3 fatty acids from fish, fish oil, and olive oil decreases carcinogenesis (Reddy & Maeura, 1984).

Marked increases in the rates of colorectal cancer in some countries have also been linked to higher levels of fat intake. A striking example is the Japanese population wherein rates have risen more than fourfold in the past 50 years in close parallel with the increase in per capita fat calories (**Figure 8.3**). Furthermore, in studies of migrants from low-risk to high-risk regions, the rates of colon cancer show dramatic increases after a single generation, suggesting that the risk for tumor development in the large bowel increases rapidly with transition to a high-fat diet (Wynder, Fujita, Harris, Hirayama, & Hiyama, 1991; Yu et al., 1991).

Mechanistically, it is theorized that diets high in fat promote secretion of bile acids from the liver and biliary tree. These bile acids are dehydrogenated by anaerobic bacteria of the colon (clostridia and bacteroides) to form the carcinogenic metabolites deoxycholic acid and lithocholic acid. In addition, diets high in fat typically contain sterols that have mitogenic activity. A key high-risk enzyme is β-glucuronidase, which is responsible for hydrolysis

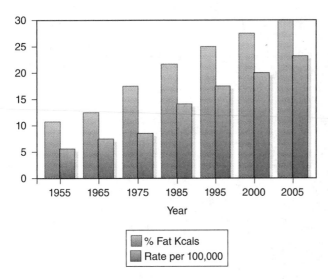

Figure 8.3 Colon Cancer Mortality and Dietary Fat in Japan: 1955–2005.

Annual mortality rates are age-adjusted to the Japanese population of 2000.

Source: Data from Center for Cancer Control and Information Services. (2010). *Cancer statistics in Japan.* Tokyo, Japan: National Cancer Center; Matsumura, Y. (2001). Emerging trends of nutrition: Transition and trade-offs. Nutrition trends in Japan. *Asia Pacific Journal of Clinical Nutrition, 10*(Suppl), S40–S47; Wynder, E. L., Fujita, Y., Harris, R. E., Hirayama, T., & Hiyama, T. (1991). Comparative epidemiology of cancer between the United States and Japan: A second look. *Cancer, 67*(3), 746–763.

of sterol conjugates so that they may be recirculated (Lipkin et al., 1999).

Dietary Fiber and Colorectal Cancer

Denis Burkitt is primarily responsible for formulating the high fat/low fiber hypothesis of colon cancer (Burkitt, 1971). This hypothesis is based on the low incidence of colon cancer and other intestinal diseases in the African countries where Burkitt conducted his surgical practice. In populations consuming a high-fiber, low-fat diet, Burkitt observed virtually none of the large bowel diseases that are commonplace in westernized societies such as hemorrhoids, diverticulosis, diverticulitis, ulcerative colitis, Crohn's disease, and colorectal cancer. His recommendations for prevention of colon cancer specify high levels of fiber intake throughout life (40 grams of fiber daily with a high proportion of bran) (Burkitt, 1973; Burkitt, Walker, & Painter, 1974).

Although many early epidemiologic investigations consistently supported the "Burkitt hypothesis" that high fiber intake reduces the risk of colorectal cancer (Greenwald, Lanza, & Eddy, 1987; Levin &

Dozois, 1991; Trock, Lanza, & Greenwald, 1990), some more recent epidemiologic investigations have failed to show protective effects of dietary fiber (Fuchs et al., 1999; Nakaji et al., 2001). A pooled analysis of 13 prospective cohort studies determined that the age-adjusted relative risk (RR) of colorectal cancer was significantly reduced by high intake of fiber (RR = 0.84), but also found that adjustment for a large profile of other factors dissipated the effect (Park, Hunter, et al., 2005). On the other hand, Howe and colleagues conducted a meta-analysis of 13 case control studies and found that the highest level of fiber intake reduced the risk of colorectal cancer by 50% (Howe et al., 1992). Furthermore, results from the large European Prospective Investigation into Cancer and Nutrition (EPIC) show that colon cancer risk declines by about 9% per quintile increase in fiber intake (multivariate adjusted RR = 0.58 for the highest versus lowest quintile) (Bingham et al., 2005, 2010). It is important to note that in most of these studies, particularly those that did not show protection, the type of fiber was not considered and the highest level of fiber consumption was far below the 40-gram daily threshold recommended by Denis Burkitt.

Several preclinical trials also have examined the impact of dietary fiber in animal models of colorectal carcinogenesis. The results suggest that colorectal protection depends on the type and level of fiber and that wheat bran inhibits tumor development more consistently than other sources of fiber (Reddy, 1995). The totality of evidence from studies of colon cancer in animals and humans remains compatible with Burkitt's original hypothesis that diets high in fiber, particularly wheat bran fiber, provide significant protection against the development of colorectal cancer.

Protective mechanisms of fiber within the large bowel can be broadly divided into those from soluble and insoluble fiber. Increasing the level of insoluble fiber increases fecal bulk, thereby reducing transit time and diluting the concentration of toxic and carcinogenic compounds. Soluble fiber binds to bile acids and bile salts that may irritate the colorectal mucosa; furthermore, soluble fiber is fermented to single-chain fatty acids such as butyrate that maintain homeostasis of cell proliferation and apoptosis (Anderson et al., 2009; Wong, de Souza, Kendall, Emam, & Jenkins, 2006).

Alcohol, Tobacco, and Colorectal Cancer

Chronic alcohol abuse is etiologically linked to colorectal carcinogenesis (Cho et al., 2004; Mizoue et al., 2008; Su & Arab, 2004). Analysis of data from the National Health and Nutrition Examination

Survey (NHANES) in the United States showed a 70% increase in colorectal cancer among individuals who consumed one or more servings of alcoholic beverages daily (Su & Arab, 2004). In a pooled analysis of eight prospective cohort studies performed in five countries, Cho and colleagues (2004) found that the risk increased by 40% at the highest level of alcohol consumption (> 45 grams of alcohol daily). Mizoue and colleagues analyzed data from five Japanese studies and estimated that one-quarter of all colorectal cancers in Japan are attributable to alcohol consumption above 23 grams daily (Mizoue et al., 2008).

Chronic tobacco addiction has also been linked to colorectal cancer development. The epidemiologic evidence shows that chronic smokers have a two- to threefold increased incidence of premalignant adenomas of the colon compared to nonsmokers (Giovannucci, 2001). In a meta-analysis of 106 studies, Botteri and colleagues concluded that smoking significantly increases both the incidence and mortality of colorectal cancer (Botteri et al., 2008). The existing evidence therefore supports the addition of colorectal cancer to the list of tobacco-associated malignancies.

Various mechanisms may be responsible for the effects of alcohol and tobacco on colorectal carcinogenesis. One mechanism involves the combination of chronic alcohol consumption and folate deficiency. As ethanol enters the large bowel, it is metabolized into acetaldehyde by anaerobic microbes; acetaldehyde, in turn, rapidly degrades folate. Because folate is essential for normal DNA synthesis and repair, its rapid degradation by acetaldehyde could readily lead to DNA instability and carcinogenesis in the colorectal mucosa (Duthie, 1999; Homann, Tillonen, & Salaspuro, 2000).

Alcohol consumption may also delay peristalsis in the large bowel and increase transit time and exposure to carcinogens and other toxic substances. Carcinogens from tobacco can reach the colorectal mucosa through the gastrointestinal tract or the circulatory system and may accentuate mutagenesis, inflammation, and carcinogenesis, particularly in the distal colon (Zisman et al., 2006). There is also speculation that tobacco and alcohol may synergistically heighten the risk of colorectal cancer.

Vitamin D, Calcium, and Colorectal Cancer

As initially noted by Garland and Garland (1980), there is a gradient of colorectal cancer rates with latitude (i.e., the rates become higher in populations that are more distant from the equator). On careful examination, the current patterns of global colorectal cancer incidence and mortality reflect a similar gradient (see Figure 8.1). This observation has given rise to the hypothesis that colon cancer development may be related to the lack of vitamin D due to decreased exposure to sunlight in populations more distant from the equator. Activated vitamin D is necessary for the absorption of dietary calcium, an important mineral for the maintenance of physiologic homeostasis in the human body, particularly the regulation and control of cell division and the cell cycle in proliferating cell populations such as the colorectal mucosa.

Higher levels of vitamin D and calcium intake have been found to reduce the risk of colorectal cancer in several epidemiologic studies (Gorham et al., 2005). For example, the relationship of vitamin D and cancer mortality was examined in the Third National Health and Nutrition Examination Survey (NHANES III). Baseline levels of serum 25-hydroxylated vitamin D were measured in 16,818 participants age 17 years or older with follow-up from 1988 to 2000. Although there was no overall effect on cancer mortality, individuals with serum vitamin D levels of 80 nmol/L or higher at baseline experienced a 72% reduction in colorectal cancer mortality compared to individuals with levels lower than 50 nmol/L (Freedman, Looker, Chang, & Graubard, 2007).

Despite the beneficial impact of vitamin D and calcium observed in epidemiologic studies, a randomized clinical trial involving postmenopausal women of the Women's Health Initiative (WHI) failed to show any benefit. In this study, daily supplementation of calcium and vitamin D for 7 years had no effect on the incidence of colorectal cancer. The long latency associated with the development of colorectal cancer and the limited 7-year duration of the trial may have contributed to this null finding (Wactawski-Wende, Morley Kotchen, & Anderson, 2006).

Insulin, Insulin-Like Growth Factors, and Colorectal Cancer

High levels of circulating insulin and insulin-like growth factors (IGFs) have been found to increase the risk of developing colorectal cancer (Giovannucci, 2007). Insulin is secreted by the beta cells in the islets of Langerhans of the pancreas and is the chief hormone that regulates blood glucose. The IGFs are polypeptide hormones that share sequence homology with insulin. They are synthesized in the liver and other organs in response to growth hormone from the pituitary gland. Although the main function of IGF is to regulate human growth and development, it also stimulates cell proliferation and angiogenesis and inhibits apoptosis in the colorectal mucosa.

Individuals who manifest clinical conditions associated with high levels of insulin and IGF-1 such as type 2 diabetes mellitus, the metabolic syndrome, and acromegaly are at increased risk for the development of colorectal cancer. Furthermore, phenotypic and lifestyle factors associated with hyperinsulinemia (physical inactivity, high body mass index, central adiposity) and high IGF-1 levels (tall stature), as well as dietary patterns that stimulate insulin resistance or secretion, including high consumption of sucrose, various sources of starch, a high glycemic index, and high intake of certain types of fat, also increase the risk (Giovannucci, 2001, 2007; Giovannucci, Colditz, Stampfer, & Willett, 1996; Terry, Miller, & Rohan, 2002). It is clear that components of the IGF axis (IGF-1, IGF-2, IGF cell membrane receptors, and binding molecules) constitute an important molecular interface with exposures that initiate and promote colorectal carcinogenesis.

Ulcerative Colitis, Crohn's Disease, and Colorectal Cancer

Chronic inflammatory conditions of the intestinal tract also predispose to the development of colorectal cancer. Ulcerative colitis is characterized by chronic inflammation and ulceration of the epithelial lining of the colon plus other extra-colonic lesions. The primary site of attack is usually in the descending (left) colon. About 1% of colorectal cancer patients have a history of chronic ulcerative colitis. The risk of developing colorectal cancer varies inversely with the age of onset of the colitis and directly with the extent of colonic involvement and the duration of active disease. It is estimated that 40–50% of individuals with longstanding ulcerative colitis eventually develop colon cancer (Kumar et al., 2009).

Crohn's disease, a granulomatous inflammatory condition of the intestinal tract, also increases the risk of colorectal cancer development, but to a lesser extent than ulcerative colitis. Many investigators have noted many similarities in ulcerative colitis and Crohn's disease. Both diseases appear to have an autoimmune basis and are characterized by similar alterations in the IGF axis (Street et al., 2004). Quite possibly these conditions represent different immune and tissue responses to one or more highly inflammatory etiologic factors.

Genetics of Colorectal Cancer

The investigation of a large multigenerational kindred by Aldred Scott Warthin in the early 1900s identified a hereditary form of colorectal cancer. Warthin documented 33 relatives with colorectal cancer or endometrial cancer among 70 members of the pedigree. Hereditary nonpolyposis colorectal cancer (HNPCC) was later named the *Lynch syndrome* after Henry T. Lynch, who documented two large kindreds with this autosomal-dominant syndrome (Lynch, Shaw, Magnuson, Larsen, & Krush, 1966). Lynch and colleagues initially designated HNPCC as the cancer family syndrome (Lynch, Guirgis, Lynch, & Harris, 1977; Lynch, Lynch, & Harris, 1977).

The cause of HNPCC is an inherited (germline) mutation in at least one of a set of genes that normally repair DNA, the mismatch repair genes. In 1993 the first of the HNPCC genes (MSH2) was discovered on chromosome 2 by a team of international investigators (Aaltonen et al., 1993). Soon after, MLH1 was discovered on chromosome 3 (Aaltonen et al., 1994). It was determined that mutations in these two genes accounted for 90% of the known HNPCC families. Carriers of either mutant gene have a lifetime colon cancer risk approaching 100%. The Lynch syndrome accounts for a small percentage of all colorectal cancer cases, perhaps 1–3%.

In 1951, Eldron J. Gardner published a report of a large Utah family containing many relatives with diffuse polyps of the colon and intestinal tract and multiple relatives with colorectal cancer (Gardner, 1951). Gardner's syndrome is a rare familial form of familial adenomatous polyposis (FAP) characterized by the presence of multiple polyps in the colon together with tumors outside the colon. In Gardner's syndrome, the extracolonic tumors may include osteomas of the skull, thyroid cancer, epidermoid cysts, fibromas, sebaceous cysts, and desmoid tumors.

FAP and Gardner's syndrome are caused by an autosomal-dominant germline mutation in the adenomatous polyposis coli (APC) gene located on chromosome 5q21 (band q21 on chromosome 5) (Leppert et al., 1987). The APC gene is a *tumor suppressor gene* that regulates cell adhesion, cell migration, and apoptosis in the colorectal epithelium. Mutations of the APC gene inactivate its protein function, leading to initiation and promotion of colorectal carcinogenesis. Inactivation of both copies of the APC is required to initiate polyp development (Fearon & Vogelstein, 2000).

The countless polyps in the colon of FAP patients predispose to the development of colon cancer with 100% probability unless the colon is removed. The onset of polyps occurs during the teenage years, and the average age at diagnosis of colon cancer is 35–40 years. Polyps can also grow in the stomach, duodenum, spleen, kidneys, liver, mesentery, and small bowel. In a small number of cases, polyps have also appeared in the cerebellum. Extracolonic cancers related to FAP commonly appear in the thyroid, liver, and kidneys.

Cooking Methods and Colorectal Cancer

Certain cooking methods can lead to carcinogenic compounds that reach the large bowel. For example, heterocyclic amines are formed on the surface of high-protein foods such as meat or fish on exposure to high-temperature cooking processes such as frying or boiling, and particularly charcoal broiling. Furthermore, mutagens other than heterocyclic amines in meats cooked at high temperature (e.g., pyridines and quinoxalines) may also play a role in increasing the risk of distal adenomas and colorectal tumors (Wu et al., 2006).

Nonsteroidal Anti-inflammatory Drugs (NSAIDs): Chemoprevention of Colorectal Cancer

The results of many epidemiologic studies provide strong evidence that regular intake of nonsteroidal anti-inflammatory drugs (NSAIDs) such as aspirin and ibuprofen reduces the risk of colorectal cancer development. In a meta-analysis of the published estimates, significant risk reductions were observed in 28 of 32 studies, and regular use of NSAIDs produced a 43% reduction in the risk (**Figure 8.4**; Harris, 2009). In randomized clinical trials, regular aspirin use also has been found to decrease the risk of colonic adenomas, the precursors of most colon cancers (Baron et al., 2003).

Molecular studies show that inflammatory biomarkers are often expressed throughout the progression of colorectal carcinogenesis. Most impressive is the overexpression of the inducible cyclooxygenase-2 (COX-2) enzyme, which is responsible for prostaglandin biosynthesis in the inflammatory cascade (Harris, 2007).

In a case control study of colon cancer, Harris and colleagues compared the effects of over-the-counter NSAIDs with prescription drugs that selectively inhibit COX-2. Their results suggest that both over-the-counter NSAIDs and selective COX-2 inhibitors produce significant reductions in the risk of colon cancer, underscoring their strong potential for colon cancer chemoprevention (Harris, Beebe-Donk, & Alshafie, 2008).

Exogenous Estrogens and Colorectal Cancer

Although postmenopausal hormone replacement therapy (HRT) has been found to increase the risk of developing cardiovascular disease, breast cancer, and endometrial cancer, there is consistent evidence from epidemiologic studies that HRT *reduces* the risk of colorectal cancer (MacLennan, MacLennan, & Ryan, 1991). A meta-analysis of 18 studies determined that current HRT use resulted in a 34% decrease in the risk (Nelson, Humphrey, Nygren, Teutsch, & Allen, 2002). This finding is supported by the results of a randomized clinical trial in the Women's Health Initiative (WHI) in which the incidence of colorectal cancer was 44% less in women receiving HRT (estrogen plus progesterone) compared to those receiving a placebo (Chlebowski et al., 2004).

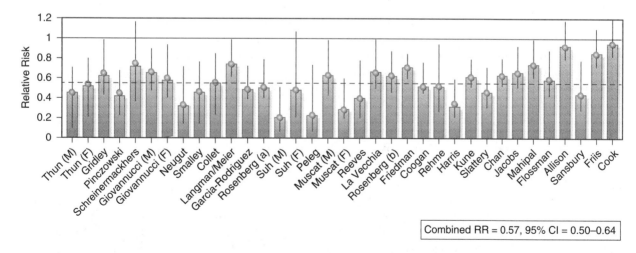

Combined RR = 0.57, 95% CI = 0.50–0.64

Figure 8.4 Colon Cancer and NSAIDs.

Note: Investigators are cited in the figure; M & F denote studies of males or females; a and b denote separate studies by same investigator.

Source: Data from Harris, R. E. (2009). Cyclooxygenase-2 (COX-2) blockade in the chemoprevention of cancers of the colon, breast, prostate, and lung. *Inflammo-pharmacology, 17,* 1–13.

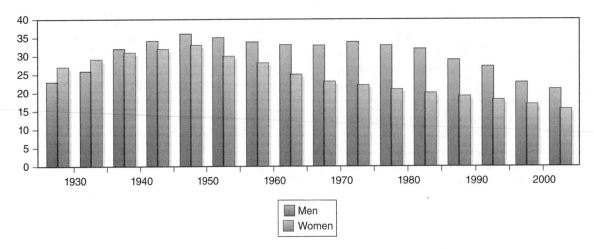

Figure 8.5 Decline in Colorectal Cancer Mortality, United States, 1930–2005.

Source: Data from Garcia, M., Jemal, A., Ward, E. M., Center, M. M., Hao, Y., Siegel, R. L., Thun, M. J. (2007). *Global cancer facts and figures, 2007*. Atlanta, GA: American Cancer Society. Retrieved from http://www.cancer.org/acs/groups/content/@nho/documents/document /globalfactsandfigures2007rev2p.pdf

SCREENING FOR COLORECTAL CANCER

In recent decades, rates of colorectal cancer have gradually increased in populations of developing nations in association with their transition to diets with higher fat and lower fiber content and lifestyle changes that heighten predisposition. In contrast, colorectal mortality rates have gradually declined in highly developed nations such as the United States (Garcia et al., 2007).

The declining trends in colorectal cancer death rates differ for U.S. men and women (**Figure 8.5**). In women, rates began to decline in the mid-twentieth century and have decreased by more than 50%. In men, rates began to decline during 1970–1980 and have decreased by about 40%. Several factors may have contributed to these declines, including greater awareness, increased screening, more efficacious treatment, improvement in diet, reduction in risk factors, and possibly greater use of chemopreventive agents such as NSAIDs. It is notable that these declines have occurred in the face of concurrent epidemics of obesity and related conditions such as type 2 diabetes.

A recent study suggests that the declining pattern of colorectal mortality in the United States is most compatible with a relatively large contribution from screening and a smaller but demonstrable impact of risk factor reductions and improved treatments (Edwards et al., 2009). Colonoscopy has gained greater acceptance in the general population and is the most reliable method of screening for the early detection of adenomatous polyps and cancer of the large bowel. In addition, visual determination of the exact location and size of existing tumors is an invaluable tool in planning and implementing definitive surgical resection. Colonoscopic imaging coupled with effective surgery has produced 5-year survival rates greater than 90% for patients whose tumors have not progressed beyond the bowel wall (National Cancer Institute, 2007).

● ● ● **REFERENCES**

Aaltonen, L. A., Peltomiki, P., Leach, F. S., Sistonen, P., Pylkkanen, L., Mecklin, J. P.,… de la Chapelle, A. (1993). Clues to the pathogenesis of familial colorectal cancer. *Science, 260,* 812–816.

Aaltonen, L. A., Peltomiki, P., Mecklin, J. P., Jirvinen, H., Jass, J. R., Green, J. S.,… de la Chapelle, A. (1994). Replication errors in benign and malignant tumors from hereditary nonpolyposis colorectal cancer patients. *Cancer Research, 54,* 1645–1648.

Anderson, J. W., Baird, P., Davis, R. H., Ferreri, S., Knudtson, M., Koraym, A.,… Williams, C. L. (2009). Health benefits of dietary fiber. *Nutrition Review, 67*(4), 188–205.

Baron, J. A., Cole, B. F., Sandler, R. S., Haile, R. W., Ahnen, D., Bresalier, R.,… van Stolk, R. U. (2003). A randomized trial of aspirin to prevent colorectal adenomas. *New England Journal of Medicine, 348,* 891–899.

Bingham, S. A., Day, N. E., Luben, R., Ferrari. P., Slimani, N., Norat, T.,... Riboli, E. (2010). Dietary fibre in food and protection against colorectal cancer in the European Prospective Investigation into Cancer and Nutrition (EPIC): An observational study. *Lancet, 361,* 1496–1501.

Bingham, S. A., Norat, T., Moskal, A., Ferrari, P., Slimani, N., Clavel-Chapelon, F.,... Riboli, E. (2005). Is the association with fiber from foods in colorectal cancer confounded by folate intake? *Cancer Epidemiology, Biomarkers and Prevention, 14,* 1552–1556.

Botteri, E., Iodice, S., Bagnardi, V., Raimondi, S., Lowenfel, A. B., & Maisonneuve, P. (2008). Smoking and colorectal cancer: A meta-analysis. *Journal of the American Medical Association, 300*(23), 2765–2778.

Boyle, P., & Langman, J. S. (2000). ABC of colorectal cancer. *British Medical Journal, 321*(7264), 805–808.

Burkitt, D. P. (1971). Epidemiology of cancer of the colon and rectum. *Cancer, 28,* 3–13.

Burkitt, D. P. (1973). Epidemiology of large bowel disease: The role of fibre. *Proceedings of the Nutrition Society, 32,* 145–149.

Burkitt, D. P., Walker, A. R. P., & Painter, N. S. (1974). Dietary fiber and disease. *Journal of the American Medical Association, 229,* 1068–1072.

Caygill, C. P., & Hill, M. J. (1995). Fish, n-3 fatty acids and human colorectal and breast cancer mortality. *European Journal of Cancer Prevention, 4,* 329–332.

Center, M. M., & Jemal, A. E. (2009). International trends in colorectal cancer incidence rates. *Cancer Epidemiology, Biomarkers, and Prevention, 18*(6), 1688–1694.

Chlebowski, R. T., Wactawski-Wende, J. W., Ritenbaugh, C., Hubbell, F. A., Ascensao, J., Rebecca, J.,... White, E. (2004). Estrogen plus progestin and colorectal cancer in postmenopausal women. *New England Journal of Medicine, 350*(10), 991–1004.

Cho, E., Smith-Warner, S. A., Ritz, J.,. van den Brandt, P. A., Colditz, G. A., Folsom, A. R.,... Hunter, D. J. (2004). Alcohol intake and colorectal cancer: A pooled analysis of 8 cohort studies. *Annals of Internal Medicine, 140*(8), 603–613.

Duthie, S. (1999). Folic acid deficiency and cancer: Mechanisms of DNA instability. *British Medical Bulletin, 55,* 578–592.

Edwards, B. K., Ward, E., Kohler, B. A., Eheman, C., Zauber, A. G., Anderson, R. N.,... Ries, L. A. (2009). Annual report to the nation on the status of cancer, 1975–2006, featuring colorectal cancer trends and impact of interventions (risk factors, screening, and treatment) to reduce future rates. *Cancer, 116*(3), 544–573.

Fearon, E. R., & Vogelstein, B. (2000). Tumor suppressor gene defects in human cancer. In Bast, R. C., et al., *Holland-Frei Cancer Medicine* (5th ed.). Retrieved from http://www.ncbi.nlm.nih.gov/books/NBK20794

Ferlay, J., Shin, H.-R., Bray, F., Forman, D., Mathers, C., & Parkin, D. M. (2010). Estimates of worldwide burden of cancer in 2008: GLOBOCAN 2008. *International Journal of Cancer, 127*(12), 2893–2917.

Ferlay, J., Soerjomataram, I., Ervik, M., Dikshit, R., Eser, S., Mathers, C.,... Bray, F. (2013). *GLOBOCAN 2012 v1.0. Cancer incidence and mortality worldwide: IARC CancerBase No. 11 [Internet].* Lyon, France: International Agency for Research on Cancer. Retrieved from http://globocan.iarc.fr

Freedman, D. M., Looker, A. C., Chang, S. C., & Graubard, B. L. (2007). Prospective study of serum vitamin D and cancer mortality in the United States. *Journal of the National Cancer Institute, 99*(21), 1594–1602.

Fuchs, C. S., Giovannucci, E. L., Colditz, G. A., Hunter, D. J., Stampfer, M. J., Rosner, B.,... Willett, W. C. (1999). Dietary fiber and the risk of colorectal cancer and adenoma in women. *New England Journal of Medicine, 340*(3), 169–176.

Garcia, M., Jemal, A., Ward, E. M., Center, M. M., Hao, Y., Siegel, R. L., & Thun, M. J. (2007). *Global cancer facts & figures 2007.* Atlanta, GA: American Cancer Society. http://www.cancer.org

/acs/groups/content/@nho/documents/document /globalfactsandfigures2007rev2p.pdf

Gardner, E. J. (1951). A genetic and clinical study of intestinal polyposis, a predisposing factor for carcinoma of the colon and rectum. *American Journal of Human Genetics, 3,* 167–176.

Garland, C. F., & Garland, F. C. (1980). Do sunlight and vitamin D reduce the likelihood of colon cancer? *International Journal of Epidemiology, 9,* 227–231.

Giovannucci, E. (2001). An updated review of the epidemiological evidence that cigarette smoking increases risk of colorectal cancer. *Cancer Epidemiology, Biomarkers, and Prevention, 10,* 725–731.

Giovannucci, E. (2007). Metabolic syndrome, hyperinsulinemia, and colon cancer: A review. *American Journal of Clinical Nutrition, 86*(3), 836–842.

Giovannucci, E., Colditz, G. A., Stampfer, M. J., & Willett, W. C. (1996). Physical activity, obesity and risk of colorectal cancer in women (United States). *Cancer Causes and Control, 7,* 253–263.

Gorham, E. D., Garland, C. F., Garland, F. C., Grant, W. B., Mohr, S. B., Lipkin, M.,... Holick, M. F. (2005). Vitamin D and prevention of colorectal cancer. *Journal of Steroid Biochemistry and Molecular Biology, 97,* 179–194.

Greenwald, P., Lanza, E., & Eddy, G. A. (1987). Dietary fiber in the reduction of colon cancer risk. *Journal of the American Dietetic Association, 87,* 1178–1188.

Harris, R. E. (2007). COX-2 and the inflammogenesis of cancer. *Subcellular Biochemistry, 42,* 193–212.

Harris, R. E. (2009). Cyclooxygenase-2 (COX-2) blockade in the chemoprevention of cancers of the colon, breast, prostate, and lung. *Inflammo-pharmacology, 17,* 1–13.

Harris, R. E., Beebe-Donk, J., & Alshafie, G. A. (2008). Similar reductions in the risk of human colon cancer by selective and non-selective cyclooxygenase-2 (COX-2) inhibitors. *BMC*

Cancer, 8(237). Retrieved from http://www .biomedcentral.com/1471-2407/8/237

Homann, N., Tillonen, J., & Salaspuro, M. (2000). Microbially produced acetaldehyde from ethanol may increase the risk of colon cancer via folate deficiency. *International Journal of Cancer, 86,* 169–173.

Howe, G. R., Benito, E., Castellato, R., Cornee, J., Esteve, J., Gallagher, R. P.,... Shu, Z. (1992). Dietary intake of fiber and decreased risk of cancers of the colon and rectum: Evidence from the combined analysis of 13 case-control studies. *Journal of the National Cancer Institute, 84,* 1887–1896.

Kumar, V., Abbas, A. K., Fausto, N., & Astor, J. (2009). *Robbins and Cotran pathologic basis of disease* (8th ed.). Philadelphia, PA: W.B. Saunders.

Leppert, M., Dobbs, M., Scambler, P., O'Connell, P., Nakamura, Y., Stauffer, D., Woodward, S.,... White, R. (1987). The gene for familial polyposis coli maps to the long arm of chromosome 5. *Science, 238*(4832), 1411–1413.

Levin, K. E., & Dozois, R. R. (1991). Epidemiology of large bowel cancer. *World Journal of Surgery, 15*(5), 562–567.

Lipkin, M., Reddy, B., Newmark, H., & Lamprecht, S. A. (1999). Dietary factors in human colorectal cancer. *Annual Review of Nutrition, 19,* 545–586.

Lynch, H. T., Guirgis, H. A., Lynch, P. M., & Harris, R. E. (1977). Familial cancer syndromes: A survey. *Cancer, 39*(4 Suppl), 1867–1881.

Lynch, H. T., Lynch, P. M., & Harris, R. E. (1977). Proximal colon cancer in familial carcinoma of the colon exclusive of familial polyposis coli. *Lancet, 1*(8025), 1306–1307.

Lynch, H. T., Shaw, M. W., Magnuson, C. W., Larsen, A. L., & Krush, A. J. (1966). Hereditary factors in cancer: A study of two large midwestern kindreds. *Archives of Internal Medicine, 117*(2), 206–212.

MacLennan, S. C., MacLennan, A. H., & Ryan, P. (1991). Colorectal cancer and oestrogen replacement therapy: A meta-analysis of epidemiological studies. *Medical Journal of Australia, 162*, 491–493.

Matsumura, Y. (2001). Emerging trends of nutrition: Transition and trade-offs. Nutrition trends in Japan. *Asia Pacific Journal of Clinical Nutrition, 10*(Suppl), S40–S47.

Mizoue, T., Inoue, M., Wakai, K., Nagata, C., Shimazu, T., Tsuji, I.,... Tsugane, S. (2008). Alcohol drinking and colorectal cancer in Japanese: A pooled analysis of results from five cohort studies. *American Journal of Epidemiology, 167*(12), 1397–1406.

Nakaji, S., Shimoyama, T., Umeda, T., Sakamoto, J., Katsura, S., Sugawara, K., & Baxter, D. (2001). Dietary fiber showed no preventive effect against colon and rectal cancers in Japanese with low fat intake: An analysis from the results of nutrition surveys from 23 Japanese prefectures. *BMC Cancer, 1*, 1–14.

National Cancer Center, Japan. (2010). *Cancer statistics in Japan, 2010*. Tokyo, Japan: Author.

National Cancer Institute. (2007). *Colon cancer PDQ: Treatment options for colon cancer.* Bethesda, MD: Author.

Nelson, H. D., Humphrey, L. L., Nygren, P., Teutsch, S. M., & Allen, J. D. (2002). Postmenopausal hormone replacement therapy: Scientific review. *Journal of the American Medical Association, 288*(7), 872–881.

Park, Y., Hunter, D. J., Spiegelman, D., Bergkvist, L., Berrino, F., van den Brandt, P. A.,... Smith-Warner, S. A. (2005). Dietary fiber intake and risk of colorectal cancer: A pooled analysis of prospective cohort studies. *Journal of the American Medical Association, 294*, 2849–2857.

Parkin, M. D., Bray, F., Ferlay, J., & Pisani, P. (2005). Global cancer statistics, 2002. *CA: A Cancer Journal for Clinicians, 55*, 74–108.

Reddy, B. S. (1995). Nutritional factors and colon cancer. *Critical Reviews in Food Science and Nutrition, 35*, 175–190.

Reddy, B. S., & Maeura, Y. (1984). Tumor promotion by dietary fat in azoxymethane induced colon carcinogenesis in female F344 rats: Influence of amount and source of dietary fat. *Journal of the National Cancer Institute, 72*, 746–750.

Street, M. E., de'Angelis, G., Camacho-Hübner, C., Giovannelli, G., Ziveri, M. A., Bacchini, P. L.,... Savage, M. O. (2004). Relationships between serum IGF-1, IGFBP-2, interleukin-1beta and interleukin-6 in inflammatory bowel disease. *Hormone Research, 61*(4), 159–164.

Su, L. J., & Arab, L. (2004). Alcohol consumption and risk of colon cancer: Evidence from the national health and nutrition examination survey I epidemiologic follow-up study. *Nutrition and Cancer, 50*(2), 111–119.

Terry, P. D., Miller, A. B., & Rohan, T. E. (2002). Obesity and colorectal cancer risk in women. *Gut, 51*, 191–194.

Trock, B., Lanza, E., & Greenwald, P. (1990). Dietary fiber, vegetables, and colon cancer: Critical review and meta-analysis of epidemiological studies. *Journal of the National Cancer Institute, 82*, 650–661.

Wactawski-Wende, J., Morley Kotchen, J., & Anderson, G. L. (2006). Calcium plus vitamin D supplementation and the risk of colorectal cancer. *New England Journal of Medicine, 354*(7), 684–696.

Willett, W. C., Stampfer, M. J., Colditz, G. A., Rosner, B. A., & Speizer, F. E. (1990). Relation of meat, fat, and fiber intake to the risk of colon cancer in a prospective study among women. *New England Journal of Medicine, 323*, 1664–1672.

Wong, J. M., de Souza, R., Kendall, C. W., Emam, A., & Jenkins, D. J. (2006). Colonic health: Fermentation and short chain fatty acids. *Journal of Clinical Gastroenterology, 40*(3), 235–243.

Wu, K., Giovannucci, E., Byrne, C., Platz, E. A., Fuchs, C., Willett, W. C., & Sinha, R. (2006). Meat mutagens and risk of distal colon Adenoma in a cohort of U.S. men. *Cancer Epidemiology, Biomarkers and Prevention, 15*(6), 1120–1125.

Wynder, E. L., Fujita, Y., Harris, R. E., Hirayama, T., & Hiyama, T. (1991). Comparative epidemiology of cancer between the United States and Japan: A second look. *Cancer, 67*(3), 746–763.

Wynder, E. L., Kajitani, T., Ishikawa, S., Dodo, H., & Takano, A. (1969). Environmental factors of cancer of the colon and rectum. II. Japanese epidemiological data. *Cancer, 23*, 1210–1220.

Yu, H., Harris, R. E., Gao, Y-T., Gao, R., & Wynder, E. L. (1991). Comparative epidemiology of cancers of the colon, rectum, prostate and breast in Shanghai, China, versus the United States. *International Journal of Epidemiology, 20*(1), 76–81.

Zisman, A. L., Nickolov, A., Brand, R. E., Gorchow, A., & Roy, H. K. (2006). Associations between the age at diagnosis and location of colorectal cancer and the use of alcohol and tobacco. *Archives of Internal Medicine, 166*, 629–634.

Epidemiology of Pancreatic Cancer

GLOBAL EPIDEMIOLOGY OF PANCREATIC CANCER

Pancreatic cancer was diagnosed in 337,892 individuals and caused 330,391 deaths in the world population during 2012. In that year, pancreatic cancer caused 3.7% of all cancer deaths among men (173,827 deaths) and 4.4% among women (156,564 deaths).

Pancreatic cancer is more common in developed countries (187,465 new cases in 2012) compared to developing countries (150,407 new cases). In developed countries, pancreatic cancer mortality (6.8 deaths per 100,000) ranks fifth among the leading causes of death from cancer, whereas in developing nations, it ranks tenth (2.7 deaths per 100,000). The male-to-female ratio of pancreatic cancer deaths for developed nations (1.02 in 2012) is lower than for developing nations (1.25) (Ferlay et al., 2013).

Regardless of gender, pancreatic cancer is usually fatal; survival rates one year after diagnosis are less than 20% even in developed nations such as the United States. As a consequence, the ratio of mortality to incidence is close to unity (~0.98 in 2012). Without treatment, survival after diagnosis is only 3 to 5 months (Hariharan, Saied, & Kocher, 2008; O'Sullivan & Kocher, 2007).

Figure 9.1 depicts the international variability in pancreatic cancer incidence and mortality rates. Regions with high incidence and mortality rates include affluent industrialized nations in North America; Northern and Western Europe, including Greenland; Northern Asia (Russia); Australia and New Zealand; and the southernmost nations of South America. Low rates are observed in Africa and Southern Asia (Ferlay et al., 2010, 2013). As

initially pointed out by Dr. Ernst Wynder, the international mortality rates of pancreatic cancer are positively correlated with per capita consumption of dietary fat, presumably from meat and dairy products (Wynder, 1975). Nevertheless, as with other forms of cancer that currently occur more often in developed nations, pancreatic cancer incidence rates are increasing in economically transitioning countries, whereas in developed countries such as the United States the rates appear to be stable or slightly declining (Parkin, 2004).

PATHOGENESIS OF PANCREATIC CANCER

The pancreas is a dual-functioning gland located deep in the abdomen just behind the stomach. Numerous pancreatic ducts communicate with the main (central) pancreatic duct that merges with the common bile duct to form the *ampulla of Vater* that empties into the duodenum (the upper small intestine). The anatomy of the pancreas is shown in **Figure 9.2**.

The pancreas functions as both an endocrine and an exocrine gland. Specialized endocrine cells of the *islets of Langerhans* are instrumental in the secretion of insulin and glucagon to maintain tight control of blood glucose. In contrast, specialized exocrine cells (called acinar cells) secrete powerful digestive enzymes as well as alkaline fluid into the pancreatic ducts that eventually drain into the main pancreatic duct and the duodenum (upper small intestine). The digestive enzymes include trypsin, lipase, and amylase, which break down protein, fats, and carbohydrates, respectively. Pancreatic fluids mix with bile from the liver in the ampulla of Vater prior to reaching the duodenum (the upper small intestine). A

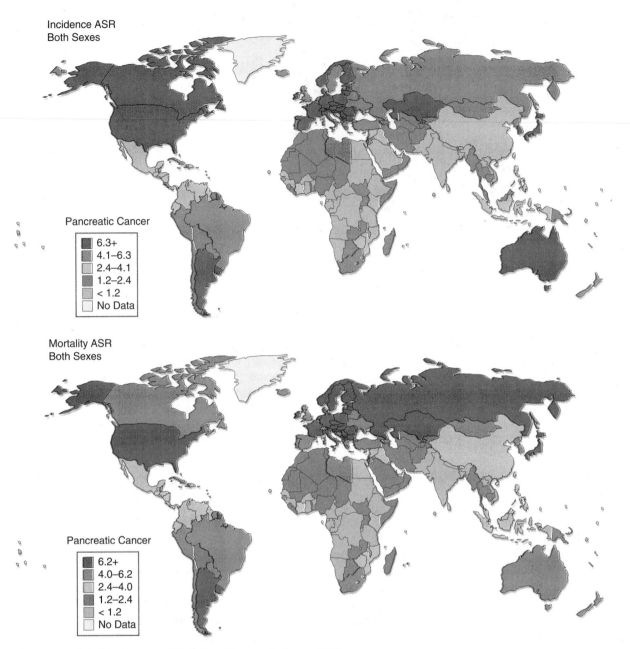

Figure 9.1 Global Incidence and Mortality of Pancreatic Cancer, 2012.

ASR: Rates per 100,000 are age-standardized to the world population, 2000–2025.

Source: Ferlay, J., Soerjomataram. I., Ervik, M., Dikshit, R., Eser, S., Mathers, C.,... Bray, F. (2013). *GLOBOCAN 2012 v1.0. Cancer incidence and mortality worldwide: IARC CancerBase No. 11* [Internet]. Lyon, France: International Agency for Research on Cancer. Retrieved from http://globocan.iarc.fr

layer of specialized columnar epithelium circumferentially lines the pancreatic ducts as well as the main pancreatic duct.

Most pancreatic cancers (approximately 99%) are adenocarcinomas that arise from the epithelial cells that line the ducts of the exocrine pancreas. The majority of this chapter is devoted to "carcinoma of the pancreas," which implies carcinoma arising

from the epithelial lining of the exocrine portion of the pancreas. Only a small fraction (perhaps 1–2%) of pancreatic tumors arise from the acinar cells of the pancreas or cells within the islets of Langerhans. These relatively rare tumors are discussed in a later section of this chapter.

Pancreatic cancer rates increase exponentially during the latter decades of the lifespan. Most cases

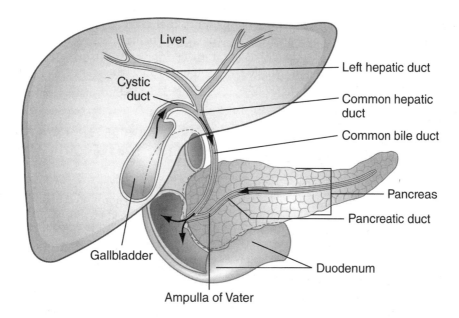

Figure 9.2 Anatomy of the Human Pancreas.

are diagnosed after the age of 50 years with peak rates occurring in the age range 65–70 years. Furthermore, the majority of cases involve the head of the pancreas (60–70%) rather than the body or tail of the gland (30–40%). Because developing pancreatic tumors are difficult to palpate and there are no valid biomarkers of impending disease, it is believed that the genesis of these malignancies spans many years. Recent cellular and molecular studies suggest that pancreatic cancer develops over time by a progression of steps in the epithelial lining of the pancreatic ducts, from dysplasia to in situ carcinoma and, ultimately, invasive cancer (Ottenhof et al., 2009).

TOBACCO SMOKING AND PANCREATIC CANCER

Tobacco smoking is a recognized risk factor for the development of pancreatic cancer. Wynder and colleagues first observed a significant dose response in the risk of pancreatic cancer with increasing number of cigarettes per day in chronic smokers (Wynder, Mabuchi, & Maruchia, 1973). As shown in **Figure 9.3**, the risk increased nearly fivefold for smokers of two or more packs per day compared to never smokers. Subsequently, many epidemiologic investigations have confirmed the etiologic impact of smoking tobacco in the development of this deadly malignancy. In a comprehensive meta-analysis of 82 studies conducted on four continents,

chronic cigarette smoking increased the risk of developing pancreatic cancer by 74% compared to never smoking (summary relative risk [RR] = 1.74, 95% confidence interval [CI] = 1.61–1.87), and the risk elevation persisted 10 years after smoking cessation (Iodice, Gandini, Maisonneuve, & Lowenfels, 2008). Results were highly consistent for case control studies (RR = 1.77) and cohort studies (RR = 1.70). The risk was also elevated for pipe or cigar smokers (RR = 1.47, 95% CI = 1.17–1.83). The public health implications of these results are enormous; for

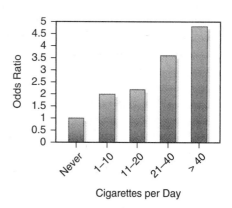

Figure 9.3 Risk of Pancreatic Cancer and Cigarette Smoking in Men.

Source: Data from Wynder, E. L. (1975). An epidemiological evaluation of the causes of cancer of the pancreas. *Cancer Research, 35*(8), 2228–2233.

example, for populations with a smoking prevalence of 30%, the proportion of pancreatic cancer attributable to smoking is approximately 20%. Recent global estimates suggest that 1 in 3 adults smoke (World Health Organization [WHO], 2009), so it is evident that at least one-fifth of all pancreatic cancers are preventable by avoidance of the smoking habit.

Carcinogens from inhaled tobacco smoke can reach the pancreas through the circulatory system or through the bile. In particular, nitrosamines are activated in the liver and detoxified by liver enzymes of the cytochrome P-450 system (e.g., *CYP1A2*) or *n*-acetyl transferase enzymes. Recall that bile is secreted by the liver through the common cystic duct into the ampulla of Vater in the head of the pancreas. Notably, carcinogenic nitrosamines and their metabolites have been found in human bile (Hecht, 1998). Conceivably, some individuals may be genetically deficient in essential detoxification enzymes and as a consequence be at high risk for the development of pancreatic cancer due to sustained exposure to inhaled or ingested carcinogens (Lowenfels & Maisonneuve, 2006). Indeed, in a recent case control investigation of genetic polymorphisms and pancreatic cancer, heavy smoking individuals genetically null for the glutathione-S-transferase enzyme (*GSTT1*) had markedly increased risk estimates compared to nonsmokers with normal *GSTT1* (Duell et al., 2002). Estimated odds ratios (OR) in the study were OR = 5.0, 95% CI = 1.8–14.5 for women, and OR = 3.2, 95% CI = 1.3–8.1 for men.

ALCOHOL AND PANCREATIC CANCER

The role of alcohol in the development of pancreatic cancer appears to be related to the dose and duration of alcohol consumption. The risk is increased by two- to threefold in heavy drinkers (i.e., consuming four or more drinks per day) (Olsen, Mandel, Gibson, Wattenberg, & Schuman, 1989; Ye et al., 2002) and the risk increase is higher per level of intake for certain ethnic groups; for example, risk estimates for African American women are higher than for Caucasian women (Silverman et al., 1995). A recent pooled analysis of 14 prospective studies found that consumption of at least 30 grams of alcohol daily (about two drinks) produced only a modest elevation in the risk (summary RR = 1.22, 95% CI = 1.03–1.45), whereas consumption of lesser amounts had no effect (Genkinger et al., 2009). Furthermore, some investigators caution that observed risk increases may be due to confounding with smoking (Ye et al., 2002; Zatonski et al., 1993). Nevertheless, there is no

doubt that chronic alcohol abuse is a major cause of chronic pancreatitis, which in turn predisposes to the development of pancreatic cancer. The association of chronic pancreatitis and pancreatic cancer is discussed in a later section of this chapter.

RISK OF PANCREATIC CANCER: COMBINED EFFECT OF TOBACCO AND ALCOHOL

Talamini and colleagues recently published the results of a case control study that examined both independent and combined effects of tobacco smoking and alcohol consumption in the development of pancreatic cancer. They compared 326 cases with incident pancreatic cancer to 652 hospital controls matched on age and gender without neoplastic disease. All subjects were ascertained and interviewed in hospitals in northern Italy during the period 1991–2008. Results revealed independent effects of tobacco smoking (OR = 2.04 for 20 or more pack years) and heavy alcohol consumption (OR = 2.03 for 21–34 drinks per week and OR = 3.42 for 35 or more drinks per week). The risk increased more than fourfold for chronic smokers and heavy drinkers (OR = 4.3) compared to never smokers who consumed less than seven drinks per week. The authors suggest that the effects of tobacco and alcohol are additive, and together they account for approximately one-third of pancreatic cancer in Italy (Talamini et al., 2010).

DIETARY FAT AND PANCREATIC CANCER

Fat and red meat consumption have been linked to the development of pancreatic cancer in a number of epidemiologic studies (Bueno de Mesquita, Moerman, Runia, & Maisonneuve, 1990; Chan, Wang, & Holly, 2007; Durbec, Chevillotte, Bidart, Berthezene, & Sarles, 1983; Farrow & Davis, 1990; Ghadirian, Simard, Baillargeon, Maisonneuve, & Boyle, 1991; Larsson, Hakanson, Permert, & Wolk, 2006; Mills, Beeson, Abbey, Fraser, & Phillips, 1988; Nöthlings et al., 2005; Raymond, Infante, Tuyns, Voirol, & Lowenfels, 1987; Stolzenberg-Solomon, Pietinen, Taylor, Virtamo, & Albanes, 2002; Wynder, 1975; Zhang, Zhao, & Berkel, 2005); however, results have not been consistent among all studies (Lin et al., 2006; Michaud, Giovannucci, Willett, Colditz, & Fuchs, 2003).

The U.S. National Institutes of Health–American Association of Retired Persons (AARP) Diet and Health Study was designed to provide definitive evidence on dietary factors and the development of a variety of chronic diseases including pancreatic cancer (Schatzkin et al., 2001). Using the NIH–AARP database, Thiébaut and colleagues (2009) examined the association between dietary fat and pancreatic cancer. Their investigation was based on the NIH–AARP cohort of 308,736 men and 216,737 women ages 51–70 years of age who completed a 124-item food frequency questionnaire in 1995–1996. Important findings of this study are summarized in the following paragraph.

Over an average follow-up of 6.3 years, 865 men and 472 women were diagnosed with exocrine pancreatic cancer (45.0 and 34.5 cases per 100 000 person-years, respectively). After multivariable adjustment and combination of data for men and women, pancreatic cancer risk was directly related to the intakes of total fat (highest versus lowest quintile, 46.8 versus 33.2 cases per 100,000 person-years, hazard ratio [HR] = 1.23, 95% CI = 1.03–1.46; P trend = 0.03), saturated fat (51.5 versus 33.1 cases per 100,000 person-years, HR = 1.36, 95% CI = 1.14 to 1.62; P trend < 0.001), and monounsaturated fat (46.2 versus 32.9 cases per 100,000 person-years, HR = 1.22, 95% CI = 1.02 to 1.46; P trend = 0.05) but not polyunsaturated fat. The associations were strongest for saturated fat from animal food sources (52.0 versus 32.2 cases per 100,000 person-years, HR = 1.43, 95% CI = 1.20–1.70; P trend < 0.001); specifically, intakes from red meat and dairy products were both statistically significantly associated with increased pancreatic cancer risk (HR = 1.27 and 1.19, respectively).

Of further note regarding findings of the NIH–AARP study of pancreatic cancer is that there were no consistent associations with polyunsaturated, saturated, or monounsaturated fats from plant food sources. Though there was no association with total intake of polyunsaturated fats (PUFAs) in this large comprehensive study, it is important to note that the high intake of dietary arachidonic acid (20:4), an omega-6 PUFA obtained primarily from animal foods, was significantly associated with the risk of developing pancreatic cancer (HR = 1.33, 95% CI = 1.12–1.59, P trend < 0.002). The investigators concluded that high intake of dietary fat of animal origin, particularly from red meat and dairy food sources, increases the risk of developing pancreatic cancer (Thiébaut et al., 2009).

Various hypotheses have been advanced to explain the link between high dietary fat and the development of pancreatic cancer. It is well known that diets with high fat content stimulate bile secretion by the liver, which in turn increases the gastrointestinal exposure to cholesterol, bile acids, and their metabolites. There is considerable experimental evidence that bile acids promote the development of gastrointestinal tumors both in vivo (Hill, 1991; Reddy, 1981; Reddy, Weisburger, & Wynder, 1978) and in vitro (Kaibara, Yurugi, & Koga, 1984). Recent evidence also suggests that bile acids promote carcinogenesis by up-regulating cyclooxygenase-2 (COX-2) and prostaglandin production (Glinghammar & Rafter, 2001; Shirvani et al., 2000; Zhang, Subbaramaiah, Altorki, & Dannenberg, 1998). Furthermore, bile acids have been found to induce COX-2 in pancreatic cancer cell lines (Tucker, Dannenberg, Yang, & Fahye, 2004). These findings, plus the significant effects of dietary fat and, specifically, arachidonic acid (the primary substrate of COX-2 in the inflammatory cascade) observed in the NIH–AARP Dietary Study (Thiébaut et al., 2009), suggest that up-regulation of COX-2 and excess production of prostaglandins may have an important role in the development of pancreatic cancer. This general process (called inflammogenesis) induces and promotes essential features of carcinogenesis (mutagenesis, mitogenesis, angiogenesis, reduced apoptosis, metastasis, and immunosuppression) (Harris, 2007).

CHRONIC PANCREATITIS AND PANCREATIC CANCER

Chronic pancreatitis refers to persistent inflammation of the pancreas, irrespective of the cause. This condition is clearly a risk factor for the development of pancreatic cancer. In an international multicenter historical cohort study of 2,015 patients diagnosed with chronic pancreatitis, 56 new cases of pancreatic cancer developed over a mean follow-up period of 7.4 years, an incidence rate more than 16 times the expected rate (standardized incidence ratio = 16.5, 95% CI = 11.1–23.7) (Lowenfels et al., 1993). The cumulative risk after 20 years of follow-up was 4.0% (95% CI = 2.0–5.9) and the risk increase was independent of gender, country of origin, and type of pancreatitis.

The main cause of chronic pancreatitis among adults is chronic alcohol abuse. More than 70% of adult patients diagnosed with chronic pancreatitis have a long-term history of frequently drinking excessive amounts of alcoholic beverages. The majority of such patients report daily consumption of at least 150 grams (more than 5 ounces) of alcohol for more than 5 years (Nair, Lawler, & Miller, 2007). The presence of gallstones (cholelithiasis) also predisposes affected individuals to the development of chronic pancreatitis. These two conditions, chronic alcohol abuse and cholelithiasis, account for about 90% of chronic pancreatitis in the United States. Autoimmune pancreatitis accounts for an additional 5–6% of cases (Finkelberg, Sahani, Deshpande, & Brugge, 2006).

The pathophysiology of chronic pancreatitis has been characterized through detailed studies of alcoholic pancreatitis in both animals and humans (Witt, Apte, Keim, & Wilson, 2007). Alcohol is directly toxic to pancreatic tissue, and chronic exposure causes significant cell damage, necrosis, and inflammation (a process known as *necroinflammation*). In addition, the alcohol-induced destruction and destabilization of the epithelial lining of the pancreatic ducts permits the release of powerful digestive enzymes, thereby predisposing the gland to *autodigestion*. The progressive cascade of pathogenic events in chronic alcoholic pancreatitis involves chronic inflammation, cell necrosis, release of digestive enzymes, cell autodigestion, formation of reactive oxygen species, collagen deposition, fibrosis, and scarring of the pancreatic tissues. The inflammatory pathophysiology of chronic pancreatitis clearly provokes multiple mechanisms of carcinogenesis such as mitogenesis, mutagenesis, and angiogenesis (Harris, 2007).

Chronic pancreatitis induced by chronic cholelithiasis (gallstone formation) appears to follow a similar course (Yan & Li, 2006). Gallstones that travel down the common bile duct and become lodged in the ampulla of Vater can cause obstruction in the outflow of pancreatic digestive fluids. Backflow of these digestive fluids into the pancreas predisposes the ductal epithelium to autodigestion. The end result is persistent necroinflammation that progresses to chronic pancreatitis.

GERMLINE MUTATIONS AND PANCREATIC CANCER

Various germline mutations have been identified that heighten the risk of developing pancreatic cancer. For example, hereditary pancreatitis is an autosomal dominant genetic condition caused by a mutation in the gene that encodes the powerful digestive enzyme trypsinogen. Carriers of the mutant gene produce abnormal trypsinogen that is resistant to autolysis, thereby causing autodigestion of the pancreas, necroinflammation, and chronic pancreatitis. Such individuals have a 40% lifetime risk of developing pancreatic cancer (Whitcomb, 1999).

Cystic fibrosis is an autosomal recessive genetic condition caused by a deleterious mutation in the transmembrane conductance regulator gene (*CFTR*) located on the long arm of chromosome 7. The protein encoded by *CFTR* is essential for normal function of the chloride ion channel of cell membranes and homeostatic regulation of concentrations of electrolytes in sweat, digestive enzymes, and mucus. The extremely viscid mucinous secretions characteristic of this condition result in cystic dilatation, necroinflammation, and fibrosis within the pancreas, lungs, and other organs, hence the name cystic fibrosis. Chronic pancreatitis develops early in patients with cystic fibrosis, with a consequent fivefold increase in the risk of early onset pancreatic cancer (Maisonneuve, Marshall, & Lowenfels, 2007). Cystic fibrosis is one of the more common genetic conditions among Caucasians, occurring in 1 of every 3,200 newborns. The median life expectancy for individuals with cystic fibrosis is only 30–35 years.

Familial breast/ovarian cancer is often caused by a heritable mutation in either of two tumor suppressor genes, *BRCA-1* or *BRCA-2*. Females who inherit mutant alleles of *BRCA-1* or *BRCA-2* are not only at high risk for developing breast cancer and/or ovarian cancer, but also at increased risk for the development of other tumors, including pancreatic cancer. Both *BRCA-1* and *BRCA-2* are tumor suppressor genes that are essential for precise DNA replication in cell division. Mutant forms of a third gene (called *PAL-B2* because it interacts with *BRCA-2*) also increase pancreatic cancer risk as well as breast cancer risk (Chen et al., 2008).

The Familial Atypical Mole and Melanoma (FAMM) syndrome is a rare genetic disorder giving rise to multiple dysplastic pigmented moles of the skin that can progress to malignant melanoma. There is also an increase in the risk of developing pancreatic cancer. One form of the FAMM syndrome is caused by a mutation in the gene that encodes *p16*, an important cell cycle regulating protein (Hussussian et al., 1994).

Peutz–Jeghers syndrome is a rare autosomal dominant disorder characterized by the development of benign hamartomatous polyps in the gastrointestinal tract and hyperpigmented macules on the lips and oral mucosa (Boardman et al., 1998). This syndrome is caused by a mutant tumor suppressor gene known as STK11 located on chromosome 19. Mutations in this gene result in an altered serine/threonine protein kinase that markedly increases the risk of gastrointestinal tumors including pancreatic cancer (Jenne et al., 1998).

Lynch syndrome (hereditary nonpolyposis coli colon cancer, HNPCC) is characterized by a high lifetime risk for the development of colon cancer. The cause of HNPCC is an inherited (germline) mutation in at least one of a set of genes that normally repair DNA, the mismatch repair genes. This genetic disorder also carries an increase in the risk of developing pancreatic cancer.

SOMATIC MUTATIONS IN PANCREATIC CANCER

Somatic mutations involving base pair changes in DNA occasionally occur in specific cells of specific tissues of the human body. The phenotypic effects of such mutations persist in the lineage of the cell of origin.

The *K-ras* gene product communicates signals from outside the cell to the nucleus, a process known as *signal transduction*. Somatic mutations of the *K-ras* gene can lead to its permanent activation, thereby causing inappropriate signaling inside the cell even in the absence of extracellular stimuli. Because *K-ras* signal transduction stimulates cell division, its deregulation may result in heightened cell proliferation and malignant transformation (Goodsell, 1999).

Somatic mutations of *K-ras* have been observed in up to 90% of certain malignancies such as colon cancer, lung cancer, and pancreatic cancer (Almoguera et al., 1988). Somatic mutations of *K-ras* have also been detected in premalignant lesions of these organs (Moskaluk, Hruban, & Kern, 1997). Molecular studies also suggest that mutational activation of *K-ras* coupled with disabling mutations in tumor suppressor genes such as *p53* and *p16* accentuate carcinogenesis (Ghaneh, Costello, & Neoptolemos, 2007; Moskaluk et al., 1997; Pellegata et al., 1994). Although specific mutagenic stimuli of persistent *K-ras* mutations have not yet been clearly identified (Crous-Bou et al., 2009), most factors that are associated with the development of pancreatic cancer (e.g., tobacco, alcohol, bile acids, reactive oxygen species, and inflammatory factors) do have significant mutagenic potential. Clearly, the oncogenic activation of *K-ras* is likely to play a key role in the initiation and promotion of pancreatic ductal adenocarcinoma.

EPIGENETICS OF PANCREATIC CANCER

Epigenetics refers to the study of changes in the expression of genes without any alteration in the base pair sequence of the DNA. Down-regulation of genetic expression has generally been linked to DNA methylation as opposed to up-regulation, which may be a result of DNA acetylation.

Because pancreatic cancer often develops subsequent to chronic pancreatitis and necroinflammation, it is notable that the inducible COX-2 gene that encodes the chief regulatory enzyme of the inflammatory cascade is markedly overexpressed in a high percentage of pancreatic adenocarcinomas; furthermore, positive immunostaining for COX-2 is localized to malignant epithelial cells whereas COX-2 staining is negative in noncancerous pancreatic tissues (Tucker et al., 1999). In addition, studies of pancreatic cancer cell lines show that bile acids effectively up-regulate the inducible COX-2 gene (Tucker et al., 2004). These findings suggest that bile acids could promote pancreatic cancer by up-regulation of the inducible COX-2 gene.

OBESITY, DIABETES MELLITUS TYPE 2, AND PANCREATIC CANCER

Twin epidemics of obesity and diabetes mellitus type 2 have emerged in many populations throughout the world. Both conditions are independently associated with the development of pancreatic cancer, and obesity is associated with the onset of diabetes.

An early meta-analysis of 20 epidemiologic studies determined a twofold elevation in the risk of pancreatic cancer among individuals with a 5-year history of diabetes mellitus type 2 (Everhart & Wright, 1995). In a more recent meta-analysis of 36 epidemiologic studies (17 case control and 19 cohort studies involving 9,220 cases), the adjusted summary odds ratio was 1.83 (95% CI = 1.66–1.89) (Huxley, Ansary-Moghaddam, Berrington de González, Barzi, & Woodward, 2005). These results support a modest causal association of type 2 diabetes in the genesis of pancreatic cancer.

A major problem with studies of the association of pancreatic cancer and diabetes is that because both conditions evolve in the same organ over a period of many years, it is difficult to determine the causal pathway. The question becomes, does diabetes predispose to pancreatic cancer or the reverse? Drawing conclusions regarding the role of diabetes in causing pancreatic cancer is thus subject to a form of bias known as *reverse causality bias*. In fact, more than 70% of pancreatic cancer cases present with glucose intolerance (Gullo, Pezzilli, & Morselli-Labate, 1994; Schwarts, Zeidler, Moossa, Kuku, & Rubenstein, 1978).

The issue of reverse causality in regard to pancreatic cancer and diabetes has been discussed in some detail by various investigators. Currently, there is no general consensus as to a cause and effect relationship between these conditions. One argument *against* such a relationship is the fact that rates of pancreatic cancer have remained constant or declined in many nations even though prevalence rates of obesity and type 2 diabetes have increased dramatically. Nevertheless, in subjects with longstanding type 2 diabetes, the pancreas is exposed to hyperinsulinemia for years, and because cultures of pancreatic cancer cells have been found to express insulin receptors, it is conceivable that hyperinsulinemia could serve as a promoter of pancreatic cancer (Wang, Herrington, Larrson, & Permert, 2003).

ISLET CELL TUMORS

Islet cell tumors of the pancreas arise from endocrine cells in the *islets of Langerhans*. Although such tumors may involve any of the hormone-producing islet cells (alpha cells produce glucagon, beta cells produce insulin, delta cells produce somatostatin, PP cells produce pancreatic polypeptide, and epsilon cells produce ghrelin), most are beta cell tumors (also called insulinomas because the beta cells elaborate insulin). Insulinomas are clinically characterized by attacks of hyperinsulinism and hypoglycemia. Islet cell tumors are a component of Zollinger–Ellison syndrome, defined by the triad of recalcitrant peptic ulcer, hypersecretion of gastrin (gastrinoma), and pancreatic islet cell tumor. Islet cell tumors also occur in multiple endocrine neoplasia syndrome (MEN I), which may include adenomas of the pituitary gland, the thyroid and parathyroid glands, and the adrenal cortex in combination with peptic ulcer. Most islet cell tumors are benign (less than 10% are malignant carcinomas). Malignant islet cell tumors constitute only about 1% of all cases of pancreatic cancer (Bellizzi & Frankel, 2004). Germline and somatic mutations and epigenetic suppression of multiple tumor suppressor genes that regulate nucleosome remodeling have been linked to the development of these rare pancreatic tumors (Elsässer, Allis, & Lewis, 2011).

PREVENTION OF PANCREATIC CANCER

There are currently no proven methods of preventing the development of pancreatic cancer, nor are there satisfactory tests or imaging procedures that can be used to screen the population for early lesions of the pancreas. Nevertheless, there are steps that can be taken to reduce the risk. These include complete avoidance of tobacco and alcohol; maintenance of a healthy weight through regular exercise; eating a diet rich in fruits, vegetables, and whole grains; and maintenance of blood glucose within normal limits.

• • • REFERENCES

Almoguera, C., Shibata, D., Forrester, K., Martin, J., Arnheim, N., & Perucho, M. (1988). Most human carcinomas of the exocrine pancreas contain mutant *c-K-ras* genes. *Cell, 53,* 549–554.

Bellizzi, A. M., & Frankel, W. L. (2004). Pancreatic pathology: A practical review. *LabMedicine, 40,* 417–426.

Boardman, L. A., Thibodeau, S. N., Schaid, D. J., Lindor, N. M., McDonnell, S. K., Burgart, L. J.,… Hartmann, L. C. (1998). Increased risk for cancer in patients with the Peutz-Jeghers syndrome. *Annals of Internal Medicine, 128*(11), 896–899.

Bueno de Mesquita, H. B., Moerman, C. J., Runia, S., & Maisonneuve, P. (1990). Are energy and energy-providing nutrients related to exocrine carcinoma of the pancreas? *International Journal of Cancer, 46*(3), 435–444.

Chan, J. M., Wang, F., & Holly, E. A. (2007). Pancreatic cancer, animal protein and dietary fat in a population-based study, San Francisco Bay Area, California. *Cancer Causes and Control, 18*(10), 1153–1167.

Chen, P., Liang, J., Wang, Z., Zhou, X., Chen, L., Li, M.,… Wang, H. (2008). Association of common PALB2 polymorphisms with breast cancer risk: A case-control study. *Clinical Cancer Research, 14*(18), 5931–5937.

Crous-Bou, M., Parta, M., Morales, E., Lopez, T., Carrato, A., Puigdome'nech, E., Readl, F. X., & PANKRAS II Study Group. (2009). Past medical conditions and K-ras mutations in pancreatic ductal adenocarcinoma: A hypothesis-generating study. *Cancer Causes and Control, 20,* 591–599.

Duell, E. J., Holly, E. A., Bracci, P. M., Liu, M., Wiencke, J. K., & Kelsey, K. T. (2002). A population-based, case control study of polymorphisms in carcinogen-metabolizing genes, smoking, and pancreatic adenocarcinoma risk. *Journal of the National Cancer Institute, 94*(4), 297–306.

Durbec, J. P., Chevillotte, G., Bidart, J. M., Berthezene, P., & Sarles, H. (1983). Diet, alcohol, tobacco and risk of cancer of the pancreas: A case-control study. *British Journal of Cancer, 47*(4), 463–470.

Elsässer, S. J., Allis, C. D., & Lewis, P. W. (2011). New epigenetic drivers of cancers. *Science, 331*(6021), 1145–1146.

Everhart, J., & Wright, D. (1995). Diabetes mellitus as a risk factor for pancreatic cancer. A meta-analysis. *Journal of the American Medical Association, 273*(20), 1605–1609.

Farrow, D. C., & Davis, S. (1990). Diet and the risk of pancreatic cancer in men. *American Journal of Epidemiology, 132*(3), 423–431.

Ferlay, J., Shin, H.-R., Bray, F., Forman, D., Mathers, C., & Parkin, D. M. (2010). Estimates of worldwide burden of cancer in 2008: GLOBOCAN 2008. *International Journal of Cancer 127*(12), 2893–2917.

Ferlay, J., Soerjomataram, I., Ervik, M., Dikshit, R., Eser, S., Mathers, C.,... Bray, F. (2013). *GLOBOCAN 2012 v1.0. Cancer incidence and mortality worldwide: IARC CancerBase No. 11* [Internet]. Lyon, France: International Agency for Research on Cancer. Retrieved from http://globocan.iarc.fr

Finkelberg, D. L., Sahani, D., Deshpande, V., & Brugge, W. R. (2006). Autoimmune pancreatitis. *New England Journal of Medicine, 355,* 2670–2676.

Genkinger, J. M., Spiegelman, D., Anderson, K. E., Bergkvist, L., Bernstein, L., van den Brandt, P. A.,... Smith-Varner, S. A. (2009). Alcohol intake and pancreatic cancer risk: A pooled analysis of fourteen cohort studies. *Cancer Epidemiology, Biomarkers and Prevention, 18*(3), 765–776.

Ghadirian, P., Simard, A., Baillargeon, J., Maisonneuve, P., & Boyle, P. (1991). Nutritional factors and pancreatic cancer in the Francophone community in Montreal, Canada. *International Journal of Cancer, 47*(1), 1–6.

Ghaneh, P., Costello, E., & Neoptolemos, J. P. (2007). Biology and management of pancreatic cancer. *Gut, 56*(8), 1134–1152.

Glinghammar, B., & Rafter, J. (2001). Colonic luminal contents induce cyclooxygenase 2 transcription in human colon carcinoma cells. *Gastroenterology, 120,* 401–410.

Goodsell, D. S. (1999). The molecular perspective: The ras oncogene. *Oncologist, 4*(3), 263–264.

Gullo, L., Pezzilli, R., & Morselli-Labate, A. M., Italian Pancreatic Cancer Study Group. (1994). Diabetes and the risk of pancreatic cancer. *New England Journal of Medicine, 331,* 81–84.

Hariharan, D., Saied, A., & Kocher, H. M. (2008). Analysis of mortality rates for pancreatic cancer across the world. *Hepato-Pancreato-Biliary Journal (Oxford), 10*(1), 58–62.

Harris, R. E. (2007). COX-2 and the inflammogenesis of cancer. *Subcellular Biochemistry, 42,* 193–212.

Hecht, S. S. (1998). Biochemistry, biology, and carcinogenicity of tobacco-specific N-nitrosamines. *Chemical Research in Toxicology, 6,* 559–603.

Hill, M. J. (1991). Bile acids and colorectal cancer: Hypothesis. *European Journal of Cancer Prevention, 2,* 69–74.

Hussussian, C. J., Struewing, J. P., Goldstein, A. M., Higgins, P. A., Ally, D. S., Sheahan, M. D., et al. (1994). Germ line p16 mutations in familial melanoma. *Nature Genetics, 8*(1), 15–21.

Huxley, R., Ansary-Moghaddam, A., Berrington de González, A., Barzi, F., & Woodward, M. (2005). Type-II diabetes and pancreatic cancer: A meta-analysis of 36 studies. *British Journal of Cancer, 92*(11), 2076–2083.

Iodice, S., Gandini, S., Maisonneuve, P., & Lowenfels, A. B. (2008). Tobacco and the risk of pancreatic cancer: A review and meta-analysis. *Langenbeck's Archives of Surgery, 393*(4), 535–545.

Jenne, D. E., Reimann, H., Nezu, J., Friedel, W., Loff, S., Jeschke, R.,... Zimmer, M. (1998). Peutz-Jeghers syndrome is caused by mutations in a novel serine threonine kinase. *Nature Genetics, 18,* 38–43.

Kaibara, N., Yurugi, E., & Koga, S. (1984). Promoting effect of bile acids on the chemical transformation of C3H/10T1/2 fibroblasts *in vitro*. *Cancer Research, 44*, 5482–5485.

Larsson, S. C., Hakanson, N., Permert, J., & Wolk, A. (2006). Meat, fish, poultry and egg consumption in relation to risk of pancreatic cancer: A prospective study. *International Journal of Cancer, 118*, 2866–2870.

Lin, Y., Kikuchi, S., Tamakoshi, A., Yagyu, K., Obata, Y., Inaba, Y.,… Ishibashi, T. (2006). Dietary habits and pancreatic cancer risk in a cohort of middle-aged and elderly Japanese. *Nutrition and Cancer, 56*, 40–49.

Lowenfels, A. B., & Maisonneuve, P. (2006). Epidemiology and risk factors for pancreatic cancer. *Best Practice and Research: Clinical Gastroenterology, 20*(2), 197–209.

Lowenfels, A. B., Maisonneuve, P., Cavallini, G., Ammann, R. W., Lankisc, P. G., Andersen, J. R.,… Domellof, L. (1993). Pancreatitis and the risk of pancreatic cancer. *New England Journal of Medicine, 328*(20), 1433–1437.

Maisonneuve, P., Marshall, B. C., & Lowenfels, A. B. (2007). Risk of pancreatic cancer in patients with cystic fibrosis. *Gut, 56*, 1327–1328.

Michaud, D. S., Giovannucci, E., Willett, W. C., Colditz, G. A., & Fuchs, C. S. (2003). Dietary meat, dairy products, fat, and cholesterol and pancreatic cancer risk in a prospective study. *American Journal of Epidemiology, 157*(12), 1115–1125.

Mills, P. K., Beeson, W. L., Abbey, D. E., Fraser, G. E., & Phillips, R. L. (1988). Dietary habits and past medical history as related to fatal pancreas cancer risk among Adventists. *Cancer, 61*(12), 2578–2585.

Moskaluk, C. A., Hruban, R. H., & Kern, S. E. (1997). p16 and K-ras gene mutations in the intraductal precursors of human pancreatic adenocarcinoma. *Cancer Research, 57*, 2140–2143.

Nair, R. J., Lawler, L., & Miller, M. R. (2007). Chronic pancreatitis. *American Family Physician, 76*(11), 1679–1688.

Nöthlings, U., Wilkens, L. R., Murphy, S. P., Hankin, J. H., Henderson, B. E., & Kolonel, L. N. (2005). Meat and fat intake as risk factors for pancreatic cancer: The Multiethnic Cohort Study. *Journal of the National Cancer Institute, 97*(19), 1458–1465.

Olsen, G. W., Mandel, J. S., Gibson, R. W., Wattenberg, L. W., & Schuman, L. M. (1989). A case-control study of pancreatic cancer and cigarettes, alcohol, coffee and diet. *American Journal of Public Health, 79*(8), 1016–1019.

O'Sullivan, A., & Kocher, H. M. (2007). Pancreatic cancer. *British Medical Journal of Clinical Evidence, 11*, 409–437.

Ottenhof, N. A., Milne, A. N., Morsink, F. H., Drillenburg, P., Ten Kate F. J., Maitra, A., & Offerhaus, G. J. (2009). Pancreatic intraepithelial neoplasia and pancreatic tumorigenesis: Of mice and men. *Archives of Pathology and Laboratory Medicine, 133*(3), 375–381. doi: 10.1043/1543-2165-133.3.375.

Parkin, D. M. (2004). International variation. *Oncogene, 23*, 6329–6340.

Pellegata, N. S., Sessa, F., Renault, B., Sonato, M., Leone, B. E., Solcia, E., & Ranzani, N. (1994). K-ras and p53 gene mutations in pancreatic cancer: Ductal and nonductal tumors. *Cancer Research, 54*, 1556–1560.

Raymond, L., Infante, F., Tuyns, A. J., Voirol, M., & Lowenfels, A. B. (1987). Alimentationet cancer du pancréas [Diet and cancer of the pancreas]. *Gastroentérologie Clinique et Biologique, 11*(6–7), 488–492.

Reddy, B. S. (1981). Diet and excretion of bile acids. *Cancer Research, 41*, 3766–3788.

Reddy, B. S., Weisburger, J. H., & Wynder, E. L. (1978). Colon cancer: Bile salts as tumor promoters. In T. J. Slaga, A. Sivak, & R. K. Boutwell (Eds.), *Carcinogenesis (Vol. 2*, pp. 1453–1464). New York, NY: Raven Press.

Schatzkin, A., Subar, A. F., Thompson, F. E., Harlan, L. C., Tangrea, J., Hollenbeck, A. R.,… Kipnis, V. (2001). Design and serendipity in establishing a large cohort with wide dietary intake distributions: The National Institutes of

Health–American Association of Retired Persons Diet and Health Study. *American Journal of Epidemiology, 154*(12), 1119–1125.

Schwarts, S. S., Zeidler, A., Moossa, A. R., Kuku, S. F., & Rubenstein, A. H. (1978). A prospective study of glucose tolerance, insulin, C-peptide, and glucagon responses in patients with pancreatic carcinoma. *Digestive Diseases, 23*, 1107–1114.

Shirvani, V. N., Ouatu-Lascar, R., Kaur, B. S., Omary. M. B., & Triadafilopoulos, G. (2000). Cyclooxygenase 2 expression in Barrett's esophagus and adenocarcinoma: *Ex vivo* induction by bile salts and acid exposure. *Gastroenterology, 118*, 487–496.

Silverman, D. T., Brown, L. M., Hoover, R. N., Schiffman, M., Lilemoe, K. D., Schoenberg, J. B., & Pottern, L. M. (1995). Alcohol and pancreatic cancer in blacks and whites in the United States. *Cancer Research, 55*(21), 4899–905.

Stolzenberg-Solomon, R. Z., Pietinen, P., Taylor, P. R., Virtamo, J., & Albanes, D. (2002). Prospective study of diet and pancreatic cancer in male smokers. *American Journal of Epidemiology, 155*(9), 783–792.

Talamini, R., Polesil, J., Gallus, S., Dal Maso, L., Zucchetto, A., Negri, E.,... La Vecchia, C. (2010). Tobacco smoking, alcohol consumption and pancreatic cancer risk: A case-control study in Italy. *European Journal of Cancer, 46*(2), 370–376.

Thiébaut, A. C. M., Jiao, L., Silverman, D. T., Cross, A. J., Thompson, F. E., Subar, A. F.,... Stolzenberg-Solomon, R. Z. (2009). Dietary fatty acids and pancreatic cancer in the NIH-AARP Diet and Health Study. *Journal of the National Cancer Institute, 101*, 1001–1011.

Tucker, O. N., Dannenberg, A. J., Yang, E. K., & Fahye, T. J. (2004). Bile acids induce cyclooxygenase-2 expression in human pancreatic cancer cell lines. *Carcinogenesis, 25*(3), 419–423.

Tucker, O. N., Dannenberg, A. J., Yang, E. K., Zhang, F., Teng, L., Daly, J. M.,... Fahey, T. J. (1999). Cyclooxygenase-2 expression is upregulated in human pancreatic cancer. *Cancer Research, 59*, 987–990.

Wang, F., Herrington, M., Larrson, J., & Permert, J. (2003). The relationship between diabetes and pancreatic cancer. *Molecular Cancer, 2*(4), 1476–4598.

Whitcomb, D. (1999). Hereditary pancreatitis: New insights into acute and chronic pancreatitis. *Gut, 45*(3), 317–322.

Witt, H., Apte, M. V., Keim, V., & Wilson, J. S. (2007). Chronic pancreatitis: Challenges and advances in pathogenesis, genetics, diagnosis, and therapy. *Gastroenterology, 132*, 1557–1573.

World Health Organization. (2009). *Report on the global tobacco epidemic, 2009.* Geneva, Switzerland: Author.

Wynder, E. L. (1975). An epidemiological evaluation of the causes of cancer of the pancreas. *Cancer Research, 35*(8), 2228–2233.

Wynder, E. L., Mabuchi, K., & Maruchia, N. (1973). Epidemiology of cancer of the pancreas. *Journal of the National Cancer Institute, 50*, 645–667.

Yan, M. X., & Li, Y. Q. (2006). Gallstones and chronic pancreatitis: The black box in between. *Postgraduate Medical Journal, 82*, 254–258.

Ye, W., Lagergren, J., Weiderpass, E., Nyrén, O., Adami, H. O., & Ekbom, A. (2002). Alcohol abuse and the risk of pancreatic cancer. *Gut, 51*(2), 236–239.

Zatonski, W. A., Boyle, P., Przewozniak, K., Maisonneuve, P., Drosik, K., & Walker, A. M. (1993). Cigarette smoking, alcohol, tea and coffee consumption and pancreas cancer risk: A case-control study from Opole, Poland. *International Journal of Cancer, 53*(4), 601–607.

Zhang, F., Subbaramaiah, K., Altorki, N., & Dannenberg, A. J. (1998). Dihydroxy bile acids activate the transcription of cyclooxygenase-2. *Journal of Biological Chemistry, 273*, 2424–2428.

Zhang, J., Zhao, Z., & Berkel, H. J. (2005). Animal fat consumption and pancreatic cancer incidence: Evidence of interaction with cigarette smoking. *Annals of Epidemiology, 15*(7), 500–508.

10

Epidemiology of Primary Liver Cancer: Hepatocellular Carcinoma and Cholangiocarcinoma

LIVER FUNCTION AND ANATOMY

The human liver is a vital organ that regulates a number of life-sustaining functions, including the synthesis of important proteins (e.g., albumin, clotting factors, and complement); metabolism and regulation of lipids, carbohydrates, and certain steroidal hormones (e.g., estrogens and androgens); synthesis and regulation of cholesterol and cholesterol byproducts (e.g., bile acids and fat-soluble vitamins A, D, E, and K); production and secretion of bile acids for digestion; the formation, storage, and release of glycogen for the regulation of blood glucose; and detoxification of chemicals and harmful substances.

The liver is located in the upper right quadrant of the abdomen. Its normal weight in adults is between 1,400 and 1,600 grams. The liver receives a dual blood supply from the hepatic portal vein and hepatic arteries. The hepatic portal vein carries venous blood drained from the spleen and gastrointestinal tract, and the hepatic arteries supply arterial blood. Oxygen is provided from both sources (approximately half from the hepatic portal vein and half from the hepatic arteries). The gallbladder, which is located just beneath the liver, stores and concentrates bile produced by the liver and regulates bile secretion into the duodenum for the digestion of dietary fat (O'Brien & Gottlieb, 1979) (**Figure 10.1**).

The liver is organized into thousands of small lobules separated by bands of connective tissue. The parenchyma (tissue) within each lobule consists primarily of polygonal hepatocytes that carry out the multiple biosynthetic and metabolic functions of the liver. The hepatocytes are arranged in microscopic functional units called acini that are distributed within the lobules. Each acinus consists of hepatocytes arranged in concentric zones about hepatic arterioles and portal venules in order to facilitate selective secretion/excretion of cellular metabolites. The products of cellular synthesis and metabolism enter the blood in

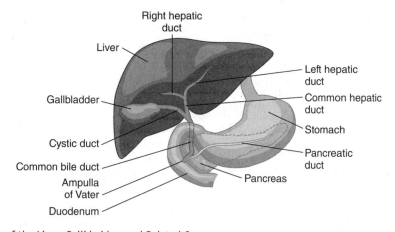

Figure 10.1 Anatomy of the Liver, Gallbladder, and Related Organs.

123

the sinusoids that are adjoined to the acini. Sinusoids are vascular channels that are lined by fenestrated endothelium and heavily populated by *Kupffer cells* (see the following description).

Hepatocytes are responsible for an amazing array of biochemical functions. Their cytoplasm is laden with mitochondria that are responsible for oxidative phosphorylation and energy production, and the oxidation of fatty acids. Also within the cytoplasm, the smooth endoplasmic reticulum is the site of synthesis of cholesterol and bile acids; conjugation of bilirubin, drugs, and steroids; for excretion, metabolism of drugs and steroids; and breakdown of glycogen. The rough endoplasmic reticulum is the site of protein synthesis. The multiple synthetic and metabolic pathways of hepatocytes are dependent upon the presence and functional integrity of a variety of essential enzymes (e.g., the mixed function oxidase system [enzymes that oxidize toxic compounds for metabolism and excretion], cytochrome oxidase [a mitochondrial enzyme essential for respiration], and cytochrome P450 enzymes [oxidizing enzymes involved in metabolism and bioactivation of lipids, steroids, and drugs]).

The liver is the detoxification center of the human body. For example, the urea cycle metabolizes ammonia, the principle byproduct of protein breakdown. Ammonia is highly toxic to cells, whereas urea is nontoxic and readily condensed in urine by the kidneys for excretion. One of the enzymes present in hepatocytes is alcohol dehydrogenase, which catalyzes the conversion of alcohol to nontoxic metabolites for excretion. As discussed later in this chapter, genetic variability in the alcohol dehydrogenase enzyme system influences the risk of developing alcoholic cirrhosis of the liver.

Kupffer cells are large phagocytic cells of the innate immune system that circulate throughout the sinusoidal network of the liver parenchyma. They were first observed by the German scientist Karl Wilhelm von Kupffer in 1876 (Haubrich, 2004). Kupffer cells phagocytize senescent red blood cells and hepatocytes and break down hemoglobin and other cellular constituents (O'Brien & Gottlieb, 1979).

In 1951, novel fat-storage cells lining the hepatic sinusoids were discovered by Ito (Ito, 1951). These *Ito cells* actively store lipids and retinoids and are apparently involved in liver fibrosis during the development and progression of cirrhosis (Geerts, 2001).

HEPATOCELLULAR CARCINOMA AND CHOLANGIOCARCINOMA

There are two separate and distinctly different forms of primary liver cancer. Hepatocellular carcinoma arises from the cells of the liver per se (called hepatocytes) whereas cholangiocarcinoma (biliary cancer) arises from the epithelial lining of the gallbladder or the biliary ducts. Hepatocellular carcinoma is much more common than biliary cancer, accounting for approximately 93% of all primary liver cancers. Each type has its own set of epidemiologic parameters, so hepatocellular carcinoma and cholangiocarcinoma are discussed individually in the following sections of this chapter.

HEPATOCELLULAR CARCINOMA

Global Epidemiology of Hepatocellular Carcinoma

Hepatocellular carcinoma is the fifth most common malignancy in the world (more than 782,451 new cases were diagnosed in 2012) and the third most common cause of death due to cancer (745,517 deaths in 2012). This malignancy has an extremely poor prognosis; nearly as many people die from the disease as are diagnosed (mortality-to-incidence ratio ~0.95). Most hepatocellular carcinomas are nonresectable at the time of diagnosis, and the disease is usually fatal within 3–6 months (American Cancer Society, 2007; Ferlay et al., 2010, 2013).

Rates are highest in sub-Saharan Africa, Eastern and Southeastern Asia, and Melanesia (South Pacific islands north of Australia) (**Figure 10.2**). More than 84% of new cases occur in developing countries in areas where oncogenic liver viruses (particularly hepatitis B virus and hepatitis C virus) are endemic. Chronic exposure to aflatoxins from moldy grains and chronic alcohol abuse are independent risk factors that can synergistically interact with oncogenic hepatitis viruses to markedly heighten the risk of developing hepatocellular carcinoma. The burden of hepatocellular carcinoma is particularly extreme in China, where more than half of new cases are diagnosed. Hepatocellular carcinoma develops two to three times more frequently in men than women (Ferlay et al., 2010, 2013; Parkin, Bray, Ferlay, & Pisani, 2005).

Global Patterns of Hepatocellular Carcinoma

Hepatocellular carcinoma shows two main epidemiologic patterns, the predominant one being in China, sub-Saharan Africa, Southeast Asia, and the Amazon basin. In these regions, liver viruses are endemic, and the initial infection usually occurs during the perinatal period. In the populations of these regions, hepatocellular carcinomas are diagnosed early in life, sometimes during adolescence, and the peak incidence occurs before the age of 50.

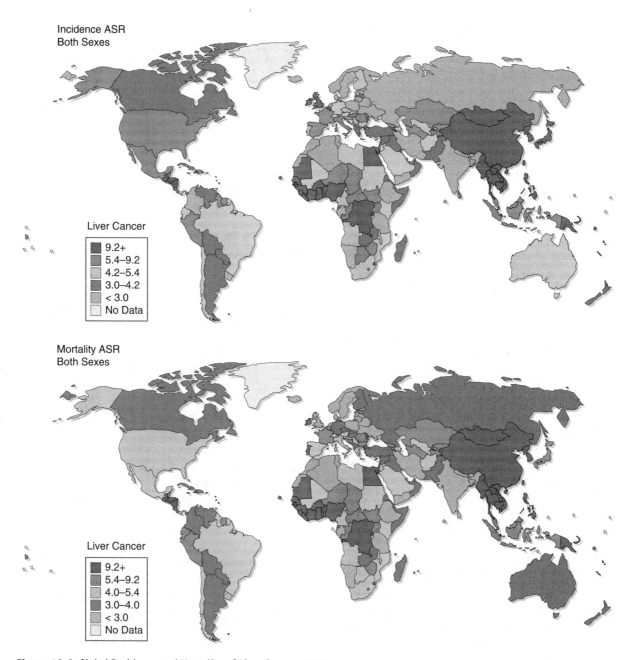

Figure 10.2 Global Incidence and Mortality of Liver Cancer, 2012.

ASR: Rates per 100,000 are age-standardized to the world population, 2000–2025.

Source: Reproduced from Ferlay, J., Soerjomataram, I., Ervik, M., Dikshit, R., Eser, S., Mathers, C., . . . Bray, F. (2013). *GLOBOCAN 2012 v1.0. Cancer incidence and mortality worldwide: IARC CancerBase No. 11* [Internet]. Lyon, France: International Agency for Research on Cancer. Retrieved from http://globocan.iarc.fr

A less common pattern of late onset is evident in North America and Western Europe. In the populations of these regions the onset of hepatocellular carcinoma occurs late in life, usually after the age of 60. This pattern is primarily a consequence of sustained damage to liver cells from chronic alcohol abuse or late onset viral hepatitis.

In the United States, the annual age-adjusted incidence rates of invasive liver cancer increased by more than twofold in women during 1975–2007 (from 1.6 to 3.6 cases per 100,000) and by nearly threefold in men (from 3.9 to 11.9 cases per 100,000). Consistent with their higher rates of chronic exposure to alcohol and liver viruses, incidence rates among African

American men and women exceed Caucasians by about 75% (Alterkruse et al., 2010).

Pathogenesis of Hepatocellular Carcinoma

Hepatocellular carcinoma is initiated and promoted by sustained recursive damage to hepatocytes due to infection by oncogenic liver viruses, chronic exposure to aflatoxins, chronic alcohol abuse, or a combination of these factors. Though the exact sequence of events may differ from person to person, the cellular mechanisms involved include early fatty change (the appearance of lipid-containing vacuoles in hepatocytes), chronic inflammation and cell necrosis (termed *necroinflammation*), wound healing and regeneration of hepatocytes, and late stage fibrosis leading to the eventual formation of fibrotic nodules (cirrhosis of the liver).

The cellular processes of necroinflammation and wound healing incite several mechanisms of cancer development (mutagenesis, cell proliferation, angiogenesis, dysfunctional apoptosis, immunosuppression, and metastasis). Hepatocelluar carcinoma may develop with or without liver cirrhosis; for example, chronic viral hepatitis alone may produce cancer in a noncirrhotic liver. Cirrhosis (scarring) of the liver is invariably associated with chronic alcohol abuse, and severe cirrhosis of the liver markedly increases the risk of developing primary liver cancer, particularly in individuals suffering from chronic active hepatitis. The fibrotic nodules characteristic of alcoholic liver cirrhosis may occur in either a micronodular pattern or as large macronodules of coalesced foci of micronodules (O'Brien & Gottlieb, 1979).

Liver Viruses and Hepatocellular Carcinoma

Two liver viruses, hepatitis B virus (HBV) and hepatitis C virus (HCV), account for 75% of the new cases of liver cancer worldwide and 85% of cases in developing countries (Parkin, Pisani, Muñoz, & Ferlay, 1999). In high-risk areas where HBV and HCV are endemic, 10–20% of young individuals become chronic carriers of HBV or HCV. Among those who suffer from chronic viral hepatitis, the annual incidence rates per 100,000 range from 400 to 800 for men and from 120 to 180 for women (Nguyen, Law, & Dore, 2009). Among such individuals, the cumulative risk of developing hepatocellular carcinoma by age 65 years is nearly 33% in men and 10% in women.

The relative risk of developing liver cancer is increased by more than 20-fold for those chronically infected with either HBV or HCV compared to noninfected individuals and more than 100-fold for those infected by both viruses (Donato, Boffetta, &

Puoti, 1998). Based on current estimates of the attributable fraction for each virus, approximately 50–55% of hepatocellular carcinomas are caused by HBV and 20–25% by HCV (Kirk, Bah, & Montesano, 2006). Because HBV causes far more infections than HCV, particularly in the younger generations, the global pattern of chronic HBV infections roughly simulates the global distribution of liver cancer (Hou, Liu, & Gu, 2005). It is important to note that HBV and HCV have both been classified as human carcinogens by the International Agency for Research on Cancer (IARC, 1994).

Hepatitis B Virus (HBV) and Hepatocellular Carcinoma

Baruch Blumberg and colleagues discovered the hepatitis B virus (HBV) by its novel "Australia antigen" in the serum of a patient with leukemia (Blumberg, Alter, & Visnich, 1965). Blumberg later developed the diagnostic test and vaccine for HBV and in 1976 was awarded the Nobel Prize in Medicine for these achievements (Blumberg, 2002). Dane first identified HBV in the serum of hepatitis patients using electron microscopy (Dane, 1970). A few years later, the genome of HBV was sequenced (Galibert, Mandart, Fitoussi, Tiollais, & Charnay, 1979) and antibody testing of viral antigens developed (Bonino, Chiaberge, Maran, & Piantino, 1987).

HBV is highly endemic in developing regions of the world that are heavily populated, such as Southeast Asia, China, sub-Saharan Africa, and the Amazon basin. In these high-risk regions, up to 95% of the population shows past or present serological evidence of HBV infection, and a significant fraction (15–20%) become chronic carriers of the HBV surface antigen (HBsAg) (Kirk et al., 2004). The global distribution of hepatocellular carcinoma correlates with the geographic prevalence of chronic carriers of HBV, who number nearly 400 million worldwide (**Figure 10.3**).

Epidemiologic studies have demonstrated that there is a consistent and specific causal association between chronic HBV infection and hepatocellular carcinoma. In a landmark study, Beasley and colleagues followed 22,707 male Taiwanese health workers for more than a decade with nearly complete follow-up. Incidence rates of hepatocellular carcinoma among carriers of the HBV surface antigen (HBsAg) were approximately 100 times higher than among noncarriers (495 versus 5 per 100,000 per year) (Beasley, Huang, Lin, & Chien, 1981). In a meta-analysis of 32 studies, Donato and colleagues determined that the overall risk of developing hepatocellular carcinoma was increased by approximately

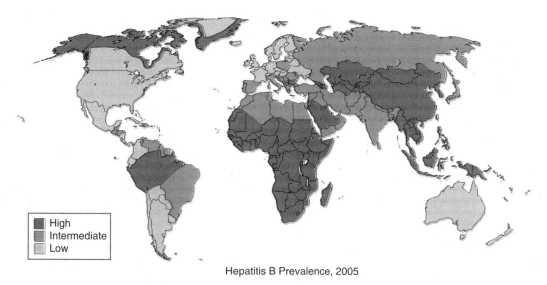

Hepatitis B Prevalence, 2005

Figure 10.3 Global Seroprevalence of Hepatitis B Virus (HBV).

Source: Data from Centers for Disease Control and Prevention. (2012). Infectious disease related to travel: Hepatitis B. In *CDC Travelers' Health Yellow Book.* Retrieved from http://wwwnc.cdc.gov/travel/yellowbook/2014/chapter-3-infectious-diseases-related-to-travel/hepatitis-b

20-fold for individuals positive for the HBV surface antigen (HBsAg) and with no evidence of coinfection by HCV (Donato et al., 1998). Nevertheless, relative risk estimates from case control and cohort studies show wide variability, ranging from 5 to 100, presumably due to genotypic differences in HBV strains (Yu & Chen, 1994). Furthermore, the risk estimates vary depending on the presence/absence of other risk factors (e.g., HCV infection, chronic alcohol abuse, and aflatoxin exposure). These risk factors and combinations of risk factors involving HBV are discussed in the following sections of this chapter.

HBV is spread through contact with infected body fluids, and the only natural host is human. Blood is the most important vehicle for transmission, but other body fluids have also been implicated including semen, breast milk, and saliva. In regions of the world where HBV is endemic, most HBV infections occur during infancy or early childhood. Vertical transmission from mother to baby can occur during childbirth when the newborn passes through the birth canal, or later through contaminated saliva or breast milk. High rates of child-to-child transmission have also been documented in certain populations. Most acute HBV infections are asymptomatic and therefore left untreated. Because babies and young children may not have fully developed immune systems, once infected they are far more susceptible to persistence of the virus than adults. Therefore, acute HBV infections acquired during the perinatal period or early in childhood often progress to chronic infections that persist for many years (Shapiro, 1993).

Antibodies against the HBV surface antigen (HBsAg) develop in exposed individuals after an incubation period of a few weeks. Individuals who remain HBsAg positive for at least 6 months are considered to be hepatitis B carriers (Shapiro, 1993; Zuckerman, 1996). In young individuals who become chronic carriers of HBV, the rates of liver cancer begin to rise during adolescence and reach peak values by age 50 (Parkin et al., 2005).

Transmission of HBV in adults occurs through unprotected sexual contact with an infected individual or by using contaminated needles and syringes for the intravenous injection of illicit drugs. The virus can also be transmitted by transfusion with contaminated blood or blood products in countries without effective screening programs for donor blood. Nevertheless, immunocompetent adults who become infected by HBV usually clear the virus without treatment; less than 1% of individuals who become infected during adulthood will develop chronic hepatitis B.

The genome of HBV is made of circular DNA, but it is unusual because the DNA is not fully double-stranded. Furthermore, HBV replicates by reverse transcriptase, similar to the RNA viruses. At least four serotypes and eight genotypic strains of HBV have been identified. The process of carcinogenesis induced by chronic HBV infection involves interaction of the HBV genotype with the host immune system and infiltration of infected foci of hepatocytes by cytotoxic (killer) T lymphocytes (Zuckerman, 1996). Integration of the viral genome into the host DNA is a prominent feature of carcinogenesis that may induce overexpression of oncogenes and dysfunction of tumor suppressor genes (Kew, 1996).

Although all strains of HBV appear to be capable of sustaining long-term infections associated with liver damage, cirrhosis, and carcinogenesis, molecular epidemiologic studies suggest that there are genotypic differences in the pathogenesis of cirrhosis, carcinogenicity, and response to therapy. For example, individuals who carry genotype C are likely to have antibodies against the viral precore antigen, HBeAg, which is indicative of a high viral load and increased cirrhosis and carcinogenesis (Cao, 2009). In a prospective study of 11,893 men conducted in Taiwan (Yang et al., 2002), investigators observed a much higher incidence rate of hepatocellular carcinoma among men positive for both HBsAg and HBeAg (1,169 cases per 100,000 person years, relative risk [RR] = 60.2) compared to men positive for HBsAg alone (324 cases per 100,000 person years, RR = 9.6). Other studies also suggest that viral load and viral replication are important determinants of liver cirrhosis and cancer risk in individuals suffering from chronic HBV infection (Chen et al., 2006; Iloeje et al., 2007). Furthermore, therapeutic trials show that individuals infected by genotypes A or B respond better to interferon therapy than individuals with other HBV genotypes (Cao, 2009). As will be discussed later in this chapter, effective vaccines that target the viral envelope (HBsAg) are now available that provide long-term immunity against HBV infection as well as protection against liver carcinogenesis (Vandamme & Van Herck, 2007).

Hepatitis C Virus (HCV) and Hepatocellular Carcinoma

The studies of Harvey J. Alter and colleagues at the U.S. National Institutes of Health during the 1970s demonstrated that most patients who developed hepatitis following transfusion were not infected by either hepatitis A or B virus (Alter, 1995, 1997). Subsequently, in the laboratories of Michael Houghton, a novel virus named hepatitis C virus (HCV) was identified in patients with non-A non-B hepatitis (Choo et al., 1989; Kuo et al., 1989). Screening methods for detecting HCV in donor blood have markedly reduced the risk of posttransfusion hepatitis (Tanaka et al., 1994).

HCV is endemic in many parts of the world, particularly in those nations with impoverished populations, poor living conditions, and substandard sanitation. In these nations, seropositive rates range from 10% to 15% and high rates of transmission have no doubt persisted for centuries. Recent estimates suggest that HCV has infected nearly 200 million people worldwide and infects 3–4 million more people per year (World Health Organization, 2009). The seroprevalence of HCV is highest in certain countries of Africa, Asia, and South America (**Figure 10.4**). Egypt has the highest seroprevalence (approximately 20%), which may have resulted from the inadvertent spread of HCV by a now-discontinued mass campaign of parenteral treatment of schistosomiasis (infection by an endemic parasitic worm) (Frank et al., 2000).

HCV is transmitted by exposure to contaminated blood. In developed countries such as the

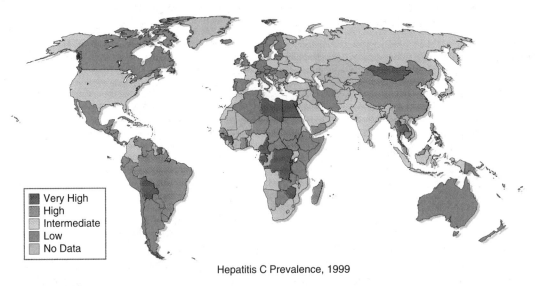

Hepatitis C Prevalence, 1999

Figure 10.4 Seroprevalence of Hepatitis C Virus (HVC).

Source: Data from Centers for Disease Control and Prevention. (2012). Infectious diseases related to travel: Hepatitis C. In *CDC Travelers' Health Yellow Book*. Retrieved from http://wwwnc.cdc.gov/travel/yellowbook/2014/chapter-3-infectious-diseases-related-to-travel/hepatitis-c

United States, most infections were once caused by transfusions with contaminated blood or blood products. Fortunately, accurate methods of screening the blood supply have been developed and are in use; as a consequence, there has not been a documented posttransfusion-related case of hepatitis C in the United States for more than a decade. Currently, the primary route of HCV transmission in the United States is by intravenous injection of illicit drugs using contaminated needles (Campbell et al., 2006).

In less developed countries, the primary sources of HCV infection are unsterilized injection equipment and transfusion of inadequately screened blood and blood products. Vertical transmission from an infected mother to her child can occur during the birthing process, particularly when the mother is coinfected by the human immunodeficiency virus (HIV).

Sexual contact with an HCV-infected individual is believed to be an inefficient method of transmission; nevertheless, circumstances and any untoward events causing exposure to contaminated blood could facilitate transmission. Prison inmates are at high risk of being infected either by injecting drugs using contaminated needles or by sexual transmission; a survey conducted in California found that 82% of subjects diagnosed with hepatitis C had previously been incarcerated (McGovern et al., 2006).

The hepatitis C virus is a small, single-stranded RNA virus (50 nanometers in diameter). Like HBV and other liver viruses, HCV has a tropism for the liver, where it tends to persist in the cytoplasm of hepatocytes. Six major genotypes of HCV have been identified, and host responses to acute HCV infection vary. The virus can be detected in the blood by polymerase chain reaction (PCR) within 1–3 weeks after infection, and antibodies against HCV usually develop within 15 weeks. The acute phase of infection lasts up to 6 months and is treatable with antiviral drugs plus interferon. Chronic hepatitis C, defined as infection persisting for more than 6 months, is much more resistant to therapy (Caruntu & Benea, 2006).

The natural course of chronic hepatitis C varies considerably from one person to another. Nevertheless, HCV usually persists in the hepatocytic cell population of the liver, even in immunocompetent individuals who become infected. It is estimated that 60–70% of infected adults will develop chronic hepatitis C. Furthermore, over a period of 10–30 years, 20–30% of chronically infected individuals progress to liver cirrhosis and some develop hepatocellular carcinoma. Without treatment, it is estimated that more than 50% of patients with chronic hepatitis C

will develop cirrhosis of the liver (National Institutes of Health, 2002). Concomitant alcohol abuse and/or coinfection with HIV are cofactors that hasten progression of liver cirrhosis. Males also tend to have more rapid disease progression than females.

Chronic hepatitis C and progressive liver cirrhosis may lead to loss of liver function and accumulation of ammonia and other toxic substances, jaundice, hepatic encephalopathy, ascites, portal hypertension, and bleeding varices. Chronic infection by HCV and subsequent cirrhosis of the liver resulting in liver failure is the leading reason for liver transplantation in the United States.

A meta-analysis of 32 studies that examined hepatocellular carcinoma and chronic hepatitis due to HBV and/or HCV provides convincing evidence that chronic infection by either virus alone markedly increases the risk of developing this malignancy and that chronic coinfection by both viruses further increases the risk (Donato et al., 1998). Two distinct patterns of risk are evident (**Figure 10.5**). In nations where HBV is highly endemic (sub-Saharan Africa, China, Taiwan, South Korea, and Vietnam), HBV risk exceeds HCV risk and the markedly increased risk due to coinfection with both viruses is consistent with synergism. A different pattern is apparent in Japan and Mediterranean nations where HCV is more prominent. In these populations, HCV risk exceeds HBV risk, but the risk due to coinfection is more consistent with an additive model.

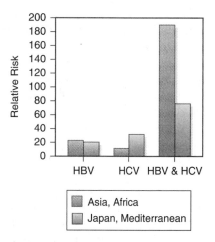

Figure 10.5 Relative Risk of Hepatocellular Carcinoma: Effects of HBV and HCV Infection.

Source: Data from Donato, F., Boffetta, P., & Puoti, M. A. (1998). Meta-analysis of epidemiological studies on the combined effect of hepatitis B and C virus infections in causing hepatocellular carcinoma. *International Journal of Cancer,* 75, 347–354.

Coinfection with HIV and HCV: Liver Cirrhosis and Hepatocellular Carcinoma

Approximately 30% of HIV-infected patients in the United States are also infected with the hepatitis C virus. The increasing rates of HIV and HCV coinfection have arisen due to blood-borne transmission of both viruses in association with high-risk behavior (e.g., IV drug use and unprotected sex with multiple partners). Even though overall survival has improved for HIV-infected individuals due to highly active antiretroviral therapy (HAART), it has been demonstrated in clinical studies that patients coinfected with HIV and HCV have more rapid progression of liver cirrhosis and are at increased risk of liver failure and hepatocellular carcinoma compared to those infected by only HCV (Ding, Gui, Zhang, Gao, & Yang, 2009; Giordano, Kramer, Souchek, Richardson, & El Serag, 2004). In a recent meta-analysis, Chen and colleagues observed that coinfected individuals have increased mortality primarily due to liver disease that is unrelated to HIV disease progression (Chen, Ding, Seage, & Kim, 2009). Indeed, hepatocellular carcinoma has become the leading cause of non-AIDS-related death among coinfected individuals (Wilcox, 2009).

Aflatoxins and Hepatocellular Carcinoma

Aflatoxins are mycotoxins produced by certain species of the fungus *Aspergillus*, most notably *Aspergillus flavus* and *Aspergillus parasiticus*. When conditions of high humidity and heat prevail, these fungi readily colonize and contaminate grain before harvest and during storage. A wide variety of crops are frequently affected including cereals (maize, sorghum, pearl millet, rice, wheat), oilseeds (peanut, soybean, sunflower, cotton), spices (chili peppers, black pepper, coriander, turmeric, ginger), and tree nuts (almond, pistachio, walnut, coconut, brazil nut). Humans are exposed to aflatoxins by consumption of moldy grains (Williams et al., 2004). Exposure rates are highest in populations with high rates of hepatocellular carcinoma, particularly in the nations of sub-Saharan Africa and in certain provinces of southern China (Montesano, Hainaut, & Wild, 1997).

Aflatoxins are toxic and potent carcinogens in the liver where they are metabolized to form reactive (highly mutagenic) epoxides. Among the many different forms of aflatoxins that have been identified, aflatoxin B_1, which is produced by both *Aspergillus flavus* and *Aspergillus parasiticus*, is considered the most toxic. Recent molecular studies have found that aflatoxin B_1 can specifically mutate and hence deactivate p53, a tumor suppressor gene that is critical

for control of cell division (Montesano et al., 1997; Stern et al., 2001).

Chronic exposure to aflatoxins independently increases the risk of developing hepatocellular carcinoma. Early epidemiologic investigations using urinary metabolites of aflatoxins as biomarkers of exposure determined five- to sixfold increases in the risk with exposure to metabolites of aflatoxin B_1 (Ross et al., 1992; Wang et al., 1996). Furthermore, aflatoxin exposure in combination with chronic hepatitis B or C has been found to synergistically increase hepatocarcinogenesis. It is estimated that chronic exposure to aflatoxins plus concomitant liver infection by HBV increases the risk of developing hepatocellular carcinoma by up to 60-fold (Groopman, 1993; Sylla, Diallo, Castegnaro, & Wild, 1999; Yeh et al., 1989).

Alcohol Abuse, Cirrhosis of the Liver, and Hepatocellular Carcinoma

Cirrhosis of the liver is characterized by replacement of necrotic liver tissue by fibrosis, scar tissue, and regenerative nodules. The most common causes of this devastating condition are chronic alcohol abuse and chronic hepatitis due to HBV and/or HCV infection. Alcoholic cirrhosis of the liver develops in 10–20% of individuals who drink heavily, usually for a decade or more. The process is accelerated when alcohol abuse is combined with chronic hepatitis.

Heavy chronic alcohol consumption (greater than 80 grams [just under 3 ounces] daily for more than a decade) is estimated to increase the risk of developing hepatocellular carcinoma by more than fivefold, and if severe alcoholic liver cirrhosis develops, the risk approaches 1% per year (Morgan, Mandayam, & Jamal, 2004). Furthermore, chronic alcohol abuse in combination with chronic hepatitis C doubles the risk compared to hepatitis C alone, and even in the absence of liver cirrhosis and hepatitis, alcohol abuse increases the risk of hepatocellular carcinoma by more than fourfold (Chiesa et al., 2000). Alcohol is the primary risk factor for hepatocellular carcinoma in the populations of many developed nations, such as the United States and Italy.

Other Risk Factors for Hepatocellular Carcinoma

Acute and chronic hepatic porphyrias are inherited genetic disorders in heme biosynthesis that predispose to the development of hepatocellular carcinoma. Heme is the oxygen-binding component of hemoglobin in red blood cells and is also a key element of many enzymes of the P-450 system in the liver. This enzyme family is important in converting potentially harmful substances such as alcohol, drugs, and carcinogens to inactive metabolites destined for excretion. Thus, the pathogenesis of hepatocellular carcinoma in genetic carriers of this heme disorder may be due to inadequate detoxification and persistence of harmful substances in the liver.

In patients with acute hepatic porphyria, the calculated risk of hepatocellular carcinoma is increased 61-fold compared to normal individuals (Kauppinen & Mustajoki, 1988); furthermore, the risk increase appears to be several-fold higher in women who carry this genetic disorder compared to men (Andant, Puy, Faivre, & Deybach, 1998). Both active and latent genetic carriers of acute hepatic porphyrias are at risk, and patients with acute hepatic porphyria should be monitored for hepatocellular carcinoma.

Several other risk factors appear to modify the risk of developing hepatocellular carcinoma. These include cigarette smoking, obesity, and certain comorbid conditions such as hemochromatosis (excess deposition of iron in the liver and other organs) and Wilson's disease (excess deposition of copper in the liver). Also, vinyl chloride, a compound used in the plastics industry, can cause a rare form of liver cancer called *hepatic angiosarcoma* that appears many years after exposure (Baxter, 1976; Chuang, La Vecchia, & Boffetta, 2009).

Prevention of Hepatocellular Carcinoma

Primary prevention of the majority of liver cancer cases worldwide is now feasible, thanks to the development of a vaccine against HBV. This has been shown to be effective in preventing infection in childhood. A dramatic demonstration of the results of community vaccination is already available from Taiwan, where HBV immunization of newborns was introduced in 1984; for children ages 6–9 years in birth cohorts receiving vaccination, there was a dramatic decrease in the incidence of liver cancer (Chang et al., 1997; Thomas & Zhu, 2005).

CHOLANGIOCARCINOMA

Epidemiology of Cholangiocarcinoma

Cholangiocarcinoma is an uncommon malignancy that arises from the epithelial lining of the gallbladder or bile ducts that drain bile from the liver into the small intestine. In 2012, 178,101 new cases of gallbladder cancer were diagnosed in the world population, and 143,823 people died from the disease. The age-standardized incidence and mortality rates per 100,000 were 2.2 and 1.7, respectively. Among afflicted individuals, approximately 58% were women, and the incidence and mortality rates for women were approximately 10% higher than for men. As discussed next, the prevalence in women may be partially attributable to their higher rates of cholelithiases (gallstones and biliary stones) compared to men.

The annual incidence of cholangiocarcinoma is high in China and other regions of Southeast Asia, which is attributable to endemic liver parasites. The annual incidence in northern Thailand was estimated at 135 per 100,000 in men and 43 per 100,000 in women compared to only 1–2 cases per 100,000 in the United States (Green et al., 1991). The incidence is also high in other regions in which liver flukes are endemic (e.g., the Caribbean, Andean nations of South America, North Africa, and the Middle East) (**Figure 10.6**). Without complete resection, cholangiocarcinoma has an extremely poor prognosis; as a consequence, the mortality/incidence ratio is high (~0.80), and mortality and incidence rates show similar patterns (Ferlay et al., 2010, 2013).

Global Trends in Cholangiocarcinoma

Cholangiocarcinoma is divisable into intrahepatic and extrahepatic disease. Intrahepatic disease refers to the gallbladder and ducts within the liver, whereas extrahepatic disease refers only to the biliary ducts outside the liver.

Patel examined chronological trends in the annual mortality rates of each subtype using data reported by the World Health Organization during 1980–1997. Mortality estimates were available for the men and women of 22 nations with population-based tumor registries. Regions represented included North America, Australia/New Zealand, Western Europe, Central Europe, Scandinavia, Asia, and the Middle East. Trend analysis revealed that the mortality rates of people with intrahepatic tumors increased on average by 6.9% per year in men and 5.1% in women, whereas the rates for those with extrahepatic tumors declined by 0.3% in men and 1.3% women. The reasons for the increasing occurrence of intrahepatic cholangiocarcinoma are unclear; improved diagnostic methods may be partially responsible, but the prevalence of potential risk factors for cholangiocarcinoma such as HBV and HCV infections have also been increasing in some populations during this time frame. The diverging trends of these two subtypes of cholangiocarcinoma may be related to the high rate of cholecystectomies to remove symptomatic gallstones in some populations (Patel, 2001, 2002).

Risk Factors for Cholangiocarcinoma

Chronic biliary tract inflammation is a major risk factor for the development of cholangiocarcinoma.

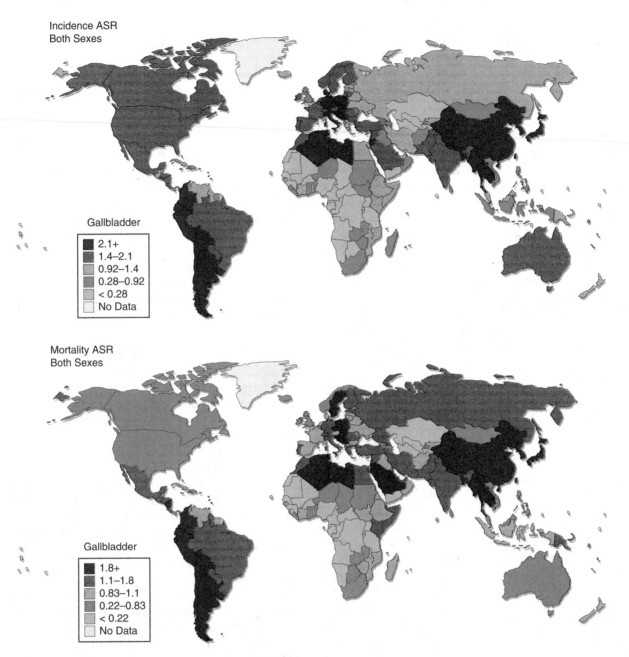

Figure 10.6 Global Incidence and Mortality Rates of Cholangiocarcinoma, 2012.

ASR: Rates per 100,000 are age-standardized to the world population, 2000–2025.

Source: Reproduced from Ferlay, J., Soerjomataram, I., Ervik, M., Dikshit, R., Eser, S., Mathers, C., ... Bray, F. (2013). *GLOBOCAN 2012 v1.0. Cancer incidence and mortality worldwide: IARC CancerBase No. 11* [Internet]. Lyon, France: International Agency for Research on Cancer. Retrieved from http://globocan.iarc.fr

The association between chronic parasitic infection of the biliary tract and cholangiocarcinoma is obvious in regions of high endemicity (e.g., in Far Eastern nations such as Taiwan). Additional risk factors in underserved nations include viral hepatitis and HIV disease. In Western nations there is a distinctly different profile of risk factors including alcoholic and nonalcoholic cirrhosis of the liver, congenital liver abnormalities (choledochal cysts), hepatolithiasis (liver stones), and cholelithiasis (gallstones).

Liver Flukes and Cholangiocarcinoma

In certain regions of Southeast Asia, North Africa, and South America, chronic colonization of the liver and biliary tract by liver flukes is a major public health problem. The technical term for this parasitic infection is *fasciolosis*. Two species of liver flukes, *Opisthorchis viverrini* (found in Thailand, Laos, and Malaysia) and *Clonorchis sinensis* (found in Japan, Korea, and Vietnam) markedly heighten the risk of developing cholangiocarcinoma (Watanapa, 1996; Watanapa & Watanapa, 2002). The highest annual incidence rates (334 and 104 per 100,000 for males and females, respectively) were observed in the northern Thailand province of Khon Kaen, where *Opisthorchis viverrini* is endemic (Green et al., 1991). In an epidemiologic study in Pusan, Korea, infection by *Clonorchis sinensis* was associated with a threefold increase in the risk (Shin et al., 1996).

Fasciolosis is also a human health problem in Central America (Puerto Rico, Cuba, and Caribbean islands), the Andean countries of South America (Bolivia, Peru, Ecuador, and Bolivia), and coastal regions of North Africa and the Middle East. The life cycle of liver flukes involves a larval stage in snails and an encysted larval stage (metacercaria) in fish. Human infection results from the consumption of uncooked (raw) freshwater fish contaminated with the metacercarial form of the parasite (Markell & Voge, 1976).

In a recent meta-analysis of case control studies of cholangiocarcinoma, the odds ratios (ORs) were highest for individuals chronically infected with liver flukes (summary OR = 4.8) but also consistently elevated for individuals with hepatitis B (summary OR = 2.6) or hepatitis C (summary OR = 1.8) (Shin et al., 2010).

Primary Sclerosing Cholangitis and Cholangiocarcinoma

In developed countries such as the United States, the most common risk factor for the development of cholangiocarcinoma is the presence of *primary sclerosing cholangitis*, a rare inflammatory disease of the bile ducts. Primary sclerosing cholangitis has a prevalence in the United States of 6 per 100,000 people. The mean age at diagnosis is 40 years of age, and 70% of cases are men. The development of primary sclerosing cholangitis is associated with other inflammatory conditions such as ulcerative colitis and Crohn's disease. Epidemiologic investigations suggest that up to 30% of individuals with primary sclerosing cholangitis may eventually develop cholangiocarcinoma (Rosen, Nagorney, Wiesner, Coffey, & LaRusso, 1991).

Cholelithiasis and Cholangiocarcinoma

Cholelithiasis refers to biliary stones in either the gallbladder or the biliary ducts. Biliary stones are formed by solidification of bile components, principally cholesterol. Cholesterol stones are predominantly found in women and obese individuals. If left untreated, these formations may cause obstruction of the biliary tree and chronic inflammation and malignant transformation of the biliary epithelium. Approximately one-third of patients who develop cholangiocarcinoma report a medical history of cholelithiasis. However, due to the high prevalence of cholelithiasis in many populations, some have argued that its association with cholangiocarcinoma is spurious rather than etiologic.

To clarify the risk factors for cholangiocarcinoma, investigators in Taiwan conducted a large case control study of 5,157 cases of cholangiocarcinoma and 20,628 disease-free controls matched to the cases by age, gender, and time of diagnosis. In the analysis, cases and their matched controls were subdivided into intrahepatic cholangiocarcinoma (within the gallbladder and liver) and extrahepatic cholangiocarcinoma (within the biliary ducts outside the liver). Results revealed that multiple inflammatory and cystic conditions are associated with substantial increases in the risk for the development of both intrahepatic and extrahepatic cholangiocarcinoma. Risk factors included medical history of choledochal cysts, cholangitis, cholecystitis, and cholelithiasis. After adjustment for other factors, cholelithiasis increased the risk of intrahepatic cholangiocarcinoma (OR = 4.3) and extrahepatic cholangiocarcinoma (OR = 3.3). Other major independent risk factors included cirrhosis of the liver and viral hepatitis (Chang, Tsai, & Chen, 2013).

Ionizing Radiation and Cholangiocarcinoma

Thorotrast, a radiologic contrast medium, was widely used throughout the world from 1920 to 1950. This ionizing compound has a half-life of 400 years and is retained in the liver, where it caused the eventual development of cholangiocarcinoma in some patients many years after their exposure. Thorotrast was banned from use in the United States in the 1950s due to its carcinogenicity (Zhu, Lauwers, & Tanabe, 2004).

Prevention and Control of Cholangiocarcinoma

Cholangiocarcinoma is difficult to diagnose and frequently presents at a late stage when no effective therapeutic intervention is possible. Primary prevention is therefore critical to reduce the risk of developing this malignancy. In areas endemic for liver flukes, effective prevention involves control of foodborne infection and/or mass anthelmintic therapy. Other strategies include avoidance of excessive alcohol intake, elimination of tobacco use, vaccination against HBV, prevention of HCV and HIV transmission, and excision of the gallbladder and common bile duct in patients with obstructive/inflammatory conditions of the biliary tree.

● ● ● **REFERENCES**

Alter, M. J. (1995). Epidemiology of hepatitis C in the West. *Semininars in Liver Disease, 15,* 5–14.

Alter, M. J. (1997). Epidemiology of hepatitis C. *Hepatology, 3*(Suppl 1), 62S–65S.

Alterkruse, S. F., Kosary, C. L., Krapcho, M., Neyman, N., Aminou, R., Waldron, W., . . . Edwards, B. K. (2010). *SEER Cancer Statistics Review, 1975-2007.* Bethesda, MD: Surveillance Epidemiology and End Results, National Cancer Institute, National Institutes of Health.

American Cancer Society. (2007). *Global Cancer Facts and Figures, 2007.* Atlanta, GA: Author.

Andant, C., Puy, H., Faivre, J., & Deybach, J. C. (1998). Acute hepatic porphyrias and primary liver cancer. *New England Journal of Medicine, 338,* 1853–1854.

Baxter, P. J. (1976). Epidemiological studies of PVC manufacturers and fabricators, and primary angiosarcoma of the liver. *Proceedings of the Royal Society of Medicine, 69*(4), 297–299.

Beasley, R. P., Huang, L. Y., Lin, C., & Chien, C. (1981). Hepatocellular carcinoma and HBV: A prospective study of 22,707 men in Taiwan. *Lancet, 2,* 1129–1133.

Blumberg, B. S. (2002). Baruch Blumberg—hepatitis B and beyond. Interviewed by Pam Das. *Lancet Infectious Diseases, 2*(12), 767–771.

Blumberg, B. S., Alter, H. J., & Visnich, S. (1965). A 'new' antigen in leukemia sera. *Journal of the American Medical Association, 252*(2), 252–257.

Bonino, F., Chiaberge, E., Maran, E., & Piantino, P. (1987). Serological markers of HBV infectivity. *Annali dell'Istituto Superiore di Sanita, 24*(2), 217–223.

Campbell, J., Hagan, H., Latka, M., Garfein, R., Golub, E., Coady, M., . . . Strathdee, S. A. (2006). High prevalence of alcohol use among hepatitis C virus antibody positive injection drug users in three US cities. *Drug and Alcohol Dependence, 81*(3), 259–265.

Cao, G. W. (2009). Clinical relevance and public health significance of hepatitis B virus genomic variations. *World Journal of Gastroenterology, 15*(46), 5761–5769.

Caruntu, F. A., & Benea, L. (2006). Acute hepatitis C virus infection: Diagnosis, pathogenesis, treatment. *Journal of Gastrointestinal and Liver Diseases, 15*(3), 249–256.

Chang, J. S., Tsai, C.-R., & Chen, L.-T. (2013). Medical risk factors associated with cholangiocarcinoma in Taiwan: A population-based case-control study. *PLoS ONE, 8*(7), e69981. doi:10.1371/journal.pone.0069981.

Chang, M. H., Chen, C. J., Lai, M. S., Hsu, H. M., Wu, T. C., Kong, M. S., . . . Chen, D. S. (1997). Universal hepatitis B vaccination in Taiwan and the incidence of hepatocellular carcinoma in children. *New England Journal of Medicine, 336*(26), 1855–1859.

Chen, C. J., Yang, H. I., Su, J., Jen, C-L., You, S. L., Lu, S. N., . . . Iloeje, U. H. (2006). Risk of hepatocellular carcinoma across a biological gradient of serum hepatitis B virus DNA level. *Journal of the American Medical Association, 295*(1), 65–73.

Chen, T. Y., Ding, E. L., Seage III, G. R., & Kim, A. Y. (2009). Meta-analysis: Increased mortality associated with hepatitis C in HIV-infected persons is unrelated to HIV disease progression. *Clinical Infectious Diseases, 49*(10), 1605–1615.

Chiesa, R., Donato, F., Tagger, A., Favret, M., Ribero, M. L., Nardi, G., . . . Callea, F. (2000). Etiology of hepatocellular carcinoma in Italian patients with and without cirrhosis. *Cancer Epidemiology, Biomarkers and Prevention, 9,* 213–216.

Choo, Q., Kuo, G., Weiner, A., Overby, L., Bradley, D., & Houghton, M. (1989). Isolation of a cDNA clone derived from a blood-borne non-A, non-B viral hepatitis genome. *Science, 244*(4902), 359–362.

Chuang, S.-C., La Vecchia, C., & Boffetta, P. (2009). Liver cancer: Descriptive epidemiology and risk factors other than HBV and HCV infection. *Cancer Letters, 286,* 9–14.

Dane, D. (1970). Virus-like particles in serum of patients with Australia-antigen-associated hepatitis. *Lancet, 295,* 695–698.

Ding, L. P., Gui, X. E., Zhang, Y. X., Gao, S. C., & Yang, R. R. (2009). Impact of human immunodeficiency virus infection on the course of hepatitis C virus infection. A meta-analysis. *World Journal of Gastroenterology*, 28(3), 996–1008.

Donato, F., Boffetta, P., & Puoti, M. A. (1998). Meta-analysis of epidemiological studies on the combined effect of hepatitis B and C virus infections in causing hepatocellular carcinoma. *International Journal of Cancer*, 75, 347–354.

Ferlay, J., Shin, H.-R., Bray, F., Forman, D., Mathers, C., & Parkin, D. M. (2010). Estimates of worldwide burden of cancer in 2008: GLOBOCAN 2008. *International Journal of Cancer*, 127(12), 2893–2917.

Ferlay, J., Soerjomataram, I., Ervik, M., Dikshit, R., Eser, S., Mathers, C., . . . Bray, F. (2013). *GLOBOCAN 2012 v1.0. Cancer incidence and mortality worldwide: IARC CancerBase No. 11* [Internet]. Lyon, France: International Agency for Research on Cancer. Retrieved from http://globocan.iarc.fr

Frank, C., Mohamed, M., Strickland, G., Lavanchy, D., Arthur, R., Magder, L., . . . Sallam, I. (2000). The role of parenteral anti-schistosomal therapy in the spread of hepatitis C virus in Egypt. *Lancet*, 355(9207), 887–891.

Galibert, F., Mandart, E., Fitoussi, F., Tiollais, P., & Charnay, P. (1979). Nucleotide sequence of the hepatitis B virus genome (subtype ayw) cloned in *E. coli. Nature*, 281(5733), 646.

Geerts, A. (2001). History, heterogeneity, developmental biology and functions of quiescent hepatic stellate cells. *Seminars in Liver Disease*, 21, 311–335.

Giordano, T. P., Kramer, J. R., Souchek, J., Richardson, P., & El Serag, H. B. (2004). Cirrhosis and hepatocellular carcinoma in HCV-infected veterans with and without hepatitis C virus: A cohort study, 1992–2001. *Archives of Internal Medicine*, 164, 2249–2254.

Green, A., Uttaravichien, T., Bhudhisawasdi, V., Chartbanchachai, W., Elkins, D. B., Marieng, E. O., . . . Haswell-Elkins, M. R. (1991). Cholangiocarcinoma in northeast Thailand. A hospital-based study. *Tropical and Geographical Medicine*, 43(1–2), 193–198.

Groopman, J. D. (1993). Molecular dosimetry methods for assessing human aflatoxin exposure. In D. L. Easton & J. D. Groopman (Eds.), *The toxicology of aflatoxins: Human health, veterinary and agricultural significance* (pp. 259–279). London: Academic Press.

Haubrich, W. S. (2004). Kupffer of Kupffer cells. *Gastroenterology*, 127(1), 16.

Hou, J., Liu, Z., & Gu, F. (2005). Epidemiology and prevention of hepatitis B virus infection. *International Journal of Medical Sciences*, 2, 50–57.

Iloeje, U. H., Yang, H. I., Jen, C. L., Su, J., Wang, L. Y., You, S. L., & Chen, C. J. (2007). Risk and predictors of mortality associated with chronic hepatitis B infection. *Clinical Gastroenterology and Hepatology*, 5(8), 921–931.

International Agency for Research on Cancer. (1994). IARC monographs on the evaluation of carcinogenic risks in humans. *International Agency for Research on Cancer*, 59.

Ito, T. (1951). Cytological studies on stellate cells of Kupffer and fat storing cells in the capillary wall of human liver (abstract). *Acta Anatomica Japan*, 26, 42.

Kauppinen, R., & Mustajoki, P. (1988). Acute hepatic porphyria and hepatocellular carcinoma. *British Journal of Cancer*, 57(1), 117–120.

Kew, M. C. (1996). Hepatitis B and C viruses and hepatocellular carcinoma. *Clinics in Laboratory Medicine*, 16, 395–406.

Kirk, G. D., Bah, E., & Montesano, R. (2006). Molecular epidemiology of human liver cancer: Insights into etiology, pathogenesis and prevention from The Gambia, West Africa. *Carcinogenesis*, 27(10), 2070–2082.

Kirk, G. D., Lesi, O. A., Mendy, M., Akano, A. O., Sam, O., Goedert, J. J., . . . Montesano, W. H. (2004). The Gambia Liver Cancer Study: Infection with hepatitis B and C and the risk of hepatocellular carcinoma in West Africa. *Hepatology*, 39(1), 211–219.

Kuo, G., Choo, Q., Alter, H., Gitnick, G., Redeker, A., Purcell, R., . . . Houghton, M. (1989). An assay for circulating antibodies to a major etiologic virus of human non-A, non-B hepatitis. *Science, 244*(4902), 362–364.

Markell, E. K, & Voge, M. (1976). *Medical parasitology* (4th ed.). Philadelphia, PA: W. B. Saunders.

McGovern, B., Wurcel, A., Kim, A., Schulze zur Wiesch, J., Bica, I., Zaman, M., . . . Lauer, G. (2006). Acute hepatitis C virus infection in incarcerated injection drug users. *Clinics in Infectious Diseases, 42*(12), 1663–1670.

Montesano, R., Hainaut, P., & Wild, C. P. (1997). Hepatocellular carcinoma: From gene to public health. *Journal of the National Cancer Institute, 898,* 1844–1851.

Morgan, T. R., Mandayam, S., & Jamal, M. M. (2004). Alcohol and hepatocellular carcinoma. *Gastroenterology, 127*(5 Suppl 1), S87–S96.

National Institutes of Health. (2002). NIH consensus statement on management of hepatitis C. *Science Statements, 19*(3), 1–46.

Nguyen, V. T. T., Law, M. G., & Dore, G. J. (2009). Hepatitis B-related hepatocellular carcinoma: Epidemiological characteristics and disease burden. *Journal of Viral Hepatitis, 16*(7), 453–463.

Parkin, D. M., Bray, F., Ferlay, J., & Pisani, P. (2005). Global cancer statistics, 2002. *CA: A Cancer Journal for Clinicians, 55,* 74–108.

Parkin, D. M., Pisani, P., Muñoz, N., & Ferlay, J. (1999). The global health burden of infection associated cancer. In R. A. Weiss, V. Beral, & R. Newton (Eds.), *Infections and human cancer. Cancer surveys, Volume 33,* pp. 5–33. New York, NY: Cold Spring Harbor Laboratory Press.

Patel, T. (2001). Increasing incidence and mortality of primary intrahepatic cholangiocarcinoma in the United States. *Hepatology, 33*(6), 1353–1357.

Patel, T. (2002). Worldwide trends in mortality from biliary tract malignancies. *BMC Cancer, 2.* doi:10.1186/1471-2407-2-10.

Rosen, C., Nagorney, D., Wiesner, R., Coffey, R., & LaRusso, N. (1991). Cholangiocarcinoma complicating primary sclerosing cholangitis. *Annals of Surgery, 213*(1), 21–25.

Ross, R. K., Yuan, J. M., Yu, M. C., Wogan, G. N., Qian, G. S., Tu, J. T., . . . Groopman, J. D. (1992). Urinary aflatoxin biomarkers and risk of hepatocellular carcinoma. *Lancet, 339*(8799), 943–946.

Shapiro, C. N. (1993). Epidemiology of hepatitis B. *Pediatric Infectious Disease Journal, 12*(5), 433–437.

Shin, H., Lee, C., Park, H., Seol, S., Chung, J., Choi, H., . . . Shigemastu, T. (1996). Hepatitis B and C virus, *Clonorchis sinensis* for the risk of liver cancer: A case-control study in Pusan, Korea. *International Journal of Epidemiology, 25*(5), 933–940.

Shin, H. R., Oh, J. K., Masuyer, E., Curado, M. P., Bouvard, V., Fang, Y. Y., . . . Hong, S. T. (2010). Epidemiology of cholangiocarcinoma: An update focusing on risk factors. *Cancer Science, 101*(3), 579–585.

Stern, M. C., Umbach, D. M., Yu, M. C., London, S. J., Zhang, Z. Q., & Taylor, J. A. (2001). Hepatitis B, aflatoxin B(1), and p53 codon 249 mutation in hepatocellular carcinomas from Guangxi, People's Republic of China, and a meta-analysis of existing studies. *Cancer Epidemiology, Biomarkers and Prevention, 10*(6), 617–625.

Sylla, A., Diallo, M. S., Castegnaro, J. J., & Wild, C. P. (1999). Interactions between hepatitis B virus infection and exposure to aflatoxins with the development of hepatocellular carcinoma: A molecular epidemiological approach. *Mutation Research, 428,* 187–196.

Tanaka, H., Hiyama, T., Tsukuma, H., Okubo, Y., Yamano, H., Kitada, A., & Fujimoto, I. (1994). Prevalence of second generation antibody to hepatitis C antibody among voluntary blood donors in Osaka, Japan. *Cancer Causes and Control, 5,* 409–413.

Thomas, M., & Zhu, A. (2005). Hepatocellular carcinoma: The need for progress. *Journal of Clinical Oncology, 23*(13), 2892–2899.

Vandamme, P., & Van Herck, K. (2007). A review of the long-term protection after hepatitis A and B vaccination. *Travel Medicine and Infectious Disease, 5*(2), 79–84.

Wang, L. Y., Hatch, M., Chen, C. J., Levin, B., You, S. L., Lu, S. N., . . . Santella, R. M. (1996). Aflatoxin exposure and risk of hepatocellular carcinoma in Taiwan. *International Journal of Cancer, 67*(5), 620–625.

Watanapa, P. (1996). Cholangiocarcinoma in patients with opisthorchiasis. *British Journal of Surgery, 83*(8), 1062–1064.

Watanapa, P., & Watanapa, W. (2002). Liver fluke-associated cholangiocarcinoma. *British Journal of Surgery, 89*(8), 962–970.

Wilcox, R. D. (2009). Hepatocellular carcinoma and HIV: Is there an association? *HIV Clinician, 21*(4), 11–12.

Williams, J. H., Phillips, T. D., Jolly, P. E., Stiles, J. K., Jolly, C. M., & Aggarwal, D. (2004). Human aflatoxicosis in developing countries: A review of toxicology, exposure, potential health consequences, and interventions. *American Journal of Clinical Nutrition, 80*(5), 1106–1122.

World Health Organization. (2009). Death and DALY estimates for 2004 by cause for WHO member states (persons, all ages)*. Geneva, Switzerland: Author.

Yang, H. I., Lu, S. N., Liaw, Y. F., You, S. L., Su, C. A., Wang, L. Y., . . . Chen, C. J. (2002). Hepatitis B e antigen and the risk of hepatocellular carcinoma. *New England Journal of Medicine, 347*(3), 168–174.

Yeh, F. S., Yu, M. C., Mo, C. C., Luo, S., Tong, M. J., & Henderson, B. E. (1989). Hepatitis B virus, aflatoxins, and hepatocellular carcinoma in southern Guangxi, China. *Cancer Research, 49,* 2506–2509.

Yu, M. W., & Chen, C. J. (1994). Hepatitis B and C viruses in the development of hepatocellular carcinoma. *Critical Reviews in Oncology/Hematology, 17,* 71–91.

Zhu, A., Lauwers, G., & Tanabe, K. (2004). Cholangiocarcinoma in association with Thorotrast exposure. *Journal of Hepato-Biliary-Pancreatic Surgery, 11*(6), 430–433.

Zuckerman, A. J. (1996). Hepatitis viruses. In S. Baron et al. (Eds.), *Baron's medical microbiology* (4th ed., pp. 849–863). Galveston, TX: University of Texas Medical Branch.

11

Epidemiology of Breast Cancer

ANATOMY AND FUNCTION OF THE MAMMARY GLAND

The human female breast consists primarily of fat and glandular tissues. Each breast contains a complex network of sac-like lobules (milk glands) that produce breast milk and ducts that carry milk from the lobules to the nipple openings during breastfeeding. Adult women have 15–20 distinct clusters of lobules in each breast, which are called the breast lobes. Each breast lobe contains 20 to 40 lobules. Small ducts emanate from the lobules of the breast and join together and branch into increasingly larger ducts that carry breast milk to openings at the surface of the nipple. Adipose tissue (fat) furnishes the energy for lactation and is the most abundant tissue of the human female breast. Connective tissue and ligaments provide structural support and nerves provide sensation to the breast. The breast also contains blood vessels, lymph vessels, and lymph nodes (**Figure 11.1**).

In both males and females, immature breast tissues develop during embryogenesis and childhood; however, further development and maturation of

the breast occurs exclusively in females in preparation for reproduction and lactation. Development and maturation of the human female breast begins at puberty concurrent with the onset of menarche, usually around 11–12 years of age. Under the primary influence of ovarian steroidal hormones (estrogen and progesterone) and the pituitary hormone prolactin, a complex network of breast lobes, milk glands (lobules), and milk ducts develops. These glandular structures are surrounded and interlaced by abundant adipose tissue. Mature breast development is typically complete by the age of 17–18 years. During the first pregnancy, the milk glands undergo further maturation in preparation for lactation. Lactation (the secretion and excretion of breast milk) following childbirth is stimulated by the pituitary hormones, oxytocin and prolactin. Concurrent with aging, the onset of menopause, and the depletion of ovarian hormones, the breast undergoes involution characterized by a decrease in glandular breast tissue and a relative increase in the surrounding adipose tissue (Hutson, Cowan, & Bird, 1985).

GLOBAL IMPACT OF BREAST CANCER

Breast cancer was diagnosed in 1.68 million women and caused 521,817 deaths in the world population during 2012. It is the most commonly diagnosed cancer and the second leading cause of cancer death among women (only lung cancer causes more deaths) (Ferlay et al., 2013).

The global burden of breast cancer has increased sharply in the 21st century. During the time span 2000–2012, the reported numbers of new cases and deaths have increased by 60% and 40%, respectively

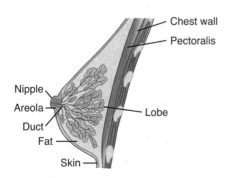

Figure 11.1 Anatomy of the Human Female Breast.

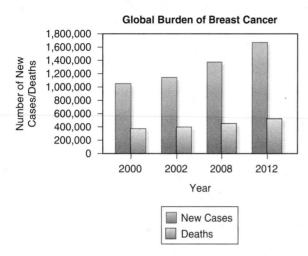

Figure 11.2 Global Increase in Breast Cancer, 2000–2012.

Sources: Data from Parkin, D. M., Bray, F., Ferlay, J., & Pisani, P. (2001). Estimating the world cancer burden: GLOBOCAN 2000. *International Journal of Cancer, 94,* 153–156; Ferlay, J., Bray, F., Pisani, P., & Parkin, D. M. (2004). *GLOBOCAN 2002. Cancer incidence, mortality, and prevalence worldwide.* IARC Cancer Base No. 5, version 2.0. Lyon, France: IARC Press. Retrieved from http://www-dep.iarc.fr; Ferlay, J., Shin, H.-R., Bray, F., Forman, D., Mathers, C., & Parkin, D. M. (2010). Estimates of worldwide burden of cancer in 2008: GLOBOCAN 2008. *International Journal of Cancer, 127*(12), 2893–2917; Ferlay, J., Soerjomataram, I., Ervik, M., Dikshit, R., Eser, S., Mathers, C., ... Bray, F. (2013). *GLOBOCAN 2012 v1.0. Cancer incidence and mortality worldwide: IARC CancerBase No. 11.* [Internet] Lyon, France: International Agency for Research on Cancer. Retrieved from http://globocan.iarc.fr

(**Figure 11.2**) (Bray, McCarron, & Parkin, 2004; Ferlay et al., 2010, 2013; Parkin, Bray, Ferlay, & Pisani, 2001). As discussed in the following sections of this chapter, the rising worldwide trend in breast cancer rates undoubtedly reflects the impact of multiple factors, including screening (mammography), therapy, and risk factors including late childbearing, lack of breastfeeding, intake of exogenous hormones, intake of diets high in fat and calories, lack of exercise, and increasing obesity (Bray et al., 2004; Harris, Casto, & Harris, 2014).

Breast cancer incidence is highly variable among populations, ranging from low rates of 20–30 per 100,000 women in China, Africa, and India to high rates of 85–105 cases per 100,000 in Scandinavia, Western Europe, the United States, Great Britain, and Australia/New Zealand. The lifetime risk of breast cancer for U.S. women is approximately 1 in 8 compared to a lifetime risk of only 1 in 66 for Chinese women. Breast cancer mortality rates show a narrower range than incidence rates, ranging from 5.4 deaths per 100,000 in Chinese women to 26 deaths per 100,000 in Nigerian women (Ferlay, Bray, Pisani & Parkin, 2004; Ferlay et al., 2010, 2013; Garcia et al., 2007). In general, incidence rates of breast cancer tend to be higher for women in developed countries compared to those in underdeveloped countries, whereas mortality rates are highest in less developed nations where access to screening and therapy is limited (**Figure 11.3**).

BREAST CANCER DETECTION, STAGING, AND SURVIVAL

Mammography is a radiographic imaging process using low-dose x-rays to assist in the detection and diagnosis of breast cancer. The goal of mammography as a screening tool is to detect breast tumors early in their growth and development so they can be completely excised by qualified breast surgeons. Screening mammography together with effective biopsy, accurate pathologic evaluation, and surgical excision of breast tumors have been shown to reduce the mortality from breast cancer by approximately 30% in women over the age of 50 years. Because of the difficulty in discriminating normal active mammary glands from abnormal neoplastic growths in women during their reproductive years, there is controversy about the value of screening for breast cancer by mammography in premenopausal women (before age 50). Currently, the American National Cancer Institute recommends that women initiate biannual screening for breast cancer by mammography at age 40–49, whereas after age 50, screening is recommended on an annual basis. Other imaging techniques such as ultrasound, magnetic resonance imaging (MRI), and positron emission tomography (PET) are now being widely used by physicians to assist in the evaluation and diagnosis of breast tumors. Breast self-examination (BSE) and physician examination are also considered essential components of regular breast care.

PATHOLOGY OF BREAST CANCER

Tumor staging refers to the microscopic evaluation of tissue by a pathologist to assess size, exact anatomic location, growth, and spread of a cancerous lesion. It is important to realize that although imaging procedures are important for the identification of suspicious lesions, the ultimate diagnosis of breast cancer (or any other malignant neoplasm) must be confirmed by microscopic examination of cancerous tissue (obtained by biopsy) by a qualified pathologist.

Breast cancer survival is highest when tumors are detected prior to breaching the basement membrane upon which most solid tumors develop and invading contiguous tissues or lymph nodes (carcinoma in situ, stage I), whereas survival is lowest with late detection after tumors have spread (metastasized) to other sites

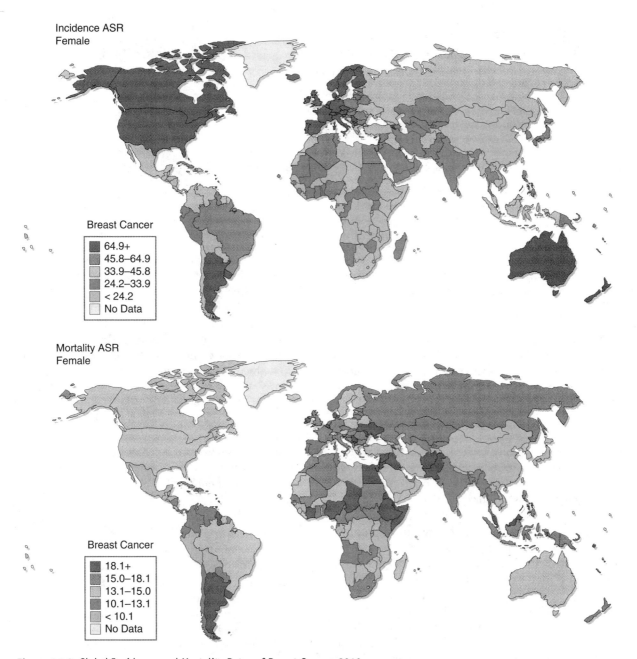

Figure 11.3 Global Incidence and Mortality Rates of Breast Cancer, 2012.

ASR: Rates per 100,000 are age-standardized to the world population, 2000–2025.

Source: Reproduced from Ferlay, J., Soerjomataram, I., Ervik, M., Dikshit, R., Eser, S., Mathers, C., . . . Bray, F. (2013). *GLOBOCAN 2012 v1.0. Cancer incidence and mortality worldwide: IARC CancerBase No. 11* [Internet]. Lyon, France: International Agency for Research on Cancer. Retrieved from http://globocan.iarc.fr

(**Table 11.1**). Early stage breast cancer is effectively "cured" by complete surgical excision with clear margins (no evidence of spread beyond the surgical margins) whereas later stage disease is much more resistant to therapy and is conventionally treated by a combination of treatment modalities including chemotherapy, radiation therapy, and hormonal therapy and immunomodulation.

MECHANISMS OF BREAST CARCINOGENESIS

Breast cancer arises from the epithelial cells that line the ductal and glandular structures of the mammary gland. Breast carcinogenesis is most probably due to excess stimulation of these cells by estrogen. Estrogen is a powerful mitogen that stimulates cell proliferation by activating estrogen receptors of the

Table 11.1	Breast Cancer Survival by Stage at Detection	
Stage at Diagnosis	**Description of Stage at Diagnosis**	**Five-Year Survival Rate (%)**
0	Carcinoma in situ (no invasion)	100%
I	Tumor < 2 cm with no lymphatic spread	100%
IIA	Tumor ≥ 2 cm with no lymphatic spread	92%
IIB	Spread to axillary lymph nodes	81%
IIIA	Spread to axillary and other lymph nodes	67%
IIIB	Spread to lymph nodes and opposite breast	54%
IV	Widespread metastatic cancer	20%

Source: Data from American Joint Committee on Cancer (AJCC). (2010). Breast cancer staging. In S. B. Edge, D. R. Byrd, C. C. Compton, A. G. Fritz, F. L. Greene, & A., Trotti (Eds)., *Cancer staging manual* (7th ed., pp. 347–376). New York, NY: Springer-Verlag.

cell surface membrane. Sustained excessive estrogen stimulation may lead to heightened proliferation and atypia of the mammary epithelium, which are believed to be forerunners of breast cancer.

Breast cancer primarily occurs in women, although occasionally breast tumors do develop in men, particularly in association with Klinefelter's syndrome, where there is an extra X chromosome in the karyotype (XXY) or following ingestion of synthetic estrogens such as diethylstilbesterol, which has been used for the treatment of cancer of the prostate.

Several theories have been proposed to explain breast carcinogenesis. Perhaps the best known of these theories relates breast cancer risk to the sustained stimulus of estrogen over many years. The "estrogen stimulus" theory of breast cancer postulates that the risk is enhanced with a sustained continuum of estrogen cycles unbroken by pregnancy or other mechanisms of estrogen ablation such as ovariectomy. As discussed later in this chapter, both endogenous and exogenous factors may potentially increase estrogen stimulus of the mammary gland in association with breast cancer development.

A derivative of the estrogen stimulus hypothesis is the "estrogen window" hypothesis (Korenman, 1980). This postulate states that human breast cancer is induced by environmental carcinogens in a susceptible mammary gland, and that susceptibility is due to unopposed estrogen stimulation early in life during the onset of puberty (menses) and later in life with the onset of menopause. By this theory, susceptibility to induction of breast cancer declines with establishment of normal luteal phase progesterone secretion and becomes very low during pregnancy.

RISK FACTORS FOR BREAST CANCER

Several risk factors have been identified that increase a woman's chance of developing breast cancer.

Nevertheless, cause and effect cannot be established in most individual cases. The classical risk factors of breast cancer were first established in an early case control study of breast cancer cases and matched controls conducted in 1923 by Dr. Janet Elizabeth Lane-Claypon in the United Kingdom. Dr. Lane-Claypon compared 500 women with breast cancer (cases) to 500 women of similar age with no history of cancer (controls) in the first documented epidemiologic case control study (Winkelstein, 2006). Her groundbreaking study was the first to elucidate the well-known profile of classical breast cancer risk factors including familial and genetic predisposition, early menses, delayed reproductive history, nulliparity, absence of lactation, late menopause, and the natural process of aging (Lane-Claypon, 1926).

Early Menarche and Late Menopause

Menarche and menopause mark the onset and cessation of ovarian activity and reproduction in women. During the reproductive years estrogens are produced by the ovaries, whereas after menopause the source of circulating estrogens is biosynthesis in fat and muscle cells catalyzed by the enzyme aromatase.

An international team of investigators recently examined data on menarche and menopause from 117 epidemiologic studies including 118,964 women with invasive breast cancer and 306,091 controls. Compared to menarche at 13 years of age or menopause at 50 years of age, breast cancer risk was found to increase slightly for each year of earlier menarche (relative risk [RR] = 1.05) and each year of older menarche (RR = 1.03) (Collaborative Group on Hormonal Factors in Breast Cancer, 2012).

Nulliparity and Age at First Pregnancy

Pregnancy induces anatomic and physiologic changes in the female breast. During gestation, the ductal network of the breast expands and the mammary epithelium differentiates into alveolar structures (glands) that secrete breast milk during lactation. In particular, the differentiation and maturation of the female breast at first pregnancy influences breast cancer risk.

MacMahon and colleagues conducted an international case control study of pregnancy and breast cancer involving 4,323 cases and 12,699 controls from seven areas of the world. Compared to nulliparous women, mothers who reported having their first full-term pregnancy before 20 years of age had a 50% reduced risk of developing breast cancer; furthermore, the risk reduction was about 60% compared to women who had their first child after 35 years of age (MacMahon et al., 1970). Recent studies provide evidence that early age at first birth is associated with reduced risk of developing only those tumors that are positive for estrogen and progesterone receptors (Ma, Bernstein, Pike, & Ursin, 2006; Ursin et al., 2005).

Genetic Predisposition to Breast Cancer

A strong family history (breast cancer in a first-degree or second-degree relative) increases the risk of breast cancer by three- to fivefold. Genetic or familial predisposition is identifiable for approximately 5–10% of women diagnosed with breast cancer. Hallmarks of familial predisposition to breast cancer include early age of onset, an excess of bilateral disease, and breast cancer in familial association with other malignancies such as ovarian cancer and endometrial cancer.

Two heritable genetic mutations have been identified that predispose to familial breast and ovarian cancer, BRCA-1 and BRCA-2. The BRCA-1 gene was discovered in 1990 by King and colleagues and is located on the long arm of chromosome 17 (Hall et al., 1990). Subsequently, a second breast cancer gene, BRCA-2, was identified on the long arm of chromosome 13 (Wooster et al., 1994). A mutation in either BRCA gene predisposes heterozygous female carriers to both breast cancer and, to a lesser extent, ovarian cancer. The lifetime risk of breast cancer among women who carry a single mutation in either BRCA-1 or BRCA-2 is approximately 85%, whereas the lifetime ovarian cancer risk for women with a BRCA-1 mutation is 54%, compared to 24% for women with a BRCA-2 mutation (King, Marks, Mandell, & New York Breast Cancer Study Group, 2003).

Both BRCA-1 and BRCA-2 are tumor suppressor genes that upon transcription form proteins essential for the repair of double-strand DNA breaks (Boulton, 2006). Mutated BRCA genes result in proteins that do not function properly in DNA repair, thereby promoting accumulation of genetic errors and carcinogenesis.

Breast cancer has also been observed in individuals with Cowden's disease and Sipple syndrome, two rare genetic conditions caused by germline autosomal dominant mutations (Eng, 1998). Cowden's disease is caused by a mutated tumor suppressor gene called PTEN located on chromosome 11 that normally helps regulate cell division and cell senescence (apoptosis). Mutations in the PTEN gene cause the development of small benign papules of the skin and mucous membranes (called hamartomas) and often result in thyroid lesions such as goiter, follicular adenomas, and thyroid cancer, as well as breast cancer, uterine cancer, and renal cancer. Sipple syndrome is caused by a variant of a proto-oncogene called RET located on chromosome 10 that regulates an important cellular growth factor (transforming growth factor beta or TGF-β). Carriers of the RET mutation develop malignancies of the endocrine system (specifically medullary thyroid cancer, pheochromocytoma, and occasionally breast cancer) (Lima & Smith, 1971).

Hormone Replacement Therapy and Postmenopausal Breast Cancer

Approximately 75% of breast cancers are diagnosed in women after they undergo menopause. A number of investigations have examined the association between hormone replacement therapy and postmenopausal breast cancer risk, and most have reported a modest increase in breast cancer risk with estrogen alone but a greater risk for estrogen plus progestin. For example, in the Million Women Study conducted in the United Kingdom, current use of estrogen alone increased the risk of invasive breast cancer by 30% compared to a twofold risk increase with current use of estrogen plus progestin (Beral & Million Woman Study Collaborators, 2003). Similar results were observed in the randomized clinical trial of estrogen plus progestin and the prospective observational cohort of postmenopausal women of the Women's Health Initiative (WHI) in the United States. The WHI results showed that breast cancer risk doubled after about 5 years of using estrogen plus progestin but declined soon after discontinuation of hormone therapy (Chlebowski et al., 2009).

Results of studies of hormone replacement therapy involving only estrogen are less clear, with some studies finding an increase in the risk of breast cancer whereas others report either no effect or a decrease in the risk. In the WHI clinical trial of conjugated equine estrogen (CEE) versus placebo for women who had undergone hysterectomy prior to enrollment, the risk of invasive breast cancer was *reduced* by 23% in women who received CEE (Anderson et al., 2004). However, 40% of the women in the trial also reported having bilateral oophorectomies prior to enrollment, and an alternative explanation of results is that discontinuation of estrogen replacement among oophorectomized women in the placebo arm may have heightened their risk by removing feedback inhibition of estrogen biosynthesis in breast tissues.

Several studies show consistency in observing an interaction between body mass and estrogen replacement therapy (ERT) in elevating the risk of breast cancer in postmenopausal women (Colditz et al., 1992; Harris, Namboodiri, Farrar, Solano, & Wynder, 1996; Kaufman et al., 1991; Palmer et al., 1991; Stanford et al., 1995). Specifically, lean women who receive ERT after menopause have been found to be at significantly higher risk than heavier women (**Figure 11.4**). One possible explanation for this is that lean women who receive ERT may have relatively higher concentrations of exogenous estrogens per unit of breast tissue, thereby increasing carcinogenesis.

Body Mass and Postmenopausal Breast Cancer

Body mass index (BMI) shows differential effects on premenopausal versus postmenopausal breast cancer risk. Before menopause, BMI shows little association with risk, whereas after menopause, the risk of breast cancer increases two- to threefold among women with high BMI, presumably due to heightened estrogen biosynthesis through conversion of other steroids to estrogen by the enzyme aromatase in adipose tissue. The elevated risk of postmenopausal disease is most evident among women who gain excessive weight throughout the reproductive years and have no exposure to exogenous estrogens after menopause (Harris, Namboodiri, & Wynder, 1992).

Dietary Fat and Breast Cancer

From an etiologic perspective, it is of interest that rates of breast cancer are changing in populations that historically have been at low risk, whereas the rates have remained relatively constant in populations at higher risk. For example, breast cancer mortality rates among Japanese, Indian, and Chinese women have increased approximately threefold in the past two decades whereas rates for women in the United States, United Kingdom, and Sweden have declined (**Figure 11.5**). Concurrently, the Japanese, Indian, and Chinese diets have also changed dramatically with higher intakes of fat and calories; however, other risk factors may also be involved because birth rates are declining, age at first pregnancy is being delayed, the practice of breastfeeding is decreasing, and nulliparity is increasing in these populations.

A well-known but controversial hypothesis of breast cancer etiology is known as the *dietary fat hypothesis*. An extension of this hypothesis states that breast cancer development is due to intake of certain types of essential polyunsaturated fatty acids (PUFAs) that increase inflammation and estrogen biosynthesis and thus promote breast cancer development (Harris,

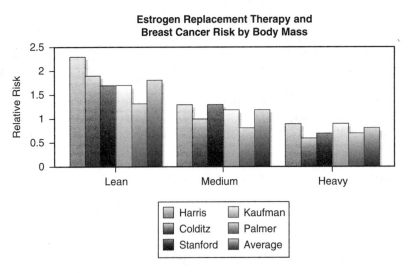

Figure 11.4 Body Mass and Breast Cancer Risk.

Source: Data from Harris, R. E., Namboodiri, K. K., Farrar, W. B., Solano, S. M., & Wynder, E. L. (1996). Hormone replacement therapy and breast cancer risk. *Journal of the American Medical Association, 275*(15), 1158.

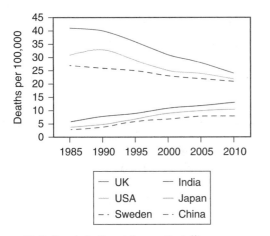

Figure 11.5 Trends in Breast Cancer Mortality.

Mortality rates are age-standardized to the world population, 2000.

Source: Data from Ferlay, J., Bray, F., Pisani, P., & Parkin, D. M. (2004). *GLOBOCAN 2002. Cancer incidence, mortality, and prevalence worldwide*. IARC Cancer Base No. 5, version 2.0. Lyon, France: IARC Press. Retrieved from http://www-dep.iarc.fr; Ferlay, J., Shin, H.-R., Bray, F., Forman, D., Mathers, C., & Parkin, D. M. (2010). Estimates of worldwide burden of cancer in 2008: GLOBOCAN 2008. *International Journal of Cancer, 127*(12), 2893–2917; Ferlay, J., Soerjomataram, I., Ervik, M., Dikshit, R., Eser, S., Mathers, C.,... Bray, F. (2013). *GLOBOCAN 2012 v1.0. Cancer incidence and mortality worldwide: IARC CancerBase No. 11* [Internet]. Lyon, France: International Agency for Research on Cancer. Retrieved from http://globocan.iarc.fr

2002). Karmali and colleagues first observed the divergent effects of omega-6 versus omega-3 PUFAs in animal models of breast carcinogenesis. Their studies clearly show that proinflammatory omega-6 fatty acids such as linoleic acid promote tumor development and metastasis whereas anti-inflammatory omega-3 fatty acids such as linolenic acid are inhibitory (Karmali, Adams, & Trout, 1993).

Important supportive evidence for the dietary fat hypothesis of breast cancer comes from chronological studies of Japanese women. Over the past half century, the age-adjusted breast cancer mortality rate among Japanese women has increased more than twofold, rising from less than 5 deaths per 100,000 in 1950 to nearly 12 deaths per 100,000 in 2006 (Kawamura & Sobue, 2005; Saika & Sobue, 2009). Notably, this gradual increase in breast cancer mortality among Japanese women closely parallels a threefold increase in per capita fat consumption over the same time period (**Figure 11.6**). In 1950, less than 10% of kilocalories were derived from fat, whereas in 2005 the level had risen to nearly 30% (Harris, 2002; Minami et al., 2004).

Although the correlated time trends of breast cancer rates and per capita dietary changes in certain populations support a role for dietary fat, analytic (case control and cohort) studies of diet and breast cancer have yielded inconsistent results, perhaps due

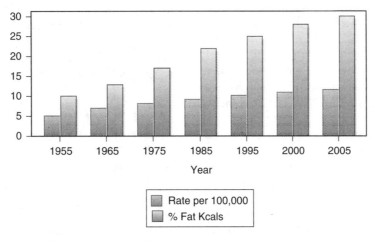

Figure 11.6 Breast Cancer and Dietary Fat, Japan, 1955–2005.

Sources: Data from Harris, R. E. (2002). Epidemiology of breast cancer and nonsteroidal anti-inflammatory drugs: Extension of the dietary fat hypothesis of breast cancer. In R. E. Harris (Ed.), *COX-2 blockade in cancer prevention and therapy* (pp. 57–68). Totowa, NJ: Humana Press; Minami, Y., Tsubono, Y., Nishino, Y., Ohuchi, N., Shibuya, D., & Hisamichi, S. (2004). The increase of female breast cancer incidence in Japan: Emergence of birth cohort effect. *International Journal of Cancer, 108*(6), 901–906; Kawamura, T., & Sobue, T. (2005). Comparison of breast cancer mortality in five countries: France, Italy, Japan, the UK, and the USA from the WHO Mortality Database (1960–2000). *Japan Journal of Clinical Oncology, 35*(12), 758–759; Saika, K., & Sobue, T. (2009). Epidemiology of breast cancer in Japan and the US. *Japanese Medical Association Journal, 52*(1), 39–44.

to the difficulty of accurately assessing dietary exposure on an individual basis. As a consequence, there is controversy among epidemiologists regarding the role of dietary fat or other dietary factors in the genesis of breast cancer.

Oral Contraceptives and Premenopausal Breast Cancer

Oral contraceptive (OC) use has been found to influence the development of breast cancer in premenopausal women but not postmenopausal women (Mills, Beeson, Phillips, & Fraser, 1989; Romieu, Berlin, & Colditz, 1990). In a meta-analysis of 34 studies, OC use was found to increase the risk of premenopausal breast cancer in parous women (odds ratio [OR] = 1.29) and nulliparous women (OR = 1.24), and the association was stronger when OCs were used before the first full-term pregnancy (OR = 1.44) (Kahlenborn, Modugno, Potter, & Severs, 2006). Conceivably, the OC content of estrogen and progestin heightens cancer risk by inducing hyperplasia of the breast epithelium in some premenopausal women.

Alcohol and Breast Cancer

Some investigations have noted a weak association between moderate alcohol consumption and breast cancer risk (Willett, Stampfer, & Colditz, 1989). However, the results of independent studies are mixed, and this too is a controversial issue in breast cancer epidemiology (Harris & Wynder, 1988; Wynder & Harris, 1989).

In a meta-analysis of the relationship of alcohol and breast cancer that included estimates of risk for drinkers versus nondrinkers from 89 separate studies, 29 studies reported odds ratios less than 1.0, 60 studies reported estimates greater than 1.0, and the combined estimate of risk was 1.11, suggesting there is a weak association. Nevertheless, the analysis also revealed the presence of significant heterogeneity among risk estimates (Key et al., 2006). Furthermore, studies of some populations reveal discordant results. For example, in a meta-analysis of studies of breast cancer and alcohol among Chinese women, alcohol consumption actually showed an *inverse* association with the risk of breast cancer (Li, Yang, & Cao, 2011).

Although alcohol per se is not carcinogenic, its primary metabolite, acetaldehyde, does have potent carcinogenic properties. Although alcohol metabolism occurs primarily in the liver, the responsible enzyme, alcohol dehydrogenase, can also be expressed in other tissues, including the mammary epithelium. Thus it is conceivable that in women who are chronic drinkers, the local metabolism of alcohol may expose breast tissues to acetaldehyde (Crabb, Matsumoto, Chang, & You, 2004).

Other Breast Cancer Risk Factors

Certain endogenous conditions may also modulate the development of cancer of the breast. Fibrocystic disease with hyperplasia and/or atypia appears, in some instances, to antedate the development of cancer of the breast. In case-control studies, this condition elevates the risk of breast cancer by about two- to threefold.

Thyroid dysfunction has also been observed in association with breast cancer in some studies (Smyth, 1997). In particular, hypothyroidism may elevate breast cancer risk in certain individuals. The physiologic basis for this is, presumptively, the antiestrogenic effect of thyroxin; that is, when thyroxin levels are diminished, estrogen levels rise, thereby enhancing breast cancer risk.

It is noteworthy that the highest risk target organ for development of breast cancer is the contralateral (opposite) breast of a woman who has already manifested unilateral disease. In addition, the familial breast cancer patient has a markedly enhanced risk for development of malignancy in the contralateral breast (about 50% over 20 years, postmastectomy) (Harris, Lynch, & Guirgis, 1978).

Many studies in biochemical epidemiology have been performed with the objective of identifying a biochemical marker of breast cancer risk. The various subtypes of estrogens (estradiol, estrone, and estriol) and their ratios, androgens and other steroids, polypeptide hormones such as prolactin, and various indices of these parameters have been tried; however, no single parameter or index of parameters has been developed that accurately predicts an individual's risk of for developing cancer of the breast.

MAMMOGRAPHIC BREAST DENSITY AND POSTMENOPAUSAL BREAST CANCER RISK

Appearance of the breast on mammogram facilitates partition of tissues into radiolucent areas consisting of primarily adipose (fat) and radiodense areas consisting of primarily fibrous and glandular tissues. John Wolfe, a radiologist in Detroit, Michigan, was the first to describe differences in breast cancer risk associated with variations in the mammographic appearance of the breast (Wolfe, 1976). Many subsequent studies have consistently found that among postmenopausal women who undergo screening mammography, those with a high ratio of dense

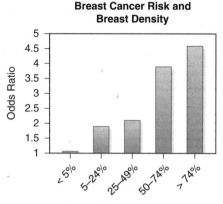

Figure 11.7 Mammographic Breast Density and Risk of Breast Cancer.

Source: McCormack, V. A., & dos Santos Silva, I. (2006). Breast density and parenchymal patterns as markers of breast cancer risk: A meta-analysis. *Cancer Epidemiology, Biomarkers and Prevention, 15*, 1159–1169.

glandular tissue to adipose tissue have an elevated risk of developing breast cancer compared to those with low ratios (Boyd et al., 2005; McCormack & dos Santos Silva, 2006; Yaghjyan, Colditz, Rosner, & Taminmi, 2013; Yaghjyan et al., 2011).

In a meta-analysis of 42 studies involving more than 14,000 cases and 226,000 controls, the composite risk estimates increased in a dose-dependent fashion with increasing breast density, and women with breast densities of 75% or more had nearly 5 times higher risk of developing breast cancer than those with breast densities less than 5% (**Figure 11.7**). The investigators concluded that "this marker has great potential to be used for research into the etiology and prevention of breast cancer" (McCormack & dos Santos Silva, 2006).

Conundrum of Mammographic Breast Density

The observed association of high mammographic breast density with the risk of breast cancer presents a conundrum. This association appears to be confounded by age and body mass, two factors that *increase* breast cancer risk but *decrease* the glandular component of mammary tissues. Furthermore, in a recent study of 9,232 women with confirmed diagnoses of invasive breast cancer, high mammographic density was *not* associated with the risk of dying from breast cancer. Instead, there was a paradoxical *increase* in the risk of dying from breast cancer associated with *low* breast density, particularly in obese women (Gierach et al., 2012).

Legislation Requiring Disclosure of Mammographic Density

Despite uncertainties regarding the biological interpretation of mammographic density, the findings relating "dense breasts" to higher breast cancer risk have prompted legislation requiring full disclosure of mammography findings to patients. In the United States, laws requiring disclosure have been passed in Connecticut, Texas, Virginia, California, and New York, and a bill calling for a federal law has been introduced in the House of Representatives. Under these laws, women who have dense breast tissue by mammography must be told not only that their risk of developing breast cancer is increased, but also that dense breast tissue can mask the detection of cancerous tumors.

Despite the association between mammographic density and the risk of breast cancer, it must be remembered that most women with radiodense breasts will *not* develop breast cancer. It is emphasized that the discrimination of small breast tumors from normal glandular tissues by mammography (or other imaging techniques) is extremely difficult because both tissues are radiodense. The only sure way of making this determination is by microscopic examination of a biopsy specimen by a trained pathologist.

PREVENTION OF BREAST CANCER

Breastfeeding and Breast Cancer

An early case control study by Janet Lane-Claypon in Great Britain found that early pregnancy and breastfeeding protect against the development of breast cancer. Recent meta-analyses provided confirmation of these effects. An international collaborative team of investigators examined data from 47 epidemiologic studies conducted in 30 different countries that included information on breastfeeding patterns and other aspects of childbearing for 50,302 women with invasive breast cancer and 96,973 controls. Results showed that each birth reduced the risk of developing breast cancer by 7.0%, and among parous women, each year of breastfeeding reduced the risk by an additional 4.3% (Collaborative Group on Hormonal Factors in Breast Cancer, 2002).

Selective Estrogen Receptor Modulators (SERMs) and Breast Cancer

Breast cancer specimens ascertained by biopsy or surgical procedures (mastectomy) are routinely subjected to laboratory analysis of estrogen receptors (ERs) and progesterone receptors (PRs). Breast tumors that are positive for ERs/PRs may respond to hormone therapy by administration of antiestrogenic compounds such as tamoxifen. Such compounds are called *selective estrogen receptor modulators (SERMs)* because they inhibit the interaction of estrogen with the estrogen receptor. Tamoxifen is now being offered to women treated for early stage breast cancer for protection against the development of second primary cancer in the contralateral breast.

Large independent clinical trials have been performed to examine the preventive activity of tamoxifen. Although a U.S. trial showed beneficial effects (Fisher et al., 1998), the results of two European trials were negative (Powles et al., 1998; Veronesi et al., 1998). In a fourth randomized clinical trial conducted in European centers, tamoxifen administration reduced the incidence of breast cancer by 32% compared to the control group, but despite this benefit, there was a significant *excess* of deaths in the tamoxifen group (25 versus 11 deaths, P < 0.03) (Cuzick et al., 2002). Nevertheless, the U.S. FDA approved tamoxifen for use as a preventive agent in high-risk women. This action tends to disregard adverse side effects of the drug including increased risks of endometrial cancer, ER-negative breast cancer, colon cancer, pulmonary embolus, and other thrombotic events.

Nonsteroidal Anti-inflammatory Drugs (NSAIDs) and Breast Cancer

Many epidemiologic studies have noted a significant preventive effect of nonsteroidal anti-inflammatory drugs (NSAIDs) against breast cancer. A meta-analysis of these investigations suggests that the risk of breast cancer is reduced by approximately 25% with regular use of common over-the-counter NSAIDs such as aspirin and ibuprofen (**Figure 11.8**) (Harris, 2009; Harris, Casto, & Harris, 2014). Studies in molecular epidemiology and in animals suggest that this effect is manifest primarily due to blockade of cyclooxygenase isoenzymes of the inflammatory cascade, particularly the inducible isoform, cyclooxygenase-2 (COX-2) (Harris, 2007).

SUMMARY OF BREAST CANCER EPIDEMIOLOGY

Breast cancer is a multifactorial disease promoted by sustained heightened exposure to endogenous or exogenous estrogens. There is a rising worldwide trend in breast cancer incidence that undoubtedly reflects the impact of multiple factors, including screening (mammography) and increases in risk factors, including late childbearing, lack of breastfeeding, intake of exogenous hormones, intake of diets high in fat and calories, lack of exercise, and obesity. Incidence rates of breast cancer vary widely and are higher in developed countries such as the United States and United Kingdom and lower in developing countries such as India and China. Breast cancer risk appears to increase with high intake of essential polyunsaturated fats that promote inflammation and estrogen biosynthesis. Reproductive risk factors include early menses, nulliparity, late first pregnancy,

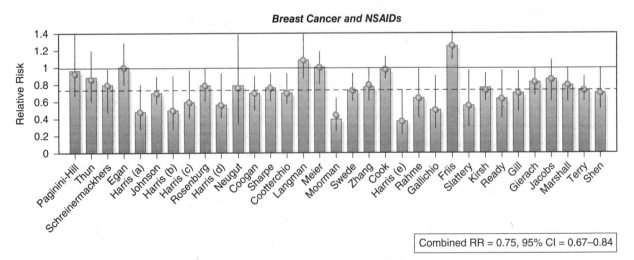

Figure 11.8 Breast Cancer and Nonsteroidal Anti-inflammatory Drugs (NSAIDs).

Source: Data from Harris, R. E. (2009). Cyclooxygenase-2 (COX-2) blockade in the chemoprevention of cancers of the colon, breast, prostate, and lung. *Inflammo-pharmacology, 17,* 1–13; Harris, R. E., Casto, B. C., & Harris, Z. M. (2014). Cyclooxygenase-2 (COX-2) and the inflammogenesis of breast cancer. *World Journal of Clinical Oncology, 5*(4), 677–692.

absence of lactation, and late menopause, all of which increase exposure to endogenous estrogens. Estrogen replacement therapy (ERT) and high body mass increase breast cancer risk in postmenopausal women. Identifiable genetic factors account for only a small fraction of breast cancer cases. Studies in cancer control show that annual screening with mammography after age 50 is effective in detecting early breast lesions when they can be surgically excised with a high probability of long-term survival. Furthermore, the risk of developing breast cancer is increased among women with higher levels of dense breast tissue based on mammography. Breast cancer prevention may be aided by taking synthetic or natural compounds with anti-inflammatory or anti-estrogenic activity. Additional studies in molecular epidemiology are needed to more clearly delineate the way in which breast cancer risk factors interact to impact the natural history of this disease.

● ● ● REFERENCES

American Joint Committee on Cancer (AJCC). (2010). Breast cancer staging. In S. B. Edge, D. R. Byrd, C. C. Compton, A. G. Fritz, F. L. Greene, & A., Trotti (Eds.), *Cancer staging manual* (7th ed., pp. 347–376). New York, NY: Springer-Verlag.

Anderson, G. L., Limacher, M., Assaf, A. R., Bassford, T., Beresford, S. A., Black, H., . . . Wassertheil-Smoller, S. (2004). Effects of conjugated equine estrogen in postmenopausal women with hysterectomy: The Women's Health Initiative randomized controlled trial. *Journal of the American Medical Association*, 291(14), 1701–1712.

Beral, V., & Million Women Study Collaborators (2003). Breast cancer and hormone-replacement therapy in the Million Women Study. *Lancet*, 362(9382), 419–427.

Boulton, S. J. (2006). Cellular functions of the BRCA tumour-suppressor proteins. *Biochemical Society Transactions*, 34(5), 633–645.

Boyd, N. F., Rommens, J. M., Vogt, K., Lee, V., Hopper, J. L., Yaffe, M. J., & Paterson, A. D. (2005). Mammographic breast density as an intermediate phenotype for breast cancer. *Lancet Oncology*, 6(10), 798–808.

Bray, F., McCarron, P., & Parkin, D. M. (2004). The changing global patterns of female breast cancer incidence and mortality. *Breast Cancer Research*, 6(6), 229–239.

Chlebowski, R. T., Kuller, L. H., Prentice, R. L., Stefanick, M. L., Manson, J. E., Gass, M., . . . Anderson, G. (2009). Breast cancer after use of estrogen plus progestin in postmenopausal women. *New England Journal of Medicine*, 360(6), 573–587.

Colditz, G. A., Stampfer, M. J., Willett, W. C., Hunter, D. J., Manson, J. E., Hennekens, C. H., . . . Speizer, F. E. (1992). Type of postmenopausal hormone use and risk of breast cancer: 12 year follow-up from the Nurses' Health Study. *Cancer Causes and Control*, 3, 433–439.

Collaborative Group on Hormonal Factors in Breast Cancer. (2002). Breast cancer and breastfeeding: Collaborative reanalysis of individual data from 47 epidemiological studies in 30 countries, including 50,302 women with breast cancer and 96,973 women without the disease. *Lancet*, 360(9328), 187–195.

Collaborative Group on Hormonal Factors in Breast Cancer. (2012). Menarche, menopause, and breast cancer risk: Individual participant meta-analysis, including 118,964 women with breast cancer from 117 epidemiological studies. *Lancet Oncology*, 13(11), 1141–1151.

Crabb, D. W., Matsumoto, M., Chang, D., & You, M. (2004). Overview of the role of alcohol dehydrogenase and aldehyde dehydrogenase and their variants in the genesis of alcohol-related pathology. *Proceedings of the Nutrition Society*, 63, 49–63.

Cuzick, J., Forbes, J., Edwards, R., Baum, M., Cawthorn, S., Coates, A., . . . IBIS Investigators (2002). First results from the International Breast Cancer Intervention Study (IBIS-I): A randomised prevention trial. *Lancet*, 360(9336), 817–824.

Eng, C. (1998). Genetics of Cowden syndrome: Through the looking glass of oncology. *International Journal of Oncology*, 12(3), 701–710.

Ferlay, J., Bray, F., Pisani, P., & Parkin, D. M. (2004). *GLOBOCAN 2002. Cancer incidence, mortality, and prevalence worldwide*. IARC Cancer Base No. 5, version 2.0. Lyon, France: IARC Press. Retrieved from http://www-dep.iarc.fr

Ferlay, J., Shin, H.-R., Bray, F., Forman, D., Mathers, C., & Parkin, D. M. (2010). Estimates of worldwide burden of cancer in 2008: GLOBOCAN 2008. *International Journal of Cancer, 127*(12), 2893–2917.

Ferlay, J., Soerjomataram, I., Ervik, M., Dikshit, R., Eser, S., Mathers, C., . . . Bray, F. (2013). *GLOBOCAN 2012 v1.0. Cancer incidence and mortality worldwide: IARC CancerBase No. 11* [Internet]. Lyon, France: International Agency for Research on Cancer. Retrieved from http://globocan.iarc.fr

Fisher, B., Costantino, J. P., Wickerham, D. L., Redmond, C. K., Kavanah, M., Cronin, W. M., . . . Wolmark, N. (1998). Tamoxifen for prevention of breast cancer: Report of the National Surgical Adjuvant Breast and Bowel Project P-1 Study. *Journal of the National Cancer Institute, 90*, 1371–1388.

Garcia, M., Jemal, A., Ward, E. M., Center, M. M., Hao, Y., Siegel, R. L., & Thun, M. J. (2007). *Global cancer facts and figures 2007*. Atlanta, GA: American Cancer Society.

Gierach, G. L., Ichikawa, L., Kerlikowske, K., Brinton, L. A., Farhat, G. N., Vacek, P. M., & Sherman, M. E. (2012). Relationship between mammographic density and breast cancer death in the Breast Cancer Surveillance Consortium. *Journal of the National Cancer Institute, 104*, 1218–1227.

Hall, J. M., Lee, M. K., Newman, B., Morrow, J. E., Anderson, L. A., Huey, B., & King, M. C. (1990). Linkage of early-onset familial breast cancer to chromosome 17q21. *Science, 250*(4988), 1684–1689.

Harris, R. E. (2002). Epidemiology of breast cancer and nonsteroidal anti-inflammatory drugs: Extension of the dietary fat hypothesis of breast cancer. In R. E. Harris (Ed.), *COX-2 blockade in cancer prevention and therapy* (pp. 57–68). Totowa, NJ: Humana Press.

Harris, R. E. (2007). COX-2 and the inflammogenesis of cancer. *Subcellular Biochemistry, 42*, 193–212.

Harris, R. E. (2009). Cyclooxygenase-2 (COX-2) blockade in the chemoprevention of cancers of the colon, breast, prostate, and lung. *Inflammopharmacology, 17*, 1–13.

Harris, R. E., Casto, B. C., & Harris, Z. M. (2014). Cyclooxygenase-2 (COX-2) and the inflammogenesis of breast cancer. *World Journal of Clinical Oncology, 5*(4), 677–692.

Harris, R. E., Lynch, H. T., & Guirgis, H. A. (1978). Familial breast cancer: Risk to the contralateral breast. *Journal of the National Cancer Institute, 60*, 955–960.

Harris, R. E., Namboodiri, K. K., Farrar, W. B., Solano, S. M., & Wynder, E. L. (1996). Hormone replacement therapy and breast cancer risk. *Journal of the American Medical Association, 275*(15), 1158.

Harris, R. E., Namboodiri, K. K., & Wynder, E. L. (1992). Breast cancer risk: Effects of estrogen replacement therapy and body mass. *Journal of the National Cancer Institute, 84*, 1575–1582.

Harris, R. E., & Wynder, E. L. (1988). Breast cancer and alcohol consumption: A study in weak associations. *Journal of the American Medical Association, 259*(19), 2867–2871.

Hutson, S. W., Cowen, P. N., & Bird, C. C. (1985). Morphometric studies of age related changes in normal human breast and their significance for evolution of mammary cancer. *Journal of Clinical Pathology, 38*, 281–287.

Kahlenborn, C., Modugno, F., Potter, D. M., & Severs, W. B. (2006). Oral contraceptive use as a risk factor for premenopausal breast cancer: A meta-analysis. *Mayo Clinic Proceedings, 81*(10), 1290–1302.

Karmali, R. A., Adams, L., & Trout, J. R. (1993). Plant and marine n-3 fatty acids inhibit experimental metastasis of rat mammary adenocarcinoma cells. *Prostaglandins Leukotrienes and Essential Fatty Acids, 48*, 309–314.

Kaufman, D. W., Palmer, J. R., de Mouzon, J., Rosenberg, L., Stolley, P. D., Warshauer, E., . . . Shapiro, S. (1991). Estrogen replacement therapy and the risk of breast cancer: Results from the case-control surveillance study. *American Journal of Epidemiology, 134*, 1375–1385.

Kawamura, T., & Sobue, T. (2005). Comparison of breast cancer mortality in five countries: France, Italy, Japan, the UK, and the USA from the WHO Mortality Database (1960–2000). *Japan Journal of Clinical Oncology, 35*(12), 758–759.

Key, J., Hodgson, S., Omar, R. Z., Jensen, T. K., Thompson, S. G., Boobis, A. R., . . . Elliott, P. (2006). Meta-analysis of studies of alcohol and breast cancer with consideration of the methodological issues. *Cancer Causes and Control, 17*(6), 759–770.

King, M. C., Marks, J. H., Mandell, J. B., & New York Breast Cancer Study Group. (2003). Breast and ovarian cancer risks due to inherited mutations in BRCA1 and BRCA2. *Science, 302*(5645), 643–646.

Korenman, S. G. (1980). Oestrogen window hypothesis of the aetiology of breast cancer. *Lancet, 315*, 700–701.

Lane-Claypon, J. E. (1926). *A further report on cancer of the breasts, with special reference to its associated antecedent conditions.* London: HMSO. Report on Public Health and Medical Subjects No. 32.

Li, Y., Yang, H., & Cao, J. (2011). Association between alcohol consumption and cancers in the Chinese population—a systematic review and meta-analysis. *PLOS One, 6*(4), e18776. doi: 10.1371/journal.pone.0018776.

Lima, J. B., & Smith, P. D. (1971). Sipple's syndrome (pheochromocytoma and thyroid carcinoma) with bilateral breast carcinoma. *American Journal of Surgery, 1*(6), 732–735.

Ma, H., Bernstein, L., Pike, M. C., & Ursin, G. (2006). Reproductive factors and breast cancer risk according to joint estrogen and progesterone receptor status: A meta-analysis of epidemiological studies. *Breast Cancer Research, 8*(4), R43.

MacMahon, B., Cole, P., Lin, T. M., Lowe, C. R., Mirra, A. P., Ravnihar, B., . . . Yuasa, S. (1970). Age at first birth and breast cancer risk. *Bulletin of the World Health Organization, 43*(2), 209–221.

McCormack, V. A., & dos Santos Silva, I. (2006). Breast density and parenchymal patterns as markers of breast cancer risk: A meta-analysis. *Cancer Epidemiology, Biomarkers and Prevention, 15*, 1159–1169.

Mills, P. K., Beeson, L., Phillips, R. L., & Fraser G. E. (1989). Prospective study of exogenous hormone use and breast cancer in Seventh-Day Adventists. *Cancer, 64*, 591–597.

Minami, Y., Tsubono, Y., Nishino, Y., Ohuchi, N., Shibuya, D., & Hisamichi, S. (2004). The increase of female breast cancer incidence in Japan: Emergence of birth cohort effect. *International Journal of Cancer, 108*(6), 901–906.

Palmer, J. R., Rosenberg, L., Clarke, E. A., Miller, D, R., & Shapiro, S. (1991). Breast cancer risk after estrogen replacement therapy: Results from the Toronto Breast Cancer Study. *American Journal of Epidemiology, 134*, 1386–1395.

Parkin, D. M., Bray, F., Ferlay, J., & Pisani, P. (2001). Estimating the world cancer burden: GLOBOCAN 2000. *International Journal of Cancer, 94*, 153–156.

Powles, T., Eeles, R., Ashley, S., Easton, D., Chang, J., Dowsett, M., . . . Davey, J. (1998). Interim analysis of the incidence of breast cancer in the Royal Marsden Hospital tamoxifen randomised chemoprevention trial. *Lancet, 352*, 98–101.

Romieu, I., Berlin, J. A., & Colditz, G. (1990). Oral contraceptives and breast cancer. Review and meta-analysis. *Cancer, 66*(11), 2253–2263.

Saika, K., & Sobue, T. (2009). Epidemiology of breast cancer in Japan and the US. *Japan Medical Association Journal, 52*(1), 39–44.

Smyth, P. P. (1997). The thyroid and breast cancer: A significant association? *Annals of Medicine, 3*, 189–191.

Stanford, J. L., Weiss, N. S., Voight, L. F., Daling, J. R., Habel, L. A., & Rossing, M. A. (1995). Combined estrogen and progestin hormone replacement therapy in relation to risk of breast cancer in middle-aged women. *Journal of the American Medical Association, 274*, 137–142.

Ursin, G., Bernstein, L., Lord, S. J., Karim, R., Deapen, D., Press, M. F., . . . Spirtas, R. (2005). Reproductive factors and subtypes of breast cancer defined by hormone receptor and histology. *British Journal of Cancer, 93*(3), 364–371.

Veronesi, U., Maisonneuve, P., Costa, A., Sacchini, V., Maltoni, C., Robertson, C., . . . Boyle, P. (1998). Prevention of breast cancer with tamoxifen: Preliminary findings from the Italian randomised trial among hysterectomised women. Italian Tamoxifen Prevention Study. *Lancet, 352,* 93–97.

Willett, W. C., Stampfer, M. J., & Colditz, G. A. (1989). Does alcohol consumption influence the risk of developing breast cancer? Two views (15a). In V. T. DeVita Jr., S. Hellman, & S. A. Rosenberg (Eds.), *Important advances in oncology, 1989* (pp. 267–281). Philadelphia, PA: J. B. Lippincott.

Winkelstein Jr., W. (2006). Janet Elizabeth Lane-Claypon: A forgotten epidemiologic pioneer. *Epidemiology, 17*(6), 705.

Wolfe, J. N. (1976). Risk for breast cancer development determined by mammographic parenchymal pattern. *Cancer, 37,* 2486–2492.

Wooster, R., Neuhausen, S. L., Mangion, J., Quirk, Y., Ford, D., Collins, N., . . . Stratton, M. R. (1994). Localization of a breast cancer susceptibility gene, BRCA2, to chromosome 13q12–13. *Science, 265*(5181), 2088–2090.

Wynder, E. L., & Harris, R. E. (1989). Does alcohol consumption influence the risk of developing breast cancer? Two views (15b). In V. T. DeVita Jr., S. Hellman, & S. A. Rosenberg (Eds.), *Important advances in oncology, 1989* (pp. 267–281). Philadelphia, PA: JB Lippincott.

Yaghjyan, L., Colditz, G. A., Collins, L. C., Schnitt, S. J., Rosner, B., Vachon, C., & Tamimi, R. M. (2011). Mammographic breast density and subsequent risk of breast cancer in postmenopausal women according to tumor characteristics. *Journal of the National Cancer Institute, 103,* 1–11.

Yaghjyan, L., Colditz, G. A., Rosner, B., & Taninmi, R. M. (2013). Mammographic breast density and subsequent risk of breast cancer in postmenopausal women according to the time since the mammogram. *Cancer Epidemiology, Biomarkers and Prevention, 22*(6), 1110–1117.

12

Epidemiology of Ovarian Cancer

GLOBAL EPIDEMIOLOGY OF OVARIAN CANCER

During 2012, ovarian cancer was diagnosed in 238,719 women and caused 151,905 deaths. This malignancy accounts for approximately 3.6% of all female cancers and about 4.2% of cancer deaths in women (Ferlay et al., 2010, 2013). Most new cases (80–90%) are diagnosed either during or after menopause, and the peak incidence occurs during the fifth decade of life (American Cancer Society, 2009; National Cancer Institute, 2009).

The global patterns of ovarian cancer incidence and mortality shown in **Figure 12.1** are somewhat similar to those of breast cancer. High incidence and mortality rates are found among Caucasian women living in industrialized areas such as the United States, Canada, Europe, Australia, New Zealand, Japan, and the Russian Federation. Nevertheless, some less developed countries (e.g., certain African countries such as Niger and Ethiopia and South American counties such as Chile, Bolivia, and Guyana) also have high rates of ovarian cancer.

OVARIAN CANCER: THE "SILENT KILLER"

Ovarian cancer develops silently over a period of many years without clinically detectable signs or symptoms. At the time of diagnosis, more than 70% of ovarian cancers have spread to lymph nodes, surrounding tissues of the peritoneum, or beyond (**Figure 12.2**). As a consequence of the failure to detect ovarian cancers at an early stage when treatment is more likely to be of benefit to the patient, ovarian cancer generally has an extremely poor

prognosis. Worldwide, the five-year survival rate for ovarian cancer is only about 30% (Parkin, Bray, Ferlay, & Pisani, 2005).

PATHOPHYSIOLOGY OF THE HUMAN OVARY

Ovarian pathophysiology is complex. The gland is covered by surface epithelium and the inner core (the cortex) consists of multiple cell types. Follicles within the cortex contain the oocytes (eggs), granulosa cells, and theca cells. Granulosa cells surround and nourish the oocytes in response to follicular stimulating hormone (FSH) secreted by the pituitary gland. Theca cells respond to luteinizing hormone (LH) and synthesize androgens that are subsequently aromatized to estrogens by the granulosa cells. On ovulation, the remnant of the follicle (the corpus luteum) secretes progesterone as well as estrogen. Various structures and cell types of the human ovary are shown in **Figure 12.3** (Kumar, Abbas, & Aster, 2014).

PATHOGENESIS OF OVARIAN CANCER

Ovarian cancer usually arises from the epithelial cells at the surface of the ovary. Dr. Mahmoud Fathalla originally proposed that the genesis of this malignancy is likely related to incessant ovulation and repetitive disruption and wound healing of the surface epithelium coincident with the menstrual cycle during the reproductive years (Fathalla, 1971). Incessant ovulation could cause sustained exposure of the ovarian epithelium to hormones and growth factors secreted by the ovarian cortex (Scully, 1995) as well as increase the inflammatory microenvironment of

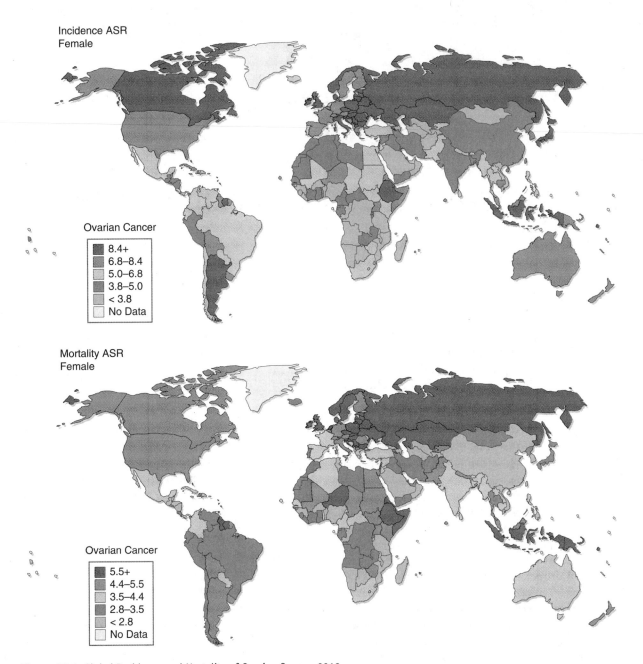

Figure 12.1 Global Incidence and Mortality of Ovarian Cancer, 2012.

ASR: Rates per 100,000 are standardized to the world population, 2000–2025.

Source: Reproduced from Ferlay, J., Soerjomataram, I., Ervik, M., Dikshit, R., Eser, S., Mathers, C., . . . Bray, F. (2013). *GLOBOCAN 2012 v1.0. Cancer incidence and mortality worldwide: IARC CancerBase No. 11* [Internet]. Lyon, France: International Agency for Research on Cancer. Retrieved from http://globocan.iarc.fr

cytokines and prostaglandins, leading to cell damage and oxidative stress (Ness & Cottreau, 1999). In support of the incessant ovulation model, several epidemiologic studies have determined that the number of successive ovulatory cycles uninterrupted by pregnancy, lactation, and/or contraception increases the risk of ovarian cancer (Risch, Marrett, & Howe, 1994). The natural repetitive cyclic process of

ovulation may thus increase the chance of spontaneous somatic mutations and/or epigenetic changes that alter the expression of tumor suppressor genes and oncogenes in favor of carcinogenesis.

However, the incessant ovulation model does not explain the increased risk of ovarian cancer in women who are infertile due to anovulation (absence of ovulation). Such women may be at risk due to

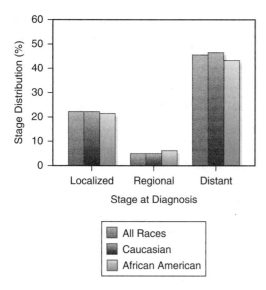

Figure 12.2 Ovarian Cancer Stage at Detection.

Source: Data from Horner, M. J., Ries, L. A. G., Krapcho, M., Neyman, N., Aminou, R., Howlader, N., . . . Edwards, B. K. (Eds). *SEER Cancer Statistics Review, 1975–2006.* Bethesda, MD: National Cancer Institute.

excessive stimulation of the ovary by gonadotropic hormones secreted by the pituitary gland, namely FSH and LH. Ovulation and ovarian secretion of estrogen and progesterone during the menstrual cycle depend upon normal functioning of the hypothalamic-pituitary-ovarian axis; reciprocally, abnormalities in this system may result in anovulation, loss of hormonal feedback control, and hypersecretion

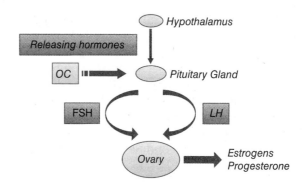

Figure 12.4 The Hypothalamus-Pituitary-Ovarian Axis.

of gonadotropins (**Figure 12.4**). Indeed, as a woman undergoes menopause, the diminished ovarian secretion of estrogen and progesterone results in loss of feedback inhibition, thereby resulting in marked elevations in FSH and LH secreted by the pituitary gland (Chakravarti et al., 1976). These perimenopausal events (diminished ovarian hormones and excess pituitary gonadotropins) are temporally related to the onset of ovarian cancer in the postmenopausal years (Choi, Wong, Huang, & Leung, 2007; Helzlsouer, Alberg, & Gordon, 1995). Furthermore, gonadotropin levels in ovarian cyst and peritoneal fluid appear to be associated with ovarian cancer incidence (Kramer, Leeker, & Jager, 1998), and cell membrane receptors for FSH are overexpressed in a high percentage of ovarian carcinomas as well as preneoplastic lesions of the ovarian surface epithelium (Choi, Choi, Auersperg, & Leung, 2004; Zheng et al.,

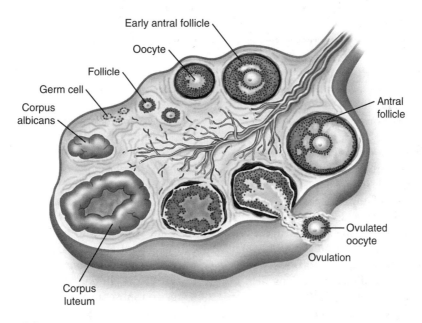

Figure 12.3 Anatomy of the Human Ovary.

2000). Up-regulation of FSH, in particular, appears to be related to the growth, survival, and metastasis of ovarian cancer cells and may involve other growth factors mediated by a complex array of intracellular signaling pathways (Choi et al., 2007). Finally, it has been hypothesized that ovarian cancer is etiologically linked to the excessive production of androgens and diminished levels of progesterone, which upset the balance of the ovarian hormonal milieu resulting in carcinogenesis (Risch, 1998).

RISK FACTORS FOR OVARIAN CANCER

Several risk factors have been identified that increase a woman's chance of developing ovarian cancer. Because the ovarian epithelium contains many of the same cell membrane receptors as the ductal epithelium of the mammary gland, the reproductive risk factor profile for ovarian cancer is similar to that of breast cancer. These risk factors include familial and genetic predisposition plus reproductive events that increase the cumulative months of ovulation, rupture of the ovarian surface epithelium, and exposure to hormones of the menstrual cycle (early menses, delayed reproductive history, nulliparity, absence of lactation, late menopause, and the natural process of aging).

Reciprocally, reproductive factors such as pregnancy, lactation, and oral contraceptive use that interrupt the menstrual cycle have consistently been observed to be protective. These factors are discussed in greater detail in a following section of this chapter.

Genetic Predisposition to Ovarian Cancer

A strong family history (ovarian cancer in a first-degree or second-degree relative) increases the risk of ovarian cancer by three- to fivefold. Genetic or familial predisposition is identifiable for approximately 5–10% of women diagnosed with ovarian cancer. Hallmarks of familial predisposition to ovarian cancer include early age of onset, an excess of bilateral disease, and ovarian cancer in familial association with other malignancies such as breast cancer, endometrial cancer, and colorectal cancer.

Two heritable genetic mutations have been identified that predispose to familial breast and ovarian cancer, *BRCA-1* and *BRCA-2*. The *BRCA-1* gene was discovered in 1990 by King and colleagues and is located on the long arm of chromosome 17 (Hall et al., 1990). Subsequently, a second breast cancer gene, *BRCA-2*, was identified on the long arm of chromosome 13 (Wooster et al., 1994). A mutation in either *BRCA* gene predisposes heterozygous female carriers to both breast cancer and, to a lesser extent,

ovarian cancer. The lifetime risk of breast cancer among women who carry a single mutation in either *BRCA-1* or *BRCA-2* is approximately 85%, whereas the lifetime ovarian cancer risk for women with a *BRCA-1* mutation is 54% compared to 24% for women with a *BRCA-2* mutation (King, Marks, Mandell, & New York Breast Cancer Study Group, 2003).

Both *BRCA-1* and *BRCA-2* are tumor suppressor genes that upon transcription form proteins essential for the repair of double-strand DNA breaks (Boulton, 2006). Mutated *BRCA* genes result in proteins that do not function properly in DNA repair, thereby promoting accumulation of genetic errors and carcinogenesis. Population studies have identified high gene frequencies of *BRCA-1* and *BRCA-2* among women of Ashkenazi Jewish descent and high frequencies of *BRCA-1* among women of Greenlander origin (Harboe et al., 2009).

Another genetic condition that predisposes to ovarian cancer is hereditary nonpolyposis colorectal cancer (HNPCC), also called Lynch syndrome (named after Henry T. Lynch, who characterized the genetic and clinical features of HNPCC). The cause of HNPCC is an inherited (germline) mutation in at least one of a set of genes that normally repair DNA, the mismatch repair genes. In 1993, the first of the HNPCC genes (*MSH2*) was discovered on chromosome 2 by a team of international investigators (Aaltonen et al., 1993). Soon after, *MLH1* was discovered on chromosome 3 (Aaltonen et al., 1994). Mutations in these two genes account for approximately 90% of the known HNPCC families. Lynch syndrome accounts for a small percentage of all colorectal cancer cases, perhaps 1–3%. Women in HNPCC families are also at increased risk of developing cancers of the uterine lining (endometrium), colon, ovary, and stomach (Offit & Kauff, 2006).

Fertility Agents and Ovarian Cancer

Results of several case control studies suggest a link between the use of fertility drugs and the development of ovarian cancer. In general, fertility drugs (e.g., clomiphene citrate) stimulate the secretion of FSH and LH by the pituitary gland in order to help stimulate ovulation. In a meta-analysis of 12 studies, Whittemore and colleagues found that infertile women who had taken any form of fertility drugs were 2.7 times more likely to develop ovarian cancer than women who had never taken these medications (Whittemore, Harris, & Itnyre, 1992). It is important to point out that there was no increase in cancer risk among the women who used fertility drugs and subsequently became pregnant. Nevertheless, a subsequent study by Rossing and colleagues also found more than a twofold increase in the risk of ovarian cancer among women who had used clomiphene citrate for at least one year (Rossing, Daling, Weiss, Moore, & Self, 1994). Controversy remains regarding the exact nature of the increased risk, and it is difficult to reconcile whether it is due to use of the fertility agent or the underlying pathologies of infertility (Holschneider & Berek, 2000).

Polycystic ovary syndrome (also called Stein–Leventhal syndrome) is a relatively common female endocrine disorder affecting approximately 5–10% of women of reproductive age. This syndrome is a leading cause of female infertility that develops when the ovaries are stimulated to produce excessive amounts of male hormones (androgens), particularly testosterone, either through the release of excessive LH by the anterior pituitary gland or through high levels of insulin in the blood (hyperinsulinemia) (Carmina, 2004). One small case control study observed a 2.5-fold increase in the risk of ovarian cancer in women with polycystic ovary syndrome (Schildkraut, Schwingl, Bastos, Evanoff, & Hughes, 1996); however, this finding has not been confirmed in prospective studies (Coulam, Annegers, & Kranz, 1983; Pierpoint, McKeigue, Isaacs, Wild, & Jacobs, 1998).

Other Risk Factors for Ovarian Cancer

Many other potential risk factors have been examined in epidemiologic investigations of ovarian cancer. One factor that has received considerable attention in the media is perineal dusting with talcum powder, a practice that has been observed to increase the risk of ovarian cancer by some investigators (Cramer et al., 1999). A meta-analyses of 16 case control studies determined a modest increase in the risk (the summary relative risk was 1.3), but also reflected heterogeneity among studies (Huncharek, Geschwind, & Kupelnick, 2003). Furthermore, the biological basis of talc carcinogenicity remains controversial because inhaled talc in mining and milling operations has not been found to be associated with the development of pulmonary tumors (Muscat & Huncharek, 2008).

Ecological studies of ovarian cancer and dietary factors have noted positive correlations between milk consumption, lactase persistence (a measure of lactose digestion), and the incidence of ovarian cancer (Cramer, 1989; Rose, Boyar, & Wynder, 1986). However, analytic studies have yielded conflicting results, some finding a positive association of lactose intake with ovarian cancer development and others finding no association (Larsson, Bergkvist, & Wolk, 2004; Risch, Jain, Marrett, & Howe, 1994). It has been hypothesized that galactose, a component sugar of the disaccharide lactose, might increase the risk of ovarian cancer either by direct toxicity to the oocytes

or by inducing high concentrations of gonadotropins, thereby stimulating the proliferation of the ovarian surface epithelium (Harlow et al., 1991).

Findings from both case control and cohort epidemiologic studies suggest there is a dose-response relationship between body mass index and the risk of developing ovarian cancer, particularly among postmenopausal women. In a large prospective study of 94,525 women ages 50–71 years, Leitzmann and colleagues observed that obesity increased the risk of ovarian cancer by 80% in postmenopausal women with no history of hormone replacement therapy (Leitzmann et al., 2009). In a meta-analysis of 28 epidemiologic studies, Olsen and colleagues found significant increases in the risk of developing ovarian cancer with obesity (summary relative risk = 1.3) or being overweight (summary relative risk = 1.2) (Olsen et al., 2007); however, there is lack of agreement regarding the timing of the development of ovarian cancer in relation to adiposity (Schouten et al., 2008). In general, the epidemiologic findings support the hypothesis that long-term adiposity enhances aromatase-catalyzed estrogen biosynthesis that in turn increases the genesis of ovarian cancer.

The use of exogenous hormones (estrogen replacement therapy [ERT]) has been studied extensively in relation to various forms of cancer, including ovarian cancer. In a meta-analysis of 19 case control studies and 8 cohort studies, the risk increase was approximately 20% in ever users versus never users, and the risk increased with the duration of use (Zhou et al., 2008). A prospective study of nearly 1 million women in the United Kingdom found that current ERT users were about 20% more likely to develop and die from ovarian cancer than never users (Beral, Million Women Study Collaborators, Bull, Green, & Reeves, 2007). Biologically, the ovarian surface epithelium has cell membrane receptors that are responsive to estrogen, and it is conceivable that ERT may stimulate cell proliferation and other cellular events related to carcinogenesis through modulation of estrogen receptors.

It has been hypothesized that circulating androgens may be involved in the development of ovarian cancer (Risch, 1998). Futhermore, in one study, the synthetic male hormone danazol was linked to the development of ovarian cancer (Cottreau, Ness, Modugno, Allen, & Goodman, 2003). Danazol is sometimes prescribed to women who suffer from endometriosis, a condition associated with dysplasia and bleeding of the endometrium. However, there is consistent evidence that endometriosis is a risk factor for the development of ovarian cancer; for example, a pooled analysis of eight case control studies found a summary relative risk of 1.7 (Ness et al., 2002), and a large cohort study of Swedish women found a 1.3-fold increase in the risk of ovarian cancer among women with endometriosis (Melin, Sparén, & Bergqvist, 2007). Because the use of danazol is confounded by the presence of endometriosis, additional studies will be required to determine whether this drug truly increases the risk of ovarian cancer.

PROTECTIVE REPRODUCTIVE FACTORS AND OVARIAN CANCER

Interruption of the menstrual cycle by a first pregnancy early in the reproductive years or by sustained use of oral contraceptives has been found to be protective against the development of ovarian cancer in a number of studies. For example, in a multicenter population-based case control study of 436 cases and 3,833 controls, the estimated relative risks of epithelial ovarian cancer were 0.6 for women who had ever been pregnant, 0.6 for women who had ever breast fed, and 0.5 for women who had ever used oral contraceptives, and there was a strong trend in decreasing risk with increasing cumulative months of pregnancy (Gwinn, Lee, Rhodes, Layde, & Rubin, 1990). Overall, women with multiple children have risk reductions in the range of 40–60% compared to nulliparous women (Adami et al., 1994; Hankinson et al., 1995; Risch et al., 1994). Lactation also confers a slight additional reduction in the risk of ovarian cancer (Rosenblatt & Thomas, 1993).

During the reproductive years, estrogens are produced by the ovaries; in contrast, after menopause, estrogen biosynthesis is catalyzed by the enzyme aromatase in fat and muscle cells. Some investigations have therefore focused on the differential impact of reproductive factors on the risk of developing ovarian cancer in the premenopausal years versus the postmenopausal years. In a large study of 896 cases and 967 controls, Moorman and colleagues observed that interruption of the menstrual cycle by either pregnancy or oral contraception conferred protection, but the effect tended to diminish with age during the postmenopausal years (Moorman et al., 2008).

ORAL CONTRACEPTIVES AND OVARIAN CANCER

A number of epidemiologic investigations have observed significant reductions in the risk of ovarian cancer in women who used oral contraceptives

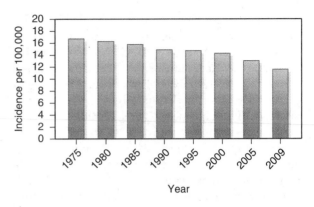

Figure 12.5 Ovarian Cancer Incidence in Caucasian Women, 1975–2006, United States.

Source: Data from American Cancer Society. (2009). *Cancer facts and figures. Statistics for 2009.* Atlanta, GA: Author; Horner, M. J., Ries. L. A. G., Krapcho, M., Neyman, N., Aminou, R., Howlader, N., ... Edwards, B. K. (Eds). *SEER Cancer Statistics Review, 1975–2006.* Bethesda, MD: National Cancer Institute.

(Franceschi et al., 1991; Gross & Schlesselman, 1994; Narod et al., 1998; Schlesselman, 1995). Recently, a comprehensive meta-analysis of 45 epidemiologic studies comparing 23,257 cases with 87,303 controls determined that the use of oral contraceptives reduced the risk by as much as 29% per five years of use (Collaborative Group on Epidemiological Studies of Ovarian Cancer, 2008). Furthermore, the rates of ovarian cancer appear to be declining in some countries as a consequence of widespread oral contraceptive use. For example, the incidence of ovarian cancer in the United States has declined by 30% and mortality rates have declined by 25% since 1975 when oral contraceptive pills were approved for use by premenopausal women (**Figure 12.5**). Oral contraceptives interfere with the pituitary hormones, FSH, and LH, thereby reducing proliferation of epithelial cells at the surface of the ovary and diminishing their potential for carcinogenesis.

SCREENING FOR OVARIAN CANCER

No screening tools have proven successful in detecting ovarian cancer at an early stage (in situ or localized, stage I) when it can be effectively treated by complete surgical excision. As a consequence, more than 70% of these tumors are diagnosed after they have metastasized to contiguous tissue and/or nearby lymph nodes. The overall survival rate is poor, with a five-year survival rate below 50%, even in developed countries such as the United States. Elevated levels of a small antigenic protein called CA-125 secreted by ovarian cancer cells are usually present and measurable at the time of diagnosis; however, this biomarker has only shown value in monitoring cancer regression or progression, and thus far has not proven useful for screening and early detection (Bast et al., 1981, 1998).

● ● ● REFERENCES

Aaltonen, L. A., Peltomiki, P., Leach, F. S., Sistonen, P., Pylkkanen, L., Mecklin, J. P., . . . de la Chapelle, A. (1993). Clues to the pathogenesis of familial colorectal cancer. *Science, 260,* 812–816.

Aaltonen, L. A., Peltomiki, P., Mecklin, J. P., Jirvinen, H., Jass, J. R., Green, J. S., . . . de la Chapelle, A. (1994). Replication errors in benign and malignant tumors from hereditary nonpolyposis colorectal cancer patients. *Cancer Research, 54,* 1645–1648.

Adami, H. O., Hsieh, C. C., Lambe, M., Persson, I., Ekbom, A., Adami, H. O., . . . Janson, P. O. (1994). Parity, age at first childbirth, and risk of ovarian cancer. *Lancet, 344*(8932), 1250–1254.

American Cancer Society. (2009). *Cancer facts and figures.* Atlanta, GA: Author.

Bast, R. C., Feeney, M., Lazarus, H., Nadler, L. M., Colvin, R. B., & Knapp, R. C. (1981). Reactivity of a monoclonal antibody with human ovarian carcinoma. *Journal of Clinical Investigations, 68*(5), 1331–1337.

Bast, R. C., Xu, F. J., Yu, Y. H., Barnhill, S., Zhang, Z., & Mills, G. B. (1998). CA 125: The past and the future. *International Journal of Biological Markers, 13*(4), 179–187.

Beral, V., Million Women Study Collaborators, Bull, D., Green, J., & Reeves, G. (2007). Ovarian cancer and hormone replacement therapy in the Million Women Study. *Lancet, 369*(9574), 1703–1710.

Boulton, S. J. (2006). Cellular functions of the BRCA tumour-suppressor proteins. *Biochemical Society Transactions, 34*(5), 633–645.

Carmina, E. (2004). Diagnosis of polycystic ovary syndrome: From NIH criteria to ESHRE-ASRM guidelines. *Minerva Ginecologica, 56*(1), 1–6.

Chakravarti, S., Collins, W. P., Forecast, J. D., Newton, J. R., Oram, D. H., & Studd, J. W. (1976). Hormonal profiles after the menopause. *British Medical Journal, 2,* 784–787.

Choi, J. H., Choi, K. C., Auersperg, N., & Leung, P. C. (2004). Overexpression of follicle-stimulating hormone receptor activates oncogenic pathways in preneoplastic ovarian surface epithelial cells. *Journal of Clinical Endocrinology and Metabolism, 89,* 5508–5516.

Choi, J. H., Wong, A. S. T., Huang, H. F., & Leung, P. C. K. (2007). Gonadotropins and ovarian cancer. *Endocrine Reviews, 28*(4), 440–461.

Collaborative Group on Epidemiological Studies of Ovarian Cancer. (2008). Ovarian cancer and oral contraceptives: Collaborative reanalysis of data from 45 epidemiological studies including 23,257 women with ovarian cancer and 87,303 controls. *Lancet, 371,* 303–314.

Cottreau, C. M., Ness, R. B., Modugno, F., Allen, G. O., & Goodman, M. T. (2003). Endometriosis and its treatment with danazol or Lupron in relation to ovarian cancer. *Clinical Cancer Research, 9,* 5142–5144.

Coulam, C. B., Annegers, J. F., & Kranz, J. S. (1983). Chronic anovulation syndrome and associated neoplasia. *Obstetrics and Gynecology, 61,* 403–407.

Cramer, D. W. (1989). Lactase persistence and milk consumption as determinants of ovarian cancer risk. *American Journal of Epidemiology, 130*(5), 904–910.

Cramer, D. W., Liberman, R. F., Titus-Ernstoff, L., Welch, W. R., Greenberg, E. R., Baron, J. A., & Harlow, B. L. (1999). Genital talc exposure and risk of ovarian cancer. *International Journal of Cancer, 81,* 351–356.

Fathalla, M. F. (1971). Incessant ovulation—A factor in ovarian neoplasia? *Lancet, 2*(7716), 163.

Ferlay, J., Shin, H.-R., Bray, F., Forman, D., Mathers, C., & Parkin, D. M. (2010). Estimates of worldwide burden of cancer in 2008: GLOBOCAN 2008. *International Journal of Cancer, 127*(12), 2893–2917.

Ferlay J, Soerjomataram I, Ervik M, Dikshit R, Eser S, Mathers C, . . . Bray, F. (2013). *GLOBOCAN 2012 v1.0. Cancer incidence and mortality worldwide: IARC CancerBase No. 11* [Internet]. Lyon, France: International Agency for Research on Cancer. Retrieved from http://globocan.iarc.fr

Franceschi, S., Parazzini, F., Negri, E., Booth, M., La Vecchia, C., Beral, V., . . . Trichopoulos, D. (1991). Pooled analysis of 3 European case-control studies of epithelial ovarian cancer: III. Oral contraceptive use. *International Journal of Cancer, 49*, 61–65.

Gross, T. P., & Schlesselman, J. J. (1994). The estimated effect of oral contraceptive use on the cumulative risk of epithelial ovarian cancer. *Obstetrics and Gynecology, 83*, 419–424.

Gwinn, M. L., Lee, N. C., Rhodes, P. H., Layde, P. M., & Rubin, G. L. (1990). Pregnancy, breast feeding, and oral contraceptives and the risk of epithelial ovarian cancer. *Journal of Clinical Epidemiology, 43*(6), 559–568.

Hall, J. M., Lee, M. K., Newman, B., Morrow, J. E., Anderson, L. A., Huey, B., & King, M. C. (1990). Linkage of early-onset familial breast cancer to chromosome 17q21. *Science, 250*(4988), 1684–1689.

Hankinson, S. E., Colditz, G. A., Hunter, D. J., Willett, W. C., Stampfer, M. J., Rosner, B., . . . Speizer, F. E. (1995). A prospective study of reproductive factors and risk of epithelial ovarian cancer. *Cancer, 76*, 284–290.

Harboe, T. L., Eiberg, E. H., Kern, E. P., Ejlertsen, B., Nedergaard, E. L., Timmermans-Wielenga, V., . . . Bisgaard, M. L. (2009). A high frequent BRCA1 founder mutation identified in the Greenlandic population. *Familial Cancer, 8*, 413–419.

Harlow, B. L., Cramer, D. W., Geller, J., Willett, W. C., Bell, D. A., & Welch, W. R. (1991). The influence of lactose consumption on the association of oral contraceptive use and ovarian cancer risk. *American Journal of Epidemiology, 134*, 445–453.

Helzlsouer, K. J., Alberg, A. J., Gordon, G. B. (1995). Serum gonadotropins and steroid hormones in the development of ovarian cancer. *Journal of the American Medical Association, 274*, 1926–1930.

Holschneider, C. H., & Berek, J. S. (2000). Ovarian cancer: Epidemiology, biology and prognostic factors. *Seminars in Surgical Oncology, 19*, 3–10.

Huncharek, M., Geschwind, J. F., & Kupelnick, B. (2003). Perineal application of cosmetic talc and risk of invasive epithelial ovarian cancer: A meta-analysis of 11,933 subjects from sixteen observational studies. *Anticancer Research, 23*, 1955–1960.

King, M. C., Marks, J. H., Mandell, J. B., & New York Breast Cancer Study Group. (2003). Breast and ovarian cancer risks due to inherited mutations in BRCA1 and BRCA2. *Science, 302*(5645), 643–646.

Kramer, S., Leeker, M., & Jager, W. (1998). Gonadotropin levels in ovarian cyst fluids: A predictor of malignancy? *International Journal of Biological Markers, 13*, 165–168.

Kumar, V., Abbas, A. K., & Aster, J. C. (2014). *Robbins and Cotran pathologic basis of disease* (9th ed.). Philadelphia, PA: Mosby & Saunders.

Larsson, S. C., Bergkvist, L., & Wolk, A. (2004). Milk and lactose intakes and ovarian cancer risk in the Swedish Mammography Cohort. *American Journal of Clinical Nutrition, 80*(5), 1353–1357.

Leitzmann, M. F., Koebnick, C., Danforth, K. N., Brinton, L. A., Moore, S. C., Hollenbeck, A. R., . . . Lacey, J. V. (2009). Body mass index and risk of ovarian cancer. *Cancer, 155*(4), 812–822.

Melin, A., Sparén, P., & Bergqvist, A. (2007). The risk of cancer and the role of parity among women with endometriosis. *Human Reproduction, 22*(11), 3021–3026.

Moorman, P. G., Calingaert, B., Palmieri, R. T., Iversen, E. S., Bentley, R. C., Halabi, S., . . . Schildkraut, J. M. (2008). Hormonal risk factors for ovarian cancer in premenopausal and postmenopausal women. *American Journal of Epidemiology, 167*(9), 1059–1069.

Muscat, J. E., & Huncharek, M. S. (2008). Perineal talc use and ovarian cancer: A critical review. *European Journal of Cancer Prevention, 17,* 139–146.

Narod, S. A., Risch, H., Moslehi, R., Dorum, A., Neuhausen, S., Olsson, H., . . . Klijn, J. G. M. (1998). Oral contraceptives and the risk of hereditary ovarian cancer. *New England Journal of Medicine, 339,* 424–428.

National Cancer Institute. (2009). *Cancer statistics, 2009.* Bethesda, MD: Author.

Ness, R. B., & Cottreau, C. (1999). Possible role of ovarian epithelial inflammation in ovarian cancer. *Journal of the National Cancer Institute, 91,* 1459–1467.

Ness, R. B., Cramer, D. W., Goodman, M. T., Kruger Kjaer, S., & Mallin, K. (2002). Infertility, fertility drugs, and ovarian cancer: A pooled analysis of case–control studies. *American Journal of Epidemiology, 155,* 217–224.

Offit, K., & Kauff, N. D. (2006). Reducing the risk of gynecologic cancer in the Lynch syndrome. *New England Journal of Medicine, 354*(3), 293–295.

Olsen, C. M., Green, A. C., Whiteman, D. C., Sadeghi, S., Kolahdooz, F., & Webb, P. M. (2007). Obesity and the risk of epithelial ovarian cancer: A systematic review and meta-analysis. *European Journal of Cancer, 43,* 690–709.

Parkin, M. D., Bray, F., Ferlay, J., & Pisani, P. (2005). Global cancer statistics, 2002. *CA: A Cancer Journal for Clinicians, 55,* 74–108.

Pierpoint, T., McKeigue, P. M., Isaacs, A. J., Wild, S. H., & Jacobs, H. S. (1998). Mortality of women with polycystic ovary syndrome at long-term follow-up. *Journal of Clinical Epidemiology, 51,* 581–586.

Risch, H. A. (1998). Hormonal etiology of epithelial ovarian cancer, with a hypothesis concerning the role of androgens and progesterone. *Journal of the National Cancer Institute, 90,* 1774–1786.

Risch, H. A., Jain, M., Marrett, L. D., & Howe, G. R. (1994). Dietary lactose intake, lactose intolerance, and the risk of epithelial ovarian cancer in southern Ontario (Canada). *Cancer Causes and Control, 5,* 540–548.

Risch, H. A., Marrett, L. D., & Howe, G. R. (1994). Parity, contraception, infertility, and the risk of epithelial ovarian cancer. *American Journal of Epidemiology, 140,* 585–597.

Rose, D. P., Boyar, A. P., & Wynder, E. L. (1986). International comparisons of mortality rates for cancer of the breast, ovary, prostate, and colon, and per capita food consumption. *Cancer, 58,* 2363–2371.

Rosenblatt, K. A., & Thomas, D. B. (1993). Lactation and the risk of epithelial ovarian cancer. The WHO Collaborative Study of Neoplasia and Steroid Contraceptives. *International Journal of Epidemiology, 22,* 192–197.

Rossing, M. A., Daling, J. R., Weiss, N. S., Moore, D. E., & Self, S. G. (1994). Ovarian tumors in a cohort of infertile women. *New England Journal of Medicine, 331,* 771–776.

Schildkraut, J. M., Schwingl, P. J., Bastos, E., Evanoff, A., & Hughes, C. (1996). Epithelial ovarian cancer risk among women with polycystic ovary syndrome. *Obstetrics and Gynecology, 88*(4 Pt 1), 554–559.

Schlesselman, J. J. (1995). Net effect of oral contraceptive use on the risk of cancer in women in the United States. *Obstetrics and Gynecology, 85*(5Pt 1), 793–801.

Schouten, L. J., Rivera, C., Hunter, D. J., Spiegelman, D., Adami, H. O., Arslan, A., . . . Smith-Warner, S. A. (2008). Height, body mass index, and ovarian cancer: A pooled analysis of 12 cohort studies. *Cancer Epidemiology, Biomarkers and Prevention, 17,* 902–912.

Scully, R. E. (1995). Pathology of ovarian cancer precursors. *Journal of Cellular Biochemistry, 23*(Suppl), 208–218.

Whittemore, A. S., Harris, R., & Itnyre, J. (1992). Characteristics relating to ovarian cancer risk: Collaborative analysis of 12 US case-control studies. II. Invasive epithelial ovarian cancers in white women. *American Journal of Epidemiology, 136,* 1184–1203.

Wooster, R., Neuhausen, S. L., Mangion, J., Quirk, Y., Ford, D., Collins, N., . . . Stratton, M. R. (1994). Localization of a breast cancer susceptibility gene, BRCA2, to chromosome 13q12–13. *Science, 265*(5181), 2088–2090.

Zheng, W., Lu, J. J., Luo, F., Zheng, Y., Feng, Y., Felix, J. C., . . . Pike, M. (2000). Ovarian epithelial tumor growth promotion by follicle-stimulating hormone and inhibition of the effect by luteinizing hormone. *Gynecologic Oncology, 76,* 80–88.

Zhou, B., Sun, Q., Cong, R., Gu, H., Tang, N., Yang, L., & Wang, B. (2008). Hormone replacement therapy and ovarian cancer risk: A meta-analysis. *Gynecologic Oncology, 108*(3), 641–651.

13

Epidemiology of Cancer of the Corpus Uteri: Endometrial Cancer, Uterine Sarcoma, and Choriocarcinoma

GLOBAL IMPACT OF CANCER OF THE CORPUS UTERI

Worldwide, cancer of the *corpus uteri* (body of the uterus) was diagnosed in 319,605 women and caused 76,155 deaths during 2012 (Ferlay et al., 2013). The annual incidence rates of corpus uteri cancer are highest in developed countries of North America, the Russian Federation, Western Europe, and Scandinavia (> 15 cases per 100,000) and lowest in underdeveloped countries of Southeast Asia and Africa (< 3 cases per 100,000) (**Figure 13.1**). Due to shared risk factors that heighten exposure to both endogenous and exogenous estrogens, the global pattern of corpus uteri cancer shows similarities to those of breast cancer and ovarian cancer.

The global burden of cancer of the corpus uteri has increased sharply in the 21st century. During the time span 2000–2012, reported numbers of new cases and deaths have increased by 69% and 70%, respectively (**Figure 13.2**) (Bray, Dos Santos Silva, Moller, & Weiderpass, 2005; Ferlay et al., 2010, 2013; Parkin, Bray, Ferlay, & Pisani, 2001, 2005). These increases are predominantly due to increasing rates of endometrial cancer, which accounts for over 90% of malignancies of the corpus uteri. As discussed in the following sections of this chapter, the rising worldwide burden of endometrial cancer undoubtedly reflects the impact of multiple factors, including better detection and therapy plus heightened exposure to certain risk factors, including late childbearing, lack of breastfeeding, intake of exogenous hormones, intake of diets high in fat and calories, lack of exercise, and in particular, increasing rates of obesity and diabetes mellitus (Bray et al., 2005).

MALIGNANT TUMORS OF THE CORPUS UTERI

Approximately 92% of malignant tumors of the corpus uteri are *endometrial carcinomas* that arise from the epithelial lining of the endometrium. Histologically, more than 90% of endometrial carcinomas are adenocarcinomas that show glandular characteristics under the microscope (Kosary, 2007).

Sarcomas derived from connective tissues of the uterus do occur, but infrequently; for example, leiomyosarcoma of smooth muscle cells and stromal sarcoma of other connective tissues account for about 3% of all uterine cancers (Kosary, 2007). Sarcomas can arise not only in the uterus, but also in many other anatomic sites such as subcutaneous tissue, the peritoneal cavity, the stomach, and omental tissues surrounding the gastrointestinal tract (Kumar, Abbas, & Aster, 2014). Uterine sarcomas are briefly discussed in a later section of this chapter.

Two additional subtypes of corpus uterine cancer, carcinosarcomas and mixed malignant Müllerian tumors, consist of a mixture of glandular and connective tissues. As a consequence, the exact histological classification of such tumors as endometrial carcinomas or sarcomas is controversial and has been debated by pathologists for many years (Kanthan & Senger, 2011). Mixed malignant Müllerian tumors and carcinosarcomas account for about 5% of corpus uteri tumors (Kosary, 2007).

Choriocarcinoma is a very rare type of uterine malignancy that occasionally develops during pregnancy. The epidemiology of choriocarcinoma is included in a later section of this chapter.

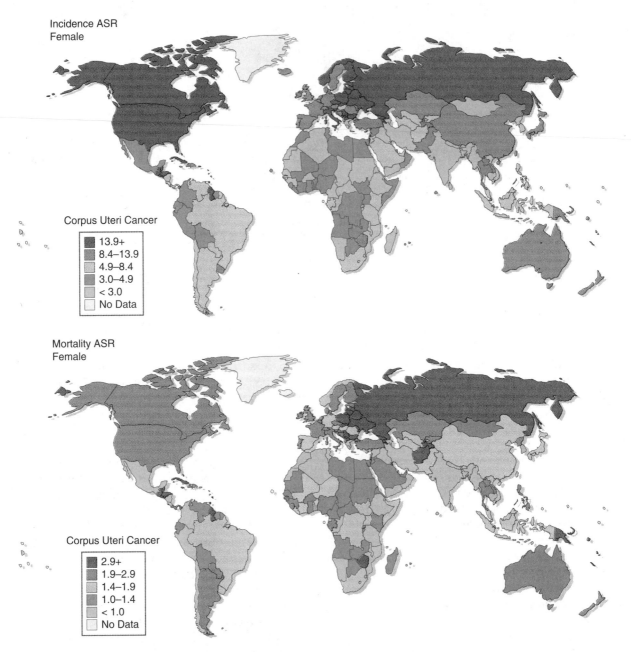

Figure 13.1 Global Rates of Cancer of the Corpus Uteri.

ASR: Rate per 100,000 standardized to the world population, 2000–2025.

Source: Reproduced from Ferlay, J., Soerjomataram, I., Ervik, M., Dikshit, R., Eser, S., Mathers, C.,... Bray, F. (2013). *GLOBOCAN 2012 v1.0. Cancer incidence and mortality worldwide: IARC CancerBase No. 11* [Internet]. Lyon, France: International Agency for Research on Cancer. Retrieved from http://globocan.iarc.fr

ENDOMETRIAL CANCER VERSUS CERVICAL CANCER: CELLULAR ORIGINS

When combined with cervical cancer, malignant neoplasms of the corpus uteri and the endometrium account for more than two-thirds of all invasive malignancies that develop in the female genital tract

(Platz & Benda, 1995). Though they border one another, the cellular populations that give rise to endometrial cancer and cervical cancer are distinctly different.

Endometrial cancer arises from the cuboidal epithelial cells that line the body of the uterus above the cervix, whereas cervical cancer arises from the

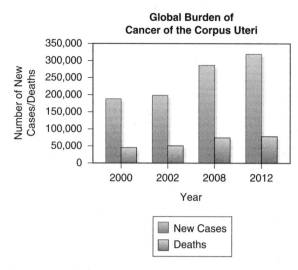

Figure 13.2 Global Increase in Cancer of the Corpus Uteri, 2000–2012.

Sources: Data from Ferlay, J., Bray, F., Pisani, P., & Parkin, D. M. (2004). *GLOBOCAN 2002. Cancer incidence, mortality, and prevalence worldwide. IARC Cancer Base No. 5, version 2.0.* Lyon, France: IARC Press. Retrieved from http://www-dep.iarc.fr; Ferlay, J., Shin, H.-R., Bray, F., Forman, D., Mathers, C., & Parkin, D. M. (2010). Estimates of worldwide burden of cancer in 2008: GLOBOCAN 2008. *International Journal of Cancer, 127*(12), 2893–2917; Ferlay, J., Soerjomataram, I., Ervik, M., Dikshit, R., Eser, S., Mathers, C.,... Bray, F. (2013). *GLOBOCAN 2012 v1.0. Cancer incidence and mortality worldwide: IARC CancerBase No. 11* [Internet]. Lyon, France: International Agency for Research on Cancer. Retrieved from http://globocan.iarc.fr; Parkin, D. M., Bray, F., Ferlay, J., & Pisani, P. (2001). Estimating the world cancer burden: GLOBOCAN 2000. *International Journal of Cancer, 94*, 153–156.

squamous epithelial cells that line the cervix. The corpus uterus is the hollow pear-shaped organ in which the placenta is implanted and the fetus develops during pregnancy. The endometrium per se refers to the innermost glandular layer of the corpus uterus. The anatomic distinction between the endometrium and the cervix can be seen in **Figure 13.3** (Kumar et al., 2014).

In world population studies by the International Association of Cancer Research (IARC), cases that are pathologically confirmed as endometrial cancer or cancer of the body of the uterus (*corpus uteri*) are all coded under the *International Code of Disease* as ICD 54. In contrast, cervical cancer is coded separately as ICD 53. It should be noted that cases of *unspecified uterine cancer* are coded as ICD 55, which are allocated to endometrial cancer or cervical cancer according to the differential age distributions of these tumors (Loos et al., 2004).

TRENDS IN ENDOMETRIAL CANCER

In developed regions of the world, endometrial cancer has surpassed cervical cancer as the leading gynecological malignancy in women (Sankaranarayanan & Ferlay, 2006). As shown in **Figures 13.4 and 13.5**, the annual incidence rates of endometrial cancer among U.S. women have trended upward

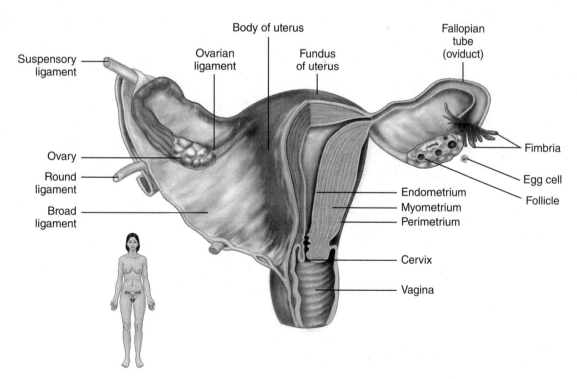

Figure 13.3 Female Reproductive Anatomy.

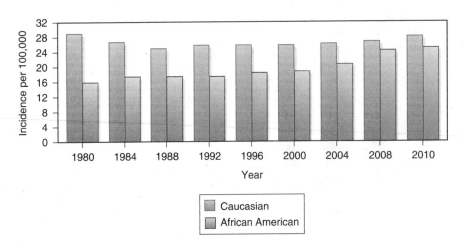

Figure 13.4 Incidence of Endometrial Cancer, United States, 1980–2010.

Source: Data from Howlader, N., Noone, A. M., Krapcho, M., Garshell, J., Neyman, N., Altekruse, S. F., . . . Cronin, K. A. (Eds.). (2012, November). *SEER cancer statistics review, 1975–2010*. Bethesda, MD: National Cancer Institute. Retrieved from http://seer.cancer.gov/csr/1975_2010/

since 2000 and are now three to four times higher than cervical cancer rates, which continue to decline (Duong, Wilson, Ajani, Singh, & Eheman, 2011; Hayat, Howlader, Reichman, & Edwards, 2007; Howlader et al., 2012). Recent increases in the incidence of endometrial cancer and declining rates of cervical cancer are also evident in Great Britain, Western Europe, Scandinavia, and Australia (Bray et al., 2005; Evans et al., 2011; Purdie & Green, 2001; Saso et al., 2011). These trends undoubtedly reflect greater exposure to major risk factors for endometrial cancer (e.g., obesity, insulin resistance, estrogen replacement therapy, tamoxifen) plus the significant impact of successful screening for precancerous cervical lesions by Papanicolaou cytological testing (the Pap test).

In contrast to the pattern in developed nations, women living in underdeveloped nations have markedly higher rates of cervical cancer than endometrial cancer. This is due to the high rates of genital infections by oncogenic strains of human papillomavirus (HPV) in women living in underdeveloped nations. Although HPV infections account for virtually all cases of cervical cancer, their role in the genesis of endometrial cancer is negligible.

ENDOMETRIAL CANCER: POSTMENOPAUSAL AGE OF ONSET

The vast majority of cases of endometrial cancer (nearly 95%) are detected in postmenopausal women

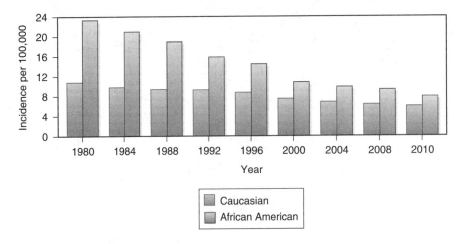

Figure 13.5 Incidence of Cervical Cancer, United States, 1980–2010.

Source: Data from Howlader, N., Noone, A. M., Krapcho, M., Garshell, J., Neyman, N., Altekruse, S. F., . . . Cronin, K. A. (Eds.). (2012, November). *SEER cancer statistics review, 1975–2010*. Bethesda, MD: National Cancer Institute. Retrieved from http://seer.cancer.gov/csr/1975_2010/

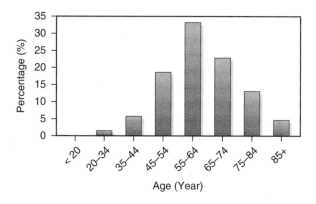

Figure 13.6 Age at Diagnosis of Endometrial Cancer.

Source: Data from National Cancer Institute. (n.d.). Fast stats. Retrieved from http://seer.cancer.gov/faststats

after the age of 45 years (**Figure 13.6**). Based on data from the United States collected during 2006–2010, the median age at diagnosis is 62 years (National Cancer Institute, n.d.).

SUBTYPES OF ENDOMETRIAL CANCER

Endometrial cancers can be classified according to their dependence (or lack of dependence) on estrogen for growth and development. Type 1 cancers are estrogen-dependent and positive for estrogen receptors (ER positive) (Bender, Buekers, & Leslie, 2011). They develop in women in association with obesity, hyperlipidemia, hyperestrogenism, anovulatory uterine bleeding, infertility, late onset of menopause, and hyperplasia of the epithelial lining of the endometrium (Bokhman, 1983). Type 1 endometrial cancers are typically low-grade, well-differentiated adenocarcinomas that have a favorable prognosis. Type 1 tumors are also called *endometrioid endometrial carcinomas*. They account for about 90% of all endometrial cancers (Felix et al., 2010).

Type 2 endometrial cancers are non-estrogen-dependent and are ER negative. Type 2 endometrial cancers are typically high-grade serous carcinomas associated with poor survival. They account for about 10% of all endometrial cancers (Amant et al., 2005).

MODELS OF ENDOMETRIAL CARCINOGENESIS

Similar molecular mechanisms may be at work in the genesis of endometrial cancer and breast cancer. Both tumors arise from epithelial cell populations that are rich in estrogen and progesterone receptors

and thus responsive to ovarian fluctuations in estrogen and progesterone during the menstrual cycle in premenopausal women and to other sources of estrogen in postmenopausal women. As a consequence, sustained exposure to estrogen, particularly in the absence of progesterone (unopposed estrogen), may lead to an increasing mitotic rate and atypical hyperplasia of the mammary epithelium or endometrial epithelium, which increases the chance of cancer development (Key & Pike, 1988a, 1988b). Sources of excessive estrogen exposure may be endogenous, exogenous, or both, as discussed later in this section.

Barry Sherman and Stanley Korenman originally proposed that heightened *endogenous* exposure to unopposed estrogen is most likely to occur during two windows of time: early in life at menarche when menstruation begins and later in life at menopause when menstrual cycles cease. They postulated that exposure to unopposed estrogen occurs in association with abnormal maturation of follicles (containing unfertilized eggs) as well as irregular or deficient progesterone production by the corpus luteum (the remnant follicle after ovulation). Their theory of corpus luteum dysfunction as the cause of unopposed estrogen and heightened breast cancer risk is called the *estrogen window hypothesis* (Korenman, 1980; Sherman & Korenman, 1974).

In considering the estrogen window hypothesis of either breast cancer or endometrial cancer, it is essential to review key features of the human female menstrual cycle, as shown in **Figure 13.7**. During the *follicular proliferative phase*, which lasts about 10 days in an ordinary 28-day cycle, follicular stimulating hormone (FSH) is secreted by the pituitary gland, which stimulates maturation of ovarian follicles containing unfertilized eggs. The maturing ovarian follicles secrete increasing amounts of estrogen, causing accelerated cell proliferation and thickening of the endometrial epithelium. Both FSH and estrogen peak at the time of ovulation, which involves the rupture of one follicle and release of its unfertilized egg into the fallopian tube. After ovulation, luteinizing hormone (LH) from the pituitary gland stimulates the *luteal secretory phase* of the cycle, which lasts for about 14 days. During this phase, the corpus luteum secretes progesterone, which induces the development of spiral arteries and stromal edema of the endometrium. In the absence of fertilization, the *menstrual phase* of the cycle occurs, which lasts about 4 days. During menses, the endometrial lining is shed, and blood and tissue are discharged from the uterus.

According to the *estrogen window hypothesis*, unopposed estrogen due to corpus luteum dysfunction during anovulatory cycles of the perimenopausal

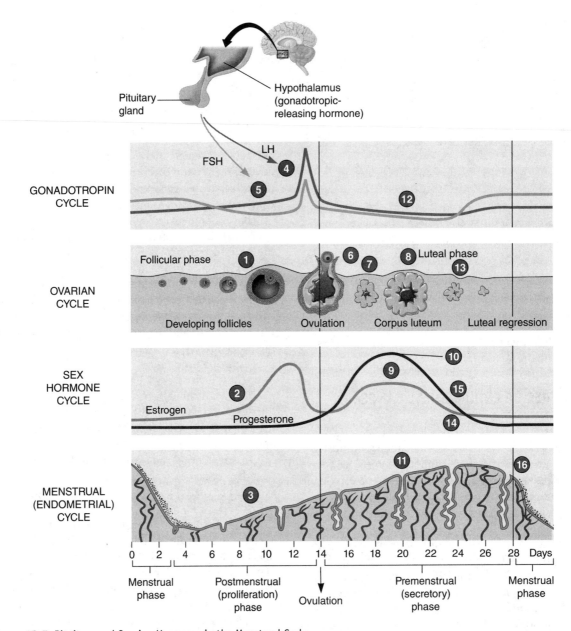

Figure 13.7 Pituitary and Ovarian Hormones in the Menstrual Cycle.

Note: Endometrial cancer risk is increased by exposure to unopposed estrogen and inflammatory factors. Inflammation and wound healing are present with the shedding and repair of the endometrium during menstruation. Unopposed estrogen is present in anovulatory cycles because no corpus luteum forms and progesterone is absent.

time window elevates the risk of cancer development in the epithelial tissues of the mammary gland and the endometrium (Korenman, 1980; Sherman & Korenman, 1974). With cessation of menstruation at menopause, the ovaries abruptly discontinue secretion of both estrogen and progesterone. However, in some women this biological phenomenon opens a window of time during which irregular or anovulatory cycles occur, resulting in heightened exposure to unopposed estrogen from either continuing production of estrogen

in the absence of progesterone or amplified enzymatic conversion of other steroids to estrogen by aromatase in fat and muscle. An earlier time window of unopposed estrogen may also occur in young women around the time of menarche when anovulatory menstrual cycles are more likely to occur (Korenman, 1980).

Several factors must be considered in assessing a woman's level of exposure to excessive levels of unopposed estrogen. These include reproductive history (pregnancy and lactation), long-term use of oral contraceptives, surgical history (e.g., hysterectomy and oophorectomy), postmenopausal estrogen replacement therapy (with or without progesterone), obesity, and chronic cigarette smoking (Key & Pike, 1988a, 1988b; Sherman, Wallace, & Korenman, 1981).

An alternative model postulates that the chronic repetitive inflammatory process of menstruation may also play an important role in the genesis of endometrial cancer. The shedding and repair of the endometrium during menstruation obviously includes inflammation and wound healing as physiologic components. Thus, in the absence of a pregnancy, the endometrium is cyclically exposed to chronic repetitive inflammation involving the release of multiple inflammatory factors (prostaglandins, cytokines, and growth factors) that could influence the initiation and progression of endometrial malignancies (Modugno, Ness, Chen, & Weiss, 2005).

RISK FACTORS FOR ENDOMETRIAL CANCER

Estrogenic risk factors for endometrial cancer are broadly divisible into (1) reproductive hallmarks and medical conditions that heighten exposure to *endogenous estrogens*, and (2) lifestyle choices that result in exposure to *exogenous estrogens*. Conversely, avoidance of excessive exposure to estrogen reduces the risk. Genetic factors play a minor role. The profile of endometrial cancer risk factors is similar to those for breast cancer and ovarian cancer.

Factors that increase the risk include early menarche, nulliparity, late menopause, obesity, type 2 diabetes mellitus, estrogen replacement therapy, and use of medications that modulate estrogen receptors. Factors that decrease the risk include high parity, late age at last pregnancy, the use of oral contraceptives, and tobacco smoking (Purdie & Green, 2001; Schottenfeld, 1995). Removal of the endometrium and/or the ovaries by hysterectomy and/or oophorectomy for conditions other than cancer must be taken into account in the assessment of risk.

Reproductive Hallmarks and Endometrial Cancer

Early menarche, nulliparity, and late menopause have all been consistently found to increase the risk of developing endometrial cancer. Conversely, late menarche, high parity, and early menopause are associated with decreases in risk. Unlike breast cancer, early age at first full-term pregnancy has no effect on the risk of endometrial cancer. Rather, *late age at a last pregnancy* appears to reduce the risk (MacMahon, 1974; McPherson, Sellers, Potter, Bostick, & Folsom, 1996; Purdie & Green, 2001).

Recently, a team of investigators analyzed data from the European Prospective Investigation into Cancer and Nutrition (EPIC) to re-examine the association of menstrual and reproductive factors and the risk of developing endometrial cancer. In the EPIC database, 1,017 incident cases of endometrial cancer were identified among 302,618 women enrolled for study from 10 European countries (Denmark, France, Germany, Greece, Italy, the Netherlands, Norway, Spain, Sweden, and the United Kingdom). Results revealed significant risk reductions associated with late menarche, early menopause, past use of oral contraceptives (OC), high parity, and shorter time since last full-term pregnancy. Compared to nulliparous women, parous women had a 35% reduction in the risk of developing endometrial cancer. Among parous women, the number of full-term pregnancies and the age at last pregnancy were inversely related to risk. After multivariate adjustment, late age at menarche, early age at menopause, and duration of OC use showed similar risk reductions of 7–8% per year of menstrual life, whereas the decreased risk associated with cumulative duration of full-term pregnancies was stronger (22% per year). The investigators concluded that "our findings confirmed a reduction in risk of endometrial cancer with factors associated with a lower cumulative exposure to estrogen and/or higher exposure to progesterone, such as increasing number of full term pregnancies and shorter menstrual lifespan and, therefore, support an important role of hormonal mechanisms in endometrial carcinogenesis" (Dossus et al., 2010).

Polycystic Ovary Syndrome and Premenopausal Endometrial Cancer

Certain menstrual cycle irregularities increase the risk of developing endometrial cancer in premenopausal women. One such condition is *polycystic ovary syndrome* (also known as Stein–Leventhal syndrome) wherein women of reproductive age develop bilateral ovarian cysts in association with prolonged anovulation, infertility, excess ovarian secretion of androgens, masculinizing symptoms (e.g., hirsutism), and endometriosis (Radosh, 2009). A recent prevalence study suggests that about 7% of U.S. women are afflicted with polycystic ovary syndrome (Azziz et al., 2004).

The link between polycystic ovary syndrome and endometrial cancer was first observed more than half a century ago (Dockerty, Loveday, & Foust, 1951; Jackson & Dockerty, 1957; Speert, 1949). In a recent study of Australian women, the medical history of polycystic ovary syndrome was assessed among

156 cases and 398 controls under the age of 50 years. Results showed that women with polycystic ovaries had a fourfold increase in risk compared to healthy women (Fearnley et al., 2010). One mechanism underlying this association is that during anovulatory menstrual cycles the endometrium receives increased exposure to estrogens unopposed by progesterone (Jafari, Javaheri, & Ruiz, 1978; Navaratnarajah, Pillay, & Hardiman, 2008).

Granulosa Cell Ovarian Tumors and Endometrial Cancer

Granulosa cell tumors of the ovary occasionally occur in association with heterogeneous symptoms of the female genital tract, including menstrual cycle irregularities, infertility, vaginal bleeding, pelvic pain, and uterine pathologies. These tumors are uncommon and account for only 2–5% of all ovarian malignancies. Because human ovarian granulosa cells secrete estrogen, women who develop granulosa cell ovarian tumors manifest marked increases in circulating estrogens, which in turn stimulate estrogen receptors in other tissues such as the endometrium. As a consequence, women who develop ovarian granulosa cell tumors are prone to the development of endometrial hyperplasia and endometrial carcinoma. Granulosa cell tumors also typically secrete inhibin, a polypeptide hormone that regulates FSH secretion by the anterior pituitary gland. Due to hyperestrogenism and hormonal imbalance, endometrial cancer develops in about 10% of women with ovarian granulosa cell tumors (Malmström, Högberg, Risberg, & Simonsen, 1994; Schumer & Cannistra, 2003).

In a molecular study of tissue samples of granulosa cell ovarian tumors, 90 of 93 cases (97%) manifested a somatic mutation that mapped to the same location in the *FOXL2* gene on chromosome 3. Because *FOXL2* is required for the normal development and function of granulosa cells in ovarian tissue, further studies of its mutant form may aid in diagnosis and provide new modalities and molecular targets for prevention and therapeutic intervention (Shah et al., 2009).

Endometriosis and Endometrial Cancer

Endometriosis is the abnormal presence of endometrial glands in the myometrium (muscle) of the female genital tract (e.g., ovaries, uterine ligaments, vagina). This is a common gynecologic condition with a prevalence of about 10% among women of reproductive age (Viganò, Parazzini, Somigliana, & Vercellini., 2004). The pathogenesis of endometriosis is most often attributed to retrograde implantation of endometrial glands external to the uterus during menstruation. Although endometriosis has been linked to the development of ovarian cancer, current evidence *does not* support an association between endometriosis and the development of endometrial cancer (Brinton, Gridley, Persson, Baron, & Bergqvist, 1997).

Obesity and Endometrial Cancer

The role of obesity as a significant risk factor for endometrial cancer has been firmly established. In a meta-analysis of 16 epidemiologic studies, the pooled relative risk (RR) for obese women compared to women of normal weight was elevated nearly twofold (RR = 1.85, 95% confidence interval 1.30–2.65, $P < 0.0001$). In the study, women with a body mass index (BMI) of 30 or more were compared to those with a BMI less than 25. The largest of the studies included in the meta-analysis was a prospective examination of 103,882 women who participated in the American Association of Retired Persons Diet and Health Study, which was designed to address the effects of dietary and lifestyle factors on cancer risk. In this investigation, similar increases in risk were observed for obese women (RR = 3.03) and women who had gained more than 20 kg (44 pounds) since age 18 (RR = 2.75) (Chang et al., 2007). The association among obesity, excess adiposity, and the development of endometrial cancer is biologically plausible because obese women tend to have higher endogenous estrogen levels than lean women due to aromatization of androstenedione in adipose tissue. Obese women have also been found to have reduced levels of sex hormone–binding globulin compared to lean women, which increases the bioavailability of estrogens (Simpson & Brown, 2011).

Diabetes Mellitus and Endometrial Cancer

Many epidemiologic investigations have observed that women with a medical history of diabetes mellitus are at increased risk of developing endometrial cancer. The role of both type 1 and type 2 diabetes was examined in a meta-analysis of 16 studies (3 cohort and 13 case control studies) including data on 96,003 subjects and 7,596 cases of endometrial cancer. Summary relative risk estimates revealed a twofold risk increase for type 2 diabetics (RR = 2.10) and a threefold increase for type 1 diabetics (RR = 3.15) (Friberg, Orsini, Mantzoros, & Wolk, 2007).

The biological basis of this association may be related to hyperinsulinemia due to the insulin resistance of type 2 diabetes or insulin therapy for type 1 diabetes; that is, chronically elevated levels of circulating insulin may stimulate the proliferation of endometrial epithelium by binding to insulin receptors in endometrial tissues (Nagamani & Stuart, 1998). Hyperinsulinemia may also increase exposure to bioactive estrogens by decreasing the activity of sex hormone–binding globulin (Nestler et al., 1991). Furthermore, obesity is a major risk factor for type 2 diabetes, and the presence of both conditions has been found to synergistically increase the risk of developing endometrial cancer (Lucenteforte et al., 2007).

Hormone Replacement and Endometrial Cancer

In the early 1970s, the incidence of endometrial cancer abruptly doubled among Caucasian women in the United States (**Figure 13.8**). This phenomenon was observed shortly after a marked increase in estrogen replacement therapy (equine estrogens) for the treatment of hot flashes at the time of menopause in some U.S. women (Purdie & Green, 2001).

Subsequent epidemiologic studies consistently revealed significant increases in the risk of developing endometrial cancer among women who received estrogen replacement therapy. In an international study of 425 cases and 792 controls, the use of estrogen replacement therapy was found to increase the risk of developing early stage endometrial cancer by more than fivefold and late stage cancer by more than threefold. Furthermore, the risk persisted for more than 10 years after discontinuation of use (Shapiro et al., 1985).

Another striking example of the link between endometrial cancer and estrogen replacement therapy comes from a longitudinal study of postmenopausal women in a California retirement community. In this investigation, women who reported any exposure to estrogen replacement therapy had a relative risk of 10 compared to women with no exposure and women with 15 years of exposure, who had a relative risk of 20 (Paganini-Hill, Ross, & Henderson, 1989). A meta-analysis of 30 studies found a summary relative risk of 2.3 among women who had ever received estrogen replacement therapy and a 10-fold risk increase after 10 or more years of use (Grady, Gebretsadik, Kerlikowske, Ernster, & Petitti, 1996).

Fortunately, the administration of progesterone in each treatment cycle has been found to mitigate the deleterious mitogenic effects of unopposed estrogen therapy. The decline in the incidence of endometrial cancer to pre-1970 levels during the 1980s (shown in Figure 13.8) is ascribed to the introduction of progesterones as part of the hormonal replacement regimen (Ziel, Finkle, & Greenland, 1998).

Despite some evidence suggesting that the estrogen plus progesterone regimens do not increase the risk of developing endometrial cancer, recent studies have provided mixed results on this controversial issue. In a study of 541 incident cases of endometrial cancer detected among 30,379 postmenopausal women enrolled in the Breast Cancer Detection Demonstration Project (BCDDP), endometrial cancer risk increased by 0.38 per year of estrogen plus progesterone use, and the risk remained elevated for more than 10 years after the cessation of use (Lacey et al., 2005).

In sharp contrast, a study of 433 incident cases of endometrial cancer among 73,211 women enrolled

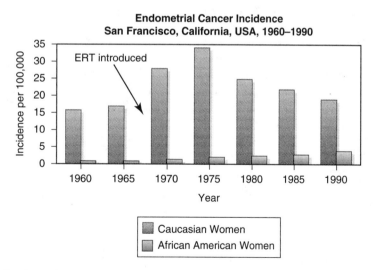

Figure 13.8 Incidence of Endometrial Cancer Among Women in San Francisco, California, United States, 1960–1990.

Source: Data from Purdie, D. M., & Green, A. C. (2001). Epidemiology of endometrial cancer. *Best Practice and Research Clinical Obstetrics and Gynaecology, 16*(3), 341–354.

in the National Institutes of Health–AARP Diet and Health Study during 1995–2000 found that estrogen plus progesterone regimens neither increased nor decreased the risk of developing endometrial cancer (Lacey et al., 2007).

Further complicating this issue is the impact of hormone replacement therapy on the risk of developing other medical conditions. In the Women's Health Initiative (WHI), a placebo-controlled randomized clinical trial in which 8,506 postmenopausal women received estrogen plus progesterone and 8,102 women received placebo, significant risk increases were noted in the treated group for coronary heart disease, stroke, pulmonary embolism, and breast cancer whereas risk reductions were observed for colorectal cancer and hip fracture. Notably, the overall health risks exceeded the health benefits. The authors stated that "despite decades of accumulated observational evidence, the balance of risks and benefits for hormone use in healthy postmenopausal women remains uncertain" (Rossouw et al., 2002).

Selective Estrogen Receptor Modulators (SERMs) and Endometrial Cancer

Randomized clinical trials of breast cancer patients conducted in the 1970s found that tamoxifen, a drug that selectively modulates estrogen receptors, reduces the risk of cancer of the contralateral breast as well as the recurrence of breast cancer. These results soon led to the approval of tamoxifen for routine use as adjuvant therapy for women with breast cancer (Jordan, 1997). However, follow-up studies of women who received tamoxifen determined that they had an increased incidence of endometrial cancer (Fisher et al., 1994). In a case control study of 324 cases of endometrial cancer and 671 controls, the use of tamoxifen for 2–4 years was found to double the risk of endometrial cancer; longer duration of use quadrupled the risk. Notably, results of this study also showed that combined exposure to tamoxifen and estrogen replacement therapy in obese women increased the risk of developing endometrial cancer by almost ninefold (Bernstein et al., 1999). Molecular studies indicate that tamoxifen has estrogenic effects on the endometrial epithelium and may also have genotoxic properties, which may account for its association with endometrial cancer (Brown, 2009).

Radiation Therapy and Endometrial Cancer

Women who develop primary cancers of the pelvic organs (kidneys, urinary bladder, colon, rectum, cervix, vulva, or vagina) may receive therapeutic radiation. Such patients have an increased risk of developing second primary malignancies in tissues that are inadvertently exposed to high dosages of ionizing radiation (Boice et al., 1985). In a study of 205 cases with radiation-associated endometrial cancer, the mean latency period between diagnosis of the primary pelvic tumor and the onset of endometrial cancer was 110 months. Radiation-associated endometrial cancers are typically poorly differentiated advanced stage malignancies that carry a grave prognosis (Kumar et al., 2009).

Oral Contraceptives and Endometrial Cancer

Standard regimens of oral contraceptives currently in use involve the administration of estrogen and progesterone during the menstrual cycle to prevent pregnancy by suppressing ovulation. In most oral contraceptive regimens, the progesterone component prevents the surge of LH from the pituitary gland that is required for the release of the ovum from the ovary.

A significant body of scientific evidence suggests that use of oral contraceptives decreases the risk of some gynecologic malignancies, including ovarian cancer and endometrial cancer. In a highly instructive meta-analysis of 11 studies of oral contraceptive use and endometrial cancer, the duration of use was found to be inversely related to the risk. Compared to women with no exposure, 12 years of using oral contraceptives was estimated to reduce the risk of developing endometrial cancer by 72% (**Figure 13.9**). Furthermore, the data suggested that the protective effect of oral contraceptive use persisted after discontinuation; for example, 20 years after stopping use, the risk in former users was 50% below that of women who never used oral contraceptives (Schlesselman, 1997).

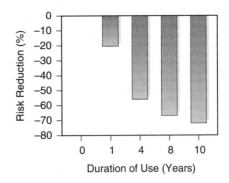

Figure 13.9 Endometrial Cancer Risk and Oral Contraceptive Use.

Source: Data from Schlesselman, J. J. (1997). Risk of endometrial cancer in relation to use of combined oral contraceptives. A practitioner's guide to meta-analysis. *Human Reproduction, 12,* 1851–1863.

Smoking and Endometrial Cancer

A number of epidemiologic studies have consistently found that women who smoke cigarettes are at *reduced risk* of developing endometrial cancer. In a meta-analysis of 34 epidemiologic studies (20 prospective and 24 case control studies), the combined relative risk for ever smokers compared to never smokers was reduced by 19% (RR = 0.81), and heavier smoking was found to be inversely related to the risk. Estimated risk reductions were stronger in postmenopausal women (RR = 0.71) and women who received estrogen replacement therapy (RR = 0.45) (Zhou et al., 2008). The biological basis of the inverse association of smoking and the risk of endometrial cancer remains to be clarified. Some studies suggest that circulating estrogens are decreased and androgens are increased in smokers (Michnovicz, Hershcopf, Naganuma, Bradlow, & Fishman, 1986); however, interactions of chronic smoking with weight, diet, and exercise make the issue highly complex.

Exercise and Endometrial Cancer

Sedentary behavior may contribute to the development of endometrial cancer, and reciprocally, physical activity may be protective. In a meta-analysis of nine prospective studies, women who reported high levels of physical activity reduced their risk of developing endometrial cancer by about 25% compared to inactive women (Moore, Gierach, Schatzkin, & Matthews, 2010). Biologically, physical activity reduces obesity and central adiposity and can lead to favorable changes in the balance of endogenous estrogens and androgens.

Diet and Endometrial Cancer

Among the dietary factors that have been studied, coffee consumption has shown the most consistent inverse association with the risk of endometrial cancer. In a meta-analysis of two cohort studies (201 cases) and seven case control studies (2,409 cases), regular coffee drinkers versus nondrinkers had an overall 20% reduction in risk, and heavy coffee consumers (four or more cups per day) reduced their risk by 36% (Bravi et al., 2009).

More recently, investigators in the Nurse's Health Study (NHS) examined coffee consumption and endometrial cancer risk among 27,470 female participants over a period of 26 years during 1980–2006. A total of 672 incident cases of endometrial cancer were diagnosed in the study. Results revealed that women consuming four or more cups of coffee daily had a 25% lower risk than women consuming less than one cup daily (Je, Hankinson, Tworoger, DeVivo, & Giovannucci, 2011).

Biologically, high concentrations of caffeine are present in most blends of coffee (60–100 mg per cup), and caffeine has antioxidant properties that may inhibit carcinogenesis. High levels of coffee and caffeine intake have also been found to improve insulin sensitivity and reduce levels of endogenous estrogens, factors thought to reduce the risk (Kotsopoulos, Eliassen, Missmer, Hankinson, & Tworoger, 2009; Wu, Willett, Hankinson, & Giovannucci, 2005).

Aspirin and Endometrial Cancer

Regular intake of aspirin and other nonsteroidal anti-inflammatory drugs (NSAIDs) appears to protect against the development of many forms of cancer. To examine the effects of NSAIDs on the development of endometrial cancer, a team of investigators examined data from the Australian National Endometrial Cancer Study (ANECS), a population-based study of 1,398 cases and 740 controls. Results revealed that women who reported taking two or more regular aspirin tablets per week reduced their risk of developing endometrial cancer by nearly 50% compared to those reporting no intake. Ever use of non-aspirin NSAIDs (e.g., ibuprofen) was also associated with a significant decrease in the risk, and the observed risk reductions with aspirin/NSAID use were similar for both type 1 and type 2 endometrial cancer. Systematic review of the published literature identified nine studies of NSAIDs and endometrial cancer. A pooled meta-analysis of these data revealed a significant risk reduction with regular aspirin use, particularly in obese women (Neill et al., 2013). These results demonstrate chemopreventive effects of aspirin and other NSAIDs against the development of endometrial cancer. Biologically, aspirin and other NSAIDs block the cyclooxygenase-2 (COX-2) enzyme that triggers the prostaglandin inflammatory cascade (Harris, 2002, 2007).

Hysterectomy and Endometrial Cancer

Hysterectomy, the surgical removal of the uterus, is a frequent major surgical procedure among women of reproductive age in developed nations such as the United States. Women who have had a hysterectomy for conditions other than cancer obviously eliminate their risk of developing endometrial cancer; failure to remove these women from the population at risk leads to an underestimate of endometrial cancer incidence (Jamison, Noone, Ries, Lee, & Edwards, 2013). Correction of incidence rates of endometrial cancer becomes very important in populations with high prevalence rates of hysterectomy.

In a study of endometrial cancer and hysterectomy utilizing data from the Surveillance, Epidemiology, and

End Results (SEER) cancer registries and the Behavioral Risk Factor Surveillance System (BRFSS) of the United States during 1992–2008, the observed prevalence of hysterectomy among women of reproductive age was 41% for Caucasians and 47% for African Americans. Correction for hysterectomy increased the annual incidence rates by 73% and 90%, respectively, 136 per 100,000 for Caucasians and 115 per 100,000 for African American women 50 years and older. The authors concluded that "comparisons of rates of endometrial cancer among racial groups may be misleading in the absence of denominator correction for hysterectomy prevalence" (Jamison et al., 2013).

Molecular Genetics of Endometrial Cancer

Tumor Suppressor Genes and Endometrial Cancer

Loss of function of the *PTEN* tumor suppressor gene located on the long arm of human chromosome 10 is a frequent event in the genesis of type 1 (estrogen-dependent) endometrial cancer. In a recent molecular study of endometrial cancer tissues, somatic *PTEN* mutations were identified by immunohistochemistry in 64% of cases (Djordjevic et al., 2012). Somatic mutations in *PTEN* have been found to elevate the risk of not only endometrial cancer, but also prostate cancer and glioblastoma (Sansal & Sellers, 2004; Steck et al., 1997).

Endometrial cancer also occurs in Cowden's disease, a rare genetic condition caused by a germline mutation in *PTEN*. Cowden's disease is characterized by a spectrum of neoplasms, including cancers of the breast, thyroid, and endometrium, plus the presence of multiple hamartomas (small benign papules of the skin and mucous membranes) (Eng, 1998).

The *PTEN* gene encodes the enzymatic protein *phosphatase and tensin homolog*, which functions as a tumor suppressor by dephosphorylating protein kinase B (*PKB*, also known as *Akt*). Normal *PTEN* function is important in regulating the intracellular *PKB/Akt* signaling pathway to maintain tight control of the rates of cell division and programmed cell death (apoptosis) (Lee et al., 1999).

Normal *PTEN* function may be compromised by germline mutations, somatic mutations, or epigenetic mechanisms such as DNA methylation (Djordjevic et al., 2012). The silencing of *PTEN* in estrogen-responsive tissues (e.g., the endometrial epithelium) leads to constitutive activation of the *PKB/Akt* signaling cascade, which results in uncontrolled cell proliferation and enhanced cell survival, thereby increasing the risk of dysplasia and cancer development. Interestingly, progesterone counteracts the loss of *PTEN* function, and the administration of progesterone-containing agents has proven effective in the treatment of endometrial dysplasia and localized endometrial cancer (Luo, Manning, & Cantley, 2003; Zheng, Baker, & Mutter, 2004).

In contrast to type 1 (estrogen-dependent) endometrial cancer, type 2 (non-estrogen-dependent) is commonly associated with *p53* mutations that result in abnormal accumulation of abnormal *p53* protein and deregulation of the cell cycle. Mutations in *p53* lead to excessive cell proliferation, hyperplasia, and malignant transformation of the endometrial epithelium (Okuda et al., 2010).

Oncogenes and Endometrial Cancer

Mutational events that enhance rather than suppress the function of certain genes have been detected in tissue studies of endometrial cancer, particularly type 1 endometrial cancer (endometrioid endometrial cancer). Genes that increase carcinogenesis by somatic mutations or epigenetic mechanisms leading to their activation or overexpression are called *proto-oncogenes*. Mutated forms of two such proto-oncogenes, *K-ras* and *β-catenin*, have been observed in excess in studies of endometrial cancer tissues. Molecular studies suggest that mutated forms of these proto-oncogenes stimulate cell proliferation and inhibit apoptosis (Okuda et al., 2010; Peifer, 1997; Sasaki et al., 1993).

Lynch Syndrome and Endometrial Cancer

Endometrial cancer is a significant component of Lynch syndrome (hereditary nonpolyposis colorectal cancer), named after Henry T. Lynch who documented two large kindreds with this autosomal dominant syndrome (Lynch, Shaw, Magnuson, Larsen, & Krush, 1966). The cause of Lynch syndrome is an inherited (germline) mutation in at least one of a set of genes that normally repair DNA, the mismatch repair genes. Mutant forms of two mismatch repair genes, *MSH2* and *MLH1*, account for over 90% of cases with Lynch syndrome (Aaltonen et al., 1993, 1994). Women who inherit either of these genes have a markedly increased lifetime risk (40 to 60%) of developing not only colorectal cancer, but also endometrial cancer. Germline mutations in mismatch repair genes account for about 2% of all prevalent cases of endometrial cancer and about 9% of cases that are diagnosed before the age of 50 years (Meyer, Broaddus, & Lu, 2009).

SUMMARY: EPIDEMIOLOGY OF ENDOMETRIAL CANCER

In developed regions of the world, endometrial cancer has surpassed cervical cancer as the leading gynecological malignancy in women, and incidence rates appear to be rising in these populations. The majority of cases (90%) are diagnosed in postmenopausal women. Factors that increase exposure to estrogen in the absence of progesterone (unopposed estrogen) increase the risk (e.g., early menarche, anovulatory menstrual cycles, nulliparity, late menopause, estrogen replacement therapy, and in particular, obesity). Reciprocally, factors that decrease estrogen exposure reduce the risk (e.g., oral contraceptives and tobacco smoking). Current evidence also suggests that women who drink coffee or take aspirin regularly are at lower risk. Therapy of breast cancer patients with tamoxifen, a selective estrogen receptor modulator (SERM), has consistently been found to increase their risk of developing endometrial cancer.

Somatic mutations causing loss of function of the *PTEN* tumor suppressor gene, which regulates cell division and apoptosis, are found in more than 60% of type 1 (estrogen-dependent) endometrial tumors whereas *p53* mutations are more common in type 2 (non-estrogen-dependent) tumors. Germline mutations in mismatch repair genes that also predispose to colorectal cancer have been observed in familial endometrial cancer.

Certain medical conditions also increase the risk (e.g., polycystic ovaries, estrogen-secreting granulosa cell ovarian tumors, and diabetes mellitus). Excision of the uterus by hysterectomy for an unrelated medical condition (e.g., fibroids) removes the target tissue and eliminates the risk.

The majority of women manifest symptoms of endometrial cancer (postmenopausal bleeding, pain, discomfort, pelvic mass) prior to the metastatic spread of cancer cells. The size and location of endometrial tumors can be precisely determined by transvaginal ultrasound; however, the presence of cancer must be confirmed by endometrial biopsy and pathologic examination of cancerous tissues under the microscope. Surgical excision by total hysterectomy and bilateral salpingo-oophorectomy is the treatment of choice for endometrial cancer. For all stages taken together, the overall 5-year survival rate is 80% among women who receive timely and appropriate treatment (Amant et al., 2005).

EPIDEMIOLOGY OF UTERINE SARCOMA

Uterine sarcomas are relatively rare forms of uterine cancer that arise from smooth muscle (myometrium) or connective tissues of the uterus. Among U.S. women, these tumors account for less than 5% of all uterine malignancies. Due to their low incidence,

very few epidemiologic investigations have been conducted to identify risk factors for these tumors. Furthermore, recent pathologic studies of uterine sarcomas have led to an important change in the classification of one type of uterine sarcoma called *uterine carcinosarcoma*. Although this malignant tumor is very aggressive with poor survival, it is now classified as a high-grade endometrial adenocarcinoma and has been renamed *malignant mixed mullerian tumor* (McCluggage, 2002).

Due to the low incidence of uterine sarcomas plus the recent change in pathologic classification and nomenclature, members of the Epidemiology of Endometrial Cancer Consortium designed an international study to combine all data from published cohort and case control studies to re-examine the risk factors for uterine sarcoma in comparison to malignant mixed mullerian tumor and endometrioid endometrial carcinoma. Data from 15 studies (10 case control studies and 5 cohort studies) were combined and analyzed for this purpose. Pooled data for 229 uterine sarcomas, 244 malignant mullerian tumors, 7,623 endometrioid endometrial carcinomas, and 28,829 controls without cancer were available for analysis (Felix et al., 2013).

Results from the analysis of this large pooled database were in general agreement with the findings from previous smaller studies. In general, the findings reflect a pattern of shared risk factors for uterine sarcoma and type 1 (endometrioid) endometrial carcinoma. Obesity and postmenopausal hormone replacement therapy were associated with increases in the risk whereas cigarette smoking, parity, and oral contraceptive use were associated with risk reductions. Notably, a history of diabetes mellitus increased the risk of developing uterine sarcoma more than twofold. Analysis by subtype of uterine sarcoma (endometrial stromal sarcoma and leiomyosarcoma) revealed associations similar to those for all uterine sarcomas combined. The risk pattern for malignant mixed mullerian tumors was not strikingly different from that of uterine sarcoma or endometrioid endometrial carcinoma. The investigators concluded that "associations between menstrual, hormonal, and anthropometric risk factors and uterine sarcoma were similar to those identified for endometrioid endometrial carcinoma" (Felix et al., 2013).

Uterine Leiomyoma (Uterine Fibroids)

Leiomyomas (colloquially known as fibroids) are benign tumors that frequently develop in the smooth muscle (myometrium) of the uterus. Uterine fibroids are, in fact, the most common of all tumors that afflict the female population. Prevalence estimates for women living in developed nations suggest that up to 25% of women develop these benign tumors, typically during their reproductive years. Uterine fibroids are the most frequent indication for hysterectomy in premenopausal women and therefore present a major public health issue (Flake, Andersen, & Dixon, 2003; Kumar, Abbas, & Aster, 2014; Stewart, 2001).

Leiomyomas usually arise during the premenopausal years in association with excessive secretion of estrogen and progesterone by the ovaries. Several lines of evidence support their dependence on stimulation of estrogen receptors (ERs) and progesterone receptors (PRs) in smooth muscle. During pregnancy, when estrogen and progesterone levels increase dramatically, existing leiomyomas experience rapid growth and development, which subsides after delivery. Conversely, oophorectomy induces atrophy of existing leiomyomas, and primary tumors rarely arise after menopause when estrogen and progesterone levels are low.

Risk factors for leiomyoma are similar to the risk factors for endometrial cancer and breast cancer. They include early menarche (before age 12 years), late first pregnancy (after age 30 years), nulliparity, late menopause, obesity, and exposure to exogenous estrogens (hormone replacement therapy) in the postmenopausal years or exposure to SERMs (e.g., tamoxifen) as adjuvant therapy for ER-positive breast cancer. Reciprocally, factors that decrease the risk appear to lower exposure to estrogen or have anti-estrogenic effects. For example, the inverse association of chronic tobacco smoking and leiomyoma risk has been attributed to the anti-estrogenic effect of nicotine exposure (Flake et al., 2003). It is important to emphasize that nearly all known risk factors for leiomyoma involve sustained excess exposure to estrogens and/or activation of cell membrane estrogen receptors.

Several epidemiologic investigations have noted that African American women have earlier average onset and two- to threefold higher rates of uterine fibroids than Caucasian women (Stewart, 2001). In a recent study, leiomyoma tissues from African American women were found to have significantly higher concentrations of aromatase than tissues from women of other ethnic groups. Because aromatase is the enzyme responsible for the conversion of androgens to estrogens in fat and muscle, this finding may help account for the higher prevalence and earlier incidence of leiomyoma in the female African American population (Ishikawa et al., 2009)

Uterine Leiomyosarcoma

Uterine leiomyosarcomas arise from the smooth muscle (myometrium) of the uterus. These tumors are extremely rare, and whether or not they are derived from preexisting benign leiomyomas (fibroids) remains a highly controversial issue (Hodge & Morton, 2007; Kumar, Abbas, & Aster, 2014). The peak incidence of leiomyosarcomas occurs during the perimenopausal years between ages 45 and 60 years. In a recent population-based study of uterine sarcomas in Scandinavian women, the annual incidence of leiomyosarcoma was estimated at about 4–5 cases per million for the time period 2003–2007 (Koivisto-Korander, Martinsen, Weiderpass, Leminen, & Pukkala, 2012). In the U.S. population, the estimated annual rates of leiomyosarcoma for women over 35 years of age during 1989–1999 were higher for African American women than women of all other ethnic groups (15 cases per million versus 9 cases per million) (Brooks, Zhan, Cote, & Baquet, 2004). Leiomyosarcomas have the capability to metastasize to distant organs (e.g., lungs, liver, bones, and brain); as a consequence, 5-year survival rates are less than 50%.

Similar to its benign counterpart leiomyoma, the etiology of leiomyosarcoma appears to be linked to excessive exposure to exogenous sources of estrogen, such as hormone replacement therapy (Schwartz et al., 1996) or sustained exposure to SERMs (e.g., tamoxifen) as adjunct therapy for breast cancer (Arenas et al., 2006). Other risk factors include a history of pelvic radiation, history of diabetes, and obesity (Felix et al., 2013).

Endometrial Stromal Sarcoma

Endometrial stromal sarcomas arise from connective tissues of the uterus. These tumors are less common than leiomyomas with annual incidence rates of about 2–3 per million in European women and 5–6 per million in U.S. women (Brooks et al., 2004; Koivisto-Korander et al., 2012). Similar patterns of risk have been observed for all uterine sarcomas, regardless of subtype. In general, risk increases are associated with chronic excessive exposure to endogenous estrogens due to reproductive factors (early menarche, late first pregnancy, nulliparity, or late menopause) or exposure to exogenous estrogens or estrogen receptor modulators (postmenopausal hormone replacement or adjunct breast cancer therapy with tamoxifen). Reciprocally, risk decreases are associated with anti-estrogenic factors such as chronic cigarette smoking and long-term use of oral contraceptives (Arenas et al., 2006; Schwartz et al., 1996). A novel finding from the analysis of a large pooled database extracted from epidemiologic studies of uterine sarcomas is a significant link with diabetes mellitus (Felix et al., 2013).

EPIDEMIOLOGY OF CHORIOCARCINOMA

Choriocarcinomas are rare tumors that develop from trophoblastic cells called *syncytiotrophoblasts* and *cytotrophoblasts* that ordinarily form the chorionic membranes of the placenta. Although the majority of choriocarcinomas develop in the uterus, they can also arise in extrauterine sites such as the ovaries or the fallopian tubes in association with an ectopic pregnancy, and even in the male testes. Approximately 50% of choriocarcinomas develop from *hydatidiform moles*, 20% in association with spontaneous abortions and miscarriages, 20–30% in normal pregnancies, and 2–3% in ectopic pregnancies (Kumar, Abbas, & Aster, 2014).

During the early stages of a normal pregnancy, projections of the chorionic membranes called *chorionic villi* invade the endometrium and absorb nutrients essential for fetal growth and development. However, the trophoblastic cells that form the chorionic membranes occasionally manifest abnormal proliferation and differentiation and form a neoplastic lesion.

The most common form of gestational choriocarcinoma arises from a precursor lesion known as a *hydatidiform mole*. Hydatidiform moles are vesicular (grapelike) tumors that arise due to the implantation of nonviable eggs in the uterus. These cells are void of maternal DNA and may contain various combinations of paternal DNA. Implantation of a nonviable egg in the uterine wall induces aberrant development of placental chorionic tissues that are swollen (hydropic) and void of circulation. About 1 in 40 hydatidiform moles eventually progress to gestational choriocarcinomas. Gestational choriocarcinomas are typically diagnosed during the fourth or fifth month of pregnancy. A key diagnostic feature is excessive secretion of β human chorionic gonadotropin by the syncytiotrophoblasts.

In a study of women of reproductive age in the United States during 1973–1982, choriocarcinomas were detected in about 1 in 24,000 pregnancies, and significant effects of race and age were observed. African American women had a twofold increase in the incidence compared to Caucasians, and women ages 40–44 years had an 8.6-fold increase compared to those ages 20–24 years. Incidence rates were also increased in teen pregnancies (Brinton, Bracken, & Connelly, 1986). Subsequent studies of diverse populations have noted increases in the incidence of gestational trophoblastic disease for women in underdeveloped areas (e.g., southeast Asia, India, and Africa) and have confirmed that women in the extreme classes of gestational age (under 20 and over 40 years) are at increased risk (Di Cintio, Parazzini, Rosa, Chatenoud, & Benzi, 1997).

Because syncytiotrophoblasts within choriocarcinomas secrete human chorionic gonadotropin (hCG), a marked elevation in the blood level of this hormone can serve as an early biomarker of tumor development. Nevertheless, choriocarcinomas are often detected after metastatic spread to other anatomic sites (e.g., lungs, liver, and bones). Fortunately, most of these tumors are extremely sensitive to treatment with methotrexate and other chemotherapeutic agents. With appropriate therapy, the cure rate for gestational choriocarcinoma exceeds 90% (Lurain & Nejad, 2005).

• • • REFERENCES

Aaltonen, L. A., Peltomiki, P., Leach, F. S., Sistonen, P., Pylkkanen, L., Mecklin, J.-P., . . . de la Chappelle, A. (1993). Clues to the pathogenesis of familial colorectal cancer. *Science, 260,* 812–816.

Aaltonen, L. A., Peltomiki, P., Mecklin, J.-P., Jirvinen, H., Jass, J. R., Green, J. S., . . . de la Chappelle, A. (1994). Replication errors in benign and malignant tumors from hereditary nonpolyposis colorectal cancer patients. *Cancer Research, 54,* 1645–1648.

Amant, F., Moerman, P., Neven, P., Timmerman, D., Van Limbergen, E., & Vergote, I. (2005). Endometrial cancer. *Lancet, 366,* 491–505.

Arenas, M., Rovirosa, A., Henandez, V., Ordi, J., Jorcano, S., Mellado, B., & Biete, A. (2006). Uterine sarcomas in breast cancer patients treated with tamoxifen. *International Journal of Gynecologic Cancer, 16,* 861–865.

Azziz, R., Woods, K. S., Reyna, R., Key, T. J., Knochenhauer, E. S., & Yildiz, B. O. (2004). The prevalence and features of the polycystic ovary syndrome in an unselected population. *Journal of Clinical Endocrinology and Metabolism, 89*(6), 2745–2749.

Bender, D., Buekers, T., & Leslie, K. K. (2011). Hormone receptors and endometrial cancer. *Proceedings in Obstetrics and Gynecology, 2*(1), 1–25.

Bernstein, L., Deapen, D., Cerhan, J. R., Schwartz, S. M., Liff, J., McGann-Maloney, E., . . . Ford, L.

(1999). Tamoxifen therapy for breast cancer and endometrial cancer risk. *Journal of the National Cancer Institute, 91,* 1654–1662.

Boice, J. D. Jr, Day, N. E., Andersen, A., Brinton, L. A., Brown, R., Choi, N. W., . . . Flannery, J. T. (1985). Second cancers following radiation treatment for cervical cancer. An international collaboration among cancer registries. *Journal of the National Cancer Institute, 74*(5), 955–975.

Bokhman, J. V. (1983). Two pathogenetic types of endometrial carcinoma. *Gynecologic Oncology, 15*(1), 10–17.

Bravi, F., Scotti, L., Bosetti, C., Gallus, S., Negri, E., La Vecchia, C., & Tavani, A. (2009). Coffee drinking and endometrial cancer risk: A metaanalysis of observational studies. *American Journal of Obstetrics and Gynecology, 200*(2), 130–135.

Bray, F., Dos Santos Silva, I., Moller, H., & Weiderpass, E. (2005). Endometrial cancer incidence trends in Europe: Underlying determinants and prospects for prevention. *Cancer Epidemiology, Biomarkers and Prevention, 14*(5), 1132–1142.

Brinton, L. A., Bracken, M. B., & Connelly, R. R. (1986). Choriocarcinoma incidence in the United States. *American Journal of Epidemiology, 123*(6), 1094–1100.

Brinton, L. A., Gridley, G., Persson, I., Baron, J., & Bergqvist, A. (1997). Cancer risk after a hospital discharge diagnosis of endometriosis. *American Journal of Obstetrics and Gynecology, 176*(3), 572–579.

Brooks, S. E., Zhan, M., Cote, T., Baquet, C. R. (2004). Surveillance, Epidemiology, and End Results analysis of 2677 cases of uterine sarcoma 1989–1999. *Gynecologic Oncology, 93,* 204–208.

Brown, K. (2009). Is tamoxifen a genotoxic carcinogen in women? *Mutagenesis, 24*(5), 391–404.

Chang, S.-C., Lacey, J. V., Brinton, L. A., Harge, P., Adams, K., Mouw, T., . . . Leitzmann, M. F. (2007). Lifetime weight history and endometrial cancer risk by type of menopausal hormone use

in the NIH-AARP Diet and Health Study. *Cancer Epidemiology, Biomarkers and Prevention, 16*(4), 723–730.

Di Cintio, E., Parazzini, F., Rosa, C., Chatenoud, L., & Benzi, G. (1997). The epidemiology of gestational trophoblastic disease. *General and Diagnostic Pathology, 143*(2–3), 103–108.

Djordjevic, B., Hennessy, B. T., Li, J., Barkoh, B. A., Luthra, R., Mills, G. B., & Broaddus, R. R. (2012). Clinical assessment of PTEN loss in endometrial carcinoma: Immunohistochemistry outperforms gene sequencing. *Modern Pathology, 25,* 699–708.

Dockerty, M. B., Loveday, S. B., & Foust, G. T. (1951). Carcinoma of the corpus uteri in young women. *American Journal of Obstetrics and Gynecology, 61,* 966–981.

Dossus, L., Allen, N., Kaaks, R., Bakken, K., Lund, E., Tjonneland, A., . . . Riboli, E. (2010). Reproductive risk factors and endometrial cancer: The European Prospective Investigation into Cancer and Nutrition. *International Journal of Cancer, 127,* 442–451.

Duong, L. M., Wilson, R. J., Ajani, U. A., Singh, S. D., & Eheman, C. R. (2011). Trends in endometrial cancer incidence rates in the United States, 1999-2006. *Journal of Women's Health, 20*(8), 1157–1163.

Eng, C. (1998). Genetics of Cowden syndrome: Through the looking glass of oncology. *International Journal of Oncology, 12*(3), 701–710.

Evans, T., Sany, O., Pearman, P., Ganesan, R., Blann, A., & Sundar, S. (2011). Differential trends in the rising incidence of endometrial cancer by type: Data from a UK population-based registry from 1994 to 2006. *British Journal of Cancer, 104*(9), 1505–1510.

Fearnley, E. J., Marquart, L., Spurdle, A. B., Weinstein, P., & Webb, P. M.; Australian Ovarian Cancer Study Group and Australian National Endometrial Cancer Study Group. (2010). Polycystic ovary syndrome increases the risk of endometrial cancer in women aged less than 50 years: An Australian case-control study. *Cancer Causes and Control, 21*(12), 2303–2308.

Felix, A. S., Cook, L. S., Gaudet, M. M., Rohan, T. E., Schouten, L. J., Setiawan, V. W., . . . Brinton, L. A. (2013). The etiology of uterine sarcomas: A pooled analysis of the Epidemiology of Endometrial Cancer Consortium. *British Journal of Cancer, 108*(3), 727–734.

Felix, A. S., Weissfeld, J. L., Stone, R. A., Bowser, R., Chivukula, M., Edwards, R. P., & Linkov, F. (2010). Factors associated with type I and type II endometrial cancer. *Cancer Causes and Control, 21*(11), 1851–1856.

Ferlay, J., Bray, F., Pisani, P., & Parkin, D. M. (2004). *GLOBOCAN 2002. Cancer incidence, mortality, and prevalence worldwide.* IARC Cancer Base No. 5, version 2.0. Lyon, France: IARC Press. Retrieved from http://www-dep.iarc.fr

Ferlay, J., Shin, H.-R., Bray, F., Forman, D., Mathers, C., & Parkin, D. M. (2010). Estimates of worldwide burden of cancer in 2008: GLOBOCAN 2008. *International Journal of Cancer, 127*(12), 2893–2917.

Ferlay, J., Soerjomataram, I., Ervik, M., Dikshit, R., Eser, S., Mathers, C., . . . Bray, F. (2013). *GLOBOCAN 2012 v1.0. Cancer incidence and mortality worldwide: IARC CancerBase No. 11* [Internet]. Lyon, France: International Agency for Research on Cancer. Retrieved from http://globocan.iarc.fr

Fisher, B., Costantino, J. P., Redmond, C. K., Fisher, E. R., Wickerham, D. L., & Cronin, W. M. (1994). Endometrial cancer in tamoxifen-treated breast cancer patients: Findings from the National Surgical Adjuvant Breast and Bowel Project (NSABP) B-14. *Journal of the National Cancer Institute, 86*, 527–537.

Flake, G. P., Andersen, J., & Dixon, D. (2003). Etiology and pathogenesis of uterine leiomyomas: A review. *Environmental Health Perspectives, 111*(8), 1037–1054.

Friberg, E., Orsini, N., Mantzoros, C. S., & Wolk, A. (2007). Diabetes mellitus and risk of endometrial cancer: A meta-analysis. *Diabetologia, 50*(7), 1365–1374.

Grady, D., Gebretsadik, T., Kerlikowske, K., Ernster, V., & Petitti, D. (1995). Hormone replacement therapy and endometrial cancer risk: A meta-analysis. *Obstetrics and Gynecology, 85*, 304–313.

Harris, R. E. (2002). Cyclooxygenase-2 blockade in cancer prevention and therapy: Widening the scope of impact. In R. E. Harris (Ed.), *Cyclooxygenase-2 blockade in cancer prevention and therapy* (pp. 341–365). Totowa, NJ: Human Press.

Harris, R. E. (2007). Cyclooxygenase-2 (COX-2) and the inflammogenesis of cancer. *Subcellular Biochemistry, 42*, 93–126.

Hayat, M. J., Howlader, N., Reichman, M. E., & Edwards, B. K. (2007). Cancer statistics, trends, and multiple primary cancer analyses from the Surveillance, Epidemiology, and End Results (SEER) program. *Oncologist, 12*(1), 20–37.

Hodge, J. C., & Morton, C. C. (2007). Genetic heterogeneity among uterine leiomyomata: Insights into malignant progression. *Human Molecular Genetics, 16*(1), 7–13.

Howlader, N., Noone, A. M., Krapcho, M., Garshell, J., Neyman, N., Altekruse, S. F., . . . Cronin, K. A. (Eds.). (2012, November). *SEER cancer statistics review, 1975–2010*. Bethesda, MD: National Cancer Institute. Retrieved from http://seer.cancer.gov/csr/1975_2010/

Ishikawa, H., Reierstad, S., Demura, M., Rademaker, A. W., Kasai, T., Inoue, M., . . . Bulun, S. E. (2009). High aromatase expression in uterine leiomyoma tissues of African-American women. *Journal of Clinical Endocrinology and Metabolism, 94*(5), 1752.

Jackson, R., & Dockerty, M. B. (1957). The Stein–Leventhal syndrome: Analysis of 43 cases with special reference to association with endometrial carcinoma. *American Journal of Obstetrics and Gynecology, 73*, 161–173.

Jafari, K., Javaheri, G., & Ruiz, G. (1978). Endometrial adenocarcinoma and the Stein-Leventhal syndrome. *Obstetrics and Gynecology, 51*, 97–100.

Jamison, P. M., Noone, A. M., Ries, L. A., Lee, N. C., & Edwards, B. K. (2013). Trends in endometrial cancer incidence by race and histology with a correction for the prevalence of hysterectomy, SEER 1992 to 2008. *Cancer Epidemiology, Biomarkers and Prevention, 22*(2), 233–241.

Je, Y., Hankinson, S. E., Tworoger, S. S., DeVivo, I., & Giovannucci, E. (2011). A prospective cohort study of coffee consumption and risk of endometrial cancer over a 26-year follow-up. *Cancer Epidemiology, Biomarkers and Prevention, 20*(12), 2487–2495.

Jordan, V. C. (1997). Tamoxifen: The herald of a new era of preventive therapeutics [editorial]. *Journal of the National Cancer Institute, 89*, 747–749.

Kanthan, R., & Senger, J. L. (2011). Uterine carcinosarcomas (malignant mixed Müllerian tumours): A review with special emphasis on the controversies in management. *Obstetrics and Gynecology International, 2011*, d470795.

Key, T. J., & Pike, M. C. (1988a). The dose-effect relationship between 'unopposed' oestrogens and endometrial mitotic rate: Its central role in explaining and predicting endometrial cancer risk. *British Journal of Cancer, 57*(2), 205–212.

Key, T. J., & Pike, M. C. (1988b). The role of oestrogens and progestagens in the epidemiology and prevention of breast cancer. *European Journal of Cancer and Clinical Oncology, 24*(1), 29–43.

Koivisto-Korander, R., Martinsen, J. I., Weiderpass, E., Leminen, A., & Pukkala, E. (2012). Incidence of uterine leiomyosarcoma and endometrial stromal sarcoma in Nordic countries: Results from NORDCAN and NOCCA databases. *Maturitas, 72*(1), 56–60.

Korenman, S. G. (1980). Oestrogen window hypothesis of the aetiology of breast cancer. *Lancet, 315*(8170), 700–701.

Kosary, C. L. (2007). Cancer of the corpus uteri. In: L. A. G. Ries, J. L. Young, G. E. Keel, M. P. Eisner, Y. D. Lin, & M.-J. Horner (Eds.), *SEER survival monograph: Cancer survival among adults: US SEER program, 1988–2001, patient and tumor characteristics*. NIH Pub. No. 07-6215. Bethesda, MD: National Cancer Institute.

Kotsopoulos, J., Eliassen, A. H., Missmer, S. A., Hankinson, S. E., & Tworoger, S. S. (2009). Relationship between caffeine intake and plasma sex hormone concentrations in premenopausal and postmenopausal women. *Cancer, 115*(12), 2765–2774.

Kumar, S., Shah, J. P., Bryant, C. S., Seward, S., Ali-Fehmi, R., Morris, R. T., & Malone, J. M. Jr. (2009). Radiation-associated endometrial cancer. *Obstetrics and Gynecology, 113*(2 Pt 1), 319–325.

Kumar, V., Abbas, A. K., & Aster J. C. (2014). *Robbins and Cotran pathologic basis of disease* (9th ed.). Philadelphia, PA: Mosby & Saunders.

Lacey, J. V. Jr, Brinton, L. A., Lubin, J. H., Sherman, M. E., Schatzkin, A., & Schairer, C. (2005). Endometrial carcinoma risks among menopausal estrogen plus progestin and unopposed estrogen users in a cohort of postmenopausal women. *Cancer Epidemiology, Biomarkers and Prevention, 14*(7), 1724–1731.

Lacey, J. V. Jr, Leitzmann, M. F., Chang, S. C., Mouw, T., Hollenbeck, A. R., Schatzkin, A., & Brinton, L. A. (2007). Endometrial cancer and menopausal hormone therapy in the National Institutes of Health-AARP Diet and Health Study cohort. *Cancer, 109*(7), 1303–1311.

Lee, J. O., Yang, H., Georgescu, M. M., Di Cristofano, A., Maehama, T., Shi, Y., . . . Pavletich, N. P. (1999). Crystal structure of the PTEN tumor suppressor: Implications for its phosphoinositide phosphatase activity and membrane association. *Cell, 99*(3), 323–334.

Loos, A. H., Bray, F., McCarron, P., Weiderpass, E., Hakama, M., & Parkin, D. M. (2004). Sheep and goats: Separating cervix and corpus uteri from imprecisely coded uterine cancer deaths, for studies of geographical and temporal variations in mortality. *European Journal of Cancer, 40*, 2794–2803.

Lucenteforte, E., Bosetti, C., Talamini, R., Montella, M., Zucchetto, A., Pelucchi, C., . . . La Vecchia, C. (2007). Diabetes and endometrial cancer: Effect modification by body weight, physical activity and hypertension. *British Journal of Cancer, 97*(7), 995–998.

Luo, J., Manning, B. D., & Cantley, L. C. (2003). Targeting the PI3K-Akt pathway in human cancer: Rationale and promise. *Cancer Cell, 4*, 257–262.

Lurain, J. R., & Nejad, B. (2005). Secondary chemotherapy for high-risk gestational trophoblastic neoplasia. *Gynecologic Oncology, 97*(2), 618–623.

Lynch, H. T., Shaw, M. W., Magnuson, C. W., Larsen, A. L., & Krush, A. J. (1966). Hereditary factors in cancer: A study of two large Midwestern kindreds. *Archives of Internal Medicine, 117*(2), 206–212.

MacMahon, B. (1974). Risk factors for endometrial cancer. *Gynecologic Oncology, 2*(2–3), 122–129.

Malmström, H., Högberg, H., Risberg, B., & Simonsen, E. (1994). Granulosa cell tumors of the ovary: Prognostic factors and outcome. *Gynecologic Oncology, 52*(1), 50–55.

McCluggage, W. G. (2002). Uterine carcinosarcomas (malignant mixed Mullerian tumors) are metaplastic carcinomas. *International Journal of Gynecologic Cancer, 12*(6), 687–690.

McPherson, C. P., Sellers, T. A., Potter, J. D., Bostick, R. M., & Folsom, A. R. (1996). Reproductive factors and risk of endometrial cancer. The Iowa Women's Health Study. *American Journal of Epidemiology, 143*(12), 1195–1202.

Meyer, L. A., Broaddus, R. R., & Lu, K. H. (2009). Endometrial cancer and Lynch syndrome: Clinical and pathologic considerations. *Cancer Control, 16*(1), 14–22.

Michnovicz, J. J., Hershcopf, R. J., Naganuma, H., Bradlow, H. L., & Fishman, J. (1986). Increased 2-hydroxylation of estradiol as a possible mechanism for the anti-estrogenic effect of cigarette smoking. *New England Journal of Medicien, 315*(21), 1305–1319.

Modugno, F., Ness, R. B., Chen, C., & Weiss, N. S. (2005). Inflammation and endometrial cancer: A hypothesis. *Cancer Epidemiology, Biomarkers and Prevention, 14*, 2480.

Moore, S. C., Gierach, G. L., Schatzkin, A., & Matthews, C. E. (2010). Physical activity, sedentary behaviours, and the prevention of endometrial cancer. *British Journal of Cancer, 103*(7), 933–938.

Nagamani, M., & Stuart, C. A. (1998). Specific binding and growth promoting activity of insulin in endometrial cancer cells in culture. *American Journal of Obstetrics and Gynecology, 179*, 6–12.

National Cancer Institute. (n.d.). Fast Stats: An interactive tool for access to SEER cancer statistics. Surveillance Research Program. Retrieved from http://seer.cancer.gov/faststats

Navaratnarajah, R., Pillay, O. C., & Hardiman, P. (2008). Polycystic ovary syndrome and endometrial cancer. *Seminars in Reproductive Medicine, 26*(1), 62–71.

Neill, A. S., Nagle, C. M., Protani, M. M., Obermair, A., Spurdle, A. B., Webb, P. M.; Australian National Endometrial Cancer Study Group. (2013). Aspirin, nonsteroidal anti-inflammatory drugs, paracetamol and risk of endometrial cancer: A case-control study, systematic review and meta-analysis. *International Journal of Cancer, 132*(5), 1146–1155.

Nestler, J. E., Powers, L. P., Matt, D. W., Steingold, K. A., Plymate, S. R., Rittmaster, R. S., . . . Blackard, W. G. (1991). A direct effect of hyperinsulinemia on serum sex hormone-binding globulin levels in obese women with the polycystic ovary syndrome. *Journal of Clinical Endocrinology and Metabolism, 72*, 83–89.

Okuda, T., Sekizawa, A., Purwosunu, Y., Nagatsuka, M., Morioka, M., Hayashi, M., & Okai, T. (2010). Genetics of endometrial cancers. *Obstetrics and Gynecology International, 2010*. doi:10.1155/2010/984013

Paganini-Hill, A., Ross, R. K., & Henderson, B. E. (1989). Endometrial cancer and patterns of use of oestrogen replacement therapy: A cohort study. *British Journal of Cancer, 59*(3), 445–447.

Parkin, D. M., Bray, F., Ferlay, J., & Pisani, P. (2001). Estimating the world cancer burden: GLOBOCAN 2000. *International Journal of Cancer, 94*, 153–156.

Parkin, D. M., Bray, F., Ferlay, J., & Pisani, P. (2005). Global cancer statistics, 2002. *CA: A Cancer Journal for Clinicians*, 55, 74–108.

Peifer, M. (1997). β-catenin as oncogene—the smoking gun. *Science*, 275(5307), 1752.

Platz, C. E., & Benda, J. A. (1995). Female genital tract cancer. *Cancer*, 75, 270–294.

Purdie, D. M., & Green, A. C. (2001). Epidemiology of endometrial cancer. *Best Practice and Research Clinical Obstetrics and Gynaecology*, 16(3), 341–354.

Radosh, L. (2009). Drug treatments for polycystic ovary syndrome. *American Family Physician*, 79(8), 671–676.

Rossouw, J. E., Anderson, G. L., Prentice, R. L., LaCroix, A. Z., Kooperberg, C., Stefanick, M. L., . . . Ockene J; Writing Group for the Women's Health Initiative Investigators. (2002). Risks and benefits of estrogen plus progestin in healthy postmenopausal women: Principal results from the Women's Health Initiative randomized controlled trial. *Journal of the American Medical Association*, 288(3), 321–333.

Sankaranarayanan, R., & Ferlay, J. (2006). Worldwide burden of gynaecological cancer: The size of the problem. *Best Practice and Research Clinical Obstetrics and Gynaecology*, 20(2), 207–225.

Sansal, I., & Sellers, W. R. (2004). The biology and clinical relevance of the PTEN tumor suppressor pathway. *Journal of Clinical Oncology*, 22(14), 2954–2963.

Sasaki, H., Nishii, H., Takahashi, H., Tada, A., Furusato, M., Terashima, Y., . . . Boyd, J. (1993). Mutation of the Ki-ras protooncogene in human endometrial hyperplasia and carcinoma. *Cancer Research*, 53(8), 1906–1910.

Saso, S., Chatterjee, J., Georgiou, E., Ditri, A. M., Smith, J. R., & Ghaem-Maghami, S. (2011). Endometrial cancer. *BMJ*, 343, d3954.

Schlesselman, J. J. (1997). Risk of endometrial cancer in relation to use of combined oral contraceptives. A practitioner's guide to

meta-analysis. *Human Reproduction*, 12, 1851–1863.

Schottenfeld, D. (1995). Epidemiology of endometrial neoplasia. *Journal of Cellular Biochemistry*, 59(Suppl 23), 151–159.

Schumer, S. T., & Cannistra, S. A. (2003). Granulosa cell tumor of the ovary. *Journal of Clinical Oncology*, 21(6), 1180–1189.

Schwartz, S. M., Weiss, N. S., Daling, J. R., Gammon, M. D., Liff, J. M., Watt, Z. J., . . . Thompson, W. D. (1996). Exogenous sex hormone use, correlates of endogenous hormone levels, and the incidence of histologic types of sarcoma of the uterus. *Cancer*, 77(4), 717–724.

Shah, S. P., Köbel, M., Senz, J., Morin, R. D., Clarke, B. A., Wiegand, K. C., & Huntsman, D. G. (2009). Mutation of *FOXL2* in granulosa-cell tumors of the ovary. *New England Journal of Medicine*, 360, 2719–2720.

Shapiro, S., Kelly, J. P., Rosenberg, L., Kaufman, D. W., Helmrich, S. P., Rosenshein, N. B., . . . Schottenfeld, D. (1985). Risk of localized and widespread endometrial cancer in relation to recent and discontinued use of conjugated estrogens. *New England Journal of Medicine*, 313, 969–972.

Sherman, B. M., & Korenman, S. G. (1974). Inadequate corpus luteum function: A pathophysiological interpretation of human breast cancer epidemiology. *Cancer*, 33, 1306–1312.

Sherman, B. M., Wallace, R. B., & Korenman, S. G. (1981). Corpus luteum dysfunction and the epidemiology of breast cancer: A reconsideration. *Breast Cancer Research and Treatment*, 1(4), 287–296.

Simpson, E. R., & Brown, K. A. (2011). Obesity, aromatase and breast cancer. *Expert Review of Endocrinology and Metabolism*, 6(3), 383–395.

Speert, H. (1949). Carcinoma of the endometrium in young women. *Journal of Surgery, Gynaecology and Obstetrics*, 88, 332–336.

Steck, P. A., Pershouse, M. A., Jasser, S. A., Yung, W. K., Lin, H., Ligon, A. H., . . . Tavtigian, S. V. (1997). Identification of a candidate tumour suppressor gene, MMAC1, at chromosome

10q23.3 that is mutated in multiple advanced cancers. *Nature Genetics, 15*(4), 356–362.

Stewart, E. A. (2001). Uterine fibroids. *Lancet, 357*(9252), 293–298.

Viganò, P., Parazzini, F., Somigliana, E., & Vercellini, P. (2004). Endometriosis: Epidemiology and etiological factors. *Best Practice and Research Clinical Obstetrics and Gynecology, 18*(2), 177–200.

Wu, T., Willett, W. C., Hankinson, S. E., & Giovannucci, E. (2005). Caffeinated coffee, decaffeinated coffee, and caffeine in relation to plasma C-peptide levels, a marker of insulin secretion, in U.S. women. *Diabetes Care, 28,* 1390–1396.

Zheng, W., Baker, H. E., & Mutter, G. L. (2004). Involution of PTEN-null endometrial glands with progestin therapy. *Gynecologic Oncology, 92*(3), 1008–1013.

Zhou, B., Yang, L., Sun, Q., Cong, R., Gu, H., Tang, N., . . . Wang, B. (2008). Cigarette smoking and the risk of endometrial cancer: A meta-analysis. *American Journal of Medicine, 121*(6), 501–508.

Ziel, H. K., Finkle, W. D., & Greenland, S. (1998). Decline in incidence of endometrial cancer following increase in prescriptions for opposed conjugated estrogens in a prepaid health plan. *Gynecologic Oncology, 68,* 253–255.

14

Epidemiology of Cervical Cancer

GLOBAL IMPACT OF CERVICAL CANCER

Cancer of the uterine cervix is the third most common cancer diagnosed among women worldwide (behind only breast cancer and colorectal cancer). During 2012, 527,624 new cases were diagnosed and 265,653 women died from cervical cancer (Ferlay et al., 2013). Nearly 85% of the new cases (444,546 new cases) were diagnosed in women living in less-developed regions where cervical cancer was the third leading cause of cancer death (230,158 deaths), ranking behind only breast cancer and lung cancer. Cervical cancer was much less common in developed countries, afflicting 83,078 women and accounting for 35,495 deaths (Ferlay et al., 2013).

The highest incidence and mortality rates were observed in sub-Saharan African, Melanesia, Latin America and the Caribbean, South Central Asia (India), certain nations of South America (Bolivia and Guyana), and Southeast Asia (**Figure 14.1**). The public health burden due to cervical cancer in these nations reflects the virtual absence of screening programs for the detection and treatment of precancerous lesions of the uterine cervix. For example, in India, where screening is still largely absent, approximately 122,844 women were diagnosed and 67,477 women died from cervical cancer (Ferlay et al., 2013).

The women of most developed nations and certain other nations such as China have relatively low rates. The incidence and mortality rates of cervical cancer have declined dramatically among women of developed countries since the introduction and widespread use of screening for cervical dysplasia in the mid-20th century (Ferlay et al., 2004, 2010, 2013).

EARLY DETECTION OF CERVICAL DYSPLASIA

The early detection and appropriate treatment of premalignant conditions of the cervical mucosa (e.g., cervical dysplasia) reflects a major triumph of modern medicine over a life-threatening disease process. In the early decades of the 20th century, cancer of the cervix was the leading cause of cancer mortality among U.S. women. Since 1955, mortality due to cervical cancer has declined by 74%; today, cancer of the cervix ranks 14th in female cancer mortality, accounting for approximately 4,000 deaths per year in the United States (Jemal et al., 2009).

The dramatic reduction in cervical cancer among women of developed nations is due largely to the effectiveness of the Papanicolaou-Traut cytological test (Papanicolaou & Traut, 1943). The *Pap test*, which was introduced in the United States around 1950, provides a quick, safe, affordable, and accurate means of detecting precancerous dysplastic lesions of the cervix that can be cured by simple surgery or other ablative techniques. It is important to note that in situ cervical cancer is 100% curable by appropriate surgical excision. Furthermore, advanced stage cervical cancer that has not spread beyond the cervix is 80–90% curable by appropriate surgery. The importance of cervical screening coupled with appropriate therapy is underscored by differences in cervical cancer mortality in populations with high versus low screening rates. Public health programs to inform and educate the population as to the efficacy of cervical screening by appropriate implementation of Papanicolaou cytological testing at an early age are therefore imperative. Evaluation of the Pap

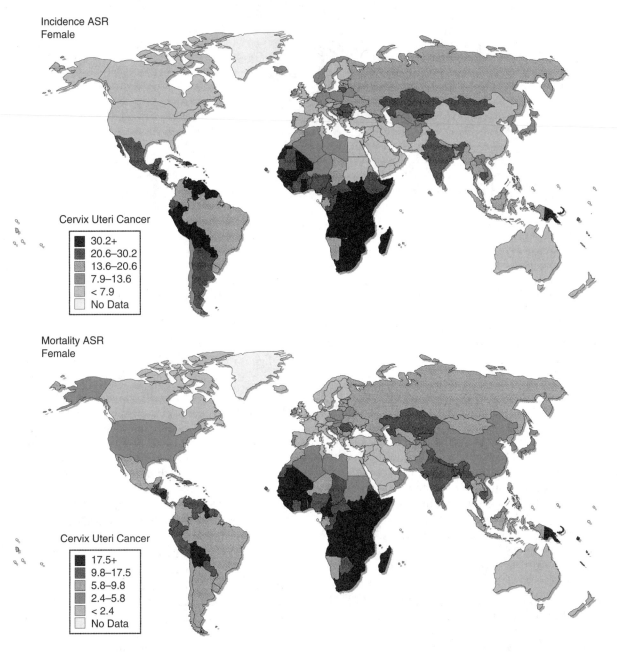

Figure 14.1 Global Incidence and Mortality Rates of Cervical Cancer, 2012.

ASR: Rates per 100,000 are age-standardized to the world population, 2000–2025.

Source: Reproduced from Ferlay, J., Soerjomataram, I., Ervik, M., Dikshit, R., Eser, S., Mathers, C., ... Bray, F. (2013). *GLOBOCAN 2012 v1.0. Cancer incidence and mortality worldwide: IARC CancerBase No. 11* [Internet]. Lyon, France: International Agency for Research on Cancer. Retrieved from http://globocan.iarc.fr

smear has also resulted in critical information regarding carcinogenesis, and in fact, more is known about the natural history of cervical cancer than about any other malignancy.

Although the Pap test has produced substantial declines in cervical cancer incidence and mortality, it is noteworthy that marked disparities persist among the subpopulations within certain nations, perhaps due to excess risk, lack of screening, and limited healthcare access (Sherman, Wang, Carreon, & Devesa, 2005). For example, among U.S. women, the incidence and mortality rates for African Americans are still nearly twice those of Caucasians (Howlader et al., 2011) (**Figure 14.2**).

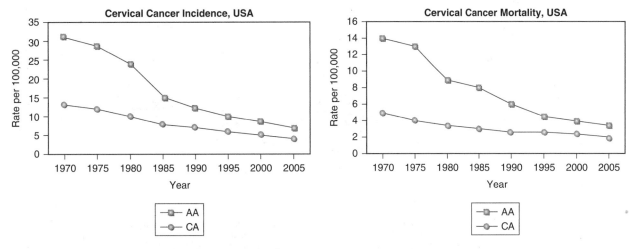

Figure 14.2 Trends in Incidence and Mortality Rates of Cervical Cancer in US Women, 1970–2005.

AA: African Americans; CA: Caucasian Americans.

Source: Data from American Cancer Society. (2007). *Cancer facts and figures, 2007.* Atlanta, GA: Author.

PATHOGENESIS OF CERVICAL CANCER

Cancer of the uterine cervix almost always originates at the squamocolumnar junction at the cervical os in the transitional area between the cervix and the vagina. It is at this border that the columnar epithelium of the cervix transforms into the squamous cell epithelium of the vagina. The vast majority (95%) of cervical cancers are of the squamous cell variety; however, a few adenocarcinomas evolve from the cervical glands, and in fact some of the cervical malignancies are of the mixed variety (i.e., adenosquamous carcinomas) (Kumar, Abbas, Nelson, & Mitchell, 2007).

Carcinoma of the cervix arises in a series of stepwise epithelial changes ranging from progressively more severe dysplasia to carcinoma in situ and, ultimately, invasive carcinoma (**Figure 14.3**). Although carcinoma of the cervix may occur at any age following puberty, the peak incidence is at about 30–40 years of age for in situ lesions and 40–50 years of age for invasive cancer.

Several questions remain regarding the risk factors associated with cervical carcinoma and cervical dysplasia. One feature of mild cervical dysplasia is the tendency for a large percentage of cases to spontaneously remiss; that is, individuals with mild dysplasia when followed over time may spontaneously undergo resolution. Although the reason for this is unknown, it is certainly a subject worthy of study by prospective epidemiologic methods.

RISK FACTORS FOR CERVICAL CANCER

Results of early epidemiologic studies of cervical cancer strongly suggested that the disease was related to the sexual transmission of an oncogenic agent, most probably a virus, from male to female at an early age. Factors that were consistently observed to increase the risk included early age at first intercourse, high parity, multiple sexual partners, contact with "high risk" (promiscuous) male sexual partners, and cigarette smoking. Observed differences in risk for certain subpopulations of women were also related to sexual behavior, including the higher incidence of cervical cancer in lower socioeconomic groups; the higher incidence in married women, which increases with the number of marriages and children; the rarity of cervical cancer in virgins and nuns; and the high incidence in prostitutes. Although herpes simplex virus type 2 (HSV2) was once suspected as the etiologic agent, it is now believed that infection by certain strains of human papillomavirus (HPV) is the most important risk factor in the genesis of cervical malignancies.

Human Papillomavirus (HPV) and Cervical Cancer

It is now quite clear that oncogenic subtypes of human papillomavirus (HPV-16 and HPV-18) are necessary agents in the pathogenesis of cervical cancer (Walboomers et al., 1999). The link between cervical cancer and HPV infection was first suggested by Harald zur Hausen in Germany (zur Hausen, 1976).

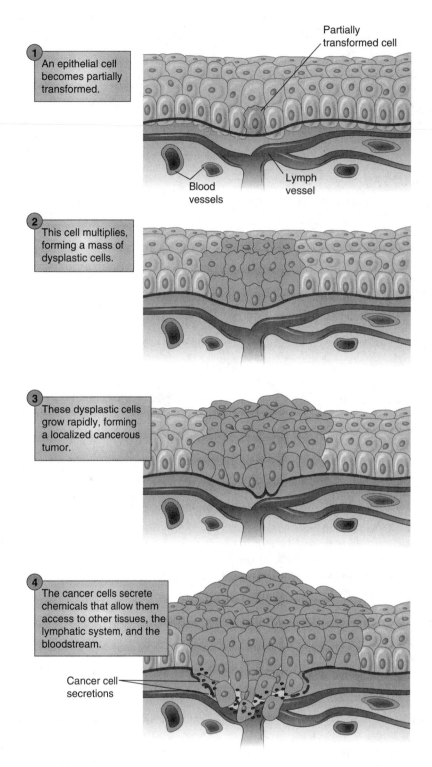

Figure 14.3 Progression of Cervical Cancer.

Professor zur Hausen and colleagues demonstrated the presence of HPV strains 16 and 18 in cancerous tissues from cervical cancer patients (Boshart et al., 1984; Dürst, Gissmann, Ikenberg, & zur Hausen, 1983). Strong etiologic evidence came from an epidemiologic case control study in which HPV DNA was detected by hybridization techniques in 75–100% of patients with cervical condylomas, precancerous cervical dysplasia, and invasive cervical carcinoma (Muñoz et al., 1992). Although there is an overlap in HPV strains, strains 6 and 11 are found most frequently in benign condylomas (vulvar condyloma acuminatum) whereas oncogenic HPV strains such as 16, 18, and 31 are more often present in carcinoma of the cervix (**Figure 14.4**). Cancer develops when the DNA from the oncogenic strains becomes integrated with the DNA of infected cervical cells, leading to overexpression of certain viral genes (E6 and E7) that in turn inactivate tumor suppressor genes such as *P53* and *Rb* (Münger & Howley, 2002).

Molecular epidemiologic studies also indicate that HPV infection coupled with low-dose nitrosamines in the cervical mucosa of cigarette smokers may accentuate carcinogenesis (Gunnell et al., 2006). It has also been shown that HPV strains 16 and 18 (but not 6 and 11) interact with the *ras* oncogene in causing transformed tumorigenic foci in cultured cervical cells (Prokopakis, Sourvinos, Koumantaki, Koumantakis, & Spandidos, 2002). Furthermore, male partners of women with cervical cancer have been found to exhibit lesions of the genitalia harboring high-risk strains HPV-16 and HPV-18. Certain strains of HPV are also suspected as oncogenic agents in a variety of other squamous cell tumors or proliferative lesions of the skin and mucous membranes.

Immunosuppression and Cervical Cancer

Immunosuppression places women at high risk for infection by oncogenic strains of HPV, thereby increasing the risk of cervical cancer (Stentella et al., 1998). Indeed, women who are seropositive for the human immunodeficiency virus (HIV) are at extremely high risk for development of cervical cancer. Apparently this is due to a synergistic interaction between HIV and onocogenic HPV strains. Antecedent infection by HIV compromises the immune system and predisposes sexually active women to co-infection by strains of HPV that cause cervical cancer.

Tobacco Use and Cervical Cancer

Although infection by high-risk strains of HPV (e.g., HPV-16 and HPV-18) is the strongest risk factor for cervical cancer, the risk appears to be modified by cigarette smoking and other forms of tobacco use. Winkelstein initially postulated that tobacco smoking may play a role in the development of cervical cancer, and several epidemiologic investigations have since found that smoking is associated with an increase in cervical cancer risk (Winkelstein, 1977, 1990). A meta-analysis of nine studies conducted between 1977 and 1990 revealed a significant effect of ever versus never smoking (odds ratio [OR] = 1.46) (Sood, 1991); a subsequent meta-analysis of 21 studies found a significant effect of current smoking (OR = 1.83) (Gandini et al., 2008). Nevertheless, with the elucidation of oncogenic HPV infection as the dominant cause of cervical cancer, these early epidemiologic results stimulated controversy as to whether the observed association with smoking was causal or simply due to confounding of smoking with sexual behavioral factors related to HPV infection.

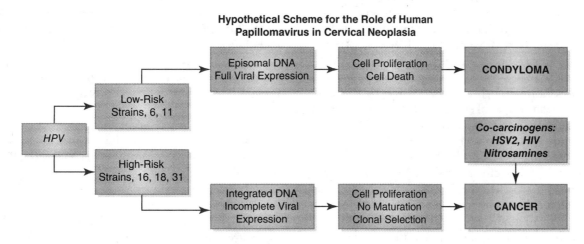

Figure 14.4 Human Papillomavirus (HPV) Infection and Cervical Cancer.

In order to rule out confounding variables, several investigators designed epidemiologic studies to estimate the effects of tobacco use in the presence of HPV infection. Castle and colleagues conducted a 10-year prospective investigation of smoking and other factors among 1,812 women who tested positive for oncogenic HPV DNA at baseline. They found that among the HPV-positive women, smoking one or more packs of cigarettes daily increased the risk more than fourfold (OR = 4.3) compared to nonsmokers (Castle et al., 2002). In a subsequent investigation, Plummer and colleagues pooled international data from 10 case control studies of invasive and in situ cervical carcinoma utilizing only those women who tested positive for HPV DNA. Their study included data on tobacco use among 1,463 cases with invasive cervical cancer, 211 cases with cervical carcinoma in situ, and 254 female controls without cancer. Compared to HPV-positive controls who were nonsmokers, the risk of developing squamous cell cervical cancer among the HPV-positive cases was significantly increased for current smokers (OR = 2.30) and ex-smokers (OR = 1.80) (Plummer et al., 2003).

A team of Swedish investigators conducted a nested population-based case control study to examine interactions between cigarette smoking and HPV-16 in the development of in situ cervical cancer. Archival cervical smears were tested for HPV-16 by polymerase chain reaction (PCR) analysis in 375 cases and 363 age-matched disease-free controls. On average, cases were diagnosed 9 years after collection of cervical smears. At time of diagnosis, data on smoking and other risk factors were collected for each participant by a telephone interview. Results revealed independent effects of smoking and HPV-16 infection and effect modification of combined exposure. Current smoking versus nonsmoking adjusted for HPV-16 status increased the risk nearly twofold (OR = 1.7), whereas HPV-16 positive versus negative status adjusted for smoking increased the risk more than eightfold (OR = 8.4). Among nonsmokers, women who were positive for HPV-16 had more than a 5-fold increase in risk (OR = 5.6) compared to women who were HPV-16 negative, whereas among smokers, HPV-16 positive women had more than a 14-fold increase in risk (OR = 14.4) compared to women who were HPV-16 negative. Nonsmoking women with a high viral load of HPV-16 had a 6-fold increase in risk (OR = 5.9) compared to women who were HPV-16 negative, whereas among smokers, women with a high viral load of HPV-16 had a 27-fold increase in risk (OR = 27.0) compared to those who were negative for HPV-16 (**Figure 14.5**). These results clearly suggest that

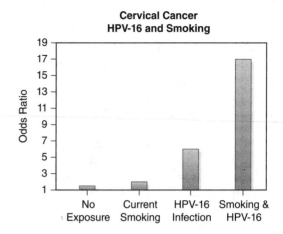

Figure 14.5 Synergism of Cigarette Smoking and HPV-16 Infection in the Pathogenesis of Cervical Cancer.

Source: Data from Gunnell, A. S., Tran, T. N., Torrång, A., Dickman, P. W., Sparén, P., Palmgren, J., & Ylitalo, N. (2006). Synergy between cigarette smoking and human papillomavirus type 16 in cervical cancer in situ development. *Cancer Epidemiology, Biomarkers and Prevention, 15*(11), 2141–2147.

smoking synergistically increases the risk of developing cervical cancer among women with HPV-16 infection (Gunnell et al., 2006).

Inflammogenesis of Cervical Cancer

Cyclooxygenase-1 and cyclooxygenase-2 (COX-1 and COX-2) are the chief rate-limiting enzymes of inflammation and the prostaglandin cascade. Low levels of the COX-1 isoform are produced constitutively in certain tissues such as the gastric mucosa, whereas much higher levels of the COX-2 isoform can be induced by a variety of pro-inflammatory stimuli, including tobacco smoke. Sustained COX-2 expression in a tissue is generally accepted as a biomarker of chronic inflammation.

In recent years, many molecular biologists have consistently and independently demonstrated that COX-2 is expressed in most epithelial neoplasms, including those of the uterine cervix. Although not detectable in normal cervical epithelium, COX-2 expression is a prominent feature of early stage premalignant lesions of the cervix as well as in situ cervical cancer and invasive cervical cancer (Harris, 2007).

Molecular studies have also shown that chronic inflammation of the cervical mucosa enhances HPV-induced carcinogenesis. According to one model, because HPV infection of the cervix by itself is not highly inflammatory, infection by other viruses (e.g., herpes simplex virus 2) and/or bacteria (e.g., *Chlamydia trachomatis*) and/or exposure to other inflammatory factors (e.g., tobacco metabolites) may be necessary to promote carcinogenesis. An important finding is that in HPV-infected women, carcinogenesis is tightly linked to *integration* of oncogenic HPV DNA into the host DNA. Notably, reactive oxygen and nitrogen species (ROS and RNS) generated by inflammation readily induce double-strand breaks in both host and viral DNA, thereby facilitating integration of HPV DNA into the DNA of infected cervical epithelium. Following integration of oncogenic HPV DNA, there is overexpression of viral oncogenes *E6* and *E7*, which accelerates carcinogenesis by interfering with key tumor suppressor genes such as *p53* and *Rb* (Williams, Filippova, Soto, & Duerksen-Hughes, 2011).

PREVENTION OF CERVICAL CANCER

Prevention of cervical cancer relies on avoidance of HPV infection and other risk factors (HIV infection and smoking) coupled with early detection and effective ablation of premalignant lesions of the uterine cervix. Strains of HPV are spread by sexual intercourse, oral sex, anal sex, or any other contact involving the genitalia. Preventive strategies include abstinence from sexual contact, monogamy, condom use, avoidance of tobacco, regular screening by Papanicolaou cytological testing (yearly Pap tests for sexually active women), and vaccination against high-risk HPV strains.

HPV Vaccination

Two effective vaccines have now been developed and are approved for use against high-risk HPV strains in the United States and Europe (McNeil, 2006). In randomized clinical trials, Gardasil (Merck) prevented infection by HPV types 6, 11, 16, and 18 in up to 98% of those vaccinated; Cervarix (GlaxoSmithKline) prevented infections by HPV strains 16 and 18 in 92% of recipients over a 4-year follow-up period. These vaccines are effective only if administered to young females prior to HPV exposure. Unfortunately, their relatively high cost may prohibit widespread HPV vaccination programs in impoverished nations (Singh, 2005). Furthermore, vaccination should not be considered a replacement for screening because the known oncogenic HPV strains account for only about 70% of cervical cancer overall.

Visual Inspection for Detection of Cervical Neoplasia

In populations with limited access to healthcare facilities, direct visual inspection of the uterine cervix after staining with acetic acid or Lugol's iodine has proven very effective in the detection of precancerous lesions (Sherris et al., 2009). Direct visual inspection procedures eliminate the need for transport of specimens and laboratory testing, require very little equipment, and provide women with immediate test results. A range of medical professionals, including doctors, nurses, and professional midwives, can effectively perform the procedure, provided they receive adequate training and supervision. Furthermore, such screening tests have been shown to perform equal to or better than cervical cytology in accurately identifying precancerous lesions. A major advantage of direct visual inspection is that women can be screened and treated in a single visit. One efficacious treatment option is cryotherapy (freezing), a relatively simple and inexpensive method by which cervical lesions can be immediately removed by the primary care physician (Denny et al., 2005).

REFERENCES

American Cancer Society. (2007). *Global cancer facts and figures, 2007*. Atlanta, GA: Author.

Boshart, M., Gissmann, L., Hans Ikenberg, H., Kleinheinz, A., Wolfram Scheurlen, W., & zur Hausen, H. (1984). A new type of papilloma virus DNA, its presence in genital cancer biopsies and in cell lines derived from cervical cancer. *EMBO Journal, 3*(5), 1151–1157.

Castle, P. E., Wacholder, S., Lorincz, A. T., Scott, D. R., Sherman, M. E., Glass, A. G., . . . Schiffman, M. (2002). A prospective study of high-grade cervical neoplasia risk among human papillomavirus-infected women. *Journal of the National Cancer Institute, 94*(18), 1406–1404.

Denny, L., Kuhn, L., De Souza, M., Pollack, A. E., Dupree, W., & Wright, T. C. Jr. (2005). Screen-and-treat approaches for cervical cancer prevention in low-resource settings: A randomized controlled trial. *Journal of the American Medical Association, 294*(17), 2173–2181.

Dürst, M., Gissmann, L., Ikenberg, H., & zur Hausen, H. (1983). A papillomavirus DNA from a cervical carcinoma and its prevalence in cancer biopsy samples from different geographic regions. *Proceedings of the National Academy of Sciences, 80*(12), 3812–3815.

Ferlay, J., Bray, F., Pisani, P., & Parkin, D. M. (2004). *GLOBOCAN 2002. Cancer incidence, mortality, and prevalence worldwide. IARC CancerBase No. 5*, version 2.0. Lyon, France: IARC Press. Retrieved from http://www-dep.iarc.fr

Ferlay, J., Shin, H.-R., Bray, F., Forman, D., Mathers, C., & Parkin, D. M. (2010). Estimates of worldwide burden of cancer in 2008: GLOBOCAN 2008. *International Journal of Cancer, 127*(12), 2893–2917.

Ferlay, J., Soerjomataram, I., Ervik, M., Dikshit, R., Eser, S., Mathers, C., . . . Bray, F. (2013). *GLOBOCAN 2012 v1.0. Cancer incidence and mortality worldwide: IARC CancerBase No. 11* [Internet]. Lyon, France: International Agency for Research on Cancer. Retrieved from http://globocan.iarc.fr

Gandini, S., Botteri, E., Iodice, S., Boniol, M., Lowenfels, A. B., Maisonneuve, P., & Boyle, P. (2008). Tobacco smoking and cancer: A meta-analysis. *International Journal of Cancer, 12*(1), 155–164.

Gunnell, A. S., Tran, T. N., Torrång, A., Dickman, P. W., Sparén, P., Palmgren, J., & Ylitalo, N. (2006). Synergy between cigarette smoking and human papillomavirus type 16 in cervical cancer in situ development. *Cancer Epidemiology, Biomarkers and Prevention, 15*(11), 2141–2147.

Harris, R. E. (2007). Cyclooxygenase-2 (COX-2) and the inflammogenesis of cancer. *Subcellular Biochemistry, 42*, 93–126.

Howlader, N., Noone, A. M., Krapcho, M., Neyman, N., Aminou, R., Waldron, W., . . . Edwards, B. K. (Eds.). (2011). *SEER Cancer Statistics Review, 1975–2008.* Bethesda, MD: National Cancer Institute.

Jemal, A., Siegel, R., Ward, E., Hao, Y., Xu, J., & Thun, M. J. (2009). Cancer statistics, 2009. *CA: A Cancer Journal for Clinicians, 59*, 225–249.

Kumar, V., Abbas, A. K., Nelson, F., & Mitchell, R. N. (2007). *Robbins basic pathology* (8th ed., pp. 718–721). Philadelphia, PA: Elsevier Saunders.

McNeil, C. (2006). Who invented the VLP cervical cancer vaccines? *Journal of the National Cancer Institute, 98*(7), 433.

Münger, K., & Howley, P. M. (2002). Human papillomavirus immortalization and transformation functions. *Virus Research, 89*(2), 213–228.

Muñoz, N., Bosch, F. X., de Sanjose, S., Tafur, L., Izarzugaza, I., Gili, M., . . . Shah, K. (1992). The causal link between human papillomavirus and invasive cervical cancer: A population-based case-control study in Colombia and Spain. *International Journal of Cancer, 52*, 743–749.

Papanicolaou, G. N., & Traut, H. F. (1943). *Diagnosis of uterine cancer by the vaginal smear.* New York, NY: Commonwealth Fund.

Plummer, M., Herrero, R., Franceschi, S., Meijer, C. J., Snijders, P., Bosch, F. X., . . . Muñoz, N.; IARC Multi-centre Cervical Cancer Study Group (2003). Smoking and cervical cancer: Pooled analysis of the IARC multi-centric case-control study. *Cancer Causes and Control, 14*(9), 805–814.

Prokopakis, P., Sourvinos, G., Koumantaki, Y., Koumantakis, E., & Spandidos, D. A. (2002). *K-ras* mutations and HPV infection in cervicitis and intraepithelial neoplasias of the cervix. *Oncology Reports, 9*, 129–133.

Sherman, M. E., Wang, S. S., Carreon, J., & Devesa, S. S. (2005). Mortality trends for cervical squamous and adenocarcinoma in the United States. Relation to incidence and survival. *Cancer, 103*, 1258–1264.

Sherris, J., Wittet, S., Kleine, A., Sellors, J., Luciani, S., Sankaranarayanan, R., & Barone, M. A. (2009). Evidence-based alternative cervical cancer screening approaches in low-resource settings. *International Perspectives on Sexual and Reproductive Health, 35*(3), 147–152.

Singh, N. (2005). HPV and cervical cancer: Prospects for prevention through vaccination. *Indian Journal of Medical and Pediatric Oncology, 26*(1), 20–23.

Sood, A. K. (1991). Cigarette smoking and cervical cancer: Meta-analysis and critical review of recent studies. *American Journal of Preventive Medicine*, 7(4), 208–213.

Stentella, P., Frega, A., Ciccarone, M., Cipriano, L., Tinari, A., Tzantzoglou, S., & Pachì, A. (1998). HPV and intraepithelial neoplasia recurrent lesions of the lower genital tract: Assessment of the immune system. *European Journal of Gynaecological Oncology*, 19(5), 466–469.

Walboomers, J. M., Jacobs, M. V., Manos, M. M., Bosch, F. X., Kummer, J. A., Shah, K. V., . . . Muñoz, N. (1999). Human papillomavirus is a necessary cause of invasive cervical cancer worldwide. *Journal of Pathology*, 189, 12–19.

Winkelstein, W. Jr. (1977). Smoking and cancer of the uterine cervix: Hypothesis. *American Journal of Epidemiology*, 106(4), 257–259.

Winkelstein, W. Jr. (1990). Smoking and cervical cancer—current status: A review. *American Journal of Epidemiology*, 131, 945–957.

Williams, V. M., Filippova, M., Soto, U., & Duerksen-Hughes, P. J. (2011). HPV-DNA integration and carcinogenesis: Putative roles for inflammation and oxidative stress. *Future Virology*, 6(1), 45–57.

zur Hausen, H. (1976). Condylomata acuminata and human genital cancer. *Cancer Research*, 36, 530.

15

Epidemiology of Vaginal, Vulvar, and Anal Cancer

GLOBAL BURDEN OF VAGINAL, VULVAR, AND ANAL CANCER

Epidemiologic features of vaginal, vulvar, and anal cancer are in many respects quite similar to those of cervical cancer because all are etiologically linked to infection of the respective tissues by oncogenic strains of human papillomavirus (HPV). However, cervical cancer is by far the most common of all HPV-related malignancies, with a global burden among women that is nearly 10-fold higher than the combined impact of malignancies of the vagina, vulva, and anus. Worldwide, invasive cervical cancer is diagnosed in approximately 530,000 women and causes 270,000 deaths annually whereas cancers of the vagina, vulva, and anus are diagnosed in about 56,000 women annually and cause 31,000 deaths. Anal cancer also afflicts about 14,000 men each year, causing an additional 8,000 deaths in the male population (de Martel et al., 2012; Ferlay et al., 2013; Forman et al., 2010, 2013; Parkin & Bray, 2006).

In contrast to cervical cancer, malignancies of the vagina and vulva are relatively rare and account for less than 0.5% of all female cancers and less than 5% of malignancies of the female genital tract. Likewise, anal cancer is an uncommon lesion of the lower gastrointestinal tract accounting for about 0.3% of all cancers and 2–3% of malignancies of the gastrointestinal tract in both men and women. Most vaginal, vulvar, and anal malignancies (90–95%) are squamous cell carcinomas that arise from the stratified epithelium that covers these anatomic sites. Adenocarcinomas are the most common of the other malignancies that arise in tissues of the vagina, vulva, or anus (Hamilton & Aaltonen, 2000; Tavassoli & Devilee, 2003a, 2003b).

HUMAN PAPILLOMAVIRUS IN VAGINAL, VULVAR, AND ANAL CARCINOMA

Human papillomaviruses are DNA viruses capable of infecting the skin and mucous membranes of humans. Although most of the more than 150 HPV subtypes do not cause disease, a few strains may cause condyloma acuminata (warts) or carcinomas of the anogenital and/or oropharyngeal mucosa. Genital infections by HPV are common, and most (~90%) resolve spontaneously over time without treatment. However, persisting infections by low-risk strains (HPV-6 and HPV-11) predispose to condyloma development, and chronic infections by high-risk strains (HPV-16 and HPV-18) predispose to carcinoma development of the anogenital tissues (cervix, vagina, vulva, and anus).

Nobel laureate Harald zur Hausen and colleagues first suggested that certain HPV strains are carcinogenic in human tissues of the cervix and elsewhere (zur Hausen, 1976, 1977). Using polymerase chain reaction (PCR) assays, they demonstrated the presence of HPV DNA in virtually all cancerous tissues from cervical cancer patients and premalignant (precursor) lesions of the uterine cervix (Boshartb et al., 1984; zur Hausen, 2002). Subsequent molecular studies have documented the presence of HPV DNA in a high proportion of other anogenital carcinomas as well as their precursor lesions. The current consensus is that virtually all cervical cancers are caused by HPV infections and that two types (HPV-16 and HPV-18) are responsible for about 70% of cases. Furthermore, chronic anogenital infections due to oncogenic HPV strains are estimated to cause approximately 88% of anal cancers, 70% of vaginal cancers, and 43% of vulvar cancers (de Martel et al., 2012; De Vuyst,

Clifford, Nascimento, Madeleine, & Franceschi, 2009; Parkin, 2006; Parkin & Bray, 2006).

Population Attributable Fraction (PAF) and HPV Infection

To gauge the overall population impact of HPV infection in the genesis of carcinomas of the vagina, vulva, and anus, investigators at the International Agency for Research on Cancer (IARC) estimated a parameter known as the population attributable fraction (PAF) for each of these malignancies. The PAF is an estimate of the proportion of cases of a specific disease (in this case, cancer) that could theoretically be avoided if exposure to a specific risk factor (in this case, HPV infection) was eliminated.

For a dichotomous risk factor, the PAF is calculated by the following formula:

$$PAF = p(\text{Incidence in exposed} - \text{Incidence in unexposed}) / \text{Total incidence}$$

where p = the prevalence of exposure in the general population at risk.

Because the relative risk (RR) is calculated by RR = Incidence in exposed / Incidence in unexposed, the PAF can also be calculated by the formula

$$PAF = p(RR - 1) / [1 + p(RR - 1)]$$

where RR = the relative risk of developing disease due to exposure to the risk factor.

An alternative estimate of the PAF is given by the formula:

$$PAF = p_c(RR - 1) / RR$$

where p_c = the prevalence of exposed cases in the population. As the RR increases, the latter formula approaches $PAF = p_c$, which can be viewed as the upper limit of the PAF. The number of cases attributable to the risk factor can be obtained by the formula

$$\text{Attributable cases} = PAF \times \text{Incident cases}$$

Estimates of the PAF and the number of cases of vaginal cancer, vulvar cancer, and anal cancer caused by HPV infection are given in **Table 15.1**. Using PAF estimates of 70%, 43%, and 88% for vaginal, vulvar, and anal cancer, respectively, the IARC investigators estimated that HPV infection accounted for nearly 45,000 new cases (66%) of these malignancies in 2008 (de Martel et al., 2012; De Vuyst et al., 2009).

Molecular Mechanisms of Carcinogenesis by Human Papillomavirus

Cancer develops when the DNA from oncogenic HPV strains, particularly HPV-16, HPV-18, HPV-31,

Table 15.1	Population Attributable Fractions (PAF) and HPV-Attributable Cases of Vaginal, Vulvar, and Anal Cancer, 2008		
Cancer Site	PAF (%)	Incident Cases	Attributable Cases
Vagina	70	13,000	9,100
Vulva	43	27,000	11,610
Anus	88	27,000	23,760
Total	66	67,000	44,470

Source: Data from de Martel, C., Ferlay, J., Franceschi, S., Vignat, J., Bray, F., Forman, D., & Plummer, M. (2012). The global burden of cancers attributable to infections in the year 2008: A review and synthetic analysis. *Lancet Oncology, 13,* 607–615.

and HPV-33, integrate with the DNA of host cells in the cervix, vagina, vulva, anus, and/or other tissues. The integration of viral genes into the genome of the invaded epithelial cell (called lysogeny) leads to the overexpression of certain viral genes (*E6* and *E7*) that in turn inactivate tumor suppressor genes such as *P53* and *Rb* (Münger, Scheffner, Huibregtse, & Howley, 1992) or up-regulate proto-oncogenes such as *ras* and *telomerase* (Kiyono et al., 1998; Matlashewskil et al., 1987; zur Hausen, 2002). Potential cofactors include chronic exposure to tobacco carcinogens, systemic HIV-related immunosuppression and co-infection by other genital viruses (such as herpes simplex virus 2 [HSV2]), and bacteria. Key steps in the carcinogenic process are illustrated in **Figure 15.1**.

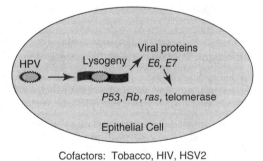

Model of HPV and Carcinogenesis

Figure 15.1 Molecular Mechanisms of HPV and Carcinogenesis.

Steps in the model: (1) HPV infection; (2) integration of HPV DNA into epithelial cell DNA (lysogeny); (3) expression of viral proteins (*E6, E7*); (4) disruption of *p53, Rb, ras,* and telomerase gene function; and (5) loss of cell cycle control, accelerated cell proliferation, failure of apoptosis, and immortalization of cell lineage.

GLOBAL PATTERN OF VAGINAL, VULVAR, AND ANAL SQUAMOUS CELL CANCERS

Because HPV is the predominant risk factor in the genesis of squamous cell carcinomas of the cervix, vagina, vulva, and anus, the global distributions of these malignancies should closely follow the global distribution of HPV genital infections. Nevertheless, marked differences in the timely diagnosis and reporting of anogenital cancers in different populations have confounded efforts to discern their true global pattern. Currently, the worldwide patterns of anogenital cancer incidence rates reflect not only the underlying risk due to factors such as HPV infection, but also the impact of screening, early detection, and curative removal of premalignant lesions in women living in more developed nations (Parkin & Bray, 2006).

Recently, data from 194 published studies were pooled to assess the global burden and pattern of HPV cervical infections in asymptomatic women. In all studies, HPV DNA was detected in cytological cervical specimens using PCR assays or hybrid capture (detection of denatured HPV DNA with complementary RNA probes). The global distribution of HPV infections is shown in **Figure 15.2**. The prevalence of HPV infection in cervical tissues is high (over 20%) among asymptomatic women living in sub-Saharan Africa,

Central America, South America, and Southeast Asia and low (less than 10%) in those living in North America, Western Europe, Scandinavia, and Oceania (Bruni et al., 2010). This pattern is a virtual image of the distribution of cervical cancer incidence and presumably approximates the global pattern of vaginal, vulvar, and anal carcinoma (Forman et al., 2012).

HUMAN IMMUNODEFICIENCY VIRUS IN VAGINAL, VULVAR, AND ANAL CARCINOMA

Patients with acquired immune deficiency syndrome (AIDS) due to infection by human immunodeficiency virus (HIV) are at markedly increased risk of developing certain malignancies, most notably Kaposi's sarcoma and non-Hodgkin's lymphoma. Chronic HIV infection also has been found to accelerate the risk of developing multiple other cancers, including those related to HPV infection.

Using data collected in the multicenter AIDS–Cancer Match Registry Study in the United States, investigators at the National Cancer Institute (NCI) examined the incidence of HPV-associated malignancies among 309,365 patients with HIV/AIDS (257,605 men and 51,760 women) during the

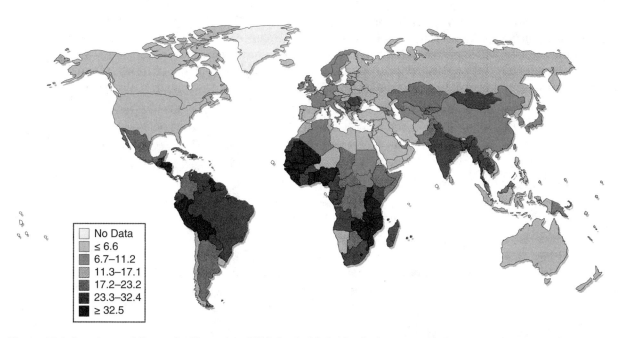

No Data
≤ 6.6
6.7–11.2
11.3–17.1
17.2–23.2
23.3–32.4
≥ 32.5

Figure 15.2 Prevalence of Human Papillomavirus (HPV) Cervical Infection in Asymptomatic Women, 2008.

Source: Data from Bruni, L., Diaz, M., Castellsagué, X., Ferrer, E., Bosch, F. X., & de Sanjosé, S. (2010). Cervical human papillomavirus prevalence in 5 continents: Meta-analysis of 1 million women with normal cytological findings. *Journal of Infectious Disease, 202,* 1789–1799; Forman, D., de Martel, C., Lacey, C. J., Soerjomataram, I., Lortet-Tieulent, J., Bruni, L.,... Franceschi, S. (2012). Global burden of human papillomavirus and related diseases. *Vaccine, 30*(Suppl 5), F12–F23.

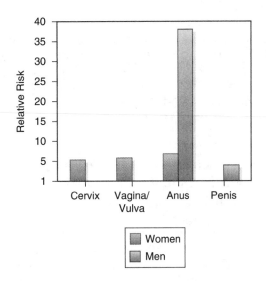

Figure 15.3 Relative Risk of HPV-Related Cancer in Women and Men With HIV/AIDS.

Source: Data from Frisch, M., Biggar, R.J., & Goedert, J. J. (2000). Human papillomavirus-associated cancers in patients with human immunodeficiency virus infection and acquired immunodeficiency syndrome. *Journal of the National Cancer Institute, 92*(18), 1500–1510.

period 1978–1996. Their study revealed that among patients with HIV/AIDS, all HPV-associated cancers occurred in significant excess of the expected rates in the general population. Invasive malignancies of the cervix, vagina, vulva, and anus were increased more than fivefold among HIV-infected women, and malignancies of the anus and penis were increased by 38-fold and 4-fold, respectively, among HIV-infected men (**Figure 15.3**). Furthermore, invasive tumors were diagnosed earlier (~10 years on average) in HIV/AIDS patients than cases from the general population, suggesting that HIV-related immuno-suppression hastens the progression of HPV-related cancer (Frisch, Biggar, & Goedert, 2000).

EPIDEMIOLOGY OF VAGINAL CANCER

Vaginal cancer is an uncommon malignancy accounting for less than 0.3% of all female cancers and about 1–2% of malignancies of the female genital tract. Estimates of the annual incidence ranged from 0.3 to 0.7 per 100,000 among populations sampled in 2002 (Parkin & Bray, 2006). During 2008, approximately 13,000 new cases of vaginal cancer were diagnosed in the world population; of these, 8,000 occurred in women living in underdeveloped countries (de Martel et al., 2012). Five-year survival rate depends on the stage at detection and is far better for women with localized tumors (70%) than those with advanced disease (15%). Based on available survival data, more than 7,000 women die annually from metastatic vaginal cancer (Ferlay et al., 2010).

Most vaginal malignancies (90–95%) are squamous cell carcinomas that arise from the vaginal epithelium distal to the opening of the cervix. The other prominent cell type of vaginal cancer is clear cell adenocarcinoma, which is caused by in utero exposure to diethylstilbesterol (DES).

Age at Diagnosis of Vaginal Cancer

The onset of vaginal cancer differs markedly according to the histologic cell type. Squamous cell carcinomas of the vagina are predominantly diagnosed late in life, whereas clear cell adenocarcinomas develop much earlier (**Figure 15.4**). This difference relates to the

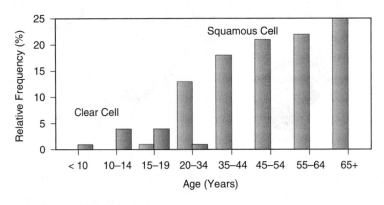

Figure 15.4 Age at Diagnosis of Vaginal Cancer by Histology.

The relative frequency of clear cell adenocarcinoma among all cases of vaginal carcinoma is approximately 10% of the level shown in the chart.

Source: Data from Howlader, N., Noone, A. M., Krapcho, M., Garshell, J., Neyman, N., Altekruse, S. F., . . . Cronin, K. A. (Eds.). (2013). *SEER cancer statistics review, 1975–2010.* Bethesda, MD: National Cancer Institute. Retrieved from http://seer.cancer.gov/csr/1975_2010/; National Cancer Institute. (2011). *Diethylstilbestrol (DES) and cancer.* Bethesda, MD: National Cancer Institute.

timing of exposure to etiologic agents. Squamous cell carcinomas are linked to exposure to oncogenic HPV strains through sexual activity with multiple partners, co-infection by HIV, and chronic cigarette smoking, whereas clear cell adenocarcinomas arise due to in utero exposure to a carcinogenic agent (DES).

Vaginal Cancer in the United States

The incidence of vaginal cancer varies by age and race. In a study of women based on 39 population-based cancer registries in the United States, 1,370 cases of in situ vaginal cancer and 5,430 cases of invasive cancer were detected during 1998–2003. The annual age-adjusted incidence estimated for all women was 0.18 per 100,000 for in situ cancer and 0.69 for invasive cancer. Cases of in situ cancer were diagnosed an average of 10 years earlier (58 years) than cases of invasive cancer (68 years). The annual incidence of invasive vaginal cancer was highest among African American women (1.06 per 100,000) and lowest among women of Asian and Pacific Island origin (0.50 per 100,000). Rates were intermediate for Caucasian and Hispanic women (0.65 and 0.87 per 100,000, respectively) (Wu et al., 2008).

Risk Factors for Squamous Cell Carcinoma of the Vagina

Squamous cell carcinoma of the vagina has a similar profile of risk factors as cervical cancer. Current evidence suggests that malignant transformation of the vaginal epithelium is most often a consequence of chronic genital infection by oncogenic strains of HPV, particularly HPV-16 and HPV-18. In fact, this type of malignancy is often diagnosed as a second primary tumor among women who were formerly treated for cervical dysplasia or cervical cancer (Brinton et al., 1990b; Choo & Anderson, 1982; Gallup, Talledo, Shah, & Hayes, 1987). Other cofactors also increase the risk, including cigarette smoking and infection by the genital herpes simplex virus (HSV2) and/or HIV.

Human Papillomavirus and Vaginal Carcinoma

Investigators at the IARC examined the prevalence of HPV in vulvar, vaginal, and anal carcinoma and premalignant lesions called intraepithelial neoplasia using the data from 93 studies conducted in 26 countries of Asia, Europe, North America, Latin America, and Oceania. In all studies included for meta-analysis, the presence of HPV DNA in tissue samples was detected by PCR assays. Prevalence estimates for vaginal lesions were obtained by pooling the data from 14 of these studies. The prevalence of HPV was 70% among 136 vaginal carcinomas and 94% among 298

vaginal intraepithelial neoplasms (VAINs). Among HPV-positive cases of vaginal carcinoma, 80% were positive for HPV-16, 10% were positive for HPV-18, and the remaining cases were positive for either HPV-6 or HPV-11. These results clearly indicate that oncogenic strains of HPV (particularly HPV-16 and HPV-18) play a significant role in the genesis of vaginal carcinoma (De Vuyst et al., 2009).

Vaginal Intraepithelial Neoplasia (VAIN)

Microscopic studies of cytological specimens of suspicious lesions of the vaginal epithelium clearly reveal the presence of premalignant foci of abnormally proliferating cells called *vaginal intraepithelial neoplasia (VAIN)*. Similar to cervical intraepithelial neoplasia (CIN), these lesions are graded as VAIN1, VAIN2, or VAIN3, reflecting the likelihood of transition to invasive carcinoma. Of these, VAIN3 is synonymous with carcinoma in situ, which may progress to invasive squamous cell carcinoma if cancer cells breach the basement membrane (National Cancer Institute, 2011).

Women who develop VAIN are most often premenopausal with coexisting CIN. In a series of 121 VAIN cases, the mean age at diagnosis was 35 years and the lesions were typically multifocal and located in the upper third of the vagina in association with CIN (Dodge, Eltabbakh, Mount, Walker, & Morgan, 2001). In a meta-analysis of tissue specimens from women with vaginal neoplasia, HPV DNA was detected in 100% of 107 cases with VAIN1, 90% of 191 cases with VAIN2 or VAIN3, and 70% of 136 cases with invasive vaginal carcinoma (De Vuyst et al., 2009). These results suggest that in some women, persisting HPV infection of the vaginal epithelium is sufficient to cause progression of VAIN to invasive vaginal carcinoma, whereas in others, additional risk factors likely contribute to malignant transformation.

Web of Causation in Vaginal Carcinoma

Factors other than HPV may be involved in the causal pathway leading to vaginal cancer. This is illustrated by the results of a population-based case control study conducted in the state of Washington in the United States. In the study, 156 women with squamous cell vaginal carcinoma were compared to 2,041 age-matched controls without cancer. Effects were quantified by estimating odds ratios (ORs). Notably, tumors of the cervix or the anus preceded the diagnosis of vaginal cancer in 30% of the cases. Women with vaginal cancer were more likely to have five or more sexual partners (OR = 3.1), first intercourse before age 17 years (OR = 2.0), and be current smokers at diagnosis (OR = 2.1) than controls. The presence of antibodies to HPV-16 was the strongest risk factor (OR = 4.3); furthermore, HPV-16 DNA was detected in 80% of cases with in situ vaginal cancer and 60% of cases with invasive vaginal cancer. Nevertheless, independent risk increases were also noted among women with antibodies to HPV-18 (OR = 2.0) and genital HSV2 (OR = 2.1). Finally, there was an increasing dose response in risk with the duration of cigarette smoking, peaking at more than 30 years of tobacco addiction (OR = 2.8). These findings suggest a web of causation that includes multiple risk factors (e.g., early sexual activity with several partners) leading to chronic infection of the cervical, anal, and vaginal epithelium by HPV-16, HPV-18, and/or HSV2 coupled with chronic tobacco smoking (Daling et al., 2002). Though not assessed in this study, immunosuppression due to HIV/AIDS also increases the risk.

Cigarette Smoking and Squamous Cell Vaginal Carcinoma

Only a small percentage (~10%) of women infected with oncogenic strains of HPV develop squamous cell carcinoma of the vagina. One cofactor that significantly heightens malignant transformation is chronic cigarette smoking.

An international team of investigators recently examined associations of HPV infection and smoking with the development of squamous cell carcinomas (SCCs) of the vulva and vagina in a case control study of Danish women. A total of 182 cases with squamous cell carcinomas of the vulva or vagina were compared to 164 women with adenocarcinomas of the corpus uteri and 518 population controls without cancer. Women with uterine adenocarcinomas and women without cancer manifested similar characteristics, and the two control groups were pooled in the final analysis of data. Tumor specimens were examined for the presence of HPV DNA by PCR assays. Univariate analyses revealed that current smoking significantly increased the risk of vulvar SCC (OR = 2.69) and vaginal SCC (OR = 1.68). However, stratification by the presence/absence of HPV DNA revealed that tobacco smoking increased the risk among HPV-positive women (OR = 2.78) *but not among HPV-negative women* (OR = 1.03). These results suggest that tobacco carcinogens interact with oncogenic strains of HPV to synergistically heighten the risk (Madsen, Jensen, van den Brule, Wohlfahrt, & Frisch, 2008).

Human Immunodeficiency Virus in Vaginal Carcinoma

Based on data from the AIDS–Cancer Match Registry Study in the United States, women with AIDS have a 5.8-fold increased incidence of developing invasive vulvar/vaginal cancer compared to women from the general population (Figure 15.3). On average, invasive tumors emerged at an earlier age in AIDS patients, suggesting that HIV-related immunosuppression markedly accelerates the progression of HPV-related in situ lesions of the vulva or vagina to invasive carcinoma (Frisch et al., 2000).

Clear Cell Adenocarcinoma of the Vagina

Clear cell adenocarcinomas of the vagina are caused by in utero exposure to diethylstilbestrol (DES). From 1940–1971, a routine practice in the United States and throughout Europe was to administer DES to pregnant women with first trimester bleeding in order to prevent miscarriage and premature labor and delivery. It is estimated that DES was prescribed to 5–10 million women in the United States and millions more in Europe. It was eventually discovered that daughters of these DES-treated women developed clear cell adenocarcinoma of the vagina at an exceptionally high rate. This tumor is extraordinarily rare and, unlike other forms of vaginal cancer that are usually diagnosed late in life, clear cell vaginal adenocarcinomas stimulated by in utero DES exposure are most often diagnosed during adolescence (Herbst & Anderson, 1991; National Cancer Institute, 2011).

In 1970, Arthur Herbst and Robert Scully reported characteristics of a series of seven rare vaginal adenocarcinomas diagnosed in young women, 15–22 years of age, during a 2-year window of time at Massachusetts General Hospital and one other hospital in Boston. Six of the tumors were pathologically classified as clear cell adenocarcinomas of the vagina. Prior to this time, there were only a few case reports of this rare type of malignancy occurring in young women (Herbst & Scully, 1970).

Shortly after the initial cluster of cases was identified, a retrospective case control investigation was conducted comparing exposures in eight young women with clear cell vaginal adenocarcinomas to four matched controls per case. Seven of the eight mothers of these patients had been treated with DES during the first trimester of pregnancy (P < 0.00001). The investigators concluded that "maternal ingestion of stilbestrol during early pregnancy appears to have enhanced the risk of vaginal adenocarcinoma developing years later in the offspring exposed" (Herbst, Ulfelder, & Poskanzer, 1971).

Following these early reports, the carcinogenic impact of in utero DES exposure was confirmed by several independent studies, and a registry of DES-exposed daughters was established. The risk of developing clear cell vaginal adenocarcinoma by age

24 years among women who were exposed to DES in utero was estimated at approximately 1 per 1,000, more than 40 times higher than among unexposed women (Herbst, 1981; Herbst & Anderson, 1991; Herbst, Cole, Colton, Robboy, & Scully, 1977). Clear cell adenocarcinoma is often preceded by a condition known as vaginal adenosis (the presence of abnormal glandular foci in the vaginal epithelium). In 1972, DES administration to pregnant women was discontinued in the United States; however, its use continued in Europe until 1978 (National Cancer Institute, 2011).

By 1981, 400 cases of clear cell adenocarcinoma of the vagina had been diagnosed among young women born after 1940. The number of cases peaked in the United States in 1975 and has since declined (**Figure 15.5**). The age-specific incidence rates of this tumor are highest among young women ages 15–22 years, with a peak incidence at age 19. Furthermore, DES-exposed women are at high risk for a multitude of other adverse reproductive events, including stillbirth, neonatal death, ectopic pregnancy, miscarriage, pre-eclampsia, and infertility (Herbst, 1981; Herbst & Anderson, 1991).

Some studies suggest that the risk of breast cancer may be elevated in DES-exposed daughters. Investigators in the United States compared the incidence of breast cancer in a cohort of 4,817 women with prenatal DES exposure to that in a matched cohort of 2,073 women with no exposure. During follow-up, 102 cases of clear cell vaginal adenocarcinoma were diagnosed among DES-exposed women compared to 26 cases in unexposed women. Exposure to DES increased the incidence of breast cancer approximately twofold by age 40 (RR = 2.05) and by nearly fourfold by age 50 (RR = 3.85) (Palmer et al., 2006). The National Cancer Institute has therefore recommended that DES-exposed daughters have regular mammograms and yearly medical checkups that include careful pelvic examination to identify pre-malignant lesions (National Cancer Institute, 2011).

EPIDEMIOLOGY OF VULVAR CANCER

Carcinoma of the vulva accounts for about 1–2% of all malignancies of the female genitalia. Estimates of the incidence of vulvar cancer ranged from 0.5 to 1.5 per 100,000 among populations sampled in 2002 (Parkin & Bray, 2006). Worldwide, vulvar cancer was diagnosed in 27,000 women during 2008 and caused nearly 15,000 deaths (de Martel et al., 2012; Ferlay et al., 2010; Parkin, 2006). This tumor rarely manifests in women under the age of 60 years and is often preceded by premalignant dysplastic lesions called *vulvar intraepithelial neoplasia (VIN)*. As is true for CIN and VAIN, higher grades of VIN increase the likelihood of progression to invasive cancer of the vulva. Carcinoma in situ of the vulva (also called *Bowen's disease*) has been found to progress to invasive cancer over a period of 5–10 years. Similar to vaginal cancer and cervical cancer, most malignant tumors (90–95%) of the vulva are squamous cell carcinomas that arise from the stratified epithelium covering the vulva. Other histologies include malignant melanomas, Bartholin gland adenocarcinomas that arise in the sweat glands, Paget tumors, sarcomas, and basal cell carcinomas.

Squamous Cell Carcinoma of the Vulva

More than 90% of vulvar malignancies are squamous cell carcinomas; however, two independent pathways of vulvar carcinogenesis have been postulated corresponding to two distinct subtypes of squamous cell

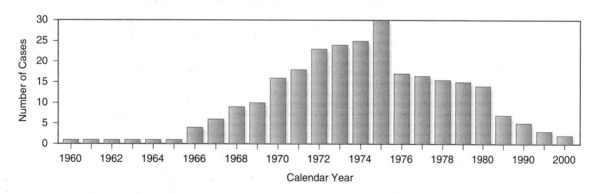

Figure 15.5 Clear Cell Vaginal Adenocarcinoma in DES-daughters.

Data points are moving averages of published numbers of cases.

Source: Data from Herbst, A. L. (1981). Clear cell adenocarcinoma and the current status of DES-exposed females. *Cancer, 48*, 484–488.

carcinomas of the vulva (Andersen, Franquemont, Williams, Taylor, & Crum, 1991; Bloss et al., 1991).

The classic, warty, or Bowenoid type is predominantly associated with chronic infection by HPV-16, HPV-18, or HPV-33 and is found in younger women (often prior to menopause). Factors associated with malignant transformation of the vulvar mucosa in HPV-infected women include early age at first intercourse, multiple sexual partners, HIV infection, genital HSV2 infection, and cigarette smoking.

The keratinizing, differentiated, or simplex type occurs in older postmenopausal women, is *not* related to HPV infection, and is associated with inflammatory vulvar dystrophies such as lichen sclerosis and chronic venereal granulomatous disease. In this type, the cancer cells are usually well differentiated and classically manifest *keratin pearls*, which are foci of keratinization within concentric layers of cancerous squamous cells.

Ethnic Differences and Time Trends in Vulvar Cancer

A team of investigators examined data from 39 population-based tumor registries in the United States covering 83% of the population during 1983–2003 and assessed patterns of vulvar cancer by age, race, ethnicity, and histology. During this time period, 12,554 in situ vulvar tumors and 18,066 invasive tumors were diagnosed. Squamous cell carcinomas accounted for 77% of in situ vulvar malignancies and 75% of invasive tumors. On average, in situ tumors were diagnosed about 20 years earlier (49 years) than invasive tumors (69 years). For all women, the annual incidence was 1.2 per 100,000 for in situ cancer and 1.7 per 100,000 for invasive cancer. The annual rate of invasive cancer was highest in Caucasians (1.8 per 100,000), intermediate in African American and Hispanic women (1.3 per 100,000), and lowest in Asian and Pacific Islanders (0.4 per 100,000). In contrast to many other forms of cancer, vulvar cancer rates are higher among Caucasian women than African American women, suggesting the presence of different risk factor profiles (Saraiya et al., 2008).

In a separate study, a rising trend was observed in the age-adjusted incidence of both invasive vulvar cancer and in situ tumors among U.S. women during 1973–2004. Based on data from nine registries of the Surveillance, Epidemiology, and End Results (SEER) program, the rate of in situ vulvar cancer increased 74% (3.5% annually), and the rate of invasive vulvar cancer increased 21% (1.0% annually) during the 21-year time period of study. The age-adjusted incidence rate of invasive vulvar cancer during 1997–2004 was 2.5 cases per 100,000 among all women, 2.8 per 100,000 among Caucasians, and 2.0 per

100,000 in African Americans. Speculative reasons for the increase in vulvar cancer rates include rising rates of infection by oncogenic strains of HPV and greater numbers of immunocompromised patients due to HIV infections (Bodelon, Madeleine, Voigt, & Weiss, 2009).

Human Papillomavirus and Vulvar Carcinoma

The prevalence of HPV in vulvar carcinoma was examined in a meta-analysis of data from 93 studies conducted on four continents using PCR assays for detection of HPV seropositivity. Prevalence estimates for vulvar lesions were obtained by pooling the data from 63 of these studies. The prevalence of HPV was 68% in 90 cases of VIN1, 85% in 1,061 cases of VIN2 or VIN3, but only 40% in 1,873 cases of invasive vulvar carcinoma. The prevalence of HPV strains differed by grade of neoplasia: HPV-6 (22%), HPV-16 (10%), and HPV-11 (9%) in VIN1; HPV-16 (72%), HPV-18 (5%), and HPV-33 (8%) in VIN2/3; and HPV-16 (32%), HPV-18 (4%), and HPV-33 (5%) in invasive carcinoma. Notably, the prevalence of HPV was markedly higher in basaloid (warty) vulvar carcinomas (70%) compared to keratinized tumors (13%). These results support the existence of different etiologies of carcinoma of the vulva, one process related to infection by HPV-16, HPV-18, or HPV-33 and another that is independent of HPV and related to different inflammatory and/or infectious agents (De Vuyst et al., 2009).

Cigarette Smoking and Vulvar Carcinoma

Cigarette smoking has been consistently implicated as a risk factor for squamous cell carcinomas of the female genital tract including the vulva (Daling et al., 1992). Effects of smoking on vulvar cancer were examined in a population-based case control study of 400 women with in situ vulvar carcinoma, 110 women with invasive carcinoma, and 1,403 age-matched controls in the Seattle, Washington, area. Serum samples were analyzed for antibodies against oncogenic HPV strains and HSV2. Current smokers were at increased risk (OR = 3.6 for in situ carcinoma and OR = 2.8 for invasive carcinoma). Independent effects were also observed for HPV infection or HSV2 infection. Notably, vulvar carcinoma risk was increased 18.8-fold among women who were current smokers and seropositive for HPV-16 compared to nonsmokers who were seronegative for HPV-16. The investigators concluded that current smoking and infection by either HPV or HSV2 are risk factors for vulvar carcinoma and that HPV-16 infection and smoking synergistically increase the risk (Madeleine, Daling, & Schwartz, 1997).

Condyloma Acuminata of the Vulva

Condyloma acuminata (genital warts) are associated with sexually transmitted viruses, particularly certain strains of HPV (e.g., HPV-6 and HPV-11) and genital HSV2. These lesions consist of proliferating squamous epithelium with atypical morphology. Though controversial, some studies suggest that their presence may heighten the risk of developing vulvar carcinoma. In a case control study of 209 vulvar cancer patients and 348 age-matched controls from the same communities, several risk factors were examined, including history of genital warts. The findings revealed a marked increase in risk (OR = 15.2) among those women who reported a medical history of condyloma acuminata. Furthermore, women with a history of this condition who were smokers had a 35-fold increase in the risk of developing vulvar cancer compared to women with neither exposure (Brinton et al., 1990a).

Human Immunodeficiency Virus and Vulvar Carcinoma

Immunosuppression due to HIV/AIDS appears to be a strong risk factor for vulvar carcinoma. In a case control study, investigators at the University of Witwatersand in Johannesburg, South Africa, compared 53 women with vulvar carcinoma to 556 women without cancer ascertained from three tertiary care hospitals in Johannesburg and Soweto. Seropositivity for HIV was found to significantly increase the vulvar cancer risk (adjusted OR = 4.8) (Sitas et al., 2000). This estimate for South African women is similar to findings from the AIDS–Cancer Match Registry Study in the United States in which women with HIV/AIDS had a 5.8-fold increased incidence of developing invasive vulvar/vaginal cancer compared to women from the general population (Figure 15.3) (Frisch et al., 2000). These results, together with several published case reports, indicate that HIV-associated immunosuppression increases the likelihood of chronic infection by high-risk HPV types that predispose to intraepithelial neoplasia and carcinoma of the vulva (Elit, Voruganti, & Simunovic, 2005).

Vulvar Lichen Sclerosis and Vulvar Carcinoma

Vulvar lichen sclerosis is an insidious inflammatory condition that is most commonly found in older postmenopausal women, but can also develop in girls prior to menarche. Characteristic signs of lichen sclerosis are leukoplakia (white glistening plaques of the vulvar mucous membranes) and unrelenting pruritus (itching). Etiologically, this condition has been linked to preexisting dermatologic autoimmune conditions, estrogen deficiency in prepubertal girls and postmenopausal women, and certain bacterial and viral infections. However, the exact cause remains enigmatic (van de Nieuwenhof, van der Avoort, & de Hullu, 2008).

Patients with vulvar lichen sclerosis are at high risk for the development of squamous cell carcinoma of the vulva. Pathologic studies of cases with vulvar carcinoma reveal that 50–60% of malignant specimens manifest lichen sclerosis (Kagie, Kenter, Herman, Trimbos, & Fleuren, 1997; Rouzier et al., 2001). In an Italian study of 211 patients with lichen sclerosis, three had developed vulvar carcinoma after 20 months, a 247-fold increase compared to age-matched women in the general population (Carli et al., 1995). Nevertheless, the absolute cancer risk in women with lichen sclerosis is small and can be attenuated with appropriate therapy (Canavan & Cohen, 2002).

Granulomatous Disease and Vulvar Carcinoma

An early report of young women with invasive vulvar carcinoma in the West Indies noted that the majority of cases (66%) had a prior history of sexually transmitted granulomatous diseases of the vulva (Hay & Cole, 1969). Similar findings were reported in a later review of 119 patients with primary invasive cancer of the vulva diagnosed during 1958–1973 at University Hospital of the West Indies, Kingston, Jamaica. Of these cases, 77 (65%) were premenopausal and in 51% of cases, vulvar carcinoma coexisted or followed previous chronic vulvar granulomatous disease and showed rapid tumor progression (Sengupta, 1980). Granuloma inguinale and lymphogranuloma venereum are granulomatous conditions caused by sexually transmitted organisms (*Donovania granulomatis* and *Chlamydia trachomatis*, respectively).

Recent studies suggest that *Chlamydia trachomatis* infection may be a component of a complex web of causation of lichen sclerosis and vulvar cancer. In a study of Polish women, 80 women with vulvar disease (30 with vulvar cancer and 50 with lichen sclerosis) were tested for the presence of *Chlamydia trachomatis* antibodies. Serum antibodies to *Chlamydia trachomatis* were detected in 50% of women with vulvar cancer and 16% of women with lichen sclerosis (Olejek et al., 2009).

EPIDEMIOLOGY OF ANAL CARCINOMA

Anal cancer is relatively uncommon, comprising only 2–3% of all gastrointestinal malignancies. Estimates of the annual incidence of anal cancer vary widely

(0.1–3.0 per 100,000), and in most populations the rates in women are approximately double the rates in men. Exceptions are populations with higher levels of male HPV transmission (e.g., San Francisco) wherein men have higher rates (Parkin & Bray, 2006). During 2008, approximately 27,000 cases were diagnosed worldwide, 15,000 in women and 12,000 in men, and in that year, 15,000 people died from anal cancer (de Martel et al., 2012; Ferlay et al., 2010; Parkin, 2006).

Most anal malignancies (~90%) are squamous cell carcinomas, with the remainder consisting predominantly of adenocarcinomas. Sarcomas and malignant melanomas very rarely develop from tissues of the anal canal (Salmo & Haboubi, 2011).

The incidence of anal cancer has more than doubled in some populations in recent years in association with increasing rates of sexually transmitted infections such as HPV, HSV2, and HIV. Other significant risk factors include receptive anal intercourse, history of condyloma acuminata (genital warts), and chronic cigarette smoking. From an etiologic perspective, anal cancer has more similarities to genital malignancies than to gastrointestinal tract cancer.

Trends in Anal Cancer

Although anal cancer is rare, the rates of squamous cell anal carcinoma have increased significantly in some populations in recent years. In the United States, population-based tumor registries of the SEER program of the National Cancer Institute reported 11,231 squamous cell anal carcinomas and 1,791 anal adenocarcinomas during the period 1973–2009. During this 26-year time period, the annual rates of squamous cell anal carcinomas increased threefold in men (from 1.0 to 3.0 per 100,000) and nearly twofold in women (1.3 to 2.4 per 100,000), whereas the rates of adenocarcinomas remained stable at approximately 0.25 per 100,000 (Johnson, Madeleine, Newcomer, Schwartz, & Daling, 2004; Nelson, Levine, Bernstein, Smith, & Lai, 2013).

Rising trends in the incidence of anal cancer and high-grade anal intraepithelial neoplasia (AIN2/3) have also been observed in the Danish population. Using data from the Danish Cancer Registry and the Danish Registry of Pathology, investigators at the Danish Cancer Society examined trends in the incidence of invasive anal carcinoma (2,198 cases) and AIN2/3 (608 cases) among Danish men and women during 1978–2008. Approximately 65% of these tumors developed in women. During the 30-year period of study, the age-standardized incidence rate of anal cancer increased from 0.68 to 1.48

per 100,000 person-years in women and from 0.45 to 0.80 per 100,000 person-years in men, and there was a corresponding 5% annual increase in AIN2/3 cases. Increases of 4% per year were noted for HPV-related squamous cell and transitional cell carcinomas in men and women, but there were no increases in the incidence of adenocarcinomas. The investigators suggest the need for intensified screening and HPV vaccination to reduce the burden of anal cancer (Nielsen, Munk, & Kjaer, 2012).

Human Papillomavirus and Anal Carcinoma

The prevalence of HPV in anal carcinoma and anal intraepithelial neoplasia (AIN) was examined in a meta-analysis of data from 93 studies conducted on four continents using PCR assays for detection of HPV DNA. Prevalence estimates for anal lesions were obtained by pooling the data from 29 of these studies. The prevalence of HPV was 84% among 955 invasive anal carcinomas and 93% among 1,280 cases of AIN. Among cases of anal carcinoma, the most frequent strains detected were HPV-16 (73%), HPV-18 (5%), and HPV-6 (5%). Notably, among cases of AIN2 or AIN3 that were co-infected with HIV, 66% were positive for multiple strains of HPV. Although the most common strains were HPV-16 (55%), HPV-18 (26%), and HPV-58 (21%), several other strains (e.g., HPV-31, HPV-33, HPV-45, HPV-58) were also detected in 10–20% of the HIV-positive AIN2/AIN3 cases. In contrast, among AIN2/3 cases that were *negative* for HIV, co-infection by multiple HPV strains was relatively infrequent (13%) and the prevalence of HPV-16 increased with increasing grade of neoplasia (e.g., 30% in AIN1, 75% in AIN2/3, and 85% in invasive carcinoma). These results support the view that immunosuppression due to HIV co-infection allows a broader range of HPV types to persist and contribute to malignant transformation of the anal mucosa, whereas in the absence of HIV, the process appears to be primarily driven by chronic infection with HPV-16 (De Vuyst et al., 2009).

Human Immunodeficiency Virus and Anal Carcinoma

The association between AIDS and anal carcinoma was examined in 309,365 men and women with AIDS (257,605 men and 51,760 women) using data collected in the multicenter AIDS–Cancer Match Registry Study during the period 1978–1996. Compared to the general population, the incidence rates of invasive and in situ anal cancers increased more than 100-fold in AIDS-afflicted men and women less than 30 years of age. Across all age groups, the incidence of invasive carcinoma of the anus increased 7-fold among HIV-infected women and 38-fold among HIV-infected men (Figrue 15.3). The relative risk (RR) among Caucasians with AIDS was more than double that of other ethnic groups (RR = 55 versus RR = 22) (Frisch et al., 2000).

To examine the impact of HIV-related immuno-suppression on the genesis of anal neoplasia, investigators in San Francisco, California, compared the progression of squamous intraepithelial neoplasia of the anal mucosa in 346 HIV-positive and 262 HIV-negative homosexual men. Subjects were examined at defined intervals using anal cytology, anoscopy with biopsy of visible lesions, HPV and HIV testing, level of CD4 lymphocytes, and data on medical history and lifestyle. After 2 years of follow-up, the incidence of anal squamous intraepithelial neoplasia among men who were free of disease at baseline was 20% in HIV-positive men and 8% in HIV-negative men. Low-grade lesions progressed to higher grade lesions in 62% of HIV-positive men and 36% of HIV-negative men. The relative risk of disease progression in HIV-positive compared to HIV-negative men was 2.4 and the risk increased to 3.1 in HIV-positive men with CD4 counts less than 200 per cubic millimeter. Infection with multiple HPV strains increased the risk of disease progression in HIV-positive men (RR = 2.0) and HIV-negative men (RR = 5.1). The findings suggest that HPV infection per se stimulates the progression of anal intraepithelial neoplasia to invasive carcinoma and that coinfection with HIV synergistically heightens the risk of malignant transformation by reducing the immune response (Palefsky et al., 1998).

Australian investigators conducted a review and meta-analysis of published data on the prevalence of HPV-16 and the incidence of anal cancer in men who have sex with men (MSM). Data were pooled from 53 studies that included 31 estimates of HPV prevalence and 9 estimates of anal cancer incidence. The prevalence of HPV-16 was threefold higher in HIV-positive MSM than HIV-negative MSM (35.4% versus 12.5%), and the incidence of anal cancer was ninefold higher among HIV-positive MSM than HIV-negative MSM (46 versus 5 per 100,000) (Machalek et al., 2012).

Investigators of the North American AIDS Cohort Collaboration on Research and Design (NA-ACCORD) compared anal cancer incidence rates among 34,189 HIV-positive and 113,260 HIV-negative individuals from 13 cohorts followed during 1996–2007. Among HIV-positive subjects, 55% were MSM, 19% were other men, and 26% were women. Among HIV-negative subjects, 90% were men and 10% were women. Anal cancer incidence rates per 100,000 person-years were considerably

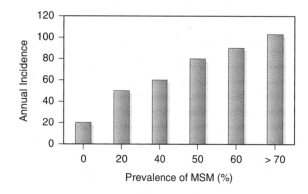

Figure 15.6 Incidence of Anal Cancer in MSM.

Annual incidence rates per 100,000 person-years are mean values estimated from 13 separate cohorts according to their prevalence of MSM. One outlier representing less than 0.5% of exposure time was omitted from the calculations.

Source: Data from Silverberg, M. J., Lau, B., Justice, A. C., Engels, E., Gill, M. J., Goedert, J. J., . . . Dubrow R; North American AIDS Cohort Collaboration on Research and Design (NA-ACCORD) of IeDEA. (2012). Risk of anal cancer in HIV-infected and HIV-uninfected individuals in North America. *Clinical Infectious Disease, 54*(7), 1026–1034.

higher among HIV-positive risk groups (131 for HIV-positive MSM, 46 for other HIV-positive men, 30 for HIV-positive women, 2 for HIV-negative men, and 0 for HIV-negative women). A striking finding was the increasing incidence of anal cancer with increasing prevalence of MSM among the 13 cohorts (**Figure 15.6**). Based on linear regression analysis, the projected incidence of anal cancer was 28 per 100,000 for a population with 0% MSM and 146 per 100,000 for a population with 100% MSM, a 5.2-fold increase in anal cancer risk. Though their study lacked data on HPV infection as well as other risk factors, the investigators suggest that HPV vaccination and enhanced cytological screening for AIN should be considered for all HIV-positive individuals (Silverberg et al., 2012).

PRIMARY PREVENTION OF HPV-RELATED VAGINAL, VULVAR, AND ANAL CANCER

Effective quadrivalent vaccines (e.g., Gardasil) have been developed against oncogenic strains of HPV (HPV-16 and HPV-18) and strains that cause genital warts (HPV-6 and HPV-11). Preliminary results of randomized clinical trials show up to 100% efficacy in preventing infection by these viruses and reducing the risk of precancerous lesions of the cervical, vaginal, and vulvar epithelium among young women who received the vaccine prior to infection. Results suggest that protection against infection by these HPV strains persists for up to 5 years after vaccination (Cutts et al., 2007; Markowitz et al., 2007).

Clinical trials have recently been conducted to assess the value of quadrivalent vaccination against HPV-16, HPV-18, HPV-6, and HPV-11 to prevent the development of anal intraepithelial neoplasia (AIN) and anal cancer in MSM. In a double-blinded international trial, 602 healthy MSM, ages 16 to 26, were randomized to receive either the quadrivalent vaccine or placebo. After 3 years of follow-up, the rates of AIN and anal carcinoma related to infection by HPV-6, HPV-11, HPV-16, or HPV-18 were reduced by 75% and 95%, respectively, in those who received the three-shot vaccine regimen compared to those receiving placebo, and no serious adverse events or reactions were reported. These findings support the use of quadrivalent HPV vaccine in high-risk groups (e.g., MSM) to reduce the anal cancer risk (Palefsky et al., 2011).

Given that a substantial proportion of cervical cancers as well as noncervical cancers are caused by HPV-16 and HPV-18, current HPV vaccines may hold great promise in reducing the burden of HPV-associated malignancies in the human population. Nevertheless, because HPV vaccines do not totally eliminate the risk of developing HPV-related malignancies, cytological screening is still recommended in order to detect premalignant lesions and minimize cancer incidence and mortality. Furthermore, it seems advisable to target certain high-risk groups such as MSM and HIV-seropositive individuals for intensified screening, even those who are well controlled on antiretroviral therapy (Cutts et al., 2007; Gillison, Chaturvedi, & Lowy, 2008; Lowy & Schiller, 2006; Palefsky, 2000).

SCREENING FOR SQUAMOUS CELL VAGINAL, VULVAR, AND ANAL CANCER

Dramatic reductions in cervical cancer incidence and mortality among women of developed nations are due largely to the effectiveness of the Papanicolaou-Traut cytological test (Papanicolaou & Traut, 1943). The *Pap test*, which was introduced in the United States around 1950, provides a quick, safe, affordable, and accurate means of detecting precancerous dysplastic lesions of the cervix that can be cured by simple surgery or other ablative techniques.

In the absence of symptoms or major risk factors, the Pap test is *not* routinely used for screening the vagina of the female genital tract. However, if symptoms are present (e.g., bleeding unrelated to the menstrual period, pelvic pain, palpable mass), the

Table 15.2	Classification of Premalignant Lesions of the Urogenital Tract
Classification	**Description**
VAIN1, VIN1, AIN1	Dysplastic cells in the outermost one-third of the epithelium
VAIN2, VIN2, AIN2	Dysplastic cells in the outermost two-thirds of the epithelium
VAIN3, VIN3, AIN3	Dysplastic cells in more than two-thirds of the epithelium without breaching the basement membrane (also called *carcinoma in situ*)

Source: Data from Holschneider, C. H. (2013). Vulvar intraepithelial neoplasia. Retrieved from http://www.uptodate.com/contents /vulvar-intraepithelial-neoplasia; Holschneider, C. H., & Berek, J. S. (2013). Vaginal intraepithelial neoplasia. Retrieved from http://www.uptodate.com/contents/vaginal-intraepithelial -neoplasia; Palefsky, J. M., & Cranston, R. D. (2013). Anal intraepithelial neoplasia: Diagnosis, screening, prevention, and treatment. Retrieved from http://www.uptodate.com/contents /anal-intraepithelial-neoplasia

Pap test is an effective diagnostic tool for the detection of dysplastic lesions of the squamous cell epithelium of the vagina (VAIN), vulva (VIN), and anus (AIN). These are similar to cervical dysplasia, and are graded according to the depth of abnormal cells in the vaginal epithelium (**Table 15.2**).

It is important to note that all VAIN, VIN, and AIN lesions including in situ carcinomas of the vagina, vulva, or anus are up to 100% curable by surgical excision or other forms of ablative therapy. Furthermore, localized tumors that have not spread to the inguinal lymph nodes are curable in 90% of cases by appropriate therapy (Batista & Martins, 2012; Holschneider, 2013; Holschneider & Berek, 2013; Palefsky & Cranston, 2013).

• • • REFERENCES

Andersen, W. A., Franquemont, D. W., Williams, H., Taylor, P. T., & Crum, C. P. (1991). Vulvar squamous cell carcinoma and papillomaviruses: Two separate entities. *American Journal of Obstetrics and Gynecology, 165*, 335–336.

Batista, T. P., & Martins, M. R. (2012). Vaginal cancer. *International Journal of Cancer Research and Prevention, 5*(3–4), 235–246.

Bloss, J. D., Liao, S. Y., Wilczynski, S. P., Macri, C., Walker, J., Peake, M., & Berman, M. L. (1991). Clinical and histologic features of vulvar carcinomas analyzed for human papillomavirus status: Evidence that squamous cell carcinoma of the vulva has more than one etiology. *Human Pathology, 22*(7), 711–718.

Bodelon, C., Madeleine, M. M., Voigt, L. F., & Weiss, N. S. (2009). Is the incidence of invasive vulvar cancer increasing in the United States? *Cancer Causes and Control, 20*(9), 1779–1782.

Boshartb, M., Gissmann, L., Ikenberg, H., Kleinheinz, A., Scheurlen, W., & zur Hausen, H. (1984). A new type of papillomavirus DNA, its presence in genital cancer biopsies and in cell lines derived from cervical cancer. *EMBO Journal, 3*(5), 1151–1157.

Brinton, L. A., Nasca, P. C., Mallin, K., Baptiste, M. S., Wilbanks, G. D., & Richart, R. M. (1990a). Case-control study of cancer of the vulva. *Obstetrics and Gynecology, 75*(5), 859–866.

Brinton, L. A., Nasca, P. C., Mallin, K., Schairer, C., Rosenthal, J., Rothenberg, R., . . . Richart, R. M. (1990b). Case-control study of *in situ* and invasive carcinoma of the vagina. *Gynecological Oncology, 38*, 49–54.

Bruni, L., Diaz, M., Castellsagué, X., Ferrer, E., Bosch, F. X., & de Sanjosé, S. (2010). Cervical human papillomavirus prevalence in 5 continents: Meta-analysis of 1 million women with normal cytological findings. *Journal of Infectious Diseases, 202*, 1789–1799.

Canavan, T. P., & Cohen, D. (2002). Vulvar cancer. *American Family Physician, 66*(7), 1269–1275.

Carli, P., Cattaneo, A., De, M. A., Biggeri, A., Taddei, G., & Giannotti, B. (1995). Squamous cell carcinoma arising in vulval lichen sclerosus: A longitudinal cohort study. *European Journal of Cancer Prevention, 4*(6), 491–495

Choo, Y. C., & Anderson, D. G. (1982). Neoplasms of the vagina following cervical carcinoma. *Gynecological Oncology, 14*, 125–132.

Cutts, F. T., Franceschi, S., Goldie, S., Castellsague, X., de Sanjose, S., Garnett, G., . . . Markowitz, L. (2007). Human papillomavirus and HPV vaccines: A review. *Bulletin of the World Health Organization, 85*(9), 719–726.

Daling, J. R., Madeleine, M. M., Schwartz, S. M., Shera, K. A., Carter, J. J., McKnight, B., . . .

Tamimi H (2002). A population-based study of squamous cell vaginal cancer: HPV and cofactors. *Gynecological Oncology, 84*(2), 263–270.

Daling, J. R., Sherman, K. J., Hislop, T. G., Mandelson, M., Beckmann, A. M., & Weiss, N. S. (1992). Cigarette smoking and the risk of anogenital cancer. *American Journal of Epidemiology, 135*, 180–189.

de Martel, C., Ferlay, J., Franceschi, S., Vignat, J., Bray, F., Forman, D., & Plummer, M. (2012). The global burden of cancers attributable to infections in the year 2008: A review and synthetic analysis. *Lancet Oncology, 13*, 607–615.

De Vuyst, H., Clifford, G. M., Nascimento, M. C., Madeleine, M. M., & Franceschi, S. (2009). Prevalence and type distribution of human papillomavirus in carcinoma and intraepithelial neoplasia of the vulva, vagina and anus: A meta-analysis. *International Journal of Cancer, 124*(7), 1626–1636.

Dodge, J. A., Eltabbakh, G. H., Mount, S. L., Walker, R. P., & Morgan, A. (2001). Clinical features and risk of recurrence among patients with vaginal intraepithelial neoplasia. *Gynecological Oncology, 83*(2), 363–369.

Elit, L., Voruganti, S., & Simunovic, M. (2005). Invasive vulvar cancer in a woman with human immunodeficiency virus: Case report and review of the literature. *Gynecological Oncology, 98*(1), 151–154.

Ferlay, J., Shin, H.-R., Bray, F., Forman, D., Mathers, C., & Parkin, D. M. (2010). Estimates of worldwide burden of cancer in 2008: GLOBOCAN 2008. *International Journal of Cancer, 127*(12), 2893–2917.

Forman, D., de Martel, C., Lacey, C. J., Soerjomataram, I., Lortet-Tieulent, J., Bruni, L., . . . Franceschi, S. (2012). Global burden of human papillomavirus and related diseases. *Vaccine, 30*(Suppl 5), F12–F23.

Frisch, M., Biggar, R. J., & Goedert, J. J. (2000). Human papillomavirus-associated cancers in patients with human immunodeficiency virus infection and acquired immunodeficiency syndrome. *Journal of the National Cancer Institute, 92*(18), 1500–1510.

Gallup, D. G., Talledo, E., Shah, K. J., & Hayes, C. (1987). Invasive squamous cell carcinoma of the vagina: A 14 year study. *Obstetrics and Gynecology, 69,* 782–785.

Gillison, M. L., Chaturvedi, A. K., & Lowy, D. R. (2008). HPV prophylactic vaccines and the potential prevention of noncervical cancers in both men and women. *Cancer, 113*(10 Suppl), 3036–3046.

Hamilton, S. R., & Aaltonen, L. A. (2000). Tumours of the anal canal. In S. R. Hamilton & L. A. Aaltonen (Eds.), *Pathology and genetics of tumours of the digestive system* (pp. 145–156). World Health Organization Classification of Tumours. Lyon, France: IARC Press.

Hay, D. M., & Cole, F. M. (1969). Primary invasive carcinoma of the vulva in Jamaica. *Journal of Obstetrics and Gynaecology of the British Commonwealth, 76*(9), 821–830.

Herbst, A. L. (1981). Clear cell adenocarcinoma and the current status of DES-exposed females. *Cancer, 48,* 484–488.

Herbst, A. L., & Anderson, D. (1991). Clear cell adenocarcinoma of the vagina and cervix secondary to intrauterine exposure to diethylstilbestrol. *Cancer, 67*(7), 1971–1978.

Herbst, A. L., Cole, P., Colton, T., Robboy, S. J., & Scully, R. E. (1977). Age-incidence and risk of diethylstilbestrol-related clear cell adenocarcinoma of the vagina and cervix. *American Journal of Obstetrics and Gynecology, 128,* 43–50.

Herbst, A. L., & Scully, R. E. (1970). Adenocarcinoma of the vagina in adolescence. A report of 7 cases including 6 clear-cell carcinomas (so-called mesonephromas). *Cancer, 25*(4), 745–757.

Herbst, A. L., Ulfelder, H., & Poskanzer, D. C. (1971). Adenocarcinoma of the vagina—association of maternal stilbestrol therapy with tumor appearance in young women. *New England Journal of Medicine, 284,* 878–881.

Holschneider, C. H. (2013). Vulvar intraepithelial neoplasia. Retrieved from http://www.uptodate.com/contents/vulvar-intraepithelial-neoplasia

Holschneider, C. H., & Berek, J. S. (2013). Vaginal intraepithelial neoplasia. Retrieved from http://www.uptodate.com/contents/vaginal-intraepithelial-neoplasia

Howlader, N., Noone, A. M., Krapcho, M., Garshell, J., Neyman, N., Altekruse, S. F., . . . Cronin, K. A. (Eds.). (2013). *SEER cancer statistics review, 1975–2010.* Bethesda, MD: National Cancer Institute. Retrieved from http://seer.cancer.gov/csr/1975_2010/

Johnson, L. G., Madeleine, M. M., Newcomer, L. M., Schwartz, S. M., & Daling, J. R. (2004). Anal cancer incidence and survival: The surveillance, epidemiology, and end results experience, 1973–2000. *Cancer, 101*(2), 281.

Kagie, M. J., Kenter, G. G., Herman, J., Trimbos, J. B., & Fleuren, G. J. (1997). The relevance of various vulvar epithelial changes in the early detection of squamous cell carcinoma of the vulva. *International Journal of Gynecological Cancer, 7*(1), 50–57.

Kiyono, T., Foster, S. A., Koop, J. I., McDougall, J. K., Galloway, D. A., & Klingelhutz, A. J. (1998). Both Rb/p16INK4a inactivation and telomerase activity are required to immortalize human epithelial cells. *Nature, 396*(6706), 84–88.

Lowy, D. R., & Schiller, J. T. (2006). Prophylactic human papillomavirus vaccines. *Journal of Clinical Investigation, 116*(5), 1167–1173.

Machalek, D. A., Poynten, M., Jin, F., Fairley, C. K., Farnsworth, A., Garland, S. M., . . . Grulich, A. E. (2012). Anal human papillomavirus infection and associated neoplastic lesions in men who have sex with men: A systematic review and meta-analysis. *Lancet Oncology, 13*(5), 487–500.

Madeleine, M. M., Daling, J. R., & Schwartz, S. M. (1997). Cofactors with human papillomavirus in a population-based study of vulvar cancer. *Journal of the National Cancer Institute, 89*(20), 1516–1523.

Madsen, B. S., Jensen, H. L., van den Brule, A. J., Wohlfahrt, J., & Frisch, M. (2008). Risk factors for invasive squamous cell carcinoma of the vulva and vagina—population-based case-control study in Denmark. *International Journal of Cancer, 122*(12), 2827–2834.

Markowitz, L. E., Dunne, E. F., Saraiya, M., Lawson, H. W., Chesson, H., & Unger, E. R.; Centers for Disease Control and Prevention Advisory Committee on Immunization Practices. (2007). Quadrivalent human papillomavirus vaccine: Recommendations of the Advisory Committee on Immunization Practices (ACIP). *Morbidity and Mortality Weekly Report Recommendation Report, 56*(RR-2), 1–24.

Matlashewskil, G., Schneider, J., Banks, L., Jones, N., Murray, A., & Crawford, L. (1987). Human papillomavirus type 16 DNA cooperates with activated *ras* in transforming primary cells. *EMBO Journal, 6*(6), 1741–1746.

Münger, K., Scheffner, M., Huibregtse, J. M., & Howley, P. M. (1992). Interactions of HPV E6 and E7 oncoproteins with tumour suppressor gene products. *Journal of Cancer Survivorship, 12*, 197–217.

National Cancer Institute. (2011). *Diethylstilbestrol (DES) and cancer.* Bethesda, MD: National Cancer Institute.

Nelson, R. A., Levine, A. M., Bernstein, L., Smith, D. D., & Lai, L. L. (2013). Changing patterns of anal canal carcinoma in the United States. *Journal of Clinical Oncology, 31*(12), 1569–1575.

Nielsen, A., Munk, C., & Kjaer, S. K. (2012). Trends in incidence of anal cancer and high-grade anal intraepithelial neoplasia in Denmark, 1978–2008. *International Journal of Cancer, 130*(5), 1168–1173.

Olejek, A., Kozak-Darmas, I., Kellas-Sleczka, S., Jarek, A., Wiczkowski, A., Krol, W., & Stencel-Gabriel, K. (2009). Chlamydia trachomatis infection in women with lichen sclerosis vulvae and vulvar cancer. *Neuro Endocrinology Letters, 30*(5), 671–674.

Palefsky, J. M. (2000). Anal squamous intraepithelial lesions in human immunodeficiency virus-positive men and women. *Seminars in Oncology, 27*(4), 471–479.

Palefsky, J. M., & Cranston, R. D. (2013). Anal intraepithelial neoplasia, diagnosis, screening, prevention and treatment. Retrieved from http://www.uptodate.com/contents/anal-intraepithelial-neoplasia

Palefsky, J. M., Giuliano, A. R., Goldstone, S., Moreira, E. D. Jr, Aranda, C., Jessen, H., . . . Garner, E. I. (2011). HPV vaccine against anal HPV infection and anal intraepithelial neoplasia. *New England Journal of Medicine, 365*(17), 1576–1585.

Palefsky, J. M., Holly, E. A., Hogeboom, C. J., Ralston, M. L., DaCosta, M. M., Botts, R., . . . Darragh, T. M. (1998). Virologic, immunologic, and clinical parameters in the incidence and progression of anal squamous intraepithelial lesions in HIV-positive and HIV-negative homosexual men. *Journal of Acquired Immune Deficiency Syndromes and Human Retrovirology, 17*(4), 314–319.

Palmer, J. R., Wise, L. A., Hatch, E. E., Troisi, R., Titus-Ernstoff, L., Stohsnitter, W., . . . Hoover, R. N. (2006). Prenatal diethylstilbestrol exposure and risk of breast cancer. *Cancer Epidemiology, Biomarkers and Prevention, 15*(8), 1509–1514.

Papanicolaou, G. N., & Traut, H. F. (1943). *Diagnosis of uterine cancer by the vaginal smear.* New York, NY: Commonwealth Fund.

Parkin, D. M. (2006). The global health burden of infection-associated cancers in the year 2002. *International Journal of Cancer, 118*(12), 3030–3044.

Parkin, D. M., & Bray, F. (2006). Chapter 2: The burden of HPV-related cancers. *Vaccine, 24*(Suppl 3), S3/11–25.

Rouzier, R., Morice, P., Haie-Meder, C., Lhomme, C., Avril, M. F., Duvillard, P., & Castaigne, D. (2001). Prognostic significance of epithelial disorders adjacent to invasive vulvar carcinomas. *Gynecological Oncology, 81*, 414–419.

Salmo, E., & Haboubi, N. (2011). Anal cancer: Pathology, staging, and evidence-based minimum data set. *Colorectal Disease, 13*, 11–20.

Saraiya, M., Watson, M., Wu, X., King, J. B., Chen, V. W., Smith, J. S., & Giuliano, A. R. (2008). Incidence of in situ and invasive vulvar cancer in the US, 1998-2003. *Cancer, 113*(10 Suppl), 2865–2872.

Sengupta, B. S. (1980). Vulvar carcinoma in premenopausal Jamaican women. *International*

Journal of Gynaecology and Obstetrics, 17(6), 526–530.

Silverberg, M. J., Lau, B., Justice, A. C., Engels, E., Gill, M. J., Goedert, J. J., . . . Dubrow, R.; North American AIDS Cohort Collaboration on Research and Design (NA-ACCORD) of IeDEA. (2012). Risk of anal cancer in HIV-infected and HIV-uninfected individuals in North America. *Clinical Infectious Diseases, 54*(7), 1026–1034.

Sitas, F., Pacella-Norman, R., Carrara, H., Patel, M., Ruff, P., Sur, R., . . . Beral, V. (2000). The spectrum of HIV-1 related cancers in South Africa. *International Journal of Cancer, 88*, 489–492.

Tavassoli, F. A., & Devilee, P. (2003a). Tumours of the vagina. In F. A. Tavassoli, & P. Devilee (Eds.), *Pathology and genetics of tumours of the breast and female genital organs* (pp. 291–311). World Health Organization Classification of Tumours. Lyon, France: IARC Press.

Tavassoli, F. A., & Devilee, P. (2003b). Tumours of the vulva. In F. A. Tavassoli, & P. Devilee (Eds.), *Pathology and genetics of tumours of the breast*

and female genital organs (pp. 313–334). World Health Organization Classification of Tumours. Lyon, France: IARC Press.

van de Nieuwenhof, H. P., van der Avoort, I. A., & de Hullu, J. A. (2008). Review of squamous premalignant vulvar lesions. *Critical Reviews in Oncology/Hematology, 68*(2), 131–156.

Wu, X., Matanoski, G., Chen, V. W., Saraiya, M., Coughlin, S. S., King, J. B., & Tao, X. G. (2008). Descriptive epidemiology of vaginal cancer incidence and survival by race, ethnicity, and age in the United States. *Cancer, 113*(10 Suppl), 2873–2882.

zur Hausen, H. (1976). Condyloma acuminata and human genital cancer. *Cancer Research, 36*, 794.

zur Hausen, H. (1977). Human papilloma viruses and their possible role in squamous cell carcinoma. *Current Topics in Microbiology and Immunology, 78*, 1–30.

zur Hausen, H. (2002). Papillomaviruses and cancer: From basic studies to clinical application. *Nature Reviews: Cancer, 2*(5), 342–350.

16

Epidemiology of Prostate Cancer

GLOBAL BURDEN OF PROSTATE CANCER

Carcinoma of the prostate is the second most common form of cancer in men (behind only lung cancer) and is now the fifth leading cause of cancer deaths worldwide. During 2012, 1,111,689 new cases were diagnosed and 307,471 men died of prostate cancer. These data reflect a marked increase in the global burden of prostate cancer. During 2000–2012, the volume of new cases of prostate cancer more than doubled, and the number of deaths increased more than 50% (Ferlay et al., 2004, 2010, 2013; Parkin, Bray, Ferlay, & Pisani, 2001, 2005) (**Figure 16.1**).

Among men living in developed countries, prostate cancer is diagnosed more often than any other form of male cancer (758,739 new cases in 2012) and is the third leading cause of death from cancer (142,004 deaths). Disease survival in developed countries is high, and the ratio of incidence to mortality is 0.19, which is primarily due to screening of asymptomatic men by prostate-specific antigen (PSA) and the early detection of small latent carcinomas of the prostate. Among men living in developing countries, prostate cancer is diagnosed less often (352,950 new cases in 2012), but tumors are usually detected late in development, resulting in a higher mortality (165,467 deaths) and a much higher incidence-to-mortality ratio (0.47) (Ferlay et al., 2013).

There is marked variability in the international incidence and mortality rates of prostate cancer. Incidence rates tend to be high in developed nations such as the United States, Canada, Australia, New Zealand, and the nations of Western Europe and Scandinavia. Rates are lowest in populations of Asia and North Africa (Ferlay et al., 2010, 2013) (**Figure 16.2**).

In sharp contrast to the global pattern of incidence rates, mortality rates tend to be higher in developing areas such as Southern and Central Africa, Central America, the Caribbean, and South America (Figure 16.2). Furthermore, certain ethnic groups

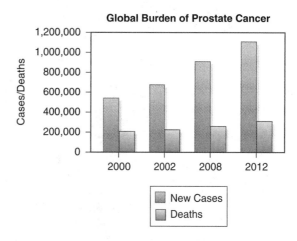

Figure 16.1 Increasing Global Burden of Prostate Cancer, 2000–2012.

Sources: Data from Ferlay, J., Bray, F., Pisani, P., & Parkin, D. M. (2004). *GLOBOCAN 2002. Cancer incidence, mortality, and prevalence worldwide.* IARC Cancer Base No. 5, version 2.0. Lyon, France: IARC Press; Ferlay, J., Shin, H.-R., Bray, F., Forman, D., Mathers, C., & Parkin, D. M. (2010). Estimates of worldwide burden of cancer in 2008: GLOBOCAN 2008. *International Journal of Cancer, 127*(12), 2893–2917; Ferlay, J., Soerjomataram, I., Ervik, M., Dikshit, R., Eser, S., Mathers, C.,... Bray, F. (2013). *GLOBOCAN 2012 v1.0. Cancer incidence and mortality worldwide: IARC CancerBase No. 11* [Internet]. Lyon, France: International Agency for Research on Cancer. Retrieved from http://globocan.iarc.fr; Parkin, D. M., Bray, F., Ferlay, J., & Pisani, P. (2001). Estimating the world cancer burden: GLOBOCAN 2000. *International Journal of Cancer, 94,* 153–156; Parkin, D. M., Bray, F., Ferlay, J., & Pisani, P. (2005). Global cancer statistics, 2002. *CA: A Cancer Journal for Clinicians, 55,* 74–108.

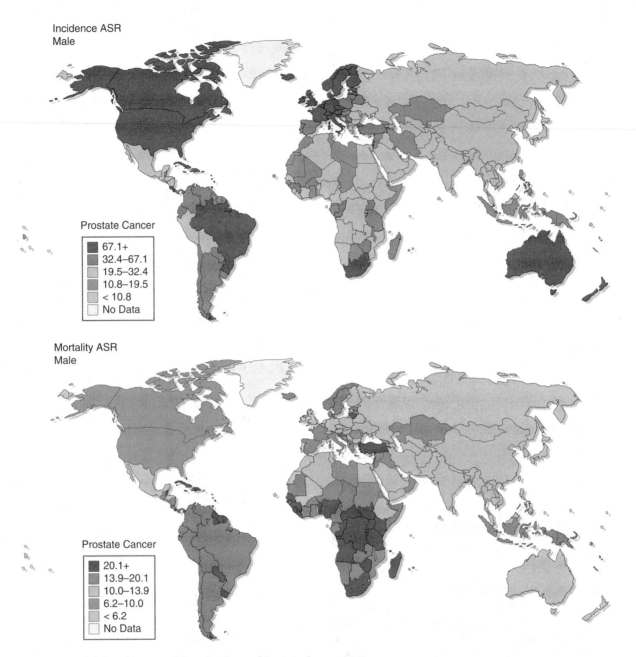

Figure 16.2 Global Incidence and Mortality Rates of Prostate Cancer, 2012.

ASR: Rates per 100,000 are age-standardized to the world population, 2000–2025.

Source: Reproduced from Ferlay, J., Soerjomataram, I., Ervik, M., Dikshit, R., Eser, S., Mathers, C., . . . Bray, F. (2013). *GLOBOCAN 2012 v1.0. Cancer incidence and mortality worldwide: IARC CancerBase No. 11* [Internet]. Lyon, France: International Agency for Research on Cancer. Retrieved from http://globocan.iarc.fr

within countries have exceedingly high mortality rates; for example, African Americans living in the United States have one of the the highest age-adjusted death rates from prostate cancer in the world (annual rate > 50 deaths per 100,000). Their rate is more than double that of Caucasian or Hispanic Americans (less than 25 deaths per 100,000) (**Figure 16.3**) (American Cancer Society [ACS], 2009). By comparison, native Asian men have annual mortality rates less than 5 deaths per 100,000 (Ito, 2014; Parkin et al., 2005). As discussed in the following sections of this chapter, the wide variation in the incidence and mortality of prostate cancer is influenced by many factors, including diet, lifestyle, genetics, screening, and therapy.

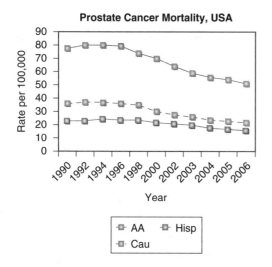

Figure 16.3 Annual Mortality Rates of Prostate Cancer by Ethnicity, United States, 1990–2006.

Rates per 100,000 are age-adjusted to the U.S. male population, 2000.

AA: African Americans; Cau: Caucasian Americans; Hisp: Hispanic Americans.

Source: Data from American Cancer Society. (2009). *Cancer facts and figures.* Atlanta, GA: Author.

AGE-SPECIFIC RISK OF PROSTATE CANCER

The incidence of invasive cancer of the prostate increases dramatically in men over the age of 50 years. The disease is rare until age 50, after which the risk increases exponentially (**Table 16.1**). The lifetime risk of developing invasive disease is approximately 1 in 6 among U.S. Caucasian men (ACS, 2009).

In addition to the clinically overt forms of prostate cancer, there is an even more frequent biologic form of prostate cancer that is discovered as

Table 16.1	Age-Specific Incidence of Prostate Cancer in U.S. Men
Age (Years)	**Cumulative Risk of Invasive Prostate Cancer**
45	1 in 2,500
50	1 in 476
55	1 in 120
60	1 in 43
65	1 in 21
70	1 in 9
75	1 in 7
Lifetime	1 in 6

Source: Data from American Cancer Society. (2009). *Cancer facts and figures.* Atlanta, GA: Author.

an incidental finding either at postmortem examination or in a surgical specimen removed for other reasons (e.g., in the treatment of benign prostatic hypertrophy [BPH]). In almost all of these incidental findings, the lesions are small and composed only of microscopic foci of malignant cells. This form of prostatic cancer is called *occult* or *latent* prostate cancer.

In postmortem studies of unselected men, occult prostate cancer can be identified in about 10% of subjects between 50 and 59 years of age, rising to a prevalence of 40–50% in those over the age of 70. It is noteworthy that in the vast majority of these subjects (95%) these occult lesions were absolutely unsuspected and clinically asymptomatic (Robbins & Cotran, 1979).

ANATOMY AND FUNCTION OF THE PROSTATE GLAND

The prostate gland encircles the urethra at the base of the urinary bladder. The normal adult gland is 3–4 centimeters in diameter, slightly larger than a walnut, and weighs 7–16 grams. The organ is composed of a network of ductules lined by epithelial cells admixed with muscular and fibrous cells. Its main function is to produce the fluid portion of semen. Prostatic fluid is continually produced and secreted by epithelial cells lining the extensive network of prostate ductules. Prostatic fluid is rich in the proteins, minerals, and other compounds necessary for maintenance and nourishment of the sperm. The anterior portion of the prostate gland also aids in the control of urine flow from the bladder.

The prostate gland is roughly divisible into four zones: the transition zone, the central zone, the peripheral zone, and the anterior fibromuscular zone. These zones are shown with other nearby structures (bladder, vas deferens, seminal vesicles, ejaculatory ducts, and verumontanum) in **Figure 16.4**. The *vas deferens* carries sperm from each testicle to the ejaculatory duct. The *seminal vesicles* are paired tubular glands that secrete seminal fluid into the ejaculatory ducts. Seminal fluid is a mixture of proteins, enzymes, fructose, and other compounds that are essential in maintaining viable sperm. The *verumontanum* refers to the union of the vas deferens with the ejaculatory duct at the point of entry of seminal fluid into the urethra.

The *transition zone* encircles the urethra as it passes through the gland just below the bladder. The transition zone contains about 5–10% of the glandular tissue of the prostate. Epithelial cells of the

Zones of the Prostate Gland

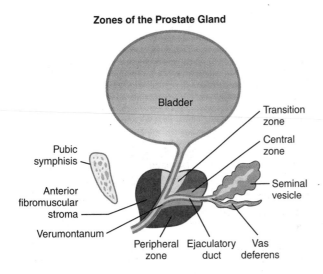

Figure 16.4 Zones of the Prostate Gland.

transition zone carry estrogen receptors and are thus predominantly responsive to estrogen stimulation. It is this zone that enlarges in the condition known as *benign prostatic hypertrophy (BPH)*. Approximately 20% of prostate adenocarcinomas arise from the epithelium of the transition zone.

The *central zone* is a cone-shaped region that surrounds the ejaculatory ducts that carry seminal fluid from the seminal vesicles into the urethra. This zone constitutes about 25% of glandular tissue of the prostate. Epithelial cells in the central zone carry primarily estrogen receptors. Less than 5% of prostate adenocarcinomas arise from the epithelium of the central zone.

The *peripheral zone* comprises the outer 70% of the prostate. This zone is situated in the posteriolateral portion of the gland and is palpable through the rectum. The epithelial cells lining the ductules of the peripheral zone are responsible for the synthesis and secretion of the majority of prostatic fluid. These cells are laden with androgen receptors and are therefore responsive to stimulation by androgens (testosterone and dihydrotestosterone). Approximately 70–75% of prostate adenocarcinomas arise from the epithelium of the peripheral zone.

The *anterolateral zone* lies in the anterior portion of the prostate and is devoid of glandular tissue. This zone consists of fibromuscular tissue, and its primary function is to propel urine and semen through the urethra during urination and ejaculation, respectively.

Benign prostatic hyperplasia (BPH) is an extremely common disorder that affects men over the age of 50. The hyperplastic nodules of BPH typically arise from the transitional zone of the prostate gland, perhaps due to the balance between androgens and estrogens. There is longstanding controversy regarding the development of cancer from BPH (Robbins & Cotran, 1979).

Dihydrotestosterone (DHT), the active form of testosterone, mediates prostatic epithelial cell division through interactions with androgen receptors (ARs) on the cell membrane. Whereas nodular hyperplasia tends to develop centrally in the prostate, prostate cancer usually arises in the posterior lobe and peripheral zone of the prostate gland (McNeal, 1981). For this reason, most experts do not believe that nodular hyperplasia is a precursor lesion of prostate cancer; rather, microscopic carcinomas appear to arise from focal areas of dysplasia in the peripheral zone of the prostate gland (McNeal, 1993). Subsequently, over a period of many years, these very small lesions increase in size and acquire invasive potential.

PATHOGENESIS OF PROSTATE CANCER

Prostate cancer arises from the epithelial lining of the prostatic ducts that channel prostatic fluids into the ejaculatory ducts of the prostate gland. Histologically, nearly all cancerous tumors are adenocarcinomas that display prominent glandular features.

The pathogenesis of prostate cancer and BPH are both related to the endocrine system. Androgens acting through ARs on the cell membranes of prostatic epithelium play critical roles in prostate development and growth as well as the pathogenesis of BPH and prostate cancer (Zhu, 2005). Studies over the years have demonstrated that there are two natural potent androgens acting at the same ARs in mammals, including humans (Zhu, Katz, & Imperato-McGinley, 1998). Although testosterone is the primary androgen synthesized and secreted by the testes, DHT converted from testosterone by the enzyme 5α-reductase (5αRD) is the main androgen in the prostate. Two forms of 5α-reductase have been identified: 5αRD-1 and 5αRD-2 (Russell & Wilson, 1994). Cellular effects of both of these enzymes are mediated by their activation of AR in prostatic tissues.

Early studies by Rose and colleagues demonstrated higher levels of the active metabolite of testosterone, dihydrotestosterone (DHT), in prostatic fluid of cases with prostate cancer compared to controls with other urologic conditions (Rose, Laaksa, Satarouta, & Wynder, 1984). International metabolic epidemiologic studies by Ross and colleagues revealed that African Americans have higher average serum levels of testosterone than Caucasian Americans (Ross et al., 1986) and that native Japanese and Chinese men have significantly lower average 5α-reductase activity than either African Americans or Caucasian Americans (Ross et al., 1992). These differences suggested a hormonal basis for the high prostate cancer rates observed in African American men compared to the relatively low rates in Asian men.

More recently, molecular studies have shown that prostate cancer tissues overexpress both the 5αRD-1 and 5αRD-2 isozymes whereas BPH tissues overexpress only the 5αRD-2 isozyme. It has also been demonstrated in animal studies that both forms of 5α-reductase can be markedly up-regulated by high intake of dietary fat (Cai, Imperato-McGinley, & Zhu, 2006). This observation provides an important mechanistic link between dietary fat intake and the genesis of prostate cancer (see the following section on "Dietary Fat and Prostate Cancer"). Furthermore, the molecular link between 5α-reductase activity and prostate carcinogenesis has motivated the development and investigation of drugs such as finasteride that inhibit 5α-reductase.

FINASTERIDE AND PROSTATE CANCER

In 1993, a large placebo-controlled randomized clinical trial, the Prostate Cancer Prevention Trial (PCPT), was initiated to determine if the 5α-reductase inhibitor, finasteride, could prevent prostate cancer. The study enrolled 18,882 men age 55 years or older randomized to receive either finasteride (5 mg daily) or placebo. About 4% of participants were African American men. After 7 years of follow-up, 18% of men receiving finasteride developed prostate cancer compared to 24% in the placebo group, a risk reduction of 25%. However, the men who did develop prostate cancer while receiving finasteride were more likely to have high-grade tumors with high metastatic potential. Furthermore, the men taking finasteride reported significantly more sexual side effects (impotence) than men on placebo. Final results were based on analysis of 9,060 participants, only about half the men who initially enrolled in the study (Thompson et al., 2003).

DIETARY FAT AND PROSTATE CANCER

Ecological correlation studies show a strong positive correlation between diets high in fat and calories with prostate cancer incidence and mortality. Within countries, chronological trends in prostate cancer rates tend to follow in close parallel with per capita trends in dietary fat intake. For example, prostate cancer rates in Japanese men have increased nearly fivefold over a 50-year period since 1955, seemingly in response to the rising level of fat in the Japanese diet (**Figure 16.5**).

West and colleagues examined associations of prostate cancer with dietary intakes of fat, protein, carbohydrate, and certain vitamins and minerals in a population-based case control study in Utah. Dietary

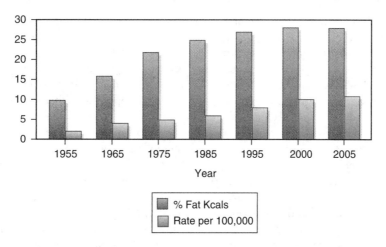

Figure 16.5 Trends in Prostate Cancer Mortality and Dietary Fat, Japan, 1955–2005.

Source: Data from Center for Cancer Control and Information Services. (2010). *Cancer statistics in Japan, 2010.* Tokyo, Japan: Author; Wynder, E. L., Fujita, Y., Harris, R. E., Hirayama, T., & Hiyama, T. (1991). Comparative epidemiology of cancer between the United States and Japan: A second look. *Cancer, 67*(3), 746–763; Matsumura, Y. (2001). Emerging trends of nutrition: Transition and trade-offs. Nutrition trends in Japan. *Asia Pacific Journal of Clinical Nutrition, 10*(Suppl), S40–S47.

data were ascertained from 358 cases and 679 controls group-matched by age and county of residence. For older cases with aggressive tumors, significant associations were observed for the highest versus lowest quartiles of intake of total fat (odds ratio [OR] = 2.9), saturated fat (OR = 2.2), monounsaturated fat (OR = 3.6), polyunsaturated fat (OR = 2.7), and total energy (OR = 2.5). Results suggest that dietary fat increases the risk of aggressive prostate cancer in elderly men (West, Slattery, Robison, Fench, & Mahoney, 1991).

Giovannucci and colleagues examined the association of dietary fat and prostate cancer in a prospective cohort of 51,529 U.S. men ages 40–75 years in the Health Professionals Follow-Up Study. After 5 years, men reporting fat intake in the highest quintile experienced a 79% increase in the risk of invasive prostate cancer compared to men in the lowest quintile. Notably, fat derived from consumption of red meat produced a 2.6-fold increase in the risk (Giovannucci et al., 1993).

Neuhouser and colleagues examined the association of prostate cancer and various dietary factors in a prospective cohort of 12,025 U.S. men followed over an 11-year period. In men with a family history of prostate cancer, high intake of essential omega-6 polyunsaturated fatty acids produced a 2.6-fold increase in the risk of invasive disease (Neuhouser et al., 2007).

Animal studies support an important etiologic link between prostate cancer development and intake of specific types of dietary fat. Zhu and colleagues found that feeding young rats a diet high in α-linoleic acid from corn oil induced high levels of plasma DHT and 5αRD-2 expression in the prostate gland, thus suggesting a potential molecular mechanism for dietary fat stimulation of prostate growth and pathogenesis (Cai et al., 2006). Their studies also suggest that insulin-like growth factor (IGF-1) increases with intake of dietary fat and may be involved in mediating the effects of androgens in the prostate gland.

Using a transgenic model of prostate cancer, Aaronson and colleagues identified strong tumor promotion by essential omega-6 polyunsaturated fats from corn oil (α-linoleic acid) that are common in the U.S. diet (Kobayashi et al., 2008). Mechanistically, omega-6 polyunsaturated fatty acids are readily converted by the cyclooxygenase and lipoxygenase pathways to eicosanoids, such as prostaglandin E2, leukotrienes, and hydroxyl derivatives of fatty acids. These inflammatory eicosanoids have long been implicated in the pathogenesis of cancer and are believed to play important roles in tumor promotion, progression, and metastasis. Reciprocally, essential omega-3 polyunsaturated fatty acids such as gamma-linolenic acid that inhibit the inflammatory cascade have been found to inhibit conversion of testosterone to its active metabolite, DHT (Pham & Ziboh, 2002; Rose & Connolly, 1991).

The differential effects of omega-6 versus omega-3 fatty acids on androgen metabolism suggest an important etiological link between the balance of essential fatty acids in the diet and prostate carcinogenesis. As discussed previously, international studies reflect marked differences in the rates of prostate cancer. African Americans have the highest rates and Asian men the lowest, but Asian men who migrate to the United States transition to higher rates after a single generation (Parkin et al., 2005). This pattern correlates with the 5α-reductase activity among ethnic groups. There is high 5α-reductase activity in African Americans and low activity in Asian men; furthermore, Asian males who live in North America have higher 5α-reductase activity when compared to males in their home countries (Ross et al., 1992). As pointed out by Yuan-Shan Zhu and Julianne Imperato-McGinley (2009), "These data indicate that differences in 5α-reductase activity may be ethnically and environmentally determined and may be related to differences in prostate cancer development." Indeed, the totality of evidence indicates that the "westernized lifestyle," which incorporates high fat/high calorie diets and, in particular, high levels of inflammatory omega-6 fatty acids, enhances the risk for malignant transformation of the prostate gland.

GENETICS OF PROSTATE CANCER

Prostatic cancer also shows a strong familial component. In studies by Meikle and Stanish (1982), brothers of cases had four times higher cumulative rates of prostate cancer than brothers-in-law or males of the general population, thereby reflecting the existence of genetic factors that increase the risk of neoplastic development in the prostate gland. Logically, discovery of mutations and genetic polymorphisms that influence prostate carcinogenesis might be expected in components of the androgen axis that regulate testosterone, dihydrotestosterone, 5α-reductase, and the androgen receptors. One such mutation has already been discovered in African American men with a family history of prostate cancer, a genetic defect in the receptor for the male hormone androgen (testosterone) that may contribute to the development of prostate cancer and its progression (Hu et al., 2010).

PROSTATE CANCER AND SEXUAL ACTIVITY

Another factor that may impact on prostate cancer risk is sexual activity. Declining activity with age may relate to changing ratios of testosterone and estrogen, which in turn may stimulate enhanced proliferation of prostatic glandular epithelium.

SUPPLEMENTAL ANTIOXIDANTS AND PROSTATE CANCER

The findings of a number of observational studies plus two randomized clinical trials indicated that supplemental intake of selenium and vitamin E might be effective in preventing the development of prostate cancer. Both agents scavenge reactive oxygen species (ROS) and are thus classifiable as *antioxidants*. In 2001, a large randomized placebo-controlled clinical trial, the Selenium and Vitamin E Cancer Prevention Trial (SELECT), was initiated to determine whether selenium, vitamin E, or both could prevent prostate cancer. A total of 35,533 men age 55 years or older were recruited for study from 427 participating sites in the United States, Canada, and Puerto Rico. After more than 5 years of follow-up, supplemental selenium or vitamin E, alone or in combination, produced no effect on the risk of developing invasive prostate cancer. In fact, the data showed two concerning trends: a slight increase in the incidence of prostate cancer in men taking supplemental vitamin E and a slight increase in the incidence of type 2 diabetes in men taking supplemental selenium (Lippman et al., 2008). Notably, with continued follow-up of men in the SELECT trial, these adverse effects of supplemental vitamin E and selenium became statistically significant (Klein et al., 2011). The results of SELECT and several other studies have shown that taking antioxidants such as vitamin E may actually accelerate the progression of cancer. Nobel laureate James Watson recently suggested that antioxidants enhance cancer progression by scavenging ROS that effectively induce apoptosis of cancer cells. In particular, the enhanced destruction of ROS by the introduction of supplemental antioxidants may spur cancer growth by disabling apoptotic cancer cell death, particularly in late stage malignancies (Watson, 2013).

NONSTEROIDAL ANTI-INFLAMMATORY DRUGS (NSAIDS) AND PROSTATE CANCER

In the past two decades, traditional nonsteroidal anti-inflammatory drugs (NSAIDs) with cyclooxygenase-2 (COX-2) blocking activity have consistently shown potential in the chemoprevention of several forms of malignant neoplasms, including prostate cancer. In a meta-analysis of 17 epidemiologic studies, regular intake of aspirin, ibuprofen, or other over-the-counter NSAIDs was found to reduce the risk of prostate cancer by 27% (Harris, 2009).

Such effects are manifest primarily through COX-2–dependent molecular mechanisms. For example, NSAIDs reduce COX-2–catalyzed formation of specific inflammatory prostaglandins (particularly PGE-2) that promote key cellular processes in cancer development, including mutagenesis, mitogenesis, angiogenesis, deregulation of apoptosis, immunosuppression, and metastasis (Harris, 2007).

SCREENING FOR PROSTATE CANCER

Screening for prostate cancer using serum prostate specific antigen (PSA) gained favor in the United States and other developed countries during the 1990s. It is estimated that 20 million PSA tests are performed annually in North America and possibly 20 million more outside of North America (De Angelis, Rittenhouse, Mikolajczyk, Blair Shamel, & Semjonow, 2007). A high level of serum PSA (> 4 nanograms per milliliter) when coupled with digital rectal examination (DRE), ultrasonography, and directed biopsy of suspicious prostatic tissue can be effective in identifying men with invasive disease confined to the prostate gland that can be completely surgically excised without recurrence. Nevertheless, PSA screening is controversial because prostate cancer often develops so slowly that it will never lead to symptoms during a man's lifetime. Furthermore, prostatectomy for removal of a cancerous prostate gland often produces major debilitating side effects such as urinary incontinence, erectile dysfunction, and impotence. The major consideration for any screening protocol is to weigh the benefits of early detection and lifesaving treatment against the risk of harm from unnecessary intervention.

Results of two large randomized clinical trials of PSA screening have now been published. The European Randomized Study of Screening for Prostate Cancer evaluated PSA testing versus no screening among 182,000 men ages 50–74 years. After 9 years of follow-up, the results did show 20% fewer deaths in the treated group; however, the study also found that a large number of men were treated unnecessarily, resulting in a high rate of major side effects (Schröder et al., 2009). Another randomized study of 76,693 men in the United States compared PSA plus

DRE to "usual care" in the detection and treatment of prostate cancer. After 7 years of follow-up, there were actually 13% fewer deaths in the "usual care" group (Andriole et al., 2009).

After careful review of the scientific evidence, the U.S. Preventive Services Task Force concluded that the data were insufficient to recommend screening for men under 75 and that men 75 and older should not be screened (U.S. Preventive Services Task Force, 2008). Rather, clinicians are now advised to use a process of shared decision making with each patient that includes candid discussion about the potential risks and benefits of screening. A telling statement from the investigator who initially discovered PSA, Dr. Richard J. Ablin, underscores the controversial nature of routinely screening asymptomatic men for prostate cancer using the PSA test. Dr. Ablin states, "I never dreamed that my discovery four decades ago would lead to such a profit-driven public health disaster. The medical community must confront reality and stop the inappropriate use of PSA screening. Doing so would save billions of dollars and rescue millions of men from unnecessary, debilitating treatments" (Ablin, 2010).

ZINC AND SURVIVAL OF PROSTATE CANCER

Zinc is an essential mineral with known antioxidant and anti-inflammatory effects. Zinc is an important cofactor in DNA repair, apoptosis, and cellular immunity. Notably, the concentration of zinc is higher in prostate tissue than any other tissue in the human body. Recently, Epstein and colleagues examined the level of dietary zinc as a potential predictor of survival among 525 Swedish men diagnosed with invasive prostate cancer during 1989–1995. Swedish men have one of the highest annual mortality rates from prostate cancer in the world (22 deaths per 100,000). After a median follow-up time of 6.4 years, 218 cases (42%) had died of prostate cancer. Zinc intake was estimated based on its average content in grains, meat, dairy products, fruits, and vegetables consumed by the individual patients. Results revealed that high dietary zinc intake (> 15.6 mg per day) was associated with a reduced risk of death due to prostate cancer (hazard ratio = 0.64), whereas zinc intake was not associated with mortality from other causes. The protective effect of high dietary zinc was stronger among men diagnosed with localized tumors (hazard ratio = 0.24). These results suggest that high intake of dietary zinc may have therapeutic benefit in men diagnosed with prostate cancer, particularly among

those with localized tumors at the time of diagnosis (Epstein et al., 2011).

• • • REFERENCES

Ablin, R. J. (2010, March 10). The great prostate mistake. *New York Times*, p. A27.

American Cancer Society. (2009). *Cancer facts and figures*. Atlanta, GA: Author.

Andriole, G. L., Crawford, E. D, Grubb, R. L., Buys, S. S., Chia, D., Church, T. R., . . . Berg, C. D. (2009). Mortality results from a randomized prostate-cancer screening trial. *New England Journal of Medicine, 360*(13), 1310–1319.

Cai, L. Q., Imperato-McGinley, J., & Zhu, Y. S. (2006). Regulation of prostate 5α-reductase-2 gene expression and prostate weight by dietary fat and caloric intake in the rat. *Prostate, 66*, 738–748.

Center for Cancer Control and Information Services. (2010). *Cancer statistics in Japan, 2010*. Tokyo, Japan: Author.

De Angelis, G., Rittenhouse, H. G., Mikolajczyk, S. D., Blair Shamel, L., & Semjonow, A. (2007). Twenty years of PSA: From prostate antigen to tumor marker. *Reviews in Urology, 9*(3), 113–123.

Epstein, M. M., Kasperzyk, J. L., Andrén, O., Giovannucci, E. L., Wolk, A., Håkansson, N., . . . Mucci, L. A. (2011). Dietary zinc and prostate cancer survival in a Swedish cohort. *American Journal of Clinical Nutrition, 93*(3), 586–593.

Ferlay, J., Bray, F., Pisani, P., & Parkin, D. M. (2004). *GLOBOCAN 2002. Cancer incidence, mortality, and prevalence worldwide*. IARC Cancer Base No. 5, version 2.0. Lyon, France: IARC Press.

Ferlay, J., Shin, H.-R., Bray, F., Forman, D., Mathers, C., & Parkin, D. M. (2010). Estimates of worldwide burden of cancer in 2008: GLOBOCAN 2008. *International Journal of Cancer, 127*(12), 2893–2917.

Ferlay, J., Soerjomataram, I., Ervik, M., Dikshit, R., Eser, S., Mathers, C., . . . Bray, F. (2013). *GLOBOCAN 2012 v1.0. Cancer incidence and mortality worldwide: IARC Cancer Base No. 11* [Internet]. Lyon, France: International Agency for Research on Cancer. Retrieved from http://globocan.iarc.fr

Giovannucci, E., Eric, B., Rimm, E. B., Colditz, G. A., Stampfer, M. J., Ascherio, A., & Willett, W. A. (1993). A prospective study of dietary fat and risk of prostate cancer. *Journal of the National Cancer Institute, 85*(19), 1571–1579.

Harris, R. E. (2007). COX-2 and the inflammogenesis of cancer. *Subcellular Biochemistry, 42,* 193–212.

Harris, R. E. (2009). Cyclooxygenase-2 (COX-2) blockade in the chemoprevention of cancers of the colon, breast, prostate and lung. *Inflammopharmacology, 17,* 1–13.

Hu, S. Y., Liu, T., Liu, Z., Ledet, E., Velasco-Gonzalez, C., Mandal, D. M., & Koochekpour, S. (2010). Identification of a novel germline missense mutation of the androgen receptor in African American men with familial prostate cancer. *Asian Journal of Andrology, 12*(3), 336–343.

Ito, K. (2014). Prostate cancer in Asian men. *Nature Reviews Urology 11,* 197–212.

Klein, E. A., Thompson, I. M., Tangen, C. M., Crowley, J. J., Lucia, M. S., Goodman, P. J., & Baker, L. H. (2011). Vitamin E and the risk of prostate cancer. The Selenium and Vitamin E Cancer Prevention Trial (SELECT). *Journal of the American Medical Association, 306*(14), 1549–1556.

Kobayashi, N., Barnard, R. J., Said, J., Hong-Gonzalez, J., Corman, D. M., Ku, M., . . . Aronson, W. J. (2008). Effect of low-fat diet on development of prostate cancer and Akt phosphorylation in the *Hi-Myc* transgenic mouse model. *Cancer Research, 68*(8), 3066–3073.

Lippman, S. M., Klein, E. A., Goodman, P. J., Lucia, M. S., Thompson, I. M., Ford, L. G., . . . Coltman, C. A. (2008). Effect of selenium and vitamin E on risk of prostate cancer and other cancers: The Selenium and Vitamin E Cancer Prevention Trial (SELECT). *Journal of the American Medical Association, 301*(1), 39–51.

Matsumura, Y. (2001). Emerging trends of nutrition: Transition and trade-offs. Nutrition trends in Japan. *Asia Pacific Journal of Clinical Nutrition, 10*(Suppl), S40–S47.

McNeal, J. (1981). Normal and pathologic anatomy of prostate. *Urology, 17*(Suppl 3), 11–16.

McNeal, J. (1993). Prostatic microcarcinomas in relation to cancer origin and the evolution to clinical cancer. *Cancer, 71,* 984–991.

Meikle, A. W., & Stanish, W. M. (1982). Familial prostatic cancer risk and low testosterone. *Journal of Clinical Endocrinology and Metabolism, 54,* 1104–1108.

Neuhouser, M. L., Barnett, M. J., Kristal, A. R., Ambrosone, C. B., King, I., Thornquist, M., & Goodman, G. (2007). Omega-6 PUFA increase and dairy foods decrease prostate cancer risk in heavy smokers. *Journal of Nutrition, 137,* 1821–1827.

Parkin, D. M., Bray, F., Ferlay, J., & Pisani, P. (2001). Estimating the world cancer burden: GLOBOCAN 2000. *International Journal of Cancer, 94,* 153–156.

Parkin, D. M., Bray, F., Ferlay, J., & Pisani, P. (2005). Global cancer statistics, 2002. *CA: A Cancer Journal for Clinicians, 55,* 74–108.

Pham, H., & Ziboh, V. A. (2002). 5 alpha-reductase-catalyzed conversion of testosterone to dihydrotestosterone is increased in prostatic adenocarcinoma cells: Suppression by 15-lipoxygenase metabolites of gamma-linolenic and eicosapentaenoic acids. *Journal of Steroid Biochemistry and Molecular Biology, 82*(4–5), 393–400.

Robbins, S. L., & Cotran, R. S. (1979). *Pathologic basis of disease* (2nd ed.). Philadelphia, PA: W. B. Saunders.

Rose, D. P., & Connolly, J. M. (1991). Effects of fatty acids and eicosanoid synthesis inhibitors on the growth of two human prostate cancer cell lines. *Prostate, 18*(3), 243–254.

Rose, D. P., Laaksa, K., Satarouta, M., & Wynder, E. L. (1984). Hormone levels in prostatic fluid in healthy Finns and prostate cancer patients. *European Journal of Cancer and Clinical Oncology, 20,* 1317–1324.

Ross, R., Bernstein, L., Judd, H., Hanisch, R., Pike, M., & Henderson, B. (1986). Serum testosterone levels in healthy young black and white men. *Journal of the National Cancer Institute, 76*(1), 45–48.

Ross, R. K., Bernstein, L., Lobo, R. A., Shimizu, H., Stanczyk, F. Z., Pike, M. C., & Henderson, B. E. (1992). 5-alpha-reductase activity and risk of prostate cancer among Japanese and US white and black males. *Lancet, 339*(8798), 887–889.

Russell, D. W., & Wilson, J. D. (1994). Steroid 5 alpha-reductase: Two genes/two enzymes. *Annual Review of Biochemistry, 63,* 25–61.

Schröder, F. H., Hugosson, J., Roobol, M. J., Tammela, T. L. J., Ciatto, S. Nelen, V., . . . Auvinen, A. (2009). Screening and prostate cancer mortality in a randomized European study. *New England Journal of Medicine, 360*(13), 1320.

Thompson, I. M., Goodman, P. J., Tangen, C. M., Lucia, M. S., Miller, G. J., Ford, L. G., . . . Coltman, C. A. (2003). The influence of finasteride on the development of prostate cancer. *New England Journal of Medicine, 349,* 215–224.

U.S. Preventive Services Task Force. (2008). Screening for prostate cancer: US Preventive Services Task Force recommendation statement. *Annals of Internal Medicine, 149*(3), 185–191.

Watson, J. (2013). Oxidants, antioxidants and the current incurability of metastatic cancers. *Open Biology, 3.* doi: 10.1098/rsob.120144.

West, D. W., Slattery, M. L., Robison, L. M., Fench, T. K., & Mahoney, A. W. (1991). Adult dietary intake and prostate cancer risk in Utah: A case-control study with special emphasis on aggressive tumors. *Cancer Causes and Control, 2,* 85–94.

World Health Organization. (2009). Death and DALY estimates for 2004 by cause for WHO member states (persons, all ages). Geneva, Switzerland: Author. Retrieved from http://www.who.int/healthinfo/global_burden_disease/estimates_country/en/

Wynder, E. L., Fujita, Y., Harris, R. E., Hirayama, T., & Hiyama, T. (1991). Comparative epidemiology of cancer between the United States and Japan: A second look. *Cancer, 67*(3), 746–763.

Zhu, Y. S. (2005). Molecular basis of steroid action in the prostate. *Cellscience, 1,* 27–55.

Zhu, Y. S., & Imperato-McGinley, J. (2009). 5α-reductase isozymes and androgen actions in the prostate. *Annals of the New York Academy of Sciences, 1155,* 43–56.

Zhu, Y. S., Katz, M. D., & Imperato-McGinley, J. (1998). Natural potent androgens: Lessons from human genetic models. *Bailliere's Clinical Endocrinology and Metabolism, 12,* 83–113.

17

Epidemiology of Testicular Cancer

ANATOMY OF THE TESTIS AND SPERMATOGENESIS

Each testis consists of approximately 250 lobules separated by fibrous strands. Each lobule consists of loose connective tissue and a network of tubules called *seminiferous tubules*. Each seminiferous tubule is lined by a basement membrane that supports the germinal epithelium. The germinal epithelium is made up of primordial germ cells or spermatogonia, from which sperm arise. Spermatogonia are stem cells that proliferate by mitosis. As spermatogonia move away from the basement membrane, they undergo meiosis to form immature sperm called *spermatids*.

Two important cell types, Sertoli cells and Leydig cells, stimulate and regulate the process of spermatogenesis. Sertoli cells are nurse cells that secrete estrogen and other hormones in response to the pituitary hormone, follicular stimulating hormone (FSH). Leydig cells secrete testosterone in response to the pituitary hormone, luteinizing hormone (LH). The process of spermatogenesis involves both mitotic and meiotic divisions of germinal epithelial cells under the influence of testosterone and estrogen.

Each day in the adult male, millions of immature spermatids travel through the seminiferous tubules into a network of efferent ductules in the central portion of the testis called the *rete testis*. Cilia within ductules of the rete testis assist the transport of spermatozoa into an extratesticular structure called the *epididymis*. The epididymis is a rich source of glucose and energy, and it is within this organ that the spermatozoa complete the maturation process to form sperm. Mature sperm cells are transported from the epididymis into a muscular tube called the *vas deferens* that transports sperm into bilateral saccular structures called

seminal vesicles near the prostate gland. Within the seminal vesicles, sperm cells are mixed with prostatic fluids to form semen for ejaculation through the urethra (**Figure 17.1**) (Kumar, Abbas, & Aster, 2014).

PATHOLOGY OF TESTICULAR CANCER

Ninety-five percent of all tumors of the testis are germcell neoplasms. The International Agency for Research on Cancer (IARC) recognizes four specific types of germ-cell tumors: seminomas, embryonal carcinomas, malignant teratomas, and choriocarcinomas. These lesions can be combined into two histologic groups: seminomas and nonseminomas. Further classification beyond the two main histologic categories (seminoma and nonseminoma) appears to have limited relevance in etiologic or clinical settings (Bray et al., 2006).

Based on pathological review, about 50% of testicular germ cell tumors are seminomas, 40% are nonseminomas, and 5–10% consist of components of both cell types. These malignancies are believed to arise from precursor carcinomas in situ (Dieckmann & Skakkebaek, 1999; Leendert, Loooijenga, & Oosterhuis, 1999; Sandberg, Meloni, & Suijkerbuijk, 1996; Skakkebaek, 1972).

Seminomas primarily occur in adult men, but rarely in infants. These tumors *do not* express fetal proteins such as alpha fetoprotein, but some *do* express human chorionic gonadotropin. Seminomas consist of sheets of round tumor cells growing in a monotonous morphologic pattern. Lymphocytic infiltration is a common feature of these tumors. They tend to be radiosensitive and are therefore usually curable by a combination of surgical excision and radiotherapy.

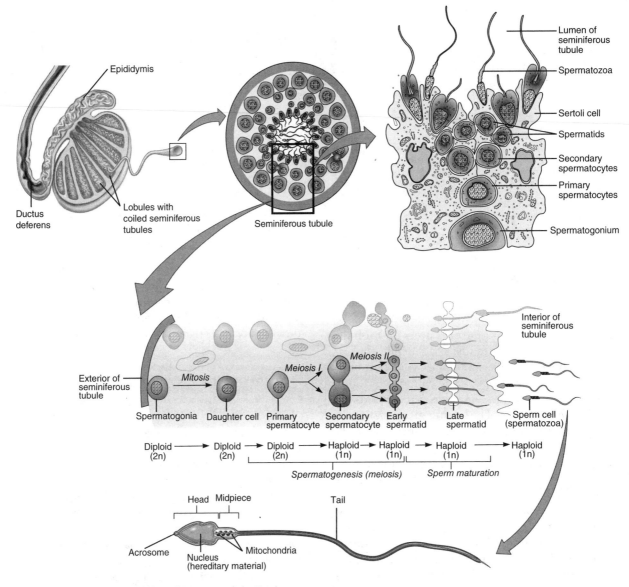

Figure 17.1 Spermatogenesis and Anatomy of the Testis.

Nonseminomas include embryonal carcinomas, immature (malignant) teratomas, and choriocarcinomas. These tumors *do* express alpha fetoprotein, and the majority are diagnosed before age 30. The morphology of nonseminomas is highly variable, and in some cases their appearance is bizarre. For example, teratomas often show characteristics of early fetal development and contain immature remnants of various body parts.

Teratomas and yolk sac tumors constitute a distinct group of rare nonseminomas of the testes that develop in prepubertal boys and are typically found during the first 4 years of life. Such tumors have been reported among male infants, usually in association with congenital anomalies and chromosomal anomalies.

Germ cell tumors are slightly more common in men than women. In women, they occasionally arise from the ovarian, placental, or uterine tissues. Choriocarcinomas are distinct from other nonseminomas in that they secrete human chorionic gonadotropin (hCG). These rare tumors can arise in the placenta or other uterine tissues during pregnancy and are composed of two specific cell types of the chorionic membranes, cytotrophoblasts and syncytiotrophoblasts. Testicular choriocarcinomas are quite rare.

GLOBAL EPIDEMIOLOGY OF TESTICULAR CANCER

Incidence and Mortality

Testicular cancer accounts for only about 1% of all malignant neoplasms in males. Nevertheless, this malignancy is the most common malignancy in young men under 40 years of age. During 2012, 55,266 incident cases were diagnosed and 10,351 deaths were attributed to testicular cancer (Ferlay et al., 2013).

The annual incidence of testicular cancer worldwide has remained stable during the last decade, at about 1.5 cases per 100,000 men. However, the incidence rates vary more than 20-fold among nations, ranging from less than 0.5 per 100,000 in some Asian and African/African American populations to over 12 per 100,000 in Norway and Switzerland (**Figure 17.2**).

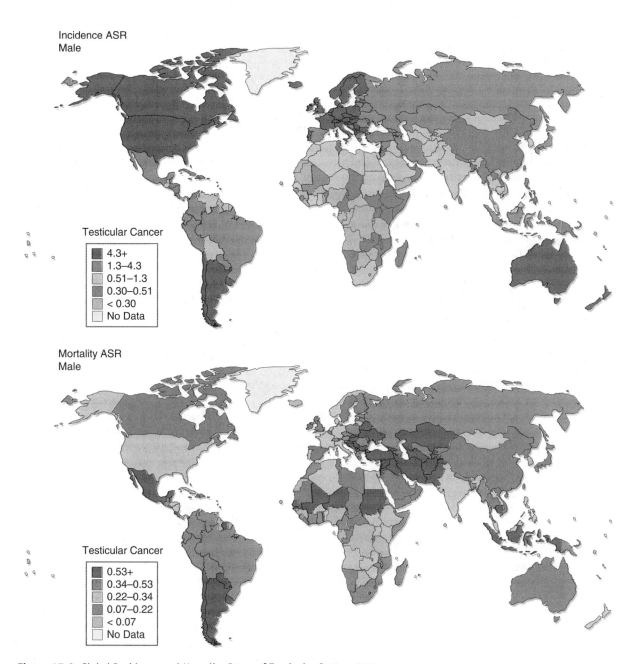

Figure 17.2 Global Incidence and Mortality Rates of Testicular Cancer, 2012.

Source: Reproduced from Ferlay, J., Soerjomataram, I., Ervik, M., Dikshit, R., Eser, S., Mathers, C., ... Bray, F. (2013). *GLOBOCAN 2012 v1.0. Cancer incidence and mortality worldwide: IARC CancerBase No. 11* [Internet]. Lyon, France: International Agency for Research on Cancer. Retrieved from http://globocan.iarc.fr

The annual mortality rate of testicular cancer worldwide has also remained stable during the last decade at about 0.3 deaths per 100,000 men. Mortality rates are highest in nations with high incidence rates and where access to therapy is limited; for example, during 2012, men living in Mexico, Argentina, the Russian Federation, and some nations of central Africa, Eastern Europe, and central Asia had mortality rates exceeding 0.5 deaths per 100,000 (Figure 17.2).

Within nations, the incidence of testicular cancer varies markedly by race, with blacks and other nonwhite races exhibiting extremely low rates in comparison to white populations. In the United States, the incidence of testicular cancer in 2012 was about five times higher among Caucasians than African Americans. Furthermore, the annual incidence has steadily increased over time in some populations, particularly in developed nations (Bray et al., 2006; Rosen, Jayram, Drazer, & Eggener, 2011; Zheng et al., 1996). For example, the incidence more than doubled in Great Britain during 1975–2010 (**Figure 17.3**).

Several investigators have examined the rising incidence of testicular cancer, which has occurred primarily in populations of the developed world, and have advanced various hypotheses to explain the trend. One possible explanation is the widespread use of scanning and imaging equipment in developed nations, which has led to earlier and more accurate detection of testicular tumors. There is also heightened awareness among urologists about the development of such tumors in adolescents and young men, particularly those with conditions of low fertility. Another hypothesis suggests that exposure to estrogenic hormones during fetal development may compromise mitosis and meiosis of the testicular germ cells (Huyghe, Matsuda, & Thonneau, 2003). One recent finding of importance is the higher rate of testicular cancer in men who are HIV-positive compared to those who are HIV-negative (Lyter, Bryant, Thackeray, Rinaldo, & Kingsley, 1995). The high rate of HIV-positive men living in underserved populations may therefore herald emerging epidemics of testicular cancer in these populations.

In the face of rising incidence rates of testicular cancer, mortality rates are steadily declining in many populations. For example, in Great Britain, testicular cancer incidence increased from 3 to 7.5 per 100,000 during 1970 to 2010, an increase of nearly 4% per year; in contrast, mortality for the same period fell from 1.2 to 0.2 per 100,000, a *decrease* of about 2% per year (Figure 17.3). Similar patterns are evident for the United States, Australia, New Zealand, China, and most Western European and Scandinavian nations (Shanmugalingam, Soultati, Chowdhury, Rudman, & Van Hemelrijck, 2013). The declining mortality rates of testicular cancer are a consequence of the high cure rates for this malignancy due to multidisciplinary therapy involving surgery, chemotherapy, and radiation.

Age Distribution of Testicular Cancer

The majority of cases of testicular cancer (more than 70%) are diagnosed in young men between the ages of 20 and 40 years. Nonseminomas tend to occur prior to age 30 whereas seminomas show a slightly later age of onset pattern (**Figure 17.4**).

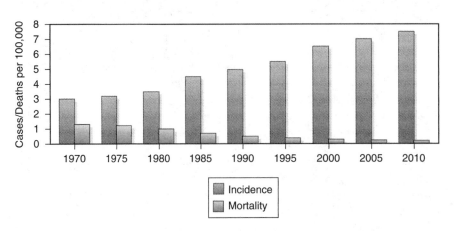

Figure 17.3 Trends in Testicular Cancer Incidence and Mortality in Great Britain, 1970–2010.

Sources: Data from Cancer Research UK. (2011). UK cancer information service. Retrieved from http://www.cancerresearchuk.org; Shanmugalingam, T., Soultati, A., Chowdhury, S., Rudman, S., & Van Hemelrijck, M. (2013). Global incidence and outcome of testicular cancer. *Journal of Clinical Epidemiology, 5,* 417–427.

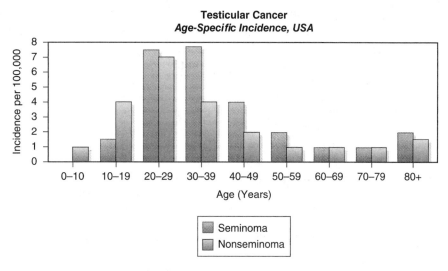

Figure 17.4 Age Distribution of Testicular Cancer, United States.

Source: Data from Zheng, T., Holford, T. R., Ma, Z., Ward, B. A., Flannery, J., & Boyle, P. (1996). Continuing increase in incidence of germ-cell testis cancer in young adults: Experience from Connecticut, USA, 1935–1992. *International Journal of Cancer, 65,* 723–729.

CYTOGENETICS AND GENETICS OF TESTICULAR GERM CELL TUMORS

Testicular germ cell tumor karyotypes are character-ized by *aneuploidy*, which means that the chromo-some number is not an exact multiple of the usual haploid number (23 in humans). The usual diploid number of chromosomes in human cells is 46 (22 autosomes plus XX in women or XY in men). In contrast, the karyotypes of germ cell tumors often approach triploidy, with chromosome numbers ranging from 50 to 70 (median ~60). According to one model, nondisjunction produces abnormal tetraploid cells that develop into carcinoma in situ. Subsequently, tetraploid cells of carcinoma in situ lose chromosomes or develop other chromosomal aberrations that result in invasive germ cell cancer (Dieckmann & Skakkebaek, 1999; Frigyesi et al., 2004).

There is a frequent appearance (~80%) of an isochromosome of the short arm of chromosome 12 called *i(12p)* in testicular germ cell tumors of all cell types. This hybrid chromosome typically consists of two combined short arms of chromosome 12. The exact role of *i(12p)* in the development of testicu-lar cancer is unknown. Notably, in tumors without *i(12p)*, other structural changes of chromosome 12 have been identified. These findings suggest that amplification of certain genes on the short arm of chromosome 12 may play a role in the genesis of germ cell tumors (Sandberg et al., 1996).

RISK FACTORS FOR TESTICULAR CANCER

Risk factors for testicular cancer include prior history of unilateral disease, familial history, cryptorchidism (maldescended testes), infertility, infection, and cer-tain congenital anomalies and germline mutations.

Cryptorchidism (Maldescended Testes)

A major risk factor for the development of testicular cancer is *cryptorchidism* or *maldescended testicle.* In a review of nine case control studies, cryptorchidism was found to increase the risk of developing testicular cancer by nearly sixfold (summary relative risk = 5.8) (Chilvers & Pike, 1992). In a large case control study conducted in Great Britain, 794 men with testicular cancer were compared to age-matched controls with-out disease. Results revealed that an undescended testis increased the risk nearly fourfold (odds ratio [OR] = 3.8), and inguinal hernia nearly doubled the risk (OR = 1.9). The risk was also elevated among men who reported infertility (OR = 2.7). Notably, the investigators found that the excess risk associ-ated with an undescended testis was eliminated in men who underwent orchiopexy (surgical reposition-ing of the testis) before the age of 10 years (Forman et al., 1994).

Orchiopexy before puberty decreases the risk of testicular cancer but may not completely attenuate excess risk. In a Swedish cohort of 16,983 men who underwent orchiopexy between 1964 and 1999 and were followed for a total of 209,984 person-years,

56 cases of testicular cancer were identified. Among those who were treated before 13 years of age, the relative risk of testicular cancer compared with the general population was 2.2. Among those who were treated at age 13 or later, the relative risk was 5.4. These findings clearly show that orchiopexy should be performed prior to puberty to minimize the risk of developing testicular cancer (Pettersson, Richiardi, Nordenskjold, Kaijser, & Akre, 2007). Furthermore, pathologic studies of biopsy specimens from patients with cryptorchidism reveal that deviations from normal spermatogenesis become more evident and the absence of germ cells more pronounced with delay of orchiopexy beyond only a few months of age (AbouZeid, Mousa, Soliman, Hamza, & Hay, 2011; Huff et al., 2001).

Familial History of Testicular Cancer

In genetic studies of index cases (probands) with testicular cancer, approximately 1.3% report having at least one blood relative (father, brother, or son) also afflicted with the disease (Dieckmann & Pichlmeier, 1997; Dong, Lönnstedt, & Hemminki, 2001). In a study of 4,659 cases among Swedish men, fathers, sons, and brothers of afflicted subjects had risk increases of 3.8, 3.9, and 8.3, respectively. An international consortium that identified 461 families with 985 cases found that the clinical and pathologic features of familial testicular germ cell tumors were similar to those of nonfamilial cases (Mai et al., 2010).

At least 25 rare hereditary disorders have been identified in isolated cases of testicular cancer. These include certain congenital and genetic anomalies such as Klinefelter's syndrome (XXY genotype), Down's syndrome (trisomy 21), the Li–Fraumeni syndrome (*p53* germline mutation), and many others; however, there is no apparent unifying role of these diverse genetic defects in malignant transformation of germ cells of the testes. One X-linked gene, *Xq27*, may heighten the risk of testicular cancer by predisposing to undescended testes (Lutke Holzik et al., 2003).

Infection and Testicular Cancer

The incidence of testicular germ cell tumors, particularly seminomas, is markedly higher among HIV-infected men compared to HIV-negative men. In the Pittsburgh component of the Multicenter AIDS Cohort Study (MACS), the rate of seminoma was 20-fold higher than expected among 430 HIV-positive patients compared to the general male population of Pennsylvania. The investigators suggest that immunosuppression due to HIV infection may heighten the risk of seminoma development (Lyter et al., 1995).

Other infectious agents have been examined in studies of testicular cancer. In a hospital-based case control study conducted in Washington, D.C., infection histories and other risk factors were examined among 271 cases with testicular cancer and 259 controls matched by age, race, and other factors. One infectious condition, mumps orchitis, occurred in six cases and only one control subject (OR = 5.8), suggesting an etiologic association (Brown, Pottern, & Hoover, 1987).

Many subsequent studies have examined the potential role of mumps orchitis and other childhood infections in the development of testicular germ cell cancer. Using existing data from the U.S. Servicemen's Testicular Tumor Environmental and Endocrine Determinants (STEED) study, a team of investigators evaluated the association between common childhood infections and testicular germ cell tumors by comparing 767 cases and 928 age-matched controls. They also conducted a meta-analysis of mumps, mumps orchitis, and testicular cancer. Results of the case control study revealed that a past history of orchitis was associated with an increase in the risk (OR = 2.4); however, this association was limited to orchitis diagnosed within 1 calendar year of the date of diagnosis (OR = 23.1) and not before that date (OR = 1.2). In the meta-analysis, estimates of testicular cancer risk due to orchitis were elevated in studies conducted prior to 1990 (pooled OR = 9.1), but the addition of more recent studies dramatically attenuated the estimate (pooled OR = 1.8). The authors of the study concluded that their data *do not* support an association between testicular cancer and mumps orchitis (Trabert, Graubard, Erickson, & McGlynn, 2012). Nevertheless, in view of recent outbreaks of mumps in the United States and other developed countries, it seems prudent to continue assessment of mumps orchitis and development of testicular cancer.

Personal History of Testicular Cancer

Patients with a history of unilateral testicular germ cell cancer carry an approximate 25- to 50-fold increased risk of developing a contralateral tumor. Follow-up studies of patients with unilateral disease consistently reveal that approximately 5% eventually develop contralateral germ cell tumors (Dieckmann & Loy, 1996; Holstein & Lauke, 1996).

Teratomas and Yolk Sac Tumors

Testicular teratomas and yolk sac tumors of prepubertal boys are rare, with an annual rate of about 1.2 per million. Most testicular teratomas are diploid without apparent chromosomal aberrations. Infantile testicular teratomas are usually benign and are curable by orchidectomy. In contrast, yolk sac tumors typically show aneuploidy (often near tetraploidy) and have invasive malignant potential, thus requiring combination therapy (Holstein & Lauke, 1996).

PREVENTION AND THERAPY OF TESTICULAR CANCER

Rapid detection of cryptorchidism (undescended testis) and timely surgical correction (orchiopexy) are essential in lowering the risk of developing testicular cancer. The optimal time of surgery is at about 6 months of age, after which spontaneous descent is rare. Males who undergo orchiopexy remain at elevated risk, particularly those who undergo surgical correction after puberty.

Regular self-examination is advised in order to detect tumors as early as possible. Suspicious testicular masses on palpation should be imaged by ultrasound and/or magnetic resonance imaging (MRI) to identify size, location, and morphological features. Biopsy and microscopic examination of tissue are necessary to confirm the presence of cancer.

Testicular cancer is treatable by surgery, radiation therapy, and chemotherapy. Data from the Surveillance, Epidemiology, and End Results (SEER) Program of the U.S. National Cancer Institute suggest that up to 95% of cases are curable with early detection and appropriate chemotherapy (Brenner, 2002); however, survival is low for patients with advanced malignancies living in regions with no access to therapy.

• • • REFERENCES

AbouZeid, A. A., Mousa, M. H., Soliman, H. A., Hamza, A. F., & Hay, S. A. (2011). Intra-abdominal testis: Histological alterations and significance of biopsy. *Journal of Urology, 85*(1), 269–274.

Bray. F., Lorenzo, R., Ekbom, A., Forman, D., Pukkala, E., Cuninkova, M., & Moller, H. (2006). Testicular seminoma and nonseminoma share the same etiology? Evidence from an age-period-cohort analysis of incidence trends in eight European countries. *Cancer Epidemiology, Biomarkers and Prevention, 15,* 652–658.

Brenner, H. (2002). Long-term survival rates of cancer patients achieved by the end of the 20th century: A period analysis. *Lancet, 360,* 1131–1135.

Brown, L. M., Pottern, L. M., & Hoover, R. N. (1987). Testicular cancer in young men: The search for causes of the epidemic increase in the United States. *Journal of Epidemiology and Community Health, 41,* 349–354.

Cancer Research UK. (2011). UK cancer information service. Retrieved from http://www.cancerresearchuk.org

Chilvers, C., & Pike, M. C. (1992). Cancer risk in the undescended testicle. *European Urology Update Series, 1,* 74–79.

Dieckmann, K.-P., & Loy, V. (1996). Prevalence of contralateral testicular intraepithelial neoplasia in patients with testicular germ cell neoplasms. *Journal of Clinical Oncology, 14,* 3126–3132.

Dieckmann, K.-P., & Pichlmeier, U. (1997). The prevalence of familial testicular cancer: An analysis of two patient populations and a review of the literature. *Cancer, 80*(10), 1954–1960.

Dieckmann, K.-P., & Skakkebaek, N. E. (1999). Carcinoma in situ of the testis: Review of biological and clinical features. *International Journal of Cancer, 83,* 815–822.

Dong, C., Lönnstedt, I., & Hemminki, K. (2001). Familial testicular cancer and second primary cancers in testicular cancer patients by histological type. *European Journal of Cancer, 37*(15), 1878–1885.

Ferlay, J., Soerjomataram, I., Ervik, M., Dikshit, R., Eser, S., Mathers, C., . . . Bray, F. (2013). *GLOBOCAN 2012 v1.0. Cancer incidence and mortality worldwide: IARC CancerBase No. 11* [Internet]. Lyon, France: International Agency for Research on Cancer. Retrieved from http://globocan.iarc.fr

Forman, D., Pike, M. C., Davey, G., Dawson, S., Baker, K., Chilvers, C. E. D., . . . Coupland, C. A. C. (1994). Aetiology of testicular cancer: Association with congenital abnormalities, age at puberty, infertility and exercise. *BMJ, 308,* 1393–1399.

Frigyesi, A., Gisselsson, D., Hansen, G. B., Soller, M., Mitelman, F., & Höglund, M. (2004). A model for karyotypic evolution in testicular germ cell tumors. *Genes, Chromosomes and Cancer, 40*(3), 172–178.

Holstein, A. F., & Lauke, H. (1996). Histologic diagnostics of early testicular germ-cell tumor. *International Journal of Urology, 3,* 165–172.

Huff, D. S., Fenig, D. M., Canning, D. A., Carr, M. G., Zderic, S. A., & Snyder, H. M. (2001). Abnormal germ cell development in cryptorchidism. *Hormone Research, 55*(1), 11–17.

Huyghe, E., Matsuda, T., & Thonneau, P. (2003). Increasing incidence of testicular cancer wordwide: A review. *Journal of Urology, 170,* 5–11.

Kumar, V., Abbas, A. K., & Aster J. C. (2014). *Robbins and Cotran pathologic basis of disease* (9th ed.). Philadelphia, PA: Mosby & Saunders.

Lutke Holzik, M. F., Sijmons, R. H., Sleijfer, D. T., Sonneveld, D. J., Hoekstra-Weebers, J. E., van Echten-Arends, J., & Hoekstra, H. J. (2003). Syndromic aspects of testicular carcinoma. *Cancer, 97*(4), 984–992.

Lyter, D. W., Bryant, J., Thackeray, R., Rinaldo, C. R., & Kingsley, L. A. (1995). Incidence of human immunodeficiency virus-related and nonrelated malignancies in a large cohort of homosexual men. *Journal of Clinical Oncology, 13*(10), 2540–2546.

Mai, P. L., Friedlander, M., Tucker, K., Phillips, K. A., Hogg, D., Jewett, M. A., . . . Greene, M. H. (2010). The International Testicular Cancer Linkage Consortium: A clinicopathologic descriptive analysis of 461 familial malignant testicular germ cell tumor kindred. *Urologic Oncology, 28*(5), 492–499.

Pettersson, A., Richiardi, L., Nordenskjold, A., Kaijser, M., & Akre, O. (2007). Age at surgery for undescended testis and risk of testicular cancer. *New England Journal of Medicine, 356*(18), 1835–1841.

Rosen, A., Jayram, G., Drazer, M., & Eggener, S. E. (2011). Global trends in testicular cancer incidence and mortality. *European Urology, 60*(2), 374–379.

Sandberg, A. A., Meloni, A. M., & Suijkerbuijk, R. F. (1996). Reviews of chromosome studies in urological tumors. III. Cytogenetics and genes in testicular tumors. *Journal of Urology, 144,* 1531–1556.

Shanmugalingam, T., Soultati, A., Chowdhury, S., Rudman, S., & Van Hemelrijck, M. (2013). Global incidence and outcome of testicular cancer. *Journal of Clinical Epidemiology, 5,* 417–427.

Skakkebaek, N. E. (1972). Possible carcinoma in situ of the testis. *Lancet, 2*(7776), 516–517.

Trabert, B., Graubard, B. I., Erickson, R. L., & McGlynn, K. A. (2012). Childhood infections, orchitis and testicular germ cell tumours: A report from the STEED study and a meta-analysis of existing data. *British Journal of Cancer, 106,* 1331–1334.

Zheng, T., Holford, T. R., Ma, Z., Ward, B. A., Flannery, J., & Boyle, P. (1996). Continuing increase in incidence of germ-cell testis cancer in young adults: Experience from Connecticut, USA, 1935–1992. *International Journal of Cancer, 65,* 723–729.

CHAPTER

18

Epidemiology of Carcinoma of the External Male Genitalia: Penis and Scrotum

GLOBAL EPIDEMIOLOGY OF PENILE CANCER

Carcinoma of the penis is an uncommon and potentially mutilating disease with a heterogeneous etiology. This malignancy is predominantly found in men who were not circumcised shortly after birth and is rarely found in populations where neonatal circumcision is routine (Maden et al., 1993; Schoen, Oehrli, Colby, & Machin, 2000). Nevertheless, sexually transmitted infectious agents such as oncogenic human papillomaviruses (HPVs) may cause disease even in circumcised men.

Approximately 26,000 new cases of penile cancer are diagnosed each year among males worldwide (IARC, 2007; Parkin & Bray, 2006). Carcinomas of the penis are rare among men living in developed countries but are relatively common among the male populations of some underdeveloped nations. Low annual incidence rates ranging from 0.3 to 1.0 per 100,000 are observed in developed nations such as the United States, Canada, Great Britain, Australia, New Zealand, and Western European and Scandinavian nations. Rates are very low among Israeli Jewish men (0.1 per 100,000) who are circumcised shortly after birth and among Muslim men (0.2 per 100,000) who are circumcised during childhood. In contrast, rates are much higher (3 to 10 per 100,000) among men living in certain parts of the world where circumcision is rare. Several high-risk populations have been identified in regions of Uganda, India, Thailand, Puerto Rico, Paraguay, Brazil, and elsewhere in which penile cancer accounts for 10–22% of all malignancies in men (Bleeker et al., 2008; Morris et al., 2011; Shabbir, Barod, Hegart, & Minhasa, 2013).

PENILE CANCER IN THE UNITED STATES

In 2013, cancer of the penis was diagnosed in 1,570 men and caused 310 deaths in the United States. A team of investigators from the University of Hawaii examined incidence and mortality rates of penile cancer among U.S. men using population-based data from the Surveillance, Epidemiology, and End Results (SEER) program of the National Cancer Institute and the National Program for Cancer Registries of the Centers for Disease Control and Prevention. During 1998–2003, 4,967 men were diagnosed with histologically confirmed squamous cell carcinoma of the penis—less than 1% of all malignant neoplasms in males. Overall, the annual age-adjusted rate was 0.81 cases per 100,000 men. Incidence rates among Caucasians and African Americans were similar to the overall rate. Pacific Islanders had the lowest rate (0.37 per 100,000) and Hispanics the highest (1.32 per 100,000). The age-adjusted annual mortality rate for all men was low (0.18 per 100,000); however, mortality rates were about 50% higher among African American and Hispanic men and those living in regions of low socioeconomic status (Hernandez et al., 2008).

AGE-SPECIFIC INCIDENCE OF PENILE CANCER

Penile cancer is diagnosed predominantly in elderly men, although onset in young adult males does occur. The median age at diagnosis of penile cancer is about 68 years of age. The incidence increases steadily throughout life, and the rates are highest for elderly men, age 70 years or older (**Figure 18.1**).

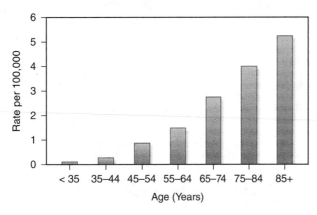

Figure 18.1 Age-Specific Annual Incidence of Penile Cancer, United States, 1973–2002.

Source: Data from Barnholtz-Sloan, J. S., Maldonado, J. L., Pow-san, J., & Guiliano, A. R. (2007). Incidence trends in primary malignant penile cancer. *Urologic Oncology: Seminars and Original Investigations, 25*(5), 361–367.

PATHOLOGY AND HISTOLOGY

The vast majority (> 95%) of penile malignancies are squamous cell carcinomas that arise from the epithelium covering the organ. Other rare forms include basal cell carcinoma, melanoma, lymphoma, and sarcoma. Approximately 75% of squamous cell carcinomas are either flat ulcerative lesions or papillary tumors that typically show keratinization. Most remaining squamous cell carcinomas exhibit wartlike features characteristic of infection by certain strains of HPV.

Pathogenesis of Squamous Cell Penile Carcinoma

Similar to other malignancies derived from epithelium, squamous cell carcinomas of the penis appear to evolve through a stepwise process. Over a period of several years, early dysplastic lesions develop and progress to carcinomas in situ. A variety of names have been given to penile carcinoma in situ, including Bowen's disease, Bowenoid papulosis, and erythroplasia of Queyrat. Subsequently, cancer cells breach the basement membrane leading to invasive carcinoma, which has the capability of disseminating to lymph nodes and other tissues.

Premalignant Lesions of Penile Carcinoma

Lichen sclerosis is characterized by white atrophic plaques on the glans and prepuce (foreskin) of the penis. These plaques may enlarge and coalesce to form sclerotic masses. In a study of 86 cases of uncircumcised Italian men with lichen sclerosis, five lesions (5.8%) exhibited malignant features and four of these were

found to be positive for HPV (Nasca, Innocenzi, & Micali, 1999). In a second study, the clinical and pathology records of 130 Italian men with confirmed lichen sclerosis were reviewed to quantify the presence of premalignant and malignant lesions. Eleven of these cases (8.4%) had lesions with malignant histopathological features (Barbagli et al., 2006).

Leukoplakia refers to solitary or multiple white scaly plaques, often involving the glans and/or meatus. Such lesions arise due to chronic irritation and inflammation and are often found in close proximity to squamous cell carcinomas. Furthermore, areas of dysplasia that can progress to cancer are present in up to 20% of cases with penile leukoplakia (Mikhail, 1980; Schellhammer, Jordan, Robey, & Spaulding, 1992).

A penile *cutaneous horn* is a keratotic lesion that develops from epithelial cells on the surface of preexisting lesions such as pigmented nevi, warts, or abrasions in response to chronic inflammation. Such lesions have been observed in association with invasive carcinoma.

Condyloma acuminata (genital warts) can arise on the penis as well as other anogenital sites of both men and women. Although usually benign, malignant transformation has been observed in association with oncogenic subtypes of HPV infection, particularly HPV-16 and HPV-18. The association of HPV infection with the development of penile carcinoma is discussed in greater detail in the section of this chapter on risk factors.

RISK FACTORS FOR CARCINOMA OF THE PENIS

Several early studies identified poor genital hygiene, smegma retention, and phimosis (unretractable foreskin) as risk factors for penile cancer. More recently, infection of the genitalia by oncogenic strains of HPV, particularly HPV-16, has been confirmed to play an etiologic role in a subset of cases. Conditions such as penile rash, abrasion, urethral stricture, and inflammation have also been found to increase the risk. Inflammation may be a key component of tumor development or progression because most penile cancers arise at sites of infection, chronic irritation, or injury (Bleeker et al., 2008).

Circumcision and Penile Cancer

Multiple studies have found that neonatal circumcision reduces the risk of carcinoma of the penis by 60–70%. The first evidence that circumcision prevented the development of penile cancer was reported in 1932 by Anthony Wolbarst from New York. In the study, 1,103 cases of penile cancer from more than 200 U.S. hospitals were reviewed and none were Jewish, despite 3% of the hospital population being Jewish and hence circumcised (Wolbarst, 1932). Based on these data, Wolbarst suggested that circumcision in early life protects against the development of penile cancer and advocated the practice of universal circumcision, which stimulated considerable controversy and debate regarding the risk versus benefit ratio of the procedure. This controversy still rages, although a recent report from the American Academy of Pediatrics (AAP) has concluded that the health benefits of infant circumcision outweigh the risks (AAP, 2012).

Figure 18.2 shows the global prevalence of circumcision by country. Overall, about one-third of all men have been circumcised. Prevalence rates of circumcision are highest among Jewish and Muslim men and men living in industrialized nations. The incidence and mortality rates of penile cancer tend to be lower in those countries with a higher prevalence of circumcision (Morris et al., 2011).

Despite the controversial nature of the practice of childhood circumcision, numerous studies provide strong evidence that early circumcision markedly reduces the risk of developing penile cancer later in life. In 1947, a hospital-based case control study was conducted among U.S. military personnel in which 139 cases with penile cancer were compared to 356 controls of similar age and ethnicity. Circumcision during childhood was infrequent among cases compared to controls (1.4% versus 17.7%, odds ratio [OR] = 0.07), suggesting a 93% reduction in risk associated with early circumcision (Schrek & Lenowitz, 1947).

A 1991 review noted that 592 cases of invasive penile cancer reported by five major cancer centers in the United States included *no* men circumcised in infancy, despite the fact that more than 80% of men surveyed during the 1960s had neonatal circumcision (Schoen, 1991).

In a systematic review of the literature on circumcision and penile carcinoma, eight studies were identified that reported estimates of odds ratios or other data suitable for meta-analysis. Study populations included men from the United States, Europe, and China. Circumcision in childhood/adolescence was found to be protective against the development of invasive cancer of the penis (summary OR = 0.33), but there was little evidence of an association with either intraepithelial neoplasia or carcinoma in situ (Larke, Thomas, dos Santos Silva, & Weiss, 2011).

Phimosis and Penile Cancer

Phimosis refers to circumferential fibrosis of preputial tissue (foreskin) in uncircumcised men that leads

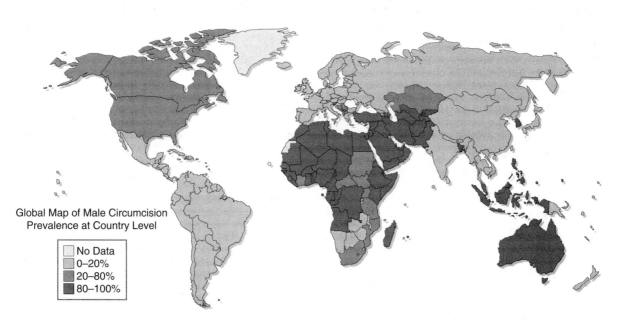

Figure 18.2 Global Prevalence of Circumcision, 2006.

Source: The World Health Organization report of 14 December 2007. Male circumcision: Global trends and determinants of prevalence, safety, and acceptability. This report is the result of collaborative work between the London School of Hygiene and Tropical Medicine, the World Health Organization, and the Joint United Nations Programme on HIV/AIDS (UNAIDS).

to narrowing and inability to retract the penile fore-skin over the glans penis. This condition leads to the accumulation of smegma beneath the foreskin and predisposes to chronic inflammation and infection. Phimosis is found in about 1% of uncircumcised men, but rarely in circumcised men. In a study of uncircumcised schoolboys conducted in Denmark, the incidence of phimosis among 3,355 adolescent boys ages 14–17 years was 1.1% (Oster, 1968).

Several studies have found that phimosis among uncircumcised men is associated with an approximate 10-fold higher risk of penile cancer, whereas uncircumcised men with no history of phimosis are not at elevated risk (Brinton et al., 1991; Daling et al., 2005; Madsen, Brule, Jensen, Wohlfahrt, & Frisch, 2008; Schoen et al., 2000; Tseng, Morgenstern, Mack, & Peters, 2001). The true predisposing factor for penile cancer associated with lack of circumcision therefore appears to be phimosis. Obviously, removal of the foreskin by circumcision virtually negates the development of phimosis, thereby reducing the risk of developing penile cancer.

Human Papillomavirus (HPV)

Investigators at the Fred Hutchinson Cancer Center in Seattle, Washington, conducted a population-based case control study of penile cancer among men living in the region. They compared 110 men with carcinoma of the penis to 355 male disease-free control subjects frequency-matched to the cases on age and date of diagnosis. Tumor tissues from 67 of the cases were tested for HPV DNA by polymerase chain reaction (PCR). Increased odds ratios (ORs) were noted for uncircumcised men compared to men circumcised at birth (OR = 3.2), smokers compared to nonsmokers (OR = 2.8), and men with a history of genital warts compared to men with no history (OR = 5.9). Among 67 tumor specimens, 49% were positive for HPV DNA, and 70% of these were positive for HPV-16 DNA. Risk increases were also noted for those men who reported persistent smegma and/or rashes and ulcerations of the penis. Notably, cases reported a greater number of sexual partners than controls (28% of cases reported 30 or more sexual partners compared to 10% of controls). These results implicate absence of early circumcision, high sexual activity, infection with HPV, and smoking as risk factors for the development of carcinoma of the penis (Maden et al., 1993).

In a subsequent case control study, investigators in Seattle compared men with carcinoma in situ (*n* = 75) or invasive cancer (*n* = 62) of the penis to 671 disease-free controls from the general population.

Blood samples were tested for HPV-16 and genital herpes simplex virus (HSV2), and tumor specimens from the cases were tested for HPV DNA. Risk factors for invasive penile cancer included smoking versus nonsmoking (OR = 4.5) and absence versus presence of circumcision in childhood (OR = 2.3). Among uncircumcised men, medical history of phimosis increased the risk of invasive penile cancer more than 11-fold (OR = 11.4), whereas those with no history of phimosis were not at increased risk. The proportion of HPV positivity was similar for carcinoma in situ and invasive cancer and did not vary with subgrouping for any of the other risk factors. Among tumor specimens from all cases, 80% were positive for HPV DNA and 69% of these were positive for HPV-16 DNA. The investigators concluded that HPV-16 infection is a strong risk factor for penile cancer and that elimination of phimosis by early circumcision is protective (Daling et al., 2005).

Investigators in Denmark conducted a case control study of penile carcinoma among Danish men, a population in which childhood circumcision is rare. They compared cases with invasive (*n* = 53) or in situ (*n* = 18) squamous cell carcinomas of the penis to 86 controls with prostate cancer and 103 disease-free population controls. Tissue samples were examined by PCR to detect HPV DNA. Overall, 24 tumors (65%) were positive for HPV, and 92% of these were positive for HPV-16. Penile cancer risk increased with lifetime number of female sex partners, number of female sex partners before age 20, early age at first intercourse, penile–oral sex, history of anogenital warts, and never having used condoms. Medical histories of phimosis or priapism (persisting painful erection) at least 5 years before diagnosis were also significant risk factors. The investigators concluded that sexually transmitted HPV-16 infection and phimosis are major risk factors for the development of squamous cell carcinoma of the penis (Madsen et al., 2008).

In a systematic review of 31 studies that included 1,466 men with penile carcinomas, 47% of cases were positive for HPV, and the majority of these were positive for either HPV-16 (60%) or HPV-18 (13%) (Miralles-Guri et al., 2009). In contrast, HPV infection in the foreskins of otherwise healthy men without penile cancer ranges from 0% to 6% (Grussendorf-Conen, Meinhof, de Villiers, & Gissmann, 1987; Varma et al., 1991).

HIV Infection

Recent case reports have documented that combined infection by HPV and human immunodeficiency virus

(HIV) may accelerate the progression of squamous cell carcinoma of the penis (Aboulafia & Gibbons, 2001; Théodore et al., 2002). These reports raise the specter of synergism between HPV and HIV due to the immunosuppressive effects of HIV.

Tobacco and Penile Cancer

Cigarette smoking has been identified as a risk factor for penile carcinoma in several epidemiologic studies. Odds ratios from these studies suggest there is an approximate two- to fourfold increase in the risk among chronic smokers compared to nonsmokers (Daling et al., 2005; Hellberg, Valentin, Eklund, & Nilsson, 1987; Maden et al., 1993). Other forms of chronic tobacco use (chewing tobacco and snuff) have also been noted to increase the risk (Harish & Ravi, 1995).

Psoralen and Ultraviolet A Radiation (PUVA)

Certain treatments have been linked to the genesis of cancer of the external male genitalia (penis and scrotum). Psoralen and ultraviolet A radiation (PUVA) is a form of photochemotherapy that is administered in several treatment sessions to patients with severe psoriasis. Long-term PUVA therapy has been found to increase the risk of developing squamous cell carcinoma of the skin and malignant melanoma (Stern, Nichols, & Väkevä, 1997). When whole-body PUVA is administered, patients are in a standing position and the external male genitalia may therefore be exposed to excess ultraviolet (UV) radiation. In a cohort of 892 U.S. men treated with PUVA and followed on average for 12 years after therapy, 14 patients (1.6%) subsequently developed penile and scrotal tumors, and the incidence of invasive squamous cell carcinoma was 286 times higher than in the general male population. Furthermore, the estimates of risk increased significantly with increasing exposure to PUVA (as well as ultraviolet B radiation), suggesting that chronic exposure to ultraviolet radiation may incite malignant transformation of the external male genitalia (Stern, 1990).

CANCER OF THE SCROTUM

Cancer of the scrotum was the first documented malignancy arising from an occupational exposure. In 1775, Percival Pott described the development of cancer of the scrotum among chimney sweeps in England. He called this tumor the "chimney-sweeper's cancer" and attributed the condition to "a lodgment of soot in the rugae of the scrotum" (Pott, 1775).

Scrotal cancer has also been reported in men with other occupational exposures (e.g., coal tar, arsenic, and mineral oil). Carcinoma of the scrotum is exceedingly rare in most populations. In the United States, the annual incidence is approximately 5–10 cases per 10 million men (Wright, Morgan, & Lin, 2008). Most cases are thought to arise as a consequence of poor genital hygiene coupled with chronic exposure to irritating and inflammatory agents. Unfortunately, patients with scrotal lesions often delay seeking medical attention for several months and even years, thereby diminishing successful therapy and survival (Azike, 2009).

MOLECULAR CARCINOGENESIS

The molecular carcinogenesis of penile cancer may involve both HPV-related and HPV-independent mechanisms. The primary mechanism of HPV-related carcinogenesis has been elucidated in studies of cervical carcinogenesis. Oncogenic strains of HPV (e.g., HPV-16) express oncoproteins E6 and E7 that bind to and inactivate $p53$ and Rb tumor suppressor gene products, respectively, resulting in loss of control of cell division and apoptosis (Scheffner et al., 1994; zur Hausen, 2002).

Other HPV-independent mechanisms may also contribute to penile carcinogenesis. For example, immunohistochemistry has demonstrated that the inducible inflammatory enzymecyclooxygenase-2 (COX-2) is overexpressed in human samples of penile intraepithelial neoplasia and carcinoma, suggesting that chronic inflammation may play a key role in the development of some penile malignancies (Golijanin et al., 2004).

PREVENTIVE STRATEGIES

Preventive strategies should target the major risk factors for penile carcinoma, including phimosis in uncircumcised men, promiscuous sexual activity, infection with HPV-16 or other oncogenic HPV strains, and cigarette smoking.

Circumcision during infancy largely negates phimosis as a risk factor for penile cancer. Furthermore, a recent meta-analysis of randomized trials of sexually active heterosexual men in Africa found that circumcision reduced the incidence of HIV by 50–60% over a period of 24 months (Doyle, Kahn, Hosang, & Carroll, 2010; Siegfried, Muller, Deeks, & Volmink, 2009; Uthman, Popoola, Uthman, & Aremu, 2010). As a consequence of these studies, the World Health

Organization (WHO) has included circumcision as a key component of a comprehensive program for HIV control in sub-Saharan Africa and other areas with high endemic rates of HIV (WHO, 2012). Other options for prevention of penile cancer include vaccination against oncogenic HPV strains, condom use to prevent virus transmission, protective clothing to prevent excess exposure to UV radiation during phototherapy for dermatologic conditions, and health education to prevent smoking, promote smoking cessation, and improve genital hygiene (Bleeker et al., 2008; Shabbir et al., 2013).

● ● ● REFERENCES

Aboulafia, D. M., & Gibbons, R. (2001). Penile cancer and human papilloma virus (HPV) in a human immunodeficiency virus (HIV)-infected patient. *Cancer Investigation*, 19(3), 266–272.

American Academy of Pediatrics. (2012). Circumcision policy statement. *Pediatrics*, 130(3), 585–586.

Azike, J. E. (2009). A review of the history, epidemiology and treatment of squamous cell carcinoma of the scrotum. *Rare Tumors*, 1(1), e17.

Barbagli, G., Palminteri, E., Mirri, F., Guazzoni, G., Turini, D., & Lazzeri, M. (2006). Penile carcinoma in patients with genital lichen sclerosus: A multicenter survey. *Journal of Urology*, 175(4), 1359–1363.

Barnholtz-Sloan, J. S., Maldonado, J. L., Pow-san, J., & Guiliano, A. R. (2007). Incidence trends I primary malignant penile cancer. *Urologic Oncology: Seminars and Original Investigations*, 25(5), 361–367.

Bleeker, M. C. G., Heideman, D. A. M., Snijders, P. J. F., Horenblas, S., Dillner, J., & Meijer, C. J. L. (2008). Penile cancer: Epidemiology, pathogenesis and prevention. *World Journal of Urology*, 27(2), 141–150.

Brinton, L. A., Li, J. Y., Rong, S. D., Huang, S., Xiao, B. S., Shi, B. G., . . . Dawsey, S. (1991). Risk factors for penile cancer: Results from a case-control study in China. *International Journal of Cancer*, 47(4), 504–509.

Daling, J. R., Madeleine, M. M., Johnson, L. G., Schwartz, S. M., Shera, K. A., Wurscher, M. A., . . . Krieger, J. N. (2005). Penile cancer: Importance of circumcision, human papillomavirus and smoking in in situ and invasive disease. *International Journal of Cancer*, 116(4), 606–616.

Doyle, S., Kahn, J., Hosang, N., & Carroll, P. (2010). The impact of male circumcision on HIV Transmission. *Journal of Urology*, 183(1), 21–26.

Golijanin, D., Tan, J. Y., Kazior, A., Cohen, E.G., Russo, P., Dalbagni, G., Auborn K.J., Subbaramaiah, K., Dannenberg, A. J. (2004) Cyclooxygenase-2 and microsomal prostaglandin E synthase-1 are overexpressed in squamous cell carcinoma of the penis. *Clinical Cancer Research*, 10(3), 1024–1031.

Grussendorf-Conen, E. I., Meinhof, W., de Villiers, E. M., & Gissmann, L. (1987). Occurrence of HPV genomes in penile smears of healthy men. *Archives of Dermatological Research*, 279(Suppl), S73–S75.

Harish, K., & Ravi, R. (1995). The role of tobacco in penile carcinoma. *British Journal of Urology*, 75(3), 375–377.

Hellberg, D., Valentin, J., Eklund, T., & Nilsson, S. (1987). Penile cancer: Is there an epidemiological role of smoking and sexual behavior? *British Medical Journal*, 295(6609), 1306–1308.

Hernandez, B. Y., Barnholtz-Sloan, J., German, R. R., Giuliano, A., Goodman, M. T., King, J. B., . . . Villalon-Gomez, J. M. (2008). Burden of invasive squamous cell carcinoma of the penis in the United States, 1998–2003. *Cancer*, 113(10 Suppl), 2883–2891.

International Agency for Research on Cancer. (2007). *Cancer incidence in five continents* (Vol. IX, IARC Scientific Publication No. 160). Lyon, France: Author.

Larke, N. L., Thomas, S. L., dos Santos Silva, I., & Weiss, H. A. (2011). Male circumcision and penile cancer: A systematic review and meta-analysis. *Cancer Causes and Control*, 22(8), 1097–1110.

Maden, C., Sherman, K. J., Beckmann, A. M., Hislop, T. G., Teh, C. Z., Ashley, R. L., & Daling, J. R. (1993). History of circumcision, medical conditions, and sexual activity and risk of penile cancer. *Journal of the National Cancer Institute, 85*(1), 19–24.

Madsen, B. S., Brule, A. J., Jensen, H. L., Wohlfahrt, J., & Frisch, M. (2008). Risk factors for squamous cell carcinoma of the penis—population-based case–control study in Denmark. *Cancer Epidemiology, Biomarkers and Prevention, 17*(10), 2683–2691.

Mikhail, G. R. (1980). Cancers, precancers, and pseudocancers on the male genitalia. A review of clinical appearances, histopathology, and management. *Journal of Dermatological Surgery and Oncology, 6*(12), 1027–1035.

Miralles-Guri, C., Bruni, L., Cubilla, A. L., Castellsagué, X., Bosch, F. X., & de Sanjosé, S. (2009). Human papillomavirus prevalence and type distribution in penile carcinoma. *Journal of Clinical Pathology, 62*(10), 870–878.

Morris, B. J., Gray, R. H., Castellsague, X., Bosch, F. X., Halperin, D. T., Waskett, J. H., & Hankins, C. A. (2011). The strong protective effect of circumcision against cancer of the penis. *Advances in Urology. 2011*, 1. doi.org/10.1155/2011/812368.

Nasca, M. R., Innocenzi, D., & Micali, G. (1999). Penile cancer among patients with genital *lichen sclerosus. Journal of the American Academy of Dermatology, 41*(6), 911–914.

Oster, J. (1968). Further fate of the foreskin: Incidence of preputial adhesions, phimosis and smegma among Danish schoolboys. *Archive of Diseases in Childhood, 43*, 200–203.

Parkin, D. M., & Bray, F. (2006). The burden of HPV-related cancer. *Vaccine, 24*(Suppl 3), 11–25.

Pott, P. (1775). Cancer scroti. In S. J. Earle (Ed.), *The chirurgical works of Percivall Pott* (Vol. III, pp.177–183). London, England: James Webster.

Scheffner, M., Romanczuk, H., Munger, K., Huibregtse, J. M., Mietz, J. A., & Howley, P. M. (1994). Functions of human papillomavirus proteins. *Current Topics in Microbiology and Immunology, 186*, 83–99.

Schellhammer, P. F., Jordan, G. H., Robey, E. L., & Spaulding, J. T. (1992). Premalignant lesions and nonsquamous malignancy of the penis and carcinoma of the scrotum. *Urologic Clinics of North America, 19*(1), 131–142.

Schoen, E. J. (1991). The relationship between circumcision and cancer of the penis. *CA: A Cancer Journal for Clinicians, 41*(5), 306–309.

Schoen, E. J., Oehrli, M., Colby, C., & Machin, G. (2000). The highly protective effect of newborn circumcision against invasive penile cancer. *Pediatrics, 105*(3), E36.

Schrek, R., & Lenowitz, H. (1947). Etiologic factors in carcinoma of the penis. *Cancer Research, 7*, 180–187.

Shabbir, M., Barod, R., Hegart, P. K., & Minhasa, S. (2013). Primary prevention and vaccination for penile cancer. *Therapeutic Advances in Urology, 5*(3), 161–169.

Siegfried, N., Muller, M., Deeks, J. J., & Volmink, J. (2009). Male circumcision for prevention of heterosexual acquisition of HIV in men. *Cochrane Database of Systematic Reviews, 2*, CD003362. doi:10.1002/14651858.

Stern, R. S. (1990). Genital tumors among men with psoriasis exposed to psoralens and ultraviolet A radiation (PUVA) and ultraviolet B radiation. The Photochemotherapy Follow-up Study. *New England Journal of Medicine, 322*(16), 1093–1097.

Stern, R. S., Nichols, K. T., & Väkevä, L. H. (1997). Malignant melanoma in patients treated for psoriasis with methoxsalen (psoralen) and ultraviolet A radiation (PUVA). *New England Journal of Medicine, 336*, 1041–1045.

Théodore, C., Androulakis, N., Spatz, A., Goujard, C., Blanchet, C. P., & Wibault, P. (2002). An explosive course of squamous cell penile cancer in an AIDS patient. *Annals of Oncology, 13*(3), 475–479.

Tseng, H. F., Morgenstern, H., Mack, T., & Peters, R. K. (2001). Risk factors for penile cancer: Results of a population-based case–control study in Los Angeles County (United States). *Cancer Causes and Control, 12*(3), 267–277.

Uthman, O. A., Popoola, T. A., Uthman, M. M., & Aremu, O. (2010). Economic evaluations of adult male circumcision for prevention of heterosexual acquisition of HIV in men in sub-Saharan Africa: A systematic review. *PLoS ONE, 5*(3), e9628.

Varma, V. A., Sanchez-Lanier, M., Unger, E. R., Clark, C., Tickman, R., Hewan-Lowe, K., . . . Swan, D. C. (1991). Association of human papillomavirus with penile carcinoma: A study using polymerase chain reaction and *in situ* hybridization. *Human Pathology, 22*(9), 908–913.

Wolbarst, A. (1932). Circumcision and penile cancer. *Lancet, 219*(5655), 150–153.

World Health Organization. (2012). *Use of devices for adult male circumcision in public health HIV prevention programmes: Conclusion and executive summary of the WHO Technical Advisory Group on Innovation in Male Circumcision.* Geneva, Switzerland: Author.

Wright, J. L., Morgan, T, M,, & Lin, D. W. (2008). Primary scrotal cancer: Disease characteristics and increasing incidence. *Urology, 72*(5), 1139–1143.

zur Hausen, H. (2002). Papillomaviruses and cancer: From basic studies to clinical application. *Nature Reviews Cancer, 2*(5), 342–350.

19

Epidemiology of Urinary Bladder Cancer

ANATOMY AND FUNCTION OF THE URINARY BLADDER

The urinary bladder is a muscular sac located in the lower pelvis. Basic structures and cell types are shown in **Figure 19.1**. Urine manufactured by the kidneys travels to the bladder through the ureters for storage prior to excretion. In normal adults, the urinary bladder holds 300–600 milliliters of urine. The bladder wall consists of smooth muscle that contracts during urination. Urine passes out of the body through the urethra, which is longer in men than women (approximately 20 centimeters versus 4 centimeters). In men, the prostate gland encircles the urethra just below the bladder. The urinary bladder is lined by multiple layers of transitional epithelium (called *urothelium*), which expands or contracts depending on the volume of urine contained. When the bladder is empty, transitional epithelial cells are cuboidal in shape; when the bladder is full, they are flat (Kumar, Abbas, & Aster, 2014).

GLOBAL EPIDEMIOLOGY OF BLADDER CANCER

Cancer of the urinary bladder afflicts 3–4 times more men than women. During 2012, 429,793 new cases were diagnosed in the world population and 165,068 died from bladder cancer. Of these, 330,380 cases (77%) and 123,043 deaths (75%) occurred in men. The annual age-adjusted incidence rate in men was 9.0 cases per 100,000 compared to 2.2 per 100,000 in women, and the mortality rate was 3.2 deaths per 100,000 in men compared to 0.9 per 100,000 in women (Ferlay et al., 2013).

Figure 19.2 shows the global distributions of incidence and mortality rates of bladder cancer among men. Although rates vary markedly among populations, the global incidence and mortality have remained stable during the last decade (Ferlay, Bray, Pisani, & Parkin, 2004; Ferlay et al., 2010, 2013; Parkin, Bray, Ferlay, & Pisani, 2001, 2005).

Incidence rates of transitional cell carcinoma of the bladder urothelium exceed 15 per 100,000 among men of North America, Western Europe, Scandinavia, and other regions where the prevalence of smoking is high. Incidence rates are also high among men of Eastern Mediterranean and North African countries, particularly in Egypt (22 per 100,000), where squamous cell bladder cancer arises due to chronic infection by the parasitic worm *Schistosoma haematobium*. Men living in regions where the incidence of bladder cancer is high and there is limited access to therapy have mortality rates in excess of 5 deaths per 100,000. These include the Russian Federation and countries in North Africa and Southern and Central Europe. Mortality is exceedingly high (over 10 deaths per 100,000) for the male populations of Turkey, Iraq, and Egypt (Figure 19.2).

PATHOGENESIS OF URINARY BLADDER CANCER

In developed countries of North America, Europe, and Australia, most bladder cancers (approximately 95%) are transitional cell carcinomas that arise from the epithelial cell lining of the bladder (called the urothelium). The progression of carcinogenesis appears similar to other forms of cancer with epithelial cell origin. The urothelium undergoes a stepwise

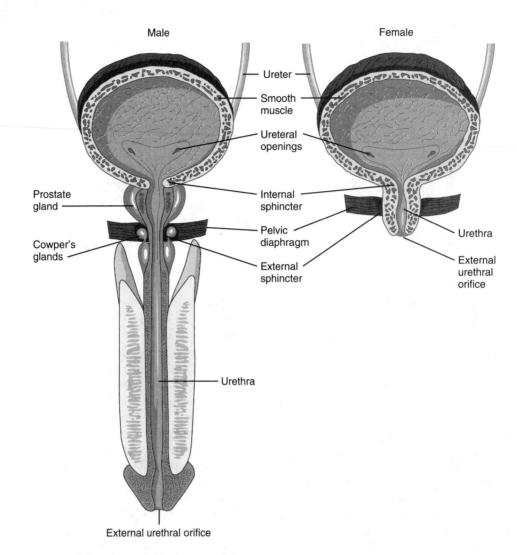

Figure 19.1 Anatomy of the Urinary Bladder in Men and Women.

progression of changes from mild to severe dysplasia that results in the formation of noninvasive papillary carcinoma in situ and ultimately invasive cancer that penetrates the basement membrane. The evolutionary progression of carcinogenesis in the urinary bladder is believed to occur over many years, usually 2 to 3 decades. Often, transitional cell carcinomas of the urinary bladder show multiple cancerous foci at the time of diagnosis, a phenomenon known as *field cancerization*.

In developing nations of Africa and Southern Asia, the predominant histological type of bladder cancer is squamous cell carcinoma, which arises due to chronic infection by the parasitic worm *Schistosoma haematobium*. Chronic infection of the bladder by these parasites (called *bilharziasis*) causes sustained local inflammation, irritation, and subsequent reparative hyperplasia and squamous metaplasia in

which the normal urothelial cells are replaced by squamous cells. These changes in the bladder mucosa eventually progress to squamous cell carcinoma.

RISK FACTORS FOR URINARY BLADDER CANCER

Tobacco Use and Urinary Bladder Cancer

The dominant risk factor for transitional cell urinary bladder cancer is cigarette smoking, which accounts for about two-thirds of new cases in men and one-third of new cases in women. Epidemiologic cohort and case control studies have consistently observed two- to threefold increases in the relative risk of developing transitional cell bladder cancer among chronic smokers compared to nonsmokers, as well as dose response relationships with the number of cigarettes

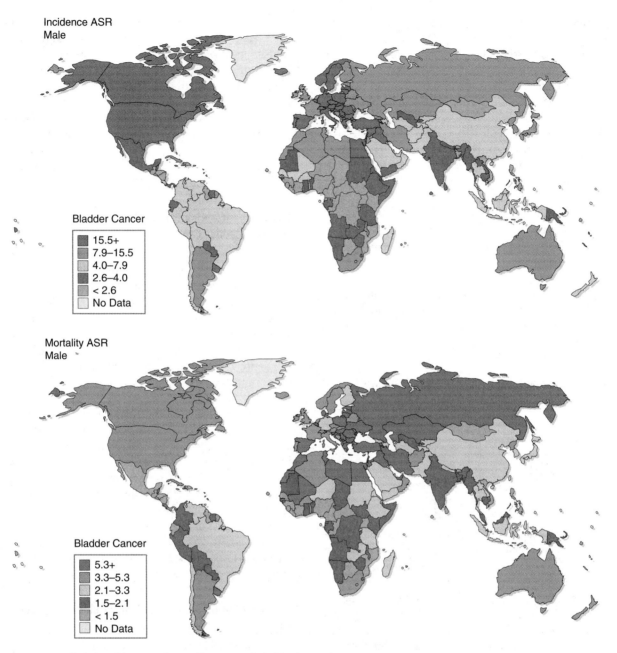

Figure 19.2 Global Incidence and Mortality Rates of Bladder Cancer in Men, 2012.

ASR: Rates per 100,000 are age-standardized to the world population, 2000–2025.

Source: Reproduced from Ferlay, J., Soerjomataram, I., Ervik, M., Dikshit, R., Eser, S., Mathers, C., . . . Bray, F. (2013). *GLOBOCAN 2012 v1.0. Cancer incidence and mortality worldwide: IARC CancerBase No. 11* [Internet]. Lyon, France: International Agency for Research on Cancer. Retrieved from http://globocan.iarc.fr

smoked and duration of smoking. Cigarette smoking shows similar effects for men and women as well as for individuals with different ethnic backgrounds (Boffetta, 2008).

Urinary bladder carcinogenesis associated with smoking is primarily the result of aromatic amines and arylamines present in cigarette smoke that reach the bladder mucosa (e.g., benzidine, 4-aminobiphenyl, 2-naphthylamine, and 4-chloro-ortho-toluidine) (Patrianakos & Hoffman, 1979). Molecular investigations show that these compounds are ultimately biotransformed (activated) in the acidic environment of the bladder to form potent DNA-reactive carcinogens (Vineis et al., 1990). Detoxification enzymes compete with activating enzymes for these procarcinogens to facilitate their excretion in the urine. Genetic differences in these enzymes are discussed in a following section on "Genetic Factors and Urinary Bladder Cancer."

Interestingly, individuals who smoke black (air-cured) tobacco are at a two- to threefold higher risk than smokers of blonde (flue-cured) tobacco, a difference attributable to the higher levels of highly carcinogenic arylamines in black tobacco (Vineis, 1994). The common practice of smoking black tobacco may thus explain the high rates of bladder cancer observed among men in Spain, Italy, the Netherlands, and Uruguay.

Notably, cigarette smoking also independently increases the risk of developing squamous cell carcinoma of the bladder and may, in fact, interact synergistically with other risk factors (Fortuny et al., 1999). As discussed in the following section, chronic schistosomiasis infection is the key risk factor for development of squamous cell carcinoma of the urinary bladder.

Schistosomiasis and Urinary Bladder Cancer

Squamous cell carcinomas of the bladder occur frequently in conjunction with infection by the trematode *Schistosoma haematobium*. The parasite is endemic in the Nile River, but is also found throughout Africa, in certain parts of Southeast Asia, on the islands of Cyprus, and in southern Portugal. It has been estimated that 85% of Egyptians become infected with this parasite in their lifetimes, which accounts for the astounding fact that bladder cancer accounts for 30% of all malignant neoplasms in Egypt (el-Mawla, el-Bolkainy, & Khaled, 2001).

Schistosome worms mature in the liver and migrate to the plexus of blood vessels that nourish the bladder and pelvic organs. The female worms may deposit their eggs in the walls of the bladder, uterus, prostate, or other pelvic organs. This parasitic infection can result in chronic inflammation of the bladder urothelium, which may ultimately produce squamous metaplasia and carcinoma.

The schistosomes are diecious, and the two sexes mature and reproduce in the vascular system. The eggs are laid in small blood vessels that are then liberated into the lumen of the intestines or the urinary bladder. Schistosome eggs subsequently hatch when they reach fresh water, and the newborn form of the worm (the miracidium) swims in search of an appropriate snail host. After infestation of the snail, the miracidium develops into another form called the cercariae, which is liberated into the fresh water again and capable of penetrating the skin of swimmers and bathers. Upon penetration of human skin, the parasite reaches the circulation and the liver, and the cycle repeats itself (**Figure 19.3**).

Molecular studies also suggest that bladder carcinogenesis associated with chronic schistosomiasis may be promoted by coinfection with certain viruses and bacteria, particularly in immunocompromised patients. For example, oncogenic strains of human papillomavirus (HPV-16, HPV-18, and HPV-52) have been found in cancerous urothelial tissues of such patients (Boucher & Anderson, 1997).

Environmental Risk Factors for Urinary Bladder Cancer

A number of environmental and occupational factors increase the risk of bladder cancer. These include occupational exposure to arylamines such as 2-naphthylamine, 4-aminobiphenyl, benzidine, and other compounds and intermediates in the synthesis of azo-dyes and pigments used in the textile, printing, plastic, rubber, and cable industries. Long-term exposure to these compounds among workers in these industries increases the risk of bladder cancer by about 50% (Scélo & Brennan, 2007).

Workers in aluminum production, auramine O (yellow) and magenta dye manufacturing, and coal gasification may also be at increased risk because of sustained exposure to a variety of chemicals that reach the bladder mucosa, including polycyclic aromatic hydrocarbons, polychlorinated biphenyls, formaldehyde, and solvents. The uncertainty surrounding the hazards posed by these occupations is partly attributable to the difficulty of measuring past exposure to specific chemical agents (Kogevinas et al., 2003; Mannetje et al., 1999).

Pharmacologic Agents and Urinary Bladder Cancer

The analgesic medication phenacetin was once widely used in European nations until the drug was linked to cancers of the renal pelvis and urinary bladder (Hoover & Fraumeni, 1981; Johansson & Wahlqvist, 1977). A case control investigation found more than a sixfold increase in the risk of bladder cancer development due to heavy phenacetin ingestion among women (Piper, Tonascia, & Matanoski, 1985). Phenactin compounds were removed from the U.S. market in 1983 and have now been discontinued worldwide.

Certain chemotherapeutic agents used in cancer therapy also increase the risk of developing bladder cancer. For example, cyclophosphamide, an alkylating agent used to treat advanced malignancies, has been linked to bladder cancer development. This

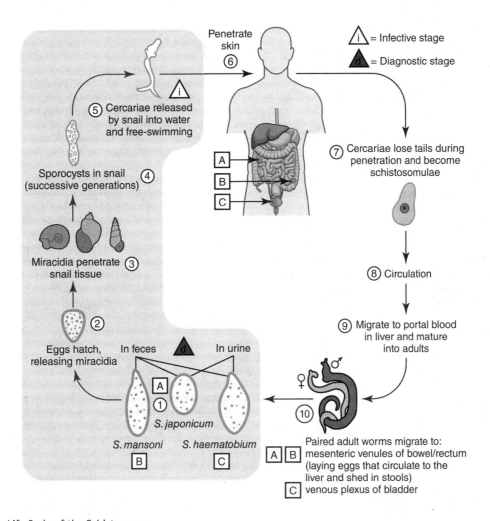

Figure 19.3 Life Cycle of the Schistosomes.

Source: Courtesy of Centers for Disease Control and Prevention, DPDx - Laboratory Identification of Parasitic Diseases of Public Health Concern-HH, http://www.cdc.gov/dpdx/schistosomiasis/

agent has strong immunosuppressive side effects and sometimes causes a disease known as hemorrhagic cystitis. This condition is associated with cellular atypia and a 10-fold increase in the risk of developing transitional cell carcinoma of the urinary bladder (Hoover & Fraumeni, 1981).

Fluid Intake, Arsenic, and Urinary Bladder Cancer

It is important to ingest plenty of water and fluids (drinking eight to ten 8-ounce glasses of water per day is recommended) to continually flush the renal system and protect against diseases of the urinary tract, including bladder cancer. In a 10-year prospective cohort study of 47,909 men, the risk of bladder cancer was reduced by about 50% among men who consumed, on average, 84 ounces of fluids daily compared to those consuming 43 ounces (Michaud

et al., 1999). Nevertheless, certain contaminants of drinking water, including chlorination disinfection by-products, nitrates, and arsenic, have been linked to bladder carcinogenesis (Cantor, 1997).

A 50-year longitudinal study documented marked increases in bladder and lung cancer mortality related to ingestion of arsenic-contaminated drinking water by the population residing in northern Chile. Observed cancer rates were highest 10–20 years after peak concentrations of arsenic were detected in the drinking water, suggesting a long latency period. Peak rates of bladder cancer were elevated by 6-fold in men and nearly 14-fold in women. Cancer rates declined dramatically following installation of water treatment plants to eliminate arsenic from the drinking water (Marshall et al., 2007; Smith, Goycolea, Haque, & Biggs, 1998).

Genetic Factors and Urinary Bladder Cancer

The relative risk of bladder cancer is influenced by the smoking habit as well as genetically determined enzymes that either activate or detoxify arylamines that enter the human system via tobacco smoke or contaminated environments. For example, first-degree relatives of patients with bladder cancer have a twofold increased risk of developing the disease compared to the general population, whereas there is a fivefold increase in the risk for individuals with a positive family history who are also chronic smokers.

Exposure to arylamines (e.g., from tobacco smoke or the environments of certain occupations) is known to increase the risk of bladder cancer. The metabolism of arylamines occurs in the liver and the urinary bladder through specific enzymatic reactions. The first step takes place in the liver, where nitrogen oxidation of arylamines is catalyzed by enzymes of the P450 system. Subsequently in the bladder, the N-hydroxylamines can be either detoxified and excreted or activated to form potent DNA-reactive carcinogens.

The enzyme arylamine N-acetyltransferase 2 (NAT2) is involved in the detoxification of various bladder carcinogens, including carcinogenic arylamines (Vineis et al., 1990). A specific dominant mutation in the *NAT2* gene results in slow metabolism of arylamines. Consequently, individuals with the *NAT2* slow-acetylation mutation are at higher risk of developing bladder cancer than those without the mutation (Risch, Wallace, Bathers, & Sim, 1995; Vineis et al., 1990). Furthermore, a synergistic interaction is present involving the *NAT2* slow-acetylation mutation and heavy smoking, which translates to a greatly increased risk of developing bladder cancer in individuals with both these risk factors compared to nonsmokers who do not carry the *NAT2* mutation (Marcus, Vineis, & Rothman, 2000).

Other enzymatic reactions also modulate the potential carcinogenicity of arylamines in the urinary bladder. Notably, levels of the ubiquitous enzyme beta-glucuronidase are present in the bladder. At urine pH 5.6, this enzyme is capable of splitting various urinary conjugates into carcinogenic elements. The glutathione-S-transferase M1 (*GSTM1*) null genotype also increases the risk of bladder cancer, although it apparently has no interaction with smoking status (Yu et al., 1995).

A team of international investigators examined *NAT2*, *GSTM1*, and smoking in a large case control study of bladder cancer in Spain involving 1,150 cases and 1,149 controls matched to the cases by age, gender, and location. The investigators also

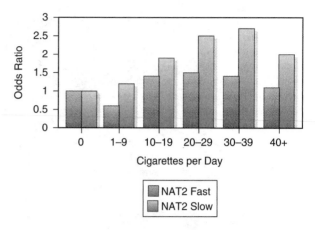

Figure 19.4 Influence of Smoking and NAT2 Genotypes on the Risk of Bladder Cancer.

Source: Data from Garcia-Closas, M., Malats, N., Silverman, D., Dosemeci, M., Kogevinas, M., Hein, D. W.,... Rothman, N. (2005). NAT2 slow acetylation and GSTM2 null genotypes increase bladder cancer risk: Results from the Spanish Bladder Cancer Study and meta-analyses. *Lancet, 36*(9486), 649–659.

conducted a meta-analysis of data on these factors from 31 studies involving 5,096 cases of bladder cancer and 6,519 disease-free controls. Results from the case control study revealed significant increases in risk associated with the slow acetylation *NAT2* genotype and the null *GSTM1* genotype. Notably, influence of the slow acetylation *NAT2* genotype became stronger with increasing intensity of smoking (**Figure 19.4**). Summary estimates of risk from the meta-analysis suggest that among smokers, the *NAT2* slow acetylation genotype increases bladder cancer risk by 40% compared to other genotypes, and the null *GSTM1* genotype increases the risk by 50% (Garcia-Closas et al., 2005).

Ethnic Variation in Urinary Bladder Cancer

In the United States, the annual incidence of bladder cancer is twice as high in Caucasian American men than African American men (41 versus 20 per 100,000 in 2007) and 24% higher in Caucasian American women compared to African American women (9.4 versus 7.6 per 100,000 in 2007) (SEER, 2007). These ethnic differences have persisted for decades (**Figure 19.5**) and they pertain primarily to transitional cell bladder cancer that is related to cigarette smoking and other sources of exposure to arylamines (Risch et al., 1995).

The persistently higher incidence rates of bladder cancer in Caucasians versus African Americans in the United States prompted investigations of genetic polymorphisms of smoking and *NAT2* in these

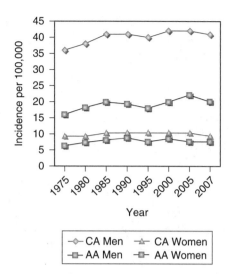

Figure 19.5 Trends in the Incidence of Bladder Cancer, United States, 1975–2007.

Source: Data from Altekruse, S. F, Kosary, C. L., Krapcho, M., Neyman, N., Aminou, R., Waldron, W., & Edwards B. K. (Eds.). (2007). *SEER cancer statistics review, 1975–2007*. Bethesda, MD: National Cancer Institute. Retrieved from http://seer.cancer.gov /csr/1975_2007/

populations. In a study restricted to smokers, Richie and colleagues demonstrated that the frequency of slow *NAT2* acetylators was twofold higher in Caucasians than African Americans (64% versus 36%). Furthermore, Caucasians smoked an average of 8 cigarettes per day more than African American smokers. These observations (high smoking-related arylamine exposure coupled with slow genetically regulated *NAT2* acetylation and delayed detoxification in Caucasians) provide a genetic by environmental basis for the ethnic divergence in the incidence rates of bladder cancer (Muscat et al., 2008).

Despite their relatively low incidence rates of bladder cancer, African Americans typically have more advanced disease at the time of diagnosis and poor survival compared to Caucasians (Underwood, Dunn, Williams, & Lee, 2009). Thus, racial disparity continues to exist in bladder cancer presentation and survival in the United States (Underwood et al., 2009).

PREVENTION OF BLADDER CANCER

For the primary prevention of urinary bladder cancer, avoid chronic exposure to tobacco or tobacco smoke, arsenic, benzene, arylamines, azo dyes, and any other chemicals known to irritate the urothelium. In regions where the schistosome parasite is endemic, protect against contracting schistosomiasis by avoiding swimming or wading in contaminated water. Infected individuals should immediately be treated with antiparasitic agents (e.g., praziquantel). It is also important to continually flush the renal system and bladder by daily intake of 8–10 glasses of clean water.

● ● ● REFERENCES

Altekruse, S. F, Kosary, C. L., Krapcho, M., Neyman, N., Aminou, R., Waldron, W., & Edwards B. K. (Eds.). (2007). *SEER cancer statistics review, 1975–2007*. Bethesda, MD: National Cancer Institute. Retrieved from http:// seer.cancer.gov/csr/1975_2007/

Boffetta, P. (2008). Tobacco smoking and risk of bladder cancer. *Scandinavian Journal of Urology and Nephrology, 42*(S218), 45–54.

Boucher, N. R., & Anderson, J. B. (1997). Human papillomavirus and bladder cancer. *International Urogynecology Journal, 8*, 354–357.

Cantor, K. P. (1997). Drinking water and cancer. *Cancer Causes and Control, 8*(3), 292–308.

el-Mawla, N. G., el-Bolkainy, M. N., & Khaled, H. M. (2001). Bladder cancer in Africa: Update. *Seminars in Oncology, 28*(2), 174–178.

Ferlay, J., Bray, F., Pisani, P., & Parkin, D. M. (2004). *GLOBOCAN 2002. Cancer incidence, mortality, and prevalence worldwide. IARC Cancer Base No. 5, version 2.0*. Lyon, France: IARC Press.

Ferlay, J., Shin, H.-R., Bray, F., Forman, D., Mathers, C., & Parkin, D. M. (2010). Estimates of worldwide burden of cancer in 2008: GLOBOCAN 2008. *International Journal of Cancer, 127*(12), 2893–2917.

Ferlay, J., Soerjomataram, I., Ervik, M., Dikshit, R., Eser, S., Mathers, C., … Bray, F. (2013). *GLOBOCAN 2012 v1.0, Cancer Incidence and Mortality Worldwide: IARC CancerBase No. 11* [Internet]. Lyon, France: International Agency for Research on Cancer. http://globocan.iarc.fr

Fortuny, J., Kogevinas, M., Chang-Claude, J., González, C. A., Hours, M., Jöckel, K. H., . . . Bofetta, P. (1999). Tobacco, occupation and non-transitional-cell carcinoma of the bladder: An international case-control study. *International Journal of Cancer, 80*(1), 44–46.

Garcia-Closas, M., Malats, N., Silverman, D., Dosemeci, M., Kogevinas, M., Hein, D. W., . . . Rothman, N. (2005). NAT2 slow acetylation and GSTM2 null genotypes increase bladdercancer risk: Results from the Spanish Bladder Cancer Study and meta-analyses. *Lancet, 36*(9486), 649–659.

Hoover, R., & Fraumeni, J. F. Jr. (1981). Drug-induced cancer. *Cancer, 47,* 1071.

Johansson, S., & Wahlqvist, L. (1977). Tumours of urinary bladder and ureter associated with abuse of phenacetin-containing analgesics. *Acta Pathologica Microbiologica Scandinavica [A], 85,* 768–774.

Kogevinas, M., 't Mannetje, A., Cordier, S., Ranft, U., González, C. A., Vineis, P., . . . Boffetta, P. (2003). Occupation and bladder cancer among men in Western Europe. *Cancer Causes and Control, 14*(10), 907–914.

Kumar, V., Abbas, A.K., & Aster J.C. (2014). *Robbins and Cotran pathologic basis of disease* (9th ed.). Philadelphia, PA: Mosby & Saunders.

Mannetje, A., Kogevinas, M., Chang-Claude, J., Cordier, S., González, C. A., Hours, M., . . . Boffetta, P. (1999). Occupation and bladder cancer in European women. *Cancer Causes and Control, 10*(3), 209–217.

Marcus, P. M., Vineis, P., & Rothman, N. (2000). NAT2 slow acetylation and bladder cancer risk: A meta-analysis of 22 case–control studies conducted in the general population. *Pharmacogenetics, 10,* 115–122.

Marshall, G., Catterina Ferreccio, C., Yuan, Y., Bates, M. N., Steinmaus, C., Selvin, S., . . . Smith, A. H. (2007). Fifty-year study of lung and bladder cancer mortality in Chile related to arsenic in drinking water. *Journal of the National Cancer Institute, 99,* 920–928.

Michaud, D. S., Spiegelman, D., Clinton, S. K., Rimm, E. B., Curhan, G. C., Willett, W. C., & Giovannucci, E. L. (1999). Fluid intake and the risk of bladder cancer in men. *New England Journal of Medicine, 340,* 1390–1397.

Muscat, J. E., Pittman, B., Kleinman, W., Lazarus, P., Steven, D., Stellman, S. D., & Richie, J. P. Jr. (2008). Comparison of CYP1A2 and NAT2 phenotypes between black and white smokers. *Biochemical Pharmacology, 76*(7), 929–937.

Parkin, D. M., Bray, F., Ferlay, J., & Pisani, P. (2001). Estimating the world cancer burden: GLOBOCAN 2000. *International Journal of Cancer, 94,* 153–156.

Parkin, D. M., Bray, F., Ferlay, J., & Pisani, P. (2005). Global cancer statistics, 2002. *CA: A Cancer Journal for Clinicians, 55,* 74–108.

Patrianakos, C., & Hoffman, D. (1979). Chemical studies of tobacco smoke. LXIV. On the analysis of aromatic amines in cigarette smoke. *Journal of Analytical Chemistry, 3,* 150–154.

Piper, J. M., Tonascia, J., & Matanoski, G. M. (1985). Heavy phenacetin use and bladder cancer in women aged 20 to 49 years. *New England Journal of Medicine, 313*(5), 292–295.

Risch, A., Wallace, D. M. A., Bathers, S., & Sim, E. (1995). Slow *N*-acetylation genotype is a susceptibility factor in occupational and smoking related bladder cancer. *Human Molecular Genetics, 4,* 231–236.

Scélo, G., & Brennan, P. (2007). The epidemiology of bladder and kidney cancer. *Nature Clinical Practice Urology, 4,* 205–217.

Smith, A.H., Goycolea, M., Haque, R., & Biggs, M.L. (1998). Marked increase in bladder and lung cancer mortality in a region of Northern Chile due to arsenic in drinking water. *American Journal of Epidemiology, 147,* 660– 669.

Underwood, W. III, Dunn, R., Williams, C., & Lee, C. (2009). Gender and geographic influence on the racial disparity in bladder cancer mortality in the US. *Journal of the American College of Surgeons, 202*(2), 284–290.

Vineis, P. (1994). Epidemiology of cancer from exposure to arylamines. *Environmental Health Perspectives, 102*(Suppl 6), 7–10.

Vineis, P., Caporaso, N., Tannenbaum, S.R., Skipper, P.L., Glogowski, J., Bartsch, H., . . .

Kadlubar, F. (1990). Acetylation phenotype, carcinogen-hemoglobin adducts, and cigarette smoking. *Cancer Research, 50,* 3002–3004.

Yu, M. C., Ross, R. K., Chan, K. K., Henderson, B. E., Skipper, P. L., Tannenbaum, S. R., & Coetzee, G. A. (1995). Glutathione *S*-transferase M1 genotype affects aminobiphenyl–hemoglobin adduct levels in white, black, and Asian smokers and nonsmokers. *Cancer Epidemiology, Biomarkers and Prevention, 4,* 861–864.

20

Epidemiology of Kidney Cancer

ANATOMY AND FUNCTION OF THE KIDNEYS

The human kidneys are paired organs that perform multiple functions that are essential for life. They excrete waste products of metabolism, regulate the body's concentration of water and salt, maintain the acid–base balance of the blood, regulate blood pressure, and secrete important hormones, including erythropoietin, renin, and prostaglandins. These physiological functions necessarily require a high degree of structural complexity (Robbins & Cotran, 1979).

Kidneys are bean-shaped organs weighing about 150 grams that are located in the retroperitoneal cavity. Individual renal arteries branching from the abdominal aorta supply blood to the kidneys. The kidneys filter about 17 liters of blood per day, producing a derived specialized filtrate of about 1 liter of urine.

Urea is the most abundant of the nitrogen-containing waste products excreted by the kidneys. Urea is formed from ammonia or amino acids by a series of reactions known as the urea cycle, which occurs primarily in the liver. Ammonia arising from the metabolism of amino acids and nitrogen-containing compounds is rapidly transported by red bloods cells to the liver, where it enters the urea cycle.

Ammonia itself is highly toxic and cannot be filtered by the kidneys. In contrast, its breakdown product, urea, is colorless, odorless, highly soluble in water, and nontoxic in humans. Urea formed in the liver is transported in the blood to the kidneys, where it is freely filtered by the glomeruli and becomes a major constituent of urine.

The basic functional unit of the kidney is the nephron (**Figure 20.1**). Each kidney contains up to 1 million nephrons that carry out the essential functions of the kidney. Each nephron receives unfiltered blood from an afferent arteriole, which divides into capillaries of the glomerulus. The glomerulus is contained in a structure known as *Bowman's capsule*. The glomerulus filters urea and other waste products from the blood. The glomerular filtrate enters Bowman's space, diffuses into the renal tubule, and then travels along the renal tubule, which is lined by a single layer of specialized endothelial cells and surrounded by capillaries. As the glomerular filtrate traverses the renal tubule, salt, water, glucose, and other small molecules are reabsorbed from the filtrate into the blood, and additional waste products (e.g., ammonia, hydrogen, and potassium ions) are secreted from the blood into the urine. Urine exits the nephron via collecting ducts at the end of the renal tubule. Filtered arteriole blood exits the nephron through the efferent arteriole.

GLOBAL EPIDEMIOLOGY OF KIDNEY CANCER

Kidney cancer causes significant morbidity and mortality worldwide. In 2012, 337,860 new cases were detected (213,924 men and 123,936 women) and 143,369 deaths were attributed to kidney cancer (90,782 men and 42,587 women). Furthermore, both the incidence and mortality have increased steadily in the past 2 decades (**Figure 20.2**) (Ferlay, Shin, Forman, Mathers, & Parkin, 2010; Ferlay et al., 2013; Parkin, Bray, Ferlay, & Pisani, 2005; Parkin, Pisani, & Ferlay, 1999a, 1999b). Although the rising incidence rates may be partially attributable to improvements in imaging techniques, better detection does *not* explain the worldwide increase in mortality (Hollingsworth, Miller, Daignault, & Hollenbeck, 2006). Rather, global increases in the three major risk factors for kidney cancer—cigarette smoking,

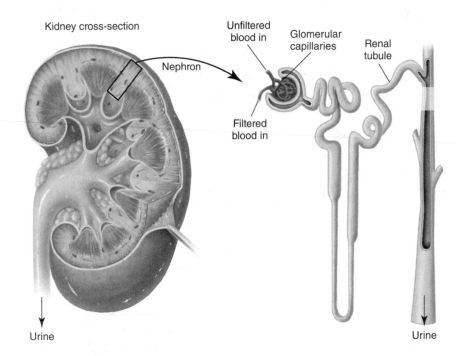

Figure 20.1 The Nephron of the Kidney.

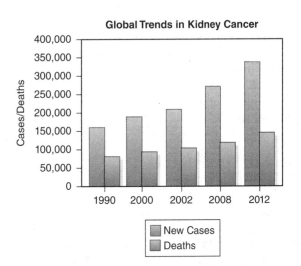

Figure 20.2 Global Trends in Kidney Cancer, 1990–2012.

Sources: Data from Ferlay, J., Shin, H. R., Forman, D., Mathers, C., & Parkin, D. M. (2010). Estimates of worldwide burden of cancer in 2008. *International Journal of Cancer, 127*(12), 2893–2917; Ferlay, J., Soerjomataram, I., Ervik, M., Dikshit, R., Eser, S., Mathers, C.,... Bray, F. (2013). *GLOBOCAN 2012 v1.0. Cancer incidence and mortality worldwide: IARC CancerBase No. 11* [Internet]. Lyon, France: International Agency for Research on Cancer. Retrieved from http://globocan.iarc.fr; Parkin, D. M., Bray, F., Ferlay, J., & Pisani, P. (2005). Global cancer statistics, 2002. *CA: A Cancer Journal for Clinicians, 55,* 74–108; Parkin, D. M., Pisani, P., & Ferlay, J. (1999a). Global cancer statistics. *CA: A Cancer Journal for Clinicians, 49*(1), 33–64, Parkin, D. M., Pisani, P., & Ferlay, J. (1999b). Estimates of the worldwide incidence of 25 major cancers in 1990. *International Journal of Cancer, 80*(6), 827–841.

obesity, and hypertension—may at least be partially responsible for the accelerating global burden of kidney cancer. The epidemiologic evidence linking these factors to the development of the most common form of kidney cancer, renal cell carcinoma, is discussed later in this chapter.

Kidney cancer afflicts about 50% more men than women. During 2012, the annual age-adjusted incidence rate in men was 4.4 cases per 100,000 compared to 3.0 per 100,000 in women, and the mortality rate was 1.8 deaths per 100,000 in men compared to 1.2 per 100,000 in women (Ferlay et al., 2013).

GLOBAL PATTERN OF KIDNEY CANCER

Figure 20.3 shows the global distributions of incidence and mortality rates of bladder cancer among men. As shown, there is considerable geographic variability in both the incidence and mortality. North American, Western European, Scandinavian, Russian, and Australian populations have the highest reported incidence rates, and Asian and African populations have the lowest. During 2002–2012, the annual incidence rates in populations of more developed nations, approximately 10 per 100,000 for men and 5 per 100,000 for women, were fivefold higher than corresponding rates in less developed

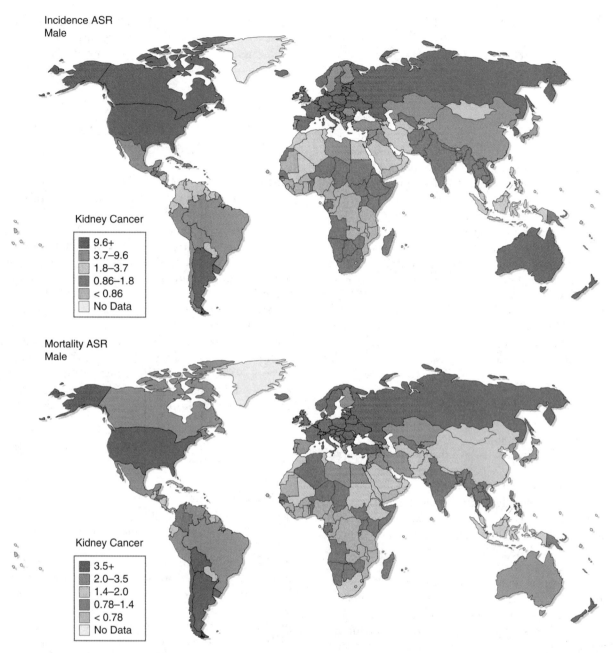

Figure 20.3 Global Incidence and Mortality Rates of Kidney Cancer in Men, 2012.

ASR: Rates per 100,000 are age-standardized to the world population, 2000–2025.

Source: Reproduced from Ferlay, J., Soerjomataram, I., Ervik, M., Dikshit, R., Eser, S., Mathers, C.,... Bray, F. (2013). *GLOBOCAN 2012 v1.0. Cancer incidence and mortality worldwide: IARC CancerBase No. 11* [Internet]. Lyon, France: International Agency for Research on Cancer. Retrieved from http://globocan.iarc.fr

nations, 2 per 100,000 for men and 1 per 100,000 for women. Mortality rates show a similar pattern; that is, rates are higher in developed nations (4.2 in men and 1.7 in women) than in developing nations (3.4 in men and 0.9 in women) (Ferlay, Bray, Pisani, & Parkin, 2004; Ferlay et al., 2013; Weikert & Ljungberg, 2010). Although such differences may partially reflect specific effects of lifestyle and environmental exposures, it is likely that they are largely attributable to underreporting due to lack of diagnostic imaging and detection in underdeveloped nations.

KIDNEY CANCER MORTALITY

Historically, the classic triad of clinical signs (flank pain, hematuria, and palpable mass) in a patient usually led to the detection of a large tumor of the kidney at a late stage of development. Such tumors had often metastasized to other anatomic sites by the time they were diagnosed, making treatment difficult and prognosis poor.

In the current practice of medicine, kidney tumors are often detected incidentally at a relatively early stage of development during imaging studies of the abdomen for other conditions. As with all forms of cancer, early detection of kidney cancer is essential for successful therapy and prolonged patient survival. Kidney tumors detected at an early stage often respond well to treatment and, as a consequence, survival rates have improved and mortality rates have stabilized or declined in many developed nations of the world (Pantuck, Zisman, & Belldegrun, 2001). Nevertheless, in less developed nations without sophisticated methods of early detection, the upward trend in mortality is continuing.

TYPES OF KIDNEY CANCER

Renal cell carcinoma, arising from epithelial cells that line the renal tubules, is the most common type of kidney cancer, accounting for approximately 85–90% of all malignant kidney tumors. Because these cells normally secrete a variety of vasoactive and regulatory hormones (e.g., renin, erythropoietin, antidiuretic hormone), such tumors often manifest symptoms of hypertension, polycythemia, and other metabolic disturbances.

Transitional cell carcinomas, arising from epithelial cells at the junction of the renal pelvis and the ureter, constitute 5–10% of malignant kidney tumors. Microscopically, transitional cell carcinomas of the renal pelvis are similar to urothelial carcinomas of the urinary bladder. Transitional epithelial cells are intermediate between flat squamous cells and tall columnar cells. This type of epithelium lines the collecting ducts in the renal pelvis, the ureters, and the urinary bladder (Kumar, Abbas, & Aster, 2014).

Wilms' tumor (named after the German surgeon, Max Wilms, who first described it) accounts for about 5% of malignant kidney tumors. This tumor occurs almost exclusively in children under the age of 10 years, usually before the age of 5 years. Wilms' tumors are composed of mixed stromal and epithelial cells with abortive configurations of renal glomeruli and tubules. As discussed in the following sections of this chapter, Wilms' tumor most often arises in children with heritable genetic susceptibility, in contrast to the adult forms of kidney cancer that are predominantly associated with exposure to certain environmental risk factors (Kim & Chung, 2006; Robbins & Cotran, 1979).

PATHOLOGIC SUBTYPES OF RENAL CELL CARCINOMA

Histological examination of renal cell carcinomas reveals four distinct subtypes: clear cell, papillary, chromophobe, and collecting duct tumors. Clear cell tumors make up about 85% of all renal cell carcinomas. They arise from the proximal tubules of the kidney and are genetically characterized by deletions and other abnormalities of the short arm of chromosome 3. An important finding in the field of cancer genetics is that the genetic abnormalities of clear cell tumors of the kidney invariably involve the von Hippel–Lindau gene. The remaining subtypes consist of papillary carcinomas (~10%), chromophobe tumors (~5%), and collecting duct (Bellini) tumors (< 1%), all of which have been found in association with a variety of chromosomal abnormalities.

RISK FACTORS FOR RENAL CELL CARCINOMA

The web of causation of renal cell carcinoma includes three major risk factors that are modifiable: cigarette smoking, obesity, and hypertension. Although epidemiologic studies have clearly established that each of these factors has an etiologic link with renal cell carcinoma, the underlying physiologic mechanisms and interactions remain to be elucidated. Specific dietary factors and certain other environmental factors have also shown effects in some studies, although the evidence supporting their role has been inconsistent. A notable finding from molecular analyses of renal cell tumors (clear cell subtype) is the presence of abnormalities in the von Hippel–Lindau gene, a tumor suppressor gene with pleiotropic (multiple) effects on tumor growth and development (Chow, Dong, & Devesa, 2010; Pascual & Borque, 2008).

Gender Differences in Kidney Cancer

Renal cell carcinoma occurs in a male-to-female ratio of approximately 1.6:1 in most populations studied. A recent analysis by the U.S. Surveillance, Epidemiology, and End Results (SEER) database also shows that men present with significantly larger and higher-grade tumors than women, and women have a slightly higher 5-year survival rate than men (69% for women versus 65% for men) (Aron, Nguyen, Stein, & Gill, 2008). Although the exact reasons for these differences have not been clarified, it is probable that men have higher levels of exposure to tobacco and other toxic compounds than women, and women are traditionally more health conscious than men.

Smoking and Renal Cell Carcinoma

There is compelling evidence to support a causal link between cigarette smoking and the development of renal cell carcinomas. Hunt and colleagues examined this association in a meta-analysis of 24 epidemiologic investigations: 19 case control studies of 8,032 cases and 13,800 controls, and 5 cohort studies of 1,326 cases among 1,457,754 participants. Combined estimates of relative risk (RR) for ever smokers compared to never smokers were RR = 1.38 for all subjects, RR = 1.54 for men, and RR = 1.22 for women. Furthermore, there were significant dose responses in the risk with increasing intensity of smoking in both men and women (**Figure 20.4**), and significant risk reductions were evident in former smokers. The investigators concluded that cigarette smoking is clearly implicated in the etiology of renal cell carcinoma (Hunt, van der Hel, McMillan, Boffetta, & Brennan, 2005). It is also noteworthy that two case control studies suggest there may be an association between exposure to environmental smoke and the risk of developing renal cell carcinoma, although further studies will be needed to confirm this (Hu & Ugnat, 2005; Theis, Dolwick Grieb, Burr, Siddiqui, & Asal, 2008).

Obesity and Renal Cell Carcinoma

Numerous epidemiologic investigations suggest there is an association between obesity and the risk of developing renal cell carcinoma. In a recent meta-analyses of 21 cohort studies involving 15,144 cases, the combined estimates of relative risk were elevated for overweight (body mass index [BMI]: 25–29.9, RR = 1.3) and obese subjects (BMI: 30–39.9, RR = 1.8) compared to those of normal weight (BMI: 20–24.9). Risk elevations were similar for obese men (RR = 1.6) and obese women (RR = 2.0), and each unit of BMI increase above 25 produced a risk increase of approximately 7% (Wang & Xu, 2014). These results are in agreement with earlier meta-analyses and suggest that obese people have a nearly twofold increase in the risk of developing renal cell carcinomas compared to those of normal weight (Ildaphonse, George, & Mathew, 2009; Mathew, George, & Ildaphonse, 2009; Bergström et al., 2001).

Hypertension and Renal Cell Carcinoma

Regulation of blood pressure is an important kidney function, and as such, hypertension has been extensively examined as a risk factor for the development of renal cell carcinoma. As discussed in the following paragraphs, several epidemiologic studies of hypertension and renal cell carcinoma in different populations show reasonable consistency in revealing an association; nevertheless, whether hypertension is a cause or an effect of this malignancy remains a topic of high controversy.

Chow and colleagues examined the health records of 363,992 Swedish men who underwent at least one physical examination during 1971–1992 and were followed until death or the end of the study in 1995. Cases of kidney cancer (759 with renal cell carcinoma and 136 with transitional cell carcinoma of the renal pelvis) were identified through cross-linkage of data with the nationwide Swedish Cancer Registry. Results revealed that obesity and hypertension independently increased the risk of developing renal cell carcinoma but not transitional cell carcinoma, whereas smoking was a risk factor for both forms of kidney cancer (Chow, Gridley, Fraumeni, & Järvholm, 2000).

Choi and colleagues examined the association between death from kidney cancer and baseline hypertension in a large cohort of 576,562 Korean

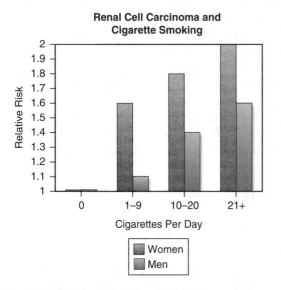

Figure 20.4 Relative Risk of Renal Cell Carcinoma by Intensity of Cigarette Smoking.

Source: Data from Hunt, J. D., van der Hel, O. L., McMillan, G. P., Boffetta, P., & Brennan, P. (2005). Renal cell carcinoma in relation to cigarette smoking: Meta-analysis of 24 studies. *International Journal of Cancer, 114*, 101–108.

men who were studied during 1992–2001. Hypertension was found to significantly increase the risk (RR = 2.43), and the risk was particularly high among cigarette smokers (RR = 8.18) (Choi, Jee, Sull, & Nam, 2005).

Flaherty and colleagues examined hypertension, thiazide use, BMI, weight change, and smoking as risk factors for renal cell carcinoma in prospective cohorts being followed in the United States. The study population included 118,191 women enrolled in the U.S. Nurses' Health Study and 48,953 men enrolled in the Health Professionals Follow-Up Study. Analysis was based on 155 incident cases reported during 24 years of follow-up for women, and 110 incident cases reported during 12 years of follow-up for men. With adjustment for other variables, hypertension significantly increased the risk of cancer development in both women (RR = 1.9) and men (RR = 1.8). Risk increases were also noted for obesity and chronic smoking, but there was no increase with thiazide use (Flaherty et al., 2005).

Vatten and colleagues conducted a prospective cohort study of blood pressure and renal cell carcinoma in 36,728 women and 35,688 men in Norway. Compared to normotensive individuals, women with elevated blood pressure (systolic blood pressure exceeding 150 mm Hg) had twice the risk of developing renal cell carcinoma (RR = 2.0); however, results were inconsistent for men (Vatten, Trichopoulos, Holmen, & Nilsen, 2007).

Weikert and colleagues examined blood pressure and renal cell carcinoma in the European Prospective Investigation into Cancer and Nutrition (EPIC). Blood pressure was measured in 296,638 men and women recruited in eight European countries during 1992–1998. Information on the use of antihypertensive medications was available for 254,935 of these individuals. During an average follow-up of more than 6 years, 250 cases of renal cell carcinoma were detected. Elevated blood pressure (systolic blood pressure exceeding 160 mm Hg) was found to be an independent risk factor (RR = 2.48). Risk estimates did not differ by gender or type of antihypertensive medication, and individuals taking antihypertensive medications were not found to be at increased risk unless blood pressure was poorly controlled (Weikert et al., 2008).

Corrao and colleagues conducted a meta-analysis of 18 studies that examined the association of renal cell carcinoma with hypertension and use of antihypertensive medications. The pooled estimate of risk for hypertension was significantly increased (odds ratio [OR] = 1.62). Risk increases were also noted for use of antihypertensive medications, although effects were attenuated with adjustment for other factors (Corrao, Scotti, Bagnardi, & Sega, 2007).

What is clear from these studies is that hypertension is independently associated with a significant increase in the risk of developing renal cell carcinoma in both men and women. What is as yet unclear is the sequence of pathogenesis. Does malignant transformation induce changes in renin and other vasoactive substances in the kidney that increase blood pressure, or does an increase in the blood pressure cause malignant transformation?

Diabetes Mellitus and Kidney Cancer

Because type 2 diabetes is etiologically linked to chronic diseases of the kidney (nephrosis and nephritis), it is logical to examine the association between diabetes and kidney cancer. Investigators at the Karolinska Institute in Sweden recently examined this association by meta-analysis of nine prospective cohort studies involving patients from Europe, Asia, and North America. Across all studies, individuals with diabetes were at increased risk for the development of kidney cancer compared to those without diabetes (combined RR = 1.42). However, there was statistically significant heterogeneity among studies, and the association with diabetes was stronger in women (RR = 1.70) than in men (RR = 1.26). Additional studies designed to assess the time interval between the onset of diabetes and development of kidney cancer are needed to provide definitive evidence of a causal link (Larsson & Wolk, 2010).

Genetic Abnormalities in Renal Cell Carcinoma

Renal cell carcinomas occasionally occur in a familial setting in association with certain genetic abnormalities; however, only a small fraction of cases (about 4%) report a positive family history of kidney cancer (Lipworth, Tarone, Lund, & McLaughlin, 2009). Familial cases often develop multifocal and/or bilateral tumors at a relatively early age. Among the heritable cancer syndromes, the most important are the von Hippel–Lindau (VHL) syndrome and Birt–Hogg–Dube syndrome.

von Hippel–Lindau Syndrome and Renal Cell Carcinoma

The von Hippel–Lindau syndrome is a rare autosomal dominant cancer syndrome with a prevalence rate of about 1 in 36,000 individuals. This syndrome is caused by a mutant tumor suppressor gene called the von Hippel–Lindau (VHL) gene. Approximately one-third of patients who carry a mutant form of the VHL gene develop renal cell carcinoma (clear cell type).

Other clinical characteristics include retinal angiomas, hemangioblastomas of the central nervous system, islet cell pancreatic tumors, and pheochromocytomas of the adrenal glands. The syndrome is named after the physicians who first described its clinical signs in afflicted patients. The German ophthalmologist Eugen von Hippel first described the angiomas of the eye (von Hippel, 1904), and the Swedish pathologist Arvid Lindau first described the angiomas of the cerebellum and spine (Lindau, 1927).

The VHL gene, which is located on the short arm of chromosome 3, regulates the transcription of other genes that encode proteins critical for cell division and function such as hypoxia-inducible factor (HIF), vascular endothelial growth factor (VEGF), platelet-derived growth factor (PDGF), and transforming growth factors (TGF-a and TGF-b). Mutations in the VHL gene accelerate tumor initiation, growth, and development.

von Hippel–Lindau Gene and Sporadic Renal Cell Carcinoma

It has recently been discovered that mutations of the VHL gene are common not only in von Hippel–Lindau syndrome, but also in sporadic (nonfamilial) cases of clear cell renal carcinoma. In a study of 187 Japanese patients with malignancy, 108 tumor samples were found to have VHL abnormalities (98 with VHL mutations and 10 with VHL hypermethylation) (Yao et al., 2002). In a more recent study of 205 clear cell tumors ascertained from patients in Central Europe, investigators found VHL abnormalities in 91% of cases (82.4% with VHL mutations and 8.3% with VHL hypermethylation). These studies suggest that most clear cell tumors of the kidney arise in association with genetic or epigenetic modifications of a single gene, the VHL gene (Nickerson et al., 2008). Indeed, the VHL gene has potential as a biomarker, a prognostic indicator, and/or a target for molecular therapy.

Birt–Hogg–Dubé Syndrome

Birt–Hogg–Dubé syndrome is a rare autosomal dominant syndrome that has been identified in about 50 families worldwide. This syndrome is characterized by renal cancer, renal and pulmonary cysts, and benign tumors of the hair follicles (Birt, Hogg, & Dubé, 1977). It is caused by mutations in the folliculin gene (FLCN), a tumor suppressor gene located on the short arm of chromosome 17 (Toro et al., 2008).

Occupational Exposures and Renal Cell Carcinoma

A few epidemiologic investigations have examined exposure to toxic compounds and the risk of developing renal cell carcinomas. Mandel and colleagues conducted an international case control study involving 1,732 incident cases of renal cell carcinoma and 2,309 controls from centers in Australia, Denmark, Germany, Sweden, and the United States. Significant associations were found for occupational exposures to asbestos (RR = 1.4), cadmium (RR = 2.0), petroleum products (RR = 1.6), and dry-cleaning solvents (RR = 1.4) (Mandel et al., 1995). Synergism involving environmental exposures have also been noted in some studies. For example, in an early case control study of cadmium exposure and renal cancer, the combination of cadmium exposure and cigarette smoking was found to increase the risk more than fourfold (Kolonel, 1976).

Development of renal cell carcinoma has been found in association with somatic genetic mutations in the von Hippel–Lindau (VHL) tumor suppressor gene. As already discussed, the VHL gene functions by controlling steps in the cell cycle and, if mutated, cell proliferation continues unabated. Brauch and colleagues studied 151 cases of renal cell carcinoma (clear cell type), 44 of whom had long-term occupational exposure to trichloroethylene, an industrial solvent, and 107 cases without exposure. Somatic mutations were detected in tumor specimens from 33 of the 44 (75%) cases exposed to trichloroethylene, whereas such mutations were totally absent in tumors from the 107 nonexposed cases. Results suggest that exposure to trichloroethylene may trigger mutational events in the VHL gene that are associated with the development of renal cell carcinoma (Brauch et al., 1999).

Acquired Cystic Kidney Disease and Renal Cell Carcinoma

Acquired cystic kidney disease develops in approximately 50% of patients who are maintained on chronic hemodialysis and peritoneal dialysis for kidney failure. A major complication of this condition is the development of renal cell carcinoma. Follow-up studies of patients with acquired cystic kidney disease suggest that their risk of developing renal cell carcinoma is 50-fold higher than in the general population. Careful surveillance of dialysis patients by periodic ultrasonagraphy and computerized tomography is recommended for the early detection of such tumors (Brennan, Stilmant, Babayan, & Siroky, 1991; Truong, Krishnan, Cao, Barrios, & Suki, 1995).

Analgesics and Renal Cell Carcinoma

Although some studies have found an association between renal cell carcinoma and heavy or long-term use of analgesics, others have not. Chow studied associations in 440 cases of renal cell carcinoma, spouses of 151 cases, and 691 control subjects. No significant excess risk was observed with regular use of aspirin, acetaminophen, or combinations of these agents. The investigators concluded that the use of analgesics is not likely to pose a significant risk for the development of renal cell carcinoma (Chow et al., 2000).

RISK FACTORS FOR TRANSITIONAL CELL CARCINOMA OF THE RENAL PELVIS

The profile of risk factors associated with the development of transitional cell carcinomas of the renal pelvis is essentially the same as for transitional cell carcinomas of the urinary bladder. The dominant risk factor is chronic exposure to tobacco smoke, which has been found to elevate the risk two- to threefold compared to nonsmokers (Boffetta, 2008). Carcinogenesis associated with smoking is primarily the result of aromatic amines and arylamines present in cigarette smoke that reach the mucosal lining of the renal pelvis, ureters, and urinary bladder.

A number of environmental and occupational factors increase the risk including occupational exposure to arylamines such as 2-naphthylamine, 4-aminobiphenyl, benzidine, and other compounds and intermediates in the synthesis of azo-dyes and pigments used in the textile, printing, plastic, rubber, and cable industries. Long-term exposure to these compounds among workers in these industries increases the risk by about 50% (Vineis, 1994).

The analgesic medication phenacetin was once widely used in European nations until the drug was linked to cancers of the renal pelvis and urinary bladder (Hoover & Fraumeni, 1981; Johansson & Wahlqvist, 1977). A case control investigation found more than a sixfold increase in the risk of bladder cancer development due to heavy phenacetin ingestion among women (Piper, Tonascia, & Matanoski, 1985). Phenactin compounds were removed from the U.S. market in 1983 and have now been discontinued worldwide (Chow, McLaughlin, Linet, Niwa, & Mandel, 1994).

PREVENTION OF KIDNEY CANCER

The rising global trajectory in the incidence and mortality rates of renal cancer during the past 25 years can be partially explained by greater use of imaging technologies such as ultrasound, computed tomography, and magnetic resonance imaging. Nevertheless, despite increased early detection and surgical excision of small renal tumors, mortality rates of kidney cancer are continuing to rise throughout the world.

Three major risk factors—smoking, hypertension, and obesity—significantly increase the risk of developing kidney cancer. These factors constitute a web of causation that has contributed to the rising global burden of kidney cancer. (The prevalence of obesity has reached pandemic proportions, and the rates of smoking and hypertension are also increasing in many populations.) Effective preventive strategies must therefore reverse the trajectory of these factors through control of weight and blood pressure and prevention of tobacco use.

• • • REFERENCES

Aron, M., Nguyen, M. M., Stein, R. J., & Gill, I. S. (2008). Impact of gender in renal cell carcinoma: An analysis of the SEER database. *European Urology, 54*(1), 133–142.

Bergström, A., Hsieh, C. C., Lindblad, P., Lu, C. M., Cook, N. R., & Wolk, A. (2001). Obesity and renal cell cancer—A quantitative review. *British Journal of Cancer, 85*(7), 984–990.

Birt, A. R., Hogg, G. R., & Dubé, W. J. (1977). Hereditary multiple fibrofolliculomas with trichodiscomas and acrochordons. *Archives of Dermatology, 113*(12), 1674–1677.

Boffetta, P. (2008). Tobacco smoking and risk of bladder cancer. *Scandinavian Journal of Urologyand Nephrology, 42*(S218), 45–54.

Brauch, H., Weirich, G., Hornauer, M. A., Störkel, S., Wöhl, T., & Brüning, T. (1999). Trichloroethylene exposure and specific somatic mutations in patients with renal cell carcinoma. *Journal of the National Cancer Institute, 91*(10), 854–861.

Brennan, J. F., Stilmant, M. M., Babayan, R. K., & Siroky, M. B. (1991). Acquired renal cystic disease: Implications for the urologist. *British Journal of Urology, 67*(4), 342–348.

Choi, M. Y., Jee, S. H., Sull, J. W., & Nam, C. M. (2005). The effect of hypertension on the risk for kidney cancer in Korean men. *Kidney International, 67*(2), 647–652.

Chow, W. H., Dong, L. M., & Devesa, S. S. (2010). Epidemiology and risk factors for kidney cancer. *Nature Reviews Urology, 7,* 245–257.

Chow, W. H., Gridley, G., Fraumeni, J. F. Jr., & Järvholm, B. N. (2000). Obesity, hypertension, and the risk of kidney cancer in men. *New England Journal of Medicine, 343*(18), 1305–1311.

Chow, W. H., McLaughlin, J. K., Linet, M. S., Niwa, S., & Mandel, J. S. (1994). Use of analgesics and risk of renal cell cancer. *International Journal of Cancer, 59*(4), 467–470.

Corrao, G., Scotti, L., Bagnardi, V., & Sega, R. (2007). Hypertension, antihypertensive therapy and renal-cell cancer: A meta-analysis. *Current Drug Safety, 2*(2), 125–133.

Ferlay, J., Bray, F., Pisani, P., & Parkin, D.M. (2004). *GLOBOCAN 2002. Cancer incidence, mortality, and prevalence worldwide. IARC Cancer Base No. 5, version 2.0.* Lyon, France: IARC Press.

Ferlay, J., Shin, H. R., Forman, D., Mathers, C., & Parkin, D. M. (2010). Estimates of worldwide burden of cancer in 2008. *International Journal of Cancer, 127*(12), 2893–2917.

Ferlay, J., Soerjomataram, I., Ervik, M., Dikshit, R., Eser, S., Mathers, C., . . . Bray, F. (2013). *GLOBOCAN 2012 v1.0, cancer incidence and mortality worldwide: IARC CancerBase No. 11* [Internet]. Lyon, France: International Agency for Research on Cancer. Retrieved from http://globocan.iarc.fr

Flaherty, K. T., Fuchs, C. S., Colditz, G. A., Stampfer, M. J., Speizer, F. E., Willett, W. C., & Curhan, G. C. (2005). A prospective study of body mass index, hypertension, and smoking and the risk of renal cell carcinoma (United States). *Cancer Causes and Control, 16*(9), 1099–1106.

Hollingsworth, J. M., Miller, D. C., Daignault, S., & Hollenbeck, B. K. (2006). Rising incidence of small renal masses: A need to reassess treatment effect. *Journal of the National Cancer Institute, 98,* 1331–1334.

Hoover, R., & Fraumeni, J. F. Jr. (1981). Drug-induced cancer. *Cancer, 47*(5 Suppl), 1071–1080.

Hu, J., & Ugnat, A. M. (2005). Active and passive smoking and risk of renal cell carcinoma in Canada. *European Journal of Cancer, 41,* 770–778.

Hunt, J. D., van der Hel, O. L., McMillan, G. P., Boffetta, P., & Brennan, P. (2005). Renal cell carcinoma in relation to cigarette smoking: Meta-analysis of 24 studies. *International Journal of Cancer, 114,* 101–108.

Ildaphonse, G., George, P. S., Mathew, A. (2009). Obesity and kidney cancer risk in men: a meta-analysis (1992–2008). *Asian Pacific Journal of Cancer Prevention, 10,* 279–286.

Johansson, S., & Wahlqvist, L. (1977). Tumours of urinary bladder and ureter associated with abuse of phenacetin-containing analgesics. *Acta Pathologica Microbiologica Scandinavica [A], 85,* 768–774.

Kim, S., & Chung, D. H. (2006). Pediatric solid malignancies: Neuroblastoma and Wilms' tumor. *Surgical Clinics of North America, 86*(2), 469–487.

Kolonel, L. N. (1976). Association of cadmium with renal cancer. *Cancer, 37,* 1782–1787.

Kumar, V., Abbas, A. K., & Aster J. C. (2014). *Robbins and Cotran pathologic basis of disease* (9th ed.). Philadelphia, PA: Mosby & Saunders.

Larsson, S. C., & Wolk, A. (2010). Diabetes mellitus and incidence of kidney cancer: A meta-analysis of cohort studies. *Diabetologia, 54*(5), 1013–1018.

Lindau, A. (1927). Zur Frage der Angiomatosis Retinae und Ihrer Hirncomplikation. *Acta Ophthalmologica, 4,* 193–226.

Lipworth, L., Tarone, R. E., Lund, L., & McLaughlin, J. K. (2009). Epidemiologic characteristics and risk factors for renal cell cancer. *Clinical Epidemiology, 2009*(1), 33–43.

Mandel, J. S., McLaughlin, J. K., Schlehofer, B., Mellemgaard, A., Helmert, U., Lindblad, P., . . . Adami, H-O. (1995). International renal-cell cancer study. IV. Occupation. *International Journal of Cancer, 61*(5), 601–605.

Mathew, A., George, P. S., Ildaphonse, G. (2009). Obesity and kidney cancer risk in women: A meta-analysis (1992–2008). *Asian Pacific Journal of Cancer Prevention, 10*, 471–478.

Nickerson, M. L., Jaeger, E., Shi, Y., Durocher, J. A., Mahurkar, S., Zaridze, D., . . . Moore, L. E. (2008). Improved identification of von Hippel-Lindau gene alterations in clear cell renal tumors. *Clinical Cancer Research, 14*(15), 4726–4734.

Pantuck, A. J., Zisman, A., & Belldegrun, A. S. (2001). The changing natural history of renal cell carcinoma. *Journal of Urology, 166*(5), 1611–1623.

Parkin, D. M., Bray, F., Ferlay, J., & Pisani, P. (2005). Global cancer statistics, 2002. *CA: A Cancer Journal for Clinicians, 55*, 74–108.

Parkin, D. M., Pisani, P., & Ferlay, J. (1999a). Global cancer statistics. *CA: A Cancer Journal for Clinicians, 49*(1), 33–64.

Parkin, D. M., Pisani, P., & Ferlay, J. (1999b). Estimates of the worldwide incidence of 25 major cancers in 1990. *International Journal of Cancer, 80*(6), 827–841.

Pascual, D., & Borque, A. (2008). Epidemiology of kidney cancer. *Advances in Urology, 2008*, 782381.

Piper, J. M., Tonascia, J., & Matanoski, G. M. (1985). Heavy phenacetin use and bladder cancer in women aged 20 to 49 years. *New England Journal of Medicine, 313*(5), 292–295.

Robbins, S. L., & Cotran, R. S. (1979). *Pathologic basis of disease* (2nd ed.). Philadelphia, PA: W. B. Saunders.

Theis, R. P., Dolwick Grieb, S. M., Burr, D., Siddiqui, T., & Asal, N. R. (2008). Smoking, environmental tobacco smoke and risk of renal cell cancer: A population-based case-control study. *BMC Cancer, 8*, 387.

Toro, J. R., Wei, M. H., Glenn, G. M., Weinreich, M., Toure, O., Vocke, C., . . . Linehan, W. M. (2008). *BHD* mutations, clinical and molecular genetic investigations of Birt–Hogg–Dubé syndrome: A new series of 50 families and a review of published reports. *Journal of Medical Genetics, 45*(6), 321–331.

Truong, L. D., Krishnan, B., Cao, J. T., Barrios, R., & Suki, W. N. (1995). Renal neoplasm in acquired cystic kidney disease. *American Journal of Kidney Diseases, 26*(1), 1–12.

Vatten, L. J., Trichopoulos, D., Holmen, J., & Nilsen, T. I. (2007). Blood pressure and renal cancer risk: The HUNT Study in Norway. *British Journal of Cancer, 97*(1), 112–114.

Vineis, P. (1994). Epidemiology of cancer from exposure to arylamines. *Environmental Health Perspectives, 102*(Suppl 6), 7–10.

Von Hippel, E. (1904). Ueber eine sehr seltene Erkrankung der Netzhaut. *Albrecht von Graefes Archiv für Ophthalmologie, 59*, 83–106.

Weikert, S., Boeing, H., Pischon, T., Weikert, C., Olsen, A., Tjonneland, A., . . . Riboli, E. (2008). Blood pressure and risk of renal cell carcinoma in the European prospective investigation into cancer and nutrition. *American Journal of Epidemiology, 167*(4), 438–446.

Weikert, S., & Ljungberg, B. (2010). Contemporary epidemiology of renal cell carcinoma: Perspectives of primary prevention. *World Journal of Urology, 28*(3), 247–252.

Yao, M., Yoshida, M., Kishida, T., Nakaigawa, N., Baba, M., Kobayashi, K., . . . Kondo, K. (2002). VHL tumor suppressor gene alterations associated with good prognosis in sporadic clear-cell renal carcinoma. *Journal of the National Cancer Institute, 94*(20), 1569–1575.

21

Epidemiology of Cancers of the Thyroid and Parathyroid

THYROID GLAND: ANATOMY AND FUNCTION

The human thyroid is a butterfly-shaped gland located in the anterior neck inferior to the thyroid cartilage (also known as the Adam's apple). The word *thyroid* means "shield," which describes the basic shape of the thyroid cartilage.

The thyroid produces iodine-containing thyroid hormones, the principal ones being triiodothyronine (T_3) and thyroxine (T_4). Triiodothyronine is 2–3 times more potent than thyroxine, and considerably more T_4 is produced than T_3 (20:1 ratio). These circulating hormones are essential in regulating the rate of metabolism in the body. Inside the cell, T_3 and T_4 stimulate energy production by the mitochondria and promote glucose catabolism, protein synthesis, lipolysis, and excretion of cholesterol. Thyroid hormones also influence growth and development in early life and participate in a number of essential physiologic functions throughout life, such as maintenance of normal cardiac rhythm, muscle tone, and neuronal function in the sympathetic nervous system (Kumar, Abbas, & Aster, 2014).

The functional unit of the thyroid is the thyroid follicle. The thyroid is composed of thousands of spherical thyroid follicles, each of which contains a material called *colloid* that contains iodide (the storage form of iodine) and thyroglobulin (the glycoprotein bound to thyroid hormones). Thyroid hormones are synthesized by cuboidal epithelial cells that line the thyroid follicles. The essential substrates for biosynthesis are the amino acid tyrosine and the mineral iodine.

The biosynthesis of thyroid hormones (T_3 and T_4) is regulated by peptide hormones secreted by the hypothalamus and the anterior pituitary gland. In response to low blood levels of thyroid hormones or neurological signals, the hypothalamus secretes a protein called *thyroid releasing hormone (TRH)* into special blood vessels connected to the pituitary gland, which in turn triggers the anterior pituitary to secrete a second protein called *thyroid stimulating hormone (TSH)* or thyrotropin into the blood. In response to TSH, receptors on the cell membranes of thyroid epithelial cells (thyrotropin receptors) activate the biosynthetic pathway for the production of thyroid hormones (T_3 and T_4). Thyroid hormones are stored in a glycoprotein called thyroglobulin, which also is synthesized in the thyroid epithelium. Thyroid hormones are secreted into the blood from the thyroglobulin (colloid) stored within thyroid follicles. Thyroid hormones (T_3 and T_4) are transported in the blood bound to a carrier protein known as *thyroxine-binding globulin*. The secretion and release of T_3 and T_4 are regulated by blood levels of thyroid hormones (i.e., low levels stimulate the release of active T_3 and T_4) (**Figure 21.1**).

Special cells of the thyroid gland called *C cells* produce a polypeptide hormone called *calcitonin* that helps regulate calcium homeostasis throughout the body. Relatively small parathyroid glands (usually four) are located at the periphery of the thyroid gland. The parathyroid glands synthesize parathyroid hormone (PTH), which together with calcitonin and the active form of vitamin D regulate levels of calcium and phosphorous in the blood, the bones, and most other tissues (Kumar et al., 2014).

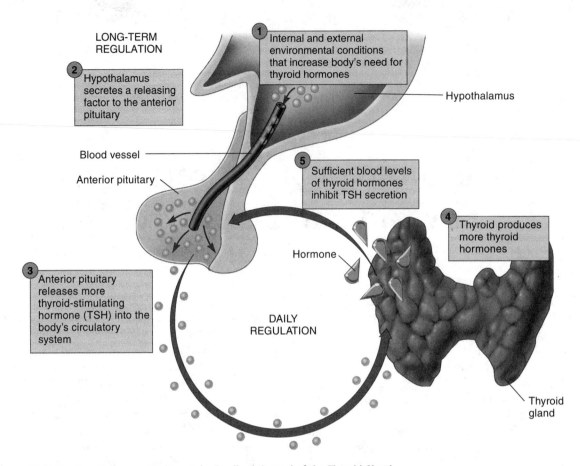

Figure 21.1 The Hypothalamus–Pituitary Axis: Feedback Control of the Thyroid Gland.

BENIGN ADENOMAS OF THE THYROID GLAND

Thyroid nodules arising from thyroid follicles are relatively common and are detected approximately 3 times more often in women than in men. Approximately 90–95% of solitary thyroid nodules are benign, and treatment by simple excision is curative; however, careful histological examination of tissue is always necessary to rule out malignant transformation. Similar to thyroid cancer (discussed in the next section), the major risk factors for thyroid adenoma include radiation exposure, iodine deficiency or excess, and personal and/or familial history of thyroid disorders.

The thyroid gland is extremely sensitive to radiation exposure. Elaine Ron and Alina Brenner at the Radiation Epidemiology Branch of the U.S. National Cancer Institute recently reviewed major studies of cohorts of individuals exposed to radiation from various sources to evaluate dosage effects on the development of thyroid adenomas and other non-malignant thyroid disorders. They found that a wide range of doses of ionizing radiation increased the risk

of developing benign thyroid adenomas and nodules in a variety of populations and settings. Their findings suggest that the elevation in risk continues for decades following exposure (Ron & Brenner, 2010). Investigators in New York monitored the incidence of thyroid adenomas in a cohort of 2,657 infants given x-ray treatment for thymus enlargement and a comparison cohort of 4,833 untreated siblings. Individuals in these cohorts were followed for up to 50 years. The observed rates of thyroid adenoma increased in a linear dose response with the level of radiation, and risk increases persisted throughout the entire follow-up period. Exposure levels of 6 Gy increased the relative risk more than sixfold. (1 Gy is approximately equivalent to 100 rads of ionizing radiation.) Other significant risk factors included a personal medical history and/or a family history of thyroid disorders (Shore, Hildreth, Dvoretsky, Pasternack, & Andresen, 1993).

The question of whether thyroid adenomas are capable of undergoing malignant transformation has been debated for decades. To address this question, Franceschi and colleagues conducted a pooled analysis of 12 case control studies including 2,094 women and 425 men with cancer of the thyroid and age-matched control groups of 3,248 women and 928 men who were disease-free. Significant risk increases were noted for history of goiter (odds ratio [OR] = 5.9) and history of benign thyroid adenomas (OR = 29.9 in women and 18 cases versus 0 controls in men). The investigators concluded that goiter and benign nodules/adenomas were strong risk factors for malignant transformation in the thyroid gland (Franceschi et al., 1999).

Recent pathological studies suggest that a subset of thyroid adenomas display atypical morphology, a pathologic entity known as *atypia*, and that such neoplasms may represent an intermediate step in the progression of adenoma to invasive carcinoma. More studies are needed to clarify the molecular features of premalignant lesions of the thyroid to determine their potential for malignant transformation and establish definitive guidelines for diagnosis and treatment (McHenry & Phitayakorn, 2011; Vasko et al., 2004).

MALIGNANT TUMORS OF THE THYROID AND PARATHYROID

Malignant tumors of the thyroid gland are rare. Nevertheless, all thyroid nodules must be carefully examined under the microscope to distinguish benign from malignant tumors. Approximately 90–95% of thyroid malignancies are carcinomas that arise from the cuboidal epithelium that lines the thyroid follicles. These cells normally synthesize thyroid hormones (T_3 and T_4) and thryoglobulin.

Pathologists routinely classify thyroid carcinomas into various subtypes. The most common subtype is *papillary carcinoma*, which constitutes about 70% of all thyroid malignancies. Papillary thyroid carcinoma is an encapsulated, well-differentiated tumor that shows a papillary growth pattern (finger-like projections) under the microscope. The second most common subtype is *follicular carcinoma*, which constitutes about 30% of thyroid cancers. Follicular thyroid carcinoma also consists of well-differentiated cells, but the growth pattern lacks papillary formations.

A small subset of thyroid malignancies consists of *medullary thyroid carcinomas*, which arise from the parafollicular C cells that secrete calcitonin (a polypeptide hormone that helps regulate calcium and phosphorous in bone remodeling). Medullary thyroid carcinomas constitute only 5–10% of all thyroid malignancies.

Malignancies of the *parathyroid glands* are distinct from thyroid cancer and are discussed in a separate section of this chapter. Parathyroid tumors arise from cells that secrete parathyroid hormone (a polypeptide hormone that increases calcium levels in the blood).

GLOBAL BURDEN OF THYROID CANCER

Cancer of the thyroid afflicts 3–4 times more women than men. During 2012, 298,102 new cases were diagnosed in the world population, and 39,769 people died from thyroid cancer. Of these, 229,923 cases (77%) and 27,142 deaths (68%) occurred in women. The annual age-adjusted incidence rate among women was 6.1 cases per 100,000 compared to 1.9 per 100,000 among men, and the mortality rate was 0.6 deaths per 100,000 among women compared to 0.3 per 100,000 among men (Ferlay et al., 2013).

During 2000–2012, the annual number of incident cases of thyroid cancer detected in the world population increased dramatically whereas the number of deaths changed relatively little (**Figure 21.2**). Age-adjusted incidence and mortality rates actually show inverse trends. During 2002–2012, the

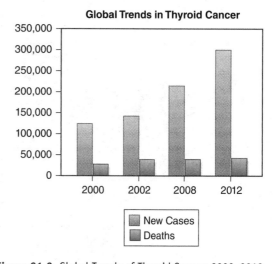

Figure 21.2 Global Trends of Thyroid Cancer, 2000–2012.

Source: Data from Ferlay, J., Shin, H. R., Forman, D., Mathers, C., & Parkin, D. M. (2010). Estimates of worldwide burden of cancer in 2008. *International Journal of Cancer, 127*(12), 2893–2917; Ferlay, J., Soerjomataram, I., Ervik, M., Dikshit, R., Eser, S., Mathers, C.,... Bray, F. (2013). *GLOBOCAN 2012 v1.0. Cancer incidence and mortality worldwide: IARC CancerBase No. 11* [Internet]. Lyon, France: International Agency for Research on Cancer. Retrieved from http://globocan.iarc.fr; Parkin, D. M., Bray, F., Ferlay, J., & Pisani, P. (2001). Estimating the world cancer burden: GLOBOCAN 2000. *International Journal of Cancer, 94*, 153–156; Parkin, D. M., Bray, F., Ferlay, J., & Pisani, P. (2005). Global cancer statistics, 2002. *CA: A Cancer Journal for Clinicians, 55*, 74–108.

incidence approximately doubled among women (6.1 versus 3.3 per 100,000), whereas the mortality declined by 25% (0.8 versus 0.6 per 100,000). As discussed in a later section of this chapter, the inverse trends of incidence and mortality may largely reflect the increased early detection of small papillary thyroid tumors that were treated by complete surgical resection (Ferlay et al., 2010, 2013; Parkin, Bray, Ferlay, & Pisani, 2005; Parkin, Pisani, & Ferlay, 1999a, 1999b).

Figure 21.3 shows the global distributions of incidence and mortality rates of thyroid cancer among women. Incidence rates are markedly higher in developed countries than developing countries; for example, the incidence in U.S. and Canadian women (~20 per 100,000) is 10–20 times higher

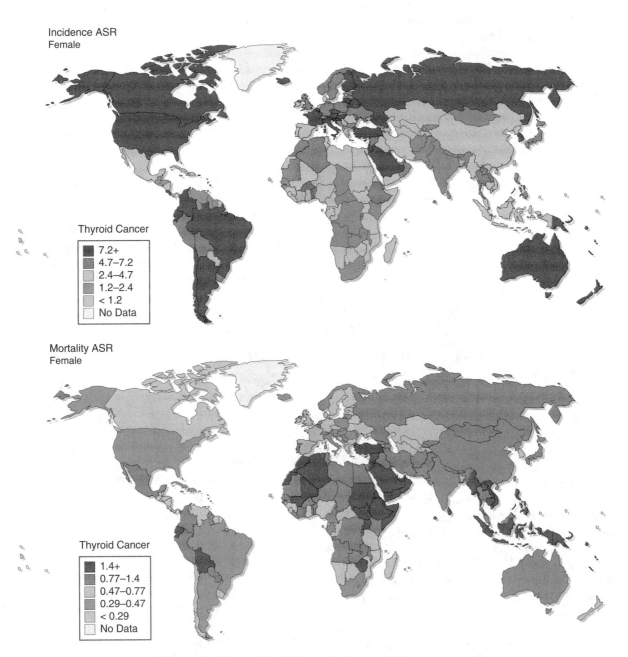

Figure 21.3 Global Incidence and Mortality Rates of Thyroid Cancer in Women, 2012.

ASR: Rates per 100,000 are age-standardized to the world population, 2000–2025.

Source: Reproduced from Ferlay, J., Soerjomataram, I., Ervik, M., Dikshit, R., Eser, S., Mathers, C.,... Bray, F. (2013). *GLOBOCAN 2012 v1.0. Cancer incidence and mortality worldwide: IARC CancerBase No. 11* [Internet]. Lyon, France: International Agency for Research on Cancer. Retrieved from http://globocan.iarc.fr

than the incidence among women living in India and sub-Saharan Africa (1–2 per 100,000). In contrast, mortality rates of thyroid cancer are markedly higher in less developed regions of the world; for example, mortality rates range from 1–3 deaths per 100,000 among women in sub-Saharan African to 0.3 deaths per 100,000 among women in Canada and the United States (Ferlay et al., 2013).

TRENDS IN PAPILLARY AND FOLLICULAR THYROID CARCINOMA

The incidence of thyroid cancer has increased dramatically in most developed countries during the past few decades; for example, in the United States the incidence rates have more than doubled since the 1970s. However, mortality has remained relatively constant over the same time period (**Figure 21.4**).

To explore reasons for the increasing incidence of thyroid cancer in the U.S. population, Davies and Welch examined the annual incidence of pathologic subtypes of thyroid cancer for the period 1973–2002 using registry data from the Surveillance, Epidemiology, and End Results (SEER) system of the U.S. National Cancer Institute. As shown in **Figure 21.5**, the annual incidence of thyroid cancer increased 142% during the study period, from 3.6 per 100,000 to 8.7 per 100,000. This increase was almost entirely

attributed to the corresponding 185% increase in the incidence of papillary thyroid carcinoma, from 2.7 per 100,000 to 7.7 per 100,000. In contrast, the incidence of follicular thyroid carcinoma did not change during the study period, and the mortality rates of thyroid cancer actually *declined* from 0.57 per 100,000 in 1973 to 0.47 per 100,000 in 2003. The investigators suggest that enhanced diagnostic scrutiny is the most likely explanation for these trends. They point out that ultrasound is routinely used to identify thyroid nodules that are only a few millimeters in diameter, and fine needle aspiration and pathologic examination of specimens from small papillary tumors has been adopted as standard practice. The observed trends are therefore largely explainable by the increased early detection of small papillary thyroid tumors that were treated by complete surgical resection (Davies & Welch, 2006).

RISK FACTORS FOR THYROID CANCER

Gender and Thyroid Cancer

Thyroid cancer as well as other thyroid disorders predominate in women. For example, iodine deficiency that causes nontoxic (simple) goiter, and autoimmune forms of thyroid disease (e.g., Graves' disease and Hashimoto's thyroiditis) are 2–3 times more common in women than in men.

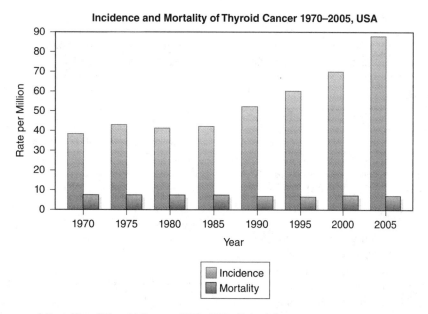

Figure 21.4 Incidence and Mortality of Thyroid Cancer, 1970–2005, United States.

Source: Data from Surveillance, Epidemiology, and End Results. *SEER Data, 1970–2005*. Bethesda, MD: U.S. National Institutes of Health, National Cancer Institute.

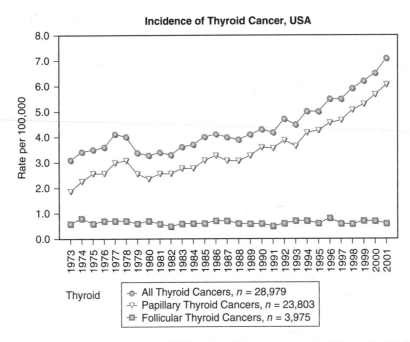

Figure 21.5 Trends in the Incidence of Papillary and Follicular Thyroid Carcinoma, 1973–2003, United States.

Source: Data from Davies, L., & Welch, H. G. (2006). Increasing incidence of thyroid cancer in the United States, 1973–2002. *Journal of the American Medical Association, 295*(18), 2164–2167.

Behavioral differences between men and women may partially explain the excess of thyroid disease in women. It is well known that women seek medical attention more often than men and may thus be more likely than men to undergo screening and diagnostic procedures that detect thyroid disorders.

Alternatively, biological gender differences may preferentially predispose women to thyroid disorders including thyroid neoplasms. For example, serum levels of thyroid stimulating hormone (TSH), a known promoter of thyroid hyperplasia, are elevated by menarche, pregnancy, surgical menopause (oophorectomy), use of oral contraceptives, and estrogen replacement therapy (Yao, Chiu, Strugnell, Gill, & Wiseman, 2011). However, the results of epidemiologic studies of these factors are mixed and do not provide clear evidence of causality (Negri et al., 1999; Sakoda & Horn-Ross, 2002; Yao et al., 2011).

The genesis of thyroid autoimmunity and its predominance in females remains enigmatic. One hypothesis postulates incompatibility of X chromosomes. Because either the paternal or the maternal X chromosome is inactivated in cell lineages early during embryogenesis, the genotype of the human female is actually a mosaic of active and inactivated paternal and maternal X chromosomes. This phenomenon was described by Mary Lyon in 1961 and is called the *Lyon hypothesis* (Lyon, 1961). Inactivated

X chromosomes are called *Barr bodies*, named after Murray Barr, who first described them (Barr & Bertram, 1949). Conceivably, incompatibility of the paternal and maternal X chromosomes might lead to immunoreactivity, particularly if thyroid tissues contain the active X chromosome from one parent and immune cells contain the active X chromosome from the other parent.

Other mechanisms might also heighten the predisposition of women to autoimmune thyroiditis as well as other forms of autoimmunity. During pregnancy, fetal cells can cross the placenta and enter the maternal circulation, and these cells may survive in maternal tissues such as the thyroid gland, a condition known as *microchimerism*. Interestingly, microchimerism in thyroid specimens and circulating fetal cells in blood samples have been found to be more common in patients with autoimmune thyroiditis than normal controls. Further research is needed to characterize the autoimmune effects of fetal cells in maternal blood and tissues (Lepez, Vandewoestyne, & Deforce, 2013).

Radiation Exposure and Thyroid Cancer

In 1950, Duffy and Fitzgerald reported that 9 out of 28 children with thyroid cancer had a history of external head and neck irradiation (Duffy & Fitzgerald, 1950). Soon after that, case reports of thyroid cancer in young atomic bomb survivors appeared in the literature (Fujimoto, Yamamoto, Numata, & Mori, 1959). There is now convincing evidence that the incidence of thyroid malignancies increased markedly in populations exposed to excessive radioactive fallout in Japan following the atomic bombing in World War II and in Russia after the Chernobyl nuclear reactor accident (Boice, 1998, 2006). Furthermore, a recent study suggests the presence of synergism between radiation exposure and iodine deficiency in elevating the risk of developing thyroid cancer (Cardis et al., 2005).

Cardis and colleagues conducted a case control study of thyroid cancer and exposure to radioactive fallout from the Chernobyl nuclear reactor accident in combination with dietary intake of iodine and iodine supplements. Cases and controls were ascertained from Belarus and the Russian Federation population living near the reactor at the time of the accident. Questionnaire data on diet were obtained from 276 patients with pathologically confirmed thyroid cancer and 1,300 healthy control subjects matched by age and gender. Radiation exposure was estimated by a comprehensive dose reconstruction program taking into account both inhaled and ingested radioactive particles. The major contribution to dose was from drinking milk contaminated with radioactive iodine isotopes, particularly I^{131}. Dietary iodine and dietary supplements containing potassium iodide were also examined as cofactors in the study. Similar to many other investigations, the overall risk of thyroid cancer increased with increasing dose of radioactivity. Notably, subjects with low iodine intake and 1 Gy of total radiation exposure had high odds ratios ranging from 4.85 to 8.44, whereas those with similar radiation exposure who took potassium iodide supplements were *not* at increased risk (OR = 1.08). These results indicate that diets deficient in iodine potentiate the risk of radiation-induced thyroid cancer and suggest that iodine supplementation has a protective effect against carcinogenesis (Cardis et al., 2005).

Dietary Factors and Thyroid Cancer

Goodman and colleagues conducted a population-based case control study of thyroid cancer, diet, and other factors in Hawaii, which has one of the highest incidence rates of thyroid cancer in the world. Cases with pathologically confirmed thyroid cancer (51 men and 140 women) were compared to 113 male and 328 female controls matched on age and gender. The risk of thyroid cancer increased with increasing body weight in both men and women. Men and women in the highest quartiles of weight had fivefold

and twofold increases in thyroid cancer risk, respectively, compared to those in the lowest quartiles. Risk increases were also observed among heavier women who used fertility drugs or experienced miscarriages or stillbirths at first pregnancy. Results suggest a dose response relationship between body weight and thyroid carcinogenesis with potential effect modification due to fertility drugs and/or reproductive failure (Goodman, Kolonel, & Wilkens, 1992; Goodman, Yoshizawa, & Kolonel, 1988). Interestingly, certain inflammatory adipokines secreted by adipocytes (fat cells) in obese individuals have been linked to carcinogenesis (Barb, Pazaitou-Panayiotou, & Mantzoros, 2006; Vona-Davis & Rose, 2007). It is therefore conceivable that the increased storage of fat associated with weight gain could induce adipocytes to secrete inflammatory adipokines that target the thyroid gland.

In another case control study conducted in the Hawaiian population, women with high iodine intake who took fertility drugs or suffered miscarriage or stillbirth at first pregnancy were found to be at exceptionally high risk for the development of thyroid cancer. Women with high iodine intake who suffered a first-pregnancy miscarriage had an odds ratio of 4.8, and women with high iodine intake who used fertility drugs had an odds ratio of 7.3 (Kolonel, Hankin, Wilkens, Fukunaga, & Hinds, 1990). These results tend to contradict the more recent findings of Cardis and colleagues (2005), who observed protective effects of supplemental potassium iodide. Clearly, additional investigations are needed in order to clarify the impact of radiation, iodine, body mass, female reproduction, and other risk factors on thyroid carcinogenesis in different populations.

Nonmalignant Thyroid Disorders and Thyroid Cancer

Several nonmalignant thyroid disorders have been found to be associated with thyroid cancer. The most prominent of these associations involve autoimmune conditions and auto-antibodies against thyroglobulin and other thyroid-specific factors.

The most commonly encountered diseases of the thyroid gland involve either an overactive gland (hyperthyroidism) or an underactive gland (hypothyroidism). Early screening surveys conducted among adults in the United States and Great Britain reflect prevalence rates of thyroid abnormalities of approximately 6% (Baldwin & Rowitt, 1978; Tunbridge et al., 1977). The most prevalent thyroid condition is enlargement of the thyroid gland, which is commonly called a *goiter*. Goiters fall into two broad categories: inflammatory (toxic) goiters that cause hyperthyroidism (e.g., Graves' disease) and noninflammatory (nontoxic) goiters that cause hypothyroidism (e.g., iodine deficiency).

Thyroiditis refers to any inflammatory condition of the thyroid gland. Thyroiditis can lead to hyperthyroidism (as in Graves' disease) or hypothyroidism (as in Hashimoto's thyroiditis). These inflammatory conditions are believed to have an autoimmune basis, and both have been linked to the development of thyroid adenomas and thyroid cancer.

Hyperthyroidism

Hyperthyroidism refers to an overactive thyroid. Symptoms of hyperthyroidism are due to the over-production of thyroid hormones (T_3 and T_4) by the thyroid gland. The most common cause of hyperthyroidism is an autoimmune form of thyroiditis known as *Graves' disease*, named after the Irish physician Robert J. Graves, who first described the condition in 1835 (Weetman, 2000).

Hypothyroidism

Hypothyroidism refers to an underactive thyroid gland, which results in a deficiency of thyroid hormones (T_3 and T_4). Hypothyroid disorders occur when the thyroid gland is inactive or underactive as a result of improper formation from birth, lack of iodine, removal or iatrogenic inactivation (ablation) of the thyroid gland, or autoimmune conditions such as Hashimoto's thyroiditis. Symptoms of hypothyroidism include abnormal weight gain, fatigue, baldness, temperature intolerance (typically cold), and in some cases thyroid enlargement (nontoxic goiter).

Human Leukocyte Antigen (HLA) Locus and Autoimmune Thyroiditis

The *human leukocyte antigen (HLA)* locus on chromosome 6 encodes a variety of molecules that are related to autoimmune conditions. The two classical forms of thyroiditis, Graves' disease (a common cause of hyperthyroidism) and Hashimoto's thyroiditis (which causes hypothyroidism), are both known to have an autoimmune basis related to specific genes of the HLA locus.

Genes of the HLA locus play a major role in the immune response to foreign antigens as well as the recognition of self versus nonself in immune reactions. The six major genes of the HLA locus are all located on the short arm of chromosome 6 (Levinson, 2006). Specific HLA genes encode cell-surface antigen-presenting proteins that regulate the processing of bacterial antigens by T lymphocytes and the formation of antibodies by B lymphocytes. The profile of cell membrane HLA proteins differentiates self from nonself in the immune response; perturbations in the system occasionally result in the formation of antibodies that are directed against self. Such autoantibodies are capable of selectively stimulating and/or destroying certain tissues of the body, thereby causing autoimmune disease.

Genetic variants at the HLA locus have been found to increase susceptibility to Graves' disease and Hashimoto's thyroiditis. For example, results of HLA genotyping studies of cases and controls suggest that individuals who carry the HLA-DR3 allele have 3–4 times higher risk of developing Graves' disease than noncarriers (Farid, Stone, & Johnson, 1980; Jacobson & Tomer, 2007b; Zamani et al., 2000) and that HLA-DR3 carriers have approximately a 2 times higher risk of developing Hashimoto's thyroiditis than noncarriers (Jacobson, Huber, & Tomer, 2008; Tandon, Zhang, & Weetman, 1991). It is hypothesized that the HLA-DR3 protein may heighten susceptibility through its special affinity for thyroid antigens, thereby creating an autoimmune response directed against the thyroid gland. Furthermore, there is increasing evidence suggesting that interactions between thyroglobulin and genetic variants of the HLA-DR3 allele enhance susceptibility to the development of Graves' disease (Jacobson & Tomer, 2007a).

Another candidate gene for conferring susceptibility to the development of autoimmune thyroid disorders is the cytotoxic T lymphocyte associated antigen-4 (*CTLA-4*). The normal *CTLA-4* gene product helps to regulate the response of T lymphocytes to antigenic stimuli. It apparently provides a negative signal to the T cell, thus limiting autoimmune responses and maintaining self-tolerance (Chambers & Allison, 1997). Significant associations have consistently been observed between Graves' disease and certain allelic forms of *CTLA-4*, whereas associations with Hashimoto's thyroiditis are less clear (Chistiakov & Turakulov, 2003).

Other susceptibility genes have also been identified. For example, variants of the gene that encodes vitamin D–binding protein have been linked to the development of Graves' disease. Vitamin D–binding protein facilitates the transport and release of vitamin D in blood and tissues, and the active form of vitamin D works in concert with calcitonin, parathyroid, and thyroid hormones to regulate calcium and phosphorous homeostasis. Graves' disease combined with low serum vitamin D leads to poor absorption of calcium and related symptoms of muscle wasting, bone resorption, and nervous system dysfunction (Herman-Bonert & Friedman, 2004).

German investigators studied genetic polymorphisms of vitamin D–binding protein among 561 individuals in families with an offspring affected by either Graves' disease (95 pedigrees) or Hashimoto's thyroiditis (92 pedigrees). They found that allelic variants of vitamin D–binding protein confer susceptibility to the development of Graves' disease but not Hashimoto's thyroiditis (Pani et al., 2002). In a subsequent genetic case control study of Graves' disease and vitamin D–binding protein, Polish investigators compared single nucleotide polymorphisms of 332 cases to 185 healthy control subjects. They found a specific polymorphism at codon 420 involving substitution of lysine for threonine that significantly increased the risk of disease and decreased the level of serum vitamin D (Kurylowicz, Ramos-Lopez, Bednarczuk, & Badenhoop, 2006). These results suggest that genetic regulation of vitamin D activity plays a role in thyroid autoimmunity and the development of Graves' disease.

Graves' Disease

Graves' disease, also called diffuse toxic goiter, is believed to arise as a consequence of autoimmune reactions. Graves' disease affects approximately 0.5% of the U.S. population and is the underlying cause of up to 80% of all cases of hyperthyroidism. The clinical signs and symptoms of this condition result from excess stimulation of the thyroid gland by autoantibodies, resulting in inflammation of the thyroid gland (thyroiditis) and overproduction of T_3 and T_4 hormones. Molecular studies suggest that circulating IgG antibodies bind to and activate thyrotropin receptors of the thyroid epithelium, causing hypertrophy and hyperplasia of thyroid follicles. This process results in increased production of thyroid hormones, thyroid enlargement, and goiter formation. The peak incidence of Graves' disease is between 20 and 40 years of age. Symptoms include enlargement of the thyroid gland (goiter), protruding eyes (exophthalmos), palpitations, excess sweating, diarrhea, weight loss, muscle weakness, and unusual sensitivity to heat. Notably, Graves' disease is diagnosed 5–10 times more often in women than men (Brent, 2008; Weetman, 2000). As shown by the age-specific rates for Swedish women and men in **Figure 21.6**, the marked female excess of this condition is evident throughout life (Hemminki, Li, Sundquist, & Sundquist, 2010).

Genetic studies suggest that Graves' disease has a significant hereditary component. A nationwide population-based study of twins ascertained from the Danish Twin Registry during 1953–1976 revealed a concordance rate of 35% among monozygous twins compared to 3% for dizygous twins. In regression models, genetic factors accounted for 79% of the liability to development of Graves' disease compared to 21% for environmental factors. Based on these findings, the investigators suggested that "genetic factors play a major role in the etiology of Graves' disease" (Brix, Kyvik, Christensen, & Hegedus, 2001).

A national genetic study of Graves' disease was conducted in Sweden using data from the Swedish Multigeneration Register linked to the Swedish Hospital Discharge Register for the years 1987–2007. Standard incidence ratios were calculated based on

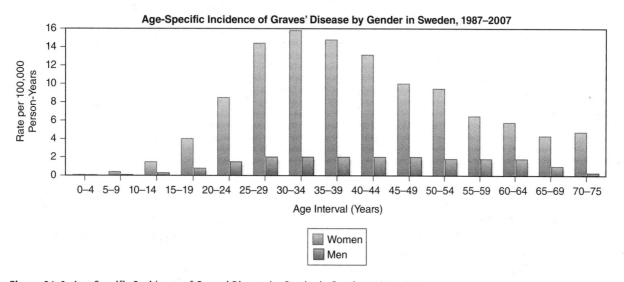

Figure 21.6 Age-Specific Incidence of Graves' Disease by Gender in Sweden, 1987–2007.

Source: Data from Hemminki, K., Li, X., Sundquist, J., & Sundquist, K. (2010). The epidemiology of Graves' disease: Evidence of a genetic and an environmental contribution. *Autoimmunity, 34*(3), J307–J313.

familial relationships of 15,743 patients hospitalized for Graves' disease during this time period. Standard incidence ratios were increased 5-fold in families with an affected sibling and more than 300-fold in families with two affected siblings. The standard incidence ratio in twins was 16.5. The incidence of Graves' disease was also increased in families with other autoimmune conditions such as Addison's disease, type 1 diabetes mellitus, Hashimoto's thyroiditis, pernicious anemia, myasthenia gravis, lupus erythematosus, and scleroderma. Surprisingly, the standard incidence ratio was also increased among spouses of affected individuals, suggesting that environmental factors may also be involved in the genesis of Graves' disease (Hemminki et al., 2010). Interestingly, cigarette smoking has been linked to the development of multiple autoimmune diseases, including rheumatoid arthritis, systemic lupus erythematosus, multiple sclerosis, and Graves' disease (Costenbader & Karlson, 2006; Manji et al., 2006). Notwithstanding, the genetic factors that influence the thyroid autoimmunity involved in Graves' disease clearly outweigh the environmental factors (Jacobson & Tomer, 2007a, 2007b).

Graves' Disease, Autoimmune Thyroiditis, and Thyroid Cancer

An association between Graves' disease and the development of thyroid cancer was reported more than 60 years ago (Pemberton & Black, 1948). Several lines of evidence suggest that patients with Graves' disease may be at increased risk for the development of benign thyroid adenomas and thyroid carcinoma. A review of 450 surgically treated patients during 1982–1994 revealed that 36 of 450 (8%) had thyroid carcinomas, 33 of which were papillary tumors (Pellegriti, Belfiore, Giuffrida, Lupo, & Vigneri, 1998). In a European multicenter study of 557 patients who were surgically treated for Graves' disease, thyroid cancer was detected among 3.9% of all patients and 15% of those patients with nodules (Kraimps et al., 2000). A review of the malignancy rate in multiple studies of surgically resected thyroid nodules suggests that approximately 1.7–2.5% of nodules from Graves' patients manifest thyroid cancer compared to only 0.25% of nodules from other patients, reflecting a 7- to 10-fold risk increase of thyroid cancer among patients with Graves' disease (Belfiore, Russo, Vigneri, & Filetti, 2001).

Specific antithyroid antibodies have been linked to the development of thyroid cancer in a number of investigations. In a U.S. study of 253 patients with thyroid cancer and 2,247 patients with benign thyroid nodules, fine needle aspiration biopsy was performed on all subjects and specimens were tested for the presence/absence of antibodies against thyroglobulin. Results revealed that thyroid cancer was significantly associated with elevated antibodies against thyroglobulin (OR = 1.57) (Azizi & Malchoff, 2011).

In an Italian study of 2,053 patients with thyroid nodules, fine needle aspirates were evaluated for the presence of a profile of antithyroid antibodies. Patients with thyroid nodules positive for antithyroid antibodies had more than double the risk of having thyroid cancer (OR = 2.2) (Boi et al., 2013).

In a retrospective study of 1,638 Korean patients with thyroid nodules, ultrasound-guided aspirates were tested for antibodies against thyroglobulin. A higher frequency of malignant nodules tested positive for auto-antibodies than did benign nodules (31% versus 21%), and patients who tested positive for thyroglobulin auto-antibodies were at increased risk (OR = 1.6) compared to those who tested negative (Kim et al., 2010).

Auto-antibodies against the receptor for TSH are a diagnostic characteristic of Graves' disease. Notably, these antibodies have been linked to the development and progression of thyroid cancer. In a study of serum samples from 27 patients with localized or metastatic thyroid cancer, 25 of 27 samples (93%) tested positive for TSH receptor antibodies compared to 0 of 51 samples from normal controls (Chinnappa et al., 2004).

In summary, evidence from both epidemiologic and immunological studies suggest that patients with Graves' disease or other forms of autoimmune thyroiditis develop antibodies against TSH receptors, thyroglobulin, and other thyroid-specific antigens that may elevate their risk of developing thyroid cancer.

Hashimoto's Thyroiditis

Hashimoto's thyroiditis is a chronic autoimmune disease in which the thyroid gland is gradually destroyed by the body's own immune system. The disorder was first described by the Japanese physician Dr. Hakaru Hashimoto in 1912 (Hashimoto, 1912). It is diagnosed by clinical symptoms plus the presence of auto-antibodies against thyroglobulin or other cellular components of the thyroid gland. Pathologic review of thyroidal tissue from patients reveals inflammation and striking infiltration by lymphocytes admixed with plasma cells, necrosis, and derangement of thyroid follicles plus goitrous enlargement of the gland. Without treatment, there is progressive depletion of thyroid follicles accompanied by hypothyroidism and loss of thyroid function (Rapoport, 1991).

Patients with Hashimoto's thyroiditis often have a family history of thyroid disorders, including Graves' disease and/or other autoimmune conditions such as type 1 diabetes, celiac disease, pernicious anemia, Addison's disease, and Sjogren's syndrome. Hashimoto's thyroiditis is typically diagnosed between the ages of 45 and 65 years and occurs 10–20 times more often in women than men (Vanderpump & Tunbridge, 2002). Certain genes of the HLA locus confer susceptibility to the development of this disorder (e.g., presence of the *HLA-DR5* gene increases the relative risk more than threefold). Furthermore, polymorphisms of the *CTLA-4* gene have also been implicated in the genesis of Hashimoto's thyroiditis (Chistiakov, 2005; Tomer, Barbesino, Greenberg, Concepcion, & Davies, 1999; Yesilkaya et al., 2008).

Hashimoto's Thyroiditis and Thyroid Cancer

The relationship between Hashimoto's thyroiditis and papillary thyroid carcinoma was first proposed by Dailey and colleagues in 1955 (Dailey, Lindsay, & Skahen, 1955). Since this initial description, the association between the two diseases has been highly debated in the literature and the relationship remains controversial. However, recent studies of patients from different populations provide evidence of a positive association.

In a study of 474 consecutive Taiwanese patients who underwent thyroidectomy and had a final pathological diagnosis of Hashimoto's thyroiditis, 133 patients (28%) had a preoperative diagnosis of thyroid cancer (based on pathologic examination of fine needle aspirates), and an additional 114 patients (24%) had a postoperative diagnosis of thyroid cancer based on pathologic examination of the surgical specimens. Most of the thyroid tumors (95%) were papillary carcinomas (Shih et al., 2008).

In a U.S. study of 217 cases with Hashimoto's thyroiditis and 1,198 controls without thyroiditis who underwent thyroid surgery, 29% of the cases had papillary thyroid carcinoma versus 23% of controls (OR = 1.3). Among patients with Hashimoto's thyroiditis, 94% of the thyroid tumors were papillary carcinomas (Repplinger et al., 2008).

In a meta-analysis of 38 studies, pathologic evidence of Hashimoto's thyroiditis was present in 938 (40.5%) of 2,317 cases with thyroid cancer compared to 634 (21%) of 3,019 controls with benign thyroid nodules or other thyroid disorders. Cases with thyroid cancer were nearly three times more likely to manifest Hashimoto's thyroiditis compared to controls with benign nodules (summary OR = 2.8) (Lee, Younghye, Choi, & Kim, 2013).

A variety of auto-antibodies have been identified in patients with Hashimoto's thyroiditis. These include antibodies against thyroglobulin, thyroid peroxidase, and to a lesser extent, antibodies against TSH receptors. Chronic influx of auto-reactive T cells in thyroid tissues and polymorphisms in the *CTLA-4* gene in response to antigenic stimuli may also be involved in thyroid carcinogenesis.

IODINE AND THYROID FUNCTION

Adequate intake of iodine is essential for the biosynthesis of thyroid hormones and maintenance of normal thyroid function. The normal range of serum iodine is approximately 40–80 nanograms per milliliter. Values consistently outside this range indicate the presence of thyroid disease: Low levels indicate hypothyroidism and high levels indicate hyperthyroidism.

Iodine Deficiency and Thyroid Disease

Nontoxic goiter, or simply "goiter," refers to enlargement of the thyroid gland in conjunction with hypothyroidism. As discussed later in this section, the dominant global cause of goiter is iodine deficiency. Enlargement of the thyroid gland in iodine-deficient children is progressive, initially involving diffuse hyperplasia and later the development of multiple nodules wherein the thyroid follicles are markedly distended by the presence of excess colloid. Goiter arising from iodine deficiency is very uncommon in developed countries because iodine is routinely added to salt and other foods for consumption. Indeed, iodized salt has been a prominent feature of the U.S. diet since 1924 (Marine, 1924; McClure, 1935).

The discovery of iodine as an essential mineral for normal function of the thyroid glands and the production of thyroid hormones provides a convincing example of the power of epidemiologic investigation. In 1905, a young physician trained at Johns Hopkins University, David Marine, began his residency training in pathology at Lakeside Hospital on the shores of Lake Erie in Cleveland, Ohio. His interest in thyroid disease was spiked by the high prevalence of goiters in dogs in the area, and he began a series of studies to elucidate the cause. Marine observed that dietary supplements of iodine in the form of iodized salt reduced the incidence of goiter in sheep and produced regression of goiters and reversal of hypothyroid symptoms in dogs (Marine, 1907). In pathologic studies, Marine found that large goitrous thyroids from dogs had lower levels of iodine than normal thyroids from healthy dogs (Marine & Williams, 1908). Marine was also called upon to investigate the high rate of "alleged thyroid carcinomas" in trout in a fish hatchery in northern Ohio. Pathologic studies revealed that the fish had goiters due to iodine deficiency, rather than thyroid carcinomas, and Marine demonstrated that goiter development was effectively prevented by the addition of iodine or foods high in iodine content to the trout hatchery water (Marine, 1914).

Marine soon translated these findings to the human population, showing in his clinic that children suffering from simple goiter responded to therapy with sodium iodide. Realizing the devastating problem of goiter in the Great Lakes region, Marine and his colleague, O. P. Kimball, organized and conducted a field intervention study using sodium iodide supplements in the diets of young girls in the Akron, Ohio, region. Girls in the fifth through eighth grades received 200 milligrams of sodium iodide for 10 consecutive days, and older girls received twice this amount. The dosing regimen was repeated every 6 months. A total of 2,305 girls received the supplemental iodine compared to 2,190 girls from a nearby region who did not. The results of this field experiment after 30 months of follow-up are summarized in **Table 21.1**.

After 30 months of observation, the chemopreventive value of the treatment with sodium iodide was remarkable. Among participants with normal thyroid glands at the beginning of the study, 347 of 1,257 girls (27.6%) who did not receive iodine developed goiters compared to only 2 of 908 girls (0.2%) who did receive iodine. Substantial therapeutic effects were also evident. Among participants with enlarged thyroid glands at baseline, progression of disease was observed in only 0.2% of treated girls compared to 14.1% of controls, whereas regression of disease was observed in 60.3% of treated girls compared to 13.8% of controls. Importantly, no toxic effects of the sodium iodide supplement were detected in the study (Marine, 1924; Marine & Kimball, 1917,

1920). The definitive evidence from this study was the crowning achievement of Marine's work on iodine deficiency as the causative factor in the development of hypothyroidism and simple goiter.

Cretinism and Iodine Deficiency

The health consequences of iodine deficiency often manifest early in life. These include abnormal neuronal development, mental retardation, congenital malformations, and hypothyroidism. Deleterious effects on reproduction such as spontaneous abortion, miscarriage, and infertility are also notable. Later in life, lack of iodine is also associated with intellectual impairment.

Cretinism is an anomaly that is caused by iodine deficiency in the developing fetus. Clinical manifestations of this condition depend on the gestational timing and severity of iodine and hormonal insufficiency in both the mother and fetus. In the absence of iodine, there is abnormal development and function of the fetal thyroid gland. This devastating condition typically manifests at birth or during infancy and is characterized by hypothyroidism, goiter, mental retardation, deaf-mutism, stunted growth, and other anomalies. Though extremely rare, there are case reports of thyroid cancer in young patients with cretinism (Fellman, Wojtowicz, & Pawlaczyk, 1968).

Endemic cretinism was once common in the Alpine populations of Southern Europe due to lack of iodine in their diets. As an example, in Switzerland, where the soil contains little iodine, cases of cretinism were once commonplace. In fact, the soils of many inland areas on all continents are iodine deficient, and plants and animals grown there are correspondingly deficient. Populations living in such areas without outside food sources are therefore at high risk for the development of iodine deficiency diseases (Gaitan & Dunn, 1992).

Fortunately, the addition of iodine to table salt has virtually eliminated cretinism in developed countries. Furthermore, early detection of thyroid insufficiency in newborns and administration of thyroxine (T_4) can often be effective in reinstating thyroid function and normal growth and development. Nevertheless, in developing nations without such programs, the lack of dietary iodine remains the leading cause of preventable mental retardation in babies and small children.

Global Impact of Iodine Deficiency

Following the pioneering research of David Marine in the early 20th century, confirming evidence of the chemopreventive value of supplemental iodine soon became available from studies in Sweden,

Table 21.1	Effects of Sodium Iodide Supplementation in School Girls of Northern Ohio	
Size of Thyroid	**Treatment Group**	**Control Group**
Initially normal	$n = 908$	$n = 1,257$
Unchanged	906 (99.8%)	910 (72.4%)
Enlarged	2 (0.2%)	347 (27.6%)
Initially enlarged	$n = 1,282$	$n = 1,048$
Unchanged	506 (39.5%)	755 (72.0%)
Increased	3 (0.2%)	148 (14.1%)
Decreased	773 (60.3%)	145 (13.8%)

Source: Data from Marine, D., & Kimball, O. P. (1920). The prevention of simple goiter in man: Fourth paper. *Archives of Internal Medicine, 25*, 661–672.

Switzerland, and many other nations. In the United States, iodized table salt containing 100 milligrams per kilogram of potassium iodide has been available since 1924. The U.S. Food and Drug Administration recommends 150 micrograms of iodine per day for both men and women.

Supplementing the diet with iodized salt is a simple, cost-effective method of ensuring adequate iodine intake, and successful population-based programs have increased around the world with the active encouragement and support of the World Health Organization (Holman & McCartney, 1960). According to recent survey data from the World Health Organization, 164 countries now have iodized salt programs, and the percentage of households in the developing world that use iodized salt rose from about 20% in 1970 to 70% in 2000. Nevertheless, these estimates also suggest that iodine deficiency impacts approximately 2 billion people worldwide and causes a high burden of disease in many developing nations. For example, in India, it is estimated that 100 million suffer from iodine deficiency, 4 million from goiter, and 500,000 from cretinism. Other pockets of iodine deficiency are evident in the Western Pacific, Southeast Asia, Africa, and the Russian Federation (Andersson, Takkouche, Egli, Allen, & de Benoist, 2005). Continuing international efforts should therefore focus on implementing and sustaining iodine supplementation programs in all nations (*Lancet*, 2008).

Iodine Deficiency and Thyroid Cancer

In 1928, the German pathologist Carl Wegelin published a report suggesting that the prevalence of occult thyroid carcinoma was 10-fold higher at autopsy among decedents from areas endemic for goiter versus those from nonendemic areas (Wegelin, 1928). Early epidemiologic data from the canton of Zurich in Switzerland provided supportive evidence of a link between iodine deficiency and thyroid cancer. Prior to the introduction of iodized salt, prevalence estimates of goiter in this region approached 100%, and up to 30% of young men were unfit for military service owing to the presence of large goiters (Bürgi, Supersaxo, & Selz, 1990; Wespi-Eggenberger, 1948). Following the introduction of iodized salt in 1923, goiters virtually disappeared in newborns and schoolchildren, and the mortality from thyroid cancer in the canton of Zurich gradually declined (the mortality rate for men was 2.1 per 100,000 before 1925, 1.4 during 1926–1935, and 0.6 after 1935), suggesting that iodized salt may have prevented not only goiter, but also thyroid cancer in this population (Wynder, 1952).

Recent ecologic studies of the two predominant histological types of thyroid cancer, papillary and follicular carcinoma, suggest there may be an inverse association with iodine levels; that is, follicular thyroid carcinoma is associated with iodine deficiency whereas papillary thyroid carcinoma is associated with iodine overload. In Poland, suspension of iodine prophylaxis (removal of iodized salt) in 1980 resulted in a rise in the incidence of follicular thyroid cancer whereas restoration of iodine prophylaxis produced a fall in the incidence of follicular tumors but a corresponding rise in the incidence of papillary tumors (Huszno et al., 2003).

Investigators in Northern California studied iodine intake and thyroid cancer in a retrospective study of 608 women with thyroid cancer and 558 age-matched controls from the same area. There were too few follicular cancers for evaluation (28 cases), so the analysis was limited to cases with papillary thyroid carcinoma. As expected, risk increases were noted for radiation exposure to the head and neck (OR = 2.3), history of goiter or thyroid nodules (OR = 3.7), and family history of thyroid disorders (OR = 2.5). After adjustment for these established risk factors, total dietary iodine intake was found to be *inversely* related to the risk of developing papillary thyroid cancer (e.g., OR = 0.49 for the highest versus the lowest quintile of intake). This protective effect of dietary iodine was primarily due to higher daily consumption of multivitamin pills containing 150 micrograms of iodine by women in the control group. Based on these findings, the investigators suggest that *moderately* high levels of dietary iodine may help *reduce* the risk of papillary thyroid cancer, possibly by maintaining normal thyroid levels of thyroxine and TSH. They also note that extraordinarily high levels of iodine consumption, which have resulted in substantially increased rates of papillary thyroid cancer in specific populations (e.g., Japanese consuming over 200 mg/day of iodine from seaweed), are more than 20 times higher than the average consumption among women in the highest quintile of iodine intake among the women in their study (Horn-Ross et al., 2001).

Iodine Overload and Thyroid Disease

In 1963, iodine prophylaxis was introduced into the severe goiter-endemic area in Salta, Argentina. Incident cases of thyroid cancer ascertained during the 15-year period before prophylaxis (59 cases) were compared to incident cases in the 16-year period after prophylaxis (85 cases). The relative frequency of papillary thyroid carcinomas rose by 80% after intervention, and thyroiditis was more frequent in patients with papillary carcinoma compared to those with nonpapillary tumors (35% versus 6%). Furthermore, three non-Hodgkin's B cell lymphomas were detected in the postintervention period, all in women over the age of 50 years. Numbers of incident cases of follicular and medullary carcinomas detected in the two periods were similar. These results indicate that high dietary intake of iodine may be associated with the development of thyroiditis, papillary thyroid carcinoma, and thyroid lymphoma (Harach, Escalante, & Day, 2002; Harach & Williams, 1995).

It is well established that excessive iodine intake is associated with thyroid autoimmunity. Several large population-based studies have demonstrated higher prevalence rates of individuals with thyroid auto-antibodies in populations in which iodine intake was supplemented. In an epidemiologic study conducted in Slovenia, 676 13-year-old schoolchildren were followed over a period of 10 years after a mandatory governmental increase in the level of iodized salt from 10 milligrams to 25 milligrams of potassium iodide per kilogram. At baseline, thyroid volume was measured by ultrasound, and the iodine concentration was measured in urine samples. During the follow-up period, all incident cases of thyroid disease among Slovenian adults were examined by ultrasonography combined with measurement of serum levels of TSH, thyroid hormones, and antibodies to thyroglobulin and thyroid peroxidase. After the increase in iodine supplementation, the prevalence of goiter among children was reduced from 11% to 1%, corresponding to average increases in urinary iodine and decreases in thyroid volume. Among adults, the incidence of diffuse goiter gradually decreased by about 80%, from 35 per 100,000 in 1999 to 7 per 100,000 in 2009, and the incidence of Graves' disease was stable throughout the follow-up period. Conversely, the incidence of solitary and multinodular goiter increased by about 60%, from 30 per 100,000 to 48 per 100,000, and the incidence of Hashimoto's thyroiditis more than doubled (from 73 per 100,000 in 1999 to 166 per 100,000 in 2009) (Zaletel et al., 2011).

These results, and those of several other studies, suggest that iodine prophylaxis effectively changes the pattern of thyroid cancer. In iodine-deficient populations, iodine prophylaxis appears to shift the incidence of papillary thyroid carcinoma upwards while decreasing the incidence of follicular carcinomas. Most studies have found increases in the incidence of Hashimoto's thyroiditis, hypothyroidism, and corresponding thyroid auto-antibodies following increased salt iodization. Nevertheless, additional studies are needed to clarify the role of iodine intake and dosage in the prevention versus pathogenesis of thyroid cancer in different populations (Knobel & Medeiros-Neto, 2007).

GOITROGENIC DIETARY FACTORS AND THYROID DISORDERS

Goitrogens are dietary agents that suppress thyroid function and induce the formation of goiters, particularly in children. The principal goitrogens are isothiocyanate and the isoflavones (a class of phytoestrogens). These compounds inhibit the activity of thyroxine peroxidase, a key enzyme in the formation of thyroid hormones from iodine and tyrosine. Cruciferous vegetables such as broccoli, cauliflower, and cabbage contain high levels of isothiocyanate. Other sources include peanuts, spinach, peaches, and strawberries (Vanderpas, 2006). Soybeans and soy-based products contain high concentrations of isoflavones (Doerge & Sheehan, 2002).

Thiocyanate overload from consumption of cassava root has been found to be goitrogenic in Central Africa, particularly in association with selenium deficiency. The cassava root has low concentrations of iodine and selenium and high concentrations of isothiocyanate. Thilly and colleagues investigated dietary factors and thyroid disorders in children ages 5–7 years from goiter-endemic areas of Central Africa. Low serum levels of thyroxine (T_4) were associated with low selenium and high thiocyanate levels in children residing in regions where cassava is the principal source of carbohydrates in the diet. Furthermore, high rates of cretinism were observed among children with severe iodine and selenium deficiencies in combination with thiocyanate overload (Thilly et al., 1993).

High consumption of soy has also been linked to thyroid disorders in children. Early case reports document goiter development in infants on a soy diet (Hydovitz, 1960). Fort and colleagues studied 59 children with autoimmune thyroid disease, their 76 healthy siblings, and 54 healthy unrelated children. They found that the frequency of feedings with soy-based milk formulas in early life (31%) was significantly higher in children with autoimmune thyroid disease compared to healthy siblings and unrelated children (12%) (Fort, Moses, & Fasano, 1990). Thus, despite some beneficial health effects of soy, the issue of goitrogenic impact remains problematic.

MEDULLARY THYROID CANCER

Medullary thyroid cancer arises from the parafollicular calcitonin-secreting cells of the thyroid gland. Although the majority of cases are sporadic (nonfamilial), approximately 25% involve heritable mutations of the *RET* gene, a proto-oncogene located on chromosome 10 (Donis-Keller et al., 1993; Eng, 1999). The *RET* gene encodes a cell membrane receptor called *receptor tyrosine kinase* that activates signal transduction and complex cascades of biochemical reactions involving tyrosine phosphorylation within cells. The exact nature of these reactions depends upon the cell type (e.g., in parafollicular C cells, *RET* signaling induces excess biosynthesis of calcitonin).

Mutations of the *RET* gene or the *MENIN* gene (a tumor suppressor gene located on chromosome 11) cause distinct heritable syndromes known as *multiple endocrine neoplasia (MEN)* (Donis-Keller et al., 1993; Guru et al., 1998). Endocrine tumors of the MEN syndromes elaborate a variety of amines and peptides, depending on the tissue of origin. Individuals who manifest MEN syndromes are classified into two major groups: *MEN I* (adenomas of the pituitary gland, islet cell tumors of the pancreas, hyperplasia of the parathyroid glands, and peptic ulcers) and *MEN II* (medullary thyroid carcinoma, pheochromocytoma, and occasionally mucocutaneous neuroma). These syndromes show an autosomal dominant inheritance pattern (Carney, 1998; Werner, 1963).

Carriers of certain mutated forms of the *RET* gene have a high lifetime risk of developing medullary thyroid carcinoma and pheochromocytoma (a malignant tumor of the adrenal glands). The familial association of medullary thyroid cancer and pheochromocytoma is called the *Sipple syndrome* after the physician who first described it (Sipple, 1961). Early onset, typically between 15 and 20 years of age, is a prominent characteristic of hereditary medullary thyroid cancer.

PREVENTION AND THERAPY OF THYROID CANCER

Strategies for the primary prevention of thyroid cancer include total avoidance of radiation exposure to the head and neck, maintenance of normal thyroid function by sufficient intake of iodine, and avoidance of goitrogens in the diet (e.g., soy products). For high-risk individuals, particularly those with a family or medical history of thyroid disorders, regular checkups by ultrasonography to detect nodules and other abnormalities of the thyroid gland may be advisable.

Fortunately, early detection of thyroid malignancies coupled with complete excision is usually curative. The 5-year survival rates for patients with stage I disease exceed 95%. Total thyroidectomy is the definitive surgery, followed by replacement of thyroid hormones with thyroxine (T_4). Graves' disease and Hashimoto's thyroiditis are often treated with oral doses of radioactive iodine, resulting in permanent destruction of cells in the thyroid and rendering them permanently inactive. Another treatment option for these conditions is surgery in which the thyroid gland is partially or fully removed. Patients who undergo thyroid ablation or thyroidectomy receive daily replacement thyroid hormone therapy.

EPIDEMIOLOGY OF PARATHYROID CANCER

Parathyroid cancer is extremely rare, accounting for about 1% of all cases of parathyroidism and only 0.005% of all cancers. Virtually all parathyroid tumors secrete parathyroid hormone (PTH) and thus cause hypercalcemia.

During 1988–2003, 224 cases of parathyroid cancer were identified from the SEER system of tumor registries in the United States. Cases were equally distributed among men and women, and most (75%) were diagnosed between 45 and 80 years of age. The crude incidence rates appeared to increase slightly over time, from 3.6 cases per 10 million in 1988–1991 to 5.7 cases per 10 million in 2000–2003 (Lee, Jarosek, Virnig, Evasovich, & Tuttle, 2007).

In a long-term study of incident cases diagnosed during 1958–2010 in Australia, 18 of the 21 cases identified were diagnosed during the last 5 years of the study. Possible reasons for the dramatic increase in new cases of parathyroid cancer include increased detection due to ultrasonography and fine needle aspiration, improved techniques of head and neck surgery, and immunohistochemistry for a protein called *parafibromin* (Brown et al., 2011).

The majority of parathyroid tumors are sporadic, but approximately 5% are associated with autosomal dominant hereditary cancer syndromes, including MEN I and MEN II, familial hyperparathyroidism, and a rare syndrome called *hyperparathyroidism jaw tumor syndrome (HPT-JT)*.

Carpten and colleagues at the U.S. National Institutes of Health discovered that HPT-JT is caused by germline mutations of a gene called *HRPT2* located on chromosome 1. The *HRPT2* gene encodes a protein called *parafibromin* that may help regulate cell division. In this syndrome, individuals develop hypercalcemia, jaw tumors, and renal lesions in childhood or early adulthood. Individuals with mutant forms of *HRPT2* have an increased risk of parathyroid cancer. Mutations of *HRPT2* were found in 14 affected families, all of which were thought to cause deficient or impaired function of parafibromin (Carpten et al., 2002).

Additional studies have confirmed the role of *HRPT2* mutations in the development of parathyroid cancer. Shattuck and colleagues identified *HRPT2* mutations in 10 of 15 sporadic parathyroid carcinomas thought to inactivate parafibromin protein (Shattuck et al., 2003), and Howell and colleagues found *HRPT2* mutations in 11 of 60 parathyroid tumors, 4 of 4 sporadic tumors, 5 of 5 tumors from patients with HPT-JT, and 2 tumors from patients with familial hyperparathyroidism (Howell et al., 2003). Mutations in the *MEN I* and *MEN II* genes have also been identified in both familial and sporadic parathyroid tumors. These genes are found primarily in medullary tumors of the thyroid gland (Carney, 1998).

Other than genetic susceptibility linked to mutant forms of *HRPT2*, *MEN I*, and *MEN II*, risk factors associated with the development of parathyroid cancer have not been identified. Hyperparathyroidism has been observed in patients irradiated for acne or other disorders, and radiation exposure may also be a risk factor for parathyroid neoplasia (Brown et al., 2011). Nevertheless, there are currently no case reports of irradiation-induced parathyroid cancer.

• • • REFERENCES

Andersson, M., Takkouche, B., Egli, I., Allen, H. E., & de Benoist, B. (2005). Current global iodine status and progress over the last decade towards the elimination of iodine deficiency. *Bulletin of the World Health Organization, 83*(7), 518–525.

Azizi, G., Malchoff, C. D. (2011). Three-dimensional ultrasound images and fine-needle aspiration biopsy of a thyroid nodule. *Endocr Pract, 17*(4), 659-661.

Baldwin, D. B., & Rowett, D. (1978). Incidence of thyroid disorders in Connecticut. *Journal of the American Medical Association, 239*, 742–744.

Barb, D., Pazaitou-Panayiotou, K., & Mantzoros, C. S. (2006). Adiponectin: A link between obesity and cancer. *Expert Opinions in Investigative Drugs, 15*, 917–931.

Barr, M. L., & Bertram, E. G. (1949). A morphological distinction between neurones of the male and female, and the behaviour of the nucleolar satellite during accelerated nucleoprotein synthesis. *Nature, 63*(4148), 676–677.

Belfiore, A., Russo, D., Vigneri, R., & Filetti, S. (2001). Graves' disease, thyroid nodules and thyroid cancer. *Clinical Endocrinology, 55*(86), 711–718.

Boi, F., Minerba, L., Lai, M. L., Marziani, B., Figus, B., Spanu, F., . . . Mariotti, S. (2013). Both thyroid autoimmunity and increased serum TSH are independent risk factors for malignancy in patients with thyroid nodules. *Journal of Endocrinological Investigation, 36*(5), 313–320.

Boice, J. D. Jr. (1998). Radiation and thyroid cancer: What more can be learned? *Acta Oncologica, 37*, 321–324.

Boice, J. D. Jr. (2006). Thyroid disease 60 years after Hiroshima and 20 years after Chernobyl. *Journal of the American Medical Association, 295*, 1060–1062.

Brent, G. (2008). Graves' disease. *New England Journal of Medicine, 358*, 2594–2605.

Brix, T. H., Kyvik, K. O., Christensen, K., & Hegedus, L. (2001). Evidence for a major role of heredity in Graves' disease: A population-based study of two Danish twin cohorts. *Journal of Clinical Endocrinology and Metabolism, 86*, 930–934.

Brown, S., O'Neill, C., Suliburk, J., Sidhu, S., Sywak, M., Gill, A., . . . Delbridge, L. (2011). Parathyroid carcinoma: Increasing incidence and changing presentation. *ANZ Journal of Surgery, 81*(7–8), 528–532.

Bürgi, H., Supersaxo, Z., & Selz, B. (1990). Iodine deficiency diseases in Switzerland one hundred years after Theodor Kocher's survey: A historical review with some new goiter prevalence data. *Acta Endocrinologica (Copenhagen), 123*(6), 577–590.

Cardis, E., Kesminiene, A., Ivanov, V., Malakhova, I., Shibata, Y., Khrouch, V., . . . Williams, D. (2005). Risk of thyroid cancer after exposure to ^{131}I in childhood. *Journal of the National Cancer Institute, 97*, 724–732.

Carney, J. A. (1998). Familial multiple endocrine neoplasia syndromes: Components, classification, and nomenclature. *Journal of Internal Medicine, 243*(6), 425–432.

Carpten, J. D., Robbins, C. M., Villablanca, A., Forsberg, L., Presciuttini, S., Bailey-Wilson, J., . . . Hobbs, M. R. (2002). *HRPT2*, encoding parafibromin, is mutated in hyperparathyroidism-jaw tumor syndrome. *Nature Genetics, 32*(4), 676–680.

Chambers, C. A., & Allison, J. P. (1997). Co-stimulation in T cell responses. *Current Opinion in Immunology, 9*, 396–404.

Chinnappa, P., Taguba, L., Arciaga, R., Faiman, C., Siperstein, A., Mehta, A. E., . . . Gupta, M. K. (2004). Detection of thyrotropin-receptor messenger ribonucleic acid (mRNA) and thyroglobulin mRNA transcripts in peripheral blood of patients with thyroid disease: Sensitive and specific markers for thyroid cancer. *Journal of Clinical Endocrinology and Metabolism, 89*(8), 3705–3709.

Chistiakov, D. A. (2005). Immunogenetics of Hashimoto's thyroiditis. *Journal of Autoimmune Diseases, 2*, 1–10.

Chistiakov, D. A., & Turakulov, R. I. (2003). *CTLA-4* and its role in autoimmune thyroid disease. *Journal of Molecular Endocrinology, 31*, 21–36.

Costenbader, K. H., & Karlson, E. W. (2006). Cigarette smoking and autoimmune disease: What can we learn from epidemiology? *Lupus, 15*, 737–745.

Dailey, M. E., Lindsay, S., & Skahen, R. (1955). Relation of thyroid neoplasms to Hashimoto disease of the thyroid gland. *Archives of Surgery, 70*, 291–297.

Davies, L., & Welch, H. G. (2006). Increasing incidence of thyroid cancer in the United States, 1973-2002. *Journal of the American Medical Association, 295*(18), 2164–2167.

Doerge, D. R., & Sheehan, D. M. (2002). Goitrogenic and estrogenic activity of soy isoflavones. *Environmental Health Perspectives, 110*(Suppl 3), 349–353.

Donis-Keller, H., Dou, S., Chi, D., Carlson, K. M., Toshima, K., Lairmore, T. C., . . . Wells, S. A. Jr. (1993). Mutations in the RET proto-oncogene are associated with MEN 2A and FMTC. *Human Molecular Genetics, 2*(7), 851–856.

Duffy, B. J. Jr., & Fitzgerald, P. J. (1950). Cancer of the thyroid in children: A report of 28 cases. *Journal of Clinical Endocrinology and Metabolism, 10*, 1296–1308.

Eng, C. (1999). RET proto-oncogene in the development of human cancer. *Journal of Clinical Oncology, 17*(1), 380–393.

Farid, N. R., Stone, E., & Johnson, G. (1980). Graves' disease and HLA: Clinical and epidemiologic associations. *Clinical Endocrinology (Oxford), 13*, 535–544.

Fellman, K., Wojtowicz, M., & Pawlaczyk, B. (1968). [Thyroid cancer with thyroidal cretinism in an 13-year-old girl.] *Endokrynologia Polska, 19*(6), 605–609.

Ferlay, J., Bray, F., Pisani, P., & Parkin, D. M. (2004). *GLOBOCAN 2002. Cancer incidence, mortality, and prevalence worldwide. IARC Cancer Base No. 5, version 2.0.* Lyon, France: IARC Press.

Ferlay, J., Shin, H. R., Forman, D., Mathers, C., & Parkin, D. M. (2010). Estimates of worldwide burden of cancer in 2008. *International Journal of Cancer, 127*(12), 2893–2917.

Ferlay, J., Soerjomataram, I., Ervik, M., Dikshit, R., Eser, S., Mathers, C., . . . Bray, F. (2013). *GLOBOCAN 2012 v1.0. Cancer incidence and mortality worldwide: IARC CancerBase No. 11* [Internet]. Lyon, France: International Agency for Research on Cancer. Retrieved from http://globocan.iarc.fr

Fort, P., Moses, N., & Fasano, M. (1990). Breast and soy-formula feedings in early infancy and the prevalence of autoimmune thyroid disease in children. *Journal of the American College of Nutrition, 9*, 164–167.

Franceschi, S., Preston-Martin, S., Dal Maso, L., Negri, E., La Vecchia, C., Mack, W. J., . . . Ron, E. (1999). A pooled analysis of case-control studies of thyroid cancer. IV. Benign thyroid diseases. *Cancer Causes and Control, 10*(6), 583–595.

Fujimoto, Y., Yamamoto, T., Numata, J., & Mori, K. (1959). Two autopsy cases of thyroid cancer in young atomic bomb survivors. *Journal of the Hiroshima Medical Association, 12,* 519–524.

Gaitan, E., & Dunn, J. T. (1992). Epidemiology of iodine deficiency. *Trends in Endocrinology and Metabolism, 3*(5), 170–175.

Goodman, M. T., Kolonel, L. N., & Wilkens, L. R. (1992). The association of body size, reproductive factors and thyroid cancer. *British Journal of Cancer, 66*(6), 1180–1184.

Goodman, M. T., Yoshizawa, C. N., & Kolonel, L. N. (1988). Descriptive epidemiology of thyroid cancer in Hawaii. *Cancer (Phila.), 61,* 1272–1281.

Guru, S. C., Manickam, P., Crabtree, J. S., Olufemi, S. E., Agarwal, S. K., & Debelenko, L. V. (1998). Identification and characterization of the multiple endocrine neoplasia type 1 (*MEN1*) gene. *Journal of Internal Medicine, 243*(6), 433–439.

Harach, H. R., Escalante, D. A., & Day, E. S. (2002). Thyroid cancer and thyroiditis in Salta, Argentina: A 40-yr study in relation to iodine prophylaxis. *Endocrine Pathology, 13*(3), 175–181.

Harach, H. R., & Williams, E. D. (1995). Thyroid cancer and thyroiditis in the goitrous region of Salta, Argentina, before and after iodine prophylaxis. *Clinical Endocrinology, 43*(6), 701–706.

Hashimoto, H. (1912). Report on lymphomatous goiter. *Archiv für klinische Chirurgie, Berlin, 97,* 219–248.

Hemminki, K., Li, X., Sundquist, J., & Sundquist, K. (2010). The epidemiology of Graves' disease: Evidence of a genetic and an environmental contribution. *Journal of Autoimmunity, 34*(3), J307–J313.

Herman-Bonert, V., & Friedman, T. C. (2004). The thyroid gland. In C. C. J. Carpenter, R. C. Griggs, & J. Loscalzo (Eds.), *Cecil essentials of medicine* (6th ed., pp. 593–602). Philadelphia: W. B. Saunders.

Holman, J. C. M., & McCartney, W. (1960). Iodized salt. In *Endemic goitre,* 1960 (pp. 411–441). Geneva, Switzerland: World Health Organization.

Horn-Ross, P. L., Morris, S., Lee, M., West, D. W., Whittemore, A. S., McDougall, I. R., . . . Krone, M. R. (2001). Iodine and thyroid cancer risk among women in a multiethnic population, The Bay Area Thyroid Cancer Study. *Cancer Epidemiology, Biomarkers and Prevention, 20,* 979–985.

Howell, V. M., Haven, C. J., Kahnoski, K., Khoo, S. K., Petillo, D., Chen, J., . . . Teh, B. T. (2003). *HRPT2* mutations are associated with malignancy in sporadic parathyroid tumours. *Journal of Medical Genetics, 40*(9), 657–663.

Huszno, B., Szybiński, Z., Przybylik-Mazurek, E., Stachura, J., Trofimiuk, M., Buziak-Bereza, M., . . . Pantoflinski, J. (2003). Influence of iodine deficiency and iodine prophylaxis on thyroid cancer histotypes and incidence in endemic goiter area. *Journal of Endocrinological Investigation, 26*(2 Suppl), 71–76.

Hydovitz, J. D. (1960). Occurrence of goiter in an infant on a soy diet. *New England Journal of Medicine, 262,* 351–353.

Jacobson, E. M., Huber, A., & Tomer, Y. (2008). The HLA gene complex in thyroid autoimmunity: From epidemiology to etiology. *Journal of Autoimmunity, 30*(1–2), 58–62.

Jacobson, E. M., & Tomer, Y. (2007a). The *CD40, CTLA-4,* thyroglobulin, TSH receptor, and *PTPN22* gene quintet and its contribution to thyroid autoimmunity: Back to the future. *Journal of Autoimmunity, 28*(2–3), 85–98.

Jacobson, E. M., & Tomer, Y. (2007b). The genetic basis of thyroid autoimmunity. *Thyroid, 17,* 949–961.

Kim, E. S., Baek, L. D. J., Lee, J. M., Kim, M. K., Kwon, H. S., Song, K. H., . . . Son, H. Y. (2010). Thyroglobulin antibody is associated with increased cancer risk in thyroid nodules. *Thyroid, 30*(9), 885–891.

Knobel, M., & Medeiros-Neto, G. (2007). Relevance of iodine intake as a reputed predisposing factor for thyroid cancer. *Archives of Endocrinology and Metabolism, 51*(5), 701–712.

Kolonel, L. N., Hankin, J. H., Wilkens, L. R., Fukunaga, F. H., & Hinds, M. W. (1990). An epidemiologic study of thyroid cancer in Hawaii. *Cancer Causes and Control, 1*(3), 223–234.

Kraimps, J. L., Bouin-Pineau, M. H., Mathonnet, M., De Calan, L., Roncery, J., Visset, J., . . . Barbier, J. (2000). Multicentre study of thyroid nodules in patients with Graves' disease. *British Journal of Surgery, 87,* 1111–1113.

Kumar, V., Abbas, A. K., & Aster, J. C. (2014). *Robbins and Cotran pathologic basis of disease* (9th ed.). Philadelphia, PA: Mosby & Saunders.

Kurylowicz, A., Ramos-Lopez, E., Bednarczuk, T., & Badenhoop, K. (2006). Vitamin D-binding protein (DBP) gene polymorphism is associated with Graves' disease and the vitamin D status in a Polish population study. *Experimental and Clinical Endocrinology and Diabetes, 114*(6), 329–335.

Lancet. (2008). Iodine deficiency—Way to go yet. *372*(9633), 88.

Lee, J.-H., Younghye, K., Choi, J.-W., & Kim, Y.-S. (2013). The association between papillary thyroid carcinoma and histologically proven Hashimoto's thyroiditis: A meta-analysis. *European Journal of Endocrinology, 168,* 343–349.

Lee, P. K., Jarosek, S. L., Virnig, B. A., Evasovich, M., & Tuttle, T. M. (2007). Trends in the incidence and treatment of parathyroid cancer in the United States. *Cancer, 109*(9), 1736–1741.

Lepez, T., Vandewoestyne, M., & Deforce, D. (2013). Fetal microchimeric cells in autoimmune thyroid diseases. *Chimerism, 4*(4), 111–118.

Levi, F., Franceschi, S., Te, V.-C., Negri, E., & La Vecchia, C. (1990). Descriptive epidemiology of thyroid cancer in the Swiss canton of Vaud. *Journal of Cancer Research and Clinical Oncology, 116,* 639–647.

Levinson, W. (2006). Major histocompatibility complex and transplantation. In *Review of medical microbiology and immunology* (9th ed., pp. 434–439). New York, NY: McGraw-Hill.

Lyon, M. F. (1961). Gene action in the X-chromosome of the mouse (*Mus musculus L.*). *Nature, 190*(4773), 372–373.

Manji, N., Carr-Smith, J. D., Boelaert, K., Allahabadia, A., Armitage, M., Chatterjee, V. K., . . . Franklyn, J. A. (2006). Influences of age, gender, smoking, and family history on autoimmune thyroid disease phenotype. *Journal of Clinical Endocrinology and Metabolism, 91,* 4873–4880.

Marine, D. (1907). On the occurrence and physiological nature of glandular hyperplasia of the thyroid (dog and sheep), together with remarks on important clinical (human) problems. *Johns Hopkins Bulletin, 18,* 359–365.

Marine, D. (1914). Further observations and experiments on goitre (so called thyroid carcinoma) in brook trout (*Salvelinus fontinalis*). *Journal of Experimental Medicine, 19,* 70–88.

Marine, D. (1924). Etiology and prevention of simple goiter. In *Harvey Lectures Series* (Vol. 19, pp. 96–122). Philadelphia, PA: Lippincott.

Marine, D., & Kimball, O. P. (1917). The prevention of simple goiter in man. *Journal of Laboratory and Clinical Medicine, 3,* 40–48.

Marine, D., & Kimball, O. P. (1920). The prevention of simple goiter in man: Fourth paper. *Archives of Internal Medicine, 25,* 661–672.

Marine, D., & Williams, W. W. (1908). The relation of iodine to the structure of the thyroid gland. *Archives of Internal Medicine, 1,* 349–384.

McClure, R. D. (1935). Goiter prophylaxis with iodized salt. *Science, 82*(2129), 370–371.

McHenry, C. R., & Phitayakorn, R. (2011). Follicular adenoma and carcinoma of the thyroid gland. *Oncologist, 16*(5), 585–593.

Negri, E., Dal Maso, L., Ron, E., La Vecchia, C., Mark, S. D., Preston-Martin, S., . . . Franceschi, S. (1999). A pooled analysis of case-control studies of thyroid cancer: II. Menstrual and reproductive factors. *Cancer Causes and Control*, *10*, 143–155.

Pani, M. A., Regulla, K., Segni, M., Hofmann, S., Hüfner, M., Pasquino, A. M., . . . Badenhoop, K. (2002). A polymorphism within the vitamin D-binding protein gene is associated with Graves' disease but not with Hashimoto's thyroiditis. *Journal of Clinical Endocrinology and Metabolism*, *87*, 2564–2567.

Parkin, D. M., Bray, F., Ferlay, J., & Pisani, P. (2001). Estimating the world cancer burden: GLOBOCAN 2000. *International Journal of Cancer*, *94*, 153–156.

Parkin, D. M., Bray, F., Ferlay, J., & Pisani, P. (2005). Global cancer statistics, 2002. *CA: A Cancer Journal for Clinicians*, *55*, 74–108.

Parkin, D. M., Muir, C. S., Whelan, S. L., Gao, Y. T., Ferlay, J., & Powell, J. (1992). *Cancer incidence in five continents*. *VI.* IARC Scientific Publ. No. 120. Lyon, France: International Agency for Research on Cancer.

Parkin, D. M., Pisani, P., & Ferlay, J. (1999a). Estimates of the worldwide incidence of 25 major cancers in 1990. *International Journal of Cancer*, *80*(6), 827–841.

Parkin, D. M., Pisani, P., & Ferlay, J. (1999b). Global cancer statistics. *CA: A Cancer Journal for Clinicians*, *49*(1), 33–64.

Pellegriti, G., Belfiore, A., Giuffrida, D., Lupo, L., & Vigneri, R. (1998). Outcome of differentiated thyroid cancer in Graves' patients. *Journal of Clinical Endocrinology and Metabolism*, *83*, 2805–2809.

Pemberton, J. D., & Black, B. M. (1948). The association of carcinoma of the thyroid gland and exophthalmic goiter. *Surgery Clinics of North America*, *28*, 935–952.

Rapoport, B. (1991). Pathophysiology of Hashimoto's thyroiditis and hypothyroidism. *Annual Review of Medicine*, *42*, 91–96.

Repplinger, D., Bargren, A., Zhang, Y.-W., Adler, J., Haymart, M., & Chen, H. (2008). Is Hashimoto's thyroiditis a risk factor for papillary thyroid cancer? *Journal of Surgical Research*, *150*(1), 49–52.

Ron, E., & Brenner, A. (2010). Non-malignant thyroid disease following a wide range of radiation exposures. *Radiation Research*, *174*(6), 877–888.

Sakoda, L. C., & Horn-Ross, P. L. (2002). Reproductive and menstrual history and papillary thyroid cancer risk: The San Francisco Bay Area Thyroid Cancer Study. *Cancer Epidemiology, Biomarkers and Prevention*, *11*(1), 1–57.

Shattuck, T. M., Välimäki, S., Obara, T., Gaz, R. D., Clark, O. H., Shoback, D., . . . Arnold, A. (2003). Somatic and germ-line mutations of the *HRPT2* gene in sporadic parathyroid carcinoma. *New England Journal of Medicine*, *349*(18), 1722–1729.

Shih, M.-L., Lee, J. A., Hsieh, C.-B., Yu, J.-C., Liu, H. D., Kebebew, E., . . ., Duh, Q.-Y. (2007). Thyroidectomy for Hashimoto's thyroiditis: Complications and associated cancers. *Thyroid*, *18*(7), 729–734.

Shore, R. E., Hildreth, N., Dvoretsky, P., Pasternack, B., & Andresen, E. (1993). Benign thyroid adenomas among persons X-irradiated in infancy for enlarged thymus glands. *Radiation Research*, *134*(2), 217–223.

Sipple, J. H. (1961). The association of pheochromocytoma with carcinoma of the thyroid gland. *American Journal of Medicine*, *31*, 163.

Surveillance, Epidemiology, and End Results. *SEER Data, 1973–2007*. Bethesda, MD: U.S. National Institutes of Health, National Cancer Institute.

Tandon, N., Zhang, L., & Weetman, A. P. (1991). HLA associations with Hashimoto's thyroiditis. *Clinical Endocrinology (Oxford)*, *34*, 383–386.

Thilly, C. H., Swennen, B., Bourdoux, P., Ntambue, K., Moreno-Reyes, R., Gillies, J., & Vanderpas, J. B. (1993). The epidemiology of iodine-deficiency disorders in relation to goitrogenic factors and thyroid-stimulating-hormone regulation. *American Journal of Clinical Nutrition, 57,* 267S–270S.

Tomer, Y., Barbesino, G., Greenberg, D. A., Concepcion, E., & Davies, T. F. (1999). Mapping the major susceptibility loci for familial Graves' and Hashimoto's diseases: Evidence for genetic heterogeneity and gene interactions. *Journal of Clinical Endocrinology and Metabolism, 84,* 4656–4664.

Tunbridge, W. M. G., Evered, D. C., Hall, R., Appleton, P. A., Brewis, M., Clark, F., . . . Smith, P. A. (1977). The spectrum of thyroid disease in a community: The Whickham survey. *Clinical Endocrinology, 7,* 481–493.

Vanderpas, J. (2006). Nutritional epidemiology and thyroid hormone metabolism. *Annual Review of Nutrition, 26,* 293–322.

Vanderpump, M. P., & Tunbridge, W. M. (2002). Epidemiology and prevention of clinical and subclinical hypothyroidism. *Thyroid, 12,* 839–847.

Vasko, V. V., Gaudart, J., Allasia, C., Savcehnko, V., Di Cristofaro, J., Saji, M., . . . De Micco, C. (2004). Thyroid follicular adenomas may display features of follicular carcinoma and follicular variant of papillary carcinoma. *European Journal of Endocrinology, 151,* 779–786.

Vona-Davis, L., & Rose, D. P. (2007). Adipokines as endocrine, paracrine, and autocrine factors in breast cancer risk and progression. *Endocrine-Related Cancer, 14,* 189–206.

Wang, C., & Crapo, L. M. (1997). The epidemiology of thyroid disease and the implications for screening. *Endocrinology and Metabolism Clinics of North America, 26*(1), 189–218.

Weetman, A. P. (2000). Graves' disease. *New England Journal of Medicine, 343,* 1236–1248.

Wegelin, C. (1928). Malignant disease of the thyroid gland and its relation to goiter in man and animal. *Cancer Review, 3,* 197–213.

Werner, P. (1963). Endocrine adenomatosis and peptic ulcer in a large kindred. Inherited multiple tumors and mosaic pleiotropism in man. *American Journal of Medicine, 35,* 205–212.

Wespi-Eggenberger, H. J. (1948). Untersuchungen über das Vorkommen und die Verhütung des Neugeborenenkropfes im Einzugsgebiet des Krankenhauses Frauenfeld. *Schweizerische medizinische Wochenschrift, 78,* 130–132.

Wynder, E. L. (1952). Some practical aspects of cancer prevention. *New England Journal of Medicine, 246,* 573–582.

Yao, R., Chiu, C. G., Strugnell, S. S., Gill, S., & Wiseman, S. M. (2011). Gender differences in thyroid cancer. *Expert Reviews in Endocrinology and Metabolism, 6*(2), 215–243.

Yesilkaya, E., Koc, A., Bideci, A., Camurdan, O., Boyraz, M., Erkal, O., . . . Cinaz, P. (2008). *CTLA4* gene polymorphisms in children and adolescents with autoimmune thyroid diseases. *Genetic Testing, 12*(3), 461–464.

Zaletel, K., Gaberšček, S., Pirnat, E., Krhin, B., Hojker, S. (2011). Ten-year follow-up of thyroid epidemiology in Slovenia after increase in salt iodization. *Croatian Medical Journal, 52*(5), 615–621.

Zamani, M., Spaepen, M., Bex, M., Bouillon, R., Cassiman, J. J. (2000). Primary role of the HLA class II DRB1*0301 allele in Graves' disease. *American Journal of Medical Genetics, 95*(5), 432–437.

22

Epidemiology of Adrenal Cancer

ANATOMY AND FUNCTION OF THE ADRENAL GLANDS

The adrenal glands are bilateral triangular structures positioned above and slightly behind the kidneys. Each gland consists of the adrenal cortex and the adrenal medulla (**Figure 22.1**).

The *adrenal cortex* consists of zones of cuboidal epithelial cells that actively synthesize and secrete steroid hormones. All steroid hormones are synthesized from cholesterol. Adrenal steroids include corticosteroids (cortisol), which regulate the metabolism of protein, fat, and carbohydrates, and mineralocorticoids (aldosterone),which regulate salt and water balance. The adrenal cortex also synthesizes low levels of androgens and estrogens that help modulate masculine and feminine characteristics.

The *adrenal medulla* consists of neuroendocrine cells called *chromaffin cells*. Chromaffin cells communicate with the sympathetic nervous system by virtue of synapses with splanchnic nerves in the adrenal medulla. These cells can be visualized by staining with chromium salts. They synthesize and secrete *catecholamines*, *epinephrine* (*adrenaline*), and *norepinephrine* (*noradrenaline*), which regulate blood pressure and modulate response to stress. When the human host is endangered, the adrenal medulla releases a burst of epinephrine (adrenaline) that spurs the body's "fight or flight" response (Kumar, Abbas, & Aster, 2014).

DETECTION OF ADRENAL TUMORS

Adrenal masses are often found incidentally during imaging studies for other conditions, such as diseases of the genitourinary and/or digestive tract. Such serendipitously discovered adrenal masses are called *incidentalomas*. Most adrenal masses are benign adenomas; only a small fraction (~10%) prove to be malignant on biopsy. Definitive differentiation of benign from malignant adrenal tumors is often problematic and requires careful evaluation of structural, clinical, hormonal, cytologic, and molecular features (Grumbach et al., 2003).

Diagnostic symptoms of adrenal tumors are often related to hormonal imbalance due to hypersecretion of specific hormones by dysplastic and malignant cells. Clinical signs and symptoms of adrenal cortical tumors include Cushing's syndrome, in which

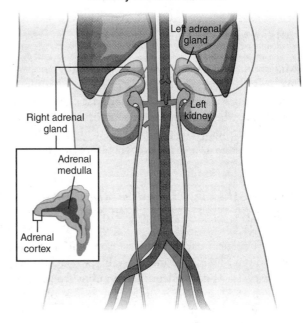

Figure 22.1 Anatomy of the Adrenal Gland.

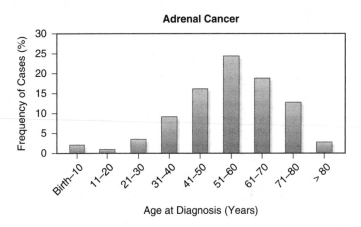

Figure 22.2 Age Distribution of Adrenal Cortical Carcinoma.

Source: Data from Kerkhofs, T. M., Verhoeven, R. H., Van der Zwan, J. M., Dieleman, J., Kerstens, M. N., Links, T. P.,... Haak, H. R. (2013). Adrenocortical carcinoma: A population-based study on incidence and survival in the Netherlands since 1993. *European Journal of Cancer,* 19(11), 2579–2586.

excessive production of cortisol influences the body's response to stress, metabolism of fat and protein, and immune function; Conn's disease, in which excessive production of aldosterone leads to increased salt retention, potassium depletion, and elevated blood pressure; and virilism due to excessive production of androgens. The dominant clinical manifestation of tumors of the adrenal medulla (neuroblastoma in children and pheochromocytoma in adults) is hypertension due to excessive production of catecholamines (epinephrine and norepinephrine). Measurement of the levels of these hormones in blood and urine aid in the differential diagnosis of adrenal tumors.

ADRENAL CORTICAL CARCINOMA

Malignant tumors that arise from the adrenal cortex are called *adrenal cortical carcinomas*. Adrenal tumors that secrete adrenal steroids are classified as functional, whereas nonsecreting tumors are classified as nonfunctional. Most adrenal cortical carcinomas (90%) secrete steroids and are therefore functional.

GLOBAL INCIDENCE AND MORTALITY OF ADRENAL CORTICAL CARCINOMA

Adrenal cortical carcinomas are rare, and accurate data on their incidence and mortality are lacking. A review of 1,891 cases identified in published reports between 1952 and 1992 found that 58.6% of cases were female, with a first peak of onset in childhood and a second peak during the fifth decade of life (Wooten & King, 1993).

In the United States, the annual incidence estimated from Surveillance, Epidemiology, and End Results (SEER) data is less than 1 case per million. Adrenal cortical carcinoma accounts for only about 0.1% of all U.S. cancer deaths (Goodman, Gurney, Smith, & Olshan, 1999). Among children younger than 15 years of age, high annual rates have been reported in southern Brazil (3–4 cases per million) compared to only 0.3 per million worldwide (Ribeiro et al., 2000; Sandrini, Ribeiro, & DeLacerda, 1997). As discussed later in this chapter, a specific germline mutation in the *p53* tumor suppressor gene is responsible for more than 90% of Brazilian childhood cases (Ribeiro et al., 2001).

In a recent population-based study conducted in the Netherlands during 1993–2010, the age-adjusted annual incidence was estimated at about 1.2 per million, and 55% of 359 cases were female. The age at diagnosis ranged from 1 to 91 years of age, with a small early peak during childhood and a much higher peak in the fifth decade of life (**Figure 22.2**). The investigators noted a slight downward trend in the incidence (from 1.3 to 1.0 per million during the period of study), but no change in survival (Kerkhofs et al., 2013).

RISK FACTORS FOR ADRENAL CORTICAL CARCINOMAS

In an exploratory study in which 176 decedent cases of adrenal cancer were compared to 352 age- and gender-matched controls, long-term use of oral contraceptives and heavy tobacco smoking were found to increase the risk of developing adrenal cortical carcinoma by approximately twofold (Hsing, Nam, Co Chien, McLaughlin, & Fraumeni, 1996).

In a subsequent study, the association between tobacco use and mortality due to adrenal cortical carcinoma was examined in a cohort of 248,046 male U.S. veterans. A total of 27 adrenal cancer deaths were observed during the period of study, 1954–1980. Relative to nonusers of any tobacco, the risk of dying from adrenal cancer was elevated more than fivefold among current cigarette smokers (relative risk [RR] = 5.1) and more than eightfold among those who smoked more than 20 cigarettes per day (RR = 8.4) (Chow, Hsing, McLaughlin, & Fraumeni, 1996).

Genetic Predisposition to Adrenal Cortical Carcinoma

Specific genetic syndromes have been identified that increase the risk of developing adrenal cortical carcinoma and several other malignant neoplasms. These include Li–Fraumeni syndrome, Beckwith–Wiedemann syndrome, Carney complex, and familial adenomatous polyposis.

Li–Fraumeni Syndrome

Li–Fraumeni syndrome is a rare hereditary condition caused by mutant forms of the *p53* tumor suppressor gene located on the short arm of chromosome 17. The protein encoded by *p53* plays a critical role in a variety of cellular processes, including cell division, DNA repair, apoptosis, response to cellular stress, and regulation of embryo implantation and fertility (Mai et al., 2012).

Multiple germline mutations of *p53* have been identified that predispose to a wide range of malignant neoplasms, including adrenal cortical carcinoma, glioma, sarcoma, and leukemia in children and cancers of the lung, breast, and lymphatic system in adults. This bizarre profile of cancers characterizes the classic Li–Fraumeni syndrome. Indeed, multigenerational pedigrees have been reported in which the risk of cancer development among carriers of such mutations approaches 100% (Schneider, Zelley, Nichols, & Garber, 1999).

In contrast to the classic Li–Fraumeni syndrome, a few *p53* mutations have been identified that show diminished penetrance and tumor development limited to specific tissues. Notably, one such *p53* mutation has been identified as the primary cause of pediatric adrenal cortical carcinomas in southern Brazil.

In the contiguous Brazilian states of São Paulo and Paraná, the incidence of adrenal cortical carcinoma in children under age 15 years is estimated at 3–4 cases per million, which is 10–15 times higher than the global incidence of this malignancy. To explore the potential role of *p53* mutations, a team of international investigators conducted a genetic study of 36 cases of childhood adrenal cortical carcinoma and members of their families ascertained from this high incidence region. Samples of DNA from cases and family members were specifically probed for *p53* mutations by polymerase chain reaction analysis. Remarkably, 35 of the 36 cases had an identical germline point mutation of the p53 gene encoding a single base pair change (*p53* mutant *R337H*). However, unlike the Li–Fraumeni syndrome, there was no excess of other cancers among family members. The investigators concluded that a single *p53* mutation is responsible for the extraordinarily high incidence of childhood adrenal cortical carcinoma in this region; nevertheless, its effect appears to be limited to the adrenal glands, in sharp contrast to the profile of malignancies observed in the classic Li–Fraumeni syndrome. They speculate that exposure to an environmental mutagen might have caused the specific germ cell mutation in this population (Ribeiro et al., 2000).

Due to the extraordinarily high incidence of pediatric adrenocortical tumors in southern Brazil, where more than 90% of patients carry the germline *p53* mutation *R337H*, free newborn screening was offered at all hospitals in the state of Paraná. Parents of positive newborns were tested, and relatives in the carrier line were offered screening. Positive newborns and their relatives under the age of 15 years were offered surveillance (periodic clinical, laboratory, and ultrasound evaluations), and adrenal cortical tumors detected by imaging were surgically resected. Of 180,000 newborns offered screening, 171,649 (95.3%) were screened and 461 were identified as carriers. Screening of relatives identified an additional 228 carriers. Surveillance resulted in early detection and successful resection of 17 adrenal cortical tumors among carriers. Cancer histories and pedigrees were also obtained for 353 families in which 48 cases of adrenal cortical carcinoma were identified among 1,704 carriers of the mutant gene. These findings provide an important example of a successful program of genetic screening and therapy for a life-threatening form of cancer in children (Custódio et al., 2013).

Beckwith–Wiedmann Syndrome

Beckwith–Wiedmann syndrome is characterized by overgrowth of certain cell populations during early human development resulting in asymmetry of legs, arms, and other bilateral structures of the body; macroglossia (large tongue); visceromegaly (enlarged abdominal organs); enlarged adrenal glands; abdominal and renal abnormalities; and hypoglycemia (low blood sugar). Children with Beckwith–Wiedmann syndrome have an approximate 20% risk of developing certain childhood cancers during the first few years of life (e.g., adrenal cortical carcinoma, neuroblastoma, retinoblastoma, Wilms tumor [nephroblastoma], and rhabdomyosarcoma). The incidence is approximately 1 per 13,700 live births (Shuman, Beckwith, Smith, & Weksberg, 2000; Weksberg, Shuman, & Smith, 2005).

Beckwith–Wiedmann syndrome has been linked to epigenetic events during childhood resulting in methylation of several genes on the short arm of chromosome 11. The affected genes encode specific growth factors, such as insulin growth factor (IGF-II), that regulate early growth and development. Overexpression of IGF-II is characteristic of adrenal cortical carcinoma in children with Beckwith–Wiedmann syndrome and is also found in 60–90% of tumor specimens from sporadic cases (Barlaskar & Hammer, 2007).

Carney Complex

The *Carney complex* is a constellation of anomalies including cardiac and cutaneous myxomas (benign tumors of connective tissue), testicular and pituitary tumors, pigmented cutaneous nodular hyperplasia, and adrenal cortical adenomas. This autosomal dominant genetic condition is caused by germline mutations in the *PRKAR1A* gene located on the long arm of chromosome 17 (Barlaskar & Hammer, 2007). The *PRKAR1A* gene encodes a subunit of the enzyme protein kinase A, which is critical for the regulation of cell division. The normal catalytic function of protein kinase A is dependent upon cyclic adenosine monophosphate (AMP) and the integrity of the *PRKAR1A* subunit. When the *PRKAR1A* gene is mutated, protein kinase A is overexpressed, which leads to uncontrolled cell proliferation and tumor formation in certain tissues (Kirschner et al., 2000).

Familial Adenomatous Polyposis

A few reports have described an association between adrenal cortical adenomas and *familial adenomatous polyposis*, a hereditary syndrome caused by a germline inactivating mutation of the *adenomatous polyposis coli (APC)* tumor suppressor gene (Gaujoux et al., 2010). The *APC* gene, which is located on the long arm of chromosome 5, regulates cadherin proteins that are involved in cell adhesion and contact inhibition of cell proliferation. Individuals who carry mutant forms of the *APC* gene develop florid adenomatous polyps of the colon and are at nearly 100% risk of developing colorectal cancer by the age of 40 years (Markowitz & Bertagnolli, 2009).

Telomerase Reverse Transcriptase (*TERT*) Mutations

A team of investigators in the Netherlands recently examined tumors of the adrenal and extra-adrenal paraganglia to assess the frequency of mutations in the promoter region of the *telomerase reverse transcriptase (TERT)* gene. They found *TERT* promoter mutations in 4 of 38 adrenal cortical carcinomas and 2 of 18 paragangliomas, whereas no mutations were found among 127 pheochromocytomas. Results suggest that activation of telomerase may be involved in the genesis of some adrenal cortical carcinomas and extra-adrenal paragangliomas (Papathomas et al., 2014).

TUMORS OF THE ADRENAL MEDULLA: NEUROBLASTOMA AND PHEOCHROMOCYTOMA

The two principal tumors of the adrenal medulla are neuroblastoma and pheochromocytoma. Both tumors arise from neuroendocrine tissues of the adrenal medulla and thus may secrete catecholamines that influence the sympathetic nervous system. Nevertheless, there are distinct differences in the clinical and pathologic features of these tumors. For example, neuroblastomas are diagnosed primarily in children whereas their counterpart, pheochromocytomas, are diagnosed in adults.

Neuroblastoma

Neuroblastomas are tumors that arise from immature neuroendocrine cells in the adrenal medulla or other neuronal tissues of the thorax or abdomen. The famous German pathologist Rudolf Virchow was the first to describe an abdominal tumor of neural tissue that developed in a child. Most neuroblastomas (~80%) are found in children before the age of 5 years, and nearly half of all cases occur before the age of 2 years. These tumors constitute about 6–10% of all childhood malignancies (Cheung & Dyer, 2013).

Neuroblastomas display unusual developmental characteristics in that they typically regress and disappear spontaneously if they appear in infants under the age of 1 year; alternatively, if they appear later in life, their prognosis is grim because they readily metastasize to other anatomic sites (e.g., bone marrow, bone, liver, brain, and lungs). Neuroblastomas secrete catecholamines, principally norepinephrine, and are thus associated with elevations in blood pressure. Unlike pheochromocytomas (discussed in the next section), neuroblastomas are *not* composed of more mature chromaffin cells that are stained brown by chromium salts.

Maternal Factors and Neuroblastoma

Because neuroblastomas are found almost exclusively in infants and children, gestational and maternal factors may be involved in their development. Preliminary studies suggest that certain gestational exposures influence the risk. These include opiates, folate deficiency, and gestational diabetes.

Investigators at the University of North Carolina evaluated associations of maternal use of specific medications during pregnancy and nursing with the risk of neuroblastoma development in offspring. The study included 504 incident cases of neuroblastoma identified from hospital records in the United States and Canada during 1992–1994 and 504 disease-free controls from the same communities. Exposure data were collected from mothers of the cases and controls by structured telephone interviews. No associations were found with maternal exposure to diuretic agents, antibiotics, estrogens, progestins, sedatives, or anticonvulsant drugs; however, there was a significant association of neuroblastoma development with maternal use of opioid agonists, particularly codeine, during pregnancy or lactation (odds ratio [OR] = 3.4) (Cook et al., 2004).

In early 1997, a program was initiated by the Canadian government to fortify cereal grains with folic acid. This intervention was aimed at reducing the rate of fetal neural tube defects and possibly other childhood conditions. Investigators at the University of Toronto examined rates of neuroblastoma before and after folate fortification in the province of Ontario, Canada. Data on incident neuroblastoma cases during 1985–2000 were retrieved from the Pediatric Oncology Group of Ontario, which captures 95% of all pediatric cancers. Time series analysis revealed a significant 61% decline in the rate of neuroblastoma from 1.57 to 0.62 cases per 10,000 live births after folic acid fortification (French et al., 2003).

Investigators at the University of Washington in Seattle conducted a population-based case control study of 240 cases of neuroblastoma and 2,400 controls ascertained from cancer registry records collected during 1980–2004. They found significant associations of neuroblastoma with major congenital abnormalities of the heart and other organs (OR = 6.9) and maternal gestational diabetes (OR = 1.8) (Chow, Friedman, & Mueller, 2007).

Genetics of Neuroblastoma

Most neuroblastomas occur sporadically in the absence of specific germline mutations or chromosomal aberrations. Exceptions include Turner syndrome (45, X genotype and gonadal dysgenesis), Hirschsprung's disease (mutant RET proto-oncogene and failure of migration of neuroblasts from the neural crest during embryogenesis), and neurofibromatosis type 1 (mutant *NF1* gene and defective neurofibromin, a protein essential for nerve development).

Alfred Knudson and Louise Strong reviewed data on the age at diagnosis and occurrence of multiple tumors in sporadic cases and familial cases of neuroblastoma and pheochromocytoma ascertained by a review of the literature. Their review included 504 sporadic and 25 familial cases of neuroblastoma and 366 sporadic and 46 familial cases of pheochromocytoma. They concluded that for both tumors, predisposed individuals do not develop a tumor until a second genetic event occurs in a somatic cell. They suggest that the data on familial incidence, age at diagnosis, and multiplicity of tumors are compatible with a two-hit mutational model of tumor development. In sporadic cases, both events occur in somatic cells whereas in familial (hereditary) cases, one mutation occurs in germinal cells and is inherited and the second occurs in somatic cells (Knudson, 1971; Knudson & Strong, 1972).

Survival of Neuroblastoma

Neuroblastomas are responsible for about 15% of deaths from cancer in children. The genetic aberration most consistently associated with poor outcome is amplification of the *N-myc* proto-oncogene, which occurs in approximately 20% of primary tumors (Slavc et al., 1990). Long-term survival in this high risk group, even with aggressive therapy, remains very low (~15%). Specific chromosomal aberrations (e.g., deletion of chromosomes 1p and 11q and gain of 17q) are also associated with poor prognosis. Stage 4S is a special category of neuroblastoma reserved for infants diagnosed before 1 year of age and who have resectable tumors and metastasis limited to the liver. Spontaneous regression of tumors in this group is high, and overall survival exceeds 85% (Brodeur, Hogarty, Mosse, & Maris, 2011).

In a recent investigation conducted by investigators of the U.S. Pediatric Cancer Genome Project, tissues from 104 patients with metastatic neuroblastoma were analyzed by polymerase chain reaction (PCR) analysis and other molecular methods to identify associated gene mutations. Notably, mutations in the α-*thalassemia/mental retardation syndrome X-linked* (*ATRX*) gene were identified in 14 of 32 tumor specimens (44%) from adolescents and young adults compared to 9 of 54 (17%) from children and 0 of 18 (0%) from infants. The *ATRX* gene encodes a protein that is intricately involved in chromatin remodeling, nucleosome assembly, and telomere maintenance. The observed *ATRX* mutations in neuroblastoma tissues were associated with the absence of the *ATRX* protein and the presence of long telomeres at the chromosomal tips. The authors suggest that the presence of *ATRX* mutations may help identify patients with progressive disease that can be targeted for new molecular therapies (Cheung et al., 2012).

Pheochromocytoma

Pheochromocytomas arise from chromaffin cells of the medulla of the adrenal gland or other anatomic sites where such cells exist in the sympathetic nervous system. Extra-adrenal pheochromocytomas (called *paragangliomas*) constitute about 10% of such tumors. These tumors are usually benign and are most often detected in adults in the age range of 20–50 years.

Pheochromocytomas hypersecrete catecholamines and thus cause marked elevations in blood pressure. Most pheochromocytomas (more than 90%) have no metastatic potential and are thus curable by excision.

Genetic Predisposition to Pheochromocytoma

A significant fraction of cases, perhaps 30%, occur in familial settings with multigenerational inheritance patterns. The most common of these hereditary conditions are von Hippel–Lindau disease (VHL) and the multiple endocrine neoplasia (MEN) syndromes.

von Hippel–Lindau (VHL) Disease   *von Hippel–Lindau disease (VHL)* is a rare, autosomal dominant genetic condition that predisposes individuals to a spectrum of benign and malignant tumors of the central nervous system and certain other tissues. The condition is caused by a germline mutation in the von Hippel–Lindau tumor suppressor gene on the short arm of chromosome 3. Carriers of the mutant gene typically develop multiple tumors, including hemangioblastomas of the retina and central nervous system, clear cell renal carcinomas, pheochromocytomas, pancreatic neuroendocrine tumors, pancreatic cysts, endolymphatic sac tumors, and epididymal papillary cystadenomas. The incidence of VHL is about 1 per 36,000 live births, and the penetrance of the mutated gene is over 90% by age 65 years (Richard, Gardie, Couvé, & Gad, 2012).

MULTIPLE ENDOCRINE NEOPLASIA (MEN) AND SIPPLE SYNDROME

Pheochromocytomas in combination with tumors of the thyroid and parathyroid glands make up a hereditary syndrome known as *multiple endocrine neoplasia (MEN)*. The MEN syndromes are caused by heritable mutations of the *MENIN* gene, a tumor suppressor gene located on chromosome 11, or the *RET* gene, a proto-oncogene located on chromosome 10 (Donis-Keller et al., 1993; Eng, 1999; Guru et al., 1998).

Endocrine tumors of the MEN syndromes elaborate a variety of amines and peptides depending upon the tissue of origin. Individuals who manifest MEN syndromes are classified into two major groups: MEN I (adenomas of the pituitary gland, islet cell tumors of the pancreas, hyperplasia of the parathyroid glands, and peptic ulcers) and MEN II (medullary thyroid carcinoma, pheochromocytoma, and occasionally mucocutaneous neuroma). These syndromes show an autosomal dominant inheritance pattern (Carney, 1998; Werner, 1963).

Mutant forms of the *MENIN* gene cause MEN I. The *MENIN* gene encodes a protein (menin) that has multiple functions within the cell nucleus. Specifically, menin regulates the transcription of certain genes involved in cell division such as telomerase reverse transcriptase (Hashimoto et al., 2008).

Mutant forms of the *RET* gene cause MEN II. The *RET* gene encodes a cell membrane receptor called receptor tyrosine kinase that activates signal transduction and complex cascades of biochemical reactions involving tyrosine phosphorylation within cells. The exact nature of these reactions depends upon the cell type; for example, in parafollicular C cells, *RET* signaling induces excess biosynthesis of calcitonin (Eng, 1999).

Carriers of certain mutated forms of the *RET* gene have a high lifetime risk of developing medullary thyroid carcinoma and pheochromocytoma. The familial association of medullary thyroid cancer (a form of thyroid carcinoma that originates from the parafollicular C cells that secrete the hormone calcitonin) and pheochromocytoma is called the *Sipple syndrome* after the physician who first described it (Sipple, 1961). Early onset, typically between 15 and 20 years of age, is a prominent characteristic of Sipple syndrome.

SUMMARY OF ADRENAL CANCER EPIDEMIOLOGY

Adrenal cancers are rare, with annual incidence rates of 1–2 per million in most populations. Adrenal tumors arise from either the cortex or the medulla of the adrenal glands. Adrenal tumors typically hypersecrete adrenal hormones specific for their cell of origin; for example, adenomas and carcinomas of the cortex secrete cortisol, aldosterone, or androgens whereas tumors of the medulla secrete catecholamines. Clinical signs and symptoms of these tumors are therefore associated with elevated levels of specific adrenal hormones.

Certain genetic syndromes caused by germline mutations are associated with the development of adrenal cortical tumors. The syndromes and mutated genes include Li–Fraumeni syndrome (*p53*), Beckwith–Wiedemann syndrome (IGF-II), Carney complex (*PRKAR1A*), and familial adenomatous polyposis (*APC*). Mutations in the promoter region of the telomerase reverse transcriptase (*TERT*) gene have also been identified in about 10% of adrenal cortical carcinomas. Chronic tobacco smoking and long-term use of oral contraceptives may also increase the risk. Notably, genetic screening for a specific germline *p53* mutation (*R337H*) conducted in southern Brazil has proven effective for the early detection and successful therapy of adrenal cortical tumors in children.

Neuroblastomas arise from immature neuroendocrine cells of the adrenal medulla. These tumors characteristically hypersecrete catecholamines that cause hypertension. They are responsible for about 15% of deaths from cancer in children. Because neuroblastomas are almost exclusively found in infants and children, gestational and maternal factors may be involved in their development. Maternal risk factors include use of opiates, folate deficiency, and gestational diabetes. Amplification of the *N-myc* proto-oncogene and disabling mutations of the X-linked *ATRX* tumor suppressor gene are associated with poor outcome in patients with neuroblastoma.

Pheochromocytomas are tumors of the adrenal medulla that arise in adults. Most pheochromocytomas (more than 90%) are benign and have no metastatic potential. Nevertheless, these tumors also hypersecrete catecholamines and thus cause marked elevations in blood pressure. A significant fraction of cases, perhaps 30%, occur in familial settings with multigenerational inheritance patterns. The most common of these hereditary conditions are von Hippel–Lindau (VHL) disease and the multiple endocrine neoplasia (MEN) syndromes.

● ● ● **REFERENCES**

Barlaskar, F. M., & Hammer, G. D. (2007). The molecular genetics of adrenal cortical carcinoma. *Reviews in Endocrine and Metabolic Disorders*, 8(4), 343–348.

Brodeur, G. M., Hogarty, M. D., Mosse, Y. P., & Maris, J. M. (2011). Neuroblastoma. In P. A. Pizzo & D. G. Poplack (Eds.), *Principles and practice of pediatric oncology* (pp. 886–922). Philadelphia, PA: Lippincott Williams & Wilkins.

Carney, J. A. (1998). Familial multiple endocrine neoplasia syndromes: Components, classification, and nomenclature. *Journal of Internal Medicine*, 243(6), 425–432.

Cheung, N. K., & Dyer, M. A. (2013). Neuroblastoma: Developmental biology, cancer genomics and immunotherapy. *Nature Reviews Cancer*, 13, 397–411.

Cheung, N. K., Zhang, J., Lu, C., Parker, M., Bahrami, A., Tickoo, S. K., . . . Dyer, M. A. (2012). Association of age at diagnosis and genetic mutations in patients with neuroblastoma. *Journal of the American Medical Association*, 307(10), 1062–1071.

Chow, E. J., Friedman, D. L., & Mueller, B. A. (2007). Maternal and perinatal characteristics in relation to neuroblastoma. *Cancer*, 109(5), 983–992.

Chow, W. H., Hsing, A. W., McLaughlin, J. K., & Fraumeni, J. F. (1996). Smoking and adrenal cancer mortality among United States veterans. *Cancer Epidemiology, Biomarkers and Prevention*, 5(2), 79–80.

Cook, M. N., Olshan, A. F., Guess, H. A., Savitz, D. A., Poole, C., Blatt, J., . . . Pollock, B. H. (2004). Maternal medication use and neuroblastoma in offspring. *American Journal of Epidemiology*, 159(8), 721–731.

Custódio, G., Parise, G. A., Kiesel Filho, N., Komechen, H., Sabbaga, C. C., Rosati, R., . . . Figueiredo, B. C. (2013). Impact of neonatal screening and surveillance for the *TP53 R337H* mutation on early detection of childhood adrenocortical tumors. *Journal of Clinical Oncology*, 31(20), 2619–2626.

Donis-Keller, H., Dou, S., Chi, D., Carlson, K. M., Toshima, K., Lairmore, T. C., . . . Wells, S. A. Jr. (1993). Mutations in the RET proto-oncogene are associated with MEN 2A and FMTC. *Human Molecular Genetics*, 2(7), 851–856.

Eng, C. (1999). RET proto-oncogene in the development of human cancer. *Journal of Clinical Oncology*, 17(1), 380–393.

French, A. E., Grant, R., Weitzman, S., Ray, J. G., Vermeulen, M. J., Sung, L., . . . Koren, G. (2003). Folic acid food fortification is associated with a decline in neuroblastoma. *Clinical Pharmacological Therapy*, 74(3), 288–294.

Gaujoux, S., Pinson, S., Gimenez-Roqueplo, A. P., Amar, L., Ragazzon, B., Launay, P., . . . Bertherat, J. (2010). Inactivation of the APC gene is constant in adrenocortical tumors from patients with familial adenomatous polyposis but not frequent in sporadic adrenocortical cancers. *Clinical Cancer Research*, 16(21), 5133–5141.

Goodman, M. T., Gurney, J. G., Smith, M. A., & Olshan, A. F. (1999). Sympathetic nervous system tumors. In L. A. Ries, M. A. Smith, J. G. Gurney, Linet, M, Young, T. T., Bunin, J. L. (Eds.), *Cancer incidence and survival among children and adolescents: United States SEER program, 1975–1995*. Bethesda, MD: National Cancer Institute.

Grumbach, M. M., Biller, B. M., Braunstein, G. D., Campbell, K. K., Carney, J. A., Godley, P. A., . . . Wieand, H. S. (2003). Management of the clinically inapparent adrenal mass ("incidentaloma"). *Annals of Internal Medicine*, 138(5), 424–429.

Guru, S. C., Manickam, P., Crabtree, J. S., Olufemi, S. E., Agarwal, S. K., & Debelenko, L. V. (1998). Identification and characterization of the multiple endocrine neoplasia type 1 (MEN1) gene. *Journal of Internal Medicine*, 243(6), 433–439.

Hashimoto, M., Kyo, S., Hua, X., Tahara, H., Nakajima, M., Takakura, M., . . . Inoue, M. (2008). Role of menin in the regulation of telomerase activity in normal and cancer cells. *International Journal of Oncology*, 33(2), 333–340.

Hsing, A. W., Nam, J. M., Co Chien, H. T., McLaughlin, J. K., & Fraumeni, J. F. Jr. (1996). Risk factors for adrenal cancer: An exploratory study. *International Journal of Cancer*, 65(4), 432–436.

Kerkhofs, T. M., Verhoeven, R. H., Van der Zwan, J. M., Dieleman, J., Kerstens, M. N., Links, T. P., . . . Haak, H. R. (2013). Adrenocortical carcinoma: A population-based study on incidence and survival in the Netherlands since 1993. *European Journal of Cancer*, 19(11), 2579–2586.

Kirschner, L. S., Carney, J. A., Pack, S. D., Taymans, S. E., Giatzakis, C., Cho, Y. S., . . . Stratakis, C. A. (2000). Mutations of the gene encoding the protein kinase A type I-alpha regulatory subunit in patients with the Carney complex. *Nature Genetics*, 26(1), 89–92.

Knudson, A. G. (1971). Mutation and cancer: Statistical study of retinoblastoma. *Proceedings of the National Academy of Sciences of the United States of America*, 68, 820–823.

Knudson, A. G. Jr, & Strong, L. C. (1972). Mutation and cancer: Neuroblastoma and pheochromocytoma. *American Journal of Human Genetics*, 24(5), 514–532.

Kumar, V., Abbas, A.K., & Aster, J. C. (2014). *Robbins and Cotran pathologic basis of disease* (9th ed.). Philadelphia, PA: Mosby & Saunders.

Mai, P. L., Malkin, D., Garber, J., Schiffman, J. D., Weitzel, J. N., Strong, L. C., . . . Savage, S. A. (2012). Li-Fraumeni syndrome: Report of a clinical research workshop and creation of a research consortium. *Cancer Genetics*, 205(10), 479–487.

Markowitz, S. D., & Bertagnolli, M. M. (2009). Molecular basis of colorectal cancer. *New England Journal of Medicine*, 361, 2449–2460.

Papathomas, T., Oudijk, L., Zwarthoff, E. C., Post, E., Duijkers, F. A., van Noesel, M., . . . Korpershoek, E. (2014). *TERT* promoter mutations in tumors originating from the adrenal gland and extra-adrenal paraganglia. *Endocrine Related Cancer*. ERC-13-0429 [Epub ahead of print].

Ribeiro, R. C., Michalkiewicz, E. L., Figueiredo, B. C., DeLacerda, L., Sandrini, F., Pianovsky, M. D., . . . Sandrini, R. (2000). Adrenocortical tumors in children. *Brazilian Journal of Medical and Biological Research*, *33*(10), 1225–1234.

Ribeiro, R. C., Sandrini, F., Figueiredo, B., Zambetti, G. P., Michalkiewicz, E., Lafferty, A. R., . . . Sandrini, R. (2001). An inherited *p53* mutation that contributes in a tissue-specific manner to pediatric adrenal cortical carcinoma. *Proceedings of the National Academy of Sciences of the United States of America*, *98*(16), 9330–9335.

Richard, S., Gardie, B., Couvé, S., & Gad, S. (2012). Von Hippel-Lindau: How a rare disease illuminates cancer biology. *Seminars in Cancer Biology*, *23*(1), 26–37.

Sandrini, R., Ribeiro, R. C., & DeLacerda, L. (1997). Childhood adrenocortical tumors. *Journal of Clinical Endocrinology and Metabolism*, *82*(7), 2027–2031.

Schneider, K., Zelley, K., Nichols, K. E., & Garber, J. (1999). Li-Fraumeni syndrome. In R. A. Pagon, M. P. Adam, H. H. Ardinger, D. Bird, C. R. Dolan, C. T. Fong, . . . K. Stephens (Eds.), *GeneReviews*. Seattle: University of Washington.

Shuman, C., Beckwith, J. B., Smith, A. C., & Weksberg, R. (2000). Beckwith-Wiedemann Syndrome. In: R. A. Pagon, M. P. Adam, H. H. Ardinger, D. Bird, C. R. Dolan, C. T. Fong, . . . K. Stephens (Eds.), *GeneReviews*. Seattle: University of Washington.

Sipple, J. H. (1961). The association of pheochromocytoma with carcinoma of the thyroid gland. *American Journal of Medicine*, *31*, 163–166.

Slavc, I., Ellenbogen, R., Jung, W. H., Vawter, G. F., Kretschmar, C., Grier, H., & Korf, B. R. (1990). *myc* gene amplification and expression in primary human neuroblastoma. *Cancer Research*, *50*, 1459–1463.

Weksberg, R., Shuman, C., & Smith, A. C. (2005). Beckwith-Wiedmann syndrome. *American Journal of Medical Genetics Part C: Seminars in Medical Genetics*, *1137C*(1), 12–23.

Werner, P. (1963). Endocrine adenomatosis and peptic ulcer in a large kindred. Inherited multiple tumors and mosaic pleiotropism in man. *American Journal of Medicine*, *35*, 205–212.

Wooten, M. D., & King, D. K. (1993). Adrenal cortical carcinoma. Epidemiology and treatment with mitotane and a review of the literature. *Cancer*, *72*(11), 3145–3155.

23

Epidemiology of Malignant Melanoma

GLOBAL EPIDEMIOLOGY OF MALIGNANT MELANOMA

During 2012, malignant melanoma of the skin was diagnosed in 232,130 individuals worldwide and caused 55,489 deaths (Ferlay et al., 2013). This potentially fatal form of skin cancer was detected slightly more frequently in men than women (120,649 new cases in men versus 111,481 in women, a male-to-female ratio of 1.08); nevertheless, the deaths from melanoma in men exceeded deaths in women by more than 30% (31,393 men and 24,096 women died from melanoma). Incidence and mortality rates of melanoma reflect a similar pattern; the incidence was 18% higher in men than women (3.3 per 100,000 in men and 2.8 per 100,000 in women), whereas the mortality was 50% higher in men (0.9 per 100,000 versus 0.6 per 100,000).

The global burden of melanoma has increased dramatically in the last decade (**Figure 23.1**). During 2000–2012, the annual number of cases increased by 45% (from 160,000 to 232,000 cases) and the annual deaths from melanoma increased by 49% (from 37,000 to 55,000 deaths).

Malignant melanoma is most common in Caucasian populations living in sunny climates. High incidence rates are observed in Caucasian populations of Australia, New Zealand, North America, Western Europe, Scandinavia, the South African Republic, Northern Chile, and Papua New Guinea (**Figure 23.2**). Melanoma incidence is particularly high (~35 per 100,000 in 2012) in Australia and New Zealand (Ferlay et al., 2010, 2013; Parkin, Bray, Ferlay, & Pisani, 2005).

Survival from malignant melanoma is nearly 100% if diagnosed prior to invasion of the dermis and metastatic spread (Balch et al., 2001). Overall, 5-year survival is 91% in the United States and 81% in Europe. Females have better survival than males, probably because the site distribution permits earlier diagnosis of noninvasive lesions that can be surgically removed prior to metastasis. Survival in developing countries is relatively poor (approximately 40%), in part due to late diagnosis and limited access to therapy, but also because melanomas often develop on the soles of the feet and thus go undetected until invasion and metastasis has occurred (Buzaid, 2004).

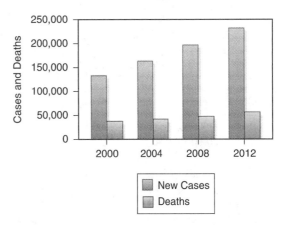

Figure 23.1 Global Trends of Malignant Melanoma, 2000–2012.

Source: Data from Ferlay, J., Shin, H. R., Forman, D., Mathers, C., & Parkin, D. M. (2010). Estimates of worldwide burden of cancer in 2008. *International Journal of Cancer, 127*(12), 2893–2917; Ferlay, J., Soerjomataram, I., Ervik, M., Dikshit, R., Eser, S., Mathers, C., . . . Bray, F. (2013). *GLOBOCAN 2012 v1.0. Cancer Incidence and Mortality Worldwide: IARC CancerBase No. 11* [Internet]. Lyon, France: International Agency for Research on Cancer. Retrieved from http://globocan.iarc.fr; Parkin, M., Bray, F., Ferlay, J., & Pisani, P. (2001). Estimating the world cancer burden: GLOBOCAN 2000. *International Journal of Cancer, 94*, 153–156; Parkin, M., Bray, F., Ferlay, J., & Pisani, P. (2005). Global cancer statistics, 2002. *CA: A Cancer Journal for Clinicians, 55*, 74–108.

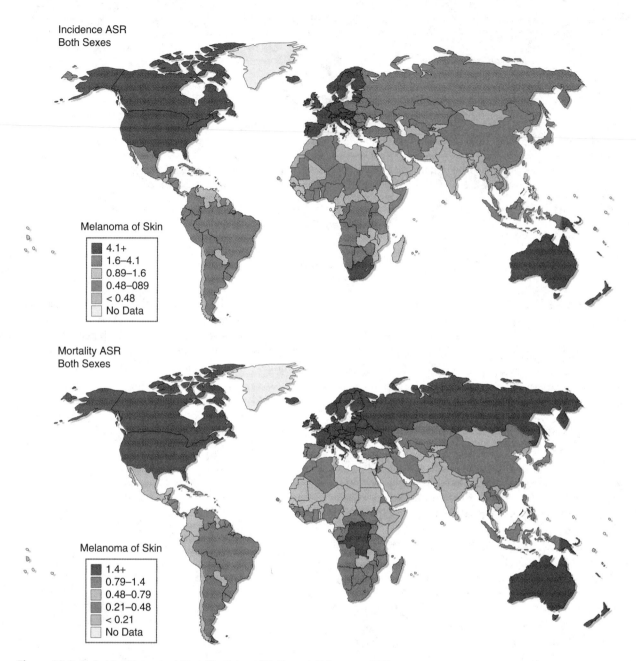

Figure 23.2 Global Incidence and Mortality Rates of Malignant Melanoma, 2012.

ASR: Rates per 100,000 are age-standardized to the world population, 2000–2025.

Source: Reproduced from Ferlay, J., Soerjomataram, I., Ervik, M., Dikshit, R., Eser, S., Mathers, C., . . . Bray, F. (2013). *GLOBOCAN 2012 v1.0. Cancer incidence and mortality worldwide: IARC CancerBase No. 11* [Internet]. Lyon, France: International Agency for Research on Cancer. Retrieved from http://globocan.iarc.fr

The global pattern of malignant melanoma reflects the interactions of susceptible genotypes and phenotypes with cumulative exposure to ionizing radiation from the sun. Due to heavy diffuse melanin skin pigmentation that forms a protective barrier against cumulative radiation damage, populations living nearest the equator are *not* at the highest risk for development of melanoma. Rather, individuals without substantial melanin pigment in the epidermis are most susceptible to cumulative damage due to ultraviolet rays and the development of this potentially fatal malignancy of the skin. The highest mortality rates are observed among the fair-skinned populations of Australia, South Africa, and certain regions of South America, and progressively lesser rates are found depending on the degree

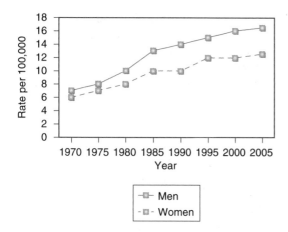

Figure 23.3 Annual Incidence of Malignant Melanoma in the United States, 1970–2005.

Incidence rates per 100,000 are age-standardized to the U.S. population in 2000.

Source: Data from Altekruse, S. F., Kosary, C. L., Krapcho, M., Neyman, N., Aminou, R., Waldron, W.,... Edwards, B. K. (Eds.). (2009). *SEER Cancer Statistics Review, 1975–2007*. Bethesda, MD: National Cancer Institute.

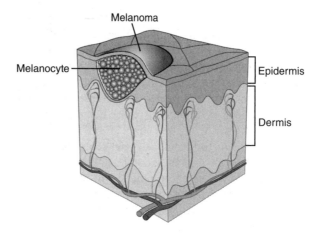

Figure 23.4 Cutaneous Malignant Melanoma.

of skin pigmentation coupled with the level of sun exposure. Furthermore, several investigators have suggested that the depletion of the ozone layer and the absence of cloud cover increase exposure to the sun and therefore heighten the risk—the Caucasian populations of Australia and New Zealand have the highest mortality, presumably as a consequence of the thinning ozone layer in the southern hemisphere over the past several decades (Carver, 1998).

In recent decades, sharp increases in incidence and mortality have been observed in both sexes in many countries, even where rates were formerly low, such as Japan. In the Nordic countries, for example, the rate of increase since 1980 has averaged approximately 30% every 5 years (Parkin et al., 2005). Similar increases are evident in the U.S. population, where the incidence of malignant melanoma has more than tripled in men and women during the last 3 decades (Altekruse et al., 2009) (**Figure 23.3**).

PATHOGENESIS OF MALIGNANT MELANOMA

The cell of origin of malignant melanoma is the melanocyte, which resides in the basal layer of the epidermis. In this location, melanocytes are in contact with keratinocytes of the epidermis. Melanocytes synthesize melanin, a brownish-black pigment that is distributed to surrounding keratinocytes through dendritic projections (Gilchrest, Eller, Geller, &

Yaar, 1999). The melanocyte population rests on a fibrous basement membrane that separates the epidermis from the dermis. When malignant melanoma first develops, the basement membrane forms a protective barrier that keeps the tumor cells confined (*in situ*). However, malignant melanocytes are unusual in their ability to breach the basement membrane and invade the underlying dermis (**Figure 23.4**). The high metastatic potential of malignant melanoma is responsible for its significant impact on cancer mortality.

Damage to melanocytes caused by ultraviolet radiation is central to the pathogenesis of malignant melanoma (Gilchrest et al., 1999). For example, patients with *xeroderma pigmentosum* have a genetically inherited defect in the repair of DNA photoproducts induced by ultraviolet radiation (Cleaver, 1968); individuals with this condition are at greatly increased risk of developing malignant melanoma as well as squamous cell and basal cell carcinomas of the skin (Lambert, Kuo, & Lambert, 1995).

Both ultraviolet A (wavelength: 320–400 nanometers) and ultraviolet B radiation (wavelength: 270–320 nanometers) have deleterious effects on the DNA of melanocytes and other cells of the skin. Ultraviolet B radiation induces the formation of pyrimidine dimers that, if incorrectly repaired, cause DNA mutations (Freeman et al., 1989). Ultraviolet A radiation causes oxidative damage to DNA that is also potentially mutagenic (Meyskens, Farmer, & Anton-Culver, 2004; Pathak, 1991).

Melanin serves *photoprotective* functions in the skin: It absorbs ultraviolet photons and reactive oxygen species generated by the interaction of photons with cell membrane lipids and other cellular components (Pathak, 1995). Within cells, melanin forms a *supranuclear protective cap* about the nucleus, thereby shielding the nuclear DNA from damaging ultraviolet radiation (Kobayashi et al., 1998). The photoprotective property of melanin is illustrated by the phenomenon of tanning in response to ultraviolet radiation. Tanning is due to enhanced proliferation of melanocytes accompanied by increased synthesis and transfer of melanin to surrounding keratinocytes (Gilchrest, Park, Eller, & Yaar, 1998).

Numerous studies suggest that repeated intense exposure to ultraviolet radiation leads to the accumulation of cancer-causing mutations in melanocytes. As discussed later in this chapter, a number of genetic mutations have already been identified that cause dysfunction in melanin biosynthesis and dissemination, cell adhesion and communication, mechanisms of DNA repair, and regulation of the cell cycle.

In addition to the potential for inducing mutagenic changes in the DNA of melanocytes, ultraviolet radiation also causes inflammation and immunosuppression in the skin, both of which may play a role in carcinogenesis as well as the metastatic spread of cancer (Gilchrest et al., 1999). Several molecular studies have noted overexpression of cyclooxygenase-2 (COX-2), the chief regulatory enzyme of the inflammatory cascade, in the progression of malignant melanoma from dysplasia to invasive cancer (Denkert et al., 2001; Goulet et al., 2003). In fact, some investigators have observed chemopreventive effects of nonsteroidal anti-inflammatory drugs against melanoma development (Gamba et al., 2013; Harris, Namboodiri, & Beebe-Donk, 2001), and selective anti-inflammatory COX-2 inhibiting agents such as celecoxib have shown significant therapeutic value in clinical trials of patients with metastatic malignant melanoma (Hakim et al., 2006).

Even low-dose ultraviolet B exposure can damage the Langerhans cells (circulating immune cells found in the epidermis) and produce significant immunosuppression (Tang & Udey, 1991). Thus, failure of the immune system to recognize and destroy malignant cells may also play a significant role in the expansion and promotion of clones of malignant melanocytes (Cruz, Paul, & Bergstresser, 1989).

A key feature in the progression of malignant melanoma is the unusual capacity of cancerous melanocytes to metastasize throughout the body. Homeostasis of the melanocytic population depends on many features of the cellular milieu in the dermis and epidermis of the skin. In particular, keratinocytes in the epidermis keep melanocytic proliferation in check, and the basement membrane prevents melanocytes from migrating into the dermis. Melanocytes that become cancerous often lose important molecules called *cadherins* that modulate cell-to-cell

adhesion and communication. Although signature mutations of malignant melanoma have not yet been identified, the metastatic potential of this form of cancer appears to be the result of complex epigenetic and genetic phenomena that result in the silencing of tumor suppressor genes (e.g., p16, *K-ras*, E-cadherin, p53, etc.) and the activation of oncogenes that stimulate cell division (*BRAF, EGFR*), angiogenesis (*VEGF*), deregulation of apoptosis (telomerase), and metastasis (*C-MET*) (Rákosy et al., 2007; Rudolph et al., 2000; Satyamoorthy & Herlyn, 2002; Soubrane et al., 2006). Recent molecular investigations have identified mutations of the *BRAF* gene in up to 80% of malignant melanomas (Davies et al., 2002). Mutant *BRAF* protein stimulates deregulation of important mechanisms of carcinogenesis in melanocytes (e.g., cell division and apoptosis) and has been proposed as a molecular target for the therapy of malignant melanoma (Garber, 2009).

RISK FACTORS FOR MALIGNANT MELANOMA

The primary risk factor for the development of malignant melanoma is excessive exposure to ultraviolet rays from the sun. Many epidemiologic investigations have also demonstrated that the risk increases with lighter pigmentation of the skin by melanin. Individuals with lightly pigmented skin are at the highest risk and individuals with darkly pigmented skin are at the lowest risk. Other phenotypic factors also increase the risk, including inability to tan, light eye color, red hair, and extensive freckling. Furthermore, the risk increases with the number of pigmented (melanocytic) nevi (see the following discussion). Although the risk of malignant melanoma development is clearly linked to cumulative exposure to the sun, the risk is heightened further by intense, intermittent exposure causing multiple sunburns, particularly during childhood and adolescence.

In contrast to other types of skin cancer, malignant melanoma frequently occurs in areas of the body that are intermittently exposed to the sun, such as the back in men and the lower legs in women, with relative sparing of more frequently exposed sites such as the face, hands, and forearms (Gilchrest et al., 1999). Furthermore, malignant melanoma is more likely to develop in persons with predominantly indoor occupations whose exposure to the sun is limited to weekends and vacations (Holman, Armstrong, & Heenan, 1986). Indeed, the marked increase in the incidence of malignant melanoma in recent decades may reflect the effects of intense intermittent exposures in individuals who vacation in sunny climates during the winter months (Westerdahl et al., 1992). The risk of malignant melanoma is specifically increased with exposures that induce sunburn; for example, a history of five or more severe sunburns during adolescence more than doubles the risk (Weinstock, 1996).

Pigmented Nevi and Malignant Melanoma

As pointed out in a review of melanoma epidemiology by Margaret Tucker, there are two broad categories of pigmented nevi, common and dysplastic, which carry different risks of melanoma development (Tucker, 2009). Dysplastic nevi, which carry a far greater risk, are characterized by size greater than 5 millimeters at largest diameter, a flat surface, irregular asymmetric shape, indiscriminant borders, and variability in the degree of pigmentation. In a meta-analysis of 46 epidemiologic studies, Gandini and colleagues examined dose responses in melanoma risk associated with the number of common or dysplastic nevi. Individuals with more than 100 common nevi had a relative risk of 6.4 compared to individuals with less than 15 common nevi, whereas even the presence of one solitary dysplastic nevus doubled the risk, and having 10 or more dysplastic nevi produced a 12-fold increase in the risk (Gandini et al., 2005).

Genetic Predisposition to Malignant Melanoma

Approximately 10% of melanoma cases diagnosed in the United States report that one or more relatives are also affected (Greene, 1998; Tucker, 2009). In case control studies, individuals with a positive family history have roughly a twofold increased risk compared to individuals with no family history.

The familial atypical mole and melanoma (FAMM) syndrome is a rare genetic disorder giving rise to multiple dysplastic pigmented moles of the skin that invariably progress to malignant melanoma. Genetic linkage studies of members of families with the FAMM syndrome have identified two major susceptibility genes, CDKN2A and CDK4, both of which are inherited in an autosomal dominant pattern. Carriers of either mutant gene are at 100% risk of developing malignant melanoma during their lifetimes (Greene, 1998).

One form of the FAMM syndrome is caused by a mutation in CDKN2A, the gene that encodes p16, an important cell cycle regulating protein (Hussussian et al., 1994). The CDKN2A gene is located on the short arm of chromosome 9 (9p21). This gene normally codes for the tumor suppressor protein p16, which is essential for the regulation of cell division

(Monzon et al., 1998). Mutant forms of CDKN2A encode dysfunctional p16 protein that leads to loss of control of cell division and enhanced proliferation of melanocytes.

A second form of the FAMM syndrome is caused by a mutation in the CDK4 gene, which maps to the long arm of chromosome 12 (12q13). This gene also codes for an oncogenic protein that is important for the regulation of cell division of melanocytes. Mutations in CDK4 are very rare and have been detected in only a few families (Greene, 1998).

Individuals who carry certain polymorphisms or mutant alleles of a gene called MC1R (melanocortin receptor) are also at increased risk for the development of malignant melanoma. The MC1R gene plays an important role in melanin biosynthesis and pigmentation of the skin and hair. Mutant forms of MC1R are extremely common and may result in a highly susceptible phenotype: red hair, fair skin, numerous freckles, and inability to tan.

Ultraviolet (UV) Radiation from Tanning Beds

Many epidemiologic investigations have focused on the association between malignant melanoma and exposure to ultraviolet rays in tanning beds. In 2009, the International Agency for Research on Cancer (IARC) released a report that categorized tanning beds as "carcinogenic to humans." This classification is based on a meta-analysis of 19 epidemiologic studies indicating that people who begin using tanning devices before age 30 are 75% more likely to develop melanoma (IARC, 2007; World Health Organization, 2009).

In a more recent meta-analysis, a team of European investigators examined data from 27 studies, including 18 conducted in Europe, 7 in the United States and Canada, and 2 in Australia. Their results are based on 11,428 cases of melanoma studied during 1981–2012. The combined results revealed that ever versus never use of tanning beds increased the risk of developing melanoma by 20% (summary relative risk [RR] = 1.20); furthermore, initiation of exposure before age 35 years nearly doubled the risk (summary RR = 1.87). Examination of data from studies that included data on frequency of using tanning beds revealed a 1.8% increase in melanoma risk for each additional annual tanning bed session. There was no evidence of heterogeneity among studies. These findings clearly link exposure to ultraviolet radiation in tanning beds to an increased risk of developing melanoma and suggest there is an urgent need to implement strict regulations regarding use of indoor tanning equipment (Beniol, Autier, Boyle, & Gandini, 2012).

A particularly disturbing finding is the increased risk of melanoma among young adults who begin using tanning beds at an early age. Investigators in Australia investigated the association between tanning bed use and the risk of early onset melanoma in a study of 604 cases diagnosed between ages 18 and 39 years and 479 controls matched by age, gender, and residence to the cases. The results revealed that ever versus never use of tanning beds significantly increased the risk of melanoma development by 41%, and more than 10 lifetime sessions doubled the risk (odds ratio [OR] = 2.01). The investigators concluded that exposure of adolescents and young adults to artificial ultraviolet radiation in tanning beds increases their risk of developing malignant melanoma at an early age (Cust et al., 2011).

Indoor tanning equipment emits primarily ultraviolet A rays and, to a lesser extent, ultraviolet B (UVB) rays. Powerful units may produce exposures 10–15 times stronger than midday sunlight, and repeated exposures delivered to the skin in 10- to 20-minute periods could enhance mutagenesis and other mechanisms of carcinogenesis.

Ozone Holes and Malignant Melanoma

The stratospheric ozone layer resides approximately 10–50 kilometers above the earth and acts as a protective shield against the sun's harmful ultraviolet rays, particularly UVB rays (wavelengths of 270–315 nanometers). The natural ozone shield has been gradually depleted by the atmospheric release of manmade chemicals such as chlorofluorocarbons (freons) and bromofluorocarbons (halons) that spark the catalytic destruction of ozone. Ozone destruction is most prominent around the polar regions of the earth, leading to "ozone holes" and penetration of the earth's atmosphere by UVB rays. Excessive exposure to UVB rays is linked to the development of malignant melanoma as well as other conditions such as cataracts (Norval et al., 2007). Such windows of UVB exposure appear to coincide roughly with the high mortality rates of malignant melanoma in the southern hemisphere of the world, particularly in the populations of Australia, New Zealand, and the southernmost tips of South America and Africa (NASA, 2006) (**Figure 23.5**).

PREVENTION OF MALIGNANT MELANOMA

The primary prevention of malignant melanoma is dependent upon minimizing exposure to intensive ultraviolet radiation from the sun, tanning beds, and

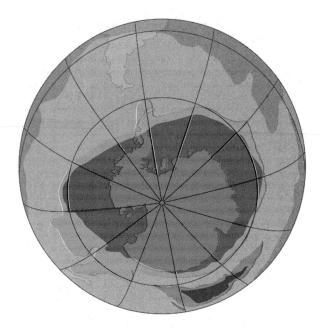

Figure 23.5 Ozone Depletion in the Southern Hemisphere, September 2006.

Source: Reproduced from National Aeronautics and Space Administration (NASA). (2006). National ozone watch. Goddard Space Flight Center. Retrieved from http://www.theozonehole .com/ozonehole2006.htm

other sources of radiation. Avoidance of intense sun exposure during peak times of the day, wearing protective clothing, and using sunscreen lotions can offer protection (Autier, 2005).

National and community programs of secondary prevention have also proven to be highly effective. The American Academy of Dermatology recommends annual inspection of the skin by a certified dermatologist for the detection and surgical removal of dysplastic pigmented nevi and other suspicious lesions prior to their progression to malignancy (American Academy of Dermatology, 2010). A special surgical technique called *Mohs surgery*, wherein repeated circumferential sections of tumor are removed and microscopically examined until cancer-free margins are evident, has been shown to be effective in treating in situ cutaneous malignant melanoma (Bene, Healy, & Coldiron, 2008).

● ● ● **REFERENCES**

Altekruse, S. F., Kosary, C. L., Krapcho, M., Neyman, N., Aminou, R., Waldron, W., . . . Edwards, B. K. (Eds.). (2009). *SEER cancer statistics review, 1975–2007*. Bethesda, MD: National Cancer Institute.

American Academy of Dermatology. (2010). *National skin cancer screening program, USA.* American Academy of Dermatology. Retrieved from https://www.aad.org

Autier, P. (2005). Cutaneous malignant melanoma: Facts about sunbeds and sunscreen. *Expert Review of Anticancer Therapy, 5*(5), 821–833.

Balch, C., Buzaid, A., Soong, S., Atkins, M., Cascinelli, N., Coit, D., . . . Thompson, J. (2001). Final version of the American Joint Committee on Cancer staging system for cutaneous melanoma. *Journal of Clinical Oncology, 19*(16), 3635–3648.

Bene, N. I., Healy, C., & Coldiron, B. M. (2008). Mohs micrographic surgery is accurate 95.1% of the time for melanoma in situ: A prospective study of 167 cases. *Dermatologic Surgery, 34*(5), 660–664.

Boniol, M., Autier, P., Boyle, P., & Gandini, S. (2012). Cutaneous melanoma attributable to sunbed use: Systematic review and meta-analysis. *BMJ, 345,* e4757.doi: 10.1136/bmj.e4757.

Buzaid, A. (2004). Management of metastatic cutaneous melanoma. *Oncology (Williston Park), 18*(11), 1443–1450.

Carver, G. (1998). *Part III. The science of the ozone hole.* Cambridge, UK: University of Cambridge, Center for Atmospheric Science.

Cleaver, J. E. (1968). Defective repair replication of DNA in xeroderma pigmentosum. *Nature, 218,* 652–656.

Cruz Jr., P. D., Paul, R., & Bergstresser, P. R. (1989). Ultraviolet radiation, Langerhans' cells and skin cancer: Conspiracy and failure. *Archives of Dermatology, 125*(7), 975–979.

Cust, A. E., Armstrong, B. K., Goumas, C., Jenkins, M. A., Schmid, H., Hopper, J. L., . . . Mann, G. J. (2011). Sunbed use during adolescence and early adulthood is associated with increased risk of early-onset melanoma. *International Journal of Cancer, 128*(10), 2425–2435.

Davies, H., Bignell, G. R., Cox, C., Stephens, P., Edkins, S., Clegg, S., . . . Futreal, P. A. (2002). Mutations of the *BRAF* gene in human cancer. *Nature, 417,* 949–954.

Denkert, C., Köbel, M., Berger, S., Siegert, A., Leclere, A., Trefzer, U., & Hauptmann, S. (2001). Expression of cyclooxygenase 2 in human malignant melanoma. *Cancer Research, 61*(1), 303–308.

Ferlay, J., Shin, H. R., Forman, D., Mathers, C., & Parkin, D. M. (2010). Estimates of worldwide burden of cancer in 2008. *International Journal of Cancer, 127*(12), 2893–2917.

Ferlay, J., Soerjomataram, I., Ervik, M., Dikshit, R., Eser, S., Mathers, C., . . . Bray, F. (2013). *GLOBOCAN 2012 v1.0. Cancer Incidence and Mortality Worldwide: IARC CancerBase No. 11* [Internet]. Lyon, France: International Agency for Research on Cancer. Retrieved from http://globocan.iarc.fr

Freeman, S. E., Hacham, H., Gange, R. W., Maytum, D. J., Sutherland, J. C., & Sutherland, B. M. (1989). Wavelength dependence of pyrimidine dimer formation in DNA of human skin irradiated *in situ* with ultraviolet light. *Proceedings of the National Academy of the Sciences of the United States of America, 86,* 5605–5609.

Gamba, C. A., Swetter, S. M., Stefanick, M. L., Kubo, J., Desai, M., Spaunhurst, K. M., . . . Tang, J. Y. (2013). Aspirin is associated with lower melanoma risk among postmenopausal women. *Cancer, 119*(8), 1562–1569.

Gandini, S., Sera, F., Cattaruzza, M. S., Pasquini, P., Abeni, D., Boyle, P., & Melchi, C. F. (2005). Meta-analysis of risk factors for cutaneous melanoma: I. Common and atypical naevi. *European Journal of Cancer, 41*(1), 28–44.

Garber, K. (2009). Cancer research. Melanoma drug vindicates targeted approach. *Science, 326*(5960), 1619.

Gilchrest, B. A., Eller, M. S., Geller, A. C., & Yaar, M. (1999). The pathogenesis of melanoma induced by ultraviolet radiation. *New England Journal of Medicine, 340*(17), 1341–1348.

Gilchrest, B. A., Park, H. Y., Eller, M. S., & Yaar, M. (1998). The photobiology of the tanning response. In J. J. Nordlund, R. E. Boissy, V. J. Hearing, R. A. King, & J. P. Ortonne (Eds.), *The pigmentary system: Physiology and pathophysiology* (pp. 359–372). New York: Oxford University Press.

Goulet, A. C., Einsphar, J. G., Alberts, D. S., Beas, A., Burk, C., Bhattacharyya, A., . . . Nelson, M. A. (2003). Analysis of cyclooxygenase 2 (COX-2) expression during malignant melanoma progression. *Cancer Biology Therapy, 2*(6), 713–718.

Greene, M. H. (1998). The genetics of hereditary melanoma and nevi. *Cancer, 86*(11), 2464–2477.

Hakim, R., Poggi, R., Pantaleo, M., Benedetti, G., Brandi, G., Zannetti, G., . . . Biasco, G. (2006). Phase II study of temozolomide and celecoxib in the treatment of metastatic melanoma. *Journal of Clinical Oncology, 24*(18S), 18015.

Harris, R. E., Namboodiri, K. A., & Beebe-Donk, J. (2001). Inverse association of malignant melanoma and non-steroidal anti-inflammatory drugs (NSAIDs) in women. *Oncology Reports, 8,* 655–657.

Holman, C. D. J., Armstrong, B. K., & Heenan, P. J. (1986). Relationship of cutaneous malignant melanoma to individual sunlight-exposure habits. *Journal of the National Cancer Institute, 76,* 403–414.

Hussussian, C. J., Struewing, J. P., Goldstein, A. M., Higgins, P. A., Ally, D. S., Sheahan, M. D., . . . Dracopoli, N. C. (1994). Germline p16 mutations in familial melanoma. *Nature Genetics, 8*(1), 15–21.

International Agency for Research on Cancer, Working Group on Artificial Ultraviolet (UV) Light and Skin Cancer. (2007). The association of use of sunbeds with cutaneous malignant melanoma and other skin cancers: A systematic review. *International Journal of Cancer, 120*(5), 1116–1122.

Kobayashi, N., Nakagawa, A., Muramatsu, T., Yamashin, Y., Shiral, T., Hashimoto, M. W., . . . Mori, T. (1998). Supranuclear melanin caps reduce ultraviolet induced DNA photoproducts in human epidermis. *Journal of Investigative Dermatology, 110,* 806–810.

Lambert, W. C., Kuo, H. R., & Lambert, M. W. (1995). Xeroderma pigmentosum. *Dermatology Clinics, 13,* 169–209.

Meyskens, F. L. Jr., Farmer, P. J., & Anton-Culver, H. (2004). Etiologic pathogenesis of melanoma: A unifying hypothesis for the missing attributable risk. *Clinical Cancer Research, 10*(8), 2581–2583.

Monzon, J., Liu, L., Brill, H., Goldstein, A. M., Tucker, M. A., From, L., . . . Lassam, N. J. (1998). *CDKN2A* mutations in multiple primary melanomas. *New England Journal of Medicine, 338*(13), 879–887.

National Aeronautics and Space Administration (NASA). (2006). National ozone watch. Goddard Space Flight Center. Retrieved from http://www .theozonehole.com/ozonehole2006.htm

Norval, M., Cullen, A. P., de Gruijl, F. R., Longstreth, J., Takizawa, Y., Lucas, R. M., . . . van der Leun, J. C. (2007). The effects on human health from stratospheric ozone depletion and its interactions with climate change. *Photochemical and Photobiological Sciences, 6*(3), 232–251.

Parkin, M., Bray, F., Ferlay, J., & Pisani, P. (2001). Estimating the world cancer burden: GLOBOCAN 2000. *International Journal of Cancer, 94,* 153–156.

Parkin, M., Bray, F., Ferlay, J., & Pisani, P. (2005). Global cancer statistics, 2002. *CA: A Cancer Journal for Clinicians, 55,* 74–108.

Pathak, M. A. (1991). Ultraviolet radiation and the development of non-melanoma and melanoma skin cancer: Clinical and experimental evidence. *Skin Pharmacology, 4*(Suppl 1), 85–94.

Pathak, M. A. (1995). Functions of melanin and protection by melanin. In L. Zeise, M. R. Chedekel, & T. B. Fitzpatrick (Eds.), *Melanin: Its role in human photoprotection* (pp. 125–134). Overland Park, KS: Valdenmar.

Rákosy, Z., Vízkeleti, L., Ecsedi, S., Vokó, Z., Bégány, A., Barok, M., . . . Balázs, M. (2007). EGFR gene copy number alterations in primary cutaneous malignant melanomas are associated with poor prognosis. *International Journal of Cancer, 121*(8), 1729–1737.

Rudolph, P., Schubert, C., Tamm, S., Heidorn, K., Hauschild, A., Michalska, I., . . . Parwaresch, R. (2000). Telomerase activity in melanocytic lesions: A potential marker of tumor biology. *American Journal of Pathology, 156*, 1425–1432.

Satyamoorthy, K., & Herlyn, M. (2002). Cellular and molecular biology of human melanoma. *Cancer Biology and Therapy, 1*(1), 12–15.

Soubrane, C., Mouawad, R., Sultan, V., Spano, J., Khayat, D., & Rixe, O. (2006). Soluble *VEGF-A* and lymphangiogenesis in metastatic malignant melanoma patients. *Journal of Clinical Oncology, 24*(18S), 8049.

Tang, A., & Udey, M. C. (1991). Inhibition of epidermal Langerhans cell function by low dose ultraviolet B radiation. Ultraviolet B radiation selectively modulates ICAM-1 (CD54) expression by murine Langerhans cells. *Journal of Immunology, 146*(10), 3347–3355.

Tucker, M. (2009). Melanoma epidemiology. *Hematology/Oncology Clinics of North America, 23*, 383–395.

Weinstock, M. A. (1996). Controversies in the role of sunlight in the pathogenesis of cutaneous melanoma. *Photochemistry and Photobiology, 63*, 406–410.

Westerdahl, J., Olsson, H., Ingvar, C., Brandt, L., Jonsson, P. E., & Moller, T. (1992). Southern travelling habits with special reference to tumour site in Swedish melanoma patients. *Anticancer Research, 12*, 1539–1542.

World Health Organization, International Agency for Research on Cancer Monograph Working Group. (2009). A review of human carcinogens—Part D: Radiation. *Lancet Oncology, 10*(8), 751–752.

24

Epidemiology of Nonmelanoma Skin Cancer: Basal Cell, Squamous Cell, and Merkel Cell Skin Cancers

ANATOMY AND FUNCTION OF THE SKIN

The skin is the largest organ of the body, covering a surface area of approximately 2 square meters (21 square feet) and weighing about 4.5 kilograms (10 pounds) in the average adult. It serves as a protective barrier that protects internal tissues from exposure to trauma, ultraviolet (UV) radiation, temperature extremes, toxins, and bacteria. Other important functions include sensory perception, immunologic surveillance, thermoregulation, and control of fluid loss. The skin is also actively involved in the biosynthesis of vitamin D. Basic anatomy of the skin is depicted in **Figure 24.1**.

The skin consists of three layers: the epidermis, the dermis, and the subcutis. The outer layer of skin is called the epidermis, and it consists of layers of cells called *keratinocytes* that produce the protein keratin. Keratin is a durable but flexible protein that provides strength and elasticity to the skin. Basal cells and squamous cells of the epidermis are collectively called *keratinocytes* because both cell types produce keratin. The epidermis also contains *melanocytes*, which produce melanin, a pigment that absorbs radiant energy from the sun and protects the skin from the harmful effects of UV radiation. Immune cells called *Langerhans cells* (so named after the German pathologist Paul Langerhans, who discovered them in 1868) circulate in the epidermis and play an important role in immunosurveillance and defense against infection. The epidermis also contains neurosensory cells called *Merkel cells* that connect with nerve

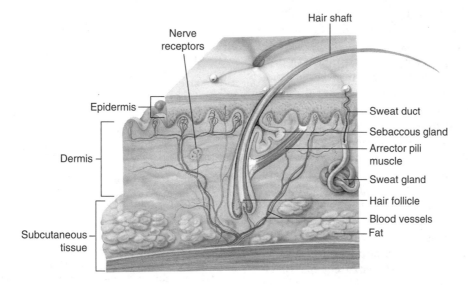

Figure 24.1 Anatomic Features of Human Skin.

endings to transmit electrical impulses in response to touch.

The epidermis is separated from the dermis by the *basement membrane*, a thin fibrous membrane composed of glycoproteins and proteoglycans. This membrane anchors the epithelial cells to the underlying dermis and provides a mechanical barrier that prevents malignant cells from invading into deeper tissues.

The *dermis* is connective tissue made of collagen, elastic fibers, and reticular fibers. Its primary function is to sustain and support the epidermis. The major cell type in the dermis is the fibroblast, which secretes collagen and elastic fibers. The dermis also contains sweat glands, hair roots, nerves, blood vessels, and lymphatic vessels.

The subcutis (or subcutaneous tissue) that underlies the dermis consists primarily of lobules of adipose (fat) separated by connective tissues. The subcutis cushions the body and provides insulation for thermoregulation of internal organs. The adipose of the subcutis also serves as an energy reserve in times of food shortage.

NONMELANOMA SKIN CANCER

This chapter focuses on nonmelanoma skin cancers, which make up about 95% of all skin cancers. Melanomas arising from melanocytes of the epidermis make up the remaining 5% of skin cancers. The two principal forms of nonmelanoma skin cancer are basal cell carcinoma and squamous cell carcinoma. These two cell types make up over 99% of all nonmelanoma skin cancers. In a German survey of 12,956 cases, 82% of nonmelanoma skin cancers were basal cell carcinomas, 17% were squamous cell carcinomas, and less than 1% were classified as other histological forms (Katalinic, Kunze, & Schäfer, 2003).

Basal cell carcinoma is the most common form of human cancer. These tumors arise from the keratinized basal cells of the epidermis, which are in contact with the basement membrane. Basal cell carcinomas most often develop from the skin of the face, neck, or upper trunk that has been damaged by intermittent blistering sunburns during childhood or adolescence. Although basal cell carcinomas rarely metastasize to distant organs, they can invade and damage contiguous tissues (de Gruijl, 1999; Miller, 1995).

Squamous cell carcinoma is the second most common human cancer. These tumors arise from keratinized squamous cells in the uppermost cell layers of the epidermis. Squamous cell carcinomas of the skin occasionally develop as a consequence of continuous sun exposure throughout life. These tumors nearly always develop due to malignant transformation of sun-induced precancerous skin lesions known as *actinic keratoses*. Exposed skin of the face, neck, and backs of the hands are the most common sites of cumulative sun damage leading to tumor development. In contrast to basal cell carcinomas, squamous cell carcinomas *do* have the potential to metastasize to other organs through the lymph and blood (Armstrong & Kricker 2001).

Merkel cell carcinoma is a rare malignancy that is briefly discussed in this chapter. This form of cancer arises from the neurosensory Merkel cells of the epidermis. Merkel cell carcinoma tends to be highly aggressive with the potential for rapid and widespread metastasis.

AGE-SPECIFIC INCIDENCE OF NONMELANOMA SKIN CANCER

Byfield and colleagues examined claims data filed during 2009–2010 in a large national managed healthcare system in the United States in order to characterize the age-specific incidence of nonmelanoma skin cancers. Estimates were based on 47,451 incident cases identified during 2010 from a population of 6.61 million individuals enrolled in the system. **Figure 24.2** shows the age-specific incidence of nonmelanoma skin cancer. The incidence rises sharply with age, ranging from approximately 1 case per 100,000 among individuals under the age of 25 years to 209 cases per 100,000 among individuals 75 years of age or older. The data revealed an excess of male cases compared to female cases (54.5% versus 45.5%), and only 16 cases (0.03%) showed

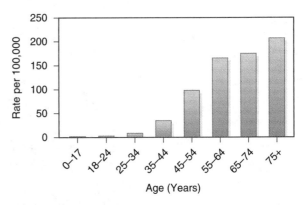

Figure 24.2 Age-Specific Incidence of Nonmelanoma Skin Cancer in Members of a U.S. Healthcare Plan, 2010.

Source: Data from Byfield, S. D., Chen, D., Yim, Y. M., & Reyes, C. (2013). Age distribution of patients with advanced non-melanoma skin cancer in the United States. *Archives of Dermatologic Research, 305*(9), 845–850.

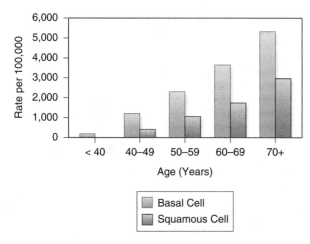

Figure 24.3 Age-Specific Incidence of Basal Cell and Squamous Cell Carcinoma in Australia.

Source: Data from Staples, M. P., Elwood, M., Burton, R. C., William, J. L., Marks, R., & Giles, G. G. (2006). Non-melanoma skin cancer in Australia: The 2002 national survey and trends since 1985. *Medical Journal of Australia, 184*, 6–10.

evidence of metastatic spread at the time of diagnosis (Byfield, Chen, Yim, & Reyes, 2013).

Staples and colleagues estimated age-specific incidence rates of the two major forms of nonmelanoma skin cancer, basal cell and squamous cell carcinomas, based on national survey data collected in Australia during 2002 (**Figure 24.3**). The Australian population has the highest rates of nonmelanoma skin cancer in the world, and it is indeed striking that the 2002 Australian rates were 10–20 times higher than the corresponding age-specific rates for the U.S. population shown in Figure 24.2 (Staples et al., 2006).

The age-specific incidence rates shown in Figure 24.3 reflect a clear difference in the pathogenesis of basal cell versus squamous cell carcinoma. Note that the rate ratio of basal cell to squamous cell carcinoma for individuals under 40 years of age is 29.0 (203 versus 7 per 100,000), whereas after age 40 the rate ratios progressively decline from 2.9 for individuals ages 40–49 years to 1.8 for individuals over 70 years of age. The sharper increase in the risk of squamous cell carcinoma compared to basal cell carcinoma with aging is a possible consequence of the effects of cumulative sun damage (Staples et al., 2006).

GLOBAL INCIDENCE OF NONMELANOMA SKIN CANCER

The incidence of nonmelanoma skin cancer is highly correlated with the level of solar radiation and varies inversely with the degree of skin pigmentation among populations. For example, among Caucasians in the United States, nonmelanoma skin cancer constitutes 20–30% of all neoplasms, whereas among African Americans such lesions are infrequent and make up less than 1% of all neoplasms (Gloster & Neal, 2005; Ridky, 2007).

Australia has the highest reported incidence of nonmelanoma skin cancer in the world. A national survey of the Australian population conducted in 2002 found an age-adjusted rate of 1,170 cases per 100,000 (884 per 100,000 for basal cell carcinoma and 387 per 100,000 for squamous cell carcinoma). The incidence of nonmelanoma skin cancer in men was 39% higher than in women (1,375 versus 991 per 100,000). Based on these data, 69% of Australian men and 58% of Australian women develop nonmelanoma skin cancer by 70 years of age. The major predisposing factors in the Australian population are light skin pigmentation, high ambient levels of ultraviolet light due to the South Polar ozone hole, and cultural emphasis on outdoor activities and sun exposure throughout life (Arthey & Clarke, 1995; Australian Institute of Health and Welfare & Cancer Australia, 2008; Staples, Marks, & Giles, 1998; Staples et al., 2006).

Incidence rates of nonmelanoma skin cancer reported for Caucasians living in the United States and other developed countries are considerably less than the Australian rates. Surveys conducted by the U.S. Surveillance, Epidemiology, and End Results (SEER) Program during 1992–1996 found an age-adjusted rate of 354 cases per 100,000 among Caucasians (310 per 100,000 for basal cell carcinoma and 54 per 100,000 for squamous cell carcinoma). The incidence of nonmelanoma skin cancer in men was twofold higher than in women (488 versus 238 per 100,000). These estimates suggest that among Caucasians, approximately 40% of men and 20% of women in the United States develop nonmelanoma skin cancer during their lifetimes (Miller & Weinstock, 1994; National Cancer Institute [NCI], 1996).

In other developed nations, reported incidence rates of nonmelanoma skin cancer for Caucasians vary between 100 and 200 cases per 100,000. For example, in Ireland, the incidence of nonmelanoma skin cancer during 1994–2011 was 156 per 100,000, 110 for basal cell carcinoma and 46 for squamous cell carcinoma (Ireland National Cancer Registry, 2013).

In Asian populations, the incidence rates of nonmelanoma skin cancer are considerably less than in Caucasian populations. Published estimates of the incidence of basal cell carcinoma are 6.4 and 5.8 per 100,000 for Chinese men and women, respectively, and 16.5 per 100,000 for Japanese men and women. Notably, the rates of skin cancer in populations with predominantly dark skin pigmentation are comparatively very low; for example, rates for African populations are in the range of 1–2 per 100,000 (Gloster & Neal, 2005).

LONGITUDINAL TRENDS IN BASAL CELL AND SQUAMOUS CELL CARCINOMAS OF THE SKIN

Basal cell and squamous cell carcinomas of the skin are rarely fatal, so physicians are not required to report cases to existing population-based tumor registries; as a consequence, definitive estimates of incidence are not routinely reported. Nevertheless, longitudinal investigations of multiple cohorts provide evidence that the incidence of nonmelanoma skin cancer (basal cell and squamous cell carcinomas) has increased among Caucasian populations of several different regions. As discussed in this section, increases have been noted for males and females of all age groups and particularly in younger individuals.

Four national surveys were conducted in the Australian population during 1985–2002 to determine trends in the incidence of nonmelanoma skin cancer. Results reflect an overall increase of 35% for basal cell carcinoma (from 657 to 884 per 100,000) and 233% for squamous cell carcinoma (from 166 to 387 per 100,000) (**Figure 24.4**). The increases were similar for men and women and tended to occur primarily among older individuals (Staples et al., 1998, 2006).

Investigators in the United States examined trends in the annual incidence of basal cell carcinoma in two large prospective cohorts of older adults: 95,743

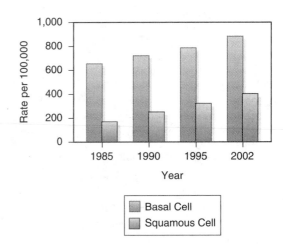

Figure 24.4 Trends in the Incidence of Basal Cell and Squamous Cell Carcinomas in Australia, 1985–2002.

Source: Data from Staples, M. P., Elwood, M., Burton, R. C., William, J. L., Marks, R., & Giles, G. G. (2006). Non-melanoma skin cancer in Australia: The 2002 national survey and trends since 1985. *Medical Journal of Australia, 184*, 6–10.

women from the Nurses' Health Study (1986–2006) and 44,428 men from the Health Professionals' Follow-up Study (1988–2006). All participants in these cohorts were between 40 and 50 years of age at baseline. During the follow-up periods, age-adjusted incidence rates increased markedly in women (from 519 to 1,019 per 100,000) and men (from 606 to 1,488 per 100,000) (**Figure 24.5**). The investigators suggested that several factors may have contributed to these trends, including increasing susceptibility with greater longevity and heightened exposure to solar radiation and/or artificial ultraviolet radiation in tanning beds (Wu, Han, Li, Li, & Qureshi, 2013).

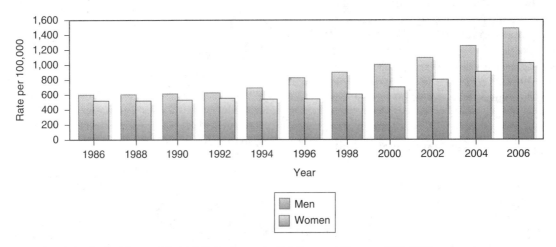

Figure 24.5 Trends in the Incidence of Basal Cell Carcinoma in U.S. Men and Women, 1986–2006.

Source: Data from Wu, S., Han, J., Li, W. Q., Li, T., & Qureshi, A. A. (2013). Basal-cell carcinoma incidence and associated risk factors in U.S. women and men. *American Journal of Epidemiology, 178*(6), 890–897.

Trends in the annual incidence rates of basal cell and squamous cell carcinomas of the skin were examined in persons younger than 40 years of age in the predominantly Caucasian population of Olmsted County, Minnesota, during 1976–2003. During the 28-year study period, 417 patients developed basal cell carcinomas and 68 patients developed squamous cell carcinomas. Overall, the age-adjusted incidence of basal cell carcinoma per 100,000 persons was 25.9 for women and 20.9 for men, whereas the incidence of squamous cell carcinoma was approximately 3.9 in men and women. The annual incidence of nonmelanoma skin cancer increased by about 60%, from 18 per 100,000 in 1976–1979 to 29 per 100,000 in 2000–2003. Notably, this trend was driven largely by the increased annual incidence among young women (13 per 100,000 in 1976–1979 versus 32 per 100,000 in 2000–2003). The investigators speculated that the increased rates of skin cancer among young women of this population may have resulted from increased exposure to solar radiation and/or artificial radiation from tanning beds, or changes in other risk factors for skin cancer such as cigarette smoking (Christenson et al., 2005).

Investigators in Great Britain examined trends in the incidence of basal cell carcinoma of the skin in a primary care population–based cohort study. They identified 11,113 cases from a total of 7.22 million person-years of follow-up data collected between 1996 and 2003. The overall age-adjusted incidence of basal cell carcinoma was 153.9 per 100,000 person-years, and the rate was slightly (~10%) higher in men compared to women. Notably, there was a 3% increase per year across the study period, with the largest increase in incidence seen in the 30- to 39-year age group (Bath-Hextall, Leonardi-Bee, Smith, Meal, & Hubbard, 2007).

In a longitudinal study of nonmelanoma skin cancer in Denmark, trends in the annual incidence rates of basal cell and squamous cell carcinomas were estimated for the period 1978–2007. During this 30-year time span, the annual incidence of basal cell carcinomas increased from 27 to 97 cases per 100,000 in women and from 34 to 91 cases per 100,000 in men. Concurrently, the incidence of squamous cell carcinomas increased from 5 to 12 cases per 100,000 in women and from 10 to 19 cases per 100,000 in men. Although increases were noted in all age groups, the rate of increase was greatest among young women. The investigators suggest that these trends may reflect effects of heightened exposure to solar radiation and artificial radiation from tanning beds (Birch-Johansen, Jensen, Mortensen, Olesen, & Kjaer, 2010).

Dutch investigators conducted a longitudinal study of basal cell carcinoma to estimate trends in the incidence rates of basal cell carcinomas by age and gender in the Netherlands. Cases were ascertained from the Eindhoven Cancer Registry in the southeast Netherlands during 1973–2009. During the entire 37-year period, the age-standardized annual rate nearly quadrupled in men (from 40 to 154 per 100,000) and more than quadrupled in women (from 34 to 157 per 100,000). The investigators suggest that heightened exposure to artificial radiation from tanning beds and/or solar radiation may partly explain the increasing trends in basal cell carcinoma of the skin in the Dutch population (Flohil et al., 2013).

In Schleswig-Holstein, the northernmost state of Germany, incidence rates of nonmelanoma skin cancer were estimated during 1998–2000 and later during 2008–2010 to assess the impact of population-based skin cancer screening implemented in the interim. Over the period of study, the incidence of nonmelanoma skin cancer increased by 47% in women (from 81 to 119 cases per 100,000) and by 31% in men (from 111 to 145 cases per 100,000). Increases were noted for all age groups in women and primarily older age groups in men (Eisemann et al., 2013; Katalinic et al., 2003).

Altogether, these findings clearly suggest that the incidence of nonmelanoma skin cancer is increasing not only among the elderly, but also in successive younger generations of several populations. Unless reversed by effective preventive measures, the consequences of leisure exposure to ultraviolet light portend an impending global epidemic in nonmelanoma skin cancer that will have a huge impact on global health in future years.

SOLAR RADIATION AND NONMELANOMA SKIN CANCER

The predominant risk factor for nonmelanoma skin cancer is solar radiation. In population studies, the incidence rises with proximity to the equator, where the ultraviolet B content of sunlight is greatest. Fair-skinned individuals have the greatest risk, and susceptibility is increased among individuals with a family history of skin cancer and those who sunburn easily. Individuals with dark skin rarely develop nonmelanoma carcinoma of the skin. The risk for malignant transformation is greatest at sites with the greatest sun exposure. Studies have consistently shown that 70–90% of basal cell carcinomas arise in sun-exposed skin of the head and neck, particularly the nose. Nevertheless, the risk is also increased for those regions of the skin with intermittent exposure to intense solar radiation (e.g., the trunk and upper portions of the arms and legs) (Armstrong & Kricker, 2001; de Gruijl, 1999; Green & Battistutta, 1990; Miller & Weinstock, 1994; Ridky, 2007).

Types of Solar Radiation

Ultraviolet radiation is divided into three types based on wavelength. UVA radiation is the longest wavelength, 315–400 nanometers (nm), and is just slightly shorter than visible light. UVB radiation has a wavelength of 280–315 nm, and UVC, the highest energy radiation, has a wavelength below 280 nm. Each of these forms of ultraviolet radiation is harmful to living cells (de Gruijl, 1999).

RISK FACTORS FOR BASAL CELL CARCINOMA OF THE SKIN

Solar Radiation and Basal Cell Carcinoma of the Skin

The evidence linking basal cell carcinoma of the skin with solar radiation is unequivocal; however, the risk is modified by genetic, phenotypic, and environmental factors (Wong, Strange, & Lear, 2003). Selected studies are discussed in this section.

In an early case control study of 2,654 cases with basal cell carcinomas of the skin and 1,938 cancer-free controls, the strongest risk factor was excessive cumulative exposure to solar radiation. Other factors that increased the risk included fair complexion, sensitivity to sunlight and inability to tan, blond hair, blue eyes, increased age, and male gender. Almost all of the tumors developed in sun-exposed areas of the skin (Kopf, 1979).

In a Canadian study, 206 male patients with basal cell carcinoma of the skin were compared to 406 age- and gender-matched control subjects without cancer. Significant risk increases were noted for individuals with light, freckled skin who suffered repeat severe sunburn in childhood (Gallagher et al., 1995).

A team of U.S. investigators examined the relation of sun exposure and other factors to the risk of developing basal cell carcinoma of the skin in a prospective cohort of 44,591 predominantly Caucasian U.S. male health professionals, 40–75 years of age and free of cancer at enrollment in 1986. During 8 years of follow-up, 3,273 cases of basal cell carcinoma were reported. Significant risk factors included inability to tan (relative risk [RR] = 2.9),

cumulative number of blistering sunburns (RR = 2.1 for 10 or more), red hair (RR = 2.4), and living in a region with high solar radiation (RR = 1.5). These findings underscore the major role of sun exposure in the genesis of basal cell skin cancer (van Dam et al., 1999).

Several published epidemiologic investigations have reported an association of *occupational* UV exposure with an increased risk of basal cell carcinoma. To gain a more thorough understanding of this association, investigators in Germany conducted a systematic review of the literature and a meta-analysis of the published risk estimates. Their analysis included data from 24 epidemiologic investigations (19 case control studies and 5 cohort studies). The combined data revealed a 43% increase in the risk of developing basal cell carcinoma among outdoor workers compared to those with indoor employment (Bauer, Diepgen, & Schmitt, 2011).

Tanning Beds and Basal Cell Carcinoma of the Skin

The use of tanning beds has been consistently found to increase the risk for early development of basal cell carcinoma and other cutaneous malignancies. Selected studies and a meta-analysis of published data are discussed here.

Investigators in Vermont conducted a population-based case control study that included 603 patients with basal cell carcinoma, 293 patients with squamous cell carcinoma, and 540 control subjects group-matched to the cases by age and gender. The study found that any use of indoor tanning devices was associated with risk increases for both basal cell carcinoma (odds ratio [OR] = 1.5) and squamous cell carcinoma (OR = 2.5). Odds ratios were higher for use initiated before 20 years of age (OR = 1.8 and 3.6 for basal cell and squamous cell carcinomas, respectively), and subjects using indoor tanning devices were more likely to be female and younger than 50 years of age (Karagas et al., 2002).

Investigators in Boston examined exposure to UV light in tanning beds and the risk of developing skin cancer in the Nurses' Health Study (NHS). The study followed 73,494 female nurses for 20 years (from 1989 to 2009) to determine whether the frequency of tanning bed use in young women influenced the incidence rates of skin cancer (basal cell carcinoma, squamous cell carcinoma, and melanoma). During follow-up, 5,506 nurses were diagnosed with basal cell carcinoma, 403 with squamous cell carcinoma, and 349 with melanoma. After adjustment for sun exposure and other risk factors, use of tanning beds more than six times per year while attending high school and college increased the risk of developing basal cell carcinoma by 73% (hazard ratio [HR] = 1.73) and, to a lesser extent, squamous cell carcinoma (HR = 1.12) and melanoma (HR = 1.28). The data suggest a greater vulnerability of younger people to the carcinogenic impact of indoor tanning, especially in the development of basal cell carcinoma (Zhang et al., 2012).

Investigators in Connecticut studied the effects of indoor tanning in a case control study of 376 young patients with basal cell carcinoma and 390 control subjects matched by age and gender. All cases in the study were younger than 40 years of age. Overall, indoor tanning increased the risk of developing basal cell carcinoma by 69%, and the risk increased in a dose response relationship with the frequency and duration of exposure (Ferrucci et al., 2012).

An international team of investigators recently conducted a systematic review and meta-analysis of the published literature on indoor tanning and non-melanoma skin cancer. They identified 12 published studies with 9,328 cases of nonmelanoma skin cancer for analysis. Summary relative risk estimates were elevated for both basal cell carcinoma (RR = 1.29) and squamous cell carcinoma (RR = 1.67). Furthermore, the summary risk estimates were higher among subjects who began using indoor tanning devices before the age of 25 years (RR = 1.40 and RR = 2.02 for basal cell and squamous cell carcinomas, respectively). The evidence suggests that indoor tanning is a significant risk factor for both basal cell and squamous cell carcinomas of the skin, especially when initiated early in life. The results underscore the need for preventive measures aimed at restricting the use of tanning beds among minors (Wehner et al., 2012).

Other Environmental Risk Factors for Basal Cell Carcinoma of the Skin

Environmental factors other than sun exposure may also contribute to the formation of basal cell carcinoma of the skin as well as other cutaneous malignancies. Factors found to increase the risk include immunosuppressive therapy (Stern & Lange, 1990), intake of psoralens in combination with exposure to ultraviolet rays (Boyd, Shyr, & Lloyd, 1988), and chronic exposure to skin irritants such as insecticides, herbicides, petroleum products, and dry cleaning agents (Gallagher et al.,1995) and arsenic-containing compounds (Hartevelt, Bavinck, Kootte, Vermeer, & Vandenbroucke, 1996). High radiation exposure has also been found to increase the risk; for example, the incidence of skin cancer is significantly increased among atomic bomb survivors (Sadamori, Mine, & Honda, 1991; Yamada et al., 1996).

Chronic arsenic poisoning appears to be a major public health problem. Arsenic exposure may occur through contact with contaminated food, water, or air. Although arsenic is ubiquitous in the environment, its ambient concentration in both food and water may be increased near smelting, mining, or coal-burning establishments. Arsenic tends to accumulate in the skin, and chronic exposure has consistently been found to increase the risk of developing basal cell and squamous cell carcinomas of the skin. Mechanistically, arsenic has been found to amplify the cytotoxicity and mutagenicity of UV radiation. Clinically, patients with arsenic-induced skin cancers are characterized by multiple recurring basal cell and squamous cell carcinomas that occur in areas of the skin usually protected from the sun (Yu, Liao, & Chai, 2006).

RISK FACTORS FOR SQUAMOUS CELL CARCINOMA OF THE SKIN

There is extensive overlap between the risk factors for squamous cell carcinoma and basal cell carcinoma, and certainly, the dominant risk factor for both malignancies is solar radiation. Nevertheless, there are distinct differences in the pathogenesis of these two forms of skin cancer, and comparative studies have elucidated distinct differences in risk depending on the frequency, duration, and type of exposure. Unlike basal cell carcinoma, squamous cell carcinoma of the skin carries a substantial risk of invasion and metastatic spread to other organs, and it often develops from a precursor lesion called *actinic keratosis* (Alam & Ratner, 2001).

Actinic Keratosis and Squamous Cell Carcinoma of the Skin

Actinic keratoses (also called *solar keratoses*) are intraepidermal skin tumors caused by chronic exposure to solar radiation. These scaly lesions are composed of highly keratinized layers of dysplastic cells that occupy the epidermal space without breaching the basement membrane. The prevailing view of actinic keratosis is that it is a precursor lesion that occasionally undergoes malignant transformation to form squamous cell carcinoma. The anatomic distribution of actinic keratosis is therefore synonymous with that of squamous cell carcinoma: Both lesions have a strong predilection for sun-exposed regions of the face, neck, hands, and upper trunk

Notably, actinic keratosis has the potential to progress to invasive squamous cell carcinoma. However, evidence from several follow-up studies of cases suggests that the risk of progression of actinic keratosis to squamous cell carcinoma is low; in a study of 1,689 cases in Australia, the annual risk of progression of individual lesions was approximately 1 per 1,000 (Marks, Rennie, & Selwood, 1988). In a more recent study of 169 U.S. male veterans with actinic keratosis, the annual risk of progression was 6 per 1,000 (Criscione et al., 2009). Progression of actinic keratosis to squamous cell carcinoma is associated with continuing exposure to solar radiation that elicits erythema, ulceration, thickening, and/or changes in size and shape of the precursor lesion (Feldman & Fleischer, 2011). In a study of 91 patients, the mean time for actinic keratosis to progress to squamous cell carcinoma was 25 months and the range was 2–76 months (Fuchs & Marmur, 2007).

Solar Radiation and Squamous Cell Carcinoma of the Skin

The largest and most comprehensive comparative study of the effects of solar radiation in the development of basal cell and squamous cell carcinomas of the skin is the European study Helios that was conducted in southern Europe. (The Greek term *Helios* means "sun.") Helios was a well-designed case control investigation of nonmelanocytic skin cancer among different populations from Southern Europe. Its primary objective was to clarify similarities and differences in risk factors for the two major forms of skin cancer, basal cell and squamous cell carcinomas. Between 1989 and 1993, investigators in 7 regions of southern Europe interviewed 1,549 incident cases of basal cell carcinoma, 228 cases of squamous cell carcinoma, and 1,795 disease-free controls matched to the cases by age, gender, and location of residence. Data were collected on sun exposure, constitutional factors, and iatrogenic and occupational exposures.

The initial results of the Helios study revealed that both forms of nonmelanoma skin cancer develop primarily in sun-exposed areas of skin on the face, head, arms, legs, and trunk. Pigmentary traits such as red hair and pale eye color as well as a tendency to sunburn were strong and independent indicators of risk for both basal cell carcinoma and squamous cell carcinoma. Self-reported susceptibility to sunburn and resistance to tanning also increased the risk for both types of malignancy (OR = 2.7 for basal cell carcinoma and OR = 2.0 for squamous cell carcinoma). A key finding was that history of sunburns and early age at first sunburn increased the risk for basal cell carcinoma (OR = 1.7) *but not squamous cell carcinoma*. The investigators concluded that basal cell carcinoma and squamous cell carcinoma are influenced by different patterns of exposure to solar radiation: Basal cell carcinoma risk is increased by periods of intense exposure, cumulative episodes of sunburn, and poor ability to tan, whereas squamous cell carcinoma risk is associated with prolonged exposure over time (Zanetti et al., 1996).

A later publication of results from the Helios study provided quantitation of the patterns of exposure to solar radiation associated with the development of basal cell and squamous cell carcinomas. The data revealed a sharp increase in the risk of developing squamous cell carcinoma beginning at a threshold level of 70,000 hours of cumulative sun exposure and maximizing at over 100,000 hours of exposure. In contrast, the risk of developing basal cell carcinoma reached a maximum at 10,000 hours of cumulative sun exposure and declined slightly with higher levels (Rosso et al., 1996) (**Figure 24.6**).

Significant associations between cumulative sun exposure and the risk of squamous cell carcinoma of the skin have been observed in other populations. In a population-based case control study conducted in Australia, investigators compared sun exposure patterns of 132 cases of squamous cell carcinoma with 1,031 controls matched by age and gender to the cases. Results revealed increasing risk with higher levels of lifetime sun exposure and a risk maximum (OR = 3.3) at 65,000 hours of exposure. History of blistering sunburns also increased the risk, whereas intermittent weekly sun exposure did not (English et al., 1998).

A case control study in Florida was designed to investigate patterns and timing of sunlight exposure that influence the development of basal cell and squamous cell carcinomas. The study included 218 cases of basal cell carcinoma, 169 cases of squamous cell carcinoma, and 316 control subjects matched to the cases by age and gender. Results showed that a history of blistering sunburn or long-term occupational sun exposure produced similar risk increases (approximately twofold) for both basal cell and squamous cell carcinomas (Iannacone et al., 2012).

To more thoroughly examine the association between occupational sun exposure and the risk of cutaneous squamous cell carcinoma, a team of German investigators conducted a systematic review of the literature and meta-analysis of the published data. The analysis included data from 18 epidemiologic investigations (12 case control studies and 6 cohort studies). The combined data showed a 77% increase in the risk of developing squamous cell carcinoma among workers who were routinely exposed to solar radiation compared to those employed in indoor occupations (Schmitt, Seidler, Diepgen, & Bauer, 2011).

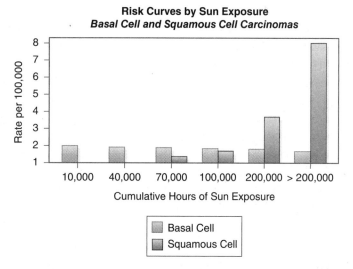

Figure 24.6 Risk of Basal Cell and Squamous Cell Carcinomas of the Skin by Cumulative Hours of Sun Exposure.

Source: Data from Rosso, S., Zanetti, R., Martinez, C., Tormo, M. J., Schraub, S., Sancho-Garnier, H., . . . Wechsler, J. (1996). The multicenter south European study 'Helios'. II: Different sun exposure patterns in the etiology of basal cell and squamous cell carcinomas of the skin. *British Journal of Cancer, 73*(11), 1447–1454.

Other Radiation Exposures and Squamous Cell Carcinoma of the Skin

Sources of radiation other than the sun also increase the risk of developing squamous cell carcinoma of the skin. In a long-term follow-up study of 4,799 Swedish patients who had received psoralen and ultraviolet A radiation (PUVA) for the treatment of skin disorders, significant risk increases were noted for both men (RR = 5.6) and women (RR = 3.6) compared to the general Swedish population (Lindelöf et al., 1999).

Similar results were observed in a cohort of 1,380 psoriasis patients treated with PUVA in Boston. At 25 years of follow-up, only 7% of individuals who underwent fewer than 200 PUVA treatments developed squamous cell carcinoma compared with more than 50% of those who underwent more than 400 treatments (Nijsten & Stern, 2003).

Skin conditions such as psoriasis may also be treated with ultraviolet B (UVB) radiation. In a cohort of 1,380 patients followed for up to 25 years, patients who received 300 or more UVB treatments had an approximately 40% increased risk of developing either squamous cell carcinoma or basal cell carcinoma compared to those who received fewer treatments (Lim & Stern, 2005).

Prolonged administration of low-dose ionizing radiation has been used in the treatment of a variety of skin disorders, including eczema, psoriasis, acne vulgaris, and tinea capitis. To examine the effects of therapeutic ionizing radiation on the development of nonmelanoma skin cancer, investigators in New Hampshire conducted a case control study of 592 cases of basal cell carcinoma, 289 cases of squamous cell carcinoma, and 536 controls matched to the cases by age and gender. Overall, the study revealed elevated risks for both squamous cell carcinoma (OR = 2.94) and basal cell carcinoma (OR = 3.30) confined to the site of radiation exposure (Lichter et al., 2000).

As already noted, the use of artificial devices that emit UV radiation, such as tanning beds, have been found to increase the risk of both squamous cell and basal cell carcinoma of the skin. Based on a meta-analysis of 12 studies, individuals who begin using indoor tanning devices before the age of 25 years increase their risk of developing squamous cell or basal cell carcinoma by 100% and 40%, respectively, compared to nonusers (Wehner et al., 2012).

Other Environmental Risk Factors for Squamous Cell Carcinoma of the Skin

Exposure to arsenic in drinking water and exposure to combustion products has been found to increase the risk of both basal cell carcinoma and squamous cell carcinoma. A biomarker of past arsenic exposure is the concentration in toenail clippings. In a case control study of skin cancer, arsenic concentrations in toenail clippings from 587 cases with basal cell carcinoma and 284 cases with squamous cell carcinoma were compared with concentrations in clippings from 524 matched controls. Compared to individuals with arsenic concentrations below the median, individuals with concentrations above the 97th percentile were found to have an approximately twofold increase in the risk of developing squamous cell carcinoma and a 44% increase in the risk of developing basal cell carcinoma. Notably, there was a long latency period from exposure to diagnosis; for example, invasive squamous cell carcinoma was diagnosed an average of 20 years after the initial reported exposure to arsenic (Karagas et al., 2001).

Smoking has been linked to certain forms of skin cancer in some studies but not in others. The available evidence on smoking and skin cancer was recently evaluated in a systematic review of the literature and meta-analysis of published risk estimates. Data were analyzed to assess the effects of current smoking on squamous cell carcinoma (6 studies) and basal cell carcinoma (16 studies). Smoking was found to increase the risk of developing squamous cell carcinoma (OR = 1.52) but not basal cell carcinoma (Leonardi-Bee, Ellison, & Bath-Hextall, 2012).

GENETICS OF NONMELANOMA SKIN CANCER

The vast majority of basal cell and squamous cell carcinomas of the skin are caused by exposure to ultraviolet light. Ultraviolet radiation, especially UVB, is absorbed by DNA and causes covalent bonding of pyrimidine bases to form dimers. If these dimers are not excised and replaced with normal bases before the DNA is replicated, the daughter cells may carry mutations at those sites that may lead to skin cancer if they disable tumor-suppressor genes. Loss of function of mutated tumor suppressor genes allows uncontrolled cell growth and division that causes tumor formation (Armstrong & Kricker 2001). Nevertheless, as discussed in the following sections, the spectrum of mutations and genetic alterations and the cellular pathways affected differ between basal cell and squamous cell carcinomas of the skin.

Somatic Mutations in Basal Cell Carcinoma of the Skin

The *Hedgehog* signaling pathway regulates spatial orientation and bilateral development of certain structures and organs during embryogenesis in all vertebrates, including humans. The pathway is called "Hedgehog" because mutated genes of the pathway cause the development of aberrant larvae in drosophila that resemble miniature hedgehogs (Nüsslein-Volhard & Wieschaus, 1980). Recent molecular studies have revealed that mutations in tumor suppressor genes that encode important proteins of the Hedgehog pathway, PTCH and SMO, are present

in about 90% of sporadic (nonheritable) basal cell carcinomas. Such mutations, which are presumably the result of UV radiation, enhance carcinogenesis of basal cells in the epidermis by disrupting the regulation of cell division, transcription, and protein synthesis (De Zwaan & Haass, 2010).

Mutations in the *p53* tumor suppressor gene are also frequently found in cases of sporadic basal cell carcinoma. Such *p53* mutations often occur together with mutations in the Hedgehog pathway. They typically arise at sites of consecutive pyrimidine DNA sequences, which is indicative of pyrimidine dimer formation due to exposure to ultraviolet B radiation (Ling et al., 2001; Rubin, Chen, & Ratner, 2005).

Germline Mutations and Basal Cell Carcinoma of the Skin

Gorlin Syndrome

A rare heritable condition known as Gorlin syndrome (also called nevoid basal cell carcinoma syndrome) is caused by a germline mutation in one allele of the *PTCH1* gene located on the long arm of human chromosome 9. Virtually all patients with this syndrome develop multiple basal cell carcinomas at an early age, and they may also develop other malignant tumors, including melanoma, medulloblastoma, meningioma, breast cancer, and non-Hodgkin's lymphoma (Gorlin, 2004).

Other Genetic Syndromes and Basal Cell Carcinoma of the Skin

Other rare genetic syndromes have been identified that predispose to multiple basal cell carcinomas of the skin. These include epidermolysis bullosa simplex (Dowling-Meara) and Rombo syndrome, which follow an autosomal dominant inheritance pattern, and Bazex–Dupre–Christol syndrome, which is an X-linked condition. These syndromes involve inheritance of defective genes that cause dysfunction of epidermal basal cells, leading to malignant transformation (NCI, 2014).

Somatic Mutations in Squamous Cell Carcinoma of the Skin

Squamous cell carcinoma of the skin characteristically develops by a multistep model of carcinogenesis. It is likely that the vast majority (~97%) of sporadic cases involve transformation of the precursor lesion, actinic keratosis, to squamous cell carcinoma (Babilas, Landthaler, & Szeimies, 2003; Ortonne, 2002).

A key factor in the development of actinic keratosis is the loss of function of the *p53* tumor suppressor gene on chromosome 17, which is essential for regulation of the cell cycle. Molecular studies have found *p53* mutations in 75–80% of actinic keratosis specimens from Caucasians and in more than 90% of cutaneous squamous cell carcinomas. Notably, mutations typically occur at dipyrimidine sites within the gene, implicating dimer formation due to UVB exposure as the mutagenic event. Additional mutations in genes encoding growth factors and DNA repair enzymes likely contribute to the multistep process. Furthermore, actinic keratoses and squamous cell carcinomas are typified by loss of heterozygosity and general chromosomal instability (Boukamp, 2005; Brash et al., 1991, 1996; Ortonne, 2002; Rass, 2005).

Germline Mutations and Squamous Cell Carcinoma of the Skin

Xeroderma Pigmentosum

Xeroderma pigmentosum is a rare genetic syndrome caused by germline mutations that regulate DNA repair. Individuals with this condition are prone to the development of multiple cutaneous malignancies, particularly squamous cell carcinomas, but also melanomas and basal cell carcinomas. The condition was initially described in four young patients by the Hungarian dermatologist Moriz Kaposi in 1874 (Hebra & Kaposi, 1874). A century later, geneticist James Cleaver discovered multiple defects in DNA excision repair genes that caused the syndrome (Cleaver, 1968).

Xeroderma pigmentosum strikes about 1 individual per million in the United States and Europe, but higher frequencies have been observed in some populations (e.g., 1 individual per 22,000 are afflicted in the Japanese population) (Tamura, DiGiovanna, & Kraemer, 2010). Classically, the condition behaves as an autosomal recessive trait whereby full phenotypic expression is manifest when there are genetic defects in both alleles of the affected gene. The median onset of nonmelanoma skin cancer in patients with xeroderma pigmentosum is under 10 years of age, and more than 50% of affected individuals die before their 40th birthday of other invasive cancers such as malignant melanoma and tumors of the brain and central nervous system (Bradford et al., 2011).

Multiple defects in DNA excision repair genes have been discovered that predispose to xeroderma pigmentosum. Patients with such defects are unable to excise pyrimidine dimers induced by ultraviolet radiation in the epidermis of the skin (Cleaver, 1968; States, McDuffie, Myrand, McDowell, & Cleaver, 1998). As a consequence, their rates of cutaneous nonmelanoma malignancies and melanoma are 10,000 and 2,000 times higher, respectively, than in the general population (DiGiovanna & Kraemer, 2012).

Other Genetic Syndromes and Squamous Cell Carcinoma of the Skin

Several rare genetic syndromes other than xeroderma pigmentosum have been discovered that predispose to the development of squamous cell carcinoma of the skin as well as other malignancies. These include Ferguson–Smith syndrome, various forms of albinism, Rothmund–Thomson syndrome, Fanconi anemia, Zinsser–Cole–Engman syndrome, Bloom syndrome, and Werner syndrome. These syndromes have been linked to a variety of germline mutations that induce chromosomal instability (NCI, 2014).

Genetic Differences in Basal Cell and Squamous Cell Carcinomas of the Skin

There appears to be a clear genetic distinction between basal cell carcinoma and squamous cell carcinoma of the skin. Typically, basal cell carcinomas exhibit a relatively simple genotype characterized by only a few key genetic mutations (e.g., Hedgehog and *p53* mutants). In contrast, although most squamous cell carcinomas do carry *p53* mutations, they tend to be more genetically heterogeneous and characteristically contain mutations of multiple genes and/or other chromosomal aberrations resulting from DNA deletions, additions, and translocations. According to one viewpoint, whereas most basal cell carcinomas develop de novo without evidence of a precursor lesion, the pathogenesis of squamous cell carcinoma of the skin appears to be a multistep process involving the intermediate precancerous lesion, actinic keratosis (Boukamp, 2005).

IMMUNOSUPPRESSION AND SKIN CANCER

Immunosuppression also contributes to the development of nonmelanoma skin cancers. Among solid-organ transplant recipients, the incidence of squamous cell carcinoma is 65 to 250 times higher and the incidence of basal cell carcinoma is 10 times higher than that observed in the general population. The risks vary with the type of transplant or therapy. For example, heart transplant recipients who require the highest rates of immunosuppression to prevent rejection are at approximately twofold higher risk of developing cutaneous malignancy than liver transplant recipients, in whom much lower levels of immunosuppression are needed to avoid rejection.

Furthermore, nonmelanoma skin cancers in solid-organ transplant recipients and chronic lymphocytic leukemia patients occur at a younger age and have a higher risk of recurrence and metastatic spread than the same malignancies in patients with intact immune systems. It is also notable that suppression of the immune system has a greater impact on the development of squamous cell carcinoma than basal cell carcinoma. For example, among transplant patients, the ratio of squamous cell carcinomas to basal cell carcinomas is approximately 2:1, whereas among patients with an intact immune system, the ratio of basal cell carcinomas to squamous cell carcinomas is approximately 4:1 (Glover, Niranjan, Kwan, & Leigh, 1994; Hartevelt et al., 1990; Jensen et al., 1999; Kaplan & Cook, 2005; Krynitz et al., 2013; Lindelöf, Sigurgeirsson, Gäbel, & Stern, 2000).

Certain infectious agents that cause immune dysfunction are also associated with the development of nonmelanoma skin cancer. In a cohort study conducted in northern California, the incidence of nonmelanoma skin cancer was compared among 6,560 HIV-positive subjects and 36,821 HIV-negative subjects monitored during 1996–2008. Results revealed that individuals who were HIV-positive had more than double the risk of developing either basal cell or squamous cell carcinoma of the skin compared to HIV-negative individuals. Furthermore, severely immunocompromised subjects with low CD4 counts (< 200 per milliliter) had more than a fourfold increase in the risk of developing squamous cell carcinoma (Silverberg et al., 2013).

Skin infections by certain strains of human papillomavirus (HPV) have also been linked to the development of nonmelanoma skin cancer. A review of the literature identified 17 studies in which HPV positivity was determined in specimens of squamous cell carcinoma compared to normal skin. Meta-analysis of the data revealed that prior infection with multiple cutaneous HPV strains was associated with a twofold increase in the risk of developing cutaneous squamous cell carcinoma. Analysis of a subset of the data also revealed that among immunocompromised individuals, HPV-positive subjects were three times more likely to develop squamous cell carcinoma than HPV-negative subjects. Based on these results, the investigators suggest that HPV infection may be a cofactor that acts in concert with other factors to heighten the risk of developing cutaneous squamous cell carcinoma (Wang, Aldabagh, Yu, & Arron, 2014).

The increased risk of nonmelanoma skin cancer in immunocompromised patients is influenced by the depletion of Langerhans cells in the epidermis. Immunologic studies suggest that one of the primary roles of these immune cells is to present antigens of invading microbes to regulatory T cells in order to stimulate the immune response. However, some recent studies suggest that the Langerhans cells may, in fact, diminish the immune response under certain conditions, and there is currently hot debate about their specific function in the immune system of the skin (Stoitzner, 2010). Regardless of the exact mechanisms involved, depletion of the Langerhans cell population by immunosuppressive drugs, UV radiation, infection, or other exposures likely plays a critical permissive role in the development of cutaneous squamous cell carcinoma (Gibson, O'Grady, Key, Leader, & Murphy, 1998; Thiers, Maize, Spicer, & Cantor, 1984). Notably, loss of function of the Langerhans cells is associated with chronic inflammation that predisposes to the development of malignancy (Bennett, Robinson, Baron, & Cooper, 2008).

INFLAMMOGENESIS OF SKIN CANCER

Chronic inflammation induced by solar UV radiation and/or other environmental exposures undoubtedly plays a critical role in the genesis of skin cancer. Molecular studies of basal cell carcinomas, squamous cell carcinomas, actinic keratosis, and malignant melanomas have identified a variety of inflammatory factors that stimulate carcinogenesis. These include genes that encode various transcription factors, cytokines, chemokines, and chemokine receptors such as cyclo-oxygenase-2 (COX-2), prostaglandin E2 (PGE2), nuclear factor kappa B (NF-κB), signal transducer and activator of transcription 3 (STAT3), and hypoxia-inducible factor alpha (HIF-1α). Chronic inflammation stimulates several mechanisms of tumor development, including mutagenesis, mitogenesis, angiogenesis, disruption of apoptosis, immunosuppression, and metastasis. Inflammatory pathways are therefore attractive molecular targets for skin cancer prevention (Maru, Gandhi, Ramchandani, & Kumar, 2014).

RISK OF MULTIPLE BASAL CELL OR SQUAMOUS CELL CARCINOMAS OF THE SKIN

Individuals who develop an initial basal cell or squamous cell carcinoma of the skin are at high risk of developing subsequent skin cancer. In a prospective study of 1,805 patients who were diagnosed with an initial basal cell or squamous cell carcinoma of the skin, 35% developed a second skin cancer within 3 years and 50% developed a second skin cancer within 5 years. For both tumor types, the risk was higher among those with severe actinic damage who sunburned easily (Robinson, 1987).

VITAMIN D AND SKIN CANCER

Because vitamin D metabolism is activated in the skin by exposure to sunlight, the level of vitamin D in the blood might be associated with the risk of skin cancer. To test this hypothesis, investigators prospectively evaluated the association between baseline levels of plasma vitamin D [measured as 25(OH)D] and the risk of incident squamous cell carcinoma and basal cell carcinoma among 4,641 women from the Nurses' Health Study. During 22 years of follow-up, 510 incident cases of basal cell carcinoma and 75 incident cases of squamous cell carcinoma were reported. The results revealed that compared to individuals with baseline vitamin D levels in the lowest quartile, women in the highest quartile were at increased risk of developing squamous cell carcinoma (OR = 3.77) or basal cell carcinoma (OR = 2.07). These data suggest that a high level of plasma vitamin D may reflect long-term sun exposure and therefore serve as a biomarker of impending nonmelanoma skin cancer (Liang, Nan, Qureshi, & Han, 2012).

EPIDEMIOLOGY OF MERKEL CELL CARCINOMA

Merkel cell carcinoma is a rare and highly aggressive form of skin cancer that develops from specialized cells of the epidermis. Merkel cells are located at terminal nerve endings in the epidermis where they regulate the sensation of touch. They were discovered in 1875 by the German pathologist Friedrick Sigmund Merkel, and have since been the subject of considerable controversy concerning their origin. Recently, molecular studies have determined that Merkel cells are specialized epithelial cells that contain mechanoreceptors on their cell membranes, thereby facilitating light touch responses in the skin (Maricich et al., 2009).

Merkel cell carcinoma occurs primarily in elderly adults who are 60–80 years of age. As with other forms of skin cancer (other than melanoma), cases of Merkel cell carcinoma are not routinely reported to tumor registries and, as a consequence, reliable estimates of incidence are sparse. In a longitudinal study of incident cases identified in the U.S. population through the SEER program of the National Cancer Institute, the annual incidence of Merkel cell carcinoma showed an approximate threefold increase during 1986–2001, from 1.5 to 4.4 cases per million (Hodgson, 2005).

Recent molecular studies conducted by investigators at the University of Pittsburgh identified a polyomavirus in tissues of Merkel cell carcinoma (Feng, Shuda, Chang, & Moore, 2008). Subsequent studies determined that the majority of Merkel cell carcinomas (~80%) contain a mutated polyomavirus gene that causes T cell anergy, depression of the immune system, and disruption of apoptosis (Shuda et al., 2008). Infection of the skin by polyomaviruses and lysogeny of viral DNA with cells in the epidermis is virtually ubiquitous among humans. Although the vast majority of these latent infections are innocuous, malignant transformation does occasionally occur, particularly in viral-infected Merkel cells of older adults with skin damage due to solar radiation and/or immunosuppressive conditions. Compared to the general population, the risk of developing Merkel cell carcinoma is increased 10-fold among organ transplant recipients, 13-fold among patients with HIV disease, and 30-fold among patients with chronic lymphocytic leukemia (Engels, Frisch, Goedert, Biggar, & Miller, 2002; Heath et al., 2008; Penn & First, 1999).

Merkel cell carcinoma typically presents clinically as a small, painless, bluish-red nodule located on the face, neck, hands, or other sun-exposed areas of skin. Nearly half of these tumors develop in the periorbital skin. Unfortunately, most Merkel cell carcinomas have already metastasized at the time of diagnosis; as a consequence, the prognosis for this form of skin cancer is grim. As with other forms of skin cancer, protection of the skin from damaging solar radiation is essential for prevention (Nghiem & James, 2007).

ENVIRONMENTAL PREVENTION OF SKIN CANCER

Ultraviolet Radiation and the Ozone Layer

The primary line of defense against harmful rays from the sun is the ozone layer in the stratosphere, 10 to 50 kilometers above the surface of the earth. Ozone (O_3) forms when molecular oxygen (O_2) in the upper atmosphere absorbs short-wave UVC radiation and decomposes to form singlet oxygen (O), which then reacts with O_2 to form O_3. The O_3 molecules effectively absorb UV radiation up to about 310 nm wavelength; the ozone layer blocks all UVC and most UVB radiation emitted by the sun, thereby protecting life on earth from these damaging rays. In 1995, Paul Crutzen, Mario Molina, and Sherwood

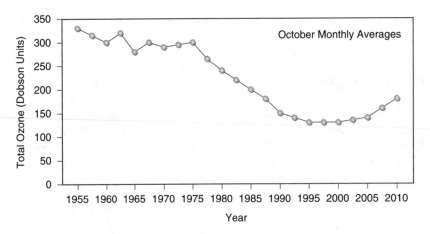

Figure 24.7 Depletion of the Ozone Layer Over Halley Bay, Antarctica.

Data points are 3-year moving averages.

Source: Data from World Meteorological Organization. (1995). Global ozone research and monitoring project: 1994. WMO No. 37. Geneva, Switzerland. Retrieved from http://ozonewatch.gsfc.nasa.gov/facts/history.html; National Aeronautics and Space Administration (NASA). (2014). Ozone hole watch. Washington, DC. Retrieved from http://ozonewatch.gsfc.nasa.gov/facts/history.html

Rowland were awarded the Nobel Prize for their pioneering work in atmospheric chemistry that elucidated the formation and decomposition of ozone (Crutzen, Molina, & Rowland, 1995).

The Ozone Hole

The *ozone hole* refers to annual thinning of the ozone layer over Antarctica due to inorganic chlorine molecules that reach the stratosphere (Farman, Gardiner, & Shanklin, 1985). Atmospheric conditions at the earth's poles favor the destruction of ozone by reactive halogen gases. In recent decades, the ozone layer over the South Pole has been depleted by the release of ozone-depleting substances that reach the stratosphere (**Figure 24.7**). These substances include chlorofluorocarbons (freons) and bromofluorocarbons (halons) that are widely used in refrigeration. Studies of the mathematical relationship among the thinning of the ozone layer, corresponding increases in ultraviolet radiation, and the development of skin cancer suggest that a 1% reduction in ozone concentration will increase UVB radiation exposure by 2%, which would increase the incidence of nonmelanoma skin cancer by 3–6% (Kripke, 1988). In Australia, where the incidence of nonmelanoma skin cancer is the highest in the world, it is estimated that the ozone layer over Australia has been depleted by 5–9% since the 1960s (World Meteorological Organization, 1995).

Protecting the Ozone Layer

Accumulating evidence that ozone is being depleted from the earth's stratosphere by manmade substances has stimulated worldwide efforts to protect the ozone layer. The Montreal Protocol is an international treaty designed to protect the ozone layer by phasing out the production of those substances (freons, halons, etc.) responsible for ozone depletion. As a result of this international agreement, the ozone hole in Antarctica appears to be slowly recovering (Anderson & Sarma, 2007).

BEHAVIORAL PREVENTION OF SKIN CANCER

The key to effective primary prevention of skin cancer is protection of the skin from damaging solar radiation. Wearing protective clothing and using sunscreen products with a sun protective factor (SPF) of 30 or higher is highly recommended for all individuals who are routinely exposed to solar radiation, and particularly those with susceptible phenotypes such as individuals with fair skin and freckles who do not readily tan and who sunburn easily, immunocompromised individuals, genetically predisposed individuals, and individuals with a history of prior skin cancer. Other chronic exposures that damage the skin or cause immunosuppression should also be avoided such as UV radiation from tanning devices, skin irritants, arsenic-containing compounds, and tobacco smoking.

Routine screening for the early detection of actinic keratoses and/or in situ malignancies of the skin is a critical component of effective secondary prevention. The vast majority of skin cancers are curable by early detection and effective therapy. *Mohs surgery* is a highly effective surgical technique that involves intraoperative microscopic examination of serial frozen sections of thin layers of tissue excised from existing lesions. The technique is designed to precisely and completely remove suspicious skin lesions with the objective of obtaining clear surgical margins in order to minimize recurrence.

Former U.S. Surgeon General Boris Lushniak released the *Call to Action to Prevent Skin Cancer* (U.S. Department of Health and Human Services, 2014), a comprehensive plea for increased awareness, policies, and research, with a goal of supporting skin cancer prevention. The five strategic goals of the report are (1) to increase opportunities for sun protection in outdoor settings; (2) to provide individuals with the information they need to make informed, healthy choices about ultraviolet radiation exposure; (3) to promote policies that advance the national goal of preventing skin cancer; (4) to reduce harms from indoor tanning; and (5) to strengthen research, surveillance, monitoring, and evaluation related to skin cancer prevention.

Despite these recommendations, there is an important caveat to restrictive advice on sun exposure habits designed to reduce the risk of skin cancer. As an example, evidence from a recent epidemiologic study of Swedish women found that those who avoided sun exposure had a twofold increase in all-cause mortality compared to those with high sun exposure, presumably due to their lower levels of vitamin D. The investigators concluded that "following sun exposure advice that is very restrictive in countries with low solar intensity might in fact be harmful to women's health" (Lindqvist et al., 2014).

Maintaining sufficient blood levels of vitamin D (at least 30 ng/ml) is important for prevention of osteoporosis, cardiovascular disease, diabetes, autoimmune disease, and some forms of cancer. More than 90% of the human vitamin D requirement comes from casual exposure to sunlight. Judicious exposure to sunlight (perhaps 10 minutes of exposure 2 to 3 times per week) is therefore necessary to meet the body's requirement for vitamin D (Holick, 2002).

• • • REFERENCES

Alam, M., & Ratner, D. (2001). Cutaneous squamous-cell carcinoma. *New England Journal of Medicine, 344,* 975–983.

Anderson, S. O., & Sarma, K. M. (2007). *Protecting the ozone layer.* London, England: The United Nations History, Earthscan Press.

Armstrong, B. K., & Kricker, A. (2001). The epidemiology of UV induced skin cancer. *Journal of Photochemistry and Photobiology B: Biology, 63,* 8–18.

Arthey, S., & Clarke, V. A. (1995). Suntanning and sun protection: A review of the psychological literature. *Social Science and Medicine, 40,* 265–274.

Australian Institute of Health and Welfare & Cancer Australia. (2008). *Non-melanoma skin cancer: General practice consultations, hospitalization and mortality.* Cancer series no. 43. Cat. no. 39. Canberra, Australia. Retrieved from http://www.aihw.gov.au/WorkArea/DownloadAsset.aspx?id=6442454591

Babilas, P., Landthaler, M., & Szeimies, R. M. (2003). Actinic keratosis. *Hautarzt, 54,* 551–562.

Bath-Hextall, F., Leonardi-Bee, J., Smith, C., Meal, A., & Hubbard, R. (2007). Trends in incidence of skin basal cell carcinoma. Additional evidence from a UK primary care database study. *International Journal of Cancer, 121*(9), 2105–2108.

Bauer, A., Diepgen, T. L., & Schmitt, J. (2011). Is occupational solar ultraviolet irradiation a relevant risk factor for basal cell carcinoma? A systematic review and meta-analysis of the epidemiological literature. *British Journal of Dermatology, 165*(3), 612–625.

Bennett, M. F., Robinson, M. K., Baron, E. D., & Cooper, K. D. (2008). Skin immune systems and inflammation: Protector of the skin or promoter of aging? *Journal of Investigative Dermatology Symposium Proceedings, 13,* 15–19.

Birch-Johansen, F., Jensen, A., Mortensen, L., Olesen, A. B., & Kjaer, S. K. (2010). Trends in the incidence of nonmelanoma skin cancer in Denmark 1978-2007: Rapid incidence increase among young Danish women. *International Journal of Cancer, 127*(9), 2190–2198.

Boukamp, P. (2005). Non-melanoma skin cancer: What drives tumor development and progression? *Carcinogenesis, 26*(10), 1657–1667.

Boyd, A. S., Shyr, Y., & Lloyd, E. K. (1991). Non-melanoma skin cancer occurring in patients treated with PUVA five to ten years after first treatment. *Journal of Investigative Dermatology, 91*(2), 120–124.

Bradford, P. T., Goldstein, A. M., Tamura, D., Khan, S. G., Ueda, T., Boyle, J., . . . Kraemer, K. H. (2011). Cancer and neurologic degeneration in xeroderma pigmentosum: Long term follow-up characterizes the role of DNA repair. *Journal of Medical Genetics, 48*(3), 168–176.

Brash, D. E., Rudolph, J. A., Simon, J. A., Lin, A., McKenna, G. J., Baden, H. P., . . . Pontén, J. (1991). A role for sunlight in skin cancer: UV-induced *p53* mutations in squamous cell carcinoma. *Proceedings of the National Academy of Sciences of the United States of America, 88*(22), 10124–10128.

Brash, D. E., Ziegler, A., Jonason, A. S., Simon, J. A., Kunala, S., & Leffell, D. J. (1996). Sunlight and sunburn in human skin cancer: *p53*, apoptosis and tumor promotion. *Journal of Investigative Dermatology Symposium Proceedings, 1*, 136–142.

Byfield, S. D., Chen, D., Yim, Y. M., & Reyes, C. (2013). Age distribution of patients with advanced non-melanoma skin cancer in the United States. *Archives of Dermatologic Research, 305*(9), 845–850.

Christenson, L. J., Borrowman, T. A., Vachon, C. M., Tellefson, M. M., Otley, C. C., Seaver, A. L., & Roenighk, R. K. (2005). Incidence of basal cell and squamous cell carcinomas in a population younger than 40 years. *Journal of the American Medical Association, 294*(6), 681–690.

Cleaver, J. (1968). Defective repair of DNA in xeroderma pigmentosum. *Nature, 218*(5142), 652–656.

Criscione, V. D., Weinstock, M. A., Naylor, M. F., Luque, C., Eide, M. J., & Bingham, S. F.; Department of Veteran Affairs Topical Tretinoin Chemoprevention Trial Group. (2009). Actinic keratoses: Natural history and risk of malignant transformation in the Veterans Affairs Topical Tretinoin Chemoprevention Trial. *Cancer, 115*(11), 2523–2530.

Crutzen, P. J., Molkina, M. J., & Sherwood, F. S. (1995). The Nobel prize in chemistry, 1995. The Royal Swedish Academy of Sciences. Retrieved from http://www.nobelprize.org/nobel_prizes /chemistry/laureates/1995/illpres/

de Gruijl, F. R. (1999). Skin cancer and solar UV radiation. *European Journal of Cancer, 35*, 2003–2009.

De Zwaan, S. E., & Haass, N. K. (2010). Genetics of basal cell carcinoma. *Australasian Journal of Dermatology, 51*(2), 81–92.

DiGiovanna, J., & Kraemer, K. H. (2012). Shining a light on xeroderma pigmentosum. *Journal of Investigative Dermatology, 132*(3), 785–796.

Eisemann, N., Waldmann, A., Geller, A. C., Weinstock, M. A., Volkmer, B., Greinert, R., . . . Katalinic, A. (2013). Non-melanoma skin cancer incidence and impact of skin cancer screening on incidence. *Journal of Investigative Dermatology, 134*, 43–50.

Engels, E. A., Frisch, M., Goedert, J. J., Biggar, R. J., & Miller, R. W. (2002). Merkel cell carcinoma and HIV infection. *Lancet, 359*, 497–498.

English, D. R., Armstrong, B. K., Kricker, A., Winter, M. G., Heenan, P. J., & Randel, P. L. (1998). Case-control study of sun exposure and squamous cell carcinoma of the skin. *International Journal of Cancer, 77*, 347–353.

Farman, J. C., Gardiner, B. G., & Shanklin, J. D. (1985). Large losses of total ozone in Antarctica reveal seasonal ClOx/NOx interaction. *Nature, 351*, 207–210.

Feldman, S. R., & Fleischer, A. B. (2011). Progression of actinic keratosis to squamous cell carcinoma revisited: Clinical and treatment implications. *Cutis, 87*(4), 201–207.

Feng, H., Shuda, M., Chang, Y., & Moore, P. S. (2008). Clonal integration of a polyomavirus in human Merkel cell carcinoma. *Science, 319*(5866), 1096–1100.

Ferrucci, L. M., Cartmel, B., Molinaro, A. M., Leffell, D. J., Bale, A. E., Mayne, S. T. (2012). Indoor tanning and risk of early-onset basal cell carcinoma. *Journal of the American Academy of Dermatology, 67*(4), 552–562.

Flohil, S. C., Seubring, I., van Rossum, M. M., Coebergh, J. W., de Vries, E., & Nijsten, T. (2013). Trends in basal cell carcinoma incidence rates: A 37-year Dutch observational study. *Journal of Investigative Dermatology, 133*(4), 913–918.

Fuchs, A. & Marmur, E. (2007). The kinetics of skin cancer: Progression of actinic keratosis to squamous cell carcinoma. *Dermatologic Surgery, 33*(9), 1099–1101.

Gallagher, R. P., Hill, G. B., Bajdik, C. D., Fincham, S., Coldman, A. J., McLean, D. I., & Threlfall, W. J. (1995). Sunlight exposure, pigmentary factors, and risk of nonmelanocytic skin cancer. I. Basal cell carcinoma. *Archives of Dermatology, 131*(2), 157–163.

Gibson, G. E., O'Grady, A., Key, E. W., Leader, M., & Murphy, G. M. (1998). Langerhans cells in benign, premalignant and malignant skin lesions of renal transplant recipients and the effect of retinoid therapy. *Journal of the European Academy of Dermatology and Venereology, 10*(2), 131–136.

Gloster, H. M. Jr., & Neal, K. (2005). Skin cancer in skin of color. *Journal of the American Academy of Dermatology, 55*(5), 741–760.

Glover, M. T., Niranjan, N., Kwan, J. T., & Leigh, I. M. (1994). Non-melanoma skin cancer in renal transplant recipients: The extent of the problem and a strategy for management. *British Journal of Plastic Surgery, 47*(2), 86–89.

Gorlin, R. J. (2004). Nevoid basal cell carcinoma (Gorlin) syndrome. *Genetics in Medicine, 6*(6), 530–539.

Green, A., & Battistutta, D. (1990). Incidence and determinants of skin cancer in a high-risk Australian population. *International Journal of Cancer, 46*(3), 356–361.

Hartevelt, M. M., Bavinck, J. N., Kootte, A. M., Vermeer, B. J., & Vandenbroucke, J. P. (1990). Incidence of skin cancer after renal transplantation in The Netherlands. *Transplantation, 49*(3), 506–509.

Hartevelt, M. M., Bavinck, J. N., Kootte, A. M., Vermeer, B. J., & Vandenbroucke, J. P. (1996). Arsenic in dermatology. *Dermatologic Surgery, 22*, 301–304.

Heath, M., Jaimes, N., Lemos, B., Mostaghimi, A., Wang, L. C., Peñas, P. F., & Nghiem, P. (2008). Clinical characteristics of Merkel cell carcinoma at diagnosis in 195 patients: The AEIOU features. *Journal of the American Academy of Dermatology, 58*, 375–381.

Hebra, F., & Kaposi, M. (1874). On diseases of the skin including exanthemata. Volume III. *The New Sydenham Society, 61*, 252–258.

Hodgson, N. C. (2005). Merkel cell carcinoma: Changing incidence trends. *Journal of Surgical Oncology, 89*(1), 1–4.

Holick, M. F. (2002). Vitamin D: The underappreciated D-lightful hormone that is important for skeletal and cellular health. *Current Opinions in Endocrinology and Diabetes, 9*, 87–98.

Iannacone, M. R., Wang, W., Stockwell, H. G., O'Rourke, K., Giuliano, A. R., Sondak, V. K., . . . Rollison, D. E. (2012). Patterns and timing of sunlight exposure and risk of basal cell and squamous cell carcinomas of the skin: A case control study. *BMC Cancer, 12*(1), 417. doi: 10.1186/1471-2407-12-417.

Ireland National Cancer Registry. (2013). Non-melanoma skin cancer. *Cancer Trends,* 20. Retrieved from http://www.ncri.ie /sites/ncri/files/pubs/CancerTrendsNo .20-NonMelanomaSkinCancer.pdf

Jensen, P., Hansen, S., Møller, B., Leivestad, T., Pfeffer, P., Geiran, O., . . . Simonsen, S. (1999). Skin cancer in kidney and heart transplant recipients and different long-term immunosuppressive therapy regimens. *Journal of the American Academy of Dermatology, 40*(2 Pt 1), 177–186.

Kaplan, A. L., & Cook, J. L. (2005). Cutaneous squamous cell carcinoma in patients with chronic lymphocytic leukemia. *SKINmed, 4*(5), 300–304.

Karagas, M. R., Stannard, V. A., Mott, L. A., Slattery, M. J., Spencer, S. K., & Weinstock, M. A. (2002). Use of tanning devices and risk of basal cell and squamous cell skin cancers. *Journal of the National Cancer Institute, 94*(3), 224–226.

Karagas, M. R., Stukel, T. A., Morris, J. S., Tosteson, T. D., Weiss, J. E., Spencer, S. K., & Greenberg, E. R. (2001). Skin cancer risk in relation to toenail arsenic concentrations in a US population-based case-control study. *American Journal of Epidemiology, 153*(6), 559–565.

Katalinic, A., Kunze, U., & Schäfer, T. (2003). Epidemiology of cutaneous melanoma and non-melanoma skin cancer in Schleswig-Holstein, Germany: Incidence, clinical subtypes, tumor stages and localization (epidemiology of skin cancer). *British Journal of Dermatology, 149*(6), 1200–1206.

Kopf, A. W. (1979). Computer analysis of 3531 basal cell carcinomas of the skin. *Journal of Dermatology, 6*(5), 267–281.

Kripke, M. L. (1988). Impact of ozone depletion on skin cancers. *Journal of Dermatologic Surgery and Oncology, 14*(8), 853–857.

Krynitz, B., Edgren, G., Lindelöf, B., Baecklund, E., Brattström, C., Wilczek, H., & Smedby, K. E. (2013). Risk of skin cancer and other malignancies in kidney, liver, heart and lung transplant recipients 1970 to 2008—a Swedish population-based study. *International Journal of Cancer, 132*(6), 1429–1438.

Leonardi-Bee, J., Ellison, T., & Bath-Hextall, F. (2012). Smoking and the risk of non-melanoma skin cancer, systematic review and meta-analysis. *Archives of Dermatology, 148*(8), 939–946.

Liang, G., Nan, H., Qureshi, A. A., & Han, J. (2012). Pre-diagnostic plasma 25-hydroxyvitamin D levels and risk of non-melanoma skin cancer in women. *PLoS One, 7*(4), e35211. doi: 10.1371/journal.pone.003521.

Lichter, M. D., Karagas, M. R., Mott, L. A., Spencer, S. K., Stukel, T. A., & Greenberg, E. R. (2000). Therapeutic ionizing radiation and the incidence of basal cell carcinoma and squamous cell carcinoma. The New Hampshire Skin Cancer Study Group. *Archives of Dermatology, 136*(8), 1007–1011.

Lim, J. L., & Stern, R. S. (2005). High levels of ultraviolet B exposure increase the risk of non-melanoma skin cancer in psoralen and ultraviolet A-treated patients. *Journal of Investigative Dermatology, 124*(3), 505–513.

Lindelöf, B., Sigurgeirsson, B., Gäbel, H., & Stern, R. S. (2000). Incidence of skin cancer in 5356 patients following organ transplantation. *British Journal of Dermatology, 143*(3), 513–519.

Lindelöf, B., Sigurgeirsson, B., Tegner, E., Larkö, O., Johannesson, A., Berne, B., . . . Emtestam, L. (1999). PUVA and cancer risk: The Swedish follow-up study. *British Journal of Dermatology, 141*(1), 108–112.

Lindqvist, P. G., Epstein, E., Landin-Olsson, M., Ingvar, C., Nielsen, K., Stenbeck, M., & Olsson, H. (2014). Avoidance of sun exposure is a risk factor for all-cause mortality: Results from the Melanoma in Southern Sweden cohort. *Journal of Internal Medicine, 176*(1), 77–86.

Ling, G., Ahmadian, A., Persson, A., Undén, A. B., Afink, G., Williams, C., . . . Pontén, F. (2001). PATCHED and *p53* gene alterations I sporadic and hereditary basal cell cancer. *Oncogene, 20*, 7770–7778.

Maricich, S. M., Wellnitz, S. A., Nelson, A. M., Lesniak, D. R., Gerling, G. J., Lumpkin, E. A., & Zoghbi, H. Y. (2009). Merkel cells are essential for light touch responses. *Science, 324*(5934), 1580–1582.

Marks, R., Rennie, G., & Selwood, T. S. (1988). Malignant transformation of solar keratoses to squamous cell carcinoma. *Lancet, 1*(8589), 795–79.

Maru, G. B., Gandhi, K., Ramchandani, A., & Kumar, G. (2014). The role of inflammation in skin cancer. *Advances in Experimental Medicine and Biology, 816*, 437–469.

Miller, D. L., & Weinstock, M. A. (1994). Nonmelanoma skin cancer in the United States: Incidence. *Journal of the American Academy of Dermatology, 30*, 774–778.

Miller, S. J. (1995). Etiology and pathogenesis of basal cell carcinoma. *Clinics in Dermatology, 13*(6), 527–536.

National Aeronautics and Space Administration (NASA). (2014). Ozone hole watch. Washington, DC. Retrieved from http://ozonewatch.gsfc.nasa.gov/facts/history.html

National Cancer Institute. (1996). *SEER rates, 1992–1996.* Bethesda, MD: U.S. Department of Health and Human Services, National Institutes of Health.

National Cancer Institute. (2014). *Genetics of skin cancer.* Bethesda, MD: U.S. Department of Health and Human Services, National Institutes of Health.

Nghiem, P., & James, N. (2008). Merkel cell carcinoma. In K. Wolff, L. A. Goldsmith, S. I. Katz, B. A. Gilchrest, A. S. Paller, & D. J. Leffell (Eds.), *Fitzpatrick's dermatology in general medicine* (7th ed., pp. 1087–1094). New York, NY: McGraw-Hill.

Nijsten, T. E., & Stern, R. S. (2003). The increased risk of skin cancer is persistent after discontinuation of psoralen+ultraviolet A: A cohort study. *Journal of Investigative Dermatology, 121*(2), 252–258.

Nüsslein-Volhard, C., & Wieschaus, E. (1980). Mutations affecting segment number and polarity in drosophila. *Nature, 287*(5785), 795–801.

Ortonne, J. P. (2002). From actinic keratosis to squamous cell carcinoma. *British Journal of Dermatology, 146*(61), 20–23.

Penn, I., & First, M. R. (1999). Merkel's cell carcinoma in organ recipients: Report of 41 cases. *Transplantation, 68,* 1717–1721.

Rass, K. (2005). UV damage and DNA repair in basal cell and squamous cell carcinomas. In J. Reichrath (Ed.), *Molecular mechanisms of basal cell and squamous cell carcinomas* (pp. 18–30). New York, NY: Springer Science.

Ridky, T. W. (2007). Nonmelanoma skin cancer. *Journal of the American Academy of Dermatology, 57*(3), 484–501.

Robinson, J. K. (1987). Risk of developing another basal cell carcinoma. A 5-year prospective study. *Cancer, 60*(1), 118–120.

Rosso, S., Zanetti, R., Martinez, C., Tormo, M. J., Schraub, S., Sancho-Garnier, H., . . . Wechsler, J. (1996). The multicentre south European study "Helios." II: Different sun exposure patterns in the aetiology of basal cell and squamous cell carcinomas of the skin. *British Journal of Cancer, 73*(11), 1447–1454.

Rubin, A. I., Chen, E. H., & Ratner, D. (2005). Basal-cell carcinoma. *New England Journal of Medicine, 353,* 2262–2269.

Sadamori, N., Mine, M., & Honda, T. (1991). Incidence of skin cancer among Nagasaki atomic bomb survivors. *Journal of Radiation Research, 32*(Suppl 2), 217–225.

Schmitt, J., Seidler, A., Diepgen, T. L., & Bauer, A. (2011). Occupational ultraviolet light exposure increases the risk forthe development of cutaneous squamous cell carcinoma: A systematic review and meta-analysis. *British Journal of Dermatology, 164*(2), 291–307.

Shuda, M., Feng, H., Kwun, H. J., Rosen, S. T., Gjoerup, O., Moore, P. S., & Chang, Y. (2008). T antigen mutations are a human tumor-specific signature for Merkel cell polyomavirus. *Proceedings of the National Academy of Sciences of the United States of America, 105,* 16272–16277.

Silverberg, M. J., Leyden, W., Warton, E. M., Quesenberry, C. P., Engels, E. A., & Asgari, M. M. (2013). HIV infection status, immunodeficiency and the incidence of non-melanoma skin cancer. *Journal of the National Cancer Institute, 105*(5), 350–360.

Staples, M., Marks, M., & Giles, G. (1998). Trends in the incidence of non-melanocytic skin cancer (NMSC) treated in Australia 1985–1995. Are primary prevention programs starting to have an effect? *International Journal of Cancer, 78,* 144–148.

Staples, M. P., Elwood, M., Burton, R. C., William, J. L., Marks, R., & Giles, G. G. (2006). Non-melanoma skin cancer in Australia: The 2002 national survey and trends since 1985. *Medical Journal of Australia, 184,* 6–10.

States, J. C., McDuffie, E. R., Myrand, S. P., McDowell, M., & Cleaver, J. E. (1998). Distribution of mutations in the human xeroderma pigmentosum group A gene and their relationships to the functional regions of the DNA damage recognition protein. *Human Mutation, 12*(2), 103–113.

Stern, R. S., & Lange, R. (1990). Incidence of skin cancer after renal transplantation in the Netherlands. *Transplantation, 49,* 506–509.

Stoitzner, P. (2010). The Langerhans cell controversy: Are they immunostimulatory or immunoregulatory cells of the skin immune system? *Immunology and Cell Biology, 88,* 348–350.

Tamura, D., DiGiovanna, J. J., & Kraemer, K. H. (2010). Founder mutations in xeroderma pigmentosum. *Journal of Investigative Dermatology, 130*(6), 1491–1493.

Thiers, B. H., Maize, J. C., Spicer, S. S., & Cantor, A. B. (1984). The effect of aging and chronic sun exposure on human Langerhans cell populations. *Journal of Investigative Dermatology, 82*(3), 223–226.

U.S. Department of Health and Human Services. (2014). *The Surgeon General's call to action to prevent skin cancer.* Washington, DC: Author.

van Dam, R. M., Huang, Z., Rimm, E. B., Weinstock, M. A., Spiegelman, D., Colditz, G. A., . . . Giovannucci, E. (1999). Risk factors for basal cell carcinoma of the skin in men: Results from the health professionals follow-up study. *American Journal of Epidemiology, 150*(5), 459–468.

Wang, J., Aldabagh, B., Yu, J., & Arron, S. T. (2014). Role of human papillomavirus in cutaneous squamous cell carcinoma, a meta-analysis. *Journal of the American Academy of Dermatology, 70*(4), 621–629.

Wehner, M. R., Shive, M. L., Chren, M. M., Han, J., Qureshi, A. A., & Linos, E. (2012). Indoor tanning and non-melanoma skin cancer: Systematic review and meta-analysis. *British Medical Journal, 345,* e5909.

Wong, C. M., Strange, R. C., & Lear, J. T. (2003). Basal cell carcinoma. *British Medical Journal, 327,* 794.

World Meteorological Organization. (1995). Global ozone research and monitoring project: 1994. WMO No. 37. Geneva, Switzerland. Retrieved from http://ozonewatch.gsfc.nasa.gov/facts/history.html

Wu, S., Han, J., Li, W. Q., Li, T., & Qureshi, A. A. (2013). Basal-cell carcinoma incidence and associated risk factors in US women and men. *American Journal of Epidemiology, 178*(6), 890–897.

Yamada, M., Kodama, K., Fujita, S., Akahoshi, M., Yamada, S., Hirose, R., & Hori, M. (1996). Prevalence of skin neoplasms among the atomic bomb survivors. *Radiation Research, 146*(2), 223–226.

Yu, H. S., Liao, W. T., & Chai, C. Y. (2006). Arsenic carcinogenesis in the skin. *Journal of Biomedical Science, 13*(5), 657–666.

Zanetti, R., Rosso, S., Martinez, C., Navarro, C., Schraub, S., Sancho-Garnier, H., . . . Wechsler, J. (1996). The multicentre south European study "Helios." I: Skin characteristics and sunburns in basal cell and squamous cell carcinomas of the skin. *British Journal of Cancer, 73,* 1440–1446.

Zhang, M., Qureshi, A. A., Geller, A. C., Frazier, L., Hunter, D. J., & Han, J. (2012). Use of tanning beds and incidence of skin cancer. *Journal of Clinical Oncology, 30*(14), 1588–1593.

25

Epidemiology of Classic Sarcoma and Kaposi Sarcoma

CLASSIFICATION OF SARCOMA

Classic sarcomas are tumors of connective tissue. These tumors are derived from mesenchymal cells that normally mature into skeletal muscle, smooth muscle, fat, fibrous tissue, bone, and cartilage. They are broadly classified as sarcomas of soft tissue or bone. Sarcomas are named after the cell of origin; Those that arise in fat are called liposarcomas, those derived from fibrous tissues are fibrosarcomas, and those that develop in bone are osteosarcomas. Other subtypes include leiomyosarcomas of smooth muscle, rhabdomyosarcomas of skeletal muscle, synovial sarcomas of joint capsule tissues, angiosarcomas of blood vessels, gastrointestinal sarcomas of the gut, chondrosarcomas of cartilage, and Ewing sarcoma of the long bones. Tumors derived from tissues of the peripheral nervous system are also included with the soft tissue sarcomas, including malignant nerve sheath tumors (schwannomas) and neurofibromas (Skubitz, 2007).

GLOBAL EPIDEMIOLOGY OF SARCOMA

Data on sarcomas of bones and soft tissues are conspicuously absent from the global data on cancer routinely reported by the World Health Organization. Although some information is available on Kaposi sarcoma, a tumor derived from blood vessels that is associated with immunosuppression and the epidemic of human immunodeficiency virus (HIV) disease, little is known about the geographic distribution of the more common forms of sarcoma, namely those arising from bone, fat, muscle, and fibrous tissues. Relevant epidemiologic data on these tumors are abstracted primarily from the U.S. Surveillance, Epidemiology, and End Results (SEER) tumor registry and the European Automated Childhood Cancer Information System (ACCIS) database.

SARCOMA IN THE U.S. POPULATION

In the U.S. population of approximately 310 million people, more than 13,000 individuals are diagnosed with sarcomas every year (2,650 with bone tumors and 10,500 with soft tissue tumors). The annual age-adjusted incidence rates of bone tumors in the U.S. population are about 10 per million in men and 8 per million in women, markedly less than the rates for soft tissue sarcomas (38 per million in men and 27 per million in women). Nevertheless, among children and adolescents under the age of 20 years, bone sarcomas and soft tissue sarcomas have relatively similar rates (about 9 per million for bone tumors and 11 per million for soft tissue tumors), and each type accounts for a significant fraction of all pediatric malignancies.

As shown in **Figure 25.1**, the U.S. age distribution of bone sarcomas differs dramatically from that of soft tissue sarcomas. Nearly 30% of bone sarcomas are diagnosed during childhood and adolescence (under 20 years of age), after which there is a general decline in the number of new cases. The incidence of these tumors peaks during times of rapid growth and development of bones, between the ages of 10 and 15 years for both boys and girls.

In contrast to bone sarcomas, soft tissue sarcomas are diagnosed at a relatively constant rate throughout the lifespan (Figure 25.1). This pattern reflects a mixture of age distributions for the various subtypes of soft tissue sarcomas. For example,

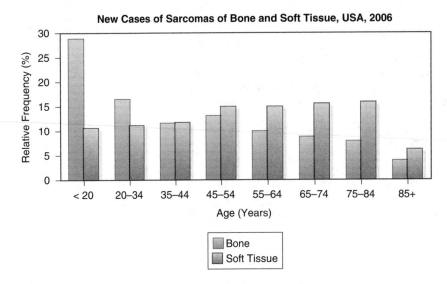

Figure 25.1 New Cases of Sarcomas of Bone and Soft Tissue, United States, 2006.

Source: Data from Altekruse, S. F., Kosary, C. L., Krapcho, M., Neyman, N., Aminou, R., Waldron, W., & Edwards, B. K. (2010). *SEER cancer statistics review, 1975–2007.* Bethesda, MD: National Cancer Institute.

rhabdomyosarcomas tend to grow and develop more rapidly and are usually detected before the age of 20 years, whereas liposarcomas, leiomyomas, and gastrointestinal sarcomas are detected more often in adults (Altekruse et al., 2010; Darling, 2007).

In the U.S. population, nearly 1,500 men and women die from bone tumors and nearly 4,000 die from soft tissue tumors every year. Similar to the pattern of incidence rates, the overall age-adjusted annual mortality rates for bone tumors (5 per million in men and 4 per million in women) are much lower

than the rates for soft tissue tumors (14 per million in men and 11 per million in women), whereas the pediatric mortality rates are relatively similar (3.5 per million for bone tumors and 4.4 per million for soft tissue tumors). The U.S. distributions of age at death for bone tumors and soft tissue tumors are compared in **Figure 25.2**. The death curve for bone tumors is bimodal with approximately 29% of deaths occurring in pediatric patients or young adults under the age of 35 years followed by an exponential rise with age and a later peak at 75–84

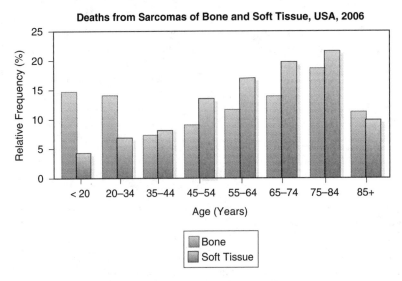

Figure 25.2 Deaths from Sarcomas of Bone and Soft Tissue, United States, 2006.

Source: Data from Altekruse, S. F., Kosary, C. L., Krapcho, M., Neyman, N., Aminou, R., Waldron, W., & Edwards, B. K. (2010). *SEER cancer statistics review, 1975–2007.* Bethesda, MD: National Cancer Institute.

years. In contrast, the death curve for soft tissue tumors rises gradually with age and peaks late in life with more than 40% of deaths occurring in the age interval 65–84 years.

It is clear from the preceding discussion that key epidemiologic features of bone tumors and soft tissue sarcomas differ dramatically for pediatric versus adult populations. In addition to the distributional differences already noted, the histological types of sarcomas that predominate among pediatric patients are replaced by other types among adult patients. Due to these striking distinctions, pediatric and adult sarcomas are discussed separately in the following sections of this chapter.

EPIDEMIOLOGY OF PEDIATRIC SARCOMAS

Bone Sarcomas in Children and Adolescents

Bone tumors account for slightly more than 6% of all pediatric malignancies. Stiller and colleagues reported rates of pediatric bone tumors among European children during 1978–1997 using the Automated Childhood Cancer Information System (ACCIS) database. Rates were similar for boys and girls up to 14 years of age (5.5 cases per million), whereas in the older adolescent age group, ages 15–19 years, boys had higher rates than girls (19.3 versus 10.7 cases per million). Combining the rates for these age categories yields estimates of 9.2 cases per million in boys, 6.9 per million in girls, and 8.0 per million for all individuals under 20 years of age. In the European database of 5,572 pediatric bone

tumors, 52% were classified as osteosarcoma, 34% as Ewing sarcoma, and 6% as chondrosarcoma. No significant time trends were detected (Stiller, Bielack, Jundt, & Steliarova-Foucher, 2006).

Data from the SEER tumor registry in the United States reflect rates of pediatric bone tumors that are similar to the European rates. For the time period 1975–1995, the annual incidence of bone tumors was 8.7 per million for individuals under the age of 20 years, and boys had higher annual rates than girls (9.4 versus 7.9 cases per million). As in Europe, no significant time trends were observed in the U.S. annual rates. **Figure 25.3** shows the age distribution of bone tumors diagnosed among U.S. children. Clearly, onset peaks at age 15 years, coinciding with the growth spurt during adolescence (Gurney, Swensen, & Bulterys, 1999; Gurney, Young, Roffers, Smith, & Bunin, 1999).

Of the approximately 700 bone tumors diagnosed among children and adolescents in the United States every year, about 56% are classified as osteosarcoma, 34% as Ewing sarcoma, and 6% as chondrosarcoma. Osteosarcomas arise most often in the metaphyseal zones near the extremities of elongating long bones (femur, tibia, and humerus), whereas Ewing sarcoma is more likely to develop in the marrow of bones of the central axis (pelvis, rib cage, ischium, sternum). Osteosarcoma occurs at approximately the same rate in African American and Caucasian children, whereas the rate of Ewing sarcoma is about six times higher in Caucasians. The relative paucity of Ewing sarcoma in children of African descent is consistent in populations other than the United States (Parkin, Stiller, Draper, & Bieber, 1988).

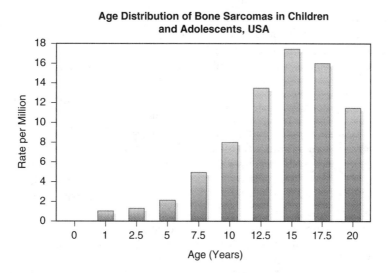

Age Distribution of Bone Sarcomas in Children and Adolescents, USA

Figure 25.3 Age Distribution of Bone Sarcomas in Children and Adolescents, United States.

Source: Data from Gurney, J. G., Swensen, A. R., & Bulterys, M. (1999). Malignant bone tumors. In L. A. G. Ries, M. A. Smith, J. G. Gurney, M. Linet, T. Tamra, J. L. Young, & G. R. Bunin (Eds.), *Cancer incidence and survival among children and adolescents: United States SEER program 1975–1995* (pp. 99–110, NIH Pub. No. 99-4649). Bethesda, MD: National Cancer Institute, SEER Program.

Subtypes of Pediatric Bone Sarcomas

Osteosarcoma   *Osteosarcoma* is the most common primary malignant tumor of bone among children and adolescents, accounting for 3–4% of all malignancies in individuals less than 20 years of age. Approximately 400 cases are diagnosed each year in the United States, most (~75%) in children and adolescents. Osteosarcomas are characterized by the production of immature bone (osteoid) by the malignant cells. The most common anatomic sites of origin are the femur, tibia, and humerus bones (Kumar, Abbas, & Aster, 2014).

Ewing Sarcoma   Nearly a century ago, James Ewing first described the pathologic features of the tumor that bears his name (Ewing, 1921). *Ewing sarcoma* is characterized as an undifferentiated tumor of the diaphyses of long bones of the extremities. In contrast to osteosarcoma, Ewing sarcoma is sensitive to radiation. As discussed in the following section, such tumors are now identified by karyotypic studies that reveal the presence of reciprocal chromosomal translocations involving the Ewing sarcoma gene (*EWSR-1*) on chromosome 22. Ewing sarcomas also occasionally arise in soft tissues. Ewing sarcoma is the second most common bone tumor among children and adolescents, accounting for more than one-third of bone sarcomas and about 2% of all malignancies in individuals less than 20 years of age. Although the peak incidence of Ewing sarcoma occurs during adolescence, molecularly confirmed cases have been discovered in adults as old as 80 years (Kumar et al., 2014).

Chondrosarcoma   Chondrosarcomas account for about 6% of bone tumors that occur in children and adolescents. These cartilaginous tumors occur more often in adults and are discussed in a later section of this chapter.

Cytogenetics of Pediatric Bone Sarcomas

Certain types of bone sarcomas have similar (nonrandom) patterns of chromosomal translocations and aberrations. For example, nearly all cases of Ewing sarcoma demonstrate one of several reciprocal chromosomal translocations involving break points within the Ewing sarcoma gene (*EWSR-1*) located on the long arm of chromosome 22. Such translocations create chimeric fusion proteins with oncogenic potential. About 95% of the *EWSR-1* translocations reposition a portion of the *EWSR-1* gene in close proximity to the Friend leukemia integration (*FLI-1*) locus on chromosome 11. The *FLI-1* gene encodes a protein involved in the regulation of cellular proliferation and differentiation. The chimeric fusion proteins encoded by *EWSR-1* and *FLI-1* reciprocal translocations stimulate tumorigenesis of bone (Ewing sarcoma); translocations of the *EWSR-1* gene to other loci have also been found in association with other types of sarcomas (e.g., myxoid liposarcoma). It is likely that these proteins act as transcription activators, deregulating genes associated with cell signaling, proliferation, angiogenesis, apoptosis, tissue invasion, and metastasis; consequently, they provide potential targets for molecular therapy (Delaney, Hornicek, Lessnick, & Mankin, 2010; Ladanyi, 1995).

Unlike Ewing sarcoma, osteosarcomas *do not* consistently manifest specific chromosomal translocations or molecular defects; rather, they tend to have a complex karyotype. Nevertheless, osteosarcomas do develop in association with certain *rare* genetic anomalies. Specifically, osteosarcomas are a component of the profile of malignancies that develop in hereditary retinoblastoma, Li–Fraumeni syndrome, and Rothmund–Thomson syndrome.

Hereditary retinoblastoma is caused by a genetic mutation in the retinoblastoma gene (*Rb1*). When the mutant *Rb1* gene is present, carriers invariably develop retinoblastoma in either one or both eyes. Treatment usually involves enucleation of the afflicted eye combined with external beam radiotherapy. Abramson and colleagues studied 817 patients who were treated for bilateral retinoblastoma during childhood. Among survivors, the cumulative risk of subsequently developing a second primary malignancy was found to cumulate at about 1% per year, reaching 53% at 50 years of age. Among the 180 second primary tumors reported, 60 were bone tumors, 36 of which developed in the skull and facial bones and 24 in bones of the extremities outside of the field of radiation. Soft tissue sarcomas of the head and neck (*n* = 60) and brain tumors (*n* = 12) also developed at high rates among survivors (Abramson & Frank, 1998). Other studies suggest that the onset of osteosarcoma following radiotherapy occurs earlier in bones within the field of radiation, possibly due to radiation-induced mutations in the second (normal) *Rb1* gene (Chauveinc et al., 2001). There is controversy as to whether the development of osteosarcoma in retinoblastoma survivors is due to the *Rb1* gene defect, radiotherapy for retinoblastoma, or the combination of both factors.

Li–Fraumeni syndrome carries a high risk for sarcomas, brain tumors, breast cancer, leukemia, lymphoma, and adrenal cortical carcinoma. This syndrome is caused by a genetic mutation in either of two tumor suppressor genes, *p53* or *CHEK2*. Individuals

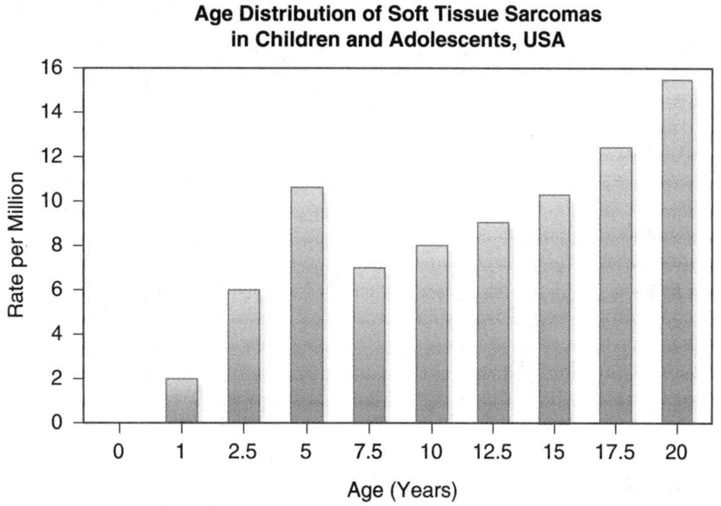

Figure 25.4 Age Distribution of Soft Tissue Sarcomas in Children and Adolescents, United States.

Source: Data from Gurney, J. G., Swensen, A. R., & Bulterys, M. (1999). Malignant bone tumors. In L. A. G. Ries, M. A. Smith, J. G. Gurney, M. Linet, T. Tamra, J. L. Young, & G. R. Bunin (Eds.), *Cancer incidence and survival among children and adolescents: United States SEER program 1975–1995* (pp. 111–122, NIH Pub. No. 99-4649). Bethesda, MD: National Cancer Institute, SEER Program.

who inherit a defective *p53* or *CHEK2* gene have an approximately 85% lifetime risk of developing one or more of the malignancies characteristic of Li–Fraumeni syndrome. Among women with the syndrome, the lifetime risk approaches 100% due to their inordinately high risk of developing premenopausal breast cancer (Li et al., 1998).

Rothmund–Thomson syndrome is an extraordinarily rare genetic disorder caused by an autosomal recessive gene defect in the helicase gene (*RECQL-4*) located on the long arm of chromosome 8. DNA helicases are enzymes that unwind DNA and are involved in many basic cellular processes (DNA replication, transcription, translation, recombination, and repair, and ribosome biogenesis). Homozygous carriers of two mutant copies of the gene have early photosensitivity and develop a skin rash known as *poikiloderma*, juvenile cataracts, and skeletal anomalies. Most individuals with this syndrome develop osteosarcomas early in life (Leonard, Craft, Moss, & Malcolm, 1996; Wang et al., 2003).

Soft Tissue Sarcomas in Children and Adolescents

Soft tissue sarcomas account for approximately 7.4% of all childhood tumors. In the United States, the annual incidence of soft tissue sarcomas in individuals under 20 years of age is 11 per million. Annual rates are about 20% higher in boys than girls (12.2 versus 10.3 per million). Of the approximately 900 soft tissue sarcomas that develop in children and adolescents in the United States every year, about 41% are

rhabdomyosarcomas of skeletal muscle and 24% are sarcomas of fibrous tissues. Other types such as histiocytomas, synovial sarcomas, and liposarcomas occur less frequently. **Figure 25.4** shows the age distribution of soft tissue tumors diagnosed in the U.S. pediatric population. The early peak in the age distribution of soft tissue sarcomas is due to the early onset of rhabdomyosarcomas followed by a nadir and then escalating rates of fibrosarcoma, synovial sarcoma, and other forms. Rare cases of congenital fibrosarcoma have also been reported. No notable ethnic differences have been observed in the pediatric rates of the various histologic subtypes of soft tissue sarcomas. Nor have there been trends in the annual rates over the past several decades (Gurney, Young, et al., 1999).

Subtypes of Pediatric Soft Tissue Sarcomas

Rhabdomyosarcoma *Rhabdomyosarcoma* is the most common pediatric solid tumor, accounting for more than half of soft tissue sarcomas and approximately 4% of all malignancies among individuals under 20 years of age. Rhabdomyosarcomas arise from primitive cells that are the precursors of striated skeletal muscle. They predominantly arise in soft tissues of the head, neck, genitourinary tract, and extremities. These tumors are divisible into two main histologic types, embryonal rhabdomyosarcoma and alveolar rhabdomyosarcoma. In embryonal rhabdomyosarcomas, which are more common in children, the malignant cells resemble embryonal cells of a typical embryo at 6–8 weeks of development. In alveolar rhabdomyosarcomas, which are more common in older children and teenagers, the malignant cells resemble pulmonary alveolar cells of the embryo at 10–12 weeks of development.

Fibrosarcoma   Fibrosarcomas are diagnosed more often in adults, but they also occur among children and adolescents and account for 20–30% of bone tumors among individuals under 20 years of age. Tumors in this category arise from fibroblasts, the precursor cells of collagen-rich connective tissues. Fibrosarcomas are most often discovered in the soft connective tissues of the trunk and extremities, but they also occasionally develop from fibroblasts of the long bones (Cordon-Cardo, 1997).

Rare cases of fibrosarcoma discovered at birth or shortly thereafter have been reported in the literature. Such *congenital fibrosarcomas* usually involve the extremities and are characterized by sheets of anaplastic spindle-shaped tumor cells and abundant deposition of collagen. They are slow growing, and although they invade other contiguous tissues, including bone, they do not readily metastasize to distant anatomic sites (Balsaver, Butler, & Martin, 1967; Exelby, Knapper, Huvos, & Beattie, 1973).

Synovial Sarcoma   *Synovial sarcomas* account for about 15–20% of soft tissue tumors in children and adolescents. These tumors arise most often in the soft tissues near the large joints of the arm (elbow) and leg (knee), but can also occur at many other anatomic sites. Histologically, the tumors are composed of two cell types, spindle cells and epithelial cells; consequently, these tumors reflect a *biphasic* pattern of growth. Synovial sarcomas are characterized by a signature chromosomal translocation involving chromosome 18 and the X chromosome, which is discussed in the following section.

Alveolar Soft-Part Sarcoma   Alveolar soft-part sarcoma is a very rare type of soft tissue sarcoma that arises mainly in children and adolescents. These tumors are usually slow growing but tend to be highly angiogenic. They are characterized by intensive ingrowth of new blood vessels (angiogenesis), thereby facilitating dissemination of tumor cells into the bloodstream. Tumor cells often metastasize to the lungs and the brain. Alveolar soft-part sarcomas most often arise in muscles and soft tissues of the thigh or leg, but can also develop from connective tissues at other anatomic sites. Histologically, the tumor cells grow in a pattern resembling pulmonary alveolar cells, leading to the name *alveolar soft-part sarcoma* (Christopherson, Foote, & Stewart, 1952).

Cytogenetics of Pediatric Soft Tissue Sarcomas

As with pediatric bone sarcomas, the various forms of soft tissue sarcomas that are diagnosed in children and adolescents are characterized by certain cytogenetic abnormalities. *Rhabdomyosarcomas* often show deletions of the short arm of chromosome 11 and loss of tumor suppressor genes, or reciprocal translocations involving the *FKHR* gene on chromosome 13 and the *PAX* genes on chromosomes 1 and 2. The *FKHR* gene regulates transcription and the *PAX* genes help regulate cell differentiation during embryogenesis. The chimeric fusion protein (called *FOX01*) encoded by the translocated gene has oncogenic potential resulting in the development of rhabdomyosarcomas consisting of cells with characteristics of pulmonary alveolar cells (Barr, 1997).

Some fibrosarcomas also involve reciprocal translocations of specific genes on specific chromosomes that result in the expression of chimeric fusion proteins with oncogenic potential. For example, congenital fibrosarcomas that are present at birth are characterized by a translocation gene product of the *ETV6* gene on chromosome 12 and the *NTRK3* gene on chromosome 13. These genes are intricately involved in the regulation of DNA mitosis and cell differentiation (Knezevich et al., 1998).

Synovial sarcoma is also characterized by the presence of a chimeric fusion protein that results from a reciprocal translocation. In this tumor, the *SYT* gene of the long arm of chromosome 18 is translocated in close proximity to one of three closely related genes (*SSX1, SSX2,* or *SSX4*) located on the X chromosome. The *SYT* gene is a transcription activator whereas the *SSX* genes are transcription repressors. The resulting chimeric fusion protein can produce one of two patterns of growth in the development of synovial sarcomas, a monophasic pattern of spindle cell growth or a biphasic pattern involving both spindle cells and epithelial cells (Clark et al., 1994).

Karyotypic and molecular studies have also revealed a characteristic reciprocal translocation and fusion protein in *alveolar soft-parts sarcoma*. The translocation involves chromosome 17 and the X chromosome, creating a fusion of the *TFE3* and *ASPA* genes and the corresponding chimeric fusion protein that enhances transcription of other genes with oncogenic potential (Ladanyi et al., 2001).

In summary, reciprocal chromosomal translocations constitute the majority of specific genetic alterations associated with pediatric sarcomas. As noted for pediatric sarcomas of both bone and soft tissues, many specific reciprocal chromosomal translocations have been identified and the chimeric fusion proteins encoded by the translocated genes characterized. It is likely that these proteins act as transcription activators—deregulating genes associated with sarcoma development. Thus, in addition to providing specific and sensitive diagnostic markers, such molecules provide potential targets for therapy with monoclonal antibodies (Ladanyi, 1995; Ladanyi & Bridge, 2000).

EPIDEMIOLOGY OF ADULT SARCOMAS

Although some reciprocal chromosomal translocations and genetic aberrations have been identified in adult sarcomas, most such tumors *do not* manifest characteristic genetic anomalies. As with other adult forms of cancer, adult sarcomas are characterized by several critical interrelated biological mechanisms, including overexpression of oncogenes and/or underexpression of tumor suppressor genes due to mutagenic and/or epigenetic effects, sustained uncontrolled cell division, angiogenesis, dysregulated apoptosis, immunosuppression, metastatic spread, and invasive potential of tumor cells. Dysregulation of the inflammatory cascade may be an important trigger and promoter of all of these biological mechanisms.

Bone Sarcomas in Adults

Subsequent to adolescence, the relative frequency of primary bone tumors gradually declines throughout the lifespan (Figure 25.1). There are four main subtypes of adult sarcomas of bone: osteosarcoma, chondrosarcoma, Ewing sarcoma, and giant cell sarcoma. Each subtype is discussed separately.

Osteosarcoma

Although about 75% of *osteosarcomas* are diagnosed in children and adolescents, such tumors are occasionally discovered in adults. Among adult cases, males exceed females (a 35% male excess was observed in one series of 47 cases diagnosed after 40 years of age) and tumors most often involve the lower limbs (55% of cases) or the axial skeleton (38% of cases) (Carsi & Rock, 2002).

Unlike other tumors of bone, osteosarcomas are characterized by the formation of osteoid matrix by tumor cells (Kumar et al., 2014). Characteristic cytogenetic or molecular aberrations have not been discovered in studies of osteosarcoma tissues; however, as already discussed in the section of this chapter on pediatric bone tumors, osteosarcomas are a component of the profile of malignancies that develop in rare genetic syndromes such as hereditary retinoblastoma, Li–Fraumeni syndrome, and Rothmund–Thomson syndrome.

Chondrosarcoma

Chondrosarcomas are tumors that produce hyaline cartilage. Most chondrosarcomas (80–90% of cases) arise de novo in older adults in the sixth or seventh decade of life without any evidence of premalignancy. Such tumors predominantly arise in and around the pelvis and scapula, although any site of cartilage formation may be involved (Azzarelli et al., 1986). Although chondrosarcomas do not ordinarily manifest specific cytogenetic abnormalities, one rare subtype, *extraskeletal myxoid chondrosarcoma*, is defined by the presence of a fusion gene between the orphan nuclear receptor *CHN1/NR4A3* and one of several partners, most commonly the Ewing sarcoma gene, *EWSR-1*.

About 10–20% of chondrosarcomas develop in young adults due to malignant transformation of benign neoplasms within bones (osteochondromas) or exterior to bones (enchondromas). Certain hereditary conditions such as Olier disease (multiple enchondromatosis) or Maffucci syndrome (multiple enchondromas and hemangiomas) predispose to the development of chondrosarcoma (Kumar et al., 2014).

Hereditary multiple exostoses is a rare genetic disorder in which multiple bony spurs (also known as exostoses or osteochondromas) develop on the bones of a child. Approximately 90% of cases with this disorder are due to inheritance of either of two mutated tumor suppressor genes, *EXT1* or *EXT2*. These genes normally encode protein components of heparan sulfate proteoglycans that are essential for normal cartilage development; mutant forms cause uncontrolled proliferation and lack of differentiation of chondrocytes, sometimes resulting in the development of chondrosarcoma.

Ewing Sarcoma

Ewing sarcoma rarely develops in adults over the age of 25 years. Nevertheless, adult cases that have been reported in the literature invariably demonstrate one of the reciprocal translocations of the Ewing sarcoma gene (*EWSR-1*) that characterize pediatric cases. Such tumors diagnosed in adults show a propensity for rapid metastatic spread and poor survival (Baldini et al., 1999)

Giant Cell Tumor of Bone

Giant cell tumors of bone, also known as *osteoclastomas*, constitute about 5% of adult bone tumors. These tumors are characterized by the presence of large (giant) multinucleated osteoclasts (cells that resorb bone matrix) admixed with spindle-shaped fibroblasts. Giant cell tumors are usually benign but can be locally aggressive. They most commonly arise in the epiphyses (growth plates) of long bones with diagnosis in the third or fourth decade of life (Mendenhall, Zlotecki, Scarborough, Gibbs, & Mendenhall, 2006).

Normal osteoclasts are large cells in bone that contain 15–20 closely packed nuclei and cytoplasm with abundant vacuoles and vesicles. The primary function of osteoclasts is to resorb bone matrix. It is notable that osteoclasts are derived from mononuclear cells (macrophages) of the blood rather than progenitor cells of bone (Walker, 1972, 1973).

Osteoclast formation requires a ligand called *RANKL (receptor activator for nuclear factor κB ligand)* that activates the receptor for nuclear factor κB (RANK). Activation of nuclear factor κB by RANKL induces the differentiation and maturation of osteoclasts from mononuclear cells (macrophages) in hematopoietic tissues. Tight homeostatic regulation of these molecules is critical for normal osteoclast development and activity because overexpression of RANKL has been found to be associated with the development of giant cell tumors of bone (Mendenhall et al., 2006; Thomas & Skubitz, 2009).

Soft Tissue Sarcomas in Adults

Soft tissue sarcomas occur with regular frequency, albeit low, throughout the lifespan (Figure 25.1). Subtypes are classified by the cell and/or anatomic site of origin: liposarcoma (adipocytes), leiomyosarcoma (smooth muscle), gastrointestinal stromal tumors (intestinal stroma), and angiosarcoma (blood or lymphatic vessels). *Malignant fibrous histiocytomas* are heterogeneous sarcomas consisting of histiocytic cells and fibroblasts. *Kaposi sarcoma*, a malignancy arising from lymphatic endothelium, is named after Moritz Kaposi (1837–1902), a Hungarian dermatologist who first described its features and symptoms (Kaposi, 1872).

Liposarcoma

Lipomas are *benign* tumors composed of adipose tissue that arise most often in the subcutaneous tissues of the neck, trunk, and extremities. They are the most common form of soft tissue tumor, with an estimated prevalence of about 1%. Lipomas have no metastatic potential, distinguishing them from liposarcomas, which are malignant neoplasms that can invade other tissues. Lipomas are typically diagnosed in adults ages 40–60 years of age, but occasionally they are discovered in children (Bancroft et al., 2006; Kumar et al., 2014).

Whether lipomas are *premalignant* tumors is controversial, because malignant transition of lipoma to liposarcoma has not been definitively demonstrated in humans. Nevertheless, liposarcomas are clearly derived from adipocytes (fat cells) and are often composed of cell populations containing both normal and malignant adipocytes.

Liposarcomas are the most common histological type of sarcoma found in adults. These malignant tumors comprise more than 20% of all adult sarcomas. In contrast to lipomas, which usually develop in subcutaneous fat, liposarcomas typically arise in deep-seated fat of muscle or other tissues. Liposarcomas are extraordinarily heterogeneous and can be histologically characterized by the mixtures of cells they contain. For example, myxoid liposarcoma is characterized by malignant adipocytes in various stages of differentiation (Kumar et al., 2014).

Leiomyosarcoma

Uterine fibroids (uterine leiomyomas) are the most common of all tumors in women. These benign tumors are typically discovered during the reproductive years, with a prevalence of about 30%. They originate from cells in the smooth muscle layer of the uterus (the myometrium). Most uterine fibroid tumors are asymptomatic and harmless, but they can enlarge causing pain, discomfort, and urinary incontinence, in which case they are usually surgically excised by hysterectomy (Wallach & Vlahos, 2004).

The malignant version of leiomyoma is *leiomyosarcoma*. These malignant tumors can arise from smooth muscle anywhere in the body, most commonly in the uterus, stomach and intestinal tract, blood vessels, and skin. Leiomyosarcomas comprise 5–10% of all soft tissue sarcomas in adults. Whether benign leiomyomas undergo malignant transformation to leiomyosarcoma is controversial. Nevertheless, cases have been reported in which malignant transformation has apparently been observed over time (Indraccolo, Luchetti, & Indraccolo, 2008). It is noteworthy that uterine leiomyomas are often surgically removed, thereby negating the chance of malignant transformation.

Gastrointestinal Stromal Tumors (GISTs)

Sarcomas arising from connective (mesenchymal) tissues in the wall of the stomach or other gastrointestinal organs are called *gastrointestinal stromal tumors (GISTs)*. Tran and colleagues utilized the U.S. SEER database to characterize distributional features of GISTs in the U.S. population during 1992–2000. During this time period, 1,458 cases were reported,

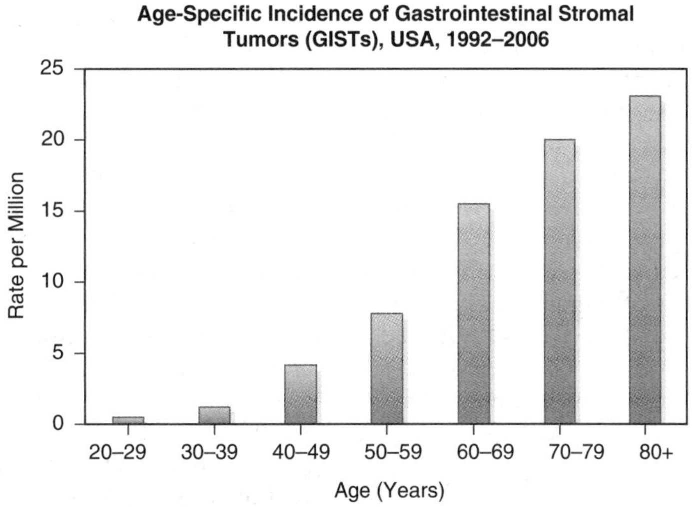

Age-Specific Incidence of Gastrointestinal Stromal Tumors (GISTs), USA, 1992–2006

Figure 25.5 Age-Specific Incidence of Gastrointestinal Stromal Tumors (GISTs), United States, 1992–2006.

Source: Data from Tran, T., Davila, J. A., & El-Serag, H. B. (2005). The epidemiology of malignant gastrointestinal stromal tumors: An analysis of 1,458 cases from 1992 to 2000. *American Journal of Gastroenterology, 100,* 162–168.

54% in men and 46% in women. Tumors were distributed throughout the gastrointestinal tract—51% in the stomach, 36% in the small intestine, 7% in the colon, 5% in the rectum, and 1% in the esophagus. Estimates of the annual age-adjusted incidence rates were 8.3 per million in men, 5.7 per million in women, and 6.8 per million overall. As shown in **Figure 25.5**, GISTs are predominantly a malignancy of old age and are rarely diagnosed before the age of 40 years. Peak onset occurs in the eighth decade of life (Tran, Davila, & El-Serag, 2005).

Gastrointestinal stromal tumors apparently arise from the interstitial cells of Cajal, cells that serve as electrical pacemakers and generate spontaneous electrical slow waves and smooth muscle contractions (peristalsis) in the walls of the gastrointestinal tract (Connolly, Gaffney, & Reynolds, 2003; Sanders, Koh, & Ward, 2006). Such cells have morphological characteristics similar to fibroblasts and express specific tyrosine kinase receptors on their cell membranes that control differentiation and maturation (Lorincz et al., 2008).

Angiosarcoma

Angiosarcoma is an uncommon subtype of soft tissue sarcoma that can arise from the endothelial cells that line blood vessels (hemangiosarcoma) or lymphatic vessels (lymphangiosarcoma). These tumors occasionally develop in the scalp or face of older adults or in patients who have undergone radiation therapy for dermatitis or other conditions. An association

with lymphedema, a complication of mastectomy for breast cancer, has also been noted. In addition, angiosarcoma of the liver has been etiologically linked to at least three chemical carcinogens: arsenic in arsenical pesticides, thorotrast (a radioactive contrast medium used prior to 1950), and polyvinyl chloride (an alkylating agent and gas used in the manufacture of plastic). Important studies of environmental risk factors for adult sarcomas are discussed later in this chapter.

Malignant Fibrous Histiocytoma

Malignant fibrous histiocytoma is a rare type of soft tissue sarcoma that is discovered most often in the elderly, usually between the ages of 50 and 70 years. Histologically, such tumors consist of a mixture of histocytes (cells derived from tissue macrophages or monocytes) and fibroblasts (cells of mesenchymal lineage). Based on early pathologic investigations, this tumor was initially characterized as the most common sarcoma in late adult life (O'Brien & Stout, 1964); however, in more recent studies, the majority of such tumors have been reclassified as poorly differentiated liposarcomas or leiomyosarcomas. In a population-based study of malignant fibrous sarcoma in Sweden, the annual incidence rate was estimated at only 4.2 per million (Rööser, Willén, Gustafson, Alvegård, & Rydholm, 1991).

Dermatofibrosarcoma Protuberans

Dermatofibrosarcoma protuberans is a rare form of fibrosarcoma that arises from the dermis (the layer of skin between the epidermis and subcutaneous tissue). This tumor can infiltrate contiguous tissues but rarely metastasizes to distant sites. Dermatofibrosarcoma protuberans is cytogenetically defined by a translocation of chromosomes 17 and 22 in which a collagen promoter gene (*COL1A1*) is juxtaposed to the platelet-derived growth factor (*PDGF*) gene, resulting in constitutive production of PDGF. This scenario creates an autocrine loop in which PDGF stimulates PDGF receptors of tumor cells, promoting their perpetual growth and survival. Monoclonal antibodies directed against the PDGF receptor have shown some benefit in the treatment of patients with this tumor (Patel et al., 2008).

Desmoid Tumor

Desmoid tumors are benign slow-growing tumors without metastatic potential. Histologically, these tumors resemble fibrosarcomas. Although most cases are sporadic, desmoid tumors develop in about 10–15% of patients with familial adenomatous polyposis (FAP) or Gardner's syndrome (adenomatous polyposis coli) in which multiple adenomatous polyps and malignant adenocarcinomas develop in the colon. This syndrome is caused by inheritance of an autosomal dominant mutant *APC* gene on chromosome 5.

An investigative team in London conducted a meta-analysis of desmoid tumors among patients with FAP. Desmoid tumors developed in 559 (12%) of 4,625 FAP patients. Peak onset was in the second and third decades, and 80% of tumors were diagnosed by age 40 years. Having a family history of desmoid tumors conferred a sevenfold increase in the risk, suggesting the existence of modifier genes (Sinha, Tekkis, Gibbons, Phillips, & Clark, 2010).

Cytogenetics of Soft Tissue Adult Sarcomas

Although not as common as in pediatric sarcomas, nonrandom genetic abnormalities have been discovered in some soft tissue sarcomas in adults. For example, translocation of the CCAAT-enhanced binding protein (*CEBP*) gene on chromosome 12 to chromosome 16 is characteristic of *myxoid liposarcoma*. The *CEBP* gene encodes a factor that is critical for normal differentiation of adipocytes, and its translocation creates a chimeric fusion protein that interferes with differentiation and leads to cancer development (Adelmant, Bilbert, & Freytag, 1998; Turc-Carel et al., 1986). A second molecular transcription factor, peroxisome proliferator-activator receptor gamma (*PPAR-γ*), is also often overexpressed in malignant liposarcoma cells (Tontonoz et al., 1997). Cytogenetic studies of liposarcomas have also revealed

the presence of ring or giant-marker chromosomes derived from the short arm of chromosome 12 with amplification of specific oncogenes in this region (Coindre et al., 2003).

The existing scientific literature reflects highly variable and inconsistent cytogenetic and molecular genetic changes in *leiomyosarcoma*. Wang and colleagues reviewed the karyotypes of 100 leiomyosarcomas and found no consistent aberrations at the chromosomal level. Because the most frequent chromosomal deletions were detected in the long arms of chromosomes 10 and 13, regions where tumor suppressor genes *PTEN* and *Rb* reside, the investigators concluded that loss of function of tumor suppressor genes and/or activation of oncogenes associated with such changes are likely involved in the development of leiomyosarcoma (Wang, Lu, Fisher, Bridge, & Shipley, 2001).

Approximately 95% of *gastrointestinal stromal tumors (GISTs)* have been found to carry mutant forms of an important tyrosine kinase receptor gene called *c-KIT*. The *c-KIT* receptor facilitates differentiation and maturation of stem cells into hematopoietic cells and several other cell lineages. It was first identified in the laboratories of the German biochemist Axel Ullrich (Yarden et al., 1987). Mutations in *c-KIT* cause overexpression of tyrosine kinase receptors in the cell membrane resulting in unregulated phosphorylation and disruption of communication pathways inside the cell. Constitutive expression of mutant forms of *c-KIT* therefore leads to malignant transformation and the development of GISTs (as well as testicular seminoma, malignant melanoma, and myeloid leukemia). Notably, a monoclonal antibody directed against the *c-KIT* protein has been found effective in the treatment of GISTs (Edling & Hallberg, 2007; Joensuu et al., 2001).

Cytogenetic studies of *angiosarcomas* reflect considerable heterogeneity and no consistent pattern of chromosomal or genetic aberrations. Literature reports based on limited sample sizes have revealed karyotypes with gains or losses of many different chromosomal regions without a common chromosomal profile (Baumhoer, Gunawan, Becker, & Füzesi, 2005). One recent study reported a reciprocal chromosomal translocation involving chromosomes 1 and 21 in a 79-year-old woman with a primary bone angiosarcoma. Although the biological significance of this translocation is unclear, it could involve abnormal expression of the gene for colony stimulating factor (*CSF-1*), which is located on chromosome 1 (Dunlap, Magenis, Davis, Himoe, & Mansoor, 2009).

Some genetic syndromes are associated with the development of soft tissue sarcoma in adults.

Neurofibromatosis type 1, or *von Recklinghausen disease*, is a rare autosomal dominant condition caused by mutation in the *NF1* gene located on chromosome 17. The *NF1* gene encodes the protein neurofibromin, which is essential for the development of fibrous nerve sheaths. Patients with this genetic disorder have a high incidence of benign schwannomas and neurofibromas as well as an increased risk of developing malignant peripheral nerve sheath tumors (malignant schwannomas and neurofibrosarcomas).

Neurofibromatosis type 2, also a rare autosomal dominant disorder, is caused by mutation in the *NF2* gene located on chromosome 22, which is essential for development of myelin nerve sheaths. This syndrome is associated with the development of meningiomas as well as schwannomas of cranial nerves, especially the vestibular nerve.

Gardner syndrome is an autosomal dominant disorder caused by mutation of the adenomatous polyposis coli (*APC*) gene located on the long arm of chromosome 5. Carriers of the mutant *APC* gene develop multiple polyps throughout the colon; without total colectomy, the probability of transformation to colon cancer is virtually 100%. Approximately 15–20% of afflicted individuals also develop other extracolonic tumors such as osteomas, fibromas, desmoid tumors, and thyroid cancer (Gardner, 1951; Johnson, Gilbert, Zimmermann, & Watne, 1972; Markowitz & Bertagnolli, 2009).

Environmental Risk Factors for Adult Sarcoma

Ionizing Radiation

There is consistent evidence that radiation exposure increases the risk of developing both bone and soft tissue sarcomas. The association was first observed by the German physician Dr. A. Beck, who commented on the unusually high incidence of sarcomas in patients who had previously been irradiated for tuberculosis arthritis (Beck, 1922). Subsequently in the United States, Martland and Humphreys reported finding 42 bone sarcomas in 1,468 female watch-dial painters exposed to radioactive luminous paint, an incidence proportion of 2.8% (Martland & Humphreys, 1929). Several more reports of excess rates of bone sarcomas soon appeared in the literature, most notably a report from investigators at Memorial Sloan-Kettering Hospital in New York City describing 50 cases of radiation-induced osteogenic sarcoma identified during 1931–1970 (Arlen et al., 1971).

Postradiation sarcomas arise more often in bones than soft tissues, perhaps due to the greater absorption of radioactivity by bone (Robinson, Neugut, & Wylie, 1988). Nevertheless, excess rates of soft tissue sarcomas have been observed subsequent to certain types of radiotherapy. For example, investigators in Sweden observed a 90% excess of soft tissue sarcomas among 122,991 women treated for breast cancer from 1958 to 1992 (standardized incidence ratio = 1.9). Furthermore, 63% of the reported sarcomas developed in the exposed region of the irradiated breast or the ipsilateral arm. Among the 116 sarcomas detected, there were 40 angiosarcomas and 76 sarcomas of other subtypes. In substudies of these tumors, angiosarcomas were found to develop in association with lymphedema of the ipsilateral axilla and arm (Karlsson, Holmberg, Samuelsson, Johansson, & Wallgren, 1998).

Chemical and Occupational Exposures

Some epidemiologic studies have noted increases in the risk of developing soft tissue or bone sarcomas among individuals with certain occupational exposures (e.g., sawdust and wood dust, cutting oils [solvents], arsenicals, phenoxyherbicides, chlorophenols, and dioxins). However, results are inconsistent from study to study, which is most likely due to the use of occupation as a proxy for exposure to broad classes of chemicals and the lack of precise information on the type, concentration, and duration of specific chemical exposures. Furthermore, inconsistencies in study results may also reflect different disease etiologies for sarcoma subtypes (Hoppin et al., 1999).

Various implant materials, including chromium, nickel, cobalt, titanium, and polyethylene, are also suspected risk factors, though epidemiologic evidence for causation is lacking. It is obvious that more precise measures of environmental exposures are needed in order to accurately quantify the risk.

Angiosarcoma of the liver is an unfortunate human model for both radiation and chemical carcinogenesis. This rare tumor has been found in excess among patients exposed to thorotrast (a radioactive contrast medium used in the past for imaging studies), workers exposed to polyvinyl chloride as a solution or gas where plastics are manufactured, and individuals exposed to arsenic in arsenical pesticides. Selected studies are discussed here.

Between September 1967 and December 1973, four cases of angiosarcoma of the liver were diagnosed among men employed in the polyvinyl chloride polymerization section of the BF Goodrich manufacturing plant near Louisville, Kentucky. This section of the plant began operations in 1938. It employed 270 people and produced polyvinyl chloride as well as a variety of copolymers by polymerization of vinyl chloride monomers. All four men had worked continuously in the section for at least 14 years prior to onset of illness and had worked directly in various phases of the polymerization process. None of the patients gave a history of prolonged alcohol use or exposure to hepatotoxins outside the workplace. In particular, none had ever had exposure to thorium dioxide (thorotrast) or to arsenic, two materials known specifically to induce hepatic angiosarcoma in humans (Creech & Johnson, 1974).

Subsequent studies in Australia, Italy, Germany, and the United Kingdom also revealed that polyvinyl chloride workers were at increased risk for the development of hepatic angiosarcoma (Mundt et al., 2000). In 1983, a team of international investigators charted the latency periods from time of exposure to vinyl chloride monomers or thorotrast to time of death due to angiosarcoma of the liver. Exposure to thorotrast occurred during 1928–1955 and exposure to polyvinyl chloride occurred during 1940–1970. Among 101 men exposed to thorotrast who later died from liver angiosarcoma, the median latency period from exposure to death was 22 years. Among 95 men exposed to polyvinyl chloride who later died from liver angiosarcoma, the median latency period was substantially longer at 29 years. The investigators suggest that their results reflect different mechanisms of radiation versus chemical carcinogenesis (Spirtas et al., 1983).

Boffetta and colleagues conducted a meta-analysis of cancer mortality and exposure to polyvinyl chloride using data from eight published studies, two multicenter cohorts, and six smaller studies. They found an increase in the standardized mortality ratio (SMR) due to soft tissue sarcoma (SMR = 2.52), the predominant cell type being angiosarcoma. Their results also showed a significant increase in mortality due to primary liver cancer (SMR = 2.96), although there was significant heterogeneity among studies (Boffetta, Matisane, Mundt, & Dell, 2003).

All known cases of angiosarcoma that have developed from exposure to vinyl chloride monomers were in workers who were regularly exposed to very high levels for many years. Most of these workers cleaned accretions in reactors, a practice that has now been replaced by automated high-pressure water jets. Other epidemiologic studies have demonstrated that the risk of developing hepatic angiosarcoma is also significantly increased with exposure to thorium dioxide (thorotrast) or arsenical pesticides (Falk, Caldwell, Ishak, Thomas, & Popper, 1981; Falk, Telles, Ishak, Thomas, & Popper, 1979)

Rous Sarcoma Virus

In the early 1900s, Dr. Peyton Rous reported a series of experiments with chicken sarcoma at Rockefeller University in New York City. He found that by injecting cell-free extracts derived from chicken sarcoma into healthy Plymouth Rock chickens, he could transfer the tumor from one chicken to another. Rous found that extracts of tumors that passed through a Berkefeld filter (which did not allow passage of bacteria) could transfer the sarcoma to other chickens. This was the first demonstration of an oncogenic virus and heralded the beginning of the field of cancer virology. Rous was awarded the Nobel Prize for his discoveries in 1966 (Rous, 1910, 1911; Rous & Huggins, 1966).

Later studies revealed that the transmissible Rous sarcoma virus (RSV) was a retrovirus containing RNA rather than DNA and that the transforming region of the virus was an oncogene (named *SRC* for *sarcoma*) (Crawford & Crawford, 1961; Oppermann, Levinson, Varmus, Levintow, & Bishop, 1979; Stehelin, Fujita, Padgett, Varmus, & Bishop, 1977). During the 1970s, J. Michael Bishop and Harold Varmus directed a series of studies showing that the SRC gene encodes a constitutively active form of the enzyme tyrosine kinase that stimulates carcinogenesis, a discovery for which they received the Nobel Prize in 1989 (Bishop & Varmus, 1989). Although the RSV that causes sarcomas in chickens was the first tumor virus found to cause solid tumors, the only virus now known to cause sarcoma in humans is human herpes virus 8 (HHV-8), which causes the development of Kaposi sarcoma.

Kaposi Sarcoma

Kaposi sarcoma is a tumor that *sometimes* develops in individuals who are severely immunocompromised. It was originally described in 1872 by Dr. Moritz Kaposi, a Hungarian dermatologist practicing at the University of Vienna (Kaposi, 1872). Before the epidemic of acquired immune deficiency syndrome (AIDS) in the 1980s, Kaposi sarcoma was practically unheard of in populations of developed nations. Only rare cases were reported, most occurring in organ transplant patients who received cyclosporin or other immunosuppressive drugs to prevent transplant rejection. But following the onset of the AIDS epidemic, the incidence of Kaposi sarcoma increased more than 1,000-fold in those subgroups at high risk for HIV. The main subgroups are homosexual and bisexual men, intravenous drug abusers, and sexually promiscuous men and women.

Due to its prevalence in individuals who are immunodeficient, Kaposi sarcoma became widely known as one of the defining conditions of AIDS during the 1980s. The etiologic agent of AIDS is HIV, and AIDS is now appropriately called HIV disease. The causal RNA retrovirus, later named the human immunodeficiency virus (HIV), was first isolated in France in 1983 by Françoise Barré-Sinoussi and colleagues in the laboratory of Luc Montaignier (Barré-Sinoussi et al., 1983). The same virus was also isolated from several AIDS patients by Robert Gallo and colleagues at the National Institutes of Health and by Jay Levy and colleagues in San Francisco (Gallo et al., 1984; Levy et al., 1984). Shortly thereafter, Montaignier's group isolated a closely related virus in West African patients; the original virus was designated HIV-1 and the West African virus HIV-2.

Although associated with HIV disease, Kaposi sarcoma is actually caused by another virus, human herpes virus 8 (HHV-8). The two viruses, HIV-2 and HHV-8, are endemic in sub-Saharan Africa, and it is in the populations of this region that Kaposi sarcoma is now the leading cause of cancer death among men.

Discovery of Human Herpes Virus 8 (HHV-8)

In 1994, Yuan Chang, Patrick Moore, and Ethel Cesarman at Columbia University in New York isolated a novel herpes virus from the tumor cells of a Kaposi sarcoma. They later sequenced the virus and identified it as the eighth human herpes virus; hence it was given the name HHV-8. This virus has since been found in all Kaposi sarcomas tested and is considered the cause of the disease. In infected lymphatic endothelial cells, HHV-8 incorporates genes from the host DNA into its own DNA, thus avoiding detection and destruction by the immune system. This process leads to active proliferation and immortalization of infected cells, resulting in the development of Kaposi sarcoma (Cesarman, Chang, Moore, Said, & Knowles, 1995; Chang et al., 1994; Moore & Chang, 1995).

Pathologic Features of Kaposi Sarcoma

Despite its name, Kaposi sarcoma does not arise from connective tissue and is therefore *not* a true sarcoma; rather, Kaposi sarcoma arises from the endothelial cells that line lymphatic vessels. The tumor is characterized by the formation of vascular channels engorged with red blood cells, giving it a dark red papular appearance. Such papules may be solitary or multifocal (Cancian, Hansen, & Boshoff, 2013).

The tumor cells of Kaposi sarcoma are spindle-shaped cells characteristic of fibroblasts in connective tissue. Detection of proteins such as latency-associated nuclear antigen (LANA) that are specific for HHV-8 in tumor cells confirms the diagnosis of Kaposi sarcoma (Moore et al., 1996). Kaposi sarcoma is typically found on the skin, but metastatic spread to other sites is common, especially the mouth, the gastrointestinal tract, and the respiratory tract.

Kaposi sarcoma is associated with significant morbidity and mortality worldwide (Parkin, Bray, Ferlay, & Pisani, 2005).

Transmission of HHV-8

Herpes viruses can be transmitted by intimate sexual contact and by transplantation of contaminated organs. In sub-Saharan Africa where high rates of HHV-8 prevail, Kaposi sarcoma is the most common of all cancers. As with other herpes viral infections, HHV-8 may persist in a dormant state for many years, only to be reactivated by conditions of severe immunosuppression such as HIV disease. Active HHV-8 infection specifically initiates and promotes malignant transformation of the lymphatic endothelium in the genesis of Kaposi sarcoma.

Global Burden of Kaposi Sarcoma

During 2012, 44,247 new cases of Kaposi sarcoma were diagnosed in the world population (29,022 in men and 15, 225 in women) and 26,974 individuals died from the disease (17,358 men and 9,616 women). Approximately 84% of all cases and 94% of all deaths occurred in sub-Saharan Africa, where HIV-2 is endemic and there is limited access to therapy. In this region, incidence rates (9.2 and 3.7 per 100,000 in men and women, respectively) and mortality rates (6.5 in men and 2.9 in women) were 10- to 400-fold higher than in other regions of the world. In Zimbabwe, the incidence of Kaposi sarcoma among men was 46.5 per 100,000 and the mortality was 40.9 per 100,000, yielding a mortality/incidence ratio of 0.89. By comparison, the incidence among U.S. men was 0.5 per 100,000 and the mortality was 0.1 per 100,000, yielding a ratio of 0.2 (**Figure 25.6**) (Ferlay et al., 2013).

Seropositivity rates for HHV-8 coincide closely with the high rates of Kaposi sarcoma in sub-Saharan Africa. Co-infection by HIV is also prominent in these same African populations. It is noteworthy that there are marked ethnic differences in the rates of Kaposi sarcoma. For example, individuals of Asian descent rarely develop the disease, even those with HIV infection. Such ethnic disparities may reflect differences in the rates of HIV and HHV-8 coinfection (Parkin et al., 2005).

During 2008–2012, the global incidence of Kaposi sarcoma *increased* from 0.5 to 0.6 per 100,000 while the global mortality *decreased* from 0.4 to 0.3 per 100,000. These changes reflect some progress in the treatment of HIV disease but an absence of progress in curbing the transmission of HIV (Ferlay et al., 2010, 2013).

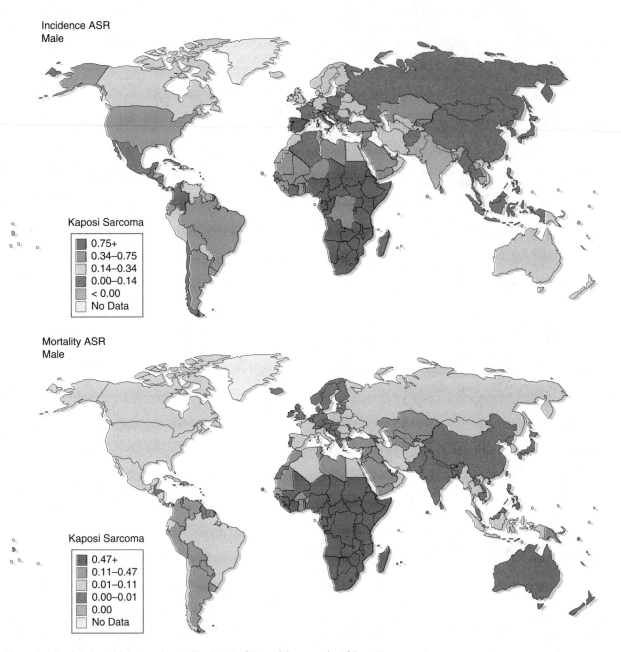

Figure 25.6 Global Incidence and Mortality Rates of Kaposi Sarcoma in African Men, 2012.

ASR: Rates per 100,000 are age-standardized to the world population, 2000–2025.

Source: Reproduced from Ferlay, J., Soerjomataram, I., Ervik, M., Dikshit, R., Eser, S., Mathers, C., . . . Bray, F. (2013). *GLOBOCAN 2012 v1.0. Cancer incidence and mortality worldwide: IARC CancerBase No. 11* [Internet]. Lyon, France: International Agency for Research on Cancer. Retrieved from http://globocan.iarc.fr

Subtypes of Kaposi Sarcoma

Several subtypes of Kaposi sarcoma have been defined. The main ones are as follows:

- *Classic Kaposi sarcoma* is a rare and relatively indolent form affecting elderly men from the Mediterranean coastal region or of Eastern European descent.

- *Endemic Kaposi sarcoma* is a moderately aggressive form found predominantly in young individuals from sub-Saharan Africa. It is *not* associated with HIV disease.

- *Transplant-related Kaposi sarcoma* is a rare form that develops in organ transplant patients who receive powerful immunosuppressive drugs such as cyclosporine.

- *AIDS-related Kaposi sarcoma* is a highly aggressive form and is one of the defining components of AIDS (HIV disease).

Impact of AIDS on Kaposi Sarcoma

A team of investigators spearheaded by Denis Burkitt investigated the geographic distributions of Kaposi sarcoma, non-Hodgkin's lymphoma, and Burkitt's lymphoma in populations of sub-Saharan Africa *prior to the AIDS epidemic*. High cumulative rates of Kaposi sarcoma (exceeding 6 per 1,000 in men ages birth–64 years) were found in equatorial Africa whereas the rates were low (nearly zero) in Northern and Southern regions. Rates were up to 10-fold higher in men than women, and in certain populations, such as in Uganda and Zaire, the estimated cumulative rates of Kaposi sarcoma (approximately 15 per 1,000) were similar to those for common malignancies of the Western world (e.g., colon cancer). These rates are hundreds of times higher than rates of Kaposi sarcoma reported for the populations of England and the United States in the pre-AIDS era. The authors noted the discovery of the etiologic viral agent of Kaposi sarcoma (HHV-8) in 1994, and suggested that the geographic and gender-related distribution of Kaposi sarcoma "may possibly mirror the distribution of the virus prior to the advent of AIDS" (Cook-Mozaffari, Newton, Beral, & Burkitt, 1998).

Before the epidemic of AIDS, Kaposi sarcoma was rare in Western countries, comprising only 0.3% of all cancers in men and 0.1% in women in the United States and Europe. During the 1970s, the cumulative (lifetime) incidence rates averaged less than 0.5 per 100,000 in U.S. men and less than 0.1 per 100,000 in U.S. women. Cases were occasionally discovered in older people of Mediterranean or Eastern European descent, often with a family history of the disease, and in immunosuppressed organ transplant recipients (Biggar, Horm, Fraumeni, Greene, & Goedert, 1984; Parkin et al., 2005).

Following the onset of the HIV epidemic, rates of Kaposi sarcoma increased dramatically among men in developed nations. In the United States, the annual incidence rates peaked in 1989 at 9.6 per 100,000 (**Figure 25.7**). Since that time, rates have declined to pre-AIDS levels, presumably in response to effective combined chemotherapy for HIV disease by highly active antiretroviral therapy (HAART) (Stebbing & Portsmouth, 2003).

Remarkably, the AIDS epidemic has had a negligible impact on the rates of Kaposi sarcoma in the U.S. female population (Figure 25.7). Although this may reflect their relatively low rates of HIV and HHV-8 coinfection, another possibility is that there are other risk factors to which women are not ordinarily exposed. For example, use of amylnitrites has been

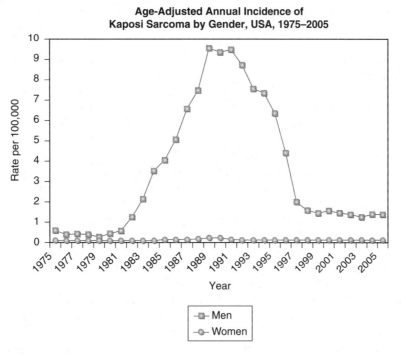

Figure 25.7 Age-Adjusted Annual Incidence of Kaposi Sarcoma by Gender, United States, 1975–2005.

Source: Data from Altekruse, S. F., Kosary, C. L., Krapcho, M., Neyman, N., Aminou, R., Waldron, W., & Edwards, B. K. (2010). *SEER cancer statistics review, 1975–2007.* Bethesda, MD: National Cancer Institute.

explored as a cofactor in the development of Kaposi sarcoma among AIDS patients (Fung & Tran, 2006).

In central Africa, post-AIDS rates of Kaposi sarcoma have continued to increase in populations with high endemic rates and little access to effective therapy, such as in Uganda, Malawi, Zimbabwe, and Swaziland. Indeed, Kaposi sarcoma is now the most common cancer in men and the second most common cancer in women in many nations of sub-Saharan Africa (Parkin et al., 2005).

CYCLOOXYGENASE-2 (COX-2) IN SARCOMAS

As in many other forms of cancer, the overexpression of cyclooxygenase-2 (COX-2) has been found to be a prominent feature of pediatric sarcomas. At the University of Cincinnati in the United States, Dickens and colleagues evaluated COX-2 expression in a series of 59 pediatric sarcomas using immunohistochemical analysis and cDNA microarray analysis. Tumor specimens included rhabdomyosarcoma, osteosarcoma, and Ewing sarcoma. Expression of COX-2 was detected in 83% of tumors by immunohistochemistry and in 89% of tumors by microarray analysis. In samples of normal osteocytes from nonmalignant bone and muscle tissues, no COX-2 expression was detected. The investigators suggest that COX-2 inhibitors should be tested in the treatment of pediatric sarcomas (Dickens, Kozielski, Khan, Forus, & Cripe, 2002).

At Helsinki University in Finland, Lassus and colleagues evaluated COX-2 expression by immunohistochemistry in 103 specimens of adult soft tissue sarcomas. They found COX-2 expression in 50 of the 103 tumors (49%) and in all 10 biphasic synovial sarcomas in the sample. They noted that COX-2 was expressed primarily by epithelial cells and in cells proximal to necrotic areas. The investigators concluded that COX-2 expression is associated with epithelial differentiation and tumor necrosis (Lassus et al., 2005).

At the University of Naples in Italy, Rossiello and colleagues evaluated COX-1 and COX-2 in tissues of Kaposi sarcoma using immunohistochemistry and western blot analysis. They investigated 35 cases of classic Kaposi sarcoma and 27 cases of epidemic Kaposi sarcoma. The results revealed that both COX-1 and COX-2 were overexpressed by tumor cells of all cases; furthermore, COX overexpression was detected in early and late stages of tumor progression, suggesting that the COX enzymes are involved in the pathogenesis of Kaposi sarcoma (Rossiello et al., 2007).

PREVENTION AND CONTROL OF KAPOSI SARCOMA

In developed nations, most cases of Kaposi sarcoma are diagnosed in patients with HIV/AIDS. Taking measures to avoid HIV infection could therefore prevent the vast majority of Kaposi sarcoma cases in these populations. Currently there is no effective vaccine against either HIV or HHV-8. Consequently, prevention depends on reducing the chance of infection by avoiding unprotected sex with HIV carriers and abstaining from injecting recreational drugs because hypodermic needles may be contaminated.

The successful prevention and control of HIV/AIDS depends on interrupting transmission of the virus. The main features of prevention are avoiding sexual contact with any HIV-infected individual, avoiding use of injectable drugs, avoiding contact with contaminated bodily fluids, and practicing universal precautions (for healthcare workers). All blood products and blood donors should be carefully screened to avoid contamination. Accurate information about HIV/AIDS prevention and control should be disseminated to the general public, preferably before sexual activity begins.

The majority of HIV infections are acquired through unprotected sexual activity between partners, one of whom has HIV. The primary mode of HIV infection worldwide is through sexual contact between members of the opposite sex. The male latex condom, if used correctly without oil-based lubricants, is the single most effective available technology to reduce the sexual transmission of HIV and other sexually transmitted infections. Studies on couples where one partner is infected show that with consistent condom use, HIV infection rates for the uninfected partner are below 1% per year (Cayley, 2004).

Antiretroviral treatment of infected patients has been found to significantly reduce the sexual transmission of HIV by reducing the level of virus in bodily fluids. In a recent multicenter study conducted in Botswana, Brazil, India, Kenya, Malawi, South Africa, Thailand, Zimbabwe, and the United States, 1,763 couples discordant for HIV positivity were randomly assigned to either a treatment group where the HIV-positive partner received antiretroviral drugs immediately or a control group where no drug was given. Out of 28 HIV infections that developed among study participants who were HIV-negative at baseline, 27 developed among members of the untreated couples. The early preventive treatment therefore led to a 96% reduction in HIV transmission to HIV-negative partners, strong evidence of the value of early intervention with antiretroviral therapy in such couples (Cohen et al., 2011).

Healthcare workers should follow universal precautions to reduce their risk of exposure to contaminated blood. These precautions include wearing gloves, masks, protective eyewear or shields, and gowns or aprons that prevent exposure of the skin or mucous membranes to blood-borne pathogens. Frequent and thorough washing of the skin immediately after being contaminated with blood or other bodily fluids reduces the chance of infection. Sharp objects like needles, scalpels, and glass must be carefully disposed of to prevent needle stick injuries with contaminated items (Kerr, Kimber, Debeck, & Wood, 2007).

Injection of illicit drugs using contaminated needles and syringes is a major mode of HIV transmission among intravenous drug abusers. Harm reduction strategies such as needle-exchange programs have been used with some success in reducing rates of HIV infection associated with intravenous drug abuse (Wodak & Cooney, 2006).

In the past, transfusions of contaminated blood and clotting factors were responsible for some HIV infections. As a result of improved HIV testing in blood banks, there is now a very low risk of HIV infection from blood products in the United States and most developed nations. Some poorer countries have not yet developed high quality screening programs of blood and blood products, leading to a higher risk of HIV infection with transfusion. The World Health Organization (WHO) has developed an integrated strategy for the provision of safe blood and blood products and safe, efficacious blood transfusion for all member nations (WHO, 2010).

To avoid mother-to-child transmission, HIV-infected mothers are encouraged to avoid breastfeeding their infant and instead use replacement feeding that is acceptable, feasible, affordable, sustainable, and safe. However, if replacement feeding is unavailable, exclusive breastfeeding is recommended during the first months of life and then should be discontinued as soon as possible (WHO, 2006).

One way to change risky behavior is health education. Several studies have shown the positive impact of culturally adapted educational programs advocating cautious sexual behavior. In 2010, a United Nations AIDS Inter-Agency Task Team encouraged more research on the actual implementation of sex-education programs (such as teacher training, access to related services through schools and the community, or parental attitudes to HIV and AIDS education), and more longitudinal studies on the deeper complexities of the relationship between education and HIV prevention and control (Lakhanpal & Ram, 2008; Rindermann & Meisenberg, 2009).

PREVENTION AND TREATMENT OF OTHER SARCOMAS

Only a few modifiable risk factors are known for other types of sarcoma, so population-based preventive strategies are generally absent. Exposure to excess radiation should be avoided and care should be taken to minimize exposure to environmental pollutants such as polyvinyl chloride, sawdust and wood dust, cutting oils (solvents), arsenicals, phenoxyherbicides, chlorophenols, and dioxins. It is also advisable to consider surgical removal of benign lesions that have potential for malignant transformation, in particular lipomas and leiomyomas.

The development of optimal treatment strategies for sarcoma is complicated by the large number of subtypes, the heterogeneity in their biological behavior, and the small number of patients with particular subtypes enrolled in trials. However, exciting new research has identified molecular markers for some sarcomas, particularly those in children, and such molecules are natural targets for therapy with monoclonal antibodies.

• • • REFERENCES

Abramson, D. H., & Frank, C. M. (1998). Second nonocular tumors in survivors of bilateral retinoblastoma: A possible age effect on radiation-related risk. *Ophthalmology, 105*(4), 573–580.

Adelmant, G., Bilbert, J. D., & Freytag, S. O. (1998). Human translocation liposarcoma-CCAAT/enhancer binding protein (C/EBP) homologous protein (TLS-CHOP) oncoprotein prevents adipocyte differentiation by directly interfering with C/EBPβ function. *Journal of Biological Chemistry, 273,* 15574–15581.

Altekruse, S. F., Kosary, C. L., Krapcho, M., Neyman, N., Aminou, R., Waldron, W., & Edwards, B. K. (2010). *SEER cancer statistics review, 1975–2007.* Bethesda, MD: National Cancer Institute.

Arlen, M., Higinbotham, N. L., Huvos, A. G., Marcove, R. C., Miller, T., & Shah, I. C. (1971). Radiation-induced sarcoma of bone. *Cancer, 28,* 1087–1099.

Azzarelli, A., Gennari, L., Quagliuolo, V., Bonfanti, G., Cerasoli, S., & Bufalino, R. (1986). Chondrosarcoma: 55 unreported cases: Epidemiology, surgical treatment and prognostic factors. *European Journal of Surgical Oncology*, *12*(2), 165–168.

Baldini, E. H., Demetri, G. D., Fletcher, C. D., Foran, J., Marcus, K. C., & Singer, S. (1999). Adults with Ewing's sarcoma/primitive neuroectodermal tumor: Adverse effect of older age and primary extraosseous disease on outcome. *Annals of Surgery*, *230*(1), 79–86.

Balsaver, A. M., Butler, J. J., & Martin, R. G. (1967). Congenital fibrosarcoma. *Cancer, 20*, 1607–1616.

Bancroft, L. W., Kransdorf, M. J., Peterson, J. J., & O'Connor, M. I. (2006). Benign fatty tumors: Classification, clinical course, imaging appearance, and treatment. *Skeletal Radiology*, *35*(10), 719–733.

Barr, F. G. (1997). Molecular genetics and pathogenesis of rhabdomyosarcoma. *Journal of Pediatric Hematology/Oncology*, *19*, 483–491.

Barré-Sinoussi, F., Chermann, J. C., Rey, F., Nugeyre, M. T., Chamaret, S., Gruest, J., . . . Montagnier, L. (1983). Isolation of a T-lymphotropic retrovirus from a patient at risk for acquired immune deficiency syndrome (AIDS). *Science, 220*, 868–871.

Baumhoer, D., Gunawan, B., Becker, H., & Füzesi, L. (2005). Comparative genomic hybridization in four angiosarcomas of the female breast. *Gynecologic Oncology*, *97*, 348–352.

Beck, A. (1922). Zur Frage des Rontgensarkoms, zugleich ein Beitrag zur Pathogenese des Sarkoms. *Münchener medizinische Wochenschrift*, *69*, 623–625.

Biggar, R. J., Horm, J., Fraumeni, J. F. Jr., Greene, M. H., & Goedert, J. J. (1984). Incidence of Kaposi's sarcoma and mycosis fungoides in the United States including Puerto Rico, 1973–81. *Journal of the National Cancer Institute*, *73*(1), 89–94.

Bishop, J. M., & Varmus, H. E. (1989). The Nobel prize in physiology or medicine, 1989. Retrieved from http://www.nobelprize.org/nobel_prizes/medicine/laureates/1989/press.html

Boffetta, P., Matisane, L., Mundt, K. A., & Dell, L. D. (2003). Meta-analysis of studies of occupational exposure to vinyl chloride on relation to cancer mortality. *Scandinavian Journal of Work, Environment and Health*, *29*, 220–229.

Cancian, L., Hansen, A., & Boshoff, C. (2013). Cellular origin of Kaposi's sarcoma and Kaposi'ssarcoma–associated herpesvirus-induced cell reprogramming. *Trends in Cell Biology*, *23*(9), 421–432.

Carsi, B., & Rock, M. G. (2002). Primary osteosarcoma in adults older than 40 years. *Clinical Orthopaedics and Related Research*, *397*, 53–61.

Cayley, W. E. Jr. (2004). Effectiveness of condoms in reducing heterosexual transmission of HIV. *American Family Physician*, *70*(7), 1268–1269.

Cesarman, E., Chang, Y., Moore, P. S., Said, J. W., & Knowles, D. M. (1995). Kaposi's sarcoma–associated herpesvirus-like DNA sequences in AIDS-related body-cavity-based lymphomas. *New England Journal of Medicine*, *332*(18), 1186–1191.

Chang, Y., Cesarman, E., Pessin, M. S., Lee, F., Culpepper, J.; Knowles, D. M., & Moore, P. S. (1994). Identification of herpesvirus-like DNA sequences in AIDS-associated Kaposi's sarcoma. *Science, 266*, 1865–1869.

Chauveinc, L., Mosseri, V., Quintana, E., Desjardins, L., Schlienger, P., Doz, F., & Dutrillaux, B. (2001). Osteosarcoma following retinoblastoma: Age at onset and latency period. *Ophthalmic Genetics*, *22*(2), 77–88.

Christopherson, W. M., Foote, F. W., & Stewart, F. W. (1952). Alveolar soft part sarcomas: Structurally characteristic tumors of uncertain histogenesis. *Cancer, 5*, 100–111.

Clark, J., Rocques, P. J., Crew, A. J., Gill, S., Shipley, J., Chan, A. L., . . . Cooper, C. S. (1994). Identification of novel genes, *SYT* and *SSX*, involved in the t(X;18)(p11.2;q11.2) translocation found in human synovial sarcoma. *Nature Genetics, 7*, 502–508.

Cohen, M. S., Chen, Y. Q., McCauley, M., Gamble, T., Hosseinipour, M. C., Kumarasamy, N., . . . Fleming, T. R. (2011). Prevention of HIV-1 infection with early antiretroviral therapy. *New England Journal of Medicine, 365*, 493–505.

Coindre, J. M., Mariani, O., Chibon, F., Maira, O., Somerhausen, N. A., Favre-Guilevin, E., . . . Aurias, A. (2003). Most malignant fibrous histiocytomas developed in the retroperitoneum are dedifferentiated liposarcomas: A review of 25 cases initially diagnosed as malignant fibrous histiocytoma. *Modern Pathology, 16*(3), 256–262.

Connolly, E., Gaffney, E., & Reynolds, J. (2003). Gastrointestinal stromal tumors. *British Journal of Surgery, 90*, 1178–1186.

Cook-Mozaffari, P., Newton, R., Beral, V., & Burkitt, D. P. (1998). The geographical distribution of Kaposi's sarcoma and of lymphomas in Africa before the AIDS epidemic. *British Journal of Cancer, 78*(11), 1521–1528.

Cordon-Cardo, C. (1997). Sarcomas of the soft tissues and bone. In V.T. DeVita, Jr. (Ed.), *Cancer principles and practice of oncology* (pp. 1731–1782). New York, NY: Lippincott-Raven.

Crawford, L. V., & Crawford, E. M. (1961). The properties of Rous sarcoma virus purified by density gradient centrifugation. *Virology, 13*, 227–232.

Creech, J. L. Jr., & Johnson, M. N. (1974). Angiosarcoma of the liver in the manufacture of polyvinyl chloride. *Journal of Occupational Medicine, 16*, 150–151.

Darling, J. (2007). A different view of sarcoma statistics. *Electronic Sarcoma Update Newsletter, 4*(6).

Delaney, T. F., Hornicek, F. J., Lessnick, S. L., & Mankin, H. J. (2010). Epidemiology, pathology, and molecular genetics of the Ewing sarcoma family of tumors. *UpToDate*, Version 18.3. Retrieved from http://www.uptodate .com/contents/epidemiology-pathology-and -molecular-genetics-of-the-ewing-sarcoma -family-of-tumors

Dickens, D. S., Kozielski, R., Khan, J., Forus, A., & Cripe, T. P. (2002). Cyclooxygenase-2 expression in pediatric sarcomas. *Pediatric and Developmental Pathology, 5*(4), 356–364.

Dunlap, J. B., Magenis, R. E., Davis, C., Himoe, E., & Mansoor, A. (2009). Cytogenetic analysis of a primary boneangiosarcoma. *Cancer Genetics and Cytogenetics, 194*(1), 1–3.

Edling, C. E., & Hallberg, B. (2007). c-Kit-a hematopoietic cell essential receptor tyrosine kinase. *International Journal of Biochemistry and Cell Biology, 39*(11), 1995–1998.

Ewing, J. (1921). Diffuse endothelioma of bone. *Proceedings of the New York Pathological Society, 21*, 17–24.

Exelby, P. R., Knapper, W. H., Huvos, A. G., & Beattie, E. J. Jr. (1973). Soft-tissue fibrosarcoma in children. *Journal of Pediatric Surgery, 8*(3), 415–420.

Falk, H., Caldwell, G. G., Ishak, K. D., Thomas, L. B., & Popper, H. (1981). Arsenic-related hepatic angiosarcoma. *American Journal of Industrial Medicine, 2*(1), 43–50.

Falk, H., Telles, N. C., Ishak, K. G., Thomas, L. B., & Popper, H. (1979). Epidemiology of thorotrast-induced hepatic angiosarcoma in the United States. *Environmental Research, 18*(1), 65–73.

Ferlay, J., Shin, H.-R., Bray, F., Forman, D., Mathers, C., & Parkin, D. M. (2010). Estimates of worldwide burden of cancer in 2008: GLOBOCAN 2008. *International Journal of Cancer, 127*(12), 2893–2917.

Ferlay, J., Soerjomataram, I., Ervik, M., Dikshit, R., Eser, S., Mathers, C., . . . Bray, F. (2013).

GLOBOCAN 2012 v1.0. Cancer incidence and mortality worldwide: IARC CancerBase No. 11 [Internet]. Lyon, France: International Agency for Research on Cancer. Retrieved from http://globocan.iarc.fr

Fung, H. L., & Tran, D. C. (2006). Effects of inhalant nitrites on VEGF expression: A feasible link to Kaposi's sarcoma? *Journal of Neuroimmune Pharmacology, 1*(3), 317–322.

Gallo, R. C., Salahuddin, S. Z., Popovic, M., Shearer, G. M., Kaplan, M., Haynes, B. F., . . . Safai, B. (1984). Frequent detection and isolation of cytopathic retroviruses (HTLV-III) from patients with AIDS and at risk for AIDS. *Science, 224*(4648), 500–503.

Gardner, E. J. (1951). A genetic and clinical study of intestinal polyposis, a predisposing factor for carcinoma of the colon and rectum. *American Journal of Human Genetics, 3*(2), 167–176.

Gurney, J. G., Swensen, A. R., & Bulterys, M. (1999). Chapter VIII. Malignant bone tumors. In L. A. G. Ries, M. A. Smith, J. G. Gurney, M. Linet, T. Tamra, J. L. Young, & G. R. Bunin (Eds.), *Cancer incidence and survival among children and adolescents: United States SEER program 1975–1995* (pp. 99–110, NIH Pub. No. 99-4649). Bethesda, MD: National Cancer Institute, SEER Program.

Gurney, J. G., Young, J. L., Roffers, S. D., Smith, M. A., & Bunin, G. R. (1999). Chapter IX. Soft tissue sarcomas. In L. A. G. Ries, M. A. Smith, J. G. Gurney, M. Linet, T. Tamra, J. L. Young, & G. R. Bunin (Eds.), *Cancer incidence and survival among children and adolescents: United States SEER program 1975–1995* (pp. 111–122, NIH Pub. No. 99-4649). Bethesda, MD: National Cancer Institute, SEER Program.

Hoppin, J. A., Tolbert, P. E., Flanders, W. D., Zhang, R. H., Daniels, D. S., Ragsdale, B. D., & Brann, E. A. (1999). Occupational risk factors for sarcoma subtypes. *Epidemiology, 10*(6), 300–306.

Indraccolo, U., Luchetti, G., & Indraccolo, S. R. (2008). Malignant transformation of uterine leiomyomata. *European Journal of Gynaecological Oncology, 29*(5), 543–534.

Joensuu, H., Roberts, P. J., Sarlomo-Rikala, M., Andersson, L. C., Tervahartiala, P., Tuveson, D., Silberman., S. L., . . . Demetri, G. D. (2001). Effect of the tyrosine kinase inhibitor STI571 in a patient with a metastatic gastrointestinal stromal tumor. *New England Journal of Medicine, 344*(14), 1052–1056.

Johnson, J. G., Gilbert, E., Zimmermann, B., & Watne, A. L. (1972). Gardner's syndrome, colon cancer, and sarcoma. *Journal of Surgical Oncology, 4*(4), 354–362.

Kaposi, M. (1872). Idiopathisches multiples pigmentsarkom der haut. *Archiv für Dermatologie und Syphilis, 4,* 265–273.

Karlsson, P., Holmberg, E., Samuelsson, A., Johansson, K. A., & Wallgren, A. (1998). Soft tissue sarcoma after treatment for breast cancer—A Swedish population-based study. *European Journal of Cancer, 34*(13), 2068–2075.

Kerr, T., Kimber, J., Debeck, K., & Wood, E. (2007). The role of safer injection facilities in the response to HIV/AIDS among injection drug users. *Current HIV/AIDS Reports, 4*(4), 158–164.

Knezevich, S. R., Garnett, M. J., Pysher, T. J., Beckwith, J. B., Grundy, P. E., & Sorensen, P. H. (1998). *ETV6-NTRK3* gene fusions and trisomy 11 establish a histogenetic link between mesoblastic nephroma and congenital fibrosarcoma. *Cancer Research, 58,* 5046–5048.

Kumar, V., Abbas, A. K., & Aster, J. C. (2014). *Robbins and Cotran pathologic basis of disease* (9th ed.). Philadelphia, PA: Mosby & Saunders.

Ladanyi, M. (1995). The emerging molecular genetics of sarcoma translocations. *Diagnostic Molecular Pathology, 4*(3), 162–173.

Ladanyi, M., & Bridge, J. A. (2000). Contribution of molecular genetic data to the classification of sarcomas. *Human Pathology, 31,* 532–538.

Ladanyi, M., Lui, M. Y., Antonescu, C. R., Krause-Boehm, A., Meindl, A., Argani, P., . . . Bridge, J. (2001). The der(17)t(X;17)(p11;q25) of human alveolar soft part sarcoma fuses the *TFE3* transcription factor gene to *ASPL*, a novel gene at 17q25. *Oncogene, 20*(1), 48–57.

Lakhanpal, M., & Ram, R. (2008). Educational attainment and HIV/AIDS prevalence: A cross-country study. *Economics of Education Review, 27*, 14–21.

Lassus, P., Ristimaki, A., Huuhtanen, R., Tukiainen, E., Asko-Seljavaara, S., Andersson, L. C., . . . Bohling, T. (2005). Cyclooxygenase-2 expression in human soft-tissue sarcomas is related to epithelial differentiation. *Anticancer Research, 25*, 2669–2674.

Leonard, A., Craft, A. W., Moss, C., & Malcolm, A. J. (1996). Osteogenic sarcoma in the Rothmund-Thomson syndrome. *Medical and Pediatric Oncology, 26*(4), 249–253.

Levy, J. A., Hoffman, A. D., Kramer, S. M., Landis, J. A., Shimabukuro, J. M., & Oshiro, L. S. (1984). Isolation of lymphocytopathic retroviruses from San Francisco patients with AIDS. *Science, 225*(4664), 840–842.

Li, F. P., Fraumeni, J. F. Jr., Mulvihill, J. J., Blattner, W. A., Dreyfus, M. G., Tucker, M. A., & Miller, R. W. (1998). A cancer family syndrome in twenty-four kindreds. *Cancer Research, 48*(18), 5358–5362.

Lorincz, A., Redelman, D., Horvath, V. J., Bardsley, M. R., Chen, H., & Ordog, T. (2008). Progenitors of interstitial cells of Cajal in the postnatal murine stomach. *Gastroenterology, 134*, 1083–1093.

Markowitz, S. D., & Bertagnolli, M. M. (2009). Molecular basis of colorectal cancer. *New England Journal of Medicine, 361*(25), 2449–2460.

Martland, H., & Humphries, R. E. (1929). Osteogenic sarcoma in dial painters using luminous paint. *Archives of Pathology, 7*, 406–417.

Mendenhall, W. M., Zlotecki, R. A., Scarborough, M. T., Gibbs, P. C., & Mendenhall, N. P. (2006). Giant cell tumor of bone. *American Journal of Clinical Oncology, 29*(1), 96–99.

Moore, P. S., & Chang, Y. (1995). Detection of herpesvirus-like DNA sequences in Kaposi's sarcoma in patients with and without HIV infection. *New England Journal of Medicine, 332*(18), 1181–1185.

Moore, P. S., Gao, S. J., Dominguez, G., Cesarman, E., Lungu, O., Knowles, D. M., . . . Chang, Y. (1996). Primary characterization of a herpesvirus agent associated with Kaposi's sarcoma. *Journal of Virology, 70*(1), 549–558.

Mundt, K. A., Dell, L. D., Austin, R. P., Luippold, R. S., Noess, R., & Bigelow, C. (2000). Historical cohort study of 10,109 men in the North American vinyl chloride industry, 1942–1972. Update of cancer mortality to 31 December. *Occupational and Environmental Medicine, 57*, 774–781.

O'Brien, J. E., & Stout, A. P. (1964). Malignant fibrous xanthomas. *Cancer, 17*, 1445–1455.

Oppermann, H., Levinson, A. D., Varmus, H. E., Levintow, L., & Bishop, J. M. (1979). Uninfected vertebrate cells contain a protein that is closely related to the product of the avian sarcoma virus transforming gene (src). *Proceedings of the National Academy of the Sciences of the United States of America, 76*(4), 1804–1808.

Parkin, D. M., Bray, F., Ferlay, J., & Pisani, P. (2005). Global cancer statistics, 2002. *CA: A Cancer Journal for Clinicians, 55*, 74–108.

Parkin, D. M., Stiller, C. A., Draper, G. J., & Bieber, C. A. (1988). The international incidence of childhood cancer. *International Journal of Cancer, 42*, 511–520.

Patel, K. U., Szabo, S. S., Hernandez, V. S., Prieto, V. G., Abruzzo, L. V., Lazar, A. J. F., & López-Terrada, D. (2008). Dermatofibrosarcoma protuberans COL1A1-PDGFB fusion is identified in virtually all dermatofibrosarcoma protuberans cases when investigated by newly developed multiplex reverse transcription polymerase chain reaction and fluorescence in situ hybridization assays. *Human Pathology, 39*(2), 184–193.

Rindermann, H., & Meisenberg, G. (2009). Relevance of education and intelligence at the national level for health: The case of HIV and AIDS. *Intelligence, 37,* 383–395.

Robinson, E., Neugut, A. I., & Wylie, P. (1988). Clinical aspects of postirradiation sarcomas. *Journal of the National Cancer Institute, 80,* 233–240.

Rööser, B., Willén, H., Gustafson, P., Alvegård, T. A., & Rydholm, A. (1991). Malignant fibrous histiocytoma of soft tissue. A population-based epidemiologic and prognostic study of 137 patients. *Cancer, 67*(2), 499–505.

Rossiello, L., Ruocco, E., Signoriello, G., Micheli, P., Rienzo, M., Napoli, C., & Rossiello, R. (2007). Evidence of COX-1 and COX-2 expression in Kaposi's sarcoma tissues. *European Journal of Cancer, 43*(8), 1232–1241.

Rous, P. (1910). A transmissable avian neoplasm. *Journal of Experimental Medicine, 12,* 696–705.

Rous, P. (1911). A sarcoma of the fowl transmissible by an agent separable from the tumor cells. *Journal of Experimental Medicine, 13,* 397–399.

Rous, P., & Huggins, C. B. (1966). The Nobel prize in physiology or medicine, 1966. Retrieved from http://www.nobelprize.org/nobel_prizes /medicine/laureates/1966/

Sanders, K., Koh, S., & Ward, S. (2006). Interstitial cells of Cajal as pacemakers in the gastrointestinal tract. *Annual Review of Physiology, 68,* 307–343.

Sinha, A., Tekkis, P. P., Gibbons, D. C., Phillips, R. K., & Clark, S. K. (2010). Risk factors predicting desmoid occurrence in patients with familial adenomatous polyposis: A meta-analysis. *Colorectal Disease, 13,* 1222–1229.

Skubitz, K. M. (2007). Sarcoma. *Mayo Clinic Proceedings, 82*(11), 1409–1432.

Spirtas, R., Beebe, G., Baxter, P., Dacey, F., Faber, M., Falk, H., . . . Stafford, J. (1983). Angiosarcoma as a model for comparative carcinogenesis. *Lancet, 322*(8347), 456.

Stebbing, J., & Portsmouth, B. (2003). How does HAART lead to the resolution of Kaposi's sarcoma? *Journal of Antimicrobial Chemotherapy, 51*(5), 1095–1098.

Stehelin, D., Fujita, D. J., Padgett, T., Varmus, H. E., & Bishop, J. M. (1977). Detection and enumeration of transformation-defective strains of avian sarcoma virus with molecular hybridization. *Virology, 76*(2), 675–684.

Stiller, C. A., Bielack, S. S., Jundt, G., & Steliarova-Foucher, E. (2006). Bone tumours in European children and adolescents, 1978–1997. Report from the Automated Childhood Cancer Information System project. *European Journal of Cancer, 42*(13), 2124–2135.

Thomas, D. M., & Skubitz, T. (2009). Giant-cell tumour of bone. *Current Opinion in Oncology, 21,* 338–344.

Tontonoz, P., Singer, S., Forman, B. M., Sarraf, P., Fletcher, J. A., Fletcher, C. D., . . . Spiegelman, B. M. (1997). Terminal differentiation of human liposarcoma cells induced by ligands for peroxisome proliferator-activated receptor gamma and the retinoid X receptor. *Proceedings of the National Academy of the Sciences of the United States of America, 94*(1), 237–241.

Tran, T., Davila, J. A., & El-Serag, H. B. (2005). The epidemiology of malignant gastrointestinal stromal tumors: An analysis of 1,458 cases from 1992 to 2000. *American Journal of Gastroenterology, 100,* 162–168.

Turc-Carel, C., Limon, J., Dal Cin, P., Rao, U., Karakousis, C., & Sandberg, A. A. (1986). Cytogenetic studies of adipose tissue tumors. II. Recurrent reciprocal translocation t(12:16) (q13;p11) in myxoid liposarcomas. *Cancer Genetics and Cytogenetics, 23*(4), 291–299.

Walker, D. G. (1972). Congenital osteopetrosis in mice cured by parabiotic union with normal siblings. *Endocrinology, 91*(4), 916–920.

Walker, D. G. (1973). Osteopetrosis cured by temporary parabiosis. *Science, 180*(88), 875.

Wallach, E. E., & Vlahos, N. F. (2004). Uterine myomas: An overview of development, clinical features, and management. *Obstetrics and Gynecology, 104,* 393–406.

Wang, L. L., Gannavarapu, A., Kozinetz, C. A., Moise, L., Levy, M. L., Lewis, R. A., . . . Zackai, E. H. (2003). Association between osteosarcoma and deleterious mutations in the *RECQL4* gene in Rothmund-Thomson syndrome. *Journal of the National Cancer Institute, 95*(9), 669–674.

Wang, R., Lu, Y. J., Fisher, C., Bridge, J. A., & Shipley, J. (2001). Characterization of chromosome aberrations associated with soft-tissue leiomyosarcomas by twenty-four-color karyotyping and comparative genomic hybridization analysis. *Genes, Chromosomes and Cancer, 31,* 54–64.

Wodak, A., & Cooney, A. (2006). Do needle syringe programs reduce HIV infection among injecting drug users: A comprehensive review of the international evidence. *Substance Use and Misuse, 41*(6–7), 777–813.

World Health Organization. (2006). *HIV and infant feeding technical consultation, consensus statement.* Geneva, Switzerland: Author.

World Health Organization. (2010). *Screening donated blood for transfusion-transmissible infections: Recommendations.* Geneva, Switzerland: Author.

Yarden, Y., Kuang, W. J., Yang-Feng, T., Coussens, L., Munemitsu, S., Dull, T. J., . . . Ullrich, A. (1987). Human proto-oncogene c-kit: A new cell surface receptor tyrosine kinase for an unidentified ligand. *EMBO Journal, 6*(11), 3341–3351.

26

Epidemiology of Lymphoma: Non-Hodgkin's Lymphoma, Hodgkin's Lymphoma, and Multiple Myeloma

CLASSIFICATION OF LYMPHOMA

The World Health Organization categorizes lymphomas into three broad groups: non-Hodgkin's lymphoma, Hodgkin's lymphoma, and multiple myeloma. Non-Hodgkin's lymphomas show considerable heterogeneity and are divisible into those arising from B cells or T cells. This chapter focuses primarily on the epidemiology of non-Hodgkin's lymphoma with brief sections devoted to Hodgkin's lymphoma and multiple myeloma.

Lymphomas are malignancies that can arise in the lymphocytes of lymphoid tissue anywhere in the body, most commonly within lymph nodes. Hodgkin's lymphoma, which is distinguishable by the presence of multinucleated Reed–Sternberg cells, constitutes 10–15% of all lymphomas (Reed, 1902). Multiple myeloma, a neoplasm of plasma cells, constitutes 15–20% of lymphomas. The remaining 65–75% of lymphomas, the non-Hodgkin's lymphomas, arise at various stages in the maturation of B lymphocytes or T lymphocytes. According to classification schemes currently used in clinical practice, non-Hodgkin's lymphomas can be subdivided into a bewildering array of subtypes. In most populations, 80–90% of non-Hodgkin's lymphomas are derived from the B-cell lineage (Harris et al., 1999).

Lymphomas are cohesive malignancies (solid tumors) composed primarily of lymphocytes. Their origin, usually in lymph nodes, may involve an arrest in differentiation of immature lymphocytes, or alternatively, retrodifferentiation of mature lymphocytes. In either case, there is sustained unrelenting proliferation of the transformed cells. As with other malignancies, the initiation, growth, development, and metastatic spread of lymphomas involves various cellular and genetic processes, including mutagenesis, mitogenesis, angiogenesis, aberrant apoptosis, immunosuppression, and metastasis.

Lymphocytes arise from hematopoietic stem cells of the bone marrow. The B lymphocytes mature and differentiate in the lymph nodes, whereas T lymphocytes do so in the thymus gland. The different types of lymphocytes display specific cell surface receptors and have characteristic morphological features and distinct functions in the immune system. For example, the maturation, differentiation, and proliferation of T lymphocytes spawn at least three distinct subpopulations: antigen-presenting T cells (also called helper T cells), suppressor T cells, and killer T cells.

With appropriate stimulation by helper T cells, mature B lymphocytes differentiate into plasma cells that secrete antibodies directed against specific antigens recognized as foreign to the human immune system. Malignancies of plasma cells are called *myelomas*, and because neoplasms of plasma cells usually involve multiple anatomic sites throughout the skeletal system and sometimes soft tissues, the condition is commonly called *multiple myeloma*.

EPIDEMIOLOGY OF NON-HODGKIN'S LYMPHOMA

Global Burden of Non-Hodgkin's Lymphoma

During 2012, 385,741 new cases of non-Hodgkin's lymphoma were diagnosed in the world population and 199,360 individuals died from the disease. Of these, 217,643 cases (56%) and 115,384 deaths (58%) occurred in men (Ferlay, Shin, Forman, Mathers, & Parkin, 2013).

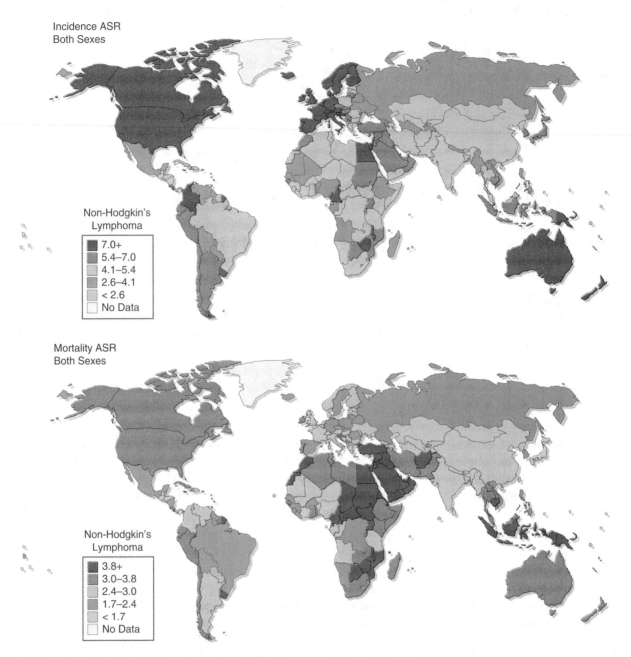

Figure 26.1 Global Incidence and Mortality Rates of Non-Hodgkin's Lymphoma, 2012.

ASR: Rates per 100,000 are age-standardized to the world population, 2000–2025.

Source: Reproduced from Ferlay, J., Soerjomataram, I., Ervik, M., Dikshit, R., Eser, S., Mathers, C., . . . Bray, F. (2013). *GLOBOCAN 2012 v1.0. Cancer incidence and mortality worldwide: IARC CancerBase No. 11* [Internet]. Lyon, France: International Agency for Research on Cancer. Retrievedfrom http://globocan.iarc.fr

Incidence rates of non-Hodgkin's lymphoma vary widely and tend to be higher in populations of developed nations (**Figure 26.1**). As in other years, the 2012 rates were high in North America, Western Europe, and Australia/New Zealand (~10 per 100,000) and low in India and China (~3 per 100,000) (Ferlay et al., 2013). High rates were also observed in some populations residing in the tropical zone of Africa, partly due to the high incidence of Burkitt's lymphoma, a particularly aggressive form of B-cell lymphoma that develops primarily in children. Of further note is that T-cell lymphomas are most common in Japan and the Caribbean (Shipp, Mauch, & Harris, 1997). Caution is advised, however, in drawing epidemiologic conclusions based on the wide variability in international rates because many nations do not have population-based cancer registries, and reporting may therefore be incomplete.

Mortality rates were highest in the populations of the Middle East and Africa (4–6 per 100,000) and lowest in India, China, and Eastern Asia (1–2 per 100,000) (Figure 26.1). In African populations where mortality is high, the available healthcare resources are generally inadequate for effective treatment. Nevertheless, relatively high death rates from non-Hodgkin's lymphoma are also evident in the populations of many developed nations. For example, mortality in U.S. men (4.5 per 100,000) was higher than in most other nations (Ferlay et al., 2013).

Global Patterns and Trends of Non-Hodgkin's Lymphoma

The global burden of non-Hodgkin's lymphoma has steadily increased during the past 2 decades (**Figure 26.2**). During 1990–2012, the annual number of new cases increased by 67% (from 230,000 in 1990 to 385,000 in 2012), and the annual number of deaths increased by 58% (from 126,000 in 1990 to 199,000 in 2012). However, the global annual *age-adjusted* mortality rates have been relatively stable during this time period, averaging approximately 3.4 per 100,000 in men and 2.1 per 100,000 in women. Likewise, the global annual age-adjusted incidence rates have also stabilized at 6.0 per 100,000 in men and 4.1 per 100,000 in women (Ferlay et al., 2010, 2013; Parkin, Bray, Ferlay, & Pisani, 2005; Parkin, Pisani, & Ferlay, 1999a, 1999b; World Health Organization, 2008).

The rising absolute numbers of new cases and deaths from non-Hodgkin's lymphoma without substantial concomitant changes in the age-adjusted rates may be largely due to increasing longevity of the world

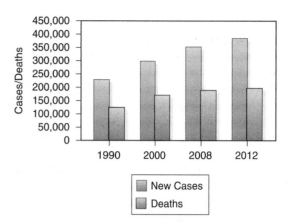

Figure 26.2 Global Trends of Non-Hodgkin's Lymphoma, 1990–2012.

Source: Data from Ferlay, J., Shin, H. R., Forman, D., Mathers, C., & Parkin, D. M. (2010). Estimates of worldwide burden of cancer in 2008. *International Journal of Cancer, 127*(12), 2893–2917; Ferlay, J., Soerjomataram, I., Ervik, M., Dikshit, R., Eser, S., Mathers, C., . . . Bray, F. (2013). *GLOBOCAN 2012 v1.0. Cancer incidence and mortality worldwide: IARC CancerBase No. 11* [Internet]. Lyon, France: International Agency for Research on Cancer. Retrieved from http://globocan.iarc.fr; Parkin, D. M., Bray, F., Ferlay, J., & Pisani, P. (2005). Global cancer statistics, 2002. *CA: A Cancer Journal for Clinicians, 55*, 74–108; Parkin, D. M., Pisani, P., & Ferlay, J. (1999a). Estimates of the worldwide incidence of 25 major cancers in 1990. *International Journal of Cancer, 80*(6), 827–841; Parkin, D. M., Pisani, P., & Ferlay, J. (1999b). Global cancer statistics. *CA: A Cancer Journal for Clinicians, 49*(1), 33–64; World Health Organization. (2008). World cancer report 2008. Lyon, France: International Agency for Research on Cancer.

population. This phenomenon has resulted in more individuals living to later ages when the risk of death from lymphoma is highest. As shown in **Figure 26.3**, lymphoma onset rises with age, and nearly 75% of deaths occur after the age of 65 years (Altekruse et al., 2010).

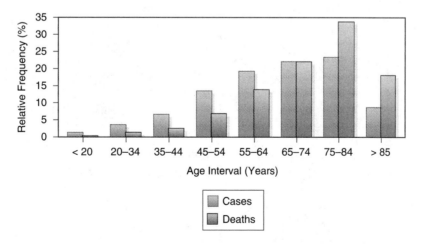

Figure 26.3 Age-Specific Frequencies of New Cases and Deaths: Non-Hodgkin's Lymphoma.

Source: Data from Altekruse, S. F., Kosary, C. L., Krapcho, M., Neyman, N., Aminou, R., Waldron, W., . . . Edwards, B. K. (2010). *SEER cancer statistics review, 1975–2007.* Bethesda, MD: National Cancer Institute.

Non-Hodgkin's Lymphoma in the United States

In nations with population-based cancer registries, marked increases were observed in the annual incidence rates of non-Hodgkin's lymphoma during the latter decades of the 20th century. For example, in the United States the incidence doubled for both men and women during 1970–1995 (**Figure 26.4**). The rising incidence rates during this time period were consistent in men and women of all ethnicities and age groups except for the very young (Devesa & Fears, 1992). Subsequently, during 1995–2010 the rates stabilized and appear to have declined slightly (Altekruse et al., 2010).

Several factors have contributed to the increasing trends in non-Hodgkin's lymphoma in populations of the United States and other developed nations. In particular, escalations in the incidence among young adult males and (to a lesser extent) females occurred following the onset of the acquired immune deficiency syndrome (AIDS) epidemic in 1981 (Hartge, Devesa, & Fraumeni, 1994). With the discovery of the human immunodeficiency virus (HIV), which is considered the causative agent of AIDS, this syndrome is currently referred to as *HIV disease* (Barré-Sinoussi et al., 1983; Gallo et al., 1983).

Other factors that have contributed to the rising incidence of non-Hodgkin's lymphoma include improvements in the detection and reporting of lymphomas and refinements in the classification system of lymphoproliferative disorders, resulting in the diagnosis of relatively more cases of non-Hodgkin's lymphoma. For example, certain extranodal lymphoproliferative conditions and T-cell neoplasms are now recognized and classified as non-Hodgkin's lymphoma. Although stomach and skin remain the most common extranodal sites, primary disease in the brain has sharply increased (Groves, Linet, Travis, & Devesa, 2000). Furthermore, the incidence of non-Hodgkin's lymphoma is also increased among cancer patients treated by chemotherapy and among subjects undergoing heart or kidney transplants, all of whom experience immunosuppression (Banks, 1992; Müller, Ihorst, Mertelsmann, & Engelhardt, 2005). Despite these coincident trends, a large portion of the increase in non-Hodgkin's lymphoma during the latter 20th century remains to be explained.

As shown in Figure 26.4, the annual incidence of non-Hodgkin's lymphoma in the United States increased until about 1995, but then subsequently declined. This pattern coincides with a decline in the development of HIV disease due to primary preventive measures and/or use of highly active antiretroviral therapy that inhibits progression of HIV infection to active disease (Eltom, Jemal, Mbulaiteye, Devesa, & Biggar, 2002). Nevertheless, the incidence of non-Hodgkin's lymphoma *not* related to HIV disease is continuing to increase, particularly among older men and women. It is well known that old age is accompanied by decreased immune function (immunosuppression) and higher susceptibility to infection, conditions that may heighten the risk of developing lymphoma as well as other malignancies (Fisher & Fisher, 2004; Müller et al., 2005).

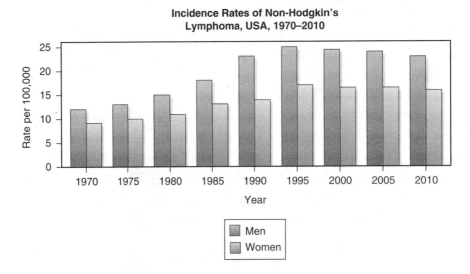

Incidence Rates of Non-Hodgkin's Lymphoma, USA, 1970–2010

Figure 26.4 Annual Incidence Rates of Non-Hodgkin's Lymphoma, United States, 1970–2010.

Rates are age-standardized to the U.S. population of 2000.

Source: Data from Altekruse, S. F., Kosary, C. L., Krapcho, M., Neyman, N., Aminou, R., Waldron, W.,... Edwards, B. K. (2010). *SEER cancer statistics review, 1975–2007.* Bethesda, MD: National Cancer Institute.

GENDER AND ETHNIC DIFFERENCES IN NON-HODGKIN'S LYMPHOMA

In the U.S. population, more than 21,000 individuals died from non-Hodgkin's lymphoma each year during 2003–2007. The age-adjusted mortality rate was 6.9 per 100,000 per year and the median age at death was 75 years of age. Death rates were 60% higher for men than women (8.7 versus 5.5) and higher among Caucasians (9.1 in men and 5.7 in women) compared to other ethnicities (5.8 in men and 4.1 in women) (Altekruse et al., 2010).

During 2003–2007, the age-adjusted incidence rate of non-Hodgkin's lymphomawas 19.6 per 100,000 per year. Incidence rates were 43% higher in men than women (23.6 versus 16.5 per 100,000), and higher in Caucasians (24.6 in men and 17.2 in women) than other ethnic groups (16.2 in men and 12.1 in women). American Indians and Alaska natives had the lowest rates (12.5 in men and 10.6 in women) (Altekruse et al., 2010).

RISK FACTORS FOR NON-HODGKIN'S LYMPHOMA

Multiple viruses and bacteria have been found in association with the development of non-Hodgkin's lymphoma (Alexander et al., 2007a; Fisher & Fisher, 2004; Melbye, Ekström Smedby, & Trichopoulos, 2008; Müller et al., 2005). These infectious agents appear to be associated with two principal biological phenomena involved in the genesis of this malignancy: immunosuppression and antigenic stimulation. Immunosuppression can be incited not only by microbes, but also by powerful drugs routinely used in transplant therapy. Indeed, the combination of drug-induced immunosuppression and heightened antigenic stimulation through reactivation of latent Epstein–Barr virus (EBV) infection appears to markedly accelerate lymphomagenesis. Selected microbes and conditions and their effects on the pathogenesis of non-Hodgkin's lymphoma are discussed in the following sections.

Genetics of Non-Hodgkin's Lymphoma

Family studies suggest that genetic susceptibility has a modest influence on the development of non-Hodgkin's lymphoma. For example, the presence of one or more first-degree relatives (parents, siblings, and offspring) afflicted with a hematopoietic malignancy has been found to increase the risk of developing non-Hodgkin's lymphoma by two- to fourfold

(Linet & Pottern, 1992; Zhu et al., 1998). Nevertheless, it is not clear whether familial clustering is truly attributable to genetic predisposition or rather to similar environmental exposures. Furthermore, familial lymphomas account for less than 5% of all cases, and it is unlikely that hereditary factors per se played a substantial role in the increasing trend in non-Hodgkin's lymphoma in the United States and other populations.

Primary congenital immunodeficiency is a rare condition that results in the absence of specific types of immunoglobulins in the immune system. This disorder arises due to point mutations in the genes controlling immunoglobulin formation, most of which are located on chromosomes 2, 14, and 22. When congenital immunodeficiency is present, the risk of developing lymphoma is high, up to 25% by the age of 25 years. This condition also shortens the lifespan considerably, because most afflicted patients die before the age of 50 years. Certain other genetic syndromes also increase the risk of developing lymphoma. These include ataxia telangiectasis, a condition marked by DNA repair defects and impaired cell-mediated immunity; Wiscott–Aldrich syndrome, a rare X-linked condition characterized by eczema, thrombocytopenia (low platelets), immunodeficiency, and bloody diarrhea; and the X-linked lymphoproliferative syndrome characterized by fatal or near-fatal infectious mononucleosis due to EBV and immunoglobulin deficiency in childhood (Filipovich, Mathur, Kamat, & Shapiro, 1992).

Lymphomas are genetically characterized by the presence of chromosomal translocations, which are usually balanced reciprocal recombinations that involve a switch of DNA between two chromosomes. Such chromosomal rearrangements are *not* heritable and are thought to occur during immune reactions against various infectious agents, particularly EBV. Rearrangements often involve the immunoglobulin genes of B cells or the receptor genes of T cells (Tycko & Sklar, 1990). At the molecular level, such translocations induce neoplastic development by either activating tumor oncogenes or inactivating tumor suppressor genes. The most common translocations found in non-Hodgkin's lymphomas involve juxtaposition of genes that regulate transcription to regions of chromosome 14 that control promotion and enhancement elements of highly active immunoglobulin genes. In studies of lymphoma karyotypes, chromosomal translocations have been detected in up to 90% of non-Hodgkin's lymphomas (Grogan & Miller, 1995; Offit, Wong, Filippa, Tao, & Chaganti, 1991; Vega & Medeiros, 2003; Ye, 2000).

HIV Disease and Non-Hodgkin's Lymphoma

Following the onset of the AIDS epidemic and the discovery of HIV in the early 1980s, population registries were established in many countries in order to monitor the number of new cases and evaluate the impact of widespread efforts to control the epidemic. Analysis of the HIV/AIDS registry data has helped elucidate important clues regarding the genesis of non-Hodgkin's lymphoma.

In 1999, a team of Italian investigators reported findings on the association of lymphoma and HIV disease based on registry data from the United States, Europe, and Australia. The study involved the analysis of datasets developed by linking registries of AIDS patients with population-based cancer registries. During 1988–1997, AIDS surveillance data from 17 Western European countries revealed that more than 7,000 cases involved non-Hodgkin's lymphoma as the AIDS-defining illness, and during the 1990s, non-Hodgkin's lymphoma was the AIDS-defining condition in approximately 5% of cases. Among adults with HIV/AIDS, the relative risks for non-Hodgkin's lymphoma ranged from 15 for low-grade disease (confined to one lymph node) to 400 for high-grade disease (affecting multiple nodes and/or sites). The relative risk (RR) of Hodgkin's lymphoma among individuals with HIV/AIDS was also increased (RR = 10). The extraordinarily high risk for the development of non-Hodgkin's lymphoma among individuals who are HIV-seropositive has led to its recognition as an AIDS-defining condition (Dal Maso & Franceschi, 2003; Franceschi, Dal Maso, & La Vecchia, 1999).

The HIV-associated non-Hodgkin's lymphomas are invariably derived from B lymphocytes, and more than 80% originate at extranodal sites, most commonly in the brain and central nervous system. These lymphomas usually present as high-grade malignancies, with 60–70% being metastatic at the time of diagnosis. An Australian case control study identified the duration of immunosuppression and the degree of B-cell stimulation as primary risk factors (Grulich et al., 2000). Although sequences of the HIV genome have never been found incorporated into the DNA of lymphoma cells, it is notable that EBV is often present in tumor tissues and/or the cerebral spinal fluid of cases. It has thus been suggested that interactions involving coinfection with EBV and/or other viruses predispose to the development of non-Hodgkin's lymphoma through immunosuppression and impairment of cell-mediated immunity in patients with HIV disease (Biggar, Frisch, Engels, & Goedert, 2001; Cinque et al., 1993).

Immunosuppression and Non-Hodgkin's Lymphoma

Immunosuppression has consistently been found to be a strong risk factor in the development of non-Hodgkin's lymphoma. Individuals with drug-induced immunodeficiency for the purpose of suppressing posttransplant organ rejection or treating autoimmune conditions, or resulting from sustained chemotherapy for cancer are among those at high risk. Enormous increases in relative risk (more than 100-fold) have been observed in organ transplant patients who receive sustained aggressive immunosuppressive regimens (Opelz & Henderson, 1993). As with HIV/AIDS patients, active infection with EBV is a common finding in posttransplant patients (Cleary, Chao, Warnke, & Sklar, 1984; Kinlen, 1992; Purtilo, 1980). Furthermore, a striking feature of some posttransplant patients who receive aggressive therapy is the short interval from the time of transplant to the diagnosis of malignancy, often within 6 months (Swinnen et al., 1990). Such rapidly evolving tumors have a predilection for the brain and are associated with sustained immunosuppression and active EBV infection (Palackdharry, 1994).

Molecular studies suggest that three host factors interact to increase the risk of developing non-Hodgkin's lymphoma in immunosuppressed individuals: active EBV infection, defects in immunoregulation and production of inflammatory cytokines, and genetic defects precipitating abnormal immunoglobulin and T-cell receptor gene rearrangement. Both congenital and acquired immunodeficiencies appear to have common features that predispose to chronic antigenic stimulus of B lymphocytes and the development of non-Hodgkin's lymphoma (Filipovich et al., 1992).

Autoimmune Disease and Non-Hodgkin's Lymphoma

The risk of developing non-Hodgkin's lymphoma is also increased in patients with autoimmune conditions such as rheumatoid arthritis, systemic lupus erythematosus, Sjogren's syndrome, and celiac disease (Harris, Cooke, Thompson, & Waterhouse, 1967; Kamel, van de Rijn, Hanasono, & Warnke, 1995; Pettersson, Pukkala, Teppo, & Friman, 1992). Although such conditions are conventionally treated with immunosuppressive drugs, persistent inflammation appears to have a dominant etiologic role in the genesis of lymphoma. For example, Baecklund and colleagues demonstrated a 25-fold increase in the risk of developing non-Hodgkin's lymphoma among patients with highly inflammatory rheumatoid arthritis compared to a similar group with low inflammation, after adjustment for treatment (Baecklund, Ekbom, Sparén, Feltelius, & Klareskog, 1998).

Epstein–Barr Virus (EBV) and Burkitt's Lymphoma

Epstein–Barr virus (EBV) is a member of the herpes family of viruses. The virus is ubiquitous in the human population. Following infection in childhood, EBV persists in a dormant state as an episomal plasmid in B lymphocytes in 80–90% of adults. When the first exposure to EBV occurs in adolescence, up to 50% of individuals manifest *infectious mononucleosis*. If an EBV-positive individual experiences sustained immunosuppression (as in HIV disease or posttransplant immunosuppressive therapy), the EBV plasmid can transform into active virus and resume proliferation in B lymphocytes. Such activity markedly heightens the risk of developing non-Hodgkin's lymphoma (Alexander et al., 2007a; Fisher & Fisher, 2004; Müller et al., 2005).

In populations residing in the tropical zone of Africa, a form of childhood B-cell lymphoma called *Burkitt's lymphoma* is endemic. This tumor typically arises in the jaw bones. Burkitt's lymphoma is named after the British investigator Denis Burkitt, who studied its epidemiology and etiology in the children of New Guinea and sub-Saharan Africa. Burkitt's lymphoma develops in children in these geographic regions with a startlingly high incidence rate, accounting for up to 25% of all childhood malignancies (Burkitt, 1958, 1983).

In pathologic studies of Burkitt's lymphoma ascertained from the endemic areas of Africa and New Guinea, EBV is detected in nearly 100% of cases. Epstein and colleagues first detected EBV in a lymphoma specimen taken from a child in New Guinea, providing the first example of a tumor-related virus (Epstein, Achong, & Pope, 1967). Most cases also have a medical history of malaria and have been found to have elevated levels of antibodies against both EBV and the malarial parasite *Plasmodium falciparum* (Carpenter et al., 2008). Burkitt initially noted the geographic clustering of EBV and malarial infection and suggested that the convergence of these two infectious agents in the same host predisposes to the development of B-cell lymphoma (Burkitt, 1971, 1983).

A defining cytogenetic feature of nearly all cases of Burkitt's lymphoma is the presence of a chromosomal translocation involving the *c-myc* gene. The *c-myc* gene, which is normally located on the long arm of chromosome 8, encodes a protein that is essential for the regulation of transcription and expression of many other genes. Translocations of the *c-myc* gene to positions in close proximity to the heavy chain immunoglobulin loci on chromosome 14 have been found in approximately 80% of cases of

Burkitt's lymphoma, and translocations of *c-myc* to immunoglobulin loci on chromosomes 2 and 12 are present in the remaining 20% of cases. These *c-myc* translocations result in hyperactivity of immunoglobulin genes and overproliferation of B cells, leading to the development of lymphoma. Transformation to malignancy involves the perpetual proliferation of B lymphocytes involving dysregulation of mitosis, differentiation, apoptosis, and cell adhesion (Blum, Lozanski, & Byrd, 2004; Ferry, 2006).

It is obvious from the preceding discussion that the pathogenesis of Burkitt's lymphoma is complex, often involving the interaction of at least three factors: EBV infection, malarial infection, and chromosomal translocation involving the *c-myc* gene. A stepwise process has been proposed in which EBV and malaria may depress the regulatory function of T cells, leading to unbridled proliferation of B cells with the *c-myc* translocation (de Thé, 1993).

The clinical variants of Burkitt's lymphoma include endemic, sporadic, and immunodeficiency-related disease. Endemic Burkitt's lymphoma occurs in young African children, ages 4–7 years, with a male-to-female ratio of 2:1. The incidence is about 13 per 100,000 in children of endemic areas such as New Guinea and sub-Saharan Africa, more than 50 times higher than in U.S. children. The tumors characteristically involve the jaw bone but can also arise in the gastrointestinal and/or urogenital tract (Ferry, 2006). EBV is present in nearly all cases, and high levels of antibodies against both EBV and *Plasmodium falciparum* have been found to increase the risk by fivefold (Carpenter et al., 2008). As initially suggested by Denis Burkitt, the immunosuppressive effect of chronic malarial infection predisposes the host to EBV-induced proliferation and malignant transformation of B lymphocytes (Burkitt, 1983).

Sporadic Burkitt's lymphoma occasionally develops in children *without* geographic or temporal clustering. The gastrointestinal tract, particularly around the ileocecal valve, is the most common anatomic site of involvement. EBV is present in only 10–30% of sporadic tumors (Ferry, 2006).

Immunodeficiency-associated Burkitt's lymphoma occurs in association with HIV/AIDS, organ transplant, and congenital immunodeficiency. Burkitt's lymphoma accounts for 30–40% of non-Hodgkin's lymphoma in patients with HIV disease and is estimated to be 1,000 times more common in such patients than in the general population. Analogous to malaria, HIV infection and other immunosuppressive conditions lead to EBV-induced proliferation and malignant transformation of B lymphocytes (Ferry, 2006).

Human T-Cell Lymphotropic Virus (HTLV-1) and Lymphoma

In 1974, Japanese investigators discovered a rare form of T-cell leukemia in two Japanese adults (Yodoi, Takatsuki, & Masuda, 1974). Further investigation soon identified a cluster of 16 patients with lymphoma or leukemia arising from T lymphocytes in the population living on the islands off the southern coast of Japan (Takatsuki, Uchiyama, Sagawa, & Yodoi, 1977; Uchiyama, Yodoi, Sagawa, Takatsuki, & Uchino, 1977). Shortly thereafter, in the laboratories of Dr. Robert Gallo at the U.S. National Institutes of Health, an RNA retrovirus was identified in malignant T cells of tumor specimens and named *human T-cell lymphotropic virus (HTLV-1)* (Poiesz et al., 1980). In studies conducted by Japanese investigators, T-cell-specific antibodies were detected in 76 of 80 patients (95%) with T-cell leukemia/lymphoma and 26% of healthy adults from endemic areas (Hinuma et al., 1981; Yoshida, Miyoshi, & Hinuma, 1982).

Subsequent epidemiologic investigations have confirmed the presence of high seroprevalence rates of HTLV-1 in populations of Southern Japan (30%), the Caribbean (7%), New Guinea (5%), and Central Africa (3%). In endemic regions, adult T-cell lymphomas and leukemias account for more than 50% of all lymphoid malignancies (Manns & Blattner, 2003).

Seropositivity for HTLV-1 develops early in life as a consequence of vertical transmission from mother to child during delivery or breastfeeding. The virus can also be transmitted sexually and through transfusion of contaminated blood. With sustained infection beginning in childhood, the cumulative lifetime risk of developing T-cell lymphoma/leukemia approaches 5% (Cleghorn et al., 1995). Carriers of HTLV-1 apparently manifest progressive immunosuppression and uncontrolled proliferation of infected helper T cells that can eventually lead to the development of adult T-cell lymphoma or leukemia (Takatsuki, 2005).

Helicobacter pylorus and Non-Hodgkin's Lymphoma

Helicobacter pylorus (*H. pylorus*) is a flagellated bacterium that infects the gastric mucosa. This unusual bacterium was discovered by Australian investigators Barry Marshall and Robin Warren in 1982, in recognition of which they were awarded the 2005 Nobel Prize in Physiology or Medicine (Marshall & Warren, 2005). It is estimated that more than 50%

of the world's population harbor *H. pylori* in their upper gastrointestinal tract (Pounder & Ng, 1995).

Since its discovery, numerous investigations have examined linkages between *H. pylori* and human disease. Chronic colonization of the gastric mucosa by *H. pylori* is associated with chronic gastritis and the development of peptic ulcer disease, gastric adenocarcinoma, and gastric lymphoma arising in mucous-associated lymphoid tissue (gastric MALT lymphoma) (Isaacson & Spencer, 1995; Kusters, van Vliet, & Kuipers, 2006).

The evidence linking chronic *H. pylori* infection to the genesis of gastric lymphoma is compelling. In a study conducted in London, Wotherspoon and colleagues detected *H. pylori* in 101 of 110 cases with primary gastric MALT lymphoma, and suggested that infection-induced gastritis provides the background lymphoid tissue in which non-Hodgkin's lymphoma develops (Wotherspoon, Ortiz-Hidalgo, Falzon, & Isaacson, 1991).

At Stanford University in California, Parsonnet and colleagues conducted a nested case control study to evaluate the potential role of *H. pylorus* in the development of non-Hodgkin's gastric lymphoma. (In a nested study design, the cases accrue over time in a specific cohort after collection of baseline data, and matched controls are ascertained from the same cohort.) The investigators compared baseline *H. pylori* seropositivity in 33 patients who developed gastric non-Hodgkin's lymphoma to controls matched 4:1 to the cases on age, gender, and time of serum collection. Results revealed more than a sixfold increase in the risk of developing gastric lymphoma related to baseline *H. pylori* seropositivity. The median interval between serum collection for *H. pylori* testing and onset of gastric lymphoma was 14 years, suggesting a long-term process of carcinogenesis (Parsonnet et al., 1994).

Subsequent in vitro experiments have demonstrated that malignant B cells proliferate only after T-cell-specific activation by *H. pylori* (Hussell, Isaacson, Crabtree, & Spencer, 1993). In clinical studies, antibiotic therapy directed against *H. pylori* infection produced regression of low-grade gastric lymphoma (Wotherspoon et al., 1993). These findings support a model of chronic *H. pylori* infection, chronic inflammation, and T-cell-modulated antigenic stimulation of B-cell proliferation in the pathogenesis of gastric MALT lymphoma (Wotherspoon, 1998).

Human Herpes Virus 8

Human herpes virus 8(HHV-8), also called *Kaposi's sarcoma–associated herpes virus (KSHV)*, was discovered by Yuan Chang, Patrick Moore, and colleagues at Columbia University in 1994 (Chang et al., 1994). This virus has been detected in the majority of patients with primary effusion lymphoma, a rare B-cell lymphoma seen almost exclusively in HIV-positive patients (Cesarman, Chang, Moore, Said, & Knowles, 1995). Such patients often present with dual EBV and HHV-8 infection; therefore, delineation of the etiologic role of each virus is difficult. Primary effusion lymphomas appear to involve monoclonal expansion of viral-infected cells (Judde et al., 2000).

Hepatitis C Virus and Non-Hodgkin's Lymphoma

Approximately 300 million people worldwide are infected with *hepatitis C virus (HCV)*, a single-strand RNA virus. The seroprevalence of HCV is high in certain populations of Asia and Africa (3%) and low in most developed countries (1%). Although not known to be oncogenic, HCV has immunomodulatory effects and has been shown to replicate in peripheral blood mononuclear cells.

Although HCV is a major etiologic factor in the development of hepatocellular carcinoma, its role in the development of non-Hodgkin's lymphoma is less clear. Early molecular studies detected anti-HCV antibodies in sera and HCV RNA sequences in biopsy specimens from some patients with B-cell non-Hodgkin's lymphoma (Luppi et al., 1998; Silvestri et al., 1996). A systematic review of HCV seroprevalence among non-Hodgkin's lymphoma patients revealed high rates in some populations (Southern and Eastern Europe, Japan, and Southern United States) but not in others (Northern Europe, Northern United States, Canada, and certain Asian countries) (Negri, Little, Boiocchi, La Vecchia, & Franceschi, 2004). Nevertheless, in a pooled analysis of 48 studies of B-cell non-Hodgkin's lymphoma, HCV infection was present in 13% of 5,542 patients; based on meta-analysis of 10 studies that included estimates of the odds ratio (OR), the overall risk was increased more than 10-fold (combined OR = 10.8) (Gisbert, García-Buey, Pajares, & Moreno-Otero, 2003). In a subsequent meta-analysis of 23 studies of HCV and non-Hodgkin's lymphoma, HCV-seropositive subjects were nearly 6 times more likely to develop non-Hodgkin's lymphoma than were seronegative subjects (combined OR = 5.7) (Matsuo et al., 2004).

Despite the increase in lymphoma risk with HCV exposure suggested by meta-analyses, it is noteworthy that some studies *do not* reflect an association between HCV and non-Hodgkin's lymphoma. For example, in a prospective study of 48,420 persons in northern California, serological evidence of HCV infection was *totally absent* in all 57 patients who

developed non-Hodgkin's lymphoma (Rabkin et al., 2002). And in Thailand, a nation with a relatively high prevalence of HCV, no link was found between HCV infection and non-Hodgkin's lymphoma (Udomsakdi-Auewarakul, Auewarakul, Sukpanichnant, & Muangsup, 2000). Furthermore, in a U.S. study of 304,411 adults with AIDS, standardized incidence ratios of non-Hodgkin's lymphoma by grade were *inversely* related to the prevalence rates of HCV infection (Engels et al., 2002). These disparities among study results may have multiple causes, including genetic, cultural, and/or environmental differences in populations; variation in HCV strains; and the different methods used for the diagnosis of lymphoma and/or assessment of HCV seropositivity (Alexander et al., 2007a).

Simian Virus 40 (SV40) and Non-Hodgkin's Lymphoma

Millions of people worldwide were inadvertently exposed to live *simian virus 40 (SV40)* between 1955 and 1963 through immunization with SV40-contaminated polio vaccines. This virus is known to induce malignancies in laboratory animals, including primary brain cancer, bone cancer, mesothelioma, and lymphoma. Recent molecular studies have shown that SV40 DNA is present in a significant fraction (~40%) of tumor specimens from patients with non-Hodgkin's lymphoma (Shivapurkar et al., 2002; Vilchez et al., 2002).

Butel and colleagues studied SV40 seropositivity in malignant lymphoid tissues from 156 patients with non-Hodgkin's lymphoma (76 HIV-positive patients and 78 HIV-negative patients), in nonmalignant lymphoid samples from 107 patients without tumors, and in colorectal tumors from 54 patients. Polymerase chain reaction and Southern blot hybridization techniques were used to detect the DNA sequences of SV40. Specific SV40 DNA sequences were detected in 64 specimens (42%) from lymphoma patients compared to *none* of the nonmalignant lymphoid specimens or colorectal tumors (Butel, Vilchez, Jorgensen, & Kozinetz, 2003). Furthermore, a retrospective study in Japan demonstrated a fourfold increase in the odds of detecting SV40 sequences in large B-cell lymphomas (19%) compared to controls (4.7%), suggesting that SV40 may be a candidate etiologic factor for lymphoma (Nakatsuka et al., 2003).

The findings of SV40 DNA sequences in human lymphoma prompted population-based studies in Denmark and the United States that compared cancer incidence rates in cohorts of children with and without exposure to the (allegedly) contaminated Salk polio vaccine. Fortunately, these studies found *no* increase in cancer rates associated with exposure (Carroll-Pankhurst et al., 2001; Engels et al., 2003).

Not all studies have found an association between SV40 and lymphoma. For example, a Spanish study that used enzyme immunoassay to detect antibodies to SV40 in sera from 520 patients with non-Hodgkin's lymphoma and 587 matched controls actually found a higher frequency of SV40 seropositivity among the controls than cases (9.5% versus 5.9%) (de Sanjose et al., 2003). In addition, a molecular study that assessed SV40 antibody reactivity found no significant difference in the frequency of seropositivity between serum samples from 724 cases of non-Hodgkin's lymphoma and 622 matched controls (Engels et al., 2004). Given these contrasting results, it seems advisable to clarify the differences in studies of SV40 DNA sequences and seropositivity through additional investigations.

Other Pathogens and Non-Hodgkin's Lymphoma

Borrelia burgdorferi is a small spirochete that can be transmitted to humans by the bite of an infected tick. Systemic human infection with this microorganism (borreliosis) causes skin rash, arthritis, and neurologic deficits, a clinical picture commonly referred to as Lyme disease. Recently, infection with *Borrelia burgdorferi* has been linked to lymphoproliferative conditions, which have been known to evolve into primary cutaneous B-cell lymphomas. The majority of these observations have come from European countries, with little evidence of such an association in North America (Cerroni, Zochling, Putz, & Kerl, 1997; Garbe, Stein, Dienemann, & Orfanos, 1991; Jelic & Filipovic-Ljeskovic, 1999; Willemze et al., 1997).

Mantle cell lymphoma, a B-cell malignancy arising in the mantle zone of lymph nodes, has also been found in association with borreliosis. Schöllkopf and colleagues conducted a Danish–Swedish case control study of 3,055 patients with non-Hodgkin's lymphoma and 3,187 population controls to evaluate the association of lymphoma subtypes with *Borrelia burgdorferi*. History of tick bite or *Borrelia* infection was ascertained through personal interviews and enzyme-linked immunosorbent assay serum analyses for antibodies against *B. burgdorferi*. Self-reported history of *B. burgdorferi* infection (OR = 2.5) and seropositivity for anti-*Borrelia* antibodies (OR = 3.6) were both found to increase the risk of mantle cell lymphoma, suggesting that *Borrelia burgdorferi* infection predisposes to the development of this malignancy (Schöllkopf et al., 2008).

Other infectious agents have also been found in association with B-cell lymphomas. *Mediterranean lymphoma* is an unusual B-cell lymphoma that arises in small intestinal mucosa-associated lymphoid tissue (MALT). Early-stage disease regresses with antibiotic treatment, suggesting a bacterial etiology. In a recent small series, five of seven tumor specimens of Mediterranean lymphoma tested positive for the intestinal bacteria *Campylobacter jejuni* (Lecuit et al., 2004).

Ocular adnexal lymphoma, a rare form of lymphoma that arises in the conjunctival membranes of the eye socket, also shows an association with an infectious microbe. In a molecular study of ocular adnexal lymphoma samples, 32 of 40 tumors (80%) carried *Chlamydia psittaci* DNA, whereas all specimens were negative for *Chlamydia trachomatis* and *Chlamydia pneumoniae*. This observation suggests that *Chlamydia psittaci* infection predisposes to the development of ocular adnexal lymphoma (Ferreri et al., 2004).

Clearly, the number of pathogens involved in the genesis of immunoproliferative lymphoid neoplasms is growing. As a rule, these infectious agents appear to enhance the initiation and promotion of malignancy by antigenic stimulation of B cells coupled with immunosuppression of T cells.

Pesticide and Insecticide Exposures in Non-Hodgkin's Lymphoma

Several cohort and case control studies have evaluated exposure to pesticides, insecticides, and/or herbicides as risk factors in the development of non-Hodgkin's lymphoma. In general, nonsignificant findings have been reported.

For example, Blair and colleagues studied a U.S. cohort of 52,393 licensed pesticide applicators and 32,345 spouses and found *no* significant associations between lymphoma mortality with the number of years handling pesticides or any other measure of exposure. The overall mortality due to non-Hodgkin's lymphoma in the cohort showed no difference from the general population (standardized mortality ratio = 1.0) (Blair et al., 2005). A number of other cohort studies also evaluated the risk of developing non-Hodgkin's lymphoma among persons employed in occupations involving potential exposure to pesticides, herbicides, and/or insecticides. Studies of occupational cohorts of farmers, pesticide-manufacturing workers, and pesticide applicators from Italy, Iceland, Sweden, Norway, Canada, and Australia have yielded mixed and generally nonsignificant results (Alexander et al., 2007a).

Meta-analyses of published studies of agricultural workers reflect the inconsistency in results. In an analysis of 14 studies that evaluated cancer risk among farmers, the combined estimate of non-Hodgkin's lymphoma risk was not significant (Blair, Zahm, Pearce, Heineman, & Fraumeni, 1992). Subsequently, a meta-analysis of 36 studies found a weak positive association overall (RR = 1.10); however, there was significant heterogeneity among studies, and the directional change in risk differed for case control studies (RR = 1.19) and cohort studies (RR = 0.95) (Khuder, Schaub, & Keller-Byrne, 1998).

Thus, although a few studies suggest there may be an increased risk of non-Hodgkin's lymphoma in occupations with heightened exposure to pesticides and related compounds, technical difficulties inherent in assessment of the intensity and duration of exposure limit any interpretation of causality. Studies that infer exposure based on occupation or job title have many limitations, most notably the lack of detailed information regarding exposure to specific environmental factors for each individual. Furthermore, complete information on other potential exposures or confounding factors is often missing or not collected. Results of these studies therefore reflect a general lack of consistent evidence to support an etiologic link between pesticide/herbicide/insecticide exposure and the development of non-Hodgkin's lymphoma (Alexander et al., 2007a; Fisher & Fisher, 2004; Müller et al., 2005).

Other Chemical Exposures and Non-Hodgkin's Lymphoma

Studies of chemical workers have also failed to delineate consistent associations with non-Hodgkin's lymphoma. Studies of workers potentially exposed to petroleum products, solvents, trichloroethylene, asbestos, occupational dusts, and other chemicals have generally been negative or inconclusive. Thus, as with pesticides and herbicides, epidemiologic investigations have not clearly identified specific occupational exposures to specific chemicals that increase the risk of developing non-Hodgkin's lymphoma (Alexander et al., 2007a; Figgs, Dosemeci, & Blair, 1995).

Hair Dye and Non-Hodgkin's Lymphoma

Hair dyes contain compounds that are mutagenic and carcinogenic in animals. Numerous human studies have therefore evaluated the relationship between exposure to these compounds and the risk of developing malignant neoplasms, including non-Hodgkin's lymphoma. Based on a meta-analysis of 14 studies, Takkouche and colleagues reported a significant increase in the risk among ever users of hair dye compared to never users (combined RR = 1.23). However, there was significant heterogeneity among studies, and the risk estimate derived from case control studies (RR = 1.27) was higher than that from cohort studies (RR = 1.10). Thus, differential recall between cases and controls may have contributed to the elevated risk estimates in the case control studies. Furthermore, dose-response relationships have not been consistently observed between lymphoma risk and the duration of use (Takkouche, Etminan, & Montes-Martinez, 2005).

Ultraviolet Radiation and Non-Hodgkin's Lymphoma

Zheng and colleagues speculated that sun exposure might increase the risk of developing non-Hodgkin's lymphoma on the following grounds: The incidence of non-Hodgkin's lymphoma has increased in parallel with that of cutaneous melanoma, antecedent skin cancer increases the risk of developing non-Hodgkin's lymphoma, sun exposure has immunosuppressive effects, and the risk of non-Hodgkin's lymphoma increases with immunosuppression (Zheng et al., 1992). In support of this hypothesis, Cartwright and colleagues reported a significant positive correlation between the incidence rates of non-Hodgkin's lymphoma and nonmelanocytic skin cancer among nine cancer registries worldwide (Cartwright, McNally, & Staines, 1994).

In opposition to this hypothesis, three case control studies of non-Hodgkin's lymphoma and sun exposure found significant *inverse* relationships (Armstrong & Kricker, 2007). Thus, the data on individual sun exposure and risk of non-Hodgkin's lymphoma are more consistent with a *protective* than a causal effect of sun exposure. Furthermore, in a geographic study of annual mortality rates reported during 1970–1989 for economic regions within the United States, the mortality rates due to non-Hodgkin's lymphoma showed a significant *inverse* association with average levels of UV exposure, whereas the rates for melanoma increased with exposure (Hartge, Devesa, Grauman, Fears, & Fraumeni, 1996).

Because these studies were not powered to examine lymphoma subtypes, it is noteworthy that some molecular investigations have found indirect evidence linking sun exposure to the development of *cutaneous* non-Hodgkin's lymphomas. For example, McGregor and colleagues examined the type and frequency of *p53* gene mutations in a series of 55 cases of primary cutaneous lymphoma and found 14 separate *p53* mutations with a mutation spectrum characteristic of DNA damage caused by ultraviolet B radiation. These mutations were most evident in the progression of a type of cutaneous T-cell lymphoma known as *mycosis fungoides* (McGregor et al., 1999). Well-designed epidemiologic studies that are powered to examine lymphoma by subtype should help resolve the present conflicting results on sun exposure and non-Hodgkin's lymphoma.

Tobacco, Alcohol, and Non-Hodgkin's Lymphoma

Tobacco and tobacco metabolites are known to be carcinogenic; however, there is little scientific evidence to support an association between tobacco use and the development of non-Hodgkin's lymphoma. Zahm and colleagues examined smoking and non-Hodgkin's lymphoma in a combined analysis of data from three population-based case control studies conducted in four Midwestern states in the United States. Data on smoking and other variables were available for 1,177 cases and 3,625 controls. Overall, there was no association between smoking and the risk of developing non-Hodgkin's lymphoma (OR = 1.0) and no clear dose-response relationships were evident (Zahm, Weisenburger, Holmes, Cantor, & Blair, 1997).

In a subsequent meta-analysis, Morton and colleagues examined the association between cigarette smoking and subtypes of non-Hodgkin's lymphoma using data collected through the International Lymphoma Epidemiology Consortium (InterLymph). The database included information on smoking and other variables for 6,594 cases and 8,892 controls ascertained in nine case control studies conducted in the United States, Europe, and Australia. Overall, smoking was associated with only a slight increase in the risk (OR = 1.07). Among subtypes of non-Hodgkin's lymphoma, only follicular lymphoma was associated with current smoking (OR = 1.31); however, the test for trend with pack-years of smoking was not significant. Risk estimates for other subtypes ranged from 0.79 to 1.11 and were nonsignificant (Morton et al., 2005a). These and many other epidemiologic investigations do not provide consistent evidence that tobacco exposure has a role in the genesis of non-Hodgkin's lymphoma.

A number of studies have detected a weak *inverse* association between alcohol consumption and the risk of developing non-Hodgkin's lymphoma. Morton and colleagues examined the relationship in a pooled analysis of nine case control studies conducted in the United States, Great Britain, Sweden, and Italy. Data on alcohol intake and other variables were available for 6,492 cases and 8,683 controls. Overall, the results suggested that people who drank alcohol had a slightly lower risk than nondrinkers (OR = 0.83), and current drinkers had a lower risk (OR = 0.73) than former drinkers (OR = 0.95). The investigators suggest the need for additional investigations to determine whether confounding by lifestyle factors or immunomodulatory effects by alcohol

are responsible for this association (Morton et al., 2005b).

Dietary Factors and Non-Hodgkin's Lymphoma

Nutritional studies of non-Hodgkin's lymphoma reflect mixed results for most dietary factors investigated. One possible exception is fish consumption, which shows a weak *inverse* association with the risk of developing non-Hodgkin's lymphoma in several studies. For example, in a U.S. study of 1,418 cases and 4,202 controls, intake in the highest quartile compared to the lowest quartile reduced the risk by 29% (Fritschi et al., 2004). Nevertheless, observed risk reductions do not reach statistical significance in all studies (Fernandez et al., 1999); additional investigations are needed to clarify if high fish consumption has preventive value.

Blood Transfusions and Non-Hodgkin's Lymphoma

Interest in blood transfusion and its relation to non-Hodgkin's lymphoma spiked after three prospective cohort studies reported increases in the risk of developing non-Hodgkin's lymphoma following transfusion. Cerhan and colleagues initially investigated this association in a prospective cohort of 37,337 older women in Iowa. Baseline information was collected in 1986, and after 5 years of follow-up, a total of 68 cases of non-Hodgkin's lymphoma were detected. Women who reported ever receiving a blood transfusion were at increased risk of developing non-Hodgkin's lymphoma (RR = 2.2) (Cerhan et al., 1993). In a subsequent study of the same cohort of women after 12 years of follow-up resulting in detection of 229 cases of non-Hodgkin's lymphoma, a significant risk increase (RR = 1.6) was again observed among women reporting a history of blood transfusion (Cerhan et al., 2001).

Shortly after publication of the initial findings from the Iowa cohort, Blomberg and colleagues reported similar increases in the risk of developing non-Hodgkin's lymphoma associated with a history of blood transfusion in two Swedish cohorts (Blomberg, Möller, Olsson, Anderson, & Jonsson, 1993), and Memon and Doll found a greater than twofold increase in mortality due to non-Hodgkin's lymphoma among subjects who had received perinatal transfusions in a cohort of 13,000 Britons (Memon & Doll, 1994). Moreover, several biological mechanisms seemed plausible to explain transfusion-related lymphoma development, including oncogenic virus transmission, transfusion-induced immunosuppression, and engraftment of malignant lymphoma cells from donors (Chow & Holly, 2002).

Nevertheless, five subsequent case control studies have since revealed inconsistent results with only one showing a significant positive association. Thus, the association between blood transfusion and development of non-Hodgkin's lymphoma remains to be clarified. As has been pointed out, future studies should be designed to collect more detailed information on the exposure variable, including the type and amount of transfusion products received by each subject. Similarly, such studies should be powered to facilitate risk estimates for lymphoma subtypes (Chow & Holly, 2002).

Breast Implants and Non-Hodgkin's Lymphoma

Anaplastic large cell lymphoma is a rare T-cell lymphoma typically seen in children and young adults. Such tumors are seldom detected in breast tissues. Nevertheless, published case reports of primary anaplastic large cell lymphoma arising in the fibrous capsules of breast implants have produced speculation that breast prostheses may increase the risk of developing this rare tumor (Bishara, Ross, & Sur, 2009).

To determine if the risk of developing anaplastic large cell lymphoma is related to breast implants, investigators in Amsterdam conducted a matched case control study among women in the Netherlands. Cases and controls were ascertained from the population-based nationwide pathology registry. Eleven cases were identified who had been diagnosed with primary anaplastic large cell lymphoma of the breast during 1990–2006. Cases were age-matched to controls with other histologic types of breast lymphomas in an overall ratio of about 3:1. Among the 11 cases, 5 had received breast prostheses for cosmetic purposes 1–23 years prior to diagnosis, whereas among the 35 control patients, only one had received a breast implant. The odds ratio linking the development of anaplastic large cell lymphoma to breast prostheses was markedly increased and statistically significant (OR = 18.2, P < 0.01). Although these preliminary findings suggest an association between breast implants and the subsequent development of anaplastic large cell lymphoma of the breast, even women with implants have an exceedingly low *absolute risk* (de Jong et al., 2008).

EPIDEMIOLOGY OF HODGKIN'S LYMPHOMA

Hodgkin's lymphoma is a B-cell lymphoma that is defined by the presence of morphologically altered immune cells called Reed–Steinberg cells. In nations with population-based tumor registries, Hodgkin's lymphoma accounts for less than 15% of all lymphomas (Altekruse et al., 2010).

The disease is named after Thomas Hodgkin, who first described elemental clinical features of lymphoid malignancies in 1832 (Hodgkin, 1832). The Reed–Sternberg cell is named after Dorothy Reed and Carl Sternberg, who discovered it in the malignant lymphoid tissues of patients with Hodgkin's lymphoma more than a century ago (Reed, 1902; Sternberg, 1898). These giant multinucleate tumor cells sometimes have the unusual appearance of "owl eyes" peering out from the microscopic field due to the presence of a double nucleus (Lukes & Collins, 1975).

Because of the coexpression of markers of several different cell types in Hodgkin's lymphoma tissues, the cellular origin of Reed–Sternberg cells remained enigmatic for many decades. Nevertheless, isolation of these cells by microscopic laser dissection and gene amplification by polymerase chain reaction have clarified their derivation through the presence of immunoglobulin gene rearrangements. Thus, nearly a century after their discovery, Reed–Sternberg cells have been definitively characterized as transformed lymphocytes arising from B cells in the germinal centers of lymph nodes (Bräuninger et al., 1997; Kanzler, Küppers, Hansmann, & Rajewsky, 1996; Küppers et al., 1994).

Global Burden of Hodgkin's Disease

Worldwide, 65,950 new cases of Hodgkin's lymphoma were diagnosed in 2012 and 25,469 died from the disease (Ferlay et al., 2013). Of these, 38,520 cases (58%) and 15,464 deaths (61%) occurred in men.

Worldwide estimates of the annual numbers of new cases and deaths from Hodgkin's lymphoma have remained relatively stable during 1990–2012. Each year, approximately 60,000 to 66,000 new cases are diagnosed and 25,000 to 30,000 individuals die from the disease (Ferlay et al., 2010, 2013; Parkin et al., 1999a, 1999b, 2001, 2005).

Incidence rates of Hodgkin's lymphoma tend to be higher in developed countries than developing countries. In 2012, rates exceeded 2 per 100,000 for the United States and Canada, Australia/New Zealand, and most nations of Western Europe and Scandinavia compared to rates less than 1 per 100,000 for China, India, and most nations of Southeast Asia and sub-Saharan Africa (Ferlay et al., 2013).

Mortality rates of Hodgkin's lymphoma show a different pattern than the incidence rates. In 2012, rates exceeded 0.5 per 100,000 in North and Central Africa, the Middle East, Northern Asia, and the Russian Federation compared to rates less than 0.5 in

North America, Europe, China, and Australia/New Zealand. Disparities in incidence and mortality likely reflect underdiagnosis and lack of access to therapy in underserved populations.

Ethnic Differences and Trends in Hodgkin's Lymphoma in the United States

Based on data from the SEER program of the U.S. National Cancer Institute, 8,490 new cases of Hodgkin's lymphoma were diagnosed in 2010 and 1,320 individuals died from the disease. The highest annual incidence rates were observed among Caucasians (3.2 per 100,000 in men and 2.5 per 100,000 in women) and the lowest were among Asian/Pacific Islanders (1.5 per 100,000 in men and 1.1 per 100,000 in women). During the time period 1998–2007, incidence rates increased among U.S. men and women by about 2% per year. Nevertheless, during the same period, mortality rates declined and 5-year survival rates now exceed 90% for patients who are diagnosed without distant metastasis (Altekruse et al., 2010).

Pathology of Hodgkin's Lymphoma

Classical Hodgkin's lymphoma always arises in lymph nodes and is classified into four subtypes. The most common of these is the *nodular sclerosing* type in which the affected lymph nodes are largely replaced by fibrotic tumor nodules. The second most common is the *mixed cellularity* subtype in which affected lymph nodes are infiltrated by inflammatory cells without fibrosis. *Lymphocyte-rich* and *lymphocyte-depleted* subtypes are rare forms (Lukes & Collins, 1975).

Recent molecular studies show that the malignant cells of Hodgkin's lymphoma often carry incapacitating mutations of the immunoglobulin genes (Bräuninger et al., 1997; Kanzler et al., 1996; Küppers et al., 1994). Furthermore, approximately 40% of Hodgkin's lymphomas are positive for EBV, and EBV-positive tumors typically carry mutations that induce aberrant signal transduction and render immunoglobulin genes ineffectual. These molecular findings suggest that viral proteins may induce mutational events in tumor suppressor genes and/or interfere with apoptosis and other processes that restrict cancer development (Bräuninger et al., 2006; Melbye, Hjalgrim, & Adami, 2008).

Genetic studies have found markedly higher concordance rates of Hodgkin's lymphoma among monozygous (identical) twins than dizygous twins, and risk increases have been observed in association with several antigens of the human leukocyte antigen (HLA) locus. Although these studies suggest that genetic variability at the HLA locus may influence the development of Hodgkin's lymphoma, it is noteworthy that familial Hodgkin's disease accounts for less than 5% of cases (Cartwright & Watkins, 2004).

Unlike non-Hodgkin's lymphoma, which shows an exponential increase in age-specific incidence, Hodgkin's lymphoma has a bimodal age of onset distribution with an early peak (15–34 years of age) and a late peak (over 55 years of age). For example, in the United States during 2003–2007, 44% of cases were diagnosed before age 35 years and 28% were diagnosed at 55 years or older. Similarly, the distribution of deaths by age also shows an early peak at 20–34 years and a late peak at 75–84 years (**Figure 26.5**) (Altekruse et al., 2010).

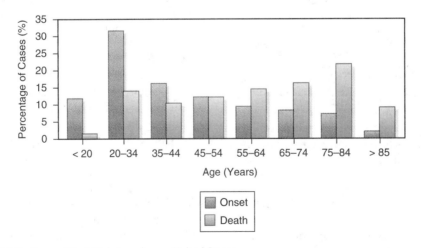

Figure 26.5 Age Distributions of Hodgkin's Lymphoma, United States.

Source: Data from Altekruse, S. F., Kosary, C. L., Krapcho, M., Neyman, N., Aminou, R., Waldron, W., ... Edwards, B. K. (2010). *SEER cancer statistics review, 1975–2007.* Bethesda, MD: National Cancer Institute.

RISK FACTORS FOR HODGKIN'S LYMPHOMA

Despite differences in their age distributions, the profile of factors that increase the risk of developing Hodgkin's lymphoma is similar to that of non-Hodgkin's lymphoma. Risk factors include male gender, family history, recent history of infectious mononucleosis or active infection with EBV, a weakened immune system due to HIV disease or use of immunosuppressive drugs, and the presence of somatic mutations and/or gene rearrangements that cause dysfunction of immunoglobulins. Nevertheless, as discussed in the following section, genetic factors have now been identified that specifically increase the risk of developing Hodgkin's lymphoma in young adults. Interestingly, one such factor is linked to the development of multiple sclerosis, an autoimmune inflammatory disease that leads to demyelination of the axons of nerves.

Genetic Predisposition to Hodgkin's Lymphoma

Comparison of the frequencies of concordance/discordance among monozygous and dizygous twins provides strong evidence that genetic factors influence the early development of Hodgkin's lymphoma. Mack and colleagues conducted a long-term follow-up study of 432 sets of twins in which one twin had developed Hodgkin's lymphoma prior to 50 years of age, in order to evaluate the concordance/discordance of Hodgkin's lymphoma in monozygous versus dizygous twins. After an average of 14 years of follow-up, both twins developed Hodgkin's lymphoma in 10 of 179 pairs of monozygous twins (5.5%) compared to none of 187 pairs of dizygous twins. The investigators estimated that Hodgkin's lymphoma in one monozygous twin increased the risk of disease in the second twin nearly 100-fold and concluded that genetic factors play a significant role in the development of this malignancy (Mack et al., 1995).

Hodgkin's Lymphoma and Multiple Sclerosis

Case reports of familial clusters of multiple sclerosis and Hodgkin's lymphoma in young adults prompted a large investigation of this familial association in Denmark. Using Danish population-based registries, Hjalgrim and colleagues identified 11,790 patients with multiple sclerosis and estimated the incidence of Hodgkin's lymphoma in 19,599 of their first-degree relatives. Reciprocally, they also identified 4,381 patients with Hodgkin's lymphoma and estimated the incidence of multiple sclerosis in 7,388 of their first-degree relatives. Results revealed a significant increase in the risk of developing Hodgkin's lymphoma among the relatives of patients with multiple sclerosis (RR = 1.40) and a significant risk increase for multiple sclerosis among relatives of patients with Hodgkin's lymphoma (RR = 1.93). Based on these results, the investigators suggested that "a common genetic and/or immunologic predisposition to the two diseases may be mediated through interaction with environmental risk factors such as EBV infection" (Hjalgrim et al., 2004).

Recently, a genome-wide association study was conducted by a team of investigators in London for the purpose of identifying genetic polymorphisms associated with Hodgkin's lymphoma. In the investigation, single nucleotide polymorphisms (SNPs) were compared among 2,024 cases with Hodgkin's lymphoma and 1,853 controls without disease. Findings revealed that susceptibility to Hodgkin's lymphoma was significantly elevated by a genetic variant of the eomesodermin (*EOMES*) gene on chromosome 3. This specific *EOMES* variant is known to disrupt cell-mediated immunity, and most notably, the same *EOMES* variant has also been found to heighten predisposition to multiple sclerosis. Thus, a specific genetic polymorphism of the *EOMES* gene appears to heighten susceptibility to both multiple sclerosis and Hodgkin's lymphoma in young adults (Frampton et al., 2013).

EPIDEMIOLOGY OF MULTIPLE MYELOMA

Multiple myeloma, also known as *plasma cell myeloma*, is a malignancy of plasma cells, which are B lymphocytes that produce antibodies. In this disease, collections of neoplastic plasma cells accumulate in bones and the bone marrow, causing bone lesions and interfering with the production of normal blood cells. Because *multiple* anatomic sites are usually involved in the same patient, the name *multiple myeloma* is appropriate. Characteristic signs and symptoms include hypercalcemia, renal failure, anemia, and bone lesions (Raab, Podar, Breitkreutz, Richardson, & Anderson, 2009).

Multiple myeloma develops from B lymphocytes that have migrated from the germinal centers of lymph nodes to other tissues. It is thus classified as a type of lymphoma. Cytogenetic features of multiple myeloma are similar to those of other B-cell lymphomas. Chromosomal translocations involving the immunoglobulin genes of chromosomes 2, 14, and 22 are often involved in the transformation of normal B cells to myeloma cells. For example, translocations and gene rearrangements involving the heavy chain immunoglobulin locus on chromosome 14 are found in approximately 50% of cases (Kyle & Rajkumar, 2004).

Global Burden of Multiple Myeloma

Both the incidence and mortality rates of multiple myeloma are increasing throughout the world. In 2012, 114,251 new cases were diagnosed and 80,015 died compared to 57,000 cases and 45,000 deaths in 1990 (Ferlay et al., 2010; Parkin et al., 1999a, 1999b). These increases are at least partly due to increasing longevity, because diagnosis is rare prior to age 40 years, and nearly 95% of cases are diagnosed in individuals 65 years and older.

Ethnic and Gender Differences in Multiple Myeloma

Striking ethnic differences are evident in U.S. rates of multiple myeloma. In particular, African American men and women have the highest reported annual rates of multiple myeloma in the world (14.3 cases per 100,000 in men and 10.0 cases per 100,000 in women), more than double the rates found among Caucasians (6.7 per 100,000 in men and 4.1 per 100,000 in women) (**Figure 26.6**).

In search of an explanation for the high multiple myeloma rates among African Americans, studies were designed to elucidate possible genetic susceptibility. These early studies targeted the human leukocyte antigen (HLA) locus on chromosome 6; in 1983, Leech and colleagues identified an HLA gene (*HLA-Cw2*) associated with excess risk among African American cases (Leech, Brown, & Scharifeld,

1985; Leech et al., 1983). Subsequently, a larger study was conducted to further evaluate associations between myeloma risk and genotypes of the HLA locus. The study examined frequencies of *HLA-Cw2* and several other HLA antigens in 46 African American cases and 88 controls, and 85 Caucasian cases and 122 controls. Findings revealed that the presence of *HLA-Cw2* significantly increased the risk in both African Americans (RR = 5.7) and Caucasians (RR = 2.6), suggesting that *HLA-Cw2* may contribute to the increased incidence among African Americans (Pottern et al., 1992).

As with other types of lymphoma, significant increases in the risk of developing multiple myeloma have been observed among patients with AIDS and certain other infectious conditions. Risk increases have been noted in cohorts of AIDS patients in the United States, Puerto Rico, and Australia (Goedert et al., 1998; Grulich, Wan, Law, Coates, & Kaldor, 1999). In a national Swedish cohort, the risk of multiple myeloma was significantly increased among individuals with hepatitis C infection (Duberg et al., 2005). In other studies, risk increases have been reported among relatives of myeloma patients, and a modest relationship has been observed between obesity and myeloma development (Alexander et al., 2007b).

Monoclonal gammopathy of undetermined significance (MGUS) refers to the presence of a high concentration of a specific monoclonal immunoglobulin protein in the blood. Such monoclonal proteins are sometimes called *paraproteins*. Patients with MGUS have been found to have a markedly increased risk of developing multiple myeloma.

In a series of 241 patients diagnosed with MGUS at the Mayo Clinic, 94 patients (39%) developed myeloma during 25 years of follow-up (Kyle et al., 2004). In a larger series of 1,384 patients with MGUS, 115 patients progressed to multiple myeloma in 11,009 person-years of follow-up, and the relative risk of developing multiple myeloma was increased by 25-fold compared to the general population. These patients developed multiple myeloma or a related disorder at a rate of 1% per year, and the initial concentration of serum monoclonal protein was found to be a significant predictor of progression (Kyle et al., 2002). The prevalence rates of MGUS in population surveys have a pattern similar to the incidence rates of multiple myeloma in the U.S. population: African Americans have twofold higher rates than Caucasians (8.4% versus 3.6%), and men have higher rates than women (4.0% versus 2.7%) (Cohen, Crawford, Rao, Pieper, & Currie, 1998; Kyle et al., 2006).

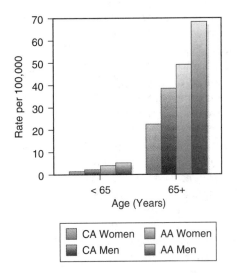

Figure 26.6 Annual Incidence of Multiple Myeloma by Age, Gender, and Race, United States.

CA = Caucasian American, AA = African American

Source: Data from Altekruse, S. F., Kosary, C. L., Krapcho, M., Neyman, N., Aminou, R., Waldron, W., . . . Edwards, B. K. (2010). *SEER cancer statistics review, 1975–2007.* Bethesda, MD: National Cancer Institute.

In a landmark study of MGUS, Landgren and colleagues followed 77,469 adults enrolled in the nationwide population-based Prostate, Lung, Colorectal, and Ovarian (PLCO) Cancer Screening Trial. During the study, 71 subjects developed multiple myeloma; serum samples had been collected from them 2–10 years prior to diagnosis. Notably, MGUS was present in 100% of patients at least 2 years prior to the diagnosis of multiple myeloma, and the concentration of monoclonal protein was found to be a significant predictor of progression. Based on these results, the investigators concluded that, "monoclonal gammopathy of undetermined significance (MGUS) is a premalignant plasma-cell proliferative disorder associated with a life-long risk of progression to multiple myeloma" (Landgren et al., 2009).

WALDENSTRÖM'S MACROGLOBULINEMIA

Waldenström's macroglobulinemia is a rare condition characterized by a monoclonal gammopathy of immunoglobulin M (IgM) plus infiltration of the bone marrow by plasma cells derived from a single clone of B lymphocytes (Kumar, Abbas, & Aster, 2014). This condition was named after the Swedish physician Jan Gosta Waldenström, who first described two patients with the condition in 1944 (Waldenström, 1944). Though similar in some respects to myeloma, Waldenström's macroglobulinemia rarely causes bone lesions and is now classified as a form of low-grade non-Hodgkin's lymphoma.

A team of investigators at the U.S. National Cancer Institute investigated associations between Waldenström's macroglobulinemia and chronic immunostimulatory conditions in a cohort of 4 million male veterans who received health care in Veteran's Administration (VA) hospitals during 1969–1996. Data on each subject were ascertained from computerized medical records maintained in the VA medical system. During an average follow-up of 12 years, a total of 361 cases of Waldenström's macroglobulinemia were identified, yielding an age-standardized incidence of 0.34 cases per 100,000 person-years. Disease risk was significantly elevated in individuals with autoimmune conditions (RR = 2.2), hepatitis (RR = 3.4), HIV disease (RR = 12.1), or rickettsiosis (RR = 3.4), a zoonotic infection transmitted by ticks and fleas. These results suggest that chronic immune stimulation plays an important role in the etiology and pathogenesis of Waldenström's macroglobulinemia (Koshiol, Gridley, Engels, McMaster, & Landgren, 2008).

In addition to chronic immune stimulation, the majority of patients with Waldenström's macroglobulinemia have been found to carry chromosomal defects. Deletion of the long arm of chromosome 6 (6q deletion) is the most commonly observed cytogenetic abnormality. In a U.S. study, bone marrow samples from 38 patients were examined by fluorescence in situ hybridization (FISH), and 6q deletions were detected in 21 of the 38 specimens (55%) (Schop et al., 2006). Subsequently, in a larger international study of 102 patients, 6q deletions were detected in 54% of bone marrow specimens and were found to be associated with a worsened prognosis (Ocio et al., 2007).

In summary, the general epidemiologic features of Waldenström's macroglobulinemia are similar to those of other forms of lymphoma. The trisomic combination of immunosuppression, chronic antigenic stimulation, and specific chromosomal aberrations stimulate the terminal differentiation of plasma cells that subsequently invade and proliferate uncontrollably in the bone marrow.

MODELS OF PATHOGENESIS OF LYMPHOMA

Biological mechanisms responsible for the genesis of lymphoma are variable and complex, and although some events and interactions have been elucidated, much remains to be discovered. In many patients, lymphomagenesis appears to involve chronic antigenic stimulation by one or more infectious agents in combination with chromosomal translocations, somatic mutations, gene rearrangements, and/or epigenetic changes that cause dysregulation and/or hyperactivity of immunoglobulin genes. Although the exact sequence of molecular events is unknown, the end result is the perpetual proliferation of lymphocytes characteristic of lymphoid malignancy. Imbalance in the function of T and B lymphocytes appears to be an important stimulus. For example, drug-induced immunosuppression of T cells in conjunction with active EBV infection and B-cell response has been found to rapidly accelerate the genesis of lymphoma in posttransplant patients and those with HIV disease. The complex nature of lymphomagenesis is perhaps best illustrated by endemic Burkitt's lymphoma, a B-cell malignancy that involves a trisomy of risk factors (chronic EBV and malarial infection in combination with chromosomal translocation of the *c-myc* oncogene to a position in close proximity to one of the immunoglobulin loci) (de Thé, 1993; Ferry, 2006; Küppers, 2005).

PREVENTION OF AIDS-RELATED LYMPHOMA

Primary prevention of AIDS-related lymphomas depends largely upon avoiding HIV infection (Thun, DeLancey, Center, Jemal, & Ward, 2010). Preventive behaviors include sexual abstinence, monogamous sex with an uninfected partner, regular condom use, and abstinence from injection drug use. Similar precautions are recommended for individuals who are HIV positive to prevent infecting others and avoid other sexually transmitted and blood-borne diseases. Screening of high-risk individuals to identify HIV seropositivity is therefore imperative for control of AIDS and AIDS-related conditions, including lymphoma.

Tertiary Prevention of Lymphoma in AIDS Patients

Key measures of immunosuppression and disease progression in patients with AIDS include the CD4 and CD8 lymphocyte counts and the viral load. In particular, severe immunosuppression reflected by a very low CD4 count is a major risk factor for the development of AIDS-related lymphoma.

In recent years, a variety of antiretroviral drugs have been developed for the treatment of patients with AIDS. In randomized clinical trials conducted in several countries, antiretroviral drugs taken in combination have proved superior to single-drug regimens in reducing the HIV viral load and improving the CD4 lymphocyte count. Such multidrug therapy is called *highly active antiretroviral therapy (HAART)*. Furthermore, following the introduction of HAART, the incidence of AIDS-related lymphoma has dramatically declined.

An example of the chemopreventive value of HAART against lymphoma development comes from the Swiss HIV Cohort Study. In this investigation, 12,959 people with HIV disease were followed during 1984–2006 to assess the long-term impact of HAART compared to single-drug regimens. For the entire cohort, 429 cases of non-Hodgkin's lymphoma were detected in 75,222 person-years of observation. Patients receiving HAART contributed 36,787 person-years in the study. The annual incidence of non-Hodgkin's lymphoma in the cohort peaked during pre-HAART years, 1993–1995 (13.6 per 1,000 person-years), and reached a nadir during post-HAART years, 2002–2006 (1.8 per 1,000 person-years). After adjustment for age, baseline CD4 count, and other variables, HAART was found to reduce the risk of developing non-Hodgkin's lymphoma by 76% (hazard ratio = 0.74). Furthermore, the reduction in risk has been sustained up to 10 years after initiation

of HAART, even among patients with a low baseline CD4 count. These findings support the efficacy of HAART regardless of immune impairment at initiation of treatment. The investigators concluded that "although it was already clear that HAART prevents [non-Hodgkin's lymphoma] through improvement of immune status, this study shows that HAART avoids the majority of [non-Hodgkin's lymphoma], even among the most severely immunosuppressed individuals" (Polesel et al., 2008).

SUMMARY

In many nations of the world, particularly those with population-based cancer registries, incidence rates of non-Hodgkin's lymphoma, Hodgkin's lymphoma, and multiple myeloma have risen steadily in the past 3 decades. These upward trends reflect increases in three immunological states: immunosuppression due to primary or acquired immunodeficiency, chronic antigenic stimulation, and disruption of normal lymphocyte function and proliferation. Other contributing factors include heightened rates of immune dysfunction in aging populations and improvements in the detection and reporting of these malignancies.

Rates of lymphoma are high in patients with acquired immunosuppression due to HIV infection, in posttransplant patients treated with immunosuppressive drugs, and in patients with autoimmune conditions or cancer who received immunosuppressive chemotherapy. Heightened antigenic stimulation often involves active infection by ubiquitous microbes such as EBV and *H. pylori* in a genetically susceptible host. Genetic errors in immunoglobulin genes due to somatic mutations and gene rearrangements are characteristic of many lymphomas, and such mutations have been found to induce aberrant signal transduction and render immunoglobulin genes ineffectual. Exposure to other exogenous factors such as agrichemicals, ultraviolet radiation, and allogeneic blood transfusions may also heighten the risk.

Prevention involves avoidance or elimination of factors known to cause immunodeficiency and/ or that inordinately heighten the antigenic response. Screening high-risk groups for the presence of HIV and *H. pylori* are advisable measures for lymphoma control. As pointed out in a review of non-Hodgkin's lymphoma, "Interdisciplinary collaborations are needed to investigate the broad scope of factors that may alter individual susceptibility and promote lymphoid malignancies" (Fisher & Fisher, 2004).

Therapy for Lymphoma

Results of clinical trials suggest that the addition of monoclonal antibodies to regimens of conventional chemotherapeutic agents has significantly improved the survival rates for patients with non-Hodgkin's lymphoma. A variety of monoclonal antibodies are under study, many of which target cell membrane receptors of lymphocytes. One example is rituximab, which specifically targets the CD20 receptors of B lymphocytes. Addition of rituximab to conventional therapeutic regimens significantly improves survival in patients with CD20-positive B-cell lymphoma (Plosker & Figgitt, 2003).

● ● ● REFERENCES

Alexander, D. D., Mink, P. J., Adami, H. O., Chang, E. T., Cole, P., Mandel, J. S., & Trichopoulos, D. (2007a). The non-Hodgkin lymphomas: A review of the epidemiologic literature. *International Journal of Cancer, 120*(S12), 1–39.

Alexander, D. D., Mink, P. J., Adami, H. O., Cole, P., Mandel, J. S., Oken, M. M., & Trichopoulos, D. (2007b). Multiple myeloma: A review of the epidemiologic literature. *International Journal of Cancer, 120*(S12), 40–61.

Altekruse, S. F., Kosary, C. L., Krapcho, M., Neyman, N., Aminou, R., Waldron, W., . . . Edwards, B. K. (2010). *SEER cancer statistics review, 1975–2007.* Bethesda, MD: National Cancer Institute.

Armstrong, B. K., & Kricker, N. (2007). Sun exposure and non-Hodgkin lymphoma. *Cancer Epidemiology, Biomarkers and Prevention, 16*(3), 396–400.

Baecklund, E., Ekbom, A., Sparén, P., Feltelius, N., & Klareskog, L. (1998). Disease activity and risk of lymphoma in patients with rheumatoid arthritis: Nested case-control study. *British Medical Journal, 317,* 180–181.

Banks, P. M. (1992). Changes in diagnosis of non-Hodgkin's lymphomas over time. *Cancer Research,52,* 5453s.

Barré-Sinoussi, F., Chermann, J. C., Rey, F., Nugeyre, M. T., Chamaret, S., Gruest, J., . . . Montagnier, L. (1983). Isolation of a T-lymphotropic retrovirus from a patient at risk for acquired immune deficiency syndrome (AIDS). *Science, 220,* 868–870.

Biggar, R. J., Frisch, M., Engels, E. A., & Goedert, J. J. (2001). Risk of T-cell lymphomas in persons with AIDS. *Journal of Acquired Immune Deficiency Syndromes, 26,* 371–376.

Bishara, M. R., Ross, C., & Sur, M. (2009). Primary anaplastic large cell lymphoma of the breast arising in reconstruction mammoplasty capsule of saline filled breast implant after radical mastectomy for breast cancer: An unusual case presentation. *Diagnostic Pathology, 2*(4), 11.

Blair, A., Sandler, D. P., Tarone, R., Lubin, J., Thomas, K., Hoppin, J. A., . . . Alavania, M. C. (2005). Mortality among participants in the agricultural health study. *Annals of Epidemiology, 15,* 279–285.

Blair, A., Zahm, S. H., Pearce, N. E., Heineman, E. F., & Fraumeni, J. F. (1992). Clues to cancer etiology from studies of farmers. *Scandinavian Journal of Work, Environment and Health, 18,* 209–215.

Blomberg, J., Möller, T., Olsson, H., Anderson, H., & Jonsson, M. (1993). Cancer morbidity in blood recipients—Results of a cohort study. *European Journal of Cancer, 29A,* 2101–2105.

Blum, K. A., Lozanski, G., & Byrd, J. C. (2004). Adult Burkitt leukemia and lymphoma. *Blood, 104,* 3009–3020.

Bräuninger, A., Küppers, R., Strickler, J. G., Wacker, H. H., Rajewsky, K., & Hansmann, M. L. (1997). Hodgkin's and Reed–Sternberg cells in lymphocyte predominant Hodgkin's disease represent clonal populations of germinal center-derived tumor B cells. *Proceedings of the National Academy of Sciences of the United States of America, 94,* 9337–9342.

Bräuninger, A., Schmitz, R., Bechtel, D., Renné, C., Hansmann, M. L., & Küppers, R. (2006). Molecular biology of Hodgkin's and Reed/Sternberg cells in Hodgkin's lymphoma. *International Journal of Cancer, 118*(8), 1853–1861.

Burkitt, D. (1958). A sarcoma involving the jaws in African children. *British Journal of Surgery*, 46(197), 218–223.

Burkitt, D. P. (1971). Epidemiology of Burkitt's lymphoma. *Proceedings of the Royal Society of Medicine*, 64(9), 909–910.

Burkitt, D. P. (1983). The discovery of Burkitt's lymphoma. *Cancer*, 51, 1777–1786.

Butel, J. S., Vilchez, R. A., Jorgensen, J. L., & Kozinetz, C. A. (2003). Association between SV40 and non-Hodgkin's lymphoma. *Leukemia and Lymphoma*, 44(Suppl 3), S33–S39.

Carpenter, L. M., Newton, R., Casabonne, D., Ziegler, J., Mbulaiteye, S., Mbidde, E., . . . Beral, V. (2008). Antibodies against malaria and Epstein-Barr virus in childhood Burkitt lymphoma: A case-control study in Uganda. *International Journal of Cancer*, 122(6), 1319–1323.

Carroll-Pankhurst, C., Engels, E. A., Strickler, H. D., Goedert, J. J., Wagner, J., & Mortimer, E. A. Jr. (2001). Thirty-five year mortality following receipt of SV40-contaminated polio vaccine during the neonatal period. *British Journal of Cancer*, 85(9), 1295–1297.

Cartwright, R., McNally, R., & Staines, A. (1994). The increasing incidence of non-Hodgkin's lymphoma (NHL): The possible role of sunlight. *Leukemia and Lymphoma*, 14, 387–394.

Cartwright, R. A., & Watkins, G. (2004). Epidemiology of Hodgkin's disease: A review. *Hematological Oncology*, 22, 11–26.

Cerhan, J. R., Wallace, R. B., Dick, F., Kemp, J., Parker, A. S., Zheng, W., . . . Folsom, A. R. (2001). Blood transfusions and risk of non-Hodgkin's lymphoma subtypes and chronic lymphocytic leukemia. *Cancer Epidemiology, Biomarkers and Prevention*, 10(4), 361–368.

Cerhan, J. R., Wallace, R. B., Folsom, A. R., Potter, J. D., Munger, R. G., & Prineas, R. J. (1993). Transfusion history and cancer risk in older women. *Annals of Internal Medicine*, 119, 8–15.

Cerroni, L., Zochling, N., Putz, B., & Kerl, H. (1997). Infection by *Borrelia burgdorferi* and cutaneous B-cell lymphoma. *Journal of Cutaneous Pathology*, 24, 457–461.

Cesarman, E., Chang, Y., Moore, P. S., Said, J. W., & Knowles, D. M. (1995). Kaposi's sarcoma–associated herpesvirus-like DNA sequences in AIDS-related body-cavity-based lymphomas. *New England Journal of Medicine*, 332(18), 1186–1191.

Chang, Y., Cesarman, E., Pessin, M. S., Lee, F., Culpepper, J., Knowles, D. M., & Moore, P. S. (1994). Identification of herpesvirus-like DNA sequences in AIDS-associated Kaposi's sarcoma. *Science*, 266(5192), 1865–1869.

Chow, E. J., & Holly, E. A. (2002). Blood transfusions and non-Hodgkin's lymphoma. *Epidemiology Reviews*, 24(2), 269–279.

Cinque, P., Brytting, M., Vago, L., Castagna, A., Parravicini, C., Zanchetta, N., . . . Linde, A. (1993). Epstein-Barr virus DNA in cerebrospinal fluid from patients with AIDS-related primary lymphoma of the central nervous system. *Lancet*, 342(8868), 398–401.

Cleary, M. L., Chao, J., Warnke, R., & Sklar, J. (1984). Immunoglobulin gene rearrangement as a diagnostic criterion of B-cell lymphoma. *Proceedings of the National Academy of Sciences of the United States of America*, 81, 593–597.

Cleghorn, F. R., Manns, A., Falk, R., Hartge, P., Hanchard, B., Jack, N., . . . Blattner, W. (1995). Effect of human T-lymphotropic virus type I infection on non-Hodgkin's lymphoma incidence. *Journal of the National Cancer Institute*, 87(13), 1009–1014.

Cohen, H. J., Crawford, J., Rao, M. K., Pieper, C. F., & Currie, M. S. (1998). Racial differences in the prevalence of monoclonal gammopathy in a community-based sample of the elderly. *American Journal of Medicine*, 104, 439–444.

Dal Maso, L., & Franceschi, S. (2003). Epidemiology of non-Hodgkin lymphomas and other haemolymphopoietic neoplasms in people with AIDS. *Lancet Oncology*, 4(2), 110–119.

de Jong, D., Vasmel, W. L. E., de Boer, J. P., Verhave, G., Barbé, E., Casparie, M. K., & van Leeuwen, F. E. (2008). Anaplastic large-cell lymphoma in women with breast implants. *Journal of the American Medical Association*, 300(17), 2030–2035.

de Sanjose, S., Shah, K. V., Domingo-Domenech, E., Engels, E. A., de Sevilla, A. F., Alvaro, T., . . . Viscidi, R. P. (2003). Lack of serological evidence for an association between simian virus 40 and lymphoma. *International Journal of Cancer*, 104, 522–524.

de Thé, G. (1993). The etiology of Burkitt's lymphoma and the history of the shaken dogmas. *Blood Cells*, 19, 667–673.

Devesa, S. S., & Fears, T. (1992). Non-Hodgkin's lymphoma time trends, United States and international data. *Cancer Research*, 52, 5432s–5440s.

Duberg, A. S., Nordstrom, M., Torner, A., Reichard, O., Strauss, R., Janzon, R., . . . Ekdahl, K. (2005). Non-Hodgkin's lymphoma and other nonhepatic malignancies in Swedish patients with hepatitis C virus infection. *Hepatology*, 41, 652–659.

Eltom, M. A., Jemal, A., Mbulaiteye, S. M., Devesa, S. S., & Biggar, R. J. (2002). Trends in Kaposi's sarcoma and non-Hodgkin's lymphoma incidence in the United States from 1973 through 1998. *Journal of the National Cancer Institute*, 94(16), 1204–1210.

Engels, E. A., Frisch, M., Lubin, J. H., Gail, M. H., Biggar, R. J., & Goedert, J. J. (2002). Prevalence of hepatitis C virus infection and risk for hepatocellular carcinoma and non-Hodgkin lymphoma in AIDS. *Journal of Acquired Immune Deficiency Syndromes*, 31, 536–541.

Engels, E. A., Katki, H. A., Nielsen, N. M., Winther, J. F., Hjalgrim, H., Gjerris, F., . . . Frisch, M. (2003). Cancer incidence in Denmark following exposure to poliovirus vaccine contaminated with simian virus 40. *Journal of the National Cancer Institute*, 95(7), 532–539.

Engels, E. A., Viscidi, R. P., Galloway, D. A., Carter, J. J., Cerhan, J. R., . . . Hartge, P. (2004). Case-control study of Simian Virus 40 and non-Hodgkin lymphoma in the United States. *Journal of the National Cancer Institute*, 96(18), 1368–1374.

Epstein, M. A., Achong, B. G., & Pope, J. H. (1967). Virus in cultured lymphoblasts from a New Guinea Burkitt lymphoma. *British Medical Journal*, 2(5547), 290–291.

Ferlay, J., Shin, H. R., Forman, D., Mathers, C., & Parkin, D. M. (2010). Estimates of worldwide burden of cancer in 2008. *International Journal of Cancer*, 127(12), 2893–2917.

Ferlay, J., Soerjomataram, I., Ervik, M., Dikshit, R., Eser, S., Mathers, C., . . . Bray, F. (2013). *GLOBOCAN 2012 v1.0. Cancer incidence and mortality worldwide: IARC CancerBase No. 11* [Internet]. Lyon, France: International Agency for Research on Cancer. Retrieved from http://globocan.iarc.fr

Fernandez, E., Chatenoud, L., La Vecchia, C., Negri, E., & Franceschi, S. (1999). Fish consumption and cancer risk. *American Journal of Clinical Nutrition*, 70(1), 85–90.

Ferreri, A. J. M., Guidoboni, M., Ponzoni, M., De Conciliis, C., Dell'Oro, S., Fleischhauer, K., . . . Dolcetti, R. (2004). Evidence for an association between *Chlamydia psittaci* and ocular adnexal lymphomas. *Journal of the National Cancer Institute*, 96, 586–594.

Ferry, J. A. (2006). Burkitt's lymphoma: Clinicopathologic features and differential diagnosis. *Oncologist*, 11(4), 375–383.

Figgs, L. W., Dosemeci, M., & Blair, A. (1995). United States non-Hodgkin's lymphoma surveillance by occupation 1984–1989: A twenty-four state death certificate study. *American Journal of Industrial Medicine*, 27, 817–835.

Filipovich, A. H., Mathur, A., Kamat, D., & Shapiro, R. S. (1992). Primary immunodeficiencies: Genetic risk factors for lymphoma. *Cancer Research*, 52, 5465s–5467s.

Fisher, S. G., & Fisher, R. I. (2004). The epidemiology of non-Hodgkin's lymphoma. *Oncogene*, 23, 6524–6534.

Frampton, M., da Silva Filho, M. I., Broderic, P., Thomsen, H., Forsti, A., Vijayakrishnan, J., . . . Houlston, R. S. (2013). Variation at 3p24.1 and 6q23.3 influences the risk of Hodgkin's lymphoma. *Nature Communications, 4,* 2549. doi: 10.1038/ncomms3549.

Franceschi, S., Dal Maso, L., & La Vecchia, C. (1999). Advances in the epidemiology of HIV-associated non-Hodgkin's lymphoma and other lymphoid neoplasms. *International Journal of Cancer, 83*(4), 481–485.

Fritschi, L., Ambrosini, G. L., Kliewer, E. V., & Johnson, K. C.; Canadian Cancer Registries Epidemiologic Research Group. (2004). Dietary fish intake and risk of leukaemia, multiple myeloma, and non-Hodgkin lymphoma. *Cancer Epidemiology, Biomarkers and Prevention, 13*(4), 532–537.

Gallo, R. C., Sarin, P. S., Gelmann, E. P., Robert-Guroff, M., Richardson, E., Kalyanaraman, V. S., . . . Popovic, M. (1983). Isolation of human T-cell leukemia virus in acquired immune deficiency syndrome (AIDS). *Science, 220*(4599), 865–867.

Garbe, C., Stein, H., Dienemann, D., & Orfanos, C. E. (1991). *Borrelia burgdorferi*–associated cutaneous B cell lymphoma: Clinical and immunohistologic characterization of four cases. *Journal of the American Academy of Dermatology, 24,* 584–590.

Gisbert, J. P., García-Buey, L., Pajares, J. M., & Moreno-Otero, R. (2003). Prevalence of hepatitis C virus infection in B cell non-Hodgkin's lymphoma: Systematic review and meta-analysis. *Gastroenterology, 125,* 1723–1732.

Goedert, J. J., Cote, T. R., Virgo, P., Scoppa, S. M., Kingma, D. W., Gail, M. H., . . . Biggar, R. J. (1998). Spectrum of AIDS-associated malignant disorders. *Lancet, 351,* 1833–1899.

Grogan, T., & Miller, T. (1995). Natural history and pre-treatment evaluation of non-Hodgkins lymphomas. In C. M. Haskell (Ed.), *Cancer treatment* (pp. 979–1005). Philadelphia, PA: W. B. Saunders.

Groves, F. D., Linet, M. S., Travis, L. B., & Devesa, S. S. (2000). Cancer surveillance series: Non-Hodgkin's lymphoma incidence by histologic subtype in the United States from 1978 through 1995. *Journal of the National Cancer Institute, 92,* 1240–1251.

Grulich, A. E., Wan, X., Law, M. G., Coates, M., & Kaldor, J. M. (1999). Risk of cancer in people with AIDS. *AIDS, 13,* 839–843.

Grulich, A. E., Wan, X., Law, M. G., Milliken, S. T., Lewis, C. R., Garsia, R. J., . . . Kaldor, J. M. (2000). B-cell stimulation and prolonged immune deficiency are risk factors for non-Hodgkin's lymphoma in people with AIDS. *AIDS, 14,* 133–140.

Harris, N. L., Jaffe, E. S., Diebold, J., Flandrin, G., Muller-Hermelink, H. K., Vardiman, J., . . . Bloomfield, C. D. (1999). World Health Organization classification of neoplastic diseases of the hematopoietic and lymphoid tissues: Report of the Clinical Advisory Committee meeting—Airlie House, Virginia, November 1997. *Journal of Clinical Oncology, 17*(12), 3835–3849.

Harris, O. D., Cooke, W. T., Thompson, H., & Waterhouse, J. A. H. (1967). Malignancy in adult coeliac disease and idiopathic steatorrhoea. *American Journal of Medicine, 42,* 899–912.

Hartge, P., Devesa, S. S., & Fraumeni, J. F. Jr. (1994). Hodgkin's and non-Hodgkin's lymphomas. *Cancer Surveys, 19–20,* 423–453.

Hartge, P., Devesa, S. S., Grauman, D., Fears, T. R., & Fraumeni, J. F. Jr. (1996). Non-Hodgkin's lymphoma and sunlight. *Journal of the National Cancer Institute, 88,* 298–300.

Hinuma, Y., Nagata, K., Hanaoka, M., Nakai, M., Matsumoto, T., Kinoshita, K. I., . . . Miyoshi, I. (1981). Adult T-cell leukemia: Antigen in an ATL cell line and detection of antibodies to the antigen in human sera. *Proceedings of the National Academy of Sciences of the United States of America, 78*(10), 6476–6480.

Hjalgrim, H., Rasmussen, S., Rostgaard, K., Nielsen, N. M., Koch-Henriksen, N., Munksgaard, L., . . . Melbye, M. (2004). Familial clustering of Hodgkin lymphoma and multiple sclerosis. *Journal of the National Cancer Institute, 96,* 780–784.

Hodgkin, T. (1832). On some morbid experiences of the absorbent glands and spleen. *Medico-Chirurgical Transactions, 17,* 69–97.

Hussell, T., Isaacson, P. G., Crabtree, J. E., & Spencer, J. (1993). The response of cells from low-grade B-cell gastric lymphomas of mucosa-associated lymphoid tissue to *Helicobacter pylori. Lancet, 342,* 571–574.

Isaacson, P. G., & Spencer, J. (1995). The biology of low grade MALT lymphoma. *Journal of Clinical Pathology, 48*(5), 395–397.

Jelic, S., & Filipovic-Ljeskovic, I. (1999). Positive serology for Lyme disease borrelias in primary cutaneous B-cell lymphoma: A study in 22 patients: Is it a fortuitous finding? *Hematological Oncology, 17,* 107–116.

Judde, J. G., Lacoste, V., Briere, J., Kassa-Kelembho, E., Clyti, E., Couppie, P., . . . Gessain, A. (2000). Monoclonality or oligoclonality of human herpesvirus 8 terminal repeat sequences in Kaposi's sarcoma and other diseases. *Journal of the National Cancer Institute, 92,* 729–736.

Kamel, O. W., van de Rijn, M., Hanasono, M. M., & Warnke, R. A. (1995). Immunosuppression-associated lymphoproliferative disorders in rheumatic patients. *Leukemia and Lymphoma, 16,* 363.

Kanzler, H., Küppers, R., Hansmann, M. L., & Rajewsky, K. (1996). Hodgkin's and Reed–Sternberg cells in Hodgkin's disease represent the outgrowth of a dominant tumor clone derived from (crippled) germinal center B cells. *Journal of Experimental Medicine, 184,* 1495–1505.

Khuder, S. A., Schaub, E. A., & Keller-Byrne, J. E. (1998). Meta-analyses of non-Hodgkin's lymphoma and farming. *Scandinavian Journal of Work, Environment and Health, 24,* 255–261.

Kinlen, L. (1992). Immunosuppressive therapy and acquired immunological disorders. *Cancer Research, 52,* 5474s–5476s.

Koshiol, J., Gridley, G., Engels, E., McMaster, M., & Landgren, O. (2008). Chronic immune stimulation and subsequent Waldenström macroglobulinemia. *Archives of Internal Medicine, 168*(17), 1903–1909.

Kumar, V., Abbas, A. K., & Aster, J. C. (2014). *Robbins and Cotran pathologic basis of disease* (9th ed.). Philadelphia, PA: Mosby & Saunders.

Küppers, R. (2005). Mechanisms of B-cell lymphoma pathogenesis. *Nature Reviews Cancer, 5*(4), 251–262.

Küppers, R., Rajewsky, K., Zhao, M., Simons, G., Laumann, R., Fischer, R., & Hansmann, M. L. (1994). Hodgkin's disease: Hodgkin's and Reed–Sternberg cells picked from histological sections show clonal immunoglobulin gene rearrangements and appear to be derived from B cells at various stages of development. *Proceedings of the National Academy of Sciences of the United States of America, 91,* 10962–10966.

Kusters, J. G., van Vliet, A. H. M., & Kuipers, E. J. (2006). Pathogenesis of *Helicobacter pylori* infection. *Clinical Microbiology Reviews, 19*(3), 449–490.

Kyle, R. A., & Rajkumar, S. V. (2004). Multiple myeloma. *New England Journal of Medicine, 351*(18), 1860–1873.

Kyle, R. A., Therneau, T. M., Rajkumar, S. V., Larson, D. R., Plevak, M. F., & Melton, L. J. III. (2004). Long-term follow-up of 241 patients with monoclonal gammopathy of undetermined significance: The original Mayo Clinic series 25 years later. *Mayo Clinic Proceedings, 79,* 859–866.

Kyle, R. A., Therneau, T. M., Rajkumar, S. V., Larson, D. R., Plevak, M. F., Offord, J. R., . . . Melton, L. J. III (2006). Prevalence of monoclonal gammopathy of undetermined significance. *New England Journal of Medicine, 354,* 1362–1369.

Kyle, R. A., Therneau, T. M., Rajkumar, S. V., Offord, J. R., Larson, D. R., Plevak, M. F., & Melton, L. J. III (2002). A long-term study of prognosis in monoclonal gammopathy of undetermined significance. *New England Journal of Medicine, 346,* 564–569.

Landgren, O., Kyle, R. A., Pfeiffer, R. M., Katzmann, J. A., Caporaso, N. E., Hayes, R. B., . . . Rajkumar, S. V. (2009). Monoclonal gammopathy of undetermined significance

(MGUS) consistently precedes multiple myeloma: A prospective study. *Blood, 113*(22), 5412–5417.

Lecuit, M., Abachin, E., Martin, A., Poyart, C., Pochart, P., Suarez, F., . . . Lortholary, O. (2004). Immunoproliferative small intestinal disease associated with *Campylobacter jejuni. New England Journal of Medicine, 350,* 239–248.

Leech, S. H., Brown, R., & Scharifeld, M. S. (1985). Genetic studies in multiple myeloma: Immunoglobulin allotype associations. *Cancer, 5,* 1473–1476.

Leech, S. H., Bryan, C. F., Elston, R. C., Rainey, J., Bickers, J. N., & Pelias, M. Z. (1983). Genetic studies in multiple myeloma: Association with HLA-Cw5. *Cancer, 51,* 1408–1411.

Linet, M. S., & Pottern, L. M. (1992). Familial aggregation of hematopoietic malignancies and risk of non-Hodgkin's lymphoma. *Cancer Research, 52S,* 5468–5473.

Lukes, R. J., & Collins, R. D. (1975). New approaches to the classification of the lymphomata. *British Journal of Cancer, Suppl. 2,* 1–28.

Luppi, M., Longo, G., Ferrari, M. G., Barozzi, P., Marasca, R., Morselli, M., . . . Torelli, G. (1998). Clinico-pathological characterization of hepatitis C virus-related B-cell non-Hodgkin's lymphomas without symptomatic cryoglobulinemia. *Annals of Oncology, 9,* 495–498.

Mack, T. M., Cozen, W., Shibata, D. K., Weiss, L. M., Nathwani, B. N., Hernandez, A. M., . . . Rappaport, E. B. (1995). Concordance for Hodgkin's disease in identical twins suggesting genetic susceptibility to the young-adult form of the disease. *New England Journal of Medicine, 332,* 413–419.

Manns, A., & Blattner, W. A. (2003). The epidemiology of the human T-cell lymphotropic virus type I and type II: Etiologic role in human disease. *Transfusion, 31*(1), 67–75.

Marshall, B. J., & Warren, R. J. (2005). The Nobel prize in physiology or medicine, 2005. Retrieved from http://www.mja.com.au/journal/2005 /183/11/2005-nobel-prize-physiology-or-medicine

Matsuo, K., Kusano, A., Sugumar, A., Nakamura, S., Tajima, K., & Mueller, N. E. (2004). Effect of hepatitis C virus infection on the risk of non-Hodgkin's lymphoma: A meta-analysis of epidemiological studies. *Cancer Science, 95,* 745–752.

McGregor, J. M., Crook, T., Fraser-Andrews, E. A., Rozycka, M., Crossland, S., Brooks, L., & Whittaker, S. J. (1999). Spectrum of *p53* gene mutations suggests a possible role for ultraviolet radiation in the pathogenesis of advanced cutaneous lymphomas. *Journal of Investigative Dermatology, 112*(3), 317–321.

Melbye, M., Ekström Smedby, K., & Trichopoulos, D. (2008). Non-Hodgkin lymphoma. In H.-O. Adami, D. Hunter, & D. Trichoupoulos (Eds.), *Textbook of cancer epidemiology* (pp. 535–555). Oxford, UK: Oxford University Press.

Melbye, M., Hjalgrim, H., & Adami, H.-O. (2008). Hodgkin's lymphoma. In H.-O. Adami, D. Hunter, & D. Trichopoulos (Eds.), *Textbook of cancer epidemiology* (pp. 520–534). Oxford, UK: Oxford University Press.

Memon, A., & Doll, R. (1994). A search for unknown blood-borne oncogenic viruses. *International Journal of Cancer, 58,* 366–368.

Morton, L. M., Hartge, P., Holford, T. R., Holly, E. A., Chiu, B. C., Vineis, P., . . . Zheng, T. (2005a). Cigarette smoking and risk of non-Hodgkin lymphoma: A pooled analysis from the International Lymphoma Epidemiology Consortium (InterLymph). *Cancer Epidemiology, Biomarkers and Prevention, 14,* 925–933.

Morton, L. M., Zheng, T., Holford, T. R., Holly, E. A., Chiu, B. C., Costantini, A. S., . . . InterLymph Consortium. (2005b). Alcohol consumption and risk of non-Hodgkin lymphoma: A pooled analysis. *Lancet Oncology, 6,* 469–476.

Müller, A. M. S., Ihorst, G., Mertelsmann, R., & Engelhardt, M. (2005). Epidemiology of non-Hodgkin's lymphoma (NHL): Trends, geographic distribution, and etiology. *Annals of Hematology, 84,* 1–12.

Nakatsuka, S., Liu, A., Dong, Z., Nomura, S., Takakuwa, T., Miyazato, H., & Aozasa, K.

(2003). Simian virus 40 sequences in malignant lymphomas in Japan. *Cancer Research, 63*, 7606–7608.

Negri, E., Little, D., Boiocchi, M., La Vecchia, C., & Franceschi, S. (2004). B-cell non-Hodgkin's lymphoma and hepatitis C virus infection: A systematic review. *International Journal of Cancer, 111*, 1–8.

Ocio, E. M., Schop, R. F. J., Gonzalez, B., Van Wier, S. A., Hernandez-Rivas, J. M., Gutierrez, N. C., . . . Fonseca, R. (2007). 6q deletion in Waldenström macroglobulinemia is associated with features of adverse prognosis. *British Journal of Haematology, 136*(1), 80–86.

Offit, K., Wong, G., Filippa, D. A., Tao, Y., & Chaganti, R. S. (1991). Cytogenetic analysis of 434 consecutively ascertained specimens of non-Hodgkin's lymphoma: Clinical correlations. *Blood, 77*(7), 1508–1515.

Opelz, G., & Henderson, R. (1993). Incidence of non-Hodgkin lymphoma in kidney and heart transplant recipients. *Lancet, 342*(8886–8887), 1514–1516.

Palackdharry, C. S. (1994). The epidemiology of non-Hodgkin's lymphoma: Why the increased incidence? *Oncology, 8*(8), 67–73; discussion 73–78.

Parkin, D. M., Bray, F., Ferlay, J., & Pisani, P. (2001). Estimating the world cancer burden, GLOBOCAN 2000. *International Journal of Cancer, 94*, 153–156.

Parkin, D. M., Bray, F., Ferlay, J., & Pisani, P. (2005). Global cancer statistics, 2002. *CA: A Cancer Journal for Clinicians, 55*, 74–108.

Parkin, D. M., Pisani, P., & Ferlay, J. (1999a). Estimates of the worldwide incidence of 25 major cancers in 1990. *International Journal of Cancer, 80*(6), 827–841.

Parkin, D. M., Pisani, P., & Ferlay, J. (1999b). Global cancer statistics. *CA: A Cancer Journal for Clinicians, 49*(1), 33–64.

Parsonnet, J., Hansen, S., Rodriguez, L., Gelb, A. B., Warnke, R. A., Jellum, E., . . . Friedman, G. D. (1994). *Helicobacter pylori* infection and gastric lymphoma. *New England Journal of Medicine, 330*, 1267–1271.

Pettersson, T., Pukkala, E., Teppo, L., & Friman, C. (1992). Increased risk of cancer in patients with systemic lupus erythematosus. *Annals of the Rheumatic Diseases, 51*(4), 437–439.

Plosker, G. L., & Figgitt, D. P. (2003). Rituximab: A review of its use in non-Hodgkin's lymphoma and chronic lymphocytic leukaemia. *Drugs, 63*(8), 803–843.

Poiesz, B. J., Ruscetti, F. W., Gazdar, A. F., Bunn, P. A., Minna, J. D., & Gallo, R. C. (1980). Detection and isolation of type C retrovirus particles from fresh and cultured lymphocytes of a patient with cutaneous T-cell lymphoma. *Proceedings of the National Academy of Sciences of the United States of America, 77*, 7415–7419.

Polesel, J., Clifford, G., Rickenbach, M., Dal Maso, L., Battegay, M., Bouchardy, C., . . . the Swiss HIV Cohort Study. (2008). Non-Hodgkin's lymphoma incidence in the Swiss HIV Cohort Study before and after highly active antiretroviral therapy. *AIDS, 22*(2), 301–306.

Pottern, L. M., Gart, J. J., Nam, J. M., Dunston, G., Wilson, J., Greenberg, R., . . . Schwartz, A. G. (1992). HLA and multiple myeloma among black and white men: Evidence of a genetic association. *Cancer Epidemiology, Biomarkers and Prevention, 1*(3), 177–182.

Pounder, R. E., Ng, D. (1995). The prevalence of *Helicobacter pylori* infection in different countries. *Alimentary Pharmacology and Therapeutics, 9 Suppl 2*, 33–39.

Purtilo, D. T. (1980). Epstein–Barr virus–induced oncogenesis in immune-deficient individuals. *Lancet, 1*, 300–303.

Raab, M. S., Podar, K., Breitkreutz, I., Richardson, P. G., & Anderson, K. C. (2009). Multiple myeloma. *Lancet, 374*(9686), 324–339.

Rabkin, C. S., Tess, B. H., Christianson, R. E., Wright, W. E., Waters, D. J., Alter, H. J., & Van Den Berg, B. J. (2002). Prospective study of hepatitis C viral infection as a risk factor for subsequent B-cell neoplasia. *Blood, 99*, 4240–4242.

Reed, D. (1902). On the pathological changes in Hodgkin's disease, with special reference to its relation to tuberculosis. *Johns Hopkins Hospital Reports, 10,* 133–196.

Schöllkopf, C., Melbye, M., Munksgaard, L., Smedby, K. E., Rostgaard, K., Glimelius, B., . . . Hjalgrim, H. (2008). *Borrelia* infection and risk of non-Hodgkin lymphoma. *Blood, 111*(12), 5524–5529.

Schop, R. F., Van Wier, S. A., Xu, R., Ghobrial, I., Ahmann, G. J., Greipp, P. R., . . . Fonseca, R. (2006). 6q deletion discriminates Waldenström macroglobulinemia from IgM monoclonal gammopathy of undetermined significance. *Cancer Genetics and Cytogenetics, 169*(2), 150–153.

Shipp, M. A., Mauch, P. M., & Harris, N. L. (1997). Non-Hodgkin's lymphomas. In V. DeVita Jr., S. Hellman, & S. A. Rosenberg (Eds.), *Cancer principles and practice of oncology* (Vol. 3, pp. 2165–2220). Philadelphia, PA: Lippincott-Raven.

Shivapurkar, N., Harada, K., Reddy, J., Scheuermann, R. H., Xu, Y., McKenna, R. W., . . . Gazdar, A. F. (2002). Presence of simian virus 40 DNA sequences in human lymphomas. *Lancet, 359,* 851–852.

Silvestri, F., Pipan, C., Barillari, G., Zaja, F., Fanin, R., Infanti, L., . . . Baccarani, M. (1996). Prevalence of hepatitis C virus infection in patients with lymphoproliferative disorders. *Blood, 87*(10), 4296–4301.

Sternberg, C. (1898). Uber eine eigenartige unter dem Bilde der Pseudoleukamie verlaufende Tuberculose des lymphatischen Apparates. *Zeitschrift fuer Heilkunde, 19,* 21–90.

Swinnen, L., Costanzo-Nordin, M. R., Fisher, S. G., O'Sullivan, E. J., Johnson, M. R., Heroux, A. L., . . . Fisher, R. I. (1990). Increased incidence of lymphoproliferative disorder after immunosuppression with the monoclonal antibody OKT3 in cardiac-transplant recipients. *New England Journal of Medicine, 323*(25), 1723–1728.

Takatsuki, K. (2005). Discovery of adult T-cell leukemia. *Retrovirology, 2,* 16.

Takatsuki, K., Uchiyama, T., Sagawa, K., & Yodoi, J. (1977). Adult T cell leukemia in Japan. In S. Seno, F. Takaku, & S. Irino (Eds.), *Topics in hematology* (pp. 73–77). Amsterdam, Netherlands: Excerpta Medica.

Takkouche, B., Etminan, M., & Montes-Martinez, A. (2005). Personal use of hair dyes and risk of cancer: A meta-analysis. *Journal of the American Medical Association, 293,* 2516–2525.

Thun, M. J., DeLancey, J. O., Center, M. M., Jemal, A., & Ward, E. M. (2010). The global burden of cancer: Priorities for prevention. *Carcinogenesis, 31*(1), 100–110.

Tycko, B., & Sklar, J. (1990). Chromosomal translocations in lymphoid neoplasia: A reappraisal of the recombinase model. *Cancer Cells, 2*(1), 1–8.

Uchiyama, T., Yodoi, J., Sagawa, K., Takatsuki, K., & Uchino, H. (1977). Adult T-cell leukemia: Clinical and hematologic features of 16 cases. *Blood, 50,* 481–492.

Udomsakdi-Auewarakul, C., Auewarakul, P., Sukpanichnant, S., & Muangsup, W. (2000). Hepatitis C virus infection in patients with non-Hodgkin lymphoma in Thailand. *Blood, 95,* 3640–3641.

Vega, F., & Medeiros, L. J. (2003). Chromosomal translocations involved in non-Hodgkin lymphomas. *Archives of Pathology and Laboratory Medicine, 127*(9), 1148–1160.

Vilchez, R. A., Madden, C. R., Kozinetz, C. A., Halvorson, S. J., White, Z. S., Orgensen, J. L., . . . Butel, J. S. (2002). Association between simian virus 40 and non-Hodgkin lymphoma. *Lancet, 359,* 817–823.

Waldenstrom, J. (1944). Incipient myelomatosis or "essential" hyperglobulinemia with fibrinogenopenia—a new syndrome? *Acta Medica Scandinavica, 117,* 216–247.

Willemze, R., Kerl, H., Sterry, W., Berti, E., Cerroni, L., Chimenti, S., . . . Meijer, C. J. L. M. (1997). EORTC classification for primary cutaneous lymphomas: A proposal from the Cutaneous Lymphoma Study Group of the European Organization for Research and Treatment of Cancer. *Blood, 90*, 354–371.

World Health Organization. (2008). *World cancer report 2008*. Lyon, France: International Agency for Research on Cancer.

Wotherspoon, A. C. (1998). *Helicobacter pylori* infection and gastric lymphoma. *British Medical Bulletin, 54*(1), 79–85.

Wotherspoon, A. C., Doglioni, C., Diss, T. C., Pan, L., Moschini, A., de Boni, M., & Isaacson, P. G. (1993). Regression of primary low-grade B-cell gastric lymphoma of mucosa-associated lymphoid tissue type after eradication of *Helicobacter pylori*. *Lancet, 342*, 575–577.

Wotherspoon, A. C., Ortiz-Hidalgo, C., Falzon, M. R., & Isaacson, P. G. (1991). *Helicobacter pylori*–associated gastritis and primary B-cell gastric lymphoma. *Lancet, 338*, 1175–1176.

Ye, B. H. (2000). Role of BCL-6 in the pathogenesis of non-Hodgkin's lymphoma. *Cancer Investigation, 18*, 356–365.

Yodoi, J., Takatsuki, K., & Masuda, T. (1974). Letter: Two cases of T-cell chronic lymphocytic leukemia in Japan. *New England Journal of Medicine, 290*(10), 572–573.

Yoshida, M., Miyoshi, I., & Hinuma, Y. (1982). Isolation and characterization of retrovirus from cell lines of human adult T-cell leukemia and its implication in the disease. *Proceedings of the National Academy of Sciences of the United States of America, 79*(6), 2031–2035.

Zahm, S. H., Weisenburger, D. D., Holmes, F. F., Cantor, K. P., & Blair, A. (1997). Tobacco and non-Hodgkin's lymphoma: Combined analysis of three case-control studies (United States). *Cancer Causes and Control, 8*, 159–166.

Zheng, T., Mayne, S. T., Boyle, P., Holford, T. R., Liu, W. L., & Flannery, J. (1992). Epidemiology of non-Hodgkin lymphoma in Connecticut. 1935–1988. *Cancer, 70*, 840–849.

Zhu, K., Levine, R. S., Gu, Y., Brann, E. A., Hall, I., Caplan, L. S., & Baum, M. K. (1998). Non-Hodgkin's lymphoma and family history of malignant tumors in a case-control study (United States). *Cancer Causes and Control, 9*, 77–82.

27

Epidemiology of Leukemia

CLASSIFICATION OF LEUKEMIA

Leukemia arises in the bone marrow from cell lineages that form the immune cells that circulate in the blood. The three basic types of immune cells are myelocytes, lymphocytes, and monocytes. Leukemias are therefore broadly categorized as either myelocytic, lymphocytic, or monocytic. A further classification is based on whether disease follows a rapidly fatal course in a matter of weeks if left untreated (acute leukemia) or persists over a period of years (chronic leukemia).

The term *leukemia*, which means "white blood," was first used by the famous German pathologist Rudolph Virchow in describing the predominance of circulating white blood cells versus red blood cells that often exists in patients with leukemia. As pointed out by Stanley Robbins and Ramzi Cotran in their classic text, leukemias are best characterized by diffuse replacement of bone marrow by proliferating leukemic cells, abnormal forms of malignant cells circulating in the blood, and infiltrates of leukemic cells in various anatomic sites such as the liver, spleen, lymph nodes, and elsewhere (Kumar, Abbas, & Aster, 2014; Robbins & Cotran, 1979).

Standard nomenclature for the leukemias is given in **Table 27.1**. The six basic types are acute and chronic forms of lymphocytic leukemia, myelocytic leukemia, and monocytic leukemia. Each can be further subdivided according to the morphology of the cell of origin and staining characteristics of cells. For example, when cells are routinely stained with hematoxylin and eosin dye, the cells are identifiable as neutrophils (neutral stain), basophils (blue stain), or eosinophils (red stain). Cell types can also be molecularly characterized by the presence of cell membrane receptors. Such receptors are used to differentiate T and B lymphocytic leukemias. Rare forms of leukemia have also been identified such as histiocytic or hairy-cell leukemia (derived from monocytes and macrophages) and erythroleukemia, in which the majority of tumor cells are of erythropoietic lineage (Vardiman et al., 2009).

HEMATOPOIESIS

Immune cells of the blood are continuously being formed in the bone marrow. They originate from progenitor (stem) cells and undergo tightly regulated differentiation into the various lineages of immune cell populations. It is estimated that more than *1 trillion* new cells are produced daily to maintain homeostasis in the peripheral circulation. Hematopoietic stem cells reside in the bone marrow and have the unique ability to differentiate into all of the mature cell types that circulate in the blood (**Figure 27.1**). There are differences of opinion regarding the cell of origin of monocytes, which are not shown in the diagram. The conventional view is that monocytes arise from myeloid precursors; however, some studies suggest that monocytes are derived from stem cells that are distinct from the myeloid lineage. Macrophages (also called phagocytes) develop from circulating monocytes that migrate into tissues of the body (Dale, Boser, & Liles, 2008; Vardiman et al., 2009).

Production of red and white blood cells is regulated with extreme precision in the human body. A plethora of growth factors, hormones, and transcription factors are involved in the differentiation and maturation of progenitor cells. For example, erythropoietin secreted by the kidneys stimulates the

Table 27.1	Classification of Leukemias
Type of Leukemia	**Common Characteristics**
Acute lymphocytic leukemia (ALL)	Predominant type in children, usually B-cell origin, T-cell origin is rare
Chronic lymphocytic leukemia (CLL)	Predominant type in adults, usually B-cell origin, T-cell origin is rare
Acute myelocytic leukemia (AML)	Occurs in young adults, usually myelocyte (granulocyte) origin
Chronic myelocytic leukemia (CML)	Adult leukemia of granulocytes due to translocation (Philadelphia chromosome)
Acute monocytic leukemia	Less common adult leukemia of monocyte origin
Chronic monocytic leukemia	Rare adult leukemia of monocyte origin

Source: Data from Vardiman, J. W., Thiele, J., Arber, D. A., Brunning, R. D., Borowitz, M. J., Porwit, A., . . . Bloomfield, C. D. (2009). The 2008 revision of the World Health Organization (WHO) classification of myeloid neoplasms and acute leukemia. *Blood, 114*(5), 937–951.

formation of red blood cells, and thrombopoietin stimulates the formation of blood platelets.

In children, hematopoiesis occurs in the marrow of the long bones such as the femur and tibia. In adults, it occurs mainly in the pelvis, cranium, vertebrae, and sternum. Differentiation and maturation of progenitor cells begin in the bone marrow and continue throughout the life cycle of immune cells. Cells of the immune system enter the blood and lymphatic systems through an extensive plexus of fenestrated capillaries that anastomose with the bone marrow. Lymphocytes differentiate into T lymphocytes in the thymus whereas the final maturation of B lymphocytes occurs in the lymph nodes.

PATHOGENESIS OF LEUKEMIA

Leukemia refers to immature immune cells in the bone marrow that are undergoing uncontrolled proliferation. Without treatment, the expanding clone of leukemic cells replaces other cell populations in the bone marrow, blood, and lymph. Cytogenetic/genetic analyses of leukemia tissues often reveal the presence of reciprocal chromosomal translocations, chromosomal deletions, and/or DNA point mutations. Reciprocal exchanges of DNA between chromosomes can form hybrid genes that encode chimeric fusion proteins that deregulate critical cellular processes such as mitosis, apoptosis, and angiogenesis. Chromosomal deletions can silence tumor suppressor genes that regulate these same processes. Point mutations may also be involved as well as epigenetic modifications in the expression of proto-oncogenes or tumor suppressor genes. Such genetic errors can be acquired at any time during the lifespan, and some undoubtedly occur during early growth and development, perhaps even in utero during embryogenesis. Inherited genetic defects are uncommon. Various models have been proposed suggesting that two or more DNA errors are required to form a leukemic clone of cells. Endogenous hormones may also play

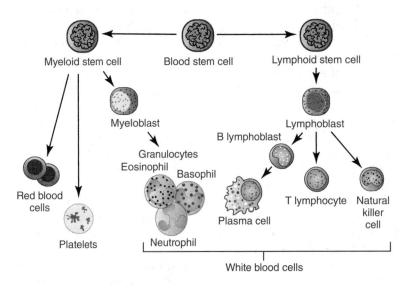

Figure 27.1 Hematopoiesis.

a role in leukemogenesis, particularly cortisol, which culls populations of immature immune cells by inducing apoptosis (Vardiman et al., 2009).

GLOBAL EPIDEMIOLOGY OF LEUKEMIA

Figure 27.2 shows the global patterns of leukemia incidence and mortality based on data collected by

the World Health Organization (WHO) in 2012 (Ferlay et al., 2013). Incidence rates are relatively high (exceeding 6.5 per 100,000) in developed areas such as the United States, Western Europe, Scandinavia, and Australia/New Zealand compared to developing nations such as India and those in sub-Saharan Africa where the rates are lower, ranging from 2 to 3 per 100,000. Underreporting may partially account for such differences,

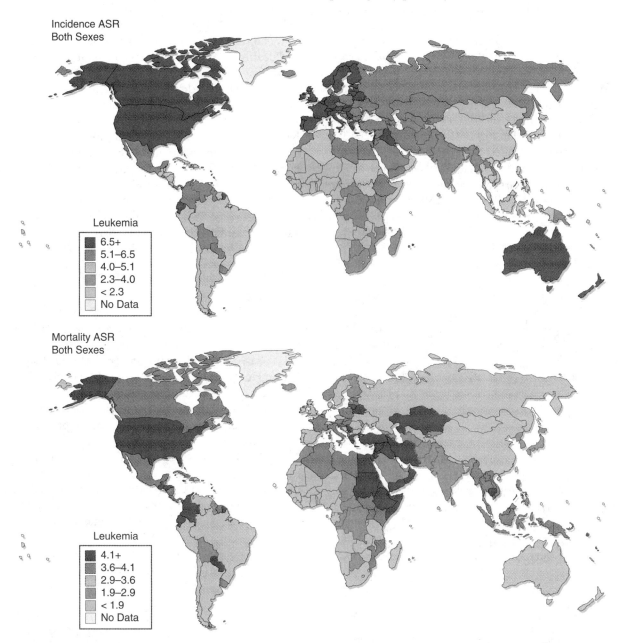

Figure 27.2 Global Incidence and Mortality Rates of Leukemia, 2012.

ASR: Rates per 100,000 are age-standardized to the world population, 2000–2025.

Source: Reproduced from Ferlay, J., Soerjomataram, I., Ervik, M., Dikshit, R., Eser, S., Mathers, C., . . . Bray, F. (2013). *GLOBOCAN 2012 v1.0. Cancer incidence and mortality worldwide: IARC CancerBase No. 11* [Internet]. Lyon, France: International Agency for Research on Cancer. Retrieved from http://globocan.iarc.fr

particularly in nations without population-based cancer registries.

In contrast to the global pattern of incidence, the highest annual mortality rates were found in Iraq and Afghanistan, whose populations have been ravaged by war and strife in recent years. High rates are also evident in Turkey and Saudi Arabia. In those populations where mortality is exceptionally high, the available healthcare resources are generally inadequate for effective treatment. Nevertheless, relatively high death rates from leukemia are also evident in the populations of many developed nations, including the United States. According to the latest WHO/International Agency for Research on Cancer (IARC) data from 2008 and 2012, leukemias in children and adults cause more than 350,000 deaths every year, approximately 3.3% of all cancer deaths (Ferlay, Shin, Forman, Mathers, & Parkin, 2010; Ferlay et al., 2013).

The global numbers of leukemia cases and deaths steadily increased during 1990–2012 (**Figure 27.3**). Over the entire time span, the annual number of new cases increased by 40% (from 250,000 in 1990 to 352,000 in 2012) and the annual number of deaths increased by 44% (from 184,000 in 1990 to 265,000 in 2012). However, the global annual *age-adjusted* mortality rates have been relatively stable during this time period, averaging approximately 4.2 per 100,000 in men and 2.8 per 100,000 in women. Likewise, the global annual age-adjusted incidence rates have also stabilized at approximately 5.6 per 100,000 in men and 3.9 per 100,000 in women (Ferlay et al., 2010, 2013; Parkin, Bray, Ferlay, & Pisani, 2005; Parkin, Pisani, & Ferlay, 1999a,1999b).

The rising absolute number of leukemia cases and deaths without substantial concomitant changes in the age-adjusted rates is largely due to increasing longevity of the world population. This phenomenon has resulted in more individuals living to later ages when the risk of death from leukemia is highest. **Figure 27.4** shows the age distribution of new cases and deaths based on data from the United States collected during 2003–2007 (43,050 cases and 21,840 deaths). Leukemia onset shows an early peak during childhood and then rises throughout the lifespan, with more than 70% of deaths occurring after the age of 65 years (Altekruse et al., 2010).

TRENDS IN LEUKEMIA INCIDENCE AND SURVIVAL

A team of Italian investigators examined trends in the age-standardized annual mortality rates for leukemia based on death certificate data collected by the World Health Organization during 1960–1997. Data were available for the European Union (consisting of 27 member nations) and other developed regions of the world. In the European Union, the peak rates for children up to 14 years of age were observed in 1960–1964, after which mortality decreased more than 70%, reaching a nadir of 1.2 per 100,000 in males and 0.9 per 100,000 in females in 1995–1997. Substantial decreases in mortality were also noted for young and middle-aged adults, ages 15–44 years (40%) and 45–59 years (25%), but not for older age groups. The observed decline in leukemia mortality over the 35-year calendar period corresponds to nearly 250,000 saved lives. Leukemia mortality rates in the United States and Japan started from different values, but trends were similar to those of the European Union in the late 1990s, indicating that the impact of therapeutic advancements has been comparable in developed areas of the world. In Eastern Europe, however, the declines in leukemia mortality occurred later and were appreciably smaller (Levi, Lucchini, Negri, Barbui, & La Vecchia, 2000).

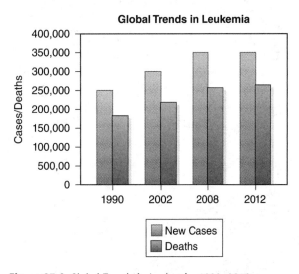

Figure 27.3 Global Trends in Leukemia, 1990–2012.

Source: Data from Ferlay, J., Shin, H. R., Forman, D., Mathers, C., & Parkin, D. M. (2010). Estimates of worldwide burden of cancer in 2008. *International Journal of Cancer, 127*(12), 2893–2917; Ferlay, J., Soerjomataram, I., Ervik, M., Dikshit, R., Eser, S., Mathers, C.,... Bray, F. (2013). *GLOBOCAN 2012 v1.0. Cancer incidence and mortality worldwide: IARC CancerBase No. 11* [Internet]. Lyon, France: International Agency for Research on Cancer. Retrieved from http://globocan.iarc.fr; Parkin, D. M., Bray, F., Ferlay, J., & Pisani, P. (2001). Estimating the world cancer burden, GLOBOCAN 2000. *International Journal of Cancer, 94*, 153–156; Parkin, D. M., Bray, F., Ferlay, J., & Pisani, P. (2005). Global cancer statistics, 2002. *CA: A Cancer Journal for Clinicians, 55*, 74–108; Parkin, D. M., Pisani, P., & Ferlay, J. (1999a). Estimates of the worldwide incidence of 25 major cancers in 1990. *International Journal of Cancer, 80*(6), 827–841; Parkin, D. M., Pisani, P., & Ferlay, J. (1999b). Global cancer statistics. *CA: A Cancer Journal for Clinicians, 49*(1), 33–64; World Health Organization. (2008). World cancer report. Geneva, Switzerland: Author.

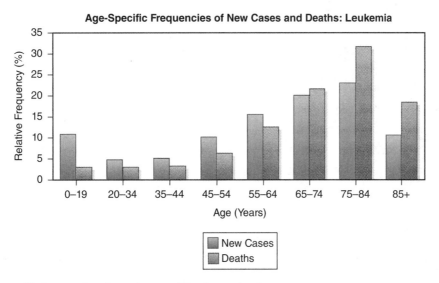

Figure 27.4 Age-Specific Frequencies of New Cases and Deaths: Leukemia.

Source: Data from Altekruse, S. F., Kosary, C. L., Krapcho, M., Neyman, N., Aminou, R., Waldron, W., ... Edwards, B. K. (2010). *SEER cancer statistics review, 1975–2007*. Bethesda, MD: National Cancer Institute.

Investigators at the University of Minnesota examined time trends in the annual age-specific incidence rates of different types of leukemia in the U.S. population during 1973–1998. Their analysis was based on 66,404 leukemia cases identified by the Surveillance, Epidemiology, and End Results (SEER) program of the U.S. National Cancer Institute. In analyses by subtype of leukemia, significant increases were observed for acute lymphocytic leukemia in all age groups except individuals over 65 years of age. Among children and adolescents under 20 years of age, the annual incidence rate of acute lymphocytic leukemia increased by 1.1% per year. Notably, 5-year survival improved by about 15% in younger age groups, presumably as a consequence of improved regimens of chemotherapy; however, there was little improvement in survival for older individuals, and survival actually worsened for elderly African Americans (Xie, Davies, Xiang, Robison, & Ross, 2003).

PEDIATRIC LEUKEMIA: TRENDS IN INCIDENCE AND MORTALITY

Approximately 11% of all cases of leukemia are diagnosed in children and adolescents under the age of 20 years. The profile of pediatric leukemia is distinctly different from that in adults. *Acute lymphocytic leukemia* accounts for approximately 75% of cases among children and adolescents younger than 15 years of age, and more than 80% of cases for children younger than 10 years of age. In contrast, the relative frequency of acute lymphocytic leukemia declines dramatically with age, and other types account for 75% of leukemias diagnosed after the age of 50 years.

Figure 27.5 shows the age-specific annual incidence of childhood leukemia in U.S. children and adolescents up to 19 years of age. There is a sharp peak for ages 2–3 years (96 cases per million), after which the incidence declines. The incidence of the predominant subtype in children, acute lymphocytic leukemia, also peaks in 2-year-olds, at 83 per million (Smith, Gloeckler-Ries, Gurney, & Ross, 1999).

In developed nations, the annual death rate from leukemia in children has fallen by more than 50% in the past 3 decades. This favorable downward trend in mortality has occurred even though the incidence of childhood leukemia has *increased* more than 30% over the same time period (Smith et al., 2010). For example, during 1975–1995, the incidence among U.S. children under age 15 years increased steadily by about 0.9% per year as the mortality rate fell by 2.4% per year (Ries, 1999; Ries et al., 1998; Smith et al., 1999). Similar trends have been noted in Europe; for example, during 1970–1999, the incidence of childhood leukemia increased by an average of 1.4% per year whereas the overall mortality rate declined by nearly 60% (Shah & Coleman, 2007). Declines in mortality have been noted for boys and girls of all ages. Trends in the incidence rates for U.S. children under 15 years of age are shown for the period 1975–2010 in **Figure 27.6**.

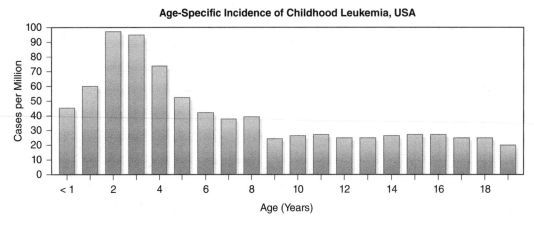

Figure 27.5 Age-Specific Incidence of Childhood Leukemia, United States.

Source: Data from Smith, M. A., Gloeckler-Ries, L. A., Gurney, J. G., & Ross, J. A. (1999). Leukemia. In L. A. G. Ries, M. A. Smith, J. G. Gurney, M. Linet, T. Tamra, J. L. Young, & G. R. Bunin (Eds.), *Cancer incidence and survival among children and adolescents: United States SEER program 1975–1995* (pp. 17–34, NIH Pub. No. 99–4649). Bethesda, MD: National Cancer Institute, SEER Program.

The falling leukemia mortality in children of developed nations reflects a marked increase in survival due to rapid detection coupled with improved therapy. In the United States, the 5-year survival rate for children who developed acute lymphocytic leukemia increased from 61% in 1975–1978 to 89% in 1999–2002 (**Figure 27.7**). As stated by Malcolm Smith and colleagues at the U.S. National Cancer Institute, "the improvement in survival for children with acute lymphocytic leukemia over the past 35 years is one of the great success stories of clinical oncology" and reflects the therapeutic benefit of combination chemotherapy, radiation therapy, and bone marrow transplantation (Smith et al., 2010).

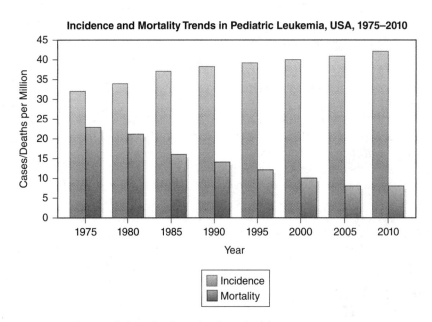

Figure 27.6 Incidence and Mortality Trends in Pediatric Leukemia, United States, 1975–2010.

Source: Data from Ries, L. A. G., Kosary, C. L., Hankey, B. F., Miller, B. A., Clegg, L., & Edwards, B. K. (Eds.). (1998). *SEER cancer statistics review 1973–1996.* Bethesda, MD: National Cancer Institute; Ries, L. A. G. (1999). Childhood cancer mortality. In L. A. G. Ries, M. A. Smith, J. G. Gurney, M. Linet, T. Tamra, J. L. Young, & G. R. Bunin (Eds.), *Cancer incidence and survival among children and adolescents: United States SEER program 1975–1995* (pp. 165–170; NIH Pub. No. 99–4649). Bethesda, MD: National Cancer Institute, SEER Program; Smith, M. A., Gloeckler-Ries, L. A., Gurney, J. G., & Ross, J. A. (1999). Leukemia. In L. A. G. Ries, M. A. Smith, J. G. Gurney, M. Linet, T. Tamra, J. L. Young, & G. R. Bunin (Eds.), *Cancer incidence and survival among children and adolescents: United States SEER program 1975–1995* (pp. 17–34; NIH Pub. No. 99–4649). Bethesda, MD: National Cancer Institute, SEER Program; Smith, M. A., Seibel, N. L., Seibel, N. L., Altekruse, S. F., Ries, L. A. G., Melbert, D. L., . . . Reaman, G. H. (2010). Outcomes for children and adolescents with cancer: Challenges for the twenty-first century. *Journal of Clinical Oncology, 28*(15), 2625–2634.

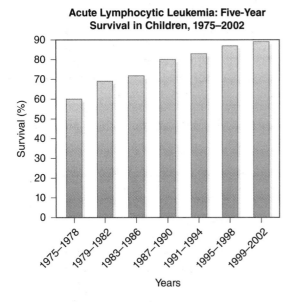

Acute Lymphocytic Leukemia: Five-Year Survival in Children, 1975–2002

Figure 27.7 Acute Lymphocytic Leukemia: Five-Year Survival in Children, 1975-2002.

Source: Data from Smith, M. A., Seibel, N. L., Seibel, N. L., Altekruse, S. F., Ries, L. A. G., Melbert, D. L.,... Reaman, G. H. (2010). Outcomes for children and adolescents with cancer: Challenges for the twenty-first century. *Journal of Clinical Oncology, 28*(15), 2625–2634.

Despite the obvious benefit of early detection and effective therapy in some parts of the world, survival remains poor for children who develop leukemia in less-developed nations. For example, the 5-year survival rate for children stricken with leukemia who live in the Philippines is only 33% compared to nearly 90% for afflicted children of the same ethnicity in the United States. Such differences highlight the deficiencies in pediatric cancer care and the need for major improvements in diagnostic and treatment facilities in developing countries (Redaniel et al., 2010).

Pediatric Leukemia: Risk Factors

Leukemia is the most common cancer in children and has been intensively investigated using molecular, genetic, clinical, and epidemiologic techniques. Nevertheless, with the exception of ionizing radiation, rare genetic syndromes, and certain chemotherapeutic drugs that are implicated in a small fraction of cases, causal factors for most cases are obscure and the etiology remains enigmatic.

Gender and Ethnic Differences of Childhood Leukemia

Marked gender and ethnic differences have been noted in the incidence rates of pediatric acute lymphocytic leukemia. For children under 15 years of age, boys have about 1.2 times higher risk than girls, and Caucasians have about 2 times higher risk than African Americans. Such differences are not spurious, because they have persisted for several decades (Harris, Harrell, Patil, & Al-Rashid, 1987; Smith et al., 1999).

Reasons for these gender and ethnic differences are speculative. The recently proposed *adrenal hypothesis* relates the higher leukemia risk in children of higher socioeconomic classes to their relatively low exposure to infectious viruses and bacteria during the early years of life. Presumably, the risk of acute lymphocytic leukemia is *reduced* when childhood infections during infancy induce the hypothalamic-pituitary-adrenal axis to secrete high levels of plasma cortisol. Corticosteroids are known to regulate the maturation and proliferation of B lymphocytes by stimulating apoptosis, and high levels may eliminate leukemic cells and/or progenitor B lymphocytes with leukemogenic potential. Furthermore, early infection and heightened cortisol secretion may favor the maturation and proliferation of T lymphocytes that secrete *anti-inflammatory* rather than *proinflammatory* cytokines, thereby reducing the risk of leukemogenesis (Schmiegelow, Vestergaard, Nielsen, & Hjalgrim, 2008).

Familial Associations of Childhood Leukemia

Some studies have noted an association between childhood leukemia and the presence of autoimmune conditions among relatives. A team of investigators in Paris designed a case control study to assess the relationship between childhood leukemia and a family history of autoimmune conditions such as type 1 diabetes mellitus, thyroid disease, and rheumatoid arthritis. Family histories of autoimmune disease in first- and second-degree relatives were ascertained for 279 incident cases of acute leukemia and 285 controls matched by age, gender, and ethnicity. The study revealed a significant association between familial autoimmune disease and the risk of leukemia (odds ratio [OR] = 1.7). The relationship was stronger for autoimmune thyroid conditions such as Grave's disease or Hashimoto's thyroiditis (OR = 3.5) but diminished for other types of thyroid diseases (goiter or adenoma). These results suggest that a family history of autoimmune thyroid disease may be associated with childhood acute leukemia (Perillat-Menegaux et al., 2003).

Investigators at the University of Montreal in Quebec explored genetic polymorphisms of the P-450 enzyme system to determine potential associations of xenobiotic-metabolizing enzymes and the risk of developing childhood leukemia. They compared polymorphisms among 177 children with acute lymphocytic leukemia to 304 controls matched by age and gender. The results revealed increased odds ratios for individuals carrying the null polymorphism of the glutathione-S transferase gene (*GSTM-1*) (OR = 1.8) or the *CYP-1A1-2A* allele (OR = 1.7). Furthermore, the odds of disease were higher for individuals carrying both genotypes (OR = 3.3). The investigators suggest that these findings have biological plausibility in that the *CYP-1A1-2A* enzyme activates polycyclic aromatic compounds that are not metabolized for excretion by individuals with the null *GSTM-1* genotype (Krajinovic, Labuda, Richer, Karimi, & Sinnett, 1999).

Genetic Syndromes and Childhood Leukemia

The risk of developing acute lymphocytic leukemia is increased in subjects with certain rare genetic syndromes and conditions. These include Down syndrome, Bloom syndrome, Shwachman syndrome, ataxia telangiectasia, neurofibromatosis, and Fanconi anemia.

Down syndrome (trisomy 21) markedly increases the risk of developing acute leukemia. The syndrome is named after the British physician John Langdon Down, who first described it in 1866 (Down, 1866). The genetic anomaly identified as an extra 21st chromosome was discovered by the French pediatrician/cytogeneticist Jérôme Lejeune in 1959 (Lejeune, 1959).

Down syndrome is a chromosomal condition caused by the presence of an extra copy of genetic material on the 21st chromosome, either in whole (trisomy 21) or in part (when due to translocations). In addition to its characteristic phenotypic, mental, and cognitive features, Down syndrome carries a high risk for development of leukemia. In particular, the risk of acute lymphoblastic leukemia is elevated at least 10-fold and the risk of acute myelogenous leukemia is increased at least 50-fold in patients with Down syndrome, perhaps due to overexpression of proto-oncogenes on the extra 21st chromosome (Hasle, Clemmensen, & Mikkelsen, 2000).

Bloom syndrome (congenital telangiectatic erythema) is a rare autosomal recessive disorder characterized by telangiectasia (clusters of small cutaneous dilated blood vessels or spider veins), photosensitivity, growth deficiency of prenatal onset, variable degrees of immunodeficiency, and increased susceptibility to various forms of cancer, including leukemia. The New York dermatologist David Bloom first described the syndrome in 1954 (Bloom, 1954). Approximately 20% of patients with Bloom syndrome develop specific malignancies (acute leukemia, lymphoma, and/or gastrointestinal adenocarcinoma). Cancer risk in such patients is increased 150–300 times compared to the general population (German, 1993).

Bloom syndrome is caused by a mutation of a tumor suppressor gene designated *BLM* (short for Bloom) traced to the long arm of chromosome 15. The protein encoded by the normal gene has DNA helicase activity and functions in the maintenance of genomic stability. Mutant forms of *BLM* increase the exchange of DNA during mitosis (sister chromatid exchange) and chromosomal instability, which are presumably responsible for the characteristic phenotypic abnormalities and cancer predisposition (Cheok et al., 2005).

Shwachman–Bodian–Diamond syndrome is a rare autosomal recessive disorder caused by a mutated gene, *SBDS*, on the long arm of chromosome 7. The *SBDS* gene appears to help regulate RNA metabolism and ribosomal assembly of proteins in the cell. Individuals homozygous for the mutant *SBDS* gene typically manifest exocrine pancreatic dysfunction, skeletal anomalies, anemia, neutropenia, and progressive bone marrow failure that may transform to acute myelogenous leukemia (Bodian, Sheldon, & Lightwood, 1964; Popovic et al., 2002; Shwachman, Diamond, Oski, & Khaw, 1964).

Ataxia telangiectasia is a rare autosomal recessive disorder caused by a mutant gene (*ATM*) located on the long arm of chromosome 11 that is critical for regulating checkpoints during cell division and for repairing errors in DNA replication. This condition is characterized by lack of coordination and cognitive control, immune deficiency, and telangiectasia (clusters of small dilated blood vessels), particularly in the sclera of the eye. Patients who are homozygous recessive for the *ATM* mutation have an approximate risk of 1% per year of developing either leukemia or lymphoma (Canman & Lim, 1998).

Neurofibromatosis type 1 (von Recklinghausen's disease) is a rare autosomal dominant disorder characterized by the development of multiple fibromas (neurofibromas) of the skin, brain, and other anatomic sites. The rare disorder was first described by the German physician Friedrich von Recklinghausen in 1882. The syndrome is due to a mutant autosomal dominant gene called *NF1* located on the long arm of chromosome 17. The mutant gene encodes a protein called neurofibromin that regulates cell division of fibrous nerve sheaths (Boyd, Korf, & Theos, 2009).

In addition to causing neurofibromas, mutant forms of *NF1* also increase the risk of developing leukemia and lymphoma. Stiller and colleagues at Oxford quantified the risk among 58 subjects with neurofibromatosis type 1 based on data ascertained from the National Registry of Childhood Tumors in Great Britain. Over the 17-year study period, 12 cases of acute lymphocytic leukemia (relative risk [RR] = 5.4), 5 cases of non-Hodgkin's lymphoma (RR = 10.0), and 5 cases of myelomonocytic leukemia (RR = 221) were detected among the 58 patients with neurofibromatosis type 1 (Stiller, Chessells, & Fitchett, 1994). These results suggest that the *NF1* gene has pleiotropic impact on the regulation of hematopoiesis.

Fanconi anemia is a rare autosomal recessive genetic disorder named after the Swiss pediatrician Guido Fanconi, who initially described it (Fanconi, 1927). Fanconi anemia is caused by mutations in any of 13 different genes that encode proteins involved in the regulation of DNA repair during replication. One of these genes is the well-known breast cancer susceptibility gene, *BRCA-2*. Up to 75% of patients have congenital defects, commonly short stature, and developmental disabilities and abnormalities at various anatomic sites. Approximately 20% of patients develop some form of cancer, the most common of which is *acute myelocytic leukemia*, and 90% suffer myelodysplasia with bone marrow failure by the age of 40 years. The median age at death for patients with Fanconi anemia is about 40 years (D'Andrea, 2010).

Drugs and Childhood Leukemia

Certain chemotherapeutic agents have been found to heighten the risk of leukemia development in children and adults. For example, the compound *epipodophyllotoxin* (etoposide and teniposide) has been linked to the development of acute myeloid leukemia. This compound interferes with the function of topoisomerases, enzymes that unwind and wind DNA for transcription and replication. Investigators at St. Jude Children's Research Hospital in Memphis, Tennessee, examined the effects of epipodophyllotoxin therapy among 734 consecutive children with acute lymphoblastic leukemia who attained completed remission and received continuation (maintenance) treatment according to specific schedules of epipodophyllotoxin administration. After 6 years of follow-up, secondary acute myelocytic leukemia was diagnosed in 21 of the 734 patients, yielding a cumulative risk of 3.8%. Within subgroups receiving higher dosages of epipodophyllotoxin, the cumulative risk increased to more than 12%. In comparative groups not treated with epipodophyllotoxin, the highest cumulative risk was 1.6%. The results indicate that maintenance therapy with epipodophyllotoxin stimulates leukemogenesis of myelocytic cells (Pui et al., 1991).

Radiation and Childhood Leukemia

The Life Span Study was initiated in 1950 to monitor the impact of radiation exposure among survivors of the atomic bomb explosions in Japan during World War II. As of the year 2000, 204 leukemia deaths had occurred among 49,204 survivors who received a bone marrow radiation dose of at least 0.005 Gy, constituting an excess of 94 cases (46%) attributable to radiation from the atomic bomb explosions. The dose response pattern in excess number of observed deaths reflects a nonlinear pattern; however, even at low doses in the range of 0.2 to 0.5 Gy, the leukemia risk is elevated (**Figure 27.8**). Risk increases have been noted for acute lymphocytic leukemia in children and acute and chronic myelocytic leukemia in adults, but not other types (Preston et al., 1994, 2004).

A recent population-based study found a marked increase in the rates of leukemia among children in Southern Iraq during the period 1993–2007. Investigators from the University of Basrah in Iraq and the University of Washington in Seattle analyzed leukemia registry data collected at Ibn Ghazwan Hospital in Basrah to evaluate leukemia trends since 1993. Annual leukemia incidence rates were estimated from 698 cases diagnosed in children age 14 years or younger. The annual incidence (cases per 100,000) increased dramatically during the period of study, from 2.6 in 1993 to 6.9 in 2007, peaking at 12.2 in 2006. Estimates for the final 3 years of the study are more than double the rates in the European Union or the United States (Hagopian et al., 2010).

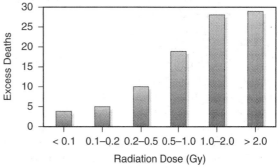

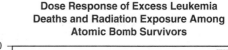

Figure 27.8 Dose Response of Excess Leukemia Deaths and Radiation Exposure Among Atomic Bomb Survivors.

Source: Data from Smith, M. A., Seibel, N. L., Seibel, N. L., Altekruse, S. F., Ries, L. A. G., Melbert, D. L., ... Reaman, G. H. (2010). Outcomes for children and adolescents with cancer: Challenges for the twenty-first century. *Journal of Clinical Oncology,* *28*(15), 2625–2634.

These results have led to speculation that heightened exposure to chemical warfare agents since 2003, in particular benzene and depleted uranium dust, may be responsible for the increased incidence of childhood leukemia, although additional investigations will be needed to definitively establish an etiologic link (Greiser & Hoffman, 2010).

Seasonal Onset of Acute Lymphocytic Leukemia

Acute lymphocytic leukemia is characterized by quick onset with rapid transition from good health to life-threatening disease, particularly in children. Typically, a newfound bleeding diathesis leads to the diagnosis by discovery of lymphoblasts in the peripheral blood and bone marrow. Due to its acute nature, onset of this form of leukemia has been examined for seasonal periodicity by a number of investigators, in the hope of elucidating etiologic factors.

Investigators at the University of Nebraska examined month-of-onset of successive cases of acute lymphocytic leukemia diagnosed during 1971–1980 in the Midwestern United States. They detected significant peaks in early winter and late summer coinciding with peak rates of influenza and hay fever from ragweed pollen, respectively (Harris & Al-Rashid, 1984). Subsequently, these same investigators examined all cases of acute lymphocytic leukemia reported in the U.S. SEER database during 1973–1980 and found that in eight of nine SEER locations, the pattern of onset fit a trimodal pattern with peaks in winter, spring, and summer, coinciding with seasonal elevations in the rates of allergenic and infectious diseases that are capable of promoting lymphocytic proliferation and transformation (Harris et al., 1987).

Investigators in the United Kingdom found a 40% excess of acute lymphocytic leukemia cases diagnosed in summer months compared to winter months based on analysis of data from the East Anglian Cancer Registry collected during 1971–1994. Seasonal patterns were not evident for other forms of leukemia. The authors suggest the data are most compatible with an infectious etiology of acute lymphocytic leukemia (Badrinath, Day, & Stockton, 1997).

Despite these results, many other investigators have *not* found evidence of seasonality in the onset of acute lymphocytic leukemia. In an attempt to resolve the question, Gao and colleagues conducted an extensive analysis of reported data on 27,000 cases from 11 countries over a wide range of latitudes. Although there was evidence of seasonal peaks and valleys in certain populations, no consistent pattern of seasonality emerged by latitude, and the investigators concluded that seasonal influences are not likely

to be of major etiologic importance (Gao, Chia, & Machin, 2007).

Cytogenetics of Pediatric Leukemia

Cytogenetic abnormalities are characteristic of pediatric acute lymphocytic leukemia. Karyotypic studies of the chromosomes reveal translocations, inversions, or deletions of chromosomes in the lymphoblasts of approximately 90% of cases. Approximately 40% of karyotypes are pseudodiploid (46 chromosomes with structural or numeric abnormalities), 35–45% are hyperdiploid (47 or more chromosomes), less than 10% are hypodiploid (fewer than 46 chromosomes), and 10–15% are diploid (46 chromosomes without detectable abnormalities) (Pui, Relling, & Downing, 2004).

Reciprocal translocations are the most common structural chromosomal aberrations found in acute lymphocytic leukemia. The first translocation discovered in pediatric acute lymphocytic leukemia was t(9;22), a reciprocal translocation involving juxtaposition of the *BCR* gene on chromosome 9 to the promoter region of the *ABL* gene on chromosome 22. The altered chromosome 22 produced by this translocation is called the *Philadelphia chromosome* because it was discovered by investigators at the University of Pennsylvania and the Fox-Chase Cancer Research Institute in Philadelphia (Nowell & Hungerford, 1960). The resulting hybrid gene, *BCR-ABL*, encodes a chimeric fusion protein that stimulates the intracellular *RAS* signal transduction pathway, leading to uncontrolled proliferation of lymphocytes and myelocytes. The Philadelphia chromosome, which is found in about 5% of pediatric acute lymphocytic leukemia cases, is the defining genetic signature of chronic myelocytic (granulocytic) leukemia in adults (Kurzrock, Kantarjian, Druker, & Talpaz, 2003).

An exciting development in leukemia research was the discovery of the *TEL-AML1* fusion gene created by the t(12;21) translocation, which is found in approximately 25% of cases of acute lymphocytic leukemia. The *TEL* gene appears to repress transcription of the *AML1* gene, thereby inhibiting normal differentiation of B lymphocytes (Golub et al., 1995). In addition to somatic rearrangements of the *TEL* gene, germline *TEL* mutations have also been discovered in pediatric acute lymphocytic leukemia that are associated with a relatively poor prognosis (Rubnitz et al., 1997, 2008).

The t(1;19) translocation is detected in 15–25% of pediatric acute lymphocytic leukemia cases. This translocation fuses the *E2A* gene on chromosome 19 with the *PBX1* gene on chromosome 1, producing a hybrid gene that encodes a chimeric fusion protein,

E2A-PBX1, that serves as a transcription activator of several other genes (Pui et al., 1994).

The most common chromosomal deletion found in pediatric acute lymphocytic leukemia involves loss of a portion of the short arm of chromosome 9. Such deletions are found in about 11% of cases and are associated with poor survival (Heerema et al., 1999).

In 35–45% of young patients with acute lymphocytic leukemia, tumor cells manifest extrachromosomes (hyperdiploidy) without apparent structural abnormalities. Chromosome 21 is the most frequently detected "extra" chromosome (Down syndrome or trisomy 21). In addition, about 5% of patients manifest hypodiploidkaryotypes characterized by the loss of certain chromosomes. An important finding is that the chromosomal pattern detected in the karyotype of children with leukemia is often an accurate predictor of survival. For example, patients with normal or hyperdiploid karyotypes respond better to treatment and have longer survival than those with translocations, deletions, or hypodiploidy (Bloomfield et al., 1986).

Genome-wide association studies of single nucleotide polymorphisms and targeted genetic polymorphism studies have also identified germline (inherited) mutations associated with the development and progression of pediatric acute lymphocytic leukemia. These include point mutations in the *TEL* gene and the *ARID5B* gene, both of which regulate transcription in embryonic development and during cell growth and differentiation (Healy, Richer, Bourgey, Kritikou, & Sinnett, 2010; Rubnitz et al., 2008).

ADULT LEUKEMIA

The relative incidence of myelocytic leukemia compared to lymphocytic leukemia increases with age and is the prominent form of leukemia in adults. In adults over the age of 50 years, approximately 60% of leukemias arise from myelocytes and 40% from lymphocytes. Leukemias diagnosed in adults (20 years or older) account for nearly 90% of all cases.

The genesis of myelocytic leukemia is similar to that of lymphocytic leukemia. Progenitor (stem) cells in the bone marrow appear to become "frozen" at a particular stage of differentiation, giving rise to a proliferative clone of leukemic cells (myeloblasts). The expanding clone of leukemic cells interrupts normal hematopoiesis, leading to neutropenia, anemia, and thrombocytopenia. Epidemiologic features of the major subtypes of adult leukemias are discussed in the following sections.

Acute Myelocytic Leukemia

Acute myelocytic (myelogenous) leukemia accounts for about 25% of adult leukemias. Several subtypes of this form of leukemia have been defined based on cellular morphology, the degree of maturation, staining characteristics, and cytogenetic findings. Following an early peak during the first year of life, the incidence of acute myelocytic leukemia remains low until age 40 years, after which it increases exponentially with age. Most cases are diagnosed after age 60 years, and the median onset is about 65 years of age (**Figure 27.9**) (Gurney, Severson, Davis, & Robison, 1995).

Worldwide, acute myelocytic leukemia causes nearly 65,000 deaths per year, approximately 25% of all deaths attributable to leukemia. The incidence is highest in developed countries such as the United States, Australia, and nations in Western Europe. In the United States, nearly 12,000 men and women were diagnosed with acute myelocytic leukemia in 2006; the average age-adjusted annual incidence during 1975–2003 was 3.4 per 100,000. No significant time trends have been noted in the past few decades

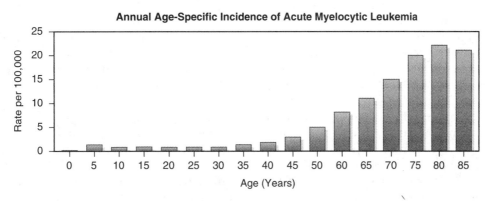

Figure 27.9 Age-Specific Incidence of Acute Myelocytic Leukemia.

Source: Data from Deschler, B., & Lübbert, M. (2006). Acute myeloid leukemia: Epidemiology and etiology. *Cancer, 107,* 2099–2107.

(American Cancer Society, 2005; Ries et al., 2003). The higher rates in developed countries partially reflect greater longevity because the elderly are at greatest risk (Figure 27.9).

Acute myelocytic leukemia shows a clear male predominance. For example, the 2006 age-adjusted rate in U.S. men (4.6 per 100,000) was about 50% higher than in women (3.0 per 100,000). The annual mortality rate was also higher in men (3.5 per 100,000) than in women (2.2 per 100,000). Survival dramatically declines with later onset of acute myelocytic leukemia. The 5-year survival rate for individuals diagnosed before age 50 years is 50% compared to only 5% for individuals diagnosed at 65 years or older (Altekruse et al., 2010).

Acute Myelocytic Leukemia: Risk Factors

Acute myelocytic leukemia is the most common type of all leukemias, yet the known risk factors account for only a small fraction of cases. One relatively common feature of this disease is the presence of cytogenetic abnormalities, which are found in up to 80% of cases. These include translocations, trisomic conditions, and other chromosomal deletions and aberrations.

The most common translocations found in acute myelocytic leukemia are t(8;21) and t(15;17). Both translocations create chimeric fusion proteins that promote leukemogenesis of immature myelocytes by deregulating nuclear binding factors and gene expression (Lavau & Dejean, 1994; McNeil et al., 1999). Significant advances have been made in the treatment of acute myelocytic leukemia with the introduction of new chemotherapeutic regimens that target specific cytogenetic markers of leukemia subtypes (Bloomfield et al., 1998).

In addition to chromosomal aberrations, some point mutations and epigenetic alterations have also been found in association with leukemia development. In England, Bowen and colleagues used polymerase chain reaction technology to examine allelic frequencies of genes encoding carcinogen-metabolizing enzymes of the P-450 enzyme system among 447 cases of acute myelocytic leukemia. They found that a variant form of the *CYP1A1* gene was associated with an increase in risk (OR = 2.36). The investigators suggest that the *CYP1A1-2B* allele may predispose to the development of certain subtypes of acute myelocytic leukemia by catalyzing the formation of carcinogenic polycyclic aromatic hydrocarbons or other reactive compounds (Bowen et al., 2003).

Epigenetic silencing of tumor suppressor genes and/or amplification of proto-oncogenes may also contribute to leukemogenesis. For example, hypermethylation of the *p15-INK4B* gene, a negative cell cycle regulator of myelocytes, has been identified in a significant fraction of cases (Christiansen, Andersen, & Pedersen-Bjergaard, 2003).

As with other forms of leukemia, the risk of developing acute myelocytic leukemia is increased by radiation exposure. The most notable example is among survivors of the atomic bomb explosions in Japan, who were found to have a fourfold increase in the risk with a peak 5–7 years after exposure (Preston et al., 1994). Excess rates of acute myelocytic leukemias have also been observed secondary to therapeutic radiation exposure (Kossman & Weiss, 2000).

Excess rates of acute myelocytic leukemia have been observed secondary to intensive chemotherapy for other forms of cancer. For example, alkylating agents such as cyclophosphamide and topoisomerase inhibitors such as epipodophyllotoxin have both been reported to significantly increase the risk (Le Beau et al., 1986a, 1986b; Pui et al., 1991). A team of Swedish investigators examined the rate of secondary leukemia in a cohort of 115 patients who received chemotherapy for other malignancies. In patients primarily treated with alkylating agents, the risk increased by approximately 1% per year over 8 years of follow-up, and in those receiving both alkylating agents and topoisomerase inhibitors, the risk increased more than 100-fold. These investigators point out that secondary development of acute myelocytic leukemia "has become the most serious long-term complication of cancer therapy" (Pedersen-Bjergaard et al., 1993).

Certain chemicals have also been implicated as risk factors for acute myelocytic leukemia, including benzene, embalming fluids (formalin), ethylene oxides, and herbicides (Deschler & Lübbert, 2006; Savitz & Andrews, 1997). Furthermore, chronic cigarette smoking has been found to increase the risk of certain subtypes of acute myelocytic leukemia (Pogoda, Preston-Martin, Nichols, & Ross, 2002).

Myelodysplastic Syndrome (Preleukemia)

It has long been recognized that individuals who develop acute myelocytic leukemia often manifest a prodromal period of anemia, myelocytic dysplasia, and abnormal erythropoiesis (red blood cell production). The first description of *preleukemia* was published in 1953 by Block and colleagues, who characterized the transformation of myelodysplasia to acute myelocytic leukemia among 12 patients (Block, Jacobson, & Bethard, 1953). In 1976, a French-American-British team of physicians and researchers defined refractory anemia in combination with myelocytic dysplasia as the *myelodysplastic syndrome*.

It is now recognized that themyelodysplastic syndrome actually consists of a diverse collection of hematological conditions characterized by various degrees of anemia, dysplasia of myeloid cells, neutropenia, and other symptoms. *Myeloid dysplasia* refers to abnormal differentiation and maturation of myeloid progenitor (stem) cells, resulting in alterations in their size, shape, organization, and function. Often, myeloid dysplasia is accompanied by excessive proliferation (hyperplasia) of deranged myelocytes.

Myeloid dysplasia is invariably associated with anemia due to ineffectual erythropoiesis and the lack of production of functional red blood cells. Over time, the disease worsens and patients develop refractory anemia, neutropenia, and thrombocytopenia. In about 30% of cases, the condition eventually transforms into acute myelocytic leukemia.

In recent years, cytogenetic, morphological, and clinical data have been reassessed to create more accurate prognostic categories of the myelodysplastic syndrome. In general, patients are classified according to the type and severity of cytopenia, the fraction of myeloblasts in the bone marrow, the appearance of multiple cytogenetic aberrations, and the likelihood of developing acute myelocytic leukemia within 1 year. In the most severe form, patients have refractory anemia and pancytopenia, 21–30% of cells in the bone marrow are myeloblasts, and the chance of transformation to acute myelocytic leukemia is very high, about 40% per year (Greenberg et al., 1997).

The incidence and prevalence rates of myelodysplastic disease have not been accurately quantified in most populations. This paucity of epidemiologic data reflects the absence of population-based screening and early detection programs, plus inconsistencies in the diagnosis and classification of disease. Nevertheless, small regional studies have provided some initial estimates and suggest that the incidence is increasing, particularly among the elderly. In a study conducted in the population of Düsseldorf in Germany during 1986–1990, the annual incidence for all ages was 3.9 per 100,000 in men and 4.3 per 100,000 in women. The peak rates occurred after 70 years of age, 33.9 per 100,000 in men and 18.0 per 100,000 in women. Among 1,759 cases, 82% were diagnosed after age 50 years, and the median age of onset was 71 years. Studies in other centers found similar patterns of onset as well as increasing numbers of cases, largely reflecting improvements in geriatric disease detection and medical care (Aul, Giagounidis, & Germing, 2001).

Certain cytogenetic abnormalities are regularly found in myeloblasts of patients with the myelodysplastic syndrome. The most common abnormality is deletion of the long arm of chromosome 5 (also called 5q– syndrome), initially discovered in 1974 (Van den Berghe et al., 1974). More recent studies have identified genes encoding colony stimulating factors and receptors (*GM-CSF, CSF-1, FMS*) and interleukin genes (*IL-3, IL-4, IL-5*) that regulate hematopoiesis, which are lost in the 5q– syndrome (Bunn, 1986; Le Beau et al., 1986a, 1986b; van Leeuwen, Martinson, Webb, & Young, 1989). A number of cytogenetic findings have been linked to the prognosis of myelodysplastic disease and/or conversion to acute myelocytic leukemia. For example, cases with single abnormalities of the long arm of chromosome 1 experience poor survival, and those with trisomy 8 have a high risk of malignant transformation; in contrast, patients with deletions in the short arm of chromosome 12 show relatively good survival. Clinical studies of cases reveal that cytogenetic features, the proportion of bone marrow myeloblasts, and hemoglobin and blood platelet levels are the main prognostic factors of survival and transformation to acute leukemia (Solé et al., 2000)

The risk factors for myeloid dysplasia are synonymous with those for acute myelocytic leukemia: exposure to ionizing radiation, benzene-containing compounds, alkylating agents and topoisomerase inhibitors used in cancer therapy, and immunosuppressive drugs used in organ transplantation (Aul et al., 2001).

Chronic Myelocytic (Granulocytic) Leukemia

Chronic myelocytic (granulocytic) leukemia is defined by the presence of the Philadelphia chromosome, which is caused by a reciprocal translocation involving juxtaposition of the *BCR* gene on chromosome 9 to the promoter region of the *ABL* gene on chromosome 22, designated t(9;22). The resulting hybrid gene, *BCR-ABL*, encodes a chimeric fusion protein that stimulates the intracellular *RAS* signal transduction pathway, leading to uncontrolled proliferation of myelocytes and other immune cells (Kurzrock et al., 2003). The Philadelphia chromosome was introduced earlier in this chapter in the section on pediatric leukemia, because it was first discovered in cells of a pediatric leukemia patient by investigators in Philadelphia (Nowell & Hungerford, 1960).

Chronic myelocytic leukemia is characterized by increased proliferation of granulocytes of all types in the bone marrow. Basophils and eosinophils are virtually always increased. Presence of the Philadelphia chromosome identified by cytogenetic or genetic analysis of tumor cells validates the diagnosis (Savage, Szydlo, & Goldman, 1997). This form of leukemia may persist in a chronic phase for many years, but eventually terminates in a blast crisis with widespread metastatic spread of myeloblasts and lymphoblasts and short survival (Kantarjian et al., 1988).

Chronic myelocytic leukemia is most commonly diagnosed in middle-aged and older adults and accounts for approximately 15–20% of adult leukemias. The only definitive risk factor for this form of leukemia is ionizing radiation. Among survivors of the atomic bomb blasts in Japan who have been followed for more than half a century, the cumulative incidence of chronic myelocytic leukemia is about sevenfold higher than in the general population (Preston et al., 1994).

Radiotherapy has also been linked to the development of chronic myelocytic leukemia. Preston-Martin and colleagues conducted a case control study of radiation exposure in 136 cases diagnosed in Los Angeles hospitals during 1979–1985 and 136 neighborhood controls. Odds ratios (ORs) were estimated by the cumulative level of bone marrow exposure to radiotherapy. Results revealed a dose response in the risk with increasing radiation dose maximizing at OR = 2.4 for the highest cumulative dose (at least 2,000 mrads) (Preston-Martin, Thomas, Yu, & Henderson, 1989).

Chronic Lymphocytic Leukemia

Chronic lymphocytic leukemia is typified by excess proliferation of small but well-differentiated (mature) lymphocytes in the bone marrow and peripheral blood. In most cases, the vast majority (98%) of malignant lymphocytes are B cells. Leukemic cells are, on average, smaller but otherwise morphologically similar to normal lymphocytes. Furthermore, the cells from most patients have membrane receptors, antigens, and immunoglobulins that are characteristic of mature B lymphocytes. However, they are functionally deficient and incapable of mounting an immune response. Hence, patients with chronic lymphocytic leukemia are predisposed to a variety of infectious conditions.

Chronic lymphocytic leukemia is a disease of older adults, with nearly 90% of cases diagnosed after the age of 55 years. The condition often takes years to progress, and patients are usually monitored for clinical and hematologic changes before initiation of treatment. However, transformation of the chronic form to an acute blast crisis carries a high risk of death.

In the United States, approximately 15,000 new cases were diagnosed in 2010 and more than 4,000 deaths were attributed to chronic lymphocytic leukemia. Annual incidence rates per 100,000 were higher in men than women (5.7 versus 3.0) and were highest in Caucasians (6.1 in men and 3.2 in women) and lowest in Asian and Pacific Islanders (1.3 in men and 0.7 in women). Annual death rates were also highest in Caucasians (2.1 in men and 1.0 in women) and lowest in Asian and Pacific Islanders (0.4 in men and 0.1 in women). Five-year survival approaches 80% for Caucasians but is less than 70% for African Americans (Altekruse et al., 2010).

Certain ethnic groups have been found to have high incidence and prevalence rates of chronic lymphocytic leukemia. For example, relatively high rates have been reported for Ashkenazi Jews in Israel compared to other ethnic groups (Bartal, Bentwich, Manny, & Izak, 1978). The relative importance of genetic and environmental factors is currently being explored in comparative studies of different ethnic groups. However, in an investigation of 302 cases of B-cell chronic lymphocytic leukemia, ethnicity per se had no discernible effects on the biological and clinical behavior of the disease (Shvidel, Shtarlid, Klepfish, Sigler, & Berrebi, 1998).

Chronic Lymphocytic Leukemia: Risk Factors

Familial history is one of the strongest risk factors for the development of chronic lymphocytic leukemia. Studies of monozygous and dizygous twins, siblings, and pedigrees with multiple generations have established that close relatives of probands (index cases) are at high risk. For example, in a Swedish study of 14,336 first-degree relatives of 5,918 probands with chronic lymphocytic leukemia and 28,876 first-degree relatives of 11,778 control subjects, first-degree relatives of the probands were found to have a 7.5-fold increase in the risk of also developing chronic lymphocytic leukemia (Goldin, Pfeiffer, Li, & Hemminki, 2004). Genome-wide association studies and linkage studies are currently being conducted to elucidate the genes responsible for the increase in familial risk of chronic lymphocytic leukemia (Goldin & Caporaso, 2007).

Chromosomal abnormalities are well documented in chronic lymphocytic leukemia. The most common of these is an interstitial deletion of the long arm of chromosome 13, which has been found in approximately 50% of cases. Other common cytogenetic findings include specific deletions of the long arm of chromosome 11 (20%), trisomy 12 (15%), specific deletions of the long arm of chromosome 6 (10%), and specific deletions of the short arm of chromosome 17 (5%) (Stilgenbauer, Dohner, & Lichter, 1993). Such nonrandom chromosomal deletions and aberrations may confer selective advantage to B lymphocytes by inactivation of tumor suppressor genes, or conversely, by amplifying the expression of proto-oncogenes.

Point mutations and epigenetic changes that alter gene expression without changing the nucleotide sequence may also be involved in the genesis of chronic lymphocytic leukemia. For example, hypermethylation and epigenetic silencing of the death-associated protein kinase (*DAPK1*) gene, which regulates apoptosis, has been noted in a large kindred affected with chronic lymphocytic leukemia (Plass, Byrd, Raval, Tanner, & De La Chapelle, 2007).

Despite compelling evidence that ionizing radiation causes most forms of leukemia, including acute lymphocytic leukemia, most studies of chronic lymphocytic leukemia have not detected risk increases with radiation exposure. These results have led some expert committees to conclude that ionizing radiation is not a significant risk factor for chronic lymphocytic leukemia (United Nations Scientific Committee on the Effects of Atomic Radiation, 2000). However, it has also been pointed out that methodological difficulties such as lack of statistical power and limited duration of follow-up have hampered efforts to detect an association (Richardson, Wing, Schroeder, Schmitz-Feuerhake, & Hoffmann, 2005).

Data are limited on the association of specific chemical exposures and the development of chronic lymphocytic leukemia. Although some individual studies suggest risk increases associated with certain occupational exposures (e.g., agrichemicals, petroleum, rubber), there is little consistency of results from study to study (Linet et al., 2007).

Agent Orange has been linked to the genesis of several lymphoproliferative disorders, including chronic lymphocytic leukemia. The compound was widely used during the Vietnam War as a defoliant. It is a 50:50 mixture of two phenoxyl herbicides, 2,4-dichlorophenoxyacetic acid (2,4-D) and 2,4,5-trichlorophenoxyacetic acid (2,4,5-T). Agent Orange was manufactured by U.S. chemical companies and given its name because it was shipped to Vietnam in orange-striped 55-gallon barrels. The 2,4,5-T used to produce Agent Orange was later discovered to be contaminated with 2,3,7,8-tetrachloro-dibenzodioxin, an extremely toxic dioxin compound.

Investigators at the Ohio State University examined computerized patient treatment files collected by the Veteran's Administration (VA) hospital system to estimate incidence rates of various malignancies among the 3.7 million U.S. veterans treated in VA hospitals during 1970–1982. During this period, 31,835 hematopoietic and lymphatic cancers were diagnosed in the VA user sample. Compared to the general U.S. population, the VA sample showed risk increases in lymphocytic leukemia (RR = 1.54), granulocytic leukemia (RR = 1.23), and monocytic leukemia (RR = 1.51). Risk increases were also noted for Hodgkin's disease (RR = 1.93), non-Hodgkin's lymphoma (RR = 1.20), and multiple myeloma (RR = 1.51). Notably, the risk of developing either leukemia or lymphatic cancer was approximately 70% higher among Vietnam-era veterans than other veterans in the sample (Namboodiri & Harris, 1991).

In 2002, the U.S. Institute of Medicine issued an update in a series of consensus reports examining the impact of chemical defoliants, including Agent Orange, on human health. The combined evidence was found sufficient to support an association between exposure to herbicides sprayed during the Vietnam War and the risk of developing chronic lymphocytic leukemia in veterans who served in Vietnam. Other Institute of Medicine consensus reports document significant associations between herbicide exposure and the development of Hodgkin's lymphoma or non-Hodgkin's lymphoma in Vietnam War veterans (Institute of Medicine, 2003).

Chronic Lymphocytic Leukemia: Survival

A devastating event in patients with chronic lymphocytic leukemia is the abrupt conversion of a chronic, relatively indolent disease into an acute, decompensated, accelerated phase with a marked increase in lymphoblasts in both the bone marrow and the peripheral circulation. As with other forms of leukemia, the blast crisis of chronic leukemia is associated with short survival, often just a few weeks. As described in the next few paragraphs, certain genetic and cytogenetic markers have been found to predict accelerated progression of chronic lymphocytic leukemia and transition into a blast crisis.

Although it seems paradoxical, a *less favorable* clinical course of chronic lymphocytic leukemia is *inversely* correlated with the presence of somatic mutations in the gene that encodes the heavy-chain variable region of immunoglobulins. Patients with the nonmutated immunoglobulin gene have a more aggressive course and shorter survival than patients with mutated genes (Van Bockstaele, Verhasselt, & Philippe, 2009).

Molecular investigations have identified an important protein, ZAP-70, that also has prognostic significance in chronic lymphocytic leukemia. The ZAP-70 protein is a tyrosine kinase encoded by a gene located on the long arm of chromosome 2. It is an integral component in cell signaling by T lymphocytes; however, the gene can also be expressed in B lymphocytes. Notably, patients who are *positive* for ZAP-70 progress about twice as rapidly as patients who are *negative* (Orchard, Ibbotson, Best, Parker, & Oscier, 2006). Gene expression profiles and clinical studies show that ZAP-70 positivity is highly correlated with the nonmutated immunoglobulin subtype, suggesting that both biomarkers influence adverse survival by the same biological mechanism (Klein et al., 2001; Rosenwald et al., 2001).

In general, the appearance of multiple chromosomal aberrations in leukemic cells (e.g., chromosomal deletions and trisomy) has been found to herald poor prognosis and an impending blast crisis in patients with chronic lymphocytic leukemia. Nevertheless, there is a lack of consistency of results from different centers, and additional investigations are needed to clarify the prognostic value of genetic and cytogenetic biomarkers.

Hairy Cell Leukemia

Hairy cell leukemia is an uncommon hematological malignancy characterized by the accumulation of abnormal B lymphocytes in the bone marrow and peripheral circulation. Hairy cell leukemia is rare, with an annual incidence of 3 cases per million in U.S. men and 0.6 cases per million in U.S. women. It is usually classified as a subtype of chronic lymphoid leukemia. Fewer than 2,000 new cases are diagnosed annually in North America and Western Europe combined. Hairy cell leukemia was first identified and pathologically characterized by Bertha Bouroncle and colleagues at the Ohio State University in 1958 (Bouroncle, Wiseman, & Doan, 1958; Vardiman et al., 2009).

Due to the rare nature of this form of leukemia, only limited data are available regarding its genesis. Nevertheless, at least 12 cases of familial hairy cell leukemia have been published, and afflicted relatives have been found to have certain human leukocyte antigen (HLA) haplotypes in common (Gramatovici, Bennett, Hiscock, & Grewal, 1993). The role of the HLA locus in the genesis of hairy cell leukemia is as yet undetermined (Cannon, Mobarek, Wegge, & Tabbara, 2008; Villemagne, Bay, Tournilhac, Chaleteix, & Travade, 2005).

In 2003, the Institute of Medicine announced there was sufficient evidence in the published literature to support an association between exposure to herbicides (such as Agent Orange) and the development of chronic B-cell leukemia, including hairy cell leukemia (Institute of Medicine, 2003).

Monocytic Leukemia

Monocytic leukemia arises from the monocytic lineage of immune cells. Monocytes are produced in the bone marrow from hematopoietic stem cell precursors called monoblasts. Monocytes circulate in the bloodstream for 1 to 3 days after which they migrate into tissues throughout the body. In the tissues, monocytes mature into highly specialized macrophages that avidly engulf and digest foreign bodies, necrotic cells, damaged or infected cells, and proteins and other debris from injured cells. The diagnosis of acute monocytic leukemia is confirmed when more than 20% of immune cells of the bone marrow are myeloblasts (Dale et al., 2008; Vardiman et al., 2009).

As in other forms of leukemia, there is an increased risk of monocytic leukemia in subjects with rare genetic disorders that impact on cell division, DNA repair, apoptosis, and angiogenesis. These include Down syndrome, Fanconi anemia, Bloom syndrome, ataxia-telangiectasia, and neurofibromatosis. Environmental risk factors for monocytic leukemia are similar to those for myelocytic leukemia and include exposure to ionizing radiation, pesticides and herbicides, alkylating agents, and topoisomerase inhibitors.

Most cases of monocytic leukemia are diagnosed in adults, usually after the age of 50 years. The disease usually presents as an acute leukemia and may develop after exposure to ionizing radiation, herbicides and pesticides, or certain chemotherapeutic agents, particularly epipodophyllotoxins and anthracyclines (Vardiman et al., 2009). *Chronic monocytic leukemia* is extraordinarily rare; only a small number of cases have been reported in the literature (Bearman, Kjeldsberg, Pangalis, & Rappaport, 1981).

Monocytic leukemia is characterized by specific chromosomal abnormalities. The most common of these involve deletions of portions of the long arm of chromosome 11 or a reciprocal translocation, t(9:11), involving chromosomes 9 and 11. These genetic rearrangements involve the *MLL* locus that encodes a methyltransferase involved in regulation of transcription (Dewald, Morrison-DeLap, Schuchard, Spurbeck, & Pierre, 1983; Guenther et al., 2005). A second translocation, t(8;16), found in some monocytic leukemia cases creates a transfusion protein that promotes leukemogenesis of immature monocytes and myelocytes by deregulating nuclear binding factors and gene expression (Borrow et al., 1996). In addition, mutations and duplications have been observed in the *Flt3* tumor suppressor gene in approximately 40% of cases (Liu, Yu, Jia, Zhang, & Guo, 2007).

Monocytic leukemia does occasionally occur in children, most often in those less than 2 years of age. The incidence in U.S. children under the age of 15 years ranges from 4.8 to 6.6 cases per million; however, in children with Down syndrome (trisomy 21), the relative risk of monocytic leukemia is increased 150-fold for ages 1–4 years (Hasle et al., 2000).

PREVENTION AND CONTROL OF LEUKEMIA

The development of leukemia is influenced by many risk factors, including inherited disorders, behavioral factors (tobacco smoking), environmental factors (exposure to radiation and toxic chemicals), chemotherapy, immune system deficiencies, and infectious agents. Other than avoidance of tobacco and high-dose radiation, no specific lifestyle changes can be recommended that are proven to lower the risk.

Many forms of leukemia can be successfully treated with chemotherapy and radiation. Bone marrow and stem cell transplants are reserved for patients who do not respond to other forms of therapy. Recent advances have been made in treating specific types of leukemia using targeted immunotherapy with monoclonal antibodies in combination with radiation and chemotherapy.

• • • REFERENCES

Altekruse, S. F., Kosary, C. L., Krapcho, M., Neyman, N., Aminou, R., Waldron, W., . . . Edwards, B. K. (2010). *SEER cancer statistics review, 1975–2007.* Bethesda, MD: National Cancer Institute.

American Cancer Society. (2005). *Cancer facts and figures, 2005.* Atlanta, GA: Author.

Aul, C., Giagounidis, A., & Germing, U. (2001). Epidemiological features of myelodysplastic syndromes: Results from regional cancer surveys and hospital-based statistics. *International Journal of Hematology, 73*(4), 405–410.

Badrinath, P., Day, N. E., & Stockton, D. (1997). Seasonality in the diagnosis of acute lymphocytic leukaemia. *British Journal of Cancer, 75*(11), 1711–1773.

Bartal, A., Bentwich, Z., Manny, N., & Izak, G. (1978). Ethical and clinical aspects of chronic lymphocytic leukemia in Israel. *Acta Hematologica, 60,* 161–171.

Bearman, R. M., Kjeldsberg, C. R., Pangalis, G. A., & Rappaport, H. (1981). Chronic monocytic leukemia in adults. *Cancer, 48,* 2239–2255.

Block, M., Jacobson, L. O., & Bethard, W. F. (1953). Preleukemic acute human leukemia. *Journal of the American Medical Association, 152,* 1018–1028.

Bloom, D. (1954). Congenital telangiectatic erythema resembling lupus erythematosus in dwarfs; probably a syndrome entity. *American Journal of Diseases of Children, 88*(6), 754–758.

Bloomfield, C. D., Goldman, A. I., Alimena, G., Berger, R., Borgstrom, G. H., Brandt, L., . . . Garson, O. M. (1986). Chromosomal abnormalities identify high-risk and low-risk patients with acute lymphoblastic leukemia. *Blood, 67*(2), 415–420.

Bloomfield, C. D., Lawrence, D., Byrd, J. C., Carroll, A., Pettenati, M. J., Tantravahi, R., . . . Mayer, R. J. (1998). Frequency of prolonged remission duration after high-dose cytarabine intensification in acute myeloid leukemia varies by cytogenetic subtype. *Cancer Research, 58*(18), 4173–4179.

Bodian, M., Sheldon, W., & Lightwood, R. (1964). Congenital hypoplasia of the exocrine pancreas. *Acta Paediatrica, 53,* 282–293.

Borrow, J., Stanton, V. P. Jr., Andresen, J. M., Becher, R., Behm, F. G., Chaganti, R. S. K., . . . Housman, D. E. (1996). The translocation t(8;16)(p11;p13) of acute myeloid leukaemia fuses a putative acetyltransferase to the CREB–binding protein. *Nature Genetics, 14,* 33–41.

Bouroncle, B. A., Wiseman, B. K., & Doan, C. A. (1958). Leukemic reticuloendotheliosis. *Blood, 13,* 609–630.

Bowen, D. T., Frew, M. E., Rollinson, S., Roddam, P. L., Dring, A., Smith, M. T., . . . Morgan, G. J. (2003). *CYP1A1*2B* (Val) allele is overrepresented in a subgroup of acute myeloid leukemia patients with poor-risk karyotype associated with *NRAS* mutation, but not associated with *FLT3* internal tandem duplication. *Blood, 101,* 2770–2774.

Boyd, K. P., Korf, B. R., & Theos, A. (2009). Neurofibromatosis type 1. *Journal of the AmericanAcademy of Dermatology, 61*(1), 1–14.

Bunn, H. F. (1986). 5q- and disordered haematopoiesis. *Clinics in Haematology, 15*(4), 1023–1035.

Canman, C. E., & Lim, D. S. (1998). The role of ATM in DNA damage responses and cancer. *Oncogene, 17*(25), 3301–3308.

Cannon, T., Mobarek, D., Wegge, J., & Tabbara, I. A. (2008). Hairy cell leukemia: Current concepts. *Cancer Investigation, 26*(8), 860–865.

Cheok, C. F., Bachrati, C. Z., Chan, K. L., Ralf, C., Wu, L., & Hickson, I. D. (2005). Roles of the Bloom's syndrome helicase in the maintenance of genome stability. *Biochemical Society Transactions, 33,* 1456–1459.

Christiansen, D. H., Andersen, M. K., & Pedersen-Bjergaard, J. (2003). Methylation of *p15INK4B* is common, is associated with deletion of genes on chromosome arm 7q and predicts a poor prognosis in therapy-related myelodysplasia and acute myeloid leukemia. *Leukemia, 17*(9), 1813–1819.

D'Andrea, A. D. (2010). Susceptibility pathways in Fanconi's anemia and breast cancer. *New England Journal of Medicine, 362*(20), 1909–1919.

Dale, D. C., Boser, L., & Liles, W. C. (2008). The phagocytes: Neutrophils and monocytes. *Blood, 112*(4), 935–945.

Deschler, B., & Lübbert, M. (2006). Acute myeloid leukemia: Epidemiology and etiology. *Cancer, 107,* 2099–2107.

Dewald, G. W., Morrison-DeLap, S. J., Schuchard, K. A., Spurbeck, J. L., & Pierre, R. V. (1983). A possible specific chromosome marker for monocytic leukemia: Three more patients with t(9;11)(p22;q24) and another with t(11;17) (q24;q21), each with acute monoblastic leukemia. *Cancer Genetics and Cytogenetics, 8*(3), 203–212.

Down, J. L. H. (1866). Observations on an ethnic classification of idiots. *Clinical Lecture Reports, London Hospital, 3,* 259–262.

Fanconi, G. (1927). Familiäre, infantile perniciosähnliche Anämie (perniziöses Blutbild und Konstitution). *Jahrbuch für Kinderheilkunde und physische Erziehung, Wien, 117,* 257–280.

Ferlay, J., Shin, H. R., Forman, D., Mathers, C., & Parkin, D. M. (2010). Estimates of worldwide burden of cancer in 2008. *International Journal of Cancer, 127*(12), 2893–2917.

Ferlay, J., Soerjomataram, I., Ervik, M., Dikshit, R., Eser, S., Mathers, C., . . . Bray, F. (2013). *GLOBOCAN 2012 v1.0. Cancer incidence and mortality worldwide: IARC CancerBase No. 11* [Internet]. Lyon, France: International Agency for Research on Cancer. Retrieved from http://globocan.iarc.fr

Gao, F., Chia, K. S., & Machin, D. (2007). On the evidence for seasonal variation in the onset of acute lymphoblastic leukemia (ALL). *Leukemia Research, 31*(10), 1327–1338.

German, J. (1993). Bloom syndrome: A mendelian prototype of somatic mutational disease. *Medicine (Baltimore), 72*(6), 393–406.

Goldin, L., Pfeiffer, R. M., Li, X., & Hemminki, K. (2004). Familial risk of lymphoproliferative tumors in families of patients with chronic lymphocytic leukemia: Results from the Swedish Family-Cancer Database. *Blood, 104,* 1850–1854.

Goldin, L. R., & Caporaso, N. E. (2007). Family studies in chronic lymphocytic leukaemia and other lymphoproliferative tumours. *British Journal of Haematology, 139*(5), 774–779.

Golub, T. R., Barker, G. F., Bohlander, S. K., Hiebert, S. W., Ward, D. C., Bray-Ward, P., . . . Gilliland, D. G. (1995). Fusion of the *TEL* gene on 12p13 to the *AML1* gene on 21q22 in acute lymphoblastic leukemia. *Proceedings of the National Academy of Sciences of the United States of America, 92*(11), 4917–4921.

Gramatovici, M., Bennett, J. M., Hiscock, J. G., & Grewal, K. D. (1993). Three cases of familial hairy cell leukemia. *American Journal of Hematology, 42*(4), 337–339.

Greenberg, P., Cox, C., LeBeau, M. M., Fenaux, P., Morel, P., Sanz, G., . . . Bennett, J. (1997). International scoring system for evaluating prognosis in myelodysplastic syndromes. *Blood, 89*(6), 2079–2088.

Greiser, E., & Hoffman, W. (2010). Questionable increase of childhood leukemia in Basrah, Iraq. *American Journal of Public Health, 100*(9), 1556–1557.

Guenther, M. G., Jenner, R. G., Chevalier, B., Nakamura, T., Croce, C. M., Canaani, E., & Young, R. A. (2005). Global and Hox-specific roles for the *MLL1* methyltransferase. *Proceedings of the National Academy of Sciences of the United States of America, 102*(24), 8603–8608.

Gurney, J. G., Severson, R. K., Davis, S., & Robison, L. L. (1995). Incidence of cancer in children in the United States. Sex-, race-, and 1-year age-specific rates by histologic type. *Cancer, 75,* 2186–2195.

Hagopian, A., Lafta, R., Hassan, J., Davis, S., Mirick, D., & Takaro, T. (2010). Trends in childhood leukemia in Basrah, Iraq, 1993–2007. *American Journal of Public Health, 100*(6), 1081–1087.

Harris, R. E., & Al-Rashid, R. A. (1984). Seasonal variation in the incidence of childhood acute lymphocytic leukemia in Nebraska. *Nebraska Medical Journal, 69,* 192–198.

Harris, R. E., Harrell, F. E. Jr., Patil, K. D., & Al-Rashid, R. (1987). The seasonal risk of pediatric/juvenile acute lymphocytic leukemia in the USA. *Journal of Chronic Diseases, 40,* 915–924.

Hasle, H., Clemmensen, I. H., & Mikkelsen, M. (2000). Risks of leukaemia and solid tumours in individuals with Down's syndrome. *Lancet, 355*(9199), 165–169.

Healy, J., Richer, C., Bourgey, M., Kritikou, E. A., & Sinnett, D. (2010). Replication analysis confirms the association of *ARID5B* with childhood B-cell acute lymphoblastic leukemia. *Haematologica, 95*(9), 1608–1611.

Heerema, N. A., Sather, H. N., Sensel, M. G., Liu-Mares, W., Lange, B. J., Bostrom, B. C., . . . Uckun, F. M. (1999). Association of chromosome arm 9p abnormalities with adverse risk in childhood acute lymphoblastic leukemia: A report from the Children's Cancer Group. *Blood, 94*(5), 1537–1544.

Institute of Medicine. (2003). *Veterans and Agent Orange: Update 2002.* Washington, DC: Institute of Medicine of the National Academies, U.S. National Academy of Science.

Kantarjian, H., Dixon, D., Keating, M., Talpaz, M., Walters, R., McCredie, K., & Freireich, E. (1988). Characteristics of accelerated disease in chronic myelogenous leukemia. *Cancer, 61*(7), 1441–1446.

Klein, U., Tu, Y., Stolovitzky, G. A., Mattioli, M., Cattoretti, G., Husson, H., . . . Dalla-Favera, R. (2001). Gene expression profiling of B cell chronic lymphocytic leukemia reveals a homogeneous phenotype related to memory B cells. *Journal of Experimental Medicine, 194,* 1625–1638.

Kossman, S. E., & Weiss, M. A. (2000). Acute myelogenous leukemia after exposure to strontium-89 for the treatment of adenocarcinoma of the prostate. *Cancer, 88,* 620–624.

Krajinovic, M., Labuda, D., Richer, C., Karimi, S., & Sinnett, D. (1999). Susceptibility to childhood acute lymphoblastic leukemia: Influence of *CYP1A1, CYP2D6, GSTM1,* and *GSTT1* genetic polymorphisms. *Blood, 93*(5), 1496–1501.

Kumar, V., Abbas, A. K., & Aster, J. C. (2014). *Robbins and Cotran pathologic basis of disease* (9th ed.). Philadelphia, PA: Mosby & Saunders.

Kurzrock, R., Kantarjian, H. M., Druker, B. J., & Talpaz, M. (2003). Philadelphia chromosome-positive leukemias: From basic mechanisms to molecular therapeutics. *Annals of Internal Medicine, 138*(10), 819–830.

Lavau, C., & Dejean, A. (1994). The t(15;17) translocation in acute promyelocytic leukemia. *Leukemia, 8*(10), 1615–1621.

Le Beau, M. M., Albain, K. S., Larson, R. A., Vardiman, J. W., Davis, E. M., Blough, R. R., . . . Rowley, J. D. (1986). Clinical and cytogenetic correlations in 63 patients with therapy-related myelodysplastic syndromes and acute nonlymphocytic leukemia: Further evidence for characteristic abnormalities of chromosomes no. 5 and 7. *Journal of Clinical Oncology, 4,* 325–345.

Le Beau, M. M., Pettenati, M. J., Lemons, R. S., Diaz, M. O., Westbrook, C. A, Larson, R. A., . . . Rowley, J. D. (1986b). Assignment of the

GM-CSF, CSF-1, and FMS genes to human chromosome 5 provides evidence for linkage of a family of genes regulating hematopoiesis and for their involvement in the deletion (5q) in myeloid disorders. *Cold Spring Harbor Symposia on Quantitative Biology, 51*(Pt 2), 899–909.

Lejeune, J. (1959). Le mongolisme. Premier example d'aberration autosomique humaine. *Annales de Genetique, 1*, 41–49.

Levi, F., Lucchini, F., Negri, E., Barbui, T., & La Vecchia, C. (2000). Trends in mortality from leukemia in subsequent age groups. *Leukemia, 14*(11), 1980–1985.

Linet, M. S., Schubauer-Berigan, M. K., Weisenburger, D. D., Richardson, D. B., Landgren, O., Blair, A., . . . Dores, G. M. (2007). Chronic lymphocytic leukaemia: An overview of aetiology in light of recent developments in classification and pathogenesis. *British Journal of Haematology, 139*(5), 672–686.

Liu, H., Yu, H., Jia, H. Y., Zhang, W., & Guo, C. J. (2007). Detection of FLT3 gene mutation in hematologic malignancies and its clinical significance. *Zhongguo Shi Yan Xue Ye Xue Za Zhi, 15*(4), 709–713.

McNeil, S., Zeng, C., Harrington, K. D., Hiebert, S., Lian, J. B., Stein, J. L., . . . Stein, G. S. (1999). The t(8;21) chromosomal translocation in acute myelogenous leukemia modifies intranuclear targeting of the AML1/CBFa2 transcription factor. *Proceedings of the National Academy of Sciences, 96*(26), 14882–14887.

Namboodiri, K. K., & Harris, R. E. (1991). Hematopoietic and lymphoproliferative cancer among male veterans using the Veterans Administration Medical System. *Cancer, 68*(5), 1123–1130.

Nowell, P., & Hungerford, D. (1960). A minute chromosome in chronic granulocytic leukemia. *Science, 132*, 1497.

Orchard, J., Ibbotson, R., Best, G., Parker, A., & Oscier, D. (2006). ZAP-70 in B cell malignancies. *Leukemia and Lymphoma, 46*(12), 1689–1698.

Parkin, D. M., Bray, F., Ferlay, J., & Pisani, P. (2001). Estimating the world cancer burden, GLOBOCAN 2000. *International Journal of Cancer, 94*, 153–156.

Parkin, D. M., Bray, F., Ferlay, J., & Pisani, P. (2005). Global cancer statistics, 2002. *CA: A Cancer Journal for Clinicians, 55*, 74–108.

Parkin, D. M., Pisani, P., & Ferlay, J. (1999a). Estimates of the worldwide incidence of 25 major cancers in 1990. *International Journal of Cancer, 80*(6), 827–841.

Parkin, D. M., Pisani, P., & Ferlay, J. (1999b). Global cancer statistics. *CA: A Cancer Journal for Clinicians, 49*(1), 33–64.

Pedersen-Bjergaard, J., Philip, P., Larsen, S. O., Andersson, M., Daugaard, G., Ersbøll, J., . . . Osterlind, K. (1993). Therapy-related myelodysplasia and acute myeloid leukemia. Cytogenetic characteristics of 115 consecutive cases and risk in seven cohorts of patients treated intensively for malignant diseases in the Copenhagen series. *Leukemia, 7*(12), 1975–1986.

Perillat-Menegaux, P., Clave, J., Auclerc, M. F., Baruchel, A., Leverger, G., Nelken, B., . . . Hémon, D. (2003). Family history of autoimmune thyroid disease and childhood acute leukemia. *Cancer Epidemiology, Biomarkers and Prevention, 12*(1), 60–63.

Plass, C., Byrd, J. C., Raval, A., Tanner, S. M., & De La Chapelle, A. (2007). Molecular profiling of chronic lymphocytic leukaemia: Genetics meets epigenetics to identify predisposing genes. *British Journal of Haematology, 139*, 744–752.

Pogoda, J. M., Preston-Martin, S., Nichols, P. W., & Ross, R. K. (2002). Smoking and risk of acute myeloid leukemia: Results from a Los Angeles County case-control study. *American Journal of Epidemiology, 155*, 546–553.

Popovic, M., Goobie, S., Morrison, J., Ellis, L., Ehtesham, N., Richards, N., . . . Rommens, J. M. (2002). Fine mapping of the locus for Shwachman–Diamond syndrome at 7q11, identification of shared disease haplotypes, and exclusion of TPST1 as a candidate gene. *European Journal of Human Genetics, 10*(4), 250–258.

Preston, D. L., Kusumi, S., Tomonaga, M., Izumi, S., Ron, E., Kuramoto, A., . . . Mabuchi, K. (1994). Cancer incidence in atomic bomb survivors. Part III. Leukemia, lymphoma and multiple myeloma, 1950–1987. *Radiation Research, 137*(2 Suppl), S68–S97.

Preston, D. L., Pierce, D. A., Shimizu, Y., Cullings, H. M., Fujita, S., Funamoto, S., & Kodama, K. (2004). Effect of recent atomic bomb survivor dosimetry changes on cancer mortality risk estimates. *Radiation Research, 162*, 377–389.

Preston-Martin, S., Thomas, D. C., Yu, M. C., & Henderson, B. E. (1989). Diagnostic radiography as a risk factor for chronic myeloid and monocytic leukaemia (CML). *British Journal of Cancer, 59*(4), 639–644.

Pui, C. H., Raimondi, S. C., Hancock, M. L., Rivera, G. K., Ribeiro, R. C., Mahmoud, H. H., . . . Behm, F. G. (1994). Immunologic, cytogenetic, and clinical characterization of childhood acute lymphoblastic leukemia with the t(1;19) (q23; p13) or its derivative. *Clinical Oncology, 12*(12), 2601–2606.

Pui, C. H., Relling, M. V., & Downing, J. R. (2004). Acute lymphoblastic leukemia. *New England Journal of Medicine, 350*, 1535–1548.

Pui, C. H., Ribeiro, R. C., Hancock, M. L., Rivera, G. K., Evans, W. E., Raimondi, S. C., . . . Crist, W. M. (1991). Acute myeloid leukemia in children treated with epipodophyllotoxins for acute lymphoblastic leukemia. *New England Journal of Medicine, 325*, 1682–1687.

Redaniel, M. T., Laudico, A., Miraol-Lumague, M. R., Alcasabas, A. P., Pulte, D., & Brenner, H. (2010). Geographic and ethnic differences in childhood leukaemia and lymphoma survival: Comparisons of Philippine residents, Asian Americans and Caucasians in the United States. *British Journal of Cancer, 103*, 149–154.

Richardson, D. B., Wing, S., Schroeder, J., Schmitz-Feuerhake, I., & Hoffmann, W. (2005). Ionizing radiation and chronic lymphocytic leukemia. *Environmental Health Perspectives, 113*, 1–5.

Ries, L. A. G. (1999). Childhood cancer mortality. In L. A. G. Ries, M. A. Smith, J. G. Gurney, M.

Linet, T. Tamra, J. L. Young, & G. R. Bunin (Eds.), *Cancer incidence and survival among children and adolescents: United States SEER program 1975–1995* (pp. 165–170). Bethesda, MD: National Cancer Institute, SEER Program. NIH Pub. No. 99-4649.

Ries, L. A. G., Kosary, C. L., Hankey, B. F., Miller, B. A., Clegg, L., & Edwards, B. K. (Eds.). (1998). *SEER cancer statistics review 1973–1996.* Bethesda, MD: National Cancer Institute.

Ries, L. A. G., Kosary, C. L., Hankey, B. F., Miller, B. A., Clegg, L., & Edwards, B. K. (Eds.). (2003). *SEER cancer statistics review, 1975–2000.* Bethesda, MD: National Cancer Institute.

Robbins, S. L., & Cotran, R. S. (1979). *Pathologic basis of disease* (2nd ed.). Philadelphia: W. B. Saunders.

Rosenwald, A., Alizadeh, A. A., Widhopf, G., Simon, R., Davis, R. E., Yu, X., . . . Staudt, L. M. (2001). Relation of gene expression phenotype to immunoglobulin mutation genotype in B cell chronic lymphocytic leukemia. *Journal of Experimental Medicine, 194*, 1639–1647.

Rubnitz, J. E., Downing, J. R., Pui, C. H., Shurtleff, S. A., Raimondi, S. C., Evans, W. E., . . . Behm, F. G. (1997). *TEL* gene rearrangement in acute lymphoblastic leukemia: A new genetic marker with prognostic significance. *Journal of Clinical Oncology, 15*(3), 1150–1157.

Rubnitz, J. E., Wichlan, D., Devidas, M., Shuster, J., Linda, S. B., Kurtzberg, J., . . . Children's Oncology Group. (2008). Prospective analysis of *TEL* gene rearrangements in childhood acute lymphoblastic leukemia: A Children's Oncology Group study. *Journal of Clinical Oncology, 26*(13), 2186–2191.

Savage, D. G., Szydlo, R. M., & Goldman, J. M. (1997). Clinical features at diagnosis in 430 patients with chronic myeloid leukaemia seen at a referral centre over a 16-year period. *British Journal of Haematology, 96*(1), 111–116.

Savitz, D. A., & Andrews, K. W. (1997). Review of epidemiologic evidence on benzene and lymphatic and hematopoietic cancers. *American Journal of Industrial Medicine, 31*, 287–295.

Schmiegelow, K., Vestergaard, T., Nielsen, S. M., & Hjalgrim, H. (2008). Etiology of common childhood acute lymphoblastic leukemia: The adrenal hypothesis. *Leukemia, 22,* 2137–2141.

Shah, A., & Coleman, M. P. (2007). Increasing incidence of childhood leukaemia: A controversy re-examined. *British Journal of Cancer, 97*(7), 1009–1012.

Shvidel, L., Shtarlid, M., Klepfish, A., Sigler, E., & Berrebi, A. (1998). Epidemiology and ethnic aspects of B cell chronic lymphocytic leukemia in Israel. *Leukemia, 12,* 1612–1617.

Shwachman, H., Diamond, L. K., Oski, F. A., & Khaw, K. T. (1964). The syndrome of pancreatic insufficiency and bone marrow dysfunction. *Journal of Pediatrics, 65,* 645–663.

Smith, M. A., Gloeckler-Ries, L. A., Gurney, J. G., & Ross, J. A. (1999). Leukemia. In L. A. G. Ries, M. A. Smith, J. G. Gurney, M. Linet, T. Tamra, J. L. Young, & G. R. Bunin (Eds.), *Cancer incidence and survival among children and adolescents: United States SEER program 1975–1995* (pp. 17–34). Bethesda, MD: National Cancer Institute, SEER Program. NIH Pub. No. 99-4649.

Smith, M. A., Seibel, N. L., Seibel, N. L., Altekruse, S. F., Ries, L. A. G., Melbert, D. L., . . . Reaman, G. H. (2010). Outcomes for children and adolescents with cancer: Challenges for the twenty-first century. *Journal of Clinical Oncology, 28*(15), 2625–2634.

Solé, F., Espinet, B., Sanz, G. F., Cervera, J., Calasanz, M. J., Luño, E., . . . Woessner, S. (2000). Incidence, characterization and prognostic significance of chromosomal abnormalities in 640 patients with primary myelodysplastic syndromes. *British Journal of Haematology, 108,* 346–356.

Stilgenbauer, S., Dohner, H., & Lichter, P. (1993). Genomic aberrations in B-cell chronic lymphocytic leukemia. In B. Cheson (Ed.), *Chronic lymphocytic leukemia* (2nd ed., pp. 353–376). New York, NY: Marcel Dekker.

Stiller, C. A., Chessells, J. M., & Fitchett, M. (1994). Neurofibromatosis and childhood leukaemia/lymphoma: A population-based UKCCSG study. *British Journal of Cancer, 70*(5), 969–972.

United Nations Scientific Committee on the Effects of Atomic Radiation. (2000). Annex I. Epidemiological evaluation of radiation-induced cancer. In *Sources and effects of ionizing radiation* (pp. 297–431). New York, NY: Author.

Van Bockstaele, F., Verhasselt, B., & Philippe, J. (2009). Prognostic markers in chronic lymphocytic leukemia: A comprehensive review. *Blood Reviews, 23*(1), 25–47.

Van den Berghe, H., Cassiman, J. J., David, G., Fryns, J. P., Michaux, J. L., & Sokal, G. (1974). Distinct haematological disorder with deletion of long arm of no. 5 chromosome. *Nature, 251*(5474), 437–438.

van Leeuwen, B. H., Martinson, M. E., Webb, G. C., & Young, I. G. (1989). Molecular organization of the cytokine gene cluster, involving the human *IL-3, IL-4, IL-5,* and *GM-CSF* genes, on human chromosome 5. *Blood, 73,* 1142–1148.

Vardiman, J. W., Thiele, J., Arber, D. A., Brunning, R. D., Borowitz, M. J., Porwit, A., . . . Bloomfield, C. D. (2009). The 2008 revision of the World Health Organization (WHO) classification of myeloid neoplasms and acute leukemia. *Blood, 114*(5), 937–951.

Villemagne, B., Bay, J. O., Tournilhac, O., Chaleteix, C., & Travade, P. (2005). Two new cases of familial hairy cell leukemia associated with HLA haplotypes A2, B7, Bw4, Bw6. *Leukemia and Lymphoma, 46*(2), 243–245.

World Health Organization. (2008). *World cancer report.* Geneva, Switzerland: Author.

Xie, Y., Davies, S. M., Xiang, Y., Robison, L. L., & Ross, J. A. (2003). Trends in leukemia incidence and survival in the United States (1973–1998). *Cancer, 97*(9), 2229–2235.

Epidemiology of Brain Tumors: Glioma, Meningioma, Acoustic Neuroma, and Pituitary Tumors

GLOBAL EPIDEMIOLOGY OF BRAIN TUMORS

Based on sequential reports from the World Health Organization (WHO), the incidence and mortality of tumors of the brain and central nervous system (CNS) are rising. Since 1990, reported new cases and deaths have more than doubled in both men and women (**Figure 28.1**). In 2012, brain/CNS tumors were diagnosed in 256,213 individuals and caused 189,394 deaths, about 2.3% of all cancer deaths. By comparison, 127,000 new cases were detected and 95,000 individuals died of brain/CNS tumors in 1990 (Ferlay, Shin, Forman, Mathers, & Parkin,

2010; Ferlay et al., 2013; Parkin, Bray, Ferlay, & Pisani, 2005; Parkin, Pisani, & Ferlay, 1999a, 1999b; Parkin, Whelan, Ferlay, Teppo, & Thomas, 2002).

Corresponding to the increasing numbers of cases and deaths, the annual age-standardized incidence and mortality rates have both increased approximately 30% in the past two decades. These increases are due in large part to the widespread use of advanced neuroimaging (computerized tomography and magnetic resonance imaging) and other diagnostic techniques (e.g., stereotactic biopsy) resulting in earlier and more accurate detection of brain tumors (Ferlay et al., 2010, 2012; Parkin et al., 1999a, 1999b, 2002, 2005).

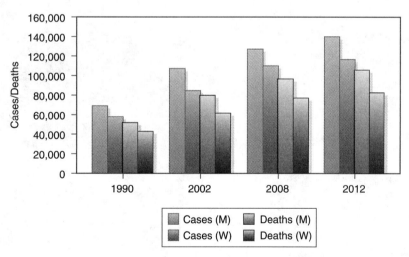

Figure 28.1 Global Trends in Malignant Tumors of the Brain and Nervous System, 1990–2012.

Source: Data from Ferlay, J., Shin, H. R., Forman, D., Mathers, C., & Parkin, D. M. (2010). Estimates of worldwide burden of cancer in 2008. *International Journal of Cancer, 127*(12), 2893–2917; Ferlay, J., Soerjomataram, I., Ervik, M., Dikshit, R., Eser, S., Mathers, C., . . . Bray, F. (2013). *GLOBOCAN 2012 v1.0. Cancer incidence and mortality worldwide: IARC CancerBase No. 11* [Internet]. Lyon, France: International Agency for Research on Cancer. Retrieved from http://globocan.iarc.fr; Parkin, D. M., Bray, F., Ferlay, J., & Pisani, P. (2001). Estimating the world cancer burden, GLOBOCAN 2000. *International Journal of Cancer, 94*, 153–156; Parkin, D. M., Bray, F., Ferlay, J., & Pisani, P. (2005). Global cancer statistics, 2002. *CA: A Cancer Journal for Clinicians, 55*, 74–108; Parkin, D. M., Pisani, P., & Ferlay, J. (1999a). Estimates of the worldwide incidence of 25 major cancers in 1990. *International Journal of Cancer, 80*(6), 827–841; Parkin, D. M., Pisani, P., & Ferlay, J. (1999b). Global cancer statistics. *CA: A Cancer Journal for Clinicians, 49*(1), 33–64.

In 2012, the global incidence was higher in men than women (3.9 per 100,000 versus 3.0 per 100,000) and higher in developed countries (5.9 per 100,000 in men and 4.4 per 100,000 in women) than developing countries (3.3 per 100,000 in men and 2.7 per 100,000 in women) (Ferlay et al., 2013). Incidence rates were relatively high (exceeding 4 per 100,000) in developed areas such as the United States, Western Europe, Scandinavia, Brazil, the Russian Federation, and Australia/New Zealand compared to developing nations such as India and those in sub-Saharan Africa, where the rates were lower, ranging from 1 to 2 per 100,000. Notably, rates exceeding 5 per 100,000 were observed in many coastal Mediterranean nations and in some less-developed countries such as Kazakhstan and Turkmenistan (**Figure 28.2**).

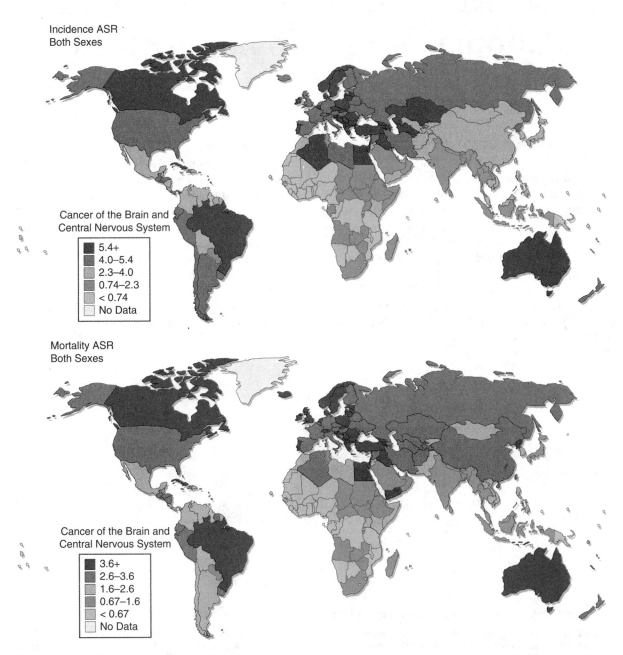

Figure 28.2 Global Incidence and Mortality Rates of Brain Tumors, 2012.

ASR: Rates per 100,000 are age-standardized to the world population, 2000–2025.

Source: Reproduced from Ferlay, J., Soerjomataram, I., Ervik, M., Dikshit, R., Eser, S., Mathers, C., . . . Bray, F. (2013).*GLOBOCAN 2012 v1.0. Cancer incidence and mortality worldwide: IARC CancerBase No. 11* [Internet]. Lyon, France: International Agency for Research on Cancer. Retrieved from http://globocan.iarc.fr

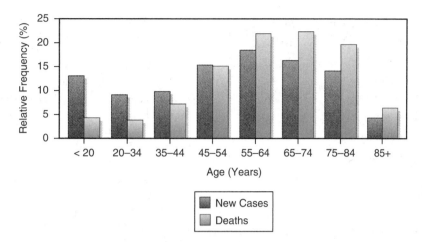

Figure 28.3 Age-Specific Frequency of New Cases and Deaths: Malignant Tumors of the Brain and Nervous System, United States.

Source: Data from Altekruse, S. F., Kosary, C. L., Krapcho, M., Neyman, N., Aminou, R., Waldron, W., . . . Edwards, B. K. (2010). *SEER cancer statistics review, 1975–2007.* Bethesda, MD: National Cancer Institute.

Global patterns of incidence and mortality are similar. Nations with high incidence rates also had high mortality rates. Men had higher mortality than women (3.0 versus 2.1 per 100,000), and the mortality/incidence ratio was only slightly higher in developed nations than in developing nations (0.65 versus 0.73).

Schwartzbaum and colleagues reported a four-fold difference in the incidence of primary malignant brain tumors between countries with a high incidence (e.g., Canada, Australia, New Zealand, Denmark, Finland, and the United States) and countries with a low incidence (e.g., India and the Philippines). Such differences are difficult to interpret because diagnostic practices, access to and quality of care, and completeness of reporting differ widely worldwide (Fisher, Schwartzbaum, Wrensch, & Wiemels, 2007; Schwartzbaum, Fisher, Aldape, & Wrensch, 2006).

BRAIN TUMORS IN THE UNITED STATES

Based on recent data from the Surveillance, Epidemiology, and End Results (SEER) program of the U.S. National Cancer Institute and the Central Brain Tumor Registry of the United States (CBTRUS), approximately 22,000 new cases of primary malignant brain tumors are diagnosed every year in the United States and more than 13,000 deaths are attributed to such tumors. During the past two decades, the age-adjusted annual incidence rate in the United States declined slightly from 7.0 cases per 100,000 in 1990 to 6.5 cases per 100,000 during 2003–2007 (Altekruse et al., 2010; CBTRUS, 2008; Horner et al., 2009).

Annual incidence and mortality rates are higher for U.S. men (7.6 and 5.6 per 100,000, respectively)

than women (5.5 and 3.5 per 100,000, respectively); however, survival differs dramatically by histology and age. For example, patients with aggressive malignant gliomas such as glioblastoma multiforme have very poor survival rates (only about 3% survive 5 years) whereas patients with low-grade gliomas have 5-year survival rates exceeding 70%.

As shown in **Figure 28.3**, the relative frequencies of newly diagnosed cases of malignant brain tumors and attributable deaths both show early peaks during adolescence. A disturbing fact is that brain cancer is the leading cause of cancer mortality among people under the age of 35 years (Bondy et al., 2008). As discussed in a separate section of this chapter, the histological profile of pediatric brain tumors differs markedly from that in adults. Following the early peak, incidence and mortality accelerate rapidly with age among adults (Altekruse et al., 2010; CBTRUS, 2008; Horner et al., 2009).

CLASSIFICATION OF BRAIN TUMORS

As pointed out by Stanley Robbins and Ramzi Cotran in their classic textbook of pathology, "the term brain tumor should be restricted only to neoplasms arising from any of the constituent cells within brain substance, neuroglial cells, neurons, cells of the blood vessels and connective tissues" (Robbins & Cotran, 1979; Kumar, Abbas, & Aster, 2014). It is also important to note that metastatic tumors from other primary anatomic sites account for 25–30% of all intracranial tumors.

The classification of primary brain tumors is based on the cell of origin. Tumors arising from glial

Table 28.1	Profile of Brain Tumors, United States
Classification of Primary Brain Tumors	**Relative Frequency (%)**
Neuroepithelial tumors (glioma)	33
Meningeal tumors (meningioma)	34
Sellar tumors (pituitary gland)	12
Nerve tumors (acoustic neuroma)	9
Embryonal tumors (medulloblastoma)	1
Lymphomas	3
Other or unclassified	8
Total	100

Total sample size = 158,088 tumors

Source: Data from Centralized Brain Tumor Registry of the United States. *CBTRUS statistical report: Primary brain and central nervous system tumors diagnosed in eighteen states in 2004–2006.* Hinsdale, IL: Author. Retrieved from http://www.cbtrus.org

cells (neuroglia) are called gliomas, those arising from neurons are called neuromas or neuroblastomas, and tumors arising from meningeal cells are called meningiomas. The most common types of primary brain tumors that develop in adults are gliomas, meningiomas, pituitary gland tumors, acoustic neuromas, and lymphomas (**Table 28.1**). These five cell types constitute approximately 90% of all primary brain tumors, with gliomas and meningiomas accounting for approximately two-thirds of all tumors that arise in the brain.

Gliomas account for more than one-third of primary brain tumors in adults. Gliomas develop from neuroepithelial cells. There are several types of gliomas. One type, the astrocytoma, arises from star-shaped cells called astrocytes and can grow anywhere in the brain or spinal cord. In adults, astrocytomas most often arise in the cerebrum, the largest part of the brain that fills most of the upper skull. Glioblastoma multiforme is an especially aggressive form of astrocytoma. Gliomas are diagnosed about twice as frequently in men compared to women.

Meningiomas also account for more than one-third of adult brain tumors. Meningiomas develop from the meninges, the protective membrane covering the brain directly underneath the skull. These tumors are usually benign and grow very slowly. Indeed, meningiomas rarely metastasize to other tissues, and symptoms such as headache, visual impairment, and focal seizures are due to compression of surrounding tissues by the expanding tumor in the confined intracranial vault. In contrast to gliomas, which predominate in men, meningiomas are diagnosed about twice as frequently in women compared

to men. As discussed in the section on risk factors, gliomas and meningiomas have distinctly different sets of risk factors.

Schwannomas are benign tumors that develop from Schwann cells in the peripheral nervous system. Schwann cells are named after the German physiologist Theodor Schwann, who first described them in 1838 (Aszmann, 2000). These cells produce the myelin that covers and protects the peripheral or cranial nerve fibers connected with the brain. Acoustic neuromas are a type of schwannoma that arise from the Schwann cells that wrap around the acoustic nerve between the brain and the ear. Acoustic neuromas account for most of the brain tumors that arise in and around the cranial nerves.

Tumors arising from tissues and structures within the bony compartment called the sella turcica in the center of the brain are called *sellar tumors*. Sellar tumors usually develop from the pituitary gland. Less common types of primary brain tumors include primary lymphomas that develop from collections of lymphocytes within the brain, vascular tumors, germ cell tumors, sarcomas, and tumors of the pineal gland.

Cell of Origin of Glioma

Glioma is a cancer that arises from the glial cells (glia) of the brain. These cells were first described by the famous German pathologist Rudolph Virchow, who named them *nervenkitt* (nerve glue) or glia (Virchow, 1846, 1854). Glial cells outnumber neurons by about 9:1, but most are unable to generate action potentials or communicate by electrical signaling. Glia are crudely divisible by size into macroglia and microglia.

Macroglia are further categorized as astrocytes and oligodendrocytes. Astrocytes nurture and support neurons, and their tentacle-like processes encircle and envelop the synapses between nerve cells, supplying energy and oxygen necessary for the transmission of nerve impulses. Astrocytes also modulate the neuronal influx and efflux of important ions such as calcium, sodium, potassium, and chloride, and serve as a conduit for waste disposal. As such, they are often juxtaposed between cerebral blood vessels and neurons, and they provide biochemical support to endothelial cells of the blood–brain barrier (**Figure 28.4**).

Oligodendrocytes are macroglia that produce and secrete myelin, the insulatory material of neurons. A single oligodendrocyte can extend its tentacle-like processes to scores of axons, wrapping a sheath of myelin around each axon.

Small glial cells (microglia) protect the brain against invading microbes through immunosurveillance and innate immune reactions, and they assist in wound healing following traumatic injury

Cells of the Central Nervous System

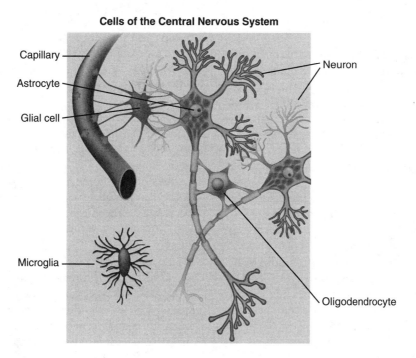

Figure 28.4 Astrocyte of the Brain.

to neurons. Microglia develop from hematopoietic stem cells rather than the neuroepithelium (Kimelberg, Jalonen, & Walz, 1993; Pollard & Earnshaw, 2008; Purves et al., 2008).

Glia were once believed to be relatively passive cells whose only purpose was to support the function of neurons. Nevertheless, in recent years, certain macroglia (particularly astrocytes) have been found to act in a partnering role with neurons in the processes of signal transduction and neurotransmission. Specifically, astrocytes are now known to play a very active role in modulating signal propagation and synaptic action by controlling the uptake of neurotransmitters at or near the synaptic cleft, and some are even capable of secreting neurotransmitters. For example, astrocytes are activated by elevated levels of calcium ions and have been found to secrete the neurotransmitter glutamate as partners in the neuronal response to excitation (Araque, Parpura, Sanzgiri, & Haydon, 1999; Santello & Volterra, 2008).

Because cancer involves uncontrolled cell division, it is important to realize that glia *do* retain the ability to undergo cell division in adulthood, whereas neurons do not. Following injury due to trauma or stroke, there is often profound proliferation of glial cells (gliosis) at or near the site of injury.

Types of Glioma

Glioma tumors are further classified by glial cell type into astrocytomas, glioblastomas multiforme, oligodendrogliomas, ependymomas, and mixed gliomas. *Glioblastoma multiforme* is the most common and most aggressive type of glioma. Patients diagnosed with glioblastoma have a median survival time of less than 1 year. Approximately 50–60% of gliomas are classified as glioblastoma. These tumors develop from cells of the cerebral white matter and tend to grow rapidly and become very large before producing symptoms that lead to diagnosis. The cell of origin of glioblastoma multiforme has long been the subject of controversy and debate. The current view is that glioblastoma arises from pluripotent neural progenitor (stem) cells in the subventricular zone of the mature brain (Quigley, Post, & Ehrlich, 2007).

Astrocytomas account for 20–30% of all gliomas. These tumors arise from astrocytes or their precursor cells. As their name implies, astrocytes are star-shaped cells that perform multiple functions, including support of endothelial cells of the blood–brain barrier, provision of nutrients and energy to neurons and maintenance of their ionic balance, and repair of nerve tissues following traumatic injury. The cytoplasm of astrocytes is densely populated with mitochondria and other organelles. These cells are highly branched and their cellular processes envelop the synapses of nerve cells to facilitate transport of glucose for energy and ions (principally calcium) to stimulate neurotransmission. Furthermore, astrocytes have been found capable of communicating with neurons by calcium-modulated release of the neurotransmitter glutamate (Santello & Volterra, 2008).

Ependymomas account for about 6% of all gliomas. They arise from the layer of neuroepithelial cells that line both the hollow cavities of the brain and the canal containing the spinal cord. Within the brain, ependymomas most often arise from the floor of the fourth ventricle, situated in the lower back portion of the brain.

Oligodendrogliomas account for less than 5% of all gliomas. They arise from the oligodendrocytes, glial cells that are primarily responsible for laying down myelin around axons of neurons.

Microglia are the predominant immune cells of the brain that normally function in a protective role against foreign microbes and agents. Paradoxically, these cells are often abundant in and around developing gliomas, particularly astrocytomas, and they may release growth-promoting factors that actually accelerate tumor development and progression (Graeber, Scheithauer, & Kreutzberg, 2002).

Risk Factors for Glioma

Gliomas account for about 75% of all *malignant* brain tumors that develop in adults. (This figure excludes meningiomas, which are invariably benign.) Only a few risk factors for glioma have been identified and corroborated through independent investigation. Established risk factors include exposure to high-dose ionizing radiation, chronic immunosuppression, and certain rare genetic syndromes. Studies of other factors, including nonionizing radiation from cellular telephones, viral and microbial agents, household chemicals, nutritional factors, and certain environmental toxins, have thus far yielded equivocal results (Fisher et al., 2007; Schwartzbaum et al., 2006).

Gender Difference in Gliomas

Gliomas are detected about 1.5 times more often in men than in women, and reciprocally, meningiomas develop about 1.5 times more often in women. These gender differences may reflect the influence of hormones. To clarify associations of reproductive factors and glioma risk in women, Whelan and colleagues conducted a case control study of 371 female glioma cases ascertained from hospitals and clinics in four Midwestern states and 527 controls randomly selected from licensed drivers and Health Care Finance Administration enrollees. All cases were confirmed by pathology. Compared with women who never breast fed, women who breast fed for 18 months or more were at increased risk (odds ratio [OR] = 1.8), and women who used estrogen

replacement therapy had a decreased glioma risk compared to nonusers (OR = 0.7). These results suggest that estrogens may provide a modest degree of protection against the development of malignant gliomas (Huang et al., 2004).

Radiation Exposure and Brain Tumors

There is consistent evidence from a number of prospective epidemiologic investigations showing that high exposure to ionizing radiation increases the risk of developing glioma and other tumors of the brain. Sources of radiation include therapeutic and diagnostic medical procedures, occupational exposures as in uranium mining and radiology, atmospheric testing of nuclear weapons, natural sources, industrial accidents, and atomic bomb explosions.

In a study of mortality among U.S. physicians over a 50-year period, Matanoski and colleagues found two- to threefold increases in brain cancer mortality among cohorts of radiologists from the 1920s and 1930s compared to cohorts of other physicians (Matanoski, Seltser, Sartwell, Diamond, & Elliott, 1975). Subsequent studies have also noted increases in the incidence of brain tumors among physicians and radiologists (Andersen et al., 1999; Yoshinaga, Mabuchi, Sigurdson, Doody, & Ron, 2004).

A team of investigators characterized the incidence of brain tumors among atomic bomb survivors in Hiroshima and Nagasaki as a function of radiation dose. Tumors diagnosed between 1958 and 1995 among 80,160 atomic bomb survivors were ascertained using the Hiroshima and Nagasaki tumor registries, medical records, and death certificates. Malignant neoplasms were confirmed by pathology. Results revealed a significant dose response in risk with increasing radiation exposure. (Each additional sievert of radiation increased the risk by 20%.) The investigators concluded that even moderate doses of radiation (< 1 sievert) increase the risk of developing nervous system tumors (Preston et al., 2002; United Nations, 2000).

A number of epidemiologic studies provide strong evidence that childhood exposure to ionizing radiation for the treatment of benign diseases increases the risk of developing a brain tumor later in life. In a study conducted in New York City, a cohort of 2,224 children given x-ray treatment and a matched cohort of 1,380 given topical medications for ringworm of the scalp (*tinea capitis*) during 1940–1959 were followed over nearly 4 decades to determine the comparative incidence of brain tumors. The average dose of ionizing radiation administered was 1.4 Gy. Sixteen intracranial tumors were detected in the irradiated cohort (7 brain cancers, 4 meningiomas, and 5 acoustic neuromas) compared to 1 acoustic neuroma in the control cohort. The standardized incidence ratio for brain cancer was 3.0, and the irradiated children also had excess incidence rates of other tumors, including basal cell carcinomas of the skin and tumors of the thyroid and parotid glands (Shore, Albert, & Pasternack, 1976; Shore, Moseson, Harley, & Pasternack, 2003).

In Israel, a team of investigators studied the relationship between radiotherapy in childhood for tinea capitis and the development of tumors of the brain and nervous system. A total of 10,834 children received ionizing radiation during 1948 and 1960 and were followed for 30 years or more. Sixty neural tumors developed in the cohort of irradiated children, a rate of 1.8 per 10,000 person-years of follow-up. Compared with a matched population control group of 10,834 nonirradiated subjects and a second control group of 5,392 nonirradiated siblings of the irradiated children, the cumulative risk of neural tumors was increased more than eightfold (relative risk [RR] = 8.4) (**Figure 28.5**). Risk increases were noted for meningiomas (RR = 9.5), gliomas (RR = 2.6), and nerve sheath tumors (RR = 18.8). The investigators found significant risk increases at exposure levels of 1–2 Gy, and they were also able to demonstrate a significant dose response in the risk with increasing exposure to ionizing radiation (Ron et al., 1988). In a subsequent investigation of these same cohorts after a median follow-up of 40 years, similar risk increases and dose responses were observed, prompting the investigators to conclude "that brain and meninges tissues are highly sensitive to radiation carcinogenesis" (Sadetzki et al., 2005).

Investigators in Sweden examined the risk of brain tumors in two cohorts containing a total of 28,008 children who received ionizing radiation therapy for hemangioma (a benign tumor of blood vessels). The average dose of radiation was low (7 cGy), but there was wide variation in exposure (up to 11.5 Gy). These cohorts were followed using the Swedish Cancer Register for detection of intracranial tumors during the period 1958–1993. For both cohorts, a total of 86 individuals developed brain tumors compared to 61 expected, yielding a standardized incidence ratio of 1.42. The excess relative risk increased by 2.7 per unit (Gy) of radiation exposure, suggesting a cause and effect dose-response relationship between the absorbed dose of ionizing radiation and brain tumor development. The findings also suggested that the risk was higher with exposure to ionizing radiation during infancy (Karlsson et al., 1998).

The development of a new primary neoplasm has long been recognized as a possible late effect of curative therapy involving ionizing radiation in combination with chemotherapy for an original childhood cancer. The Childhood Cancer Survivor Study (CCSS) is a large, retrospective cohort study of long-term survivors of childhood cancer. Participants were ascertained from 26 centers in the United States and Canada. To quantify the relative impact of radiation, chemotherapy, and other factors, Neglia and colleagues conducted a nested case control study of secondary primary neoplasms of the brain and nervous system in the CCSS cohort of 14,361 five-year survivors of childhood cancers (leukemia or primary brain tumors). Each patient with a second primary was matched to four control subjects who

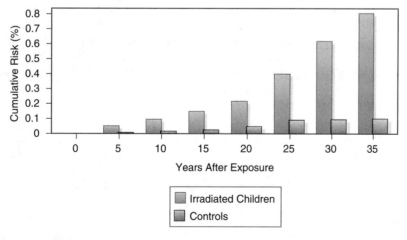

Figure 28.5 Cumulative Risk of Neural Tumors After Radiation for Tinea Capitis.

Source: Data from Ron, E., Modan, B., Boice, J. D. Jr., Alfandary, E., Stovall, M., Chetrit, A., & Katz, L. (1988). Tumors of the brain and nervous system after radiotherapy in childhood. *New England Journal of Medicine, 319*(16), 1033–1039.

had not developed a second primary by age, gender, and time since the original cancer diagnosis. Detailed information on the dose of ionizing radiation and the types and dosages of chemotherapeutic agents were ascertained from the medical records, and conditional logistic regression was used to estimate odds ratios. A total of 40 gliomas and 66 meningiomas were detected in the cohort. The median interval from the original diagnosis to detection was shorter for gliomas (9 years) than meningiomas (17 years). Radiation exposure was associated with increased risk of glioma (OR = 6.78) and meningioma (OR = 9.94), and there was a significant dose response in risk with increasing dosage of ionizing radiation. After adjustment for radiation dose, chemotherapeutic agents were *not* found to be associated with the risk of developing a subsequent primary brain tumor. The investigators concluded that exposure to radiation therapy is the most important risk factor for the development of a new primary brain tumor. They also noted that irradiation during infancy carries the highest risk for the development of a subsequent glioma (Neglia et al., 2006).

Mobile Phones and Brain Tumors

Mobile (cellular) phones have become an integral part of modern telecommunications and are now routinely used by nearly 4.6 billion people throughout the world. Since these devices are low-powered radiofrequency transmitters, several expert groups have expressed concerns about the health and safety of low-level exposure to radio-frequency electromagnetic fields with long-term mobile phone use (World Health Organization, 2014). As a consequence, an international case control study, INTERPHONE, was launched to investigate possible associations between mobile phone use and the development of brain tumors. The study included interviews with 2,708 patients with glioma, 2,409 patients with meningioma, and matched controls ascertained from 13 countries. The results actually showed that regular mobile phone use was associated with a *decrease* in the odds ratios for both glioma (OR = 0.81) and meningioma (OR = 0.79). Odds ratios were less than 1.0 for all deciles of lifetime number of phone calls and nine deciles of cumulative call time. However, in the 10th decile of "recalled" cumulative call time (51,640 hours), the OR was significantly increased for glioma (OR = 1.40) but not for meningioma (OR = 1.15). However, the investigators state that "there were implausible values of reported use in this group." Although they could not rule out an effect at the highest exposure level, biases and error prevented a causal interpretation (INTERPHONE Study Group, 2010).

Several investigators have analyzed subsets of the INTERPHONE database. For example, investigators in Sweden examined detailed information on mobile phone use among 371 cases of glioma and 273 cases of meningioma compared to 574 control subjects matched by age, gender, and residential area. For regular mobile phone use, the odds ratios were reduced for both glioma (OR = 0.8) and meningioma (OR = 0.7), and no increases in risk were observed for any type or anatomic location of brain tumor after more than 10 years of exposure. The authors concluded that "the data do not support the hypothesis that mobile phone use is related to an increased risk of glioma or meningioma"(Lönn, Ahlbom, Hall, Feychting, & Swedish Interphone Study Group, 2005).

Other investigators examined the use of mobile phones and the risk of *acoustic neuromas* because of the proximity of the ipsilateral acoustic nerve to the handset. In a case control study conducted in four Nordic countries and the United Kingdom, 678 cases of acoustic neuroma were compared to 3,553 controls. In the pooled dataset, there was no overall association between regular mobile phone use and the risk of acoustic neuroma (OR = 0.9); furthermore, subgroup analyses by duration of use, lifetime cumulative hours of exposure, total number of calls made, and type of mobile phone failed to reveal significant associations. Interestingly, the risk of acoustic neuroma development on the *same* side of the head as reported phone use was increased with use for 10 years or more (OR = 1.8); but reciprocally, the risk to the *opposite* side decreased by a corresponding amount, making interpretation difficult (Schoemaker et al., 2005).

It is important to note that case control studies are prone to differential reporting bias whereby the cases (with disease) may report differently than the controls (without disease). Thus, in case control studies of self-reported environmental exposures that are perceived by the general public to present a health risk, such bias may artificially increase the risk.

Allergy, Asthma, and Glioma

Hochberg and colleagues (1990) conducted a case control study of 160 patients with brain tumors ascertained from hospitals in Boston, Massachusetts; Providence, Rhode Island; and Baltimore, Maryland. Controls were 128 healthy persons who were friends of the cases. Their results suggested an inverse association between the development of glioblastoma and susceptibility to allergies (OR = 0.60).

Subsequently, several other epidemiologic studies examined the association between allergic conditions such as asthma and the development of brain tumors, and the majority of these investigations also found an inverse association (Schwartzbaum et al., 2003). To quantify the risk and check for heterogeneity among studies, Linos and colleagues identified eight observational studies that examined associations between atopic diseases (asthma, eczema, hay fever, or allergy) and glioma or meningioma and performed a meta-analysis by pooling estimates according to the inverse of their variances. Their analysis involved 3,450 patients with gliomas and 1,070 patients with meningiomas. Pooled estimates revealed that the risk of glioma development was significantly reduced for each atopic condition (RR = 0.61 for allergy, RR = 0.68 for asthma, and RR = 0.69 for eczema). There was no association between atopic disease and the risk of meningioma. The investigators concluded that there is a strong inverse association between atopic disease and the development of glioma that is not likely explainable by methodological bias (Linos, Raine, Alonso, & Michaud, 2007).

More recently, Chen and colleagues (2010) identified four additional published studies for inclusion in a meta-analysis to evaluate the association between allergic conditions and glioma risk. Their analysis was based on 12 studies (10 case control and 2 cohort studies) containing 6,408 glioma patients and a total of 61,090 participants. Compared to subjects without allergies, those with reported allergic conditions had a 40% reduced risk of glioma (pooled OR = 0.60). The risk reductions were consistent for specific conditions (OR = 0.70 for asthma, OR = 0.69 for eczema, and OR = 0.78 for hay fever).

Although the results of these meta-analyses show consistency of effects, it has been pointed out that in most of the studies, spouses or close relatives were often called upon to provide information about the medical histories of patients with brain tumors; as a consequence, the inverse association with allergic conditions may be an artifact of general underreporting of asthmatic conditions for cases. In a novel investigation, Schwartzbaum and colleagues attempted to rule out such reporting bias by examining the distributions of asthma and allergy-related genetic polymorphisms in 111 patients with glioblastoma multiforme and 421 controls. Similar to other studies, their results revealed that *self-reported* history of allergic conditions reduced the risk of glioma development (OR = 0.64). But what is most important about this study is that the risk was independently modified by single nucleotide polymorphisms related to asthma susceptibility (interleukin-4 receptor a and interleukin-13), and these genetic effects could not have been influenced by reporting bias. Specifically, genetic polymorphisms that heighten asthma risk

were found to reduce the risk of glioma development and vice versa. For example, interleukin-4 receptor a polymorphisms, which are known to decrease the risk of asthma, were found to increase the risk of glioma (OR = 1.61), and an interleukin-13 polymorphism that is known to increase the risk of asthma was found to decrease glioma risk (OR = 0.56). The investigators suggest that because germline mutations were used as biomarkers of susceptibility to asthma and allergic conditions, these results cannot be attributed to recall bias. As such, these findings tend to validate the inverse associations between adult glioma and self-reported histories of allergies that have been consistently observed in epidemiologic research over the past 20 years (Schwartzbaum et al., 2005, 2006).

Nonsteroidal Anti-inflammatory Drugs (NSAIDs) and Glioma

Evidence from epidemiologic and experimental studies suggests that use of nonsteroidal anti-inflammatory drugs (NSAIDs) reduces the risk of a number of malignant neoplasms, including cancers of the colon, breast, prostate, and lung (Harris, 2009). These results prompted an investigation of the association between use of aspirin and other NSAIDs and risk of adult glioblastoma multiforme. The association was evaluated among 236 incident cases and 401 population-based controls frequency-matched on age, gender, and ethnicity from the San Francisco Bay Area Adult Glioma Study. Cases (or proxies) and controls were interviewed in person between 1997 and 2000. Cases with glioblastoma multiforme reported less use of at least 600 pills of all types of NSAIDs combined during the 10-year prediagnostic period than did controls (OR = 0.53). Findings were consistent for aspirin (OR = 0.51), ibuprofen (OR = 0.41), and naproxen or other NSAIDs (OR = 0.34). Eliminating participants who initiated NSAID use within 2 years of diagnosis yielded similar results. These findings show an inverse association between NSAID use and the risk of developing glioblastoma multiforme. The authors suggest the need for further studies to determine whether NSAIDs might be effective in the inhibition of glioma development or progression (Sivak-Sears, Schwartzbaum, Miike, Moghadassi, & Wrensch, 2004).

U.S. STUDY OF BRAIN TUMORS

A team of U.S. investigators conducted a comprehensive multicenter study of adult brain tumors to identify, compare, and quantify the risk factors for glioma, meningioma, and acoustic neuroma (Inskip et al., 2001). The study included 782 brain tumor cases and 799 controls ascertained from medical centers in Phoenix, Arizona; Brigham and Women's Hospital in Boston, Massachusetts; and Western Pennsylvania Hospital in Pittsburgh. Cases included 489 patients with gliomas, 197 patients with meningiomas, and 96 patients with acoustic neuromas. The controls were ascertained from the same hospitals with matching to the cases on gender, race, age, and location of residence. Data were collected by research nurses using standardized questionnaires. Furthermore, blood samples were collected to explore associations of germline mutations and polymorphisms with the development of brain tumors.

The study found no evidence of higher brain tumor risk among people who use handheld cellular phones compared to those who did not use them. The risk of developing brain tumors did not increase with increasing years of use or average minutes of use per day, nor did brain tumors among cellular phone users occur more often than expected on the side of the head on which people reported using their phone. There was no evidence for an increased risk of any of the three major categories of tumors (glioma, meningioma, or acoustic neuroma) among persons who used cellular telephones 60 or more minutes per day, or regularly for up to 5 years (Inskip et al., 2001).

There was evidence that people with a history of allergies or autoimmune diseases were at reduced risk for developing glioma. Allergies evaluated included asthma, eczema, hay fever, and allergies to medicine, insects, food, and chemicals. Autoimmune diseases included rheumatoid arthritis, lupus erythematosus, multiple sclerosis, diabetes, and pernicious anemia. The reduced risk associated with history of allergies was specific for gliomas (OR = 0.67), but there was no significant association between history of allergies and risk of meningioma or acoustic neuroma. History of autoimmune disease, however, was associated with a reduced risk of both glioma (OR = 0.49) and meningioma (OR = 0.59). The exact nature of the immunological basis for these associations remains to be determined (Brenner et al., 2002).

Genetic data from the study were also examined to determine effects of polymorphisms in glutathione S-transferase and the cytochrome P450 system, two families of genes involved in the metabolism of solvents that may play a role in the development of brain tumors. One polymorphism of GSTP1 was found associated with an 80% increase in glioma risk, but results for other polymorphisms were indeterminate (De Roos et al., 2003).

GENETIC ANOMALIES AND BRAIN TUMORS

A few genetic syndromes have been found that heighten the risk of developing a brain tumor. These include neurofibromatosis 1 and 2, tuberous sclerosis, retinoblastoma, Li–Fraumeni syndrome, Turcot's syndrome, and Cowden syndrome. These genetic syndromes are caused by heritable mutations in certain tumor suppressor genes that are critical to the processes of normal cell division and function. Furthermore, certain brain tumors such as retinoblastoma and oligodendroglioma are also characterized by specific gene mutations or chromosomal deletions.

Neurofibromatosis Types 1 and 2

Neurofibromatosis type 1 (von Recklinghausen's disease) is a rare autosomal dominant disorder first described by the German physician Friedrech von Recklinghausen in 1882. This condition is characterized by the development of multiple fibromas (neurofibromas) of the skin, brain, and other anatomic sites. Some patients also develop gliomas of the optic nerve. The syndrome is due to a mutant autosomal dominant gene called *NF1* located on the long arm of chromosome 17. The gene encodes a protein called neurofibromin that regulates cell division of fibrous nerve sheaths. Mutant forms of *NF1* result in the development of neurofibromas (Boyd, Korf, & Theos, 2009).

Neurofibromatosis type 2 is a rare autosomal dominant disorder caused by a mutation of a tumor suppressor gene called *NF2* located on the long arm of chromosome 22. The gene encodes a protein called *merlin* that is essential for the formation of the myelin sheaths of nerves. Mutant forms of *NF2* result in the development of *schwannomas* of the vestibular branch of the eighth cranial nerve as well as tumors of other cranial nerves. Furthermore, approximately 50% of *NF2* mutant carriers develop meningiomas (Asthagiri et al., 2009).

Li–Fraumeni Syndrome

Li–Fraumeni syndrome is a rare autosomal dominant hereditary disorder (Li & Fraumeni, 1969). The syndrome is linked to germline mutations of the *p53* tumor suppressor gene located on the short arm of chromosome 17. Such mutations can be inherited or arise de novo early in embryogenesis or in one of the parents' germ cells (Varley, 2003). Patients who carry the *p53* mutant gene are at risk for a wide range of malignancies, including breast cancer, brain tumors, acute leukemia, soft tissue and bone sarcomas, and adrenal cortical carcinoma. A genetic variant of the

Li–Fraumeni syndrome may be due to a mutation of another gene called *CHEK2* located on the long arm of chromosome 22 (Bell et al., 1999). Mutant forms of *CHEK2* lead to dysfunctional DNA repair during cell division, thereby increasing the risk of certain malignancies. However, there is controversy about whether *CHEK2* mutations cause a similar profile of cancer as *p53* mutations in the Li–Fraumeni syndrome (Evans, Birch, & Narod, 2008).

Turcot's Syndrome

Turcot's syndrome is a rare genetic disorder characterized clinically by the concurrence of a primary brain tumor and multiple colorectal adenomas. The condition is caused by mutations in the *APC* gene located on chromosome 5 or mismatch repair genes on chromosomes 2 and 3. The *APC* gene plays a critical role in a number of cellular processes, and the mismatch repair genes are responsible for the detection and repair of errors that occur during DNA replication. Mutant forms of these genes cause adenomatous polyps of the colon and medulloblastomas of the cerebellum (Hamilton et al., 1995). Mutations of the *APC* gene and the mismatch repair genes also cause familial adenomatous polyposis (FAP) and other hereditary colon cancer syndromes.

Tuberous Sclerosis

Tuberous sclerosis is a rare genetic disorder that causes development of nonmalignant fibromas in the brain and other anatomic sites, including the kidneys, heart, eyes, lungs, and skin. This condition is caused by mutations in either of two tumor suppressor genes, *TSC1* or *TSC2*, located on chromosomes 9 and 16, respectively. These genes encode two proteins, *hamartin* and *tuberin*, that regulate cell proliferation and differentiation. Mutant forms of *TSC1* and *TSC2* result in the development of giant cell astrocytomas, fibrous cortical tumors in the brain, and subependymal tumors in the walls of the ventricles of the brain (Yates, 2006).

Cowden Syndrome

Cowden syndrome (also known as *multiple hamartoma syndrome*) is a rare autosomal dominant inherited disorder characterized by multiple tumor-like growths called hamartomas and an increased risk of certain forms of cancer. The characteristic hamartomas of Cowden syndrome are small, noncancerous growths that are most commonly found on the skin and mucous membranes (such as the lining of the mouth and nose), but they can also occur in the intestinal tract and other parts of the body. This syndrome is caused by a mutant gene known as *PTEN* located on the long arm of chromosome 10. The *PTEN* gene encodes a protein known as *phosphatase and tensin homolog* that helps regulate normal cell division and growth. Mutant forms of *PTEN* result in the development of hamartomas and increase the risk of developing thyroid cancer, breast cancer, and endometrial cancer. In addition, individuals with Cowden syndrome sometimes develop slow-growing benign tumors of the cerebellum (Eng, 1998).

Retinoblastoma

Retinoblastoma is a rare malignant tumor that arises from the retinal cells of the eye. In a study of U.S. SEER data for 1975–2004, the age-adjusted annual rate of retinoblastoma for males and females was 12 cases per million. Most cases occurred in children (~90% before 5 years of age), and about one-third of cases developed bilateral disease in the first 2 years of life (Broaddus, Topham, & Sigh, 2009).

Retinoblastomas are caused by mutations of the retinoblastoma gene (*Rb1*) located on the short arm of chromosome 13. The *Rb1* gene was discovered by a team of investigators in 1986 (Dryja, Friend, & Weinberg, 1986). In its nonmutated form, *Rb1* encodes a tumor suppressor protein that regulates DNA replication during cell division. Mutations in *Rb1* cause retinoblastoma of the eye, and occasionally malignant tumors of the pineal gland (Du & Pogoriler, 2006; Parsam, Kannabiran, Honavar, Vemuganti, & Ali, 2009).

In 1971, Alfred Knudson hypothesized that retinoblastoma arises from two mutational events. In the heritable form, a mutated *Rb1* gene is inherited from one parent and the second occurs in somatic cells of the retina. In the nonheritable form, both *Rb1* mutations occur in somatic cells of the retina (Knudson, 1971). The *Rb1* gene was the first tumor suppressor gene ever discovered, and Knudson's two-hit mutation theory of retinoblastoma has been generalized as the *two-hit somatic mutation theory of cancer*.

The original multi-hit theory of cancer was proposed by Carl Nordling in 1953, who stated that "the cancerous cell contains not one but a number of mutated genes. The occurrence of such accumulations of mutations may be expected to increase according to a certain exponent of age as well as according to the increase of cell proliferation" (Nordling, 1953).

Oligodendroglioma

Oligodendrogliomas are believed to originate from the oligodendrocytes of the brain or their precursor cells. These tumors constitute less than 5% of all malignant brain tumors. A common genetic structural deformity found in oligodendroglioma is codeletion of chromosomal arms 1p and 19q. In fact, this striking feature is considered to be the "genetic signature" of oligodendroglioma. In a recent study, 1p loss was present in 35 of 42 tumors (83%), 9q loss was present in 28 of 39 tumors (72%), both 1p and 9q losses were present in 27 of 39 tumors (69%), and at least one deletion was present in all tumors. Such deletions may silence the expression of important tumor suppressor genes such as the *CAMTA1* gene, a transcription regulator on chromosome 1 (Barbashina, Salazar, Holland, Rosenblum, & Ladanyi, 2005).

Cellular Signaling Pathways and Brain Tumors

Genetic alterations found to be associated with the development of brain tumors tend to disrupt cellular signaling pathways that regulate key processes of carcinogenesis such as cell division, DNA repair, angiogenesis, and apoptosis. Expression of growth factors such as epidermal growth factor (*EGFR*), protein kinase activators (*RAS*), vascular endothelial growth factor (*VEGF*), and/or inactivation of tumor suppressor genes such as *p53*, *Rb1*, and *PTEN* are currently under intense investigation to elucidate mechanisms of carcinogenesis. Elucidation of such mechanisms could obviously reveal targets for effective molecular therapy.

As pointed out by many investigators, inflammation is a powerful contributing factor to the development of cancer, including brain tumors (Harris, 2009; Kaluz & Van Meir, 2011). For example, glioblastoma multiforme tissues are characterized by the presence of immune cell infiltrates and the expression of inflammatory cytokines. In a study of the immunohistochemistry of 47 glioblastomas, 35 tumors (74.4%) stained positive for cyclooxygenase-2 (COX-2), the rate-limiting enzyme of the prostaglandin inflammatory cascade, and tumors with a high rate of proliferation tended to have greater COX-2 expression (Prayson, Castilla, Vogelbaum, & Barnett, 2002).

Many studies have implicated hypoxia (lack of oxygen) and sustained activation of hypoxia inducible factor (HIF-1) as key events in carcinogenesis. It is therefore noteworthy that *HIF-1* can be induced by factors other than hypoxia, primarily proinflammatory mediators such as interleukin-1b and NF-κB. According to one model of glioblastoma development, activation of *HIF-1* is sustained by an autocrine loop that involves the protein kinase (*RAS*) cascade and amplified expression of interleukin-1b (Kaluz & Van Meir, 2011; Sharma, Dixit, Koul, Mehta, & Sen, 2010).

RISK FACTORS FOR MENINGIOMAS

Intracranial meningiomas account for more than one-third of all brain tumors. Although most meningiomas are benign (~95%), their expansion in the closed cranial vault can produce serious neurological symptoms and even death.

Meningiomas arise from cells of the meninges, the membranous tissue that covers the surface of the brain beneath the skull. Meningeal membranes also line the ventricles of the brain and cover certain structures and glands within the brain such as the pineal gland and the thalamus. The exact cell of origin is thought to be the arachnoid cap cell, a progenitor (stem) cell of mature meningeal tissue (Bondy et al., 2008).

Meningiomas are diagnosed roughly twice as often in women compared to men. In the United States, the age-adjusted rates of meningioma are 8.4 per 100,000 in women and 3.6 per 100,000 in men. In contrast to gliomas, which can occur in children, meningiomas are infrequently diagnosed before the age of 20 years, and the age-specific incidence rises steadily throughout the adult life span (**Figure 28.6**).

As with malignant gliomas of the brain, ionizing radiation is the major environmental risk factor for meningioma. A number of studies have consistently found that exposure to high doses of ionizing radiation markedly elevates the risk of developing meningioma. For example, in the well-known cohort study of 10,834 Israeli children who received ionizing radiation to the scalp for the treatment of tinea capitis (ringworm) during 1948–1960, the risk of subsequent development of meningioma over 40 years of follow-up was increased nearly 10-fold (RR = 9.5). The mean latency period from radiation exposure to detection was 36 years, reflecting the extremely slow growth of most meningiomas (Ron et al., 1988; Sadetzki et al., 2005). It is also notable that multiple sources of radiation have been found to increase the risk of meningioma development, including radiation therapy for certain intracranial malignancies such as lymphoma and leukemia (Neglia et al., 2006), and full mouth dental x-rays (Longstreth et al., 2004).

The excess female risk for meningioma compared to males has been linked to reproductive factors and hormone (estrogen) exposure. Women have more than a threefold higher incidence than men during the reproductive years, and a few epidemiologic studies have linked exogenous estrogens to the relatively high female risk. In the Nurse's Health Study, current use of exogenous estrogens was found to increase the risk in both premenopausal women (RR = 2.48) and postmenopausal women (RR = 1.86) (Jhawar, Fuchs,

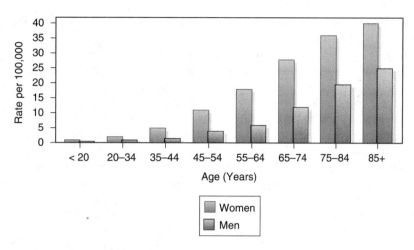

Figure 28.6 Age-Specific Incidence of Meningioma, United States, 2002–2006.

Source: Data from Central Brain Tumor Registry of the United States. (2010). *CBTRUS statistical report: Primary brain and central nervous system tumors diagnosed in eighteen states in 2002–2006.* Hinsdale, IL: Author; Wiemels, J., Wrensch, M., & Claus, E. B. (2010). Epidemiology and etiology of meningioma. *Journal of Neurooncology, 99*(3), 307–314.

Colditz, & Stampfer, 2003). In the INTERPHONE case control study of brain tumors, an increased risk of meningioma was observed among postmenopausal women who had ever received hormone replacement therapy (OR = 1.7) (Wigertz et al., 2008). In a retrospective cohort study of the Mayo Clinic database, the incidence of meningioma among women who received hormone replacement therapy was more than twofold higher than among women with no exposure (865 versus 366 per 100,000, adjusted OR = 2.2) (Blitshteyn, Crook, & Jaeckle, 2008). To clarify the effects of estrogen and other hormones on the pathogenesis of meningioma, it is suggested that future studies incorporate information on both hormonal exposures and the molecular expression of hormone receptors in meningeal tumor tissues (Wiemels, Wrensch, & Claus, 2010).

Although epidemiologic studies have consistently found that allergic conditions reduce the risk of developing *glioma*, it is unclear whether these conditions influence *meningioma* development. To help clarify the issue, Schoemaker and colleagues (2005) conducted a pooled analysis of two population-based case control studies of meningioma and allergic conditions. The analysis included 475 cases and 1,716 controls ascertained during 2001–2004 in the United Kingdom. The analysis revealed that meningioma risk was significantly reduced by individual allergic conditions, including asthma (OR = 0.85), hay fever (OR = 0.81), and eczema (OR = 0.72). Interestingly, the risk reductions were greatest among children with allergic conditions (OR = ~0.50) whereas the estimates of risk were close to unity for adults (Schoemaker et al., 2005).

Familial clustering of meningioma is uncommon, although some studies suggest that relatives of affected cases are at increased risk. For example, Malmer and colleagues examined the risk to relatives of index cases of meningioma (probands) ascertained through the Swedish National Cancer Registry and found a twofold increase in the risk among first-degree relatives compared to unrelated spouses (OR = 2.2) (Malmer, Henriksson, & Gronberg, 2003). In a similar analysis incorporating data from both the Swedish and Norwegian Registry databases, Hemminiki and colleagues also found an increase in meningioma risk among offspring of probands (OR = 1.6) (Hemminki, Tretli, Sundquist, Johannesen, & Granstrom, 2009). Although these results suggest the existence of genetic factors that heighten susceptibility to meningioma development, at present, no linkage and/or segregation studies of familial meningioma have been reported (Wiemels et al., 2010).

As already noted, the currently available evidence suggests that certain risk factors for meningioma are similar to those for breast cancer (e.g., exposure to exogenous estrogens). Furthermore, several studies have demonstrated that breast cancer and meningioma develop in the *same* patient more often than expected. For example, in a study of second primary tumors that developed among women with either a first primary breast cancer or meningioma, the risk was increased for breast cancer after meningioma (RR = 1.54), and reciprocally, for meningioma after breast cancer (RR = 1.64). The investigators concluded that shared risk factors may account for this association (Custer, Koepsell, & Mueller, 2002).

In a genome-wide association study designed to examine single nucleotide polymorphisms (SNPs) in genes that regulate DNA repair, several polymorphisms were identified that were significantly associated with meningioma. Notably, three of these genetic variants were located in a gene called *BRIP1* that is also associated with breast cancer. The *BRIP1* gene interacts with the breast cancer gene, *BRCA1*, in the repair of DNA double-strand breaks. This finding suggests that the association between meningioma and breast cancer may be due to shared genetic susceptibility (similar polymorphisms in DNA repair genes) in addition to shared environmental risk factors (estrogen replacement therapy) (Bethke et al., 2008).

PITUITARY TUMORS

Pituitary gland tumors account for about 15% of intracranial tumors in adults and 11% in children. These tumors are usually benign but can secrete excessive amounts of prolactin or growth hormone. Furthermore, enlargement of the pituitary gland in the confined bony compartment in the center of the brain, the *sella turcica*, can produce compressive injury and also result in substantial morbidity. The etiology of pituitary tumors is largely unknown.

Schoemaker and Swerdlow (2009) conducted a population-based case control study in Southeast England to examine potential risk factors for pituitary tumors. Data on medical and reproductive history, female hormones, and cigarette smoking were collected by personal interview from 299 cases and 630 controls ages 18–59 years. Tumor risk was reduced in subjects reporting a past diagnosis of hay fever (OR = 0.7) but not asthma or eczema. Among women, certain features of menopause were found to increase the risk. Women who underwent surgical menopause within 1 year of diagnosis or experienced menopause before the age of 40 years were found to be at markedly increased risk (OR = 6.7 and OR = 7.5, respectively). The effect of early menopause remained when evaluating menopausal status 10 years before diagnosis. The risk was also increased among women who delivered their first child before the age of 20 years compared with nulliparous women (OR = 3.4). No significant associations were observed for ever use of oral contraceptives, hormone replacement therapy, cigarette smoking, past head injury, or past diagnosis of epilepsy. This study suggests an elevated risk of pituitary tumors in relation to surgically induced menopause, early postmenopausal age, and young age at first childbirth, and possibly a reduced risk with allergic conditions such as hay fever. Reasons for these associations need further investigation, but among women, abrupt or early changes in the hormonal milieu appear to play a role in the genesis of pituitary tumors (Schoemaker & Swerdlow, 2009).

An international team of researchers based in Finland examined three clusters of familial pituitary adenomas using chip-based technologies to characterize germline mutations. Within these families, mutant forms of the aryl hydrocarbon receptor interacting protein (*AIP*) gene were identified by linkage and segregation analysis in those individuals who developed pituitary adenomas. The aryl hydrocarbon receptor activates certain genes of the P450 system involved in a variety of metabolic pathways, including xenobiotic and drug metabolism. In a series of pituitary adenomas ascertained from cases in Northern Finland, the investigators found that two *AIP* mutations accounted for 16% of all pituitary adenomas and 40% of pituitary adenomas diagnosed in patients under the age of 35 years. Based on these results, they suggest that inherited tumor susceptibility due to low penetrance genes, such as *AIP*, may be more common than previously thought (Vierimaa et al., 2006).

PRIMARY LYMPHOMA OF THE BRAIN

Immunosuppressed patients have an inordinately high risk of developing a primary lymphoma of the brain. Patients with progressive human immunodeficiency virus (HIV) infection complicated by Epstein-Barr virus (EBV) reactivation and posttransplant patients receiving powerful immunosuppressive drugs are at greatest risk.

BRAIN TUMORS IN CHILDREN

The profile of brain tumors that occur in children and adolescents up to 19 years of age differs markedly from that in adults. More than 70% of childhood tumors are malignant gliomas arising from astrocytes, oligodendrocytes, ependymoma cells, or primitive neuroectoderm cells. Pituitary tumors account for about 11% of childhood tumors and are more commonly found in late adolescence. Meningiomas, which account for about 34% of adult brain tumors, comprise only about 4% of childhood brain tumors. The remaining histological types (neuroblastomas, nerve sheath tumors, germ cell tumors) each account for less than 5% of childhood tumors (CBTRUS, 2010).

Medulloblastomas are derived from progenitor (stem) cells of the neuroectoderm and are often referred to as *primitive neuroectodermal tumors (PNET)*. Medulloblastomas are one type of PNET that are found near the midline of the cerebellum. These tumors are more common in children under the age of 5 years. They tend to grow rapidly and often block drainage of the cerebral spinal fluid, causing symptoms associated with increased intracranial pressure. Medulloblastoma cells can spread (metastasize) to other areas of the central nervous system, especially around the spinal cord.

Nonrandom patterns of chromosomal deletions and aberrations have been discovered in several histologic types of childhood brain tumors. These findings suggest that the loss or inactivation of tumor suppressor genes are critical events in tumorigenesis. For example, deletions and aberrations involving chromosome 17 are characteristic cytogenetic findings in medulloblastoma cells. Elucidation of key cellular events that are disrupted by such genetic changes is critical to finding molecular targets for effective therapeutic intervention (Biegel, 1999).

In the United States, the annual incidence of childhood brain tumors "jumped" from 2.3 cases per 100,000 in 1975 to 3.2 cases per 100,000 in 1985, and since that time the rates have remained relatively stable. Malcolm Smith and colleagues at the National Cancer Institute attributed this rapid increase to improved detection of brain tumors with the advent of magnetic resonance imaging (MRI) during the early 1980s. There have also been refinements in the pathological classification of brain tumors due to improved neurosurgical techniques for obtaining biopsy specimens of brain tumors (Smith, Freidlin, Ries, & Simon, 1998).

As pointed out by an Ohio pediatrician, Dr. Arthur Varner:

In the report by Smith et al., the authors' conclusion is that the increasing incidence of brain tumors in children is best explained by a "jump model" with the optimum point of change being around 1985, the time of rapidly increasing availability of magnetic resonance imaging. The authors discount environmental factors, since the change seemed to occur rapidly. (Smith et al., 1998; Varner, 1999)

Nevertheless, as noted by Dr. Varner, an abrupt change in drug use among children *did occur* at that time, namely, a large fraction of parents switched their children from pediatric aspirin to acetaminophen due to concern about aspirin as a potential cause of Reye's syndrome, and this led to a rapid and substantial decline in the use of pediatric aspirin in the early 1980s. According to U.S. marketing data for the period 1979–1985, annual purchases of pediatric aspirin declined from 600 million pills in 1979 to less than 200 million pills in 1985, coincident with a marked increase in sales of acetaminophen products (Arrowsmith, Kennedy, Kuritsky, & Faich, 1987). Varner (1999) states that "the anti-inflammatory effects of aspirin, as opposed to acetaminophen, may have been an unrecognized protective factor in the development of brain tumors, as has been demonstrated for other cancers." Indeed, it is now well known that aspirin and other NSAIDs have chemopreventive activity against many solid tumors through inhibition of the COX-2 prostaglandin inflammatory cascade, whereas acetaminophen is *not* a COX-2 inhibitor (Harris, 2009). Furthermore, recent molecular studies have shown that the tumor cells of high-grade gliomas and medulloblastomas diagnosed in children markedly overexpress COX-2 and related inflammatory cytokines (Bodey, Siegel, & Kaiser, 2006).

THERAPEUTIC APPROACHES TO GLIOMA AND OTHER BRAIN TUMORS

Diagnosis of Brain Tumors

Brain tumors can present clinically by a myriad of neurological signs and symptoms such as headache, nausea, vomiting, altered consciousness, visual disturbances, impaired hearing, loss of smell, emotional changes, paralysis, and other losses of function. Radiologically, these neoplasms present as masses with partial contrast enhancement due to limited disruption of the blood–brain barrier. Noninvasive, high-resolution techniques, such as computed tomography (CT) scans and especially magnetic resonance imaging (MRI), have enhanced the detection of brain tumors. Histologically, malignant tumors are classified and staged based on the morphology and staining characteristics of tumor cells, nuclear atypia, and mitotic activity.

Prognosis of Malignant Brain Tumors

In general, the prognosis for a patient diagnosed with a malignant brain tumor such as glioma is quite poor. Of 10,000 Americans diagnosed each year with malignant gliomas, only about 50% are alive 1 year after diagnosis, and survival drops to less than 25% after 2 years. Glioblastoma has a 14-month median survival after diagnosis. Tumor histology and grade are important prognostic factors. For example, patients diagnosed with anaplastic astrocytoma typically survive 3 or more years.

Van Meir and colleagues have recently published an excellent review of exciting new advances in neuro-oncology with emphasis on malignant glioma. They state that

> . . . new discoveries are being made in basic and translational research, which are likely to improve this situation further in the next 10 years. These include agents that block one or more of the disordered tumor proliferation signaling pathways, and that overcome resistance to already existing treatments. Targeted therapies such as antiangiogenic therapy with antivascular endothelial growth factor antibodies (bevacizumab) are finding their way into clinical practice. Large-scale research efforts are ongoing to provide a comprehensive understanding of all the genetic alterations and gene expression changes underlying glioma formation. These have already refined the classification of glioblastoma into four distinct molecular entities that may lead to different treatment regimens. The role of cancer stem-like cells is another area of active investigation. There is definite hope that by 2020, new cocktails of drugs will be available to target the key molecular pathways involved in gliomas and reduce their mortality and morbidity, a positive development for patients, their families, and medical professionals alike. (Van Meir et al., 2010)

● ● ● **REFERENCES**

Altekruse, S. F., Kosary, C. L., Krapcho, M., Neyman, N., Aminou, R., Waldron, W., . . . Edwards, B. K. (2010). *SEER cancer statistics review, 1975–2007*. Bethesda, MD: National Cancer Institute.

Andersen, A., Barlow, L., Engeland, A., Kjærheim, K., Lynge, E., & Pukkala, E. (1999). Work-related cancer in the Nordic countries. *Scandinavian Journal of Work, Environment and Health, 25*(Suppl 2), 1–116.

Araque, A., Parpura, V., Sanzgiri, R. P., & Haydon, P. G. (1999). Tripartite synapses: Glia, the unacknowledged partner. *Trends in Neuroscience, 22*(5), 208–215.

Arrowsmith, J. B., Kennedy, D. L., Kuritsky, J. N., & Faich, G. A. (1987). National patterns of aspirin use and Reye's syndrome reporting, United States, 1980 to 1985. *Pediatrics, 79*, 858–863.

Asthagiri, A. R., Parry, D. M., Butman, J. A., Kim, H. J., Tsilou, E. T., Zhuang, Z., & Lonser, R. R. (2009). Neurofibromatosis type 2. *Lancet, 373*(9679), 1974–1986.

Aszmann, O. C. (2000). The life and work of Theodore Schwann. *Journal of Reconstructive Microsurgery, 16*(4), 291–295.

Barbashina, V., Salazar, P., Holland, E. C., Rosenblum, M. K., & Ladanyi, M. (2005). Allelic losses at 1p36 and 19q13 in gliomas: Correlation with histologic classification, definition of a 150-kb minimal deleted region on 1p36, and evaluation of *CAMTA1* as a candidate tumor suppressor gene. *Clinical Cancer Research, 11*(3), 1119–11128.

Bell, D. W., Varley, J. M., Szydlo, T. E., Kang, D. H., Wahrer, D. C., Shannon, K. E., . . . Haber, D. A. (1999). Heterozygous germ line *hCHK2* mutations in Li-Fraumeni syndrome. *Science, 286*, 2528–2531.

Bethke, L., Murray, A., Webb, E., Schoemaker, M., Muir, K., McKinney, P., . . . Houlston, R. (2008). Comprehensive analysis of DNA repair gene variants and risk of meningioma. *Journal of the National Cancer Institute, 100*, 270–276.

Biegel, J. A. (1999). Cytogenetics and molecular genetics of childhood brain tumors. *Oncology, 1*, 139–151.

Blitshteyn, S., Crook, J. E., & Jaeckle, K. A. (2008). Is there an association between meningioma and hormone replacement therapy? *Journal of Clinical Oncology, 26*, 279–282.

Bodey, B., Siegel, S. E., & Kaiser, H. E. (2006). Cyclooxygenase-2 (COX-2) overexpression in childhood brain tumors. *In Vivo, 20*(4), 519–525.

Bondy, M. L., Scheurer, M. E., Malmer, B., Barnholtz-Sloan, J. S., Davis, F. G., Il'yasova, D., . . . Brain Tumor Epidemiology Consortium. (2008). Brain tumor epidemiology: Consensus from the Brain Tumor Epidemiology Consortium. *Cancer, 113*(7 Suppl), 1953–1968.

Boyd, K. P., Korf, B. R., & Theos, A. (2009). Neurofibromatosis type 1. *Journal of the American Academy of Dermatology, 61*(1), 1–14.

Brenner, A. V., Linet, M. S., Fine, H. A., Shapiro, W. R., Selker, R. G., Black, P. M., & Inskip, P. D. (2002). History of allergies and autoimmune diseases and risk of brain tumors in adults. *International Journal of Cancer*, 99, 252–259.

Broaddus, E., Topham, A., & Sigh, A. D. (2009). Incidence of retinoblastoma in the USA: 1975-2004. *British Journal of Ophthalmology*, 93, 21–23.

Central Brain Tumor Registry of the United States. (2008). *Statistical report: Primary brain tumors in the United States, 2000–2004*. Hinsdale, IL: Author.

Central Brain Tumor Registry of the United States. (2010). *Statistical report: Primary brain and central nervous system tumors diagnosed in eighteen states in 2002–2006*. Hinsdale, IL: Author.

Chen, C., Xu, T., Chen, J., Zhou, J., Yan, Y., Lu, Y., & Wu, S. (2010). Allergy and risk of glioma: A meta-analysis. *European Journal of Neurology*, 18(3), 387-395.

Custer, B. S., Koepsell, T. D., & Mueller, B. A. (2002). The association between breast carcinoma and meningioma in women. *Cancer*, 94, 1626–1635.

De Roos, A. J., Rothman, N., Inskip, P. D., Linet, M. S., Shapiro, W. R., Selker, R. G., . . . Bell, D. A. (2003). Genetic polymorphisms in *GSTM1, -P1, -T1* and *CYP2E1* and the risk of adult brain tumors. *Cancer Epidemiology, Biomarkers and Prevention*, 12, 14–27.

Dryja, T. P., Friend, S., & Weinberg, R. A. (1986). Genetic sequences that predispose to retinoblastoma and osteosarcoma. *Symposium on Fundamental Cancer Research*, 39, 115–119.

Du, W., & Pogoriler, J. (2006). Retinoblastoma family genes. *Oncogene*, 25(38), 5190–5200.

Eng, C. (1998). Genetics of Cowden syndrome: Through the looking glass of oncology. *International Journal of Oncology*, 12(3), 701–710.

Evans, D. G., Birch, J. M., & Narod, S. A. (2008). Is *CHEK2* a cause of the Li–Fraumeni syndrome? *Journal of Medical Genetics*, 45, 63–64.

Ferlay, J., Shin, H. R., Forman, D., Mathers, C., & Parkin, D. M. (2010). Estimates of worldwide burden of cancer in 2008. *International Journal of Cancer*, 127(12), 2893–2917.

Ferlay, J., Soerjomataram, I., Ervik, M., Dikshit, R., Eser, S., Mathers, C., . . . Bray, F. (2013). *GLOBOCAN 2012 v1.0. Cancer incidence and mortality worldwide: IARC CancerBase No. 11* [Internet]. Lyon, France: International Agency for Research on Cancer. Retrieved from http://globocan.iarc.fr

Fisher, J. L., Schwartzbaum, J. A., Wrensch, M., & Wiemels, J. L. (2007). Epidemiology of brain tumors. *Neurologic Clinics*, 25, 867–890.

Graeber, M. B., Scheithauer, B. W., & Kreutzberg, G. W. (2002). Microglia in brain tumors. *Glia*, 40(2), 252–259.

Hamilton, S. R., Liu, B., Parsons, R. E., Papadopoulos, N., Jen, J., Powell, S. M., . . . Kinzler, K. W. (1995). The molecular basis of Turcot's syndrome. *New England Journal of Medicine*, 332, 839–847.

Harris, R. E. (2009). Cyclooxygenase-2 (COX-2) blockade in the chemoprevention of cancers of the colon, breast, prostate, and lung. *Inflammopharmacology*, 17, 1–13.

Hemminki, K., Tretli, S., Sundquist, J., Johannesen, T. B., & Granstrom, C. (2009). Familial risks in nervous-system tumours: A histology-specific analysis from Sweden and Norway. *Lancet Oncology*, 10, 481–488.

Hochberg, F., Toniolo, P., Cole, P., & Salcman, M. (1990). Non-occupational risk indicators of glioblastoma in adults. *Journal of Neurooncology*, 8, 55–60.

Horner, M. J., Ries, L. A. G., Krapcho, M., Neyman, N., Aminou, R., Howlader, N., . . . Edwards, B. K. (Eds.). (2009). *SEER cancer statistics review, 1975–2006*. Bethesda, MD: National Cancer Institute.

Huang, K., Whelan, E. A., Ruder, A. M., Ward, E. M., Deddens, J. A., Davis-King, K. E., . . . Brain Cancer Collaborative Study Group. (2004). Reproductive factors and risk of glioma in women. *Cancer Epidemiology, Biomarkers and Prevention, 13*(10), 1583–1588.

Inskip, P. D., Tarone, R. E., Hatch, E. E., Wilcosky, T. C., Shapiro, W. R., Selker, R. G., . . . Linet, M. S. (2001). Cellular telephone use and brain tumors. *New England Journal of Medicine, 344*, 79–86.

INTERPHONE Study Group. (2010). Brain tumour risk in relation to mobile telephone use: Results of the INTERPHONE international case–control study. *International Journal of Epidemiology, 39*(3), 1–20.

Jhawar, B. S., Fuchs, C. S., Colditz, G. A., & Stampfer, M. J. (2003). Sex steroid hormone exposures and risk for meningioma. *Journal of Neurosurgery, 99*, 848–853.

Kaluz, S., & Van Meir, E. G. (2011). At the crossroads of cancer and inflammation: *RAS* rewires an HIF-driven IL-1 autocrine loop. *Journal of Molecular Medicine, 89*, 91–94.

Karlsson, P., Holmberg, E., Lundell, M., Mattsson, A., Holm, L. E., & Wallgren, A. (1998). Intracranial tumors after exposure to ionizing radiation during infancy: A pooled analysis of two Swedish cohorts of 28,008 infants with skin hemangioma. *Radiation Research, 150*, 357–364.

Kimelberg, H. K., Jalonen, T., & Walz, W. (1993). Regulation of the brain microenvironment: Transmitters and ions. In S. Murphy (Ed.), *Astrocytes: Pharmacology and function* (pp. 193–222). San Diego, CA: Academic Press.

Knudson, A. G. (1971). Mutation and cancer: Statistical study of retinoblastoma. *Proceedings of the National Academy of Sciences of the United States of America, 68*(4), 820–823.

Kumar, V., Abbas, A. K., & Aster, J. C. (2014). *Robbins and Cotran pathologic basis of disease* (9th ed.). Philadelphia, PA: Mosby & Saunders.

Li, F. P., & Fraumeni, J. F. (1969). Soft-tissue sarcomas, breast cancer, and other neoplasms. A familial syndrome? *Annals of Internal Medicine, 71*(4), 747–752.

Linos, E., Raine, T., Alonso, A., & Michaud, D. (2007). Atopy and risk of brain tumors: A meta-analysis. *Journal of the National Cancer Institute, 99*, 1544–1550.

Longstreth, W. T., Jr., Phillips, L. E., Drangsholt, M., Koepsell, T. D., Custer, B. S., Gehrels, J. A., & Belle, G. (2004). Dental x-rays and the risk of intracranial meningioma: A population-based case–control study. *Cancer, 100*, 1026–1034.

Lönn, S., Ahlbom, A., Hall, P., Feychting, M., & Swedish Interphone Study Group. (2005). Long-term mobile phone use and brain tumor risk. *American Journal of Epidemiology, 161*(6), 526–535.

Malmer, B., Henriksson, R., & Gronberg, H. (2003). Familial brain tumours—genetics or environment? A nationwide cohort study of cancer risk in spouses and first-degree relatives of brain tumour patients. *International Journal of Cancer, 106*, 260–263.

Matanoski, G. M., Seltser, R., Sartwell, P. E., Diamond, E. L., & Elliott, E. A. (1975). The current mortality rates of radiologists and other physician specialists: Specific causes of death. *American Journal of Epidemiology, 101*, 199–210.

Neglia, J. P., Robison, L. L., Stovall, M., Liu, Y., Packer, R. J., Hammond, S., . . . Inskip, P. D. (2006). New primary neoplasms of the central nervous system in survivors of childhood cancer: A report from the Childhood Cancer Survivor Study. *Journal of the National Cancer Institute, 98*(21), 1528–1537.

Nordling, C. O. (1953). A new theory on the cancer-inducing mechanism. *British Journal of Cancer, 7*, 68–72.

Parkin, D. M., Bray, F., Ferlay, J., & Pisani, P. (2005). Global cancer statistics, 2002. *CA: A Cancer Journal for Clinicians, 55*, 74–108.

Parkin, D. M., Pisani, P., & Ferlay, J. (1999a). Estimates of the worldwide incidence of 25 major cancers in 1990. *International Journal of Cancer, 80*(6), 827–841.

Parkin, D. M., Pisani, P., & Ferlay, J. (1999b). Global cancer statistics, 1990. *CA: A Cancer Journal for Clinicians, 49*(1), 33–64.

Parkin, D. M., Whelan, S. L., Ferlay, J., Teppo, L., & Thomas, D. B. (2002). *Cancer incidence in five continents* (vol. 5). Lyon, France: IARC Press.

Parsam, V. L., Kannabiran, C., Honavar, S., Vemuganti, G. K., & Ali, M. J. (2009). A comprehensive, sensitive and economical approach for the detection of mutations in the *RB1* gene in retinoblastoma. *Journal of Genetics, 88*(4), 517–527.

Pollard, W., & Earnshaw, W. C. (2008). *Cell biology.* Philadelphia, PA: Saunders Elsevier.

Prayson, R. A., Castilla, E. A., Vogelbaum, M. A., & Barnett, G. H. (2002). Cyclooxygenase-2 (COX-2) expression by immunohistochemistry in glioblastoma multiforme. *Annals of Diagnostic Pathology, 6*(3), 148–153.

Preston, D. L., Ron, E., Yonehara, S., Kibuke, T., Fjuii, H., Kishikawa, M., . . . Mabuchi, K. (2002). Tumors of the nervous system and pituitary gland associated with atomic bomb radiation exposure. *Journal of the National Cancer Institute, 94,* 1555–1563.

Purves, D., Augustine, G. J., Fitzpatrick, D., Hall, W. C., LaMantia, A., McNamara, J. O., & White, L. E. (2008). *Neuroscience.* Sunderland, MA: Sinauer Associates.

Quigley, M. R., Post, C., & Ehrlich, G. (2007). Some speculation on the origin of glioblastoma. *Neurosurgery Review, 30,* 16–21.

Robbins, S. L., & Cotran, R. S. (1979). *Pathologic basis of disease* (2nd ed.). Philadelphia: W. B. Saunders.

Ron, E., Modan, B., Boice, J. D. Jr., Alfandary, E., Stovall, M., Chetrit, A., & Katz, L. (1988). Tumors of the brain and nervous system after radiotherapy in childhood. *New England Journal of Medicine, 319*(16), 1033–1039.

Sadetzki, S., Chetrit, A., Freedman, L., Stovall, M., Modan, B., & Novikov, I. (2005). Long-term follow-up for brain tumor development after childhood exposure to ionizing radiation for tinea capitis. *Radiation Research, 163,* 424–432.

Santello, M., & Volterra, A. (2008). Synaptic modulation by astrocytes via Ca(2+)-dependent glutamate release. *Neuroscience, 158*(1), 253–259.

Schoemaker, M. J., & Swerdlow, A. J. (2009). Risk factors for pituitary tumors: A case-control study. *Cancer Epidemiology, Biomarkers and Prevention, 18*(5), 1492–1500.

Schoemaker, M. J., Swerdlow, A. J., Ahlbom, A., Auvinen, A., Blaasaas, K. G., Cardis, E., . . . Tynes, T. (2005). Mobile phone use and risk of acoustic neuroma: Results of the Interphone case–control study in five North European countries. *British Journal of Cancer, 93,* 842–848.

Schwartzbaum, J., Ahlbom, A., Malmer, B., Lönn, S., Brookes, A. J., Doss, H., . . . Feychting, M. (2005). Polymorphisms associated with asthma are inversely related to glioblastoma multiforme. *Cancer Research, 65,* 6459–6465.

Schwartzbaum, J., Fonsson, F., Ahlbom, A., Preston-Martin, S., Lönn, S., Söderberg, K. C., & Feychting, M. (2003). Cohort studies of association between self-reported allergic conditions, immune-related diagnoses and glioma and meningioma risk. *International Journal of Cancer, 106*(3), 423–428.

Schwartzbaum, J. A., Fisher, J. L., Aldape, K. D., & Wrensch, M. (2006). Epidemiology and molecular pathology of glioma. *Nature Clinical Practice Neurology, 2,* 494–503.

Sharma, V., Dixit, D., Koul, N., Mehta, V., & Sen, E. (2010). *RAS* regulates interleukin-1β-induced HIF-1α transcriptional activity in glioblastoma. *Journal of Molecular Medicine, 89*(1), 1–14.

Shore, R. E., Albert, R. E., & Pasternack, B. S. (1976). Follow-up study of patients treated by x-ray epilation for tinea capitis; Resurvey of post-treatment illness and mortality experience. *Archives of Environmental Health, 31*(1), 21–28.

Shore, R. E., Moseson, M., Harley, N., & Pasternack, B. S. (2003). Tumors and other diseases following childhood x-ray treatment for ringworm of the scalp (tinea capitis). *Health Physics, 85*(4), 404–408.

Sivak-Sears, N. R., Schwartzbaum, J. A., Miike, R., Moghadassi, M., & Wrensch, M. (2004). Case-control study of use of nonsteroidal antiinflammatory drugs and glioblastoma multiforme. *American Journal of Epidemiology, 159,* 1131–1139.

Smith, M. A., Freidlin, B., Ries, L. A., & Simon, R. (1998). Trends in reported incidence of primary malignant brain tumors in children in the United States. *Journal of the National Cancer Institute, 90*(17), 1269–1277.

United Nations. (2000). *Scientific Committee on the Effects of Atomic Radiation Sources and Effects of Ionizing Radiation: UNSCEAR 2000 report to the general assembly, with scientific annexes.* New York, NY. Retrieved from http://www.unscear.org/unscear/en/publications/2000_1.html

Van Meir, E. G., Hadjipanayis, C. G., Norden, A. D., Shu, H. K., Wen, P. Y., & Olson, J. J. (2010). Exciting new advances in neuro-oncology: The avenue to a cure for malignant glioma. *CA: A Cancer Journal for Clinicians, 60,* 166–193.

Varley, J. M. (2003). Germline *TP53* mutations and Li-Fraumeni syndrome. *Human Mutation, 21*(3), 313–320.

Varner, A. (1999). Letter to the editor: Re: Trends in reported incidence of primary malignant brain tumors in children in the United States. *Journal of the National Cancer Institute, 91*(11), 973.

Vierimaa, O., Georgitsi, M., Lehtonen, R., Vahteristo, P., Kokko, A., Raitila, A., . . . Aaltonen, L. A. (2006). Pituitary adenoma p redisposition caused by germ line mutations in the *AIP* gene. *Science, 312,* 1228–1230.

Virchow, R. (1846). Ueber das granulirte aussehen der wandungen der gehirnventrikel. *Allgeimene Zeitschrift Fur Psychiatrie, 3,* 242–250.

Virchow, R. (1854). Ueber das ausgebreitete Vorkommen einer dem Nervenmark analogen substanz in den tierischen Geweben. *Virchows Archive Fur Pathologische Anatomie, 6,* 562.

World Health Organization. (2014). Electromagnetic fields and public health: Mobile phones. Geneva, Switzerland: Author. Retrieved from http://www.who.int/mediacentre/factsheets/fs193/en/

Wiemels, J., Wrensch, M., & Claus, E. B. (2010). Epidemiology and etiology of meningioma. *Journal of Neurooncology, 99*(3), 307–314.

Wigertz, A., Lonn, S., Hall, P., Auvinen, A., Christensen, H. C., Johansen, C., . . . Feychting, M. (2008). Reproductive factors and risk of meningioma and glioma. *Cancer Epidemiology, Biomarkers and Prevention, 17,* 2663–2670.

Yates, J. R. (2006). Tuberous sclerosis. *European Journal of Human Genetics, 14*(10), 1065–1073.

Yoshinaga, S., Mabuchi, K., Sigurdson, A. J., Doody, M. M., & Ron, E. (2004). Cancer risks among radiologists and radiologic technologists: Review of epidemiologic studies. *Radiology, 233,* 313–321.

Index

Note: Page numbers followed by *f* or *t* indicate materials in figures or tables, respectively.